G000146602

MEANING AND FORM: SYSTEMIC FUNCTIONAL INTERPRETATIONS

Meaning and Choice in Language: Studies for Michael Halliday

edited by

Margaret Berry
Nottingham University,
UK

Christopher Butler
College of Ripon and York St John,
Leeds University, UK

Robin Fawcett
University of Wales,
Cardiff, UK

Guowen Huang
University of Wales,
Cardiff, UK

Volume LVII in the Series

Advances in Discourse Processes

Roy O. Freedle, Editor

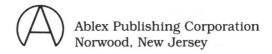

Ablex Publishing Corporation
Norwood, New Jersey

Copyright © 1996 by Ablex Publishing Corporation

All rights reserved. No part of this publication may be reproduced, stored in a retrieval system, or transmitted, in any form or by any means, electronic, mechanical, photocopying, microfilming, recording or otherwise, without permission of the publisher.

Printed in the United States of America

Library of Congress Cataloging-in-Publication Data

Meaning and form : systematic functional interpretations /
    Margaret Berry . . . [et al.].
        p.   cm. — (Advances in discourse processes ; v. 57)
    (Meaning and choice in language : studies for Michael Halliday)
    Includes bibliographical references and indexes.
    ISBN 1-56750-254-7 (cloth). — ISBN 1-56750-255-5 (pbk.)
    1. Systemic grammar. 2. Functionalism (Linguistics).
I. Berry, Margaret, 1918– . II. Halliday, M. A. K. (Michael
Alexander Kirkwood), 1925– . III. Series. IV. Series:
Meaning and choice in language.
P149.M4   1996
415—dc20   96-991
                                                                    CIP

Ablex Publishing Corporation
355 Chestnut Street
Norwood, New Jersey 07648

Contents

Preface to the Series

Roy O. Freedle

Series Editor

This series of volumes provides a forum for the cross-fertilization of ideas from a diverse number of disciplines, all of which share a common interest in discourse—be it prose comprehension and re-call, dialogue analysis, text grammar construction, computer sim-ulation of natural language, cross-cultural comparisons of commu-nicative competence or other related topics. The problems posed by multisentence contexts and the methods required to investigate them, while not always unique to discourse, are still sufficiently distinct as to benefit from the organized model of scientific interac-tion made possible by this series.

Scholars working in the discourse area from the perspective of sociolinguistics, psycholinguistics, ethnomethodology and the soci-ology of language, educational psychology (e.g., teacher–student in-teraction), the philosophy of language, computational linguistics, and related sub-areas are invited to submit manuscripts of mono-graph or book length to the series editor. Edited collections of origi-nal papers resulting from conferences will also be considered.

VOLUMES IN THE SERIES

Vol. I   Discourse Production and Comprehension. Roy O. Freedle (Ed.), 1977.

Introduction

This is the third—and last—of the three volumes in the series entitled *Meaning and Choice in Language: Studies for Michael Halliday.* Volume 1, edited by Ruqaiya Hasan and Jim Martin, was called *Language Development: Learning Language, Learning Culture.* A second volume, *Discourse in Society: Systemic Functional Perspectives,* was edited by Peter Fries and Michael Gregory. The present volume completes the trio, offering a range of "systemic functional interpretations" of "meaning and form" in lexicogrammar.[1]

This particular series of festschrift volumes was originally conceived almost a decade ago, the original planning group consisting of Berry, Fawcett, Fries, Gregory, Hasan, and Martin. The volumes consist of specially invited contributions from those whose work, in the views of the editors, belonged most closely in what one might call "the Hallidayan tradition."

But what is "the Hallidayan tradition"? Rather as Michael himself is fond of pointing out in relation to language, there are no hard and fast lines to be drawn here. Indeed, Michael's influence has been

---

[1]The three original editors of this volume (Berry, Butler, and Fawcett) are very grateful to Dr. Guowen Huang for coming to our help at this time of ever-increasing administrative work in British—and no doubt other—universities. It is his editorial work in collaboration with RPF that has finally brought this important volume through to its successful publication. It is peculiarly fitting, in a publication that was prepared in the year when we paid tribute to the important place of China in the family of systemic linguists by holding the 22nd International Systemic Functional Congress in Beijing (1995), that a representative of China should be an editor of this volume. Two other gains from the otherwise regrettable delay are (a) that the *Second Edition* of Halliday's *Introduction to Functional Grammar* (IFG) appeared in 1994, thus making most references to IFG in this volume more up to date, and (b) it has enabled us to include a number of important new contributors to systemic functional lexicogrammar who would otherwise have been unrepresented.

such that the world of linguistics and the many worlds of applied linguistics are full of scholars and teachers who could justifiably say they work in the "Hallidayan tradition"—or at least say "I have been strongly influenced by Halliday." It is for this reason that a second series of volumes has also appeared, enabling many more of those who know Michael and who appreciate the vital role that he has played in 20th-century linguistics to pay their respects to him through the traditional academic ritual-genre of the festschrift. Thus we would recommend to readers of this volume not only the two sister volumes of *Meaning and Choice in Language: Studies for Michael Halliday*, but also the two volumes of *Language Topics: Essays in Honour of Michael Halliday* (Vols. 1 and 2, edited by Ross Steele and Terry Threadgold).

Michael Halliday's interests have ranged widely through many aspects of language, as the chapters in his five volumes of festschrift demonstrate more clearly than could any mere list of topics. But it was in grammar that his impact on the field of linguistics was first felt, about 35 years ago, with his seminal "Categories of the Theory of Grammar" (1961). And it is interesting to find him writing in the Introduction of *An Introduction to Function Grammar: Second Edition* (1994) as follows:

> Twenty years ago, when the mainstream of linguistics was in what has been called its 'syntactic age', it was necessary to argue against grammar, pointing out that it was not the beginning and end of all study of language and that one could go a long way towards understanding the nature and functions of language without any understanding of language at all. . . .
>
> Now, however, it is necessary to argue the opposite case, and to insist on the importance of grammar in linguistic analysis. If I now appear as a champion of grammar, it is not because I have changed my mind on the issue, but because the issue has changed. The current preoccupation is with discourse analysis, or 'text linguistics'; and it is sometimes assumed that it can be carried on without grammar—or as an alternative to grammar. But this is an illusion. A discourse analysis that is not based on grammar is not an analysis at all, but simply a running commentary on a text. (p. xvi)

In the last decade, Michael Halliday's major contribution to asserting the centrality of grammar in understanding the nature of language has been through writing the book that is affectionately known to most of its users simply as "IFG." First we had the original *An Introduction to Functional Grammar*, published in 1985, and then the *Second Edition*, published in 1994, which incorporates a number of significant minor changes and clarifications, and is now the definitive version.

We have asked the contributors to this volume to relate their work, where it is natural to do so, to the equivalent portion of IFG (preferably the *Second Edition*). Similarly, we have followed the structure of IFG—as far as we could—in relating the contributions to this volume to each other. Thus you will find chapters on transitivity in Tagalog and Gooniyandi alongside chapters on transitivity in English, and chapters on time and tense in Polish, Spanish and English grouped together. This illustrates nicely the way that SFG is increasingly being used for work on other languages than English—an important facet of the current developments in the theory. The languages represented here are Chinese, English, German, Gooniyandi, Polish, and Spanish (with references to other European languages besides German in Steiner's chapter). Descriptive work in SFG is currently going on in many other languages, including Arabic, Hindi, Japanese and the other major languages of the world—as well as in many of those that are less widely spoken. And we even have a chapter by Davies that illustrates the other physical dimension along which languages vary from each other—i.e., the dimension of time.

Thus Part I of this volume is on the *clause*, exactly as in IFG. There are three chapters on *textual meaning and form*—all, as it happens, on theme. Berry states her "personal" views on this topic; Huang introduces the "non-contrastive" type of "experiential enhanced theme" (the reasons for this new terminology for "predicted theme" and "cleft-construction" being explained); and Davies traces theme at earlier stages of the English language.

The section on *interpersonal meaning and form* includes an assessment by Butler of the status of the interpersonal component as a meta-function; a chapter on modality in Chinese by Zhu; and one by Poynton on the so far under-studied area of "attitude" (including "affective" meaning). Even though the realizations of "attitude" are mainly in the nominal group, we place it here because she also points to the "prosodic" realizations throughout a text.

In the part entitled *Experiential Meaning and Form* the chapters provide discussions of transitivity in Tagalog (Martin), of relational processes in Gooniyandi and English by McGregor and Davidse, and "complementation" by Fawcett—who offers here the first SFG account of this important phenomenon. Davidse's chapter takes up Halliday's concern with the relationship between "grammar" and "grammatics" in this context.

Following the IFG view that matters such as time and tense belong *below the clause,* we have placed in Part II three chapters on this topic: one on English by Matthiessen, one on Polish by Gotteri, and one on Spanish and English by Downing.

There then follows a section on *lexis and the nominal group.* This includes a chapter by Tucker describing the first large-scale attempt to implement Halliday's (1961) proposal that we should treat "lexis as most delicate grammar" (see also Fawcett's chapter), and also one by Prakasam on *of*-constructions in the nominal group.

In Part III, *Above the Clause,* Parsons describes a quantitative study of the relations between cohesion and coherence.

Finally, in Part IV, we have had to step outside the framework of IFG—while continuing its spirit—as we go *across languages.* In this chapter Steiner shows a number of fascinating glimpses of the value of SFG in machine translation.

Michael Halliday's contribution to linguistics is unique. It is not just the immense fruitfulness and challenge of his linguistic insights that gives him this pre-eminent position, nor is it simply the combination of these and the way that he has been able to develop simplifying models of the extraordinarily complex phenomenon that a human language is. It is also the way he presents his ideas, the way in which he "does linguistics" with those around him—the "interpersonal" side of language, in the metaphor of the lexicogrammar.[2]

One of the greatest gifts that Michael has given to those of us who are proud to call ourselves "Hallidayan" linguists is that he does not place a straightjacket on us. He himself is always willing to try a new way of looking at some phenomenon, and even at times disappoints those students who want a clear answer to the question: "Is it this or is it that?" The fact that he will often say, with all the authority of his immense experience of analyzing and thinking about language, "It could be either," can be both frustrating and, at the same time, liberating. It is because this spirit of open-minded inquiry is now an integral part of the systemic functional way of "doing linguistics" that you will find, in these pages, good "paid-up" systemic functional linguists who are nevertheless exploring a somewhat different approach to some phenomenon from that proposed in IFG.

A linguistic theory should be a living, growing thing, which none-

---

[2]Notice that this really is a "metaphorical" use of the term; what we are actually referring to here is the "interactional" USE, or PURPOSE, or FUNCTION of language, i.e., something that lies "above" the meta-functional organization of language itself. This distinction is brought out clearly in Halliday's *Learning How to Mean* (1975).

theless remains true to its essential principles. The principles of systemic functional linguistics are captured in the name we have chosen for this series: *Meaning and Choice in Language*. And it is in large measure due to the spirit in which Michael does his linguistics that systemic functional linguistics is flourishing today more strongly than ever. Not many scholars deserve—let alone receive—five volumes of festschrift. Michael Halliday does and, when the present volume is finally placed in his hands, he will have achieved yet another rare—and richly deserved—distinction.

RF, MB, CB, GH

February 7, 1995

REFERENCES

Fries, P., & Gregory, M. (Eds.). (1995). *Discourse in society: Systemic functional perspectives.* Volume in the series *Meaning and Choice in Language: Studies for Michael Halliday.* Norwood, NJ: Ablex.

Halliday, M.A.K. (1961). Categories of the theory of grammar. *Word, 17,* 241–292.

Halliday, M.A.K. (1975). *Learning how to mean.* London: Arnold.

Halliday, M.A.K. (1985). *An introduction to functional grammar.* London: Arnold.

Halliday, M.A.K. (1994). *An introduction to functional grammar (Second edition).* London: Arnold.

Hasan, R., & Martin, J.R. (Eds.). (1989). *Language development: Learning language, learning culture.* Volume in the series *Meaning and Choice in Language: Studies for Michael Halliday.* Norwood, NJ: Ablex.

Steele, R. & Threadgold, T. (Eds.). (1987). *Language topics: Essays in honour of Michael Halliday* (Vols. 1 and 2). Amsterdam: Benjamins.

Part I
The Clause

A:
Textual Meaning and Form

1

What Is Theme?— A(nother) Personal View[1]*

Margaret Berry

University of Nottingham

1. INTRODUCTION

Huddleston (1991: 95) distinguishes between "Theme$_E$" (Theme considered as expression) and "Theme$_C$" (Theme considered as content) and asks the questions: How is Theme$_E$ determined? What

*I am grateful to fellow members of the Nottingham research team for discussion of points relevant to this chapter: Ronald Carter (co-director of the main project), Caroline Stainton (principal researcher), James Bones, Ching-Hui Chi, Carmen Foz, Timothy Gibson, Hilary Hillier, Abdulla Isa, Philippa Jeffrey, Dirk Noel, Almein O'Neal, Gerald Parsons, Dawn Wright, Jiafeng Zhang. Thanks are also due to those of my M.A. and B.A. students who have discussed Theme with me and who have carried out project work in this area, and to members of audiences to whom I have given earlier versions of this paper. I am also very grateful to those who provided the evidence on which the chapter is based: the University of Nottingham for permitting me to use passages from their publications; the members of the University who consented to be interviewed about the publications; and above all to the Bristol University Writing Research Group, who volunteered to act as informants. Thank you too to Ann Collins for her assistance with the word-processing of the table. Finally I would like to express my thanks to Huddleston (1991) and to Matthiessen and Martin (1991) for engaging in the debate which acted as the point of departure for my own discussion here.

[1]Fries (1995) is subtitled *A personal view of Theme*. I *think* I shall be largely in agreement with Fries in what I shall be saying in the present chapter. However, Theme is a field in which one can never be entirely sure whether or not one is agreeing with someone else. Hence the brackets in my title.

does it mean to say of some "x" that "x" is $Theme_C$? How is $Theme_C$ determined, and what is the relation between $Theme_C$ and $Theme_E$? What is the constituent structure assigned to a clause with multiple $Theme_E$? What is the nature of the empirical evidence supporting the analysis? The present chapter will consider lines along which such questions might be answered.[2]

A cautionary note is necessary immediately, however. My own perspective on language and language study is very different from that of Huddleston. I am a systemic functional linguist who is also a text linguist—a text linguist, furthermore, who is interested in the applications of text linguistics. Huddleston, as I read him, is a syntactician. It is my view that his questions about Theme are important questions from my perspective as well as from his; otherwise, I would not be attempting to answer them. However, it is likely that they are important to my concerns in a slightly different way from the way in which they are important to Huddleston's. In order to alert first myself and then readers to possible problems that may arise from these differences in perspective, I will first outline what I consider the main differences to be, before reconsidering the questions in the light of the differences, and then proceeding to the matter of how to provide answers.

The discussion of differences in perspective also has a further purpose. This article is to appear in a volume that is one of a series designed to celebrate the work of Michael Halliday. It is generally recognized that one of the great strengths of Halliday's work is its applicability to text analysis. Hudson (1986: 793), for instance, notes that Halliday's work, when viewed from the perspective of text analysis, provides "something which no other school has to offer." While it is not true that all those who analyze texts are text linguists in the sense in which I shall be using the term here, the reverse does apply; all text linguists must be able to analyze texts. It is not surprising, therefore, that text linguists such as myself are conscious of

---

[2]Fries (1995) had a rather different list of questions regarding Theme: (a) Exactly what does Theme mean? Is there a single unified meaning for all the sorts of information which have thematic status? (b) Which units have Themes and what is the relation between Themes at the various ranks? (c) Exactly how much of a clause (or other unit) counts as Theme? (d) How does Theme interact with other functions (e.g. Subject, Topic, Given, New)? (e) How is Theme realized and used in languages other than Modern English? (f) How should Theme be integrated into the Systemic networks? I shall be discussing matters relevant to some of Fries' questions, but I shall mainly be focusing on Huddleston's questions. It would clearly be overambitious to attempt to address two sets of questions in one paper.

a debt to Halliday. In the course of my discussion of a text linguistic perspective, I hope to show something of the enormous debt that I, like so many other text linguists, owe to Halliday and to his innovatory approach to text analysis.

2. THE DIFFERENCES BETWEEN THE AIMS AND OBJECTIVES OF A SYSTEMIC FUNCTIONAL TEXT LINGUIST AND THOSE OF A SYNTACTICIAN

In this section, I will first indicate what I take to be the aims and objectives of a text linguist, then consider the special needs of a text linguist concerned with the applications of text linguistics. I will then go on to show how Halliday's systemic functional approach is ideally suited to meet these needs.

2.1. The Aims and Objectives of a Text Linguist

De Beaugrande and Dressler (1981: 3), in their *Introduction to Text Linguistics*, described their aims as follows: "We ought to find out what standards texts must fulfill, how they might be produced or received, what people are using them for in a given setting of occurrence." From this it is clear that text linguistics is about *texts*. This might seem to be a self-evident observation, but it needs to be emphasized since it so often seems to be assumed by linguists that all linguistic inquiry is, or should be, about *syntax* as evidenced in *sentences*. The following points need to be made clear:

1. In text linguistics, what is being investigated is the nature of *texts*, not the nature of syntax. One of the main long-term aims of a text linguist is to show what makes the difference between a text and a miscellaneous set of sentences.

2. The typology that concerns a text linguist is the typology of *texts*, not the typology of languages. Typology does in fact play a large part in text linguistic studies. De Beaugrande and Dressler (1981: 1–3) emphasize this by opening their first chapter with a set of six texts that they say "appear to be alike in some ways and different in others." They then comment, "It seems reasonable to require that a science of texts should be able to describe or explain both the shared features and the distinctions among these texts or text types."

3. Text linguistics is a contextualizing, not a decontextualizing study. As my first quotation from de Beaugrande and Dressler makes clear, the aim is to explain the nature of texts and the similarities and differences between text types *in relation to* the people who produce and receive the texts, the purposes for which the texts are used, and the settings in which the texts occur.

4. Informant intuitions play an important part in text linguistics, as they do in syntax. However, the informant intuitions that are relevant to text linguistics are evaluations of *texts* rather than judgements as to the grammaticality of sentences. For example, a particular study may have as its objective the identification of textual features that would account for the views of informants that Texts X and Y of a particular set are more suitable for a particular purpose or for a particular audience than Texts W and Z.

5. Whenever possible in text linguistics, the informants are genuine producers or receivers of the text type under consideration.

In emphasizing the differences between text linguistics and syntax, I do not, of course, intend to suggest that the work of syntacticians is *irrelevant* to text linguistics—far from it. But it is important to make clear that, in text linguistics, sentence-based work is a means to an end, not an end in itself.

2.2. The Needs of an Applied Text Linguist

I have described myself as a text linguist who is interested in the applications of text linguistics. More accurately, perhaps, I should have described myself as an applied text linguist. Widdowson (1984: 21) distinguished between "applied linguistics" and "linguistics applied." In linguistics applied one does one's linguistics first and, when one comes to apply the work, "the informing principles which define this area of enquiry, already pre-established, must remain intact," regardless of the fact that the models of description derived from these principles are often not suitable for the applicational work in which one is engaged. In applied linguistics one *starts* by considering what models of language are relevant to the applicational ends of one's study. In particular, one considers what models of description are relevant to the intended *users* of one's work. There is little point in presenting the findings of one's study if they are such that they have no meaning for the intended recipients. Although accepting that linguistics applied can be of *some* benefit in applied language work, Widdowson concluded (1984: 27) "that it is only by preferring applied linguistics to linguistics applied that we shall achieve something which is relevant and accountable in terms of usefulness and avoid the kind of ethnocentrism and cultural imposition that has marked so much of language study and teaching in the past."

The applicational work in which I am myself currently engaged, together with colleagues in Nottingham, is a description of the written language of business and industry intended to assist teachers in British schools, colleges and universities to prepare students for work in business and industrial fields (see e.g. Berry 1995, in press; Gibson, 1993; Stainton in press a, b, c, d, e, f). The intended *users* of the description are thus teachers. The gathering of the information also entails talking to other non-linguists, to professionals in the fields of business and industry. It is therefore essential that the inquiry be conducted in such a way that it will have meaning for teachers, and it is at least desirable that it have meaning also for professionals in business and industry.

Dixon, for long regarded—since the publication of his influential book *Growth through English* (1967)—as a leader of and spokesman for British teachers, in a more recent publication (1987) set out his own aims for English teaching and made clear what kind of assistance he would like from linguists. The following points would seem to be particularly worth noting:

1. Dixon's observations were in the context of a discussion of *genre*. He was evidently happy with an approach that focused on texts—he expressed gratitude (1987: 11) for an analysis of a text by Christie (1985)—and on different types of texts.

2. However, he wanted the discussion to be in terms of "making meanings," rather than in terms of linguistic forms (1987: 12–13 and 16–17). This is in line with a view that teachers frequently express in conversation. Like many other non-linguists, teachers are impatient with what they see as linguists' preoccupation with *form;* for them what language is all about is *meaning*. This does not mean that they show no interest at all in form. Dixon (1987: 14) made it clear that he was prepared to take an interest in forms if these were presented as the realizations of meanings—if their status as means to the end of making meanings was made evident.

3. Dixon (1987: 10) also emphasized the importance of viewing language as *choice*. For him, a teacher's aims include becoming aware of "the wide range of . . . choices available in the language" and then helping students similarly to become aware of this wide range of choices.
4. He added that he further wished to help students by "teaching them (on specific occasions) the difficulties or constraints entailed by a given choice." This must surely involve distinguishing different "occasions" (contexts) and relating the different choices to these different occasions.

The views of professionals in the fields of business and industry are perhaps rather less clear. Usually, initially they just want to talk about spelling or "grammar" (by which they mean such things as subject–verb agreements, or lack of them). However once one gets beyond this stage and begins to look with them at actual instances of writing intended for a business/industrial context, the criticisms they offer of the writing are frequently of the following types: that the writing is too personal/impersonal; that the structure of the text is not sufficiently clearly signalled for readers to be able to process it quickly—speed being essential in a business or industrial setting. Here they seem to be touching on matters that Dixon would regard as relevant to making meanings. Impersonality is discussed (Dixon 1987: 15) in association with consideration of the construction of a "tone of voice." Structuring writing also receives a mention (1987: 17–18). Both seem to be issues that have to do with "sense of audience" or "communicative role" (1987: 14).

Encouraging for the text linguist is the fact that often the judgements expressed by business and industrial professionals are context and text-type related. A piece of writing may be criticized, for example, as too personal for a report intended for the Board of Directors, or too impersonal for a letter intended to persuade someone to cooperate.

It would seem that, for both teachers and professionals in business and industry, a text linguistic approach, with its concern for text types and their relation to producers, receivers and settings, does stand some chance of being perceived as relevant to their own concerns. Additional requirements, particularly for the teachers, are: that meaning must be emphasized rather than form; and that the study must contribute to an understanding of the choices available in the language.

2.3. The Relevance of Systemic Functional Linguistics

Anyone familiar with Halliday's work will already have realized that his systemic functional linguistics is just such an approach as is required. It is designed to be applicable to texts, it comes complete with a theory of text—context relations, it gives priority to meaning, it provides a theory of language as choice. I will discuss each of these points in turn.

2.3.1. Applicability of systemic functional linguistics (SFL) to texts

Not many linguists set out specifically to write a grammar that bears in mind the needs of those who wish to analyze texts. Halliday does. The aim of his *Introduction to Functional Grammar* (1985/94: xv) (IFG) was explicitly stated to be "to construct a grammar for purposes of text analysis: one that would make it possible to say sensible and useful things about any text, spoken or written, in modern English."

As I have said, not all text analysts are necessarily text linguists in the sense in which I am using the term here. It is, for instance, perfectly possible to analyze texts with a view to investigating the nature of syntax. It just so happens that as a text linguist I am more interested in investigating the nature of texts. In IFG, Halliday had in mind the needs of a wide variety of text analysts. He discussed possible uses of text analysis briefly (page xv) and then later (pages xxix–xxx) in more detail lists 21 different potential purposes. One of these comes very close to the aims I have listed above for text linguistics: "To understand the quality of texts: why a text means what it does, and why it is valued as it is." Text linguists share with other text analysts their gratitude to Halliday for designing a grammar suited to the needs of text analysis, and are pleased to be included among the kinds of text analysts whose aims he has in mind.

Elsewhere, particularly in his work with Ruqaiya Hasan (Halliday and Hasan, 1976, 1985/89), Halliday's own aims were, to a large extent, those of a text linguist. The opening paragraph of Halliday and Hasan (1976) made this quite explicit: "If a speaker of English hears or reads a passage of the language which is more than one sentence in length, he can normally decide without difficulty whether it forms a unified whole or is just a collection of unrelated sentences. This book is about what makes the difference between the two."

2.3.2. SFL as a theory of text–context relations

An inquiry into what makes the difference between a text and a set of miscellaneous sentences very soon leads to a consideration of context. For Halliday and Hasan (1976: 23), "A text is a passage of discourse which is coherent in these two regards: it is coherent with respect to the context of situation, and therefore consistent in register; and it is coherent with respect to itself, and therefore cohesive." In the 1976 book, Halliday and Hasan were concerned with the second of these two aspects of text. Alongside this work (see especially Halliday 1975, 1977; Halliday and Hasan 1985/89; Hasan 1978) they were developing a theory of the relations between texts and their contexts.

If I am to assist Dixon and other teachers in alerting students to "the difficulties and constraints" associated with "specific occasions," I must not only be able to describe texts; I must also be able to describe occasions of use (i.e. contexts) and relations and interactions between the texts and the contexts. Halliday and Hasan provided a theory in the framework of which such a description may be attempted.

In its theory of text–context relations, then, SFL is relevant both to the theoretical aims of text linguistics and, more particularly, to the applicational work in which I am myself at present engaged.

2.3.3. Meaning-centered inquiry as opposed to form-centered

The point that comes out strongest of all from Dixon's article and from discussions with British teachers is that, for them, language is a matter of *meaning.* Form is only of interest in so far as it is a means to the end of making/discovering meaning. This is indeed the point of view of most non-linguists. My English department students make it very clear to me that they are only prepared to pay any attention to linguistic forms if I can show them that there is some relevance to what they take to be the main purpose of language, namely meaning. If I am to make any sense at all when I come to present my findings to teachers, I am going to have to start with meanings, introducing matters of form only when I can show how the forms are related to the meanings.

Here again, Halliday's work is ideally suited to my purpose. He himself drew attention to precisely this issue of directionality. In IFG (1985/1994: xiv) he discussed the difference in directionality between the investigations of syntacticians and those of functional linguists such as systemicists. In syntax, "a language is interpreted as a system of forms, to which meanings are then attached." In a systemic functional grammar, on the other hand, "the direction is reversed. A language is interpreted as a system of meanings, accompanied by forms through which the meanings can be realized." As Halliday pointed out, "This puts the forms of a language in a different perspective: as means to an end, rather than as an end in themselves."

Halliday, then, is in complete accord with the teachers for whom my description is intended. Furthermore, Halliday's particular approach to the study of meaning looks very promising from the point of view of accounting for the judgements of the professionals in business and industry whose evaluations of texts I am hoping to explain to the teachers. In my view one of the most valuable of Halliday's contributions has been to distinguish different types of meaning. These are sometimes presented under the heading of a threefold distinction: ideational, interpersonal, textual (e.g. IFG 1985: 53); sometimes under the heading of a fourfold distinction: experiential, interpersonal, textual, logical (e.g. IFG 1994: 36). The two that look most promising for my purpose remain constant. As I indicated above, the most frequent judgements of professionals in business and industry have to do with (a) (im)personality and (b) clarity of text structure. When attempting to account for the former type of judgement, it would seem sensible to begin with interpersonal meaning, defined by Halliday (IFG 1994: 36) as "enacting social relationships." When attempting to account for the latter type of judgement, it would seem sensible to begin with textual meaning, defined by Halliday (IFG 1994: 36) as "creating relevance to context." (I am assuming that here "relevance to context" includes relevance to co-text—relevance to surrounding text—as well as relevance to context of situation as discussed above.)

Most approaches to the study of meaning privilege ideational meaning ("meaning in the sense of 'content'"—IFG 1985: 53). Halliday not only distinguishes other types of meaning, he gives them parity of treatment. As a text linguist, I am generally more concerned with interpersonal meaning and textual meaning than with ideational meaning, and interpersonal and textual meaning certainly look more relevant than ideational meaning to my current research.

2.3.4. SFL as a theory of meaning as choice

The second point about which Dixon feels particularly strongly (1987: 10–11, 16–17)—and again this is backed up by discussions with teachers—is that language should be discussed in such a way as to reveal linguistic choices and consequently to open up choices for students, not in such a way as to give the impression of prescribing structures and consequently to appear to be closing things down. In linguistic terms, what seems to be required is an approach that emphasizes paradigmatic relations rather than syntagmatic relations. Teachers can no doubt be persuaded to take an interest in syntagmatic relations, but, as in the case of form and meaning, only if the investigation of syntagmatic relations can be shown to be a means to the end of shedding light on paradigmatic relations.

Changing the emphasis in linguistic description from syntagmatic relations to paradigmatic relations is another innovation for which text analysts and others are indebted to Halliday. As Hudson (1986: 810) noted, "features (i.e. paradigmatic categories) have been one of the main focuses of interest" in SFL "since the early days" and the SFL treatment of such categories "is superior to what we find in other current theories." Halliday himself (IFG 1985/1994: xiv) described SFL as "a theory of meaning as choice, by which a language, or any other semiotic system, is interpreted as networks of interlocking options." In Halliday's early work (e.g. 1967, 1968), networks of options were central to his description. This is perhaps slightly less true of his later work; for instance, there are few networks of options in IFG. However, even here the networks of options are implied, if not expressed, and can be reconstructed. It is indeed the underlying systemic description that has motivated the structural description.[3]

Certainly, I would myself still wish the paradigmatically related options to be central to any inquiry. I have always seen it as one of the most useful aspects of systemic linguistics that it enables one to model speaker/writer choice (see e.g. Berry 1975: 61). Not only are system networks useful in applicational work; they also make possible visual representation of the similarities and differences between texts and text types which de Beaugrande and Dressler indicated (see section 2.1. above) are central to the work of the theoretical text linguist. Halliday once said that systemic linguistics is all about showing that things are alike but different.[4] It is the system network that makes this possible.

---

[3]Hudson (1986: 801) similarly commented on the apparent change of emphasis in Halliday (1985). The fact that for a while it was the fashion not to include system networks in SFL writings may explain why Dixon, though asking for an approach that emphasized meaning and choice, apparently did not recognize that SFL is such an approach. I should probably admit immediately that there will be no system networks in the present chapter. However, see Berry (1995) for related discussions that do include systemic networks.

[4]In a talk to the Nottingham Linguistic Circle.

All in all, it can be of no surprise that text linguists find Halliday's work so useful, or that Widdowson (1984: 26), asking for a move from linguistics applied to applied linguistics, regards Halliday as "pointing us . . . in the direction we might go." In this connection, Widdowson cites particularly Halliday (1964) and (1969).

3. HUDDLESTON'S QUESTIONS RECONSIDERED IN THE LIGHT OF THE DIFFERENCES

In light of the above discussion, let me now return to Huddleston's questions about Theme, first considering aspects of the questions that are in keeping with the approach I have outlined above, and then proceeding to aspects over which there is likely to be difficulty.

If as a text linguist I am going to be able to analyze the clauses of texts in terms of Theme and Rheme, I am certainly going to need to know what it means to say that something is Theme and I am certainly going to need to know how Theme is determined. Furthermore, it is helpful for my purpose that Huddleston's questions make clear that there is a meaning aspect to Theme and also a formal aspect. Indeed this is implied by Halliday himself (IFG 1985: 39; 1994: 38). Clearly one also needs to know the relation between the meaning aspect and the formal aspect. And in any study, if one is going to draw conclusions—particularly in my case where the conclusions are to be the basis of advice to teachers—one needs to know the nature of the empirical evidence on which the conclusions are based.

However, the following problems would seem to arise, the first two being relatively easy to solve, the third much more difficult:

1. In my discussion of Theme, for the reasons given above, I would want to be seen to be proceeding in the direction of meaning to form. I shall therefore reorder Huddleston's questions so that the meaning aspect of Theme is, at least in the first instance, addressed before the formal aspect.

2. I would also want to be seen to be addressing matters of interpersonal and textual meaning as much as, if not more than, matters of ideational meaning. It is possible that Huddleston's term *content*, as in *Theme$_C$*, may be interpreted as privileging ideational meaning. As I have shown above, in at least one of his own glosses, Halliday associates the term *content* with ideational meaning, and certainly my students regularly seem to interpret it in this way. The term *expression* also

seemed to cause confusion in one seminar at which I gave an earlier version of this paper. Therefore, while accepting, indeed welcoming, Huddleston's distinction, I shall prefer to use the terms Theme$_M$ (Theme considered as meaning) and Theme$_F$ (Theme considered as form).

3.   Much more difficult to solve are problems relating to my wish to give priority to paradigmatic relations rather than syntagmatic relations. I suspect that this is the point on which I am most at variance with Huddleston. Certainly I am not concerned, as he is, with constituency per se. Nevertheless I cannot afford to ignore issues of constituency; one can never totally separate an investigation of paradigmatic relations from an investigation of syntagmatic relations, and in any case I have already indicated above that I would wish to make use of an investigation into syntagmatic relations as a means to the end of shedding light on paradigmatic relations. This indeed is how a text linguist usually does work; one's end may be to reveal the meaning choices made by the producer(s) of a text/text-type, but one of the means to this end is usually a syntagmatic analysis of the text. A regular problem in SFL is how to reconcile the wish to give priority to issues of choice with the need to analyze texts syntagmatically. Halliday (IFG 1985: xxxii–xxxiv, 1994: xxxii–xxxiii) discussed the problem of how to define syntagmatic categories when they are motivated by paradigmatic distinctions. This is particularly a problem in relation to interpersonal and textual meaning (Halliday IFG 1994: 36) since it is hypothesized that these types of meaning are not realized by constituent structures, but by "prosodic" and "culminative" structures that cannot in the same way be analyzed into discrete segments. I expect to encounter this problem in my subsequent discussion. However, problematic or not, segmentable or not, if I want to be able to analyze texts in terms of interpersonal and textual meaning, I *have* to be able to work out some way of relating the structures of the texts to the interpersonal and textual meaning choices they are assumed to be representing. Huddleston's question about constituency may well prove to be a catalyst in this endeavor.

The slightly revised version of Huddleston's questions that I shall be considering is thus as follows:

1.   What does it mean to say of some x that x is Theme$_M$?
2.   How is Theme$_M$ determined?

3. What does it mean to say of some x that x is Theme$_F$?
4. How is Theme$_F$ determined?
5. What is the relation between Theme$_M$ and Theme$_F$?
6. What is the constituent structure of a clause with multiple Theme$_F$?
7. What is the nature of the empirical evidence supporting the analysis?

Throughout the discussion it should be remembered that I am not claiming fully to answer the questions, merely to consider lines along which answers might be attempted. A vast amount more research will be necessary before answers can be confidently given.

4. THE PASSAGES FOR EXEMPLIFICATION

4.1. The Texts From Which the Passages Will Be Taken

The main exemplification will be from a set of texts published by the University of Nottingham: the University's *Prospectus*, the Department of English Studies' booklet *English Studies at Nottingham*, and the Faculty of Arts' *Handbook*. As I have said, text linguistics is a contextualizing rather than a decontextualizing study and it is therefore necessary to say something of the background to the texts. The discussion here will be brief, however, as this is intended primarily as a theoretical article rather than as a discussion of the texts per se. These texts have been discussed in greater detail in Berry (in press).

The *Prospectus* is normally the university publication that prospective students see first; usually they will consult copies available in their schools when deciding to which universities to apply. Sometimes prospective students write in for individual copies.

Those prospective students who apply to the Department of English Studies and to whom places are offered are invited to attend open days in the department. *English Studies at Nottingham* is given out at these open days. It is possible that a few of the prospective students will already have seen it as it is sometimes sent out in reply to individual enquiries addressed to the department. The booklet was originally drafted by one member of the department staff, circulated for comment and revised. Further revisions have been made since to take account of course changes. The main author of the booklet, when interviewed, said that his aims were "not just to convey information, but to communicate a tone of voice, an atmosphere; to try not to sound like an official publication, but to sound accessible." When asked to characterize the tone of voice at which he was aiming, he said "non-stuffy, feet on the ground, prepared to be interested in other people, not ivory towered, familiar, friendly."

The *Handbook* is given out to students when they first arrive at the university to begin their courses. The Secretary of the Faculty of Arts, when asked what were the aims of the *Handbook*, said first, "Do you mean the Regulations?" The publication frequently is referred to in this way, although the title that appears on its cover is simply *Handbook*. Once this had been agreed, the aims were said to be "to provide factual information on basic requirements of the course." It was emphasized that the approach was a "minimalist" one—only the "barebones" of the courses were given, but with indications as to where to find further information. The work is multiply authored. A sub-committee of the Board for Undergraduate Studies (known locally as BUGS) devised the format for departmental entries; it was considered important that there should be a member of the Law Department on this sub-committee. Departments draft their own entries and revise them each year. The entries/revisions are considered by the Faculty Board or the Business Committee of the Faculty Board and referred back to departments if not in accordance with general requirements. The Faculty Secretary coordinates these activities.

4.2. Informant Judgements Relevant to the Texts

Three types of interviewing/informant testing are planned/in process in connection with these texts:

1. As will be clear from what has been said already, interviews with producers of the texts are already in progress. The main objectives of these interviews are to elicit information on: (a) the methods and procedures of production; and (b) the main aims and purposes of the texts as viewed by the producers.

2. Interviews/informant tests for genuine readers of the texts—students and prospective students—are currently being designed. The main aim of these will be to see to what extent, in the view of the readers, the producers have succeeded in their aims, to what extent they have produced texts appropriate to their purposes.

3. A further type of informant test would seem to be necessary. Since I am going to be concerned particularly with the interpersonal and textual meaning conveyed by the texts, with amounts, degrees and types of interpersonal and textual meaning, I need to know whether other readers perceive the same amounts, degrees and types as I do myself and, for the purpose of relating the meanings to the forms, whether they perceive the meanings as expressed in the same places in the texts. This is proving a difficult type of informant test to design. Eventually I would hope to find a way of eliciting the views of genuine writers and readers of the texts on these matters. However, in the meantime, it would seem sensible to experiment with tests for fellow linguists—to elicit the judgements of expert witnesses, as it were. Eight members of the Writing Research Group at the University of Bristol kindly volunteered to take part in an experiment. This was conducted as follows:

   a. Each member of the group was given a copy of passages from the texts and asked to underline the words and phrases that they perceived to be contributing to the communication of interpersonal meaning. The only clue they were given at this stage to what was intended by this instruction was Halliday's (IFG 1994: 36) definition of interpersonal meaning as "enacting social relationships."

   b. They were then invited to compare notes and discuss the judgements they had made. The main effect of the discussion seemed to be to broaden views of what could come under the heading of "enacting social relationships." Collectively they were aware of more types of interpersonal meaning than most members of the group had been individually.

   c. They were then given an opportunity to record changes in their own thinking that had resulted from the discussion by using broken underlining to add further words and phrases to those perceived as communicating interpersonal meaning, and/or by annotating their judgements.

(4), (5), (6) The three steps—(1), (2) and (3)—were then repeated for textual meaning.

Brief references to this experiment will be made in the present chapter. More detailed discussion can be found in Berry (in press).

For a discussion of the desirability of combining different methods of obtaining informants' views, see Gibson (1993: chapter 2).

4.3. The Passages to be Discussed
in the Present Chapter

One passage from each publication will be discussed here in some detail. The passages for detailed discussion are the passages in which the respective publications introduce the third year courses of the Department of English Studies. Since the content of the passages is basically the same, it will be possible to focus on ways in which the handling of the content differs in relation to aims and purposes.

The passages for detailed discussion are as follows:

Passage 1, from the *Prospectus*
Passage 2, from *English Studies at Nottingham*
Passage 3, from the *Handbook*

(It should perhaps be explained that in the Faculty of Arts at Nottingham, the Part II course is normally the third year course.)

Passage 1, from the *Prospectus*

In the third year all students are required to take two modules in Medieval English Literature. They then choose a further six core modules either from nineteenth and twentieth century literature and drama, or from early English literature and English language. In addition a choice of special subjects and an optional dissertation encourage students to develop interests which may be starting points for graduate research. The special subjects vary from year to year but always include modules focusing on specialist areas in modern English language and in medieval and modern literature. For example, courses may be taken in D H Lawrence studies, language and gender, Viking runes and writing for the media.

Passage 2, from *English Studies at Nottingham*

Year 3
In your third year you may choose whether to concentrate on Nineteenth and Twentieth Century Literature and Drama, Modern English Language or Early English, or a combination. Additionally, you study medieval English Literature and four modules from a wide range of special options.
In any year the special options may vary: current modules include the

Novel in Southern Africa, Irish Studies, D.H. Lawrence, Sexuality and Culture, Writing for the Media, English Place-names, Major Modern Novels, and Viking Age Runes.

Instead of taking a special option you may write a dissertation on a subject that particularly interests you—it could be a feminist study of the Icelandic sagas, exploration of the Arthurian tradition, or work on the language of children's books.

The advantage of the optional scheme in the third year is that after two years students tend to know where in the study of English their special interest or vocational interests and enjoyment lie, and thus the third year work enables them to develop skills and knowledge in their own preferred areas.

Passage 3, from the Faculty of Arts *Handbook*

Part II
120 credits of which at least 80 shall be in English.
The following modules must be taken:

    i.   Medieval English Literature: I (Q33211) (10 credits)

    ii. Medieval English Literature: II (Q33208) (10 credits)

    iii. 60 credits chosen from a range of Level B and Level 3 English Studies literature modules (Romantics to present day literature) and English Studies modules in Modern English Language, early language and medieval literature as specified by the Department.

Notes to (iii):

    a. Note: With the consent of the Head of Department, a candidate may substitute a dissertation in English of from 7,000 to 10,000 words in place of 20 credits' worth of Level B or Level 3 modules. (Q33403 or Q33401 and Q33402)

    b. With the consent of the Head of Department, a candidate may substitute one or two Project Modules (Q3B208 and Q3B216) in place of 10 or 20 credits worth of level B or Level 3 modules. Project modules must be based on modules which form part of the Part I or Part II English Studies course.

    c. No student may take both a dissertation and Project module(s) during one academic session.

5. POSSIBLE LINES ALONG WHICH THE QUESTIONS MIGHT BE ANSWERED

The preliminaries to answering the questions now being completed, let me turn to the questions themselves.

5.1. What Does it Mean to Say of Some "x" That "x" Is Theme$_M$?

Halliday (IFG 1985: 36) defines Theme as "what the message is concerned with: the point of departure for what the speaker is going to say."[5] At the end of his analysis of an actual text in terms of Theme and different types of Theme (IFG 1985/1994: 67), he says "by analysing the thematic structure of a text clause by clause, we can . . . understand how the writer made clear to us the nature of his underlying concerns."

Two points would seem to be particularly important here: that Theme has to do with the concerns of the speaker or writer; and that it is the cumulative force of the Themes of the clauses of a text that indicates these concerns, rather than the Theme of any one clause individually. It might in fact be useful to do for Theme what discourse analysts have done for Topic. Brown and Yule (1983: 71), citing Morgan (1975: 434), emphasize that "it is not sentences that have topics, but speakers." They go on, this time citing Keenan and Schieffelin (1976), to distinguish between *sentential topic,* the topic for an individual sentence, and *discourse topic,* the topic for a whole text, or at least a large section of a text, such as a paragraph. By analogy, I shall distinguish between discourse Theme$_M$ and clause Theme$_M$.[6] I shall assume that discourse Theme$_M$ is something that a speaker or writer has in relation to a text or large section of a text, a priority set of types of meaning that reflects his/her underlying concerns for the duration of the text or large section of text, and that clause Theme$_M$ is something that a speaker or writer has in relation to a particular clause, a (set of) meaning(s) that reflects his/her priority for that particular clause. If the overall priorities are to be communicated, it would seem likely that at least some of the clause priorities will reflect the overall priorities, but one would not expect it to be necessary for *all* the individual clauses to indicate the overall priorities. Indeed the writing might be regarded as rather heavy-handed if all the individual clauses *did* reflect the overall pri-

---

[5]I have selected this gloss of Halliday's in preference to glosses that include the word *about,* since the latter would seem to be in danger of being interpreted as privileging ideational meaning.

[6]In SFL the term *clause* is used where other approaches use the term *sentence.*

orities. Some of the clause Theme$_M$s may be reflecting merely very local priorities.

A further important general point, before I begin to exemplify, is that the priority concerns, discoursal or clausal, of a speaker or writer need not be ideational. This has been recognized by Brown and Yule (1983: 141–3). They first discuss passages in which the concerns do seem to be ideational, but then turn to a passage of spoken English and comment, "It is a characteristic of primarily interactional conversational speech in our data that the interactional aspect, marked by *I* and *you*, is frequently thematized. . . . This marking gives a clear indication of the speaker's view of what he is using language to do." The concerns of the speaker of Brown and Yule's data would seem to be primarily interpersonal.[7] It follows from this that discourse Theme$_M$ is in principle distinct from discourse topic, which I take to be an ideational phenomenon. The two *may* coincide. A speaker or writer's primary concerns *may* be to establish and develop a topic, or at least to include the establishment and development of a topic, but they may be quite other. Topic may be relatively unimportant. The speaker or writer's primary concerns may be interpersonal, in which case discourse Theme$_M$ has nothing to do with topic. The same applies to clause Theme$_M$ and sentential (i.e. clause) topic; these too are in principle distinct. It *may* be a priority for a particular clause to refer to an aspect of the topic, but again it need not be.[8]

Most of the exemplification of the general points in this subsection will be found in later subsections; it is difficult to exemplify at this stage until I have discussed other aspects of Theme. However, since in my experience, if one leaves one's readers for too long without exemplification, they begin to lose confidence in one, I will at least begin to exemplify here. Passage 2 above, from *English Studies at Nottingham*, would seem to be an example of a text whose writer has concerns that are primarily interpersonal. He has ideational concerns too, the communication of information, but, in his own words, his concerns are "not just to do with information," rather

---

[7]Downing (1991) also recognized interpersonal concerns, as did Davies (1988 and 1991).

[8]This would appear to be relevant to one of the examples cited by Huddleston (1988: 158): *You could buy a bar of chocolate like this for 6d before the war*, spoken to someone born after the war. It would seem likely that such an example would occur in interactional conversational speech and that therefore the same concerns would apply as in the case cited by Brown and Yule. *You* seems to be interpreted by informants as interactional even when it is not clear that it does refer to the reader/hearer (see e.g. Berry (1995: note 12).)

with "communicating a tone of voice or atmosphere." Since the tone-of voice he is communicating is "non-stuffy . . . prepared to bein-terested in other people . . . familiar, friendly," one might expect that his discourse Theme$_M$ would be/include the general typeof in-teractional meaning ascribed by Brown and Yule to their speaker. One might further expect that for at least some of his clauses it would be a priority for him to express the type of specific meaning that Brown and Yule associate with overall interactional priorities: references to participants in the discourse; in other words, one would expect some of his clause Theme$_M$s to be/include references to participants in the discourse. It therefore comes as no surprise that in the first two main clauses in the passage we find instances of one of the actual formal items—*you*—cited by Brown and Yule. However, I am now straying onto matters of form, which belong in section 5.3. and will be discussed further there.

As a preliminary answer to question 1, then, I am suggesting that, when one says of some "x" that "x" is Theme$_M$, one means that "x" is a priority meaning for the speaker or writer, reflecting con-cerns relevant to the text/section of text as a whole, or concerns relevant to a particular clause, or both.

5.2. How is Theme$_M$ Determined?

In the light of the discussion of the first question, the second ques-tion now breaks down into a series of further questions. The main questions are clearly: For any given text, or section of text, how is discourse Theme$_M$ determined? For any given clause, how is clause Theme$_M$ determined? The first of these questions splits into two more questions, since it is necessary first to determine the main concerns of the speaker/writer, and then to determine the general types of meaning that would reflect these concerns. The questions to be considered in this section are thus:

2. a. For any given text, or section of text, how is discourse Theme$_M$ determined?

       i. How are the speaker/writer's main concerns deter-mined?

      ii. On the basis of these main concerns, how can we determine the general types of meaning to be priori-tized?

  b. For any given clause, how is clause Theme$_M$ deter-mined?

5.2.1. How are the speaker/writer's main concerns determined?

The simplest way of discovering speaker/writer's main concerns is to ask the speakers/writers, the producers of the texts. As I have already indicated, the main author of *English Studies at Nottingham* was able to articulate his concerns very clearly. To recapitulate: He was concerned with conveying information, but not just with conveying information; he placed more emphasis on his concern to communicate a tone of voice, to appear friendly, willing to engage in interaction. He also said that he wanted to "sound accessible." Presumably he not only wanted his text to seem friendly, but also reader-friendly in the sense of easy to read, easy to follow.

The coordinator of the producers of the Faculty *Handbook* was similarly able to respond instantly to my questions. Again there was a concern with conveying information, but again this was not the concern that surfaced most strongly. The immediate association of the publication with "Regulations," the emphasis on the importance of involving a lawyer in the processes of production, and the need for individual entries to be approved by Faculty Board/Faculty Business Committee before publication suggest that the tone of voice here is to be regulatory, official, formal.

The coordinator of the producers of the *Prospectus* was less able to reply immediately. Certain basic matters were discussed, such as how prospective students obtained access to the publication, but further time was requested to think about questions relating to main aims and purposes and priorities in selecting style of writing. This was in part because the coordinator was busy when my first request for information was made—though so, it should be said, were the representatives of the other two publications when I approached them—and also in part because the coordinator of the *Prospectus* had only recently assumed this role and wished to consult more experienced colleagues. I am in fact still waiting for a further discussion.

Asking the producers themselves is the simplest way of discovering their main concerns, but, as has just been shown, there are sometimes problems with this procedure. Indeed, in some cases, if for instance one is working on an Old English text, asking the producer(s) of the text is even less practicable. A second possibility is to ask readers. Ideally one would ask genuine readers, those for whom the text is written, but again this may not always be practicable. As Dixon (1987: 14–15) has pointed out, reading is a matter of constructing, or reconstructing, meaning from a text, of reconstructing the writer's concerns. One needs readers who are fairly experienced at this type of reconstruction if one is to have confidence in what they say. It seems reasonable to ask less experienced readers to evaluate texts in a general way, to say whether texts written for them are appropriate to them and their concerns, but rather less reasonable to expect them to engage in the finer points of interpretation.

Fortunately I am able to draw here on the views of expert witnesses in relation to the texts I am discussing, the observations of the Bristol University Writing Research Group who took part in the experiment outlined in section 4.2. The members of the group were not told anything of what the producers had said until after the experiment was over. They were not even told what publications/type of publication the passages were from. To what extent were they able to reconstruct the concerns of the producers?

In step (b) the discussion initially focused on passage 2, the passage from *English Studies at Nottingham*. This was the passage the group had found easiest to mark up in terms of interpersonal meaning, the passage they found most obviously interpersonal.

One member of the group then suggested that it was possible to be negatively interpersonal—impersonal, lacking in any indication of interactiveness. Discussion then began to center on passage 3, from the *Handbook*. This passage was regarded as so impersonal that it was actually off-putting. Halliday's definition of interpersonal meaning (IFG 1994: 36)—"enacting social relationships"—was reconsidered. It was suggested that the writer(s) of passage 3 were enacting very different social relationships from the writer(s) of passage 2. Social relationships discussed in relation to passage 2 were those of friend–friend and teacher–taught. Social relationships discussed in relation to passage 3 were those of regulator–regulatee, examiner–examinee. There was some discussion of whether some of these relationships were ideational matters or interpersonal matters, but it was agreed that even if some of the relationships were basically ideational, nevertheless they all had interpersonal implications.

The passage that seemed to puzzle the group most was passage 1, from the *Prospectus*. This was neither as obviously interpersonal and interactive as passage 2, nor as off-puttingly impersonal as passage 3. A possible social relationship suggested for passage 1 was that of university as seller–prospective student as buyer, but the point was not made very strongly or by many voices. If such a relationship were being enacted, it would seem to be based on "soft sell" rather than "hard sell."

A further suggestion made, relevant to both passages 1 and 2, was that writer–reader should be regarded as a social relationship. This, it was thought, might be basically a textual relationship, but again it was thought to have interpersonal implications. On this basis, any words and phrases designed to help readers, or to improve the flow of the discourse were considered by some members of the group to be expressing interpersonal meaning.

It should be remembered that I did not in this experiment specifically ask members of the group to reconstruct the concerns of the writers. Nevertheless, it would seem reasonable to suggest that they came close to doing so. The recognition of the overt and positive interpersonalness of passage 2 would seem to reflect the writer's concern to communicate a "familiar" and "friendly" tone of voice. The regulatory nature of passage 3 was recognized and the extreme nature of the impersonality presumably marks it out as the language of officialdom. The fact that the group found it difficult to characterize passage 1 may suggest a further reason why I have not yet had a reply from the representative of the producers whom I attempted to question. Maybe this publication simply *is* more difficult to characterize than the other two, having less specific, more neutral concerns, this reflected in a more neutral tone of voice.

Further observations from the Bristol group that are likely to prove useful in my subsequent discussion concerned the topic—discourse topic—of the passages. Again I did not specifically ask the members of the group to characterize the topic, but characterizations were offered. The three passages were all thought to be on the same topic. The topic was generally thought to be "courses," "modules," "types of courses and modules."

My suggested answer to question 2ai, then, is: By asking the producers and, if this is not possible, by asking readers—genuine readers if practicable, but if not then "expert witness" readers. Indeed it would seem sensible to ask readers even when it *has* been possible to interview producers—as a check on the extent to which the producers have communicated their concerns to the readers. There is little point in trying to relate speaker/writer concerns to the forms of the language if the concerns have not been successfully communicated; in that case the forms probably do *not* relate to the concerns.

5.2.2. On the basis of the speaker/writer's main concerns, how can we determine the general types of meaning to be prioritized?

Of course it is necessary to do some interpretive work on the observations of producers and readers. I would suggest that the next step in the research would be to set up hypotheses on the basis of the observations, hypotheses about the general types of meaning that one would expect to be prioritized.

I have already given one example of this in section 5.1. On the basis of the stated concern of the main author of *English Studies at Nottingham* to communicate a "friendly," "familiar" tone of voice, this having now been checked by the Bristol readers' recognition of the passage from this publication as overtly and positively interpersonal, it would seem reasonable to hypothesize that the same type of meaning will be prioritized as Brown and Yule (1983: 71) noted in connection with their conversational speaker. This type of meaning would seem to consist of references to participants in the discourse. In Berry (1995), Brown and Yule's descriptive term *interactional* was used as a technical term to refer to this type of interpersonal meaning, *interactional meaning* being defined as *reference to the writer or reader(s) of the passage, or to a group of people that included the writer or reader(s).* (The definition could of course be extended to include speakers and hearers.) To make this first hypothesis explicit, then: the hypothesis is that passages from *English Studies at Nottingham* will be found to prioritize *interactional* meaning, interactional meaning being defined as *references to writer(s) or reader(s), or to groups of people that include writer(s) or reader(s).*

There are many other hypotheses that could be set up on the basis of the producer/reader observations already gathered but, since this is not intended to be an exhaustive discussion of these texts, merely an illustration of a particular line of argument, I will offer just two hypotheses more. First, the regulatory nature of passage 3, evident from the Faculty Secretary's counter-question to my initial enquiry (see section 4.1) and the Bristol readers' discussion of social roles (see section 5.2.1), might be expected to entail meanings of obligation or prohibition. If one is regulating someone, one is presumably telling them either that they should do something or that they should not. This leads to the hypothesis that passages from the *Handbook* will prioritize meanings of *obligation/prohibition,* where this type of meaning is defined as *an indication that someone should do something or should not do something.* Second, the concern of the main author of *English Studies at Nottingham* to be "accessible," which I have interpreted as meaning "reader-friendly," together with the suggestion from the Bristol group that the writer–reader relationship was more in evidence in passages 1 and 2, might lead one to expect that in passages 1 and 2 there will be indications of a greater attempt to help the reader by leading him/her from one part of the text to the next. A third possible hypothesis might therefore be that the *Prospectus* and *English Studies at Nottingham* will be found to prioritize what one might call *signposting* meaning (i.e. indications of how one part of a text fits together with other parts of a text).

(If it is to be possible to set up worthwhile hypotheses along these lines, it is clearly going to be necessary to work at distinguishing and defining relevant types of meaning. The descriptions in the preceding paragraph of the types of meaning relevant to the second and third hypotheses were rather of a rough and ready nature. Work on refining the description of types of meaning relevant to the first hypothesis has already begun. In Berry (1995: section 8) it was found necessary not only to recognize and define interactional meaning, as discussed above, but also to recognize and define various subtypes of interactional meaning.)

It is perhaps important to indicate that hypotheses such as those discussed here can fail. A hypothesis is not truly a hypothesis if it is not in principle possible for it to be wrong just as much as it is in principle possible for it to be right.[9] On the basis of reader observations that descriptions of places in travel brochures were (a) more directly addressed to the reader (b) more subjective than descriptions of places in guide books, I hypothesized that passages of children's writing judged by teachers and others to be suitable for inclusion in a travel brochure would be found to prioritize (i) interactional meaning (as defined above) and (ii) attitudinal meaning, defined as *indication of speaker/writer attitude to ensuing message* (Downing 1991: 129). There was considerable support for the first hypothesis, but no support for the second.

The short answer to question 2aii is thus: Empirically, by setting up hypotheses and seeing whether they are right or wrong.

5.2.3. For any given text, or section of text, how is discourse Theme$_M$ determined?

Now that questions 2ai and 2aii have been discussed it is possible to give an answer to question 2a, since the answers to 2ai and 2aii are intended jointly to provide an answer to the superordinate question. The answer to 2a is thus: first by means of interviews, discussions and more formal informant tests with writers and readers or their representatives, and then by setting up and testing hypotheses as to the types of meanings likely to be prioritized; hypotheses, that

---

[9]cf. Hudson (1986: 798).

is, as to the meanings that constitute discourse Theme$_M$ for each of the texts/sections of texts under consideration.

On the basis of the discussion so far it is being hypothesized that: discourse Theme$_M$ for the *Prospectus* will include what has been called *signposting* meaning; discourse Theme$_M$ for *English Studies at Nottingham* will include both *interactional* meaning and *signposting* meaning; discourse Theme$_M$ for the *Handbook* will include *obligation/prohibition* meaning. It remains to be seen whether there is any support for these hypotheses.

5.2.4. For any given clause, how is clause Theme$_M$ determined?

So much for discourse Theme$_M$. What about clause Theme$_M$?

The determination of clause Theme$_M$ is based partly on expectations about meaning and partly on expectations about form. Question 2b cannot, therefore, be fully discussed until after formal aspects of Theme have been considered. I will here outline the line of reasoning to be pursued, then move to questions 3 and 4, which have to do with Theme$_F$, then return to Question 2b in section 5.5.

Briefly, after an introductory discussion of Theme$_F$, the steps in the argument will be as follows:

1. An attempt will be made to see whether the hypotheses set up in connection with discourse Theme$_M$ seem likely to be supported or refuted.

2. If there seems to be some support for the hypotheses, the next step will be to see whether there is any systematic association of the meanings hypothesized to constitute the relevant discourse Theme$_M$s with a particular formal feature, such as position in clause, or postpositional particle. (The word *feature* is not being used here in the technical sense in which it was used in section 2.3.4.)

3. If such a systematic association is found, the formal feature concerned will be regarded as Theme$_F$.

4. It will be argued that the existence of such a systematic association with discourse priority meanings would confer upon Theme$_F$ a special status as conveyer of important meanings. It might then be expected that readers would interpret *anything* conveyed by Theme$_F$ as a priority meaning, even if it were not associated with discourse Theme$_M$, but had a more local importance.

5. If this were the case, it would then seem reasonable to regard as clause Theme$_M$ whatever in a clause was conveyed by Theme$_F$.

It should perhaps be said that, to a text linguist, the most interesting aspects of Theme are discourse Theme$_M$ and Theme$_F$ and the relationship between them. Clause Theme$_M$ is a by-product, as it were, of this relationship. If of course such a relationship exists, which has still to be determined.

5.3. What Does It Mean to Say of Some x That x Is Theme$_F$?

Under the reasoning just outlined, to say that x was Theme$_F$ would be to say that it was an instance of the formal feature associated with conveying prioritized meanings of discourse Theme$_M$s. Let us begin to consider whether there *is* a systematic association of meaning with form, such that a formal feature of this description can be identified.

First it is necessary to say something about what is meant by *prioritizing* meaning. This term was deliberately chosen as the most neutral term available; neutral, that is, between different aspects of form. An alternative term, *foregrounding*, was considered, but rejected because it might have been thought to imply a particular type of formal realization. *Prioritizing* is intended to cover all and any means of indicating that a particular type of meaning is specially important.

What are the available means of prioritizing meanings? The following would seem to qualify for inclusion in any list under this heading:

1. *Repetition.* Fries (1983: 135), for instance, argues that topic is realized simply by frequency of mention.[10]
2. *Intonation.* Halliday (IFG 1985: 275; 1994: 296) identifies *information focus* as something which is phonologically realized.

---

[10] I would in fact question whether topic is realized *simply* by frequency of mention. In the passage that Fries cites as example, "the English Constitution," which he took to be the topic, is referred to by the grammatical subjects of the first two main clauses and by the grammatical subject of the last main clause. Certainly not by *all* the grammatical subjects, but one could argue that it *is* referred to by strategically placed grammatical subjects.

3. *A special particle.* Halliday (IFG 1985: 38; 1994: 37) suggests that, in Japanese, Theme is realized by a postposition -*wa*.[11]

4. *Unusual position.* This is assumed to be the realization of *marked theme* (Halliday IFG 1985: 45; 1994: 44).

5. *Fronting* (i.e. placing at the beginning). This is Halliday's proposal (IFG 1985: 39; 1994: 38) for the general realization of Theme in English.

Of the items in this list, presumably only 3, 4 and 5 would qualify as *grammatical* means of prioritizing meanings. It is no coincidence that Theme receives a mention in connection with these three items because Theme is proposed as a grammatical means of prioritizing meaning. When the hypotheses of sections 5.2 and 5.3 are tested, it will be first considered whether the hypothesized meanings are prioritized by some means *other than* grammatical means. In effect, since I am dealing with written texts, this will mean considering whether the meanings are prioritized by frequency of mention. If the answer to this question is yes, this will be regarded as encouraging for the view of discourse Theme$_M$ that is being put forward here; it will be regarded as an indication that the meanings hypothesized to be prioritized really are being prioritized. It will then be considered whether the meanings are also being prioritized by some grammatical means, whether the meanings prioritized by frequency of mention are consistently associated with some grammatical feature such as position in clause. If the answer to this second question is yes, this will be regarded as encouraging for the view that there is such a thing as Theme$_F$.

To repeat the answer to question 3 given at the beginning of this section, but now adjusting it slightly to enable the substitution of

---

[11]Huddleston (1991: 96) questioned whether what is marked by -*wa* in Japanese is identifiable with what is regarded as Theme in Hallidayan analysis. Experiments I have carried out suggest that it is not. Japanese M.A. students were asked to take Halliday's examples and translate them into Japanese, paying particular attention to whether the Japanese equivalents of Halliday's Themes received the attachment of -*wa*. In some cases they did, in some cases they did not. It was difficult to see any pattern in the results that could be interpreted in terms of Halliday's account of Theme. It was certainly not as simple, for instance, as that topical Themes took -*wa*, while interpersonal and textual Themes did not. Some of the equivalents of the phrases that Halliday regarded as interpersonal and textual were assigned -*was*. Some of the equivalents of Halliday's topical Themes were not. I am grateful to the M.A. students who took part in these experiments, particularly to Kazuko Shimizu, who continued the investigation in her dissertation.

the more specific term *grammatical* for the more general term *formal:* to say that some x was Theme$_F$ would be to say that x was an instance of a grammatical means of prioritizing the meanings of discourse Theme$_M$s.

5.4. How is Theme$_F$ Determined?

I would like to think that the short answer to question 4 could again be: Empirically (i.e. by setting up hypotheses and investigating them). In this section, I will first set up some hypotheses with regard to Theme$_F$, then consider the evidence for the earlier hypotheses with regard to discourse Theme$_M$, then consider the evidence for the Theme$_F$ hypotheses in the light of the (tentative) conclusions about discourse Theme$_M$.

5.4.1. Some hypotheses about Theme$_F$

Halliday clearly envisages different hypotheses for different languages, hypotheses about postpositions for Japanese, hypotheses about position in clause for English (see section 5.3 above). Since the texts I am using for exemplifications are in English, I will take Halliday's hypotheses for English as my starting point. The general hypothesis would seem to be that Theme (for me discourse Theme$_M$) is realized by positioning at the beginning of the clause; in other words that Theme$_F$ is the beginning of the clause.

However, what is meant by the beginning of the clause? Different systemic functional linguists have put forward different views on this. It would seem to be possible to distinguish the following sub-hypotheses:

1. Halliday's own first hypothesis (IFG 1985: 39; 1994: 38) is that Theme is realized by first position in clause. I shall refer to this as *the first position hypothesis.*[12]

2. Halliday's second hypothesis (IFG 1985: 54; 1994: 53) is that Theme is realized by the part of the clause that extends up to and includes the first ideational element (i.e. the first element that has a function in transitivity). I shall refer to this as *the first ideational element hypothesis.*

---

[12]This is the position I adopted as a temporary measure, as it were, in Berry (1987).

3. Enkvist (1973) proposed that everything up to and including the Subject of a main clause should be treated as Theme.[13] I shall refer to this as *the subject hypothesis.*[14]

4. Berry (1989/1995) was based on the view that Theme was realized by the portion of a main clause that preceded the verb. This will be termed *the preverb hypothesis.*

5. Stainton (1993) proposed that auxiliary verbs, as well as what preceded them, should be included in the Theme. This will be termed *the auxiliary verb hypothesis.*

6. As far as I am aware, no one has yet proposed that Theme$_F$ includes all parts of a main clause up to and including the lexical verb, but I shall need to consider that possibility later in this article. I will therefore include in this list *the lexical verb hypothesis.*

7. Matthiessen (1992: 51) argued that "the thematic prominence of the clause gradually decreases as the clause unfolds." There is, he suggested, a "diminuendo effect." According to this view, to draw a boundary between Theme and Rheme is to impose discreteness on a phenomenon that is really non-discrete. Presumably, then, Theme–Rheme can be regarded as forming a continuum; the early part of a clause is clearly thematic, the later part of a clause clearly rhematic, but the two shade into each other, it not being possible to say precisely where the boundary occurs. I shall refer to this as *the continuum hypothesis.*

8. Another way of interpreting Matthiessen's views is to say that it *is* possible to say where Theme ends and Rheme begins, but that the two overlap. Ravelli (in press), who also discussed Matthiessen's views, related the Theme–Rheme structure of a clause to the three metafunctions,

---

[13] I am grateful to Rachel Whittaker for drawing my attention to this.

[14] Downing (1991: 127) suggested that a problem with Enkvist's proposal was that, in an example such as *Chief among these young men was Plato,* the whole clause would have to be regarded as Theme, since the subject is at the end. While I agree that there are problems with Enkvist's proposal (see section 5.4.3.3 below), the fact that the subject occurs at the end in some examples need not necessarily be a problem. Structures of this type frequently occur in what used to be called *topic sentences* (i.e. sentences whose meanings mark a new aspect of the topic or a new step in an argument). One might well want to argue that the whole of such a sentence is thematic. Other items usually found at the beginning frequently move to the end in such sentences—such as *however* and *therefore.*

suggesting that the thematic portion of a clause carries the main weight of the interpersonal and textual meaning, while the rhematic portion of a clause carries the main weight of the ideational meaning. The two meet somewhere in the neighborhood of the verb. I shall refer to this as *the overlapping hypothesis*. The Matthiessen–Ravelli proposal is an attractive one. The gradually extending list of hypotheses has been beginning to seem rather ad hoc. Here we have a suggestion of a general pattern to which some of the more specific hypotheses could be related.

9. It should not be forgotten that unusual position is regarded as a factor in English, at least in the realization of marked theme (see section 5.3 above). It will not be possible to discuss this adequately in the present paper. Nevertheless, I will include *the unusual position hypothesis* in this list of hypotheses as a reminder that it will need investigating in the future.

10. A further hypothesis is implied by a number of the earlier hypotheses: that position in a main clause is more likely to be a means of realizing prioritized meanings than position in a subordinate clause. Again it will not be possible to investigate this hypothesis in the present article, but again I will include it in the list—as *the main clause hypothesis*—as a reminder that it will need investigating in the future.

There would seem, then, to be a number of different possibilities for Theme$_F$. However, before the hypotheses listed here can be tested, it is necessary to test the hypotheses set up earlier in sections 5.2.2 and 5.2.3. Since it is being assumed that Theme$_F$, if it exists, is a grammatical means of prioritizing the meanings of discourse Theme$_M$s, it must first be established whether it is possible to determine the meanings of discourse Theme$_M$s.

5.4.2. Testing the hypotheses about discourse Theme$_M$s

The conclusions to be drawn in this section will have to be extremely tentative since such a small amount of data is being discussed. It should be remembered that the main purpose of the present paper is to develop a line of argument that can be used in future research rather than to draw conclusions as such. The purpose of the present subsection is to explore the feasibility of drawing conclusions about discourse Theme$_M$s, rather than actually to arrive at such conclusions. Even to draw conclusions about just the three texts under discussion would entail looking at more passages from those texts and considering more types of meaning in relation to the passages. The important point here is to establish whether it is possible to determine that a meaning is a prioritized meaning, in a manner that is independent of recognition of Theme$_F$. I am claiming that determination of Theme$_F$ is dependent on determination of discourse Theme$_M$, in which case I cannot also claim that the determination of discourse Theme$_M$ is dependent on determination of Theme$_F$, or the reasoning becomes circular.

The procedure to be adopted will be as follows: Each of the three types of hypothesized priority meanings will be considered in turn. A simple count will be made of the number of occurrences in each passage of the type of meaning under consideration. It will be regarded as encouraging for the hypothesis if more instances are found in the passage hypothesized to be prioritizing this type of meaning than in the passages not hypothesized to be prioritizing it. With a larger amount of data, of course, statistical tests could be used to see if the differences in frequency were significant. If (significantly) more instances are found in the predicted passage, this will be regarded as an indication that the meaning has indeed been prioritized, by the frequency of mention method. It will be remembered that frequency of mention was one of the available means of prioritizing meanings listed in section 5.3. However, frequency of mention was not one of the means regarded as a grammatical means of prioritizing meanings; in other words, it was not a candidate for the status of Theme$_F$. Hopefully it can be agreed that to establish whether a meaning is a prioritized meaning on the basis of frequency of mention is to establish it on the basis of evidence that is independent of any possible Theme$_F$.

5.4.2.1. Testing the hypothesis that English Studies at Nottingham will prioritize interactional meaning.

The first hypothesis set up in section 5.2.2 was that *English Studies at Nottingham* would prioritize interactional meaning (i.e. references to writer(s) or reader(s) or groups of people that included writer(s) or reader(s)). The passage from this publication which is under discussion here includes five references that members of the Bristol group interpreted as direct references to the reader (four realized by *you*, one by *your*). This compares with no such references in the other two passages. (There were no direct references to writers in any of the three passages.)

Because I am interested in paradigmatic relations (see section 2.3.4 above), I will also briefly mention the meanings that the Bristol group perceived to be contrasting with the direct references to the reader. The items *student* and *candidate* were regarded as indirectly/obliquely referring to the reader in that they were referring to roles into which readers might be expected to project themselves. The contrast between the direct and indirect references to reader seemed to be largely responsible for the differences in (im)personality that the Bristol group perceived between the passages. (The contrast between active and passive was also mentioned in this connection.)

On the basis of the five direct references to reader in the *English Studies at Nottingham* passage, compared with none in the other passages, it would seem reasonable to conclude that, at least in the passages discussed here, *English Studies at Nottingham* is prioritizing interactional meaning to a greater degree than the other publications. It will be remembered that this hypothesis was set up in the first place because the writer indicated that it was a major concern for him to communicate a tone of voice that was different from that of official publications in that it was "friendly" and "familiar." The discussion of contrasts suggests that, for the Bristol group, interactional meaning did play a part in distinguishing the tone of voice of *English Studies at Nottingham* from that of the other publications.

5.4.2.2. Testing the hypothesis that the Handbook will prioritize meanings of obligation/prohibition.   The second hypothesis set up in section 5.2.2 was that the *Handbook* would prioritize meanings of obligation/prohibition (i.e indications that someone should do something or should not do something). The first items mentioned by the Bristol group as conveying this type of meaning were the modal auxiliaries *shall* and *must*, the former occurring once in the *Handbook* passage, the latter twice. Some members of the group interpreted *Note* at the beginning of Note (a) as an imperative with the meaning "you should/must take note." Although *may* is more usually associated with the meaning of permission than obligation, in collocation with *With the consent of the Head of Department* it too seems to imply obligation, an obligation to seek the consent of the Head of Department if wishing to take up the relevant option. This combination occurs twice. The combination *No* with *may* in Note (c) can presumably be regarded as conveying prohibition.[15] If all

---

[15]This is reminiscent of Huddleston's (1988: 158) example *Nothing will satisfy you*. Here, *No student may take both* . . . has been chosen instead of *A student may not take both* . . . presumably because the concern is to emphasise the negativeness of the prohibition. It would seem likely that in Huddleston's example the concern is similarly to emphasise the negativeness.

these can be admitted as instances of obligation/prohibition meanings, then the passage from the *Handbook* has seven such instances. Only one instance of such meaning was found in the other two passages: *are required*, in the first line of the *Prospectus* passage was interpreted by the Bristol group as having this meaning.

Two sets of relevant contrasts were discussed by the Bristol group. The use of *may* in the *Handbook* passage was contrasted with the use of *may* in *you may write* (paragraph 3 of the *English Studies at Nottingham* passage) where the implication was of free choice as opposed to regulated choice. Also—and this was something that surprised me since I had not anticipated it—members of the Bristol group felt strongly that the meanings of lexical verbs were important here. The meanings of verbs such as *choose* and *encourage* were thought to indicate the opposite of regulatoriness, to contrast therefore with meanings of obligatoriness and prohibition.

Again, then, on the basis of numerical supremacy it would seem fair to conclude that the passage from the *Handbook* really *is* prioritizing meanings of obligation/prohibition to a greater extent than the other passages. And again the discussion of contrasts would seem to suggest that this really does have something to do with the concerns of the writers that I took as the starting point of my discussion.

5.4.2.3. *Testing the hypothesis that the* Prospectus *and* English Studies at Nottingham *will prioritize signposting meaning.* The third hypothesis relevant to discourse Theme$_M$ was that the *Prospectus* and *English Studies at Nottingham* would prioritize signposting meaning (i.e. indications of how one part of a text fitted together with other parts of a text). I have to be rather cautious here how I interpret the views of the Bristol group; the discussion of textual meaning was not as clear as the discussion of interpersonal meaning, partly I think because it came second and the participants, including myself, were tired. It seemed to be agreed that there were four different types of textual meaning manifested in the passages, and it was not always clear which items were being cited in which connection. (It must be remembered that the experiment on which I am drawing here was actually set up in connection with a rather different piece of research (see Berry in press).) I *think* the following items from the *Prospectus* were regarded as having what I am calling *signposting* meaning: *in the third year, then, in addition, for example.* I *think* the following items from *English Studies at Nottingham* were regarded as having this type of meaning: *in your third year, additionally, in any year, instead of taking a special option, thus.* No items with this type of meaning were identified in the passage from the *Handbook*.

The only contrast that was discussed was with the two instances of *with the consent of the Head of Department*. These phrases were considered in connection with signposting meaning, but it was agreed that their function was not that of helping the reader to see how the text fitted together.

There were problems, then, with the testing of the third hypothesis. While it looks as if the passages predicted to be prioritizing signposting meaning have a numerical advantage over the third passage, if the instances have been correctly identified, the discussion of contrasts is this time discouraging rather than encouraging. The only reason I can think of why *with the consent of the Head of Department* should have been even mentioned in connection with signposting meaning is that, like most of the other items discussed, it occurs in the first place of a main clause. In other words, identification of this type of meaning may *not* have been independent of matters relevant to $Theme_F$.

All this would seem to add up to two for and one against the view that discourse $Theme_M$ can be identified independently of $Theme_F$. In the case of the first two hypotheses, the predictions were numerically borne out and, since the items cited were not all in some easily detectable same place in structure, it would seem reasonable to suggest that identification of the meanings was independent of matters relevant to $Theme_F$. In the case of the third hypothesis further work is clearly necessary on defining signposting meaning and on devising suitable informant tests for identifying it. One small crumb of comfort here is that *then*, in the second sentence of the *Prospectus* passage, seems to be regarded as having signposting meaning. This item is not in first position in its main clause, which perhaps suggests that *in principle* even signposting meaning is identifiable in some way unrelated to preconceived views of $Theme_F$.

5.4.3. Testing the hypotheses about $Theme_F$

Hopefully, enough was said in the previous subsection to indicate that discourse $Theme_M$ is at least in principle identifiable independently of $Theme_F$, so that we may now proceed to consider whether discourse $Theme_F$ may be identified on the basis of discourse $Theme_M$. It will be remembered (section 5.2.4) that I am attempting to see whether recognition of $Theme_F$ can be justified on the basis of some systematic association with discourse $Theme_M$. Is there any indication of a systematic association of any particular grammatical feature with the meanings I have been discussing, particularly the first two types of meaning, about which it is possible to have greater confidence? The hypotheses listed in section 5.4.1 will be discussed in turn, to see if there is any evidence of systematic association of the part of the clause/other grammatical feature mentioned in the hypothesis with any of the meanings. The meanings seem, on the evidence of section 5.4.2, to have been prioritized by relative frequency of mention (see section 5.3). Have they also been prioritized by any grammatical means? It must again be remembered that the purpose of the present article is to develop a line of argument rather than to draw conclusions. Clearly, for conclusions to be drawn, *much* more evidence is necessary than will be considered here. The purpose of the present subsection is merely to consider the *type* of evidence that might be brought to bear on hypotheses such as those in section 5.4.1.

5.4.3.1. Testing the first position hypothesis.

Is there any systematic association of any of the prioritized meanings with first position in clause? Certainly not in the case of interactional meaning; the instance of interactional meaning conveyed by *your* is associated with the first constituent in the clause, but the four instances of interactional meaning conveyed by *you* are not located in first constituents.

The position is slightly better with regard to obligation/prohibition meaning. It could be argued that four of the instances are at least in part realized by items that occur in first constituents, but the other three—the clearest examples, in fact, of this type of meaning, the ones realized by *shall* and the two instances of *must*—are not located in first constituents. At best, then, the proportion is only slightly better than fifty–fifty.

Signposting meaning looks more promising, since all but two of the instances are realized in first position. However, as already discussed (section 5.4.2.3), the evidence here is suspect. And, in any case, due consideration must be given to the two instances that are not realized by first constituents; although there happen only to be two instances in the brief passages I am considering here, they may well be representative of large numbers of such instances to be found elsewhere. *Then* in the second sentence of the *Prospectus* passage is a problem for the first position hypothesis; although it appears to have exactly the same textual function as, for example, *additionally,* and to be equally important in that connection, it does not appear in first position. If one takes the first position hypothesis literally, then *thus* in the fourth paragraph of the *English Studies at Nottingham* passage is also a problem since it occurs after *and*.

On the basis of the evidence here, it would not seem possible to claim that there is a systematic association of prioritized meanings with first position in clause. The best that could be said is that it *might* be possible at some later date to show that *one* type of prioritized meaning, signposting meanings, *usually* occur in first position, if a reliable way can be found of identifying such meanings that is independent of first position itself.

5.4.3.2. Testing the first ideational element hypothesis. In fact, Halliday soon moved on from the first hypothesis to the second. To what extent are prioritized meanings associated with the portion of the clause up to and including the first ideational element?

Under this hypothesis, one more of the instances of interactional meaning moves into the thematic portion of the clause. *Additionally*, in the second sentence of the *English Studies at Nottingham* passage, presumably has the same meaning as *in addition*, which appears in Halliday's list of conjunctive adjuncts (IFG 1985: 50; 1994: 49). This would mean that it would be treated as non-ideational. The *you* that follows it could then, under this second hypothesis, be regarded as thematic. However, the other three instances of interactional meaning realized by *you* would still be regarded as being outside the Theme—in spite of the fact that they very clearly relate to the concerns of the writer and have been recognized as such by readers. This is indeed a very frequent problem with the type of text with which I deal. Interactional meanings judged by writers and readers to be important to the particular type of text are located, according to this hypothesis, some inside, some outside the Theme. Under the assumptions of the first ideational element hypothesis, it is impossible to capture the generalizations that one would want to be able to capture.

The second hypothesis represents no improvement over the first with regard to obligation/prohibition meaning. There would still be a four–three split between instances realized (partly) inside the Theme and those realized outside the Theme.

There is one improvement with regard to signposting meaning: the instance realized by *thus* can now be regarded as located inside the Theme. However, the instance realized by *then* is still a problem for this hypothesis, as it was for the first hypothesis.

On the basis of the evidence here, then, the second hypothesis represents a slight improvement over the first hypothesis. However, there are still seven instances of prioritized meanings unaccounted for out of a total of 21. It would seem to be time to move on again and consider other hypotheses regarding candidates for the status of Theme$_F$.

5.4.3.3. Testing the subject hypothesis. If one assumes that Theme$_F$ consists of the portion of the clause up to and including the subject, two more of the instances of interactional meaning move into the Theme, those realized by the *yous* in the first lines of the first and third paragraphs of the *English Studies at Nottingham* passage. Only one instance of interactional meaning now remains outside the Theme.

However the improvement from the point of view of interactional meaning is counter-balanced by deterioration from the point of view of obligation/prohibition meaning. The third hypothesis creates a new problem. What does one do about *Note* in Note (a) of the *Handbook* passage? The Bristol group seemed to want to interpret it as an imperative, in which case there is no subject. Does this mean that, according to this hypothesis, there is no Theme, or that the clause is simply unanalyzable from this point of view?

Then remains a problem for the third hypothesis.

Moving from the second hypothesis to the third has some advantages, then, but also some disadvantages. Let us move on again.

5.4.3.4. Testing the preverb hypothesis. Assuming that Theme$_F$ consists of the portion of the clause that precedes the verb element makes no difference from the point of view of interactional meaning. The effect is the same as for the subject hypothesis.

This is also the case for obligation/prohibition meaning. *Note* is still a problem. Also, there are still three other instances of this type of meaning that are outside the Theme.

Where this hypothesis does make a difference is in the case of *then*, which now for the first time moves into the Theme. *They* and *then*, from the beginning of the second sentence of the *Prospectus* passage, are now both considered to be within Theme$_F$. While *then* is the only representative of this particular type of problem in the passages I am discussing here, it is a type of problem that frequently occurs elsewhere. Items judged to be equally important from the point of view of indicating how a text fits together are, under the first three hypotheses, treated unequally, some inside the Theme, some outside. It is not until we come to the fourth hypothesis that we find a hypothesis that enables them to be given parity of treatment.[16]

The preverb hypothesis, then, accounts for all the instances of signposting meaning, if these have been correctly identified, and all

---

[16]Vande Kopple (1991: 319), writing of Halliday's approach to Theme, comments, "Some writing researchers might wonder whether such small differences in position can justifiably underlie differences in functional classifications." He does not say what examples he has in mind, but it would seem likely that his remark applies to examples that he cites elsewhere in his article. Certainly it seems unsatisfactory to me that *For example* should be regarded as thematic in *For example, Act I Scene i of Julius Caesar is not part of the plot*, but should not be regarded as thematic in *Act I Scene i of Julius Caesar, for example, is not part of the plot*.

but one of the instances of interactional meaning. If this were all, one might have been prepared to accept that there was a systematic association between prioritized meanings and the preverb portion of the clause; one might have been prepared to allow *one* exception to the general pattern, at least if there were no evidence that the one exception was representing a whole host of similar problems from other sources. However, the one instance of interactional meaning not yet accounted for is *not* the only exception; four of the seven instances of obligation/prohibition meaning are still outside the Theme.

5.4.3.5. *Testing the auxiliary verb hypothesis.* The auxiliary verb hypothesis, that Theme$_F$ consists of the portion of the clause up to and including the auxiliary verb, allows into the Theme three of the hitherto excluded instances of obligation/prohibition meaning, those represented by *shall* and the two *musts* in the *Handbook* passage.

However, *Note* is still a problem. And again, while *Note* is the only example, and a rather dubious example, of this problem to be found in the passages under discussion here, it is worth continuing to discuss it, for the sake of all the less dubious instances of imperatives that raise the same problem elsewhere.

5.4.3.6. *Testing the lexical verb hypothesis.* Allowing Theme$_F$ to continue through the lexical verb, so that the whole of the verbal group is within the Theme, would solve the problem of *Note*; a meaning perceived by the Bristol group to be an instance of an important type of meaning would now be realized within the Theme. It would also solve a problem for imperatives generally.

Is there anything else that can be said in favor of this sixth hypothesis? The Bristol group were emphatically of the opinion that the meanings of lexical verbs played a large part in the enacting of the social relationships relevant to the passages discussed here. For instance, the meanings of *choose* and *encourage* were considered to indicate a non-regulatory tone, in contrast with the meaning of *require*, which was considered to be regulatory. The meaning of *take* was thought to be associated with an examiner–examinee relationship, in contrast with the meaning of *study*, which seemed to be more in keeping with a teacher–taught relationship.

The lexical verb hypothesis, then, accounts for 20 out of 21 of the instances of prioritized meaning that are being used as the focus for this discussion—there is still one instance of interactional meaning outside the Theme—and it also accounts for other reader intuitions relevant to writers' concerns.

The problem is that one is perhaps beginning to be a little uneasy at the apparent ad-hoc nature of a set of hypotheses that keeps extending Theme$_F$. Is this going to go on indefinitely? Is the whole of the clause eventually going to get swallowed up in Theme$_F$? Hypotheses should not just describe what happens, but seek to *explain* what happens. We are about to move on to a rather different type of hypothesis. It will be interesting to see whether there is anything in the later hypotheses that can rescue the sixth hypothesis from its apparent ad-hoc nature.

5.4.3.7. *Testing the continuum hypothesis.* As indicated above (section 5.4.1), Matthiessen (1992: 51) wrote of a "diminuendo effect," arguing that "the thematic prominence of the clause gradually decreases as the clause unfolds." Is there anything in the evidence I have been reviewing here to support or cast doubt on this hypothesis?

If one makes a count of the number of prioritized meanings accounted for at each of the main positions in the clause, the results are as follows:

Initial constituent other than subject or verb:	11
Subject:	4
Position between subject and verb:	1
Verb (including both auxiliary and lexical verbs):	4
Still to be accounted for (i.e. realized in a constituent that follows the verb):	1

(In interpreting these figures it should be borne in mind that: Eight of the meanings accounted for by the initial constituent are of the problematic signposting meaning type; *thus* has been counted as a first constituent, though strictly speaking it is not; one of the subjects is itself an initial constituent, as is also one of the verbs.) There would certainly seem to be a decrease as one goes through the clause, if not perhaps a very smooth decrease.

Perhaps a numerical count is the wrong way to test this hypothesis. Perhaps an informant test would be better, if one could be devised, to see whether informants perceive meanings realized toward the beginning of a clause as more prominent than those later on, there being a gradual decrease in perceived degree of prominence. The meanings the Bristol group discussed most readily, most vociferously and most unanimously were the meanings conveyed by the auxiliary and lexical verbs, which would seem to go against the hypothesis. However, again it must be remembered that the experiment was not set up to investigate this particular point. An experiment specifically designed for this purpose would be necessary.

Clearly, more evidence is necessary, and probably a different kind of evidence from that which is available here, before one can even begin to draw a conclusion with regard to this seventh hypothesis.

5.4.3.8. Testing the overlapping hypothesis. The eighth hypothesis, derived in part from Matthiessen (1992), in part from Ravelli (in press), is complex and needs to be factorized before it can be tested.

The basic idea is that the weight of interpersonal and textual meaning is to be found in the early part of a clause, while the weight of ideational meaning is to be found in the later part of a clause. This idea may perhaps be linked to Fries' (1995) description of the function of Theme as "to orient the reader/listener to what is to follow." Before the main ideational meaning can be communicated, it is necessary to get the hearer/reader into the right frame of mind. From an interpersonal point of view this would mean, for instance, communicating an appropriate tone of voice, indicating what types of social relation were relevant, indicating speaker/writer's attitude to the information to be conveyed. From a textual point of view it would mean indicating the relation of the coming information to preceding information, for instance signalling whether there would be continuation of topic or change of topic, signalling the part to be played by the coming information in the overall structure of an argument or position in a chronological sequence of events. Under this interpretation, what I have been referring to in this article as the "speaker/writer's main concerns" would be the speaker/writer's main *communicative* concerns. Only when the reader/hearer had generally been smoothed down and pointed in the correct direction, as it were, would it be possible to proceed with the main meat of the information. Or, to use a slightly more consistent metaphor, only after the diner had been greeted, shown to the table and presented with the menu, could the meal actually begin.

Assuming that the general idea sounds plausible, it would then be necessary to set up precise hypotheses as to the particular point in the clause by which the preliminaries should be completed, and indeed hypotheses as to the particular point at which the main ideational meaning could begin. The hypothesis I am in the middle of discussing is actually that the two will overlap. To go back to the restaurant analogy, sometimes one only gets to see the wine menu after one has started eating one's bread roll, or in posh restaurants, one's canapes!

Given the list of preliminaries suggested above, if all this has to happen before at any rate *most* of the main ideational meaning is to appear, one would expect a transition point later rather than earlier in the clause. If we now assume that Theme$_F$ is the part of the clause associated with the speaker/writer's main *communicative* concerns, with the main interpersonal and textual preliminaries, the sixth hypothesis above begins to look rather less strange. I will take the sixth hypothesis as the basis for the hypotheses to be discussed in this section. It is important to emphasize, however, that this is only by way of example. Other hypotheses are possible along the same lines.

I shall assume, then, that to test the overlapping hypothesis one needs to factorize it into a set of hypotheses such as the following:

8a.   that the weight of the interpersonal meaning will be located in the portion of the clause up to and including the lexical verb;

8b.   that the weight of the textual meaning will be located in the portion of the clause up to and including the lexical verb;

8c.   that the weight of the ideational meaning will be located in the portion of the clause consisting of the lexical verb and all that follows it.

The small amount of evidence I have been able to present in this paper would certainly support the first of these hypotheses. Eleven out of twelve of the meanings assumed to be prioritized interpersonal meanings are located in the specified portion of the clause. To put this in perspective, readers may wish to see how much of the clause is left over, after the lexical verb. Table 1.1 shows on the lefthand side the main parts of the main clause up to and including the lexical verb, and on the righthand side what is left of the clause after the lexical verb. Hopefully, it will be agreed that there is quite a large amount of text on the righthand side and that therefore it is interesting that all this text appears to contain only one instance of the prioritized interpersonal meanings I have been discussing.

With regard to the second hypothesis, I am back to the problem of determining what counts as textual meaning. The signposting meanings, such as they are, are certainly located in the specified portion of the clause. In fact most occur well before the lexical verb; all but the instance realized by *then* occur well before the lexical verb. Is this hypothesis perhaps too generous in the extent of the clause that it specifies? It may be worth remembering that in certain types of text a favorite position for signposting meaning is between an auxiliary and a lexical verb (e.g. *The sixth hypothesis may at first*

TABLE 1.1
Passage 1, from the *Prospectus*

1	2	3	4	
In the third year	all students		are required	to take two modules in Medieval English Literature.
	They	then	choose	a further six core modules *either* from nineteenth and twentieth century literature and drama, or from early English literature and English language.
In addition	a choice of special subjects and an optional dissertation		encourage	students to develop interests which may be starting points for graduate research.
but always?	The special subjects	always?	vary	from year to year.
			include	modules focusing on specialist areas in modern English language and in medieval and modern literature.
For example	courses		may be taken	in D H Lawrence studies, language and gender, Viking runes and writing for the media.

(continued)

TABLE 1.1 (Continued)

Passage 2, from *English Studies at Nottingham*

1	2	3	4	
In your third year	you		may choose	whether to concentrate on Nineteenth and Twentieth Century Literature and Drama, Modern English Language or Early English, or a combination.
Additionally	you		study	medieval English Literature and four modules from a wide range of special options.
In any year	the special options current modules		may vary: include	the Novel in Southern Africa, Irish Studies, D.H. Lawrence, Sexuality and Culture, Writing for the Media, English Place-Names, Major Modern Novels, and Viking Age Runes.
Instead of taking a special option	you		may write	a dissertation on a subject that particularly interests you.
	it		could be	a feminist study of the Icelandic sagas, exploration of the Arthurian tradition, or work on the language of children's books.
	The advantage of the optional scheme in the third year		is	that after two years students tend to know where in the study of English their special interest or vocational interests and enjoyment lie,
and thus	the third year work		enables	them to develop skills and knowledge in their own preferred areas.

Passage 3, from *The Handbook*

1	2	3	4
	The following modules		must be taken: (i) Medieval English Literature: I (Q33211) (10 credits) (ii) Medieval English literature: II (Q33208) (10 credits) (iii) 60 credits chosen from a range of Level B and Level 3 English Studies literature modules (Romantics to present day literature) and English Studies modules in Modern English language, early language and medieval literature as specified by the Department.
With the consent of the Head of Department	a candidate		may substitute a dissertation in English of from 7,000 to 10,000 words in place of 20 credits worth of Level B or Level 3 modules. (Q33403 or Q33401 and Q33402)
With the consent of the Head of Department	a candidate		may substitute one or two Project Modules (Q3B208 and Q3B216) in place of 10 or 20 credits worth of Level B or Level 3 modules.
	Project modules		must be based on modules which form part of the Part I or Part II English Studies course.
	No student		may take both a dissertation and Project module(s) during one academic session.

(Note: Only complete main clauses have been included in this table.)

sight however appear a little ad hoc—in other words before the lexical verb, but not very far before it).

I have no direct evidence to bring to bear on the third hypothesis, since I have not been discussing ideational meaning.

5.4.3.9. A reminder of the remaining hypotheses.   As indicated in section 5.4.1, there will be no room in the present article adequately to discuss the unusual position hypothesis, or the main clause hypothesis, but they should not be forgotten. The former will be considered briefly in section 5.6. In connection with the latter, it may be worth noting that the one instance of a prioritized interpersonal meaning to occur after the lexical verb is in fact in a subordinate clause.

5.4.4. An extremely tentative conclusion with regard to Theme$_F$

As already said, *much* more evidence is necessary before confident conclusions can be drawn. However, it is presumably permissible to draw a very tentative conclusion on the basis of the evidence so far. Of the more specific hypotheses, the sixth, the lexical verb hypothesis, looks most promising since it accounts for 20 out of 21 of the prioritized meanings under discussion. (As has just been indicated, it *may* be possible to explain the apparent exception on the basis of the main clause hypothesis.) Furthermore, the sixth hypothesis looks plausible in connection with the assumptions underlying the eighth hypothesis. If Theme$_F$ is assumed to be the part of the clause associated with the speaker/writer's main communicative concerns, with the weight of the interpersonal and textual meaning, one might expect it to be fairly extensive. If Rheme$_F$ is now assumed to be the part of the clause associated with the weight of the ideational meaning, the main matter to be communicated, one might expect that too to be fairly extensive. It would not be too surprising if Theme$_F$ and Rheme$_F$ were found to intersect near the middle of the clause.

5.5. What is the Relation Between Theme$_M$ and Theme$_F$?

I have now discussed what is meant by Theme$_M$ and Theme$_F$ and have considered the procedure by which each might be determined. Huddleston's next question asks what is the relation between them. As has already been implied, it is assumed that the relation between them is a realization relation.

Hasan (1995) emphasizes that realization is a two-way relation; it subsumes both an "activational" relation and a "construal" relation. From the activational perspective, "choices at the stratum of context in turn activate choices at the stratum of semantics which in its turn activate choices from the systems at the stratum of lexicogrammar." From the construal perspective, "lexicogrammar orders, forms, articulates semantics, the latter orders, forms, articulates context of situation."

So far I have mainly been illustrating the activational relation. Choices by writers as to the relevant social relations and the appropriate tone of voice were assumed to be activating choices as to particular types of meaning to be prioritized and these in turn were assumed to be activating choices as to particular formal items and the positioning of these formal items. What of the construal perspective? Can Theme be considered from this point of view? Presumably the hypothesis would be that Theme$_F$, whatever that was determined to be, would by its very existence influence the construal of meanings, which would in turn influence the construal of context of situation. Since the assumption is that Theme$_F$ is associated with *prioritization* of meaning, what would be influenced would be perceptions of the relative importance of meanings, which in turn would influence perceptions of the relative importance of aspects of the context of situation.

This is where we return to the line of reasoning sketched in section 5.2.4. I have been arguing that it only makes sense to recognize something called Theme$_F$ if it is possible to identify a portion of a clause/other grammatical feature that is *systematically* associated with independently identifiable components of discourse Theme$_M$s. Let us suppose for the moment that this *is* possible, that we have effectively identified a Theme$_F$ in this way. Let us further suppose that *systematically* associated does not mean that every single instance of a prioritized meaning will be realized by Theme$_F$ or that every single instance of Theme$_F$ will be realizing a prioritized meaning, but that the coincidence of the two will be sufficiently frequent for the two to become associated in the minds of language users. It would seem reasonable to expect that, if the association in the minds of language users were sufficiently strong, this would influence their interpretation of Theme$_F$ even on those occasions when Theme$_F$ had nothing to do with discourse Theme$_M$. The prediction would be that they would *try* to associate whatever was expressed by Theme$_F$ with their evolving conception of discourse Theme$_M$ for the text. If this failed, they might consider whether the meaning was important for some other reason, perhaps to highlight some purely local contrast. Only if this failed too, would they conclude that this particular Theme$_F$ was not expressing meaning of any importance.[17]

It would be in this connection that it would make sense for analysts to recognize a concept of clause, as opposed to discourse, Theme$_M$. If the association between prioritized meanings and Theme$_F$ were so strong that there were a tendency for language users to regard whatever-was-expressed-by-Theme$_F$ as potentially a priority meaning, it would seem sensible to give whatever-was-expressed-by-Theme$_F$ a name: clause Theme$_M$. As I said at the end of section 5.2.4, however, to me as a text linguist, what is interesting is discourse Theme$_M$ and its possible relation to a Theme$_F$. I shall therefore not be discussing clause Theme$_M$ in detail.

Something along the lines of the interpretive process predicted in this section did in fact happen in the Bristol discussion. As I have already indicated (section 5.4.2.3), members of the group cited the two instances of *With the consent of the Head of Department* in connection with signposting meaning, although later it was agreed that these phrases did not have the function of helping readers to see how one part of the text fits together with other parts of the text. There seemed to be an *attempt* to interpret the phrases as having signposting meaning, presumably because of an association of signposting meaning with first position, and only after this attempt failed were other interpretations considered. It is important to emphasize, however, that this cannot be seen as evidence of a general association of prioritized meanings with first position, only perhaps of one particular type of prioritized meaning, the problematic signposting meaning.

I have no evidence at present that can be brought to bear on the more general hypotheses introduced in this section.

5.6. What is the Constituent Structure of a Clause with Multiple Theme$_F$?

It was over the sixth of Huddleston's questions that I anticipated greatest difficulty (see section 3). I probably do not mean the same thing as Huddleston does by *constituent structure*. Since I am not a

---

[17]This may be what happens in the case of existential *there*, another type of construction that Huddleston (1988: 158) regarded as problematic. One of my informants spontaneously commented, "I just read over the *theres*." (See Berry 1995: note 9.)

syntactician, I am not concerned, for instance, with whether stretches of clauses can be moved around independently, or whether they can be coordinated or substituted by pro-forms. My own concern with constituent structure lies in the question of which bits of clauses are the location for the realizations of what types of meaning. Since I am particularly interested in paradigmatic relations, I am specially concerned to discover which bits of clauses are the location for the realizations of *contrasting* meanings (i.e. meaning choices).

This does not mean that I do not regard constituent structure in the syntactic sense as interesting; it means that I do not regard it as my job, as an SFL text linguist, to determine syntactic constituent structure. It would, in fact, be extremely interesting if constituents arrived at by the SFL route I am about to adopt were found to coincide with constituents independently arrived at on syntactic grounds. It is already interesting, for instance, in view of the discussion in section 5.4.3.8, that the verb element, hypothesized there to be the transition point between the main interpersonal and textual meaning and the main ideational meaning, should be regarded by Quirk et al. (1985: 50), on syntactic grounds, as central to the clause. It would also be interesting, if evidence can be found to support the view that the main ideational meaning is carried by the portion of the clause consisting of the lexical verb to the end, that Quirk et al. (1985: 81) called this portion of the clause the *predication* and argued on syntactic grounds that it is "a constituent of some importance in the English clause."[18]

In my discussion of constituent structure I will take as my starting point Halliday's hypotheses (e.g. IFG 1994: 36) as to the main method of realization associated with each of the main types of meaning. For this purpose, Halliday subdivides ideational meaning into experiential meaning, "construing a model of experience," and logical meaning "constructing logical relations," these together with interpersonal meaning and textual meaning making four main types of meaning in all. I will discuss each of these four types of meaning in the order in which Halliday lists them.

---

[18]It is interesting to note that Prague School linguists also regard the verb element of a clause as the usual transition between Theme and Rheme (e.g., Firbas 1986: 60). However, one has to be wary about drawing parallels between Hallidayan and Prague School approaches to Theme, because Theme is defined very differently by the two schools, and it is not clear that the same phenomena are being investigated. See Fries (1983, 1995) for discussion of the differences between them.

5.6.1. The realization of experiential meaning

It is experiential meaning that Halliday associates with constituent structure. The hypothesis is that it is experiential meaning that gives rise to and is realized through the segments of a grammatical unit, such as a clause. Other types of meaning are mapped on to/realized through segments that already exist, as it were, as a result of the experiential meaning. It is important, therefore, in any discussion of constituent structure to begin with experiential meaning.

The assumption is that experience is modelled (Halliday: IFG 1994: 106–7) in terms of processes, participants in those processes, and circumstances attendant on the processes. Each clause will represent one process, together with the relevant participants and circumstances. The process itself will be realized by one constituent of the clause, as will each participant and each circumstance.

To what extent can these assumptions account for the distribution of the types of meaning I have been discussing in this chapter? This question cannot really be considered until the following subsections, since it is interpersonal and textual meaning that I have been discussing. However certain preliminary points need to be made here. Table 1.1 represents a rather rough and ready attempt to group together like meanings in relation to the positions in the clause suggested by the hypotheses of section 5.4.1. Is it now possible to reinterpret this table in the light of what has just been said about experiential meaning and constituent structure?

Column 4 can presumably be regarded as the column representing the location for the realization of the process. Other meanings also appear in this column, but that is only to be expected, given what has been said about the mapping of other types of meaning onto the experientially derived segments.

Column 2 represents the location for the realization of a participant, the first participant to appear in the clause. The first participant to be realized in a clause will be referred to as participant A. (In passive clauses, participant A will not be the first participant in the sense in which Halliday (IFG 1985: 155; 1994: 173) uses the term *first participant.*) In traditional grammatical terms of course, column 2 represents the grammatical subject. While it is now recognized that not every subject in a text will refer to the discourse topic, one might expect that this grammatical constituent will still bear some responsibility for establishing and maintaining the topic. Indeed, informants seem to prefer texts in which the subjects sometimes refer to aspects of the discourse topic, but not too often. For instance, of the passages discussed in Berry (1995), Child A's passage, in which the subjects very rarely refer to aspects of the topic, is the passage valued least highly. Child C's passage, in which the subjects refer to aspects of the topic very frequently indeed, is criticized as repetitive in structure. Child B's passage, in which a happy medium is struck, is preferred to both Child A's and Child C's. It is interesting in this connection that, as column 2 of Table 1.1 shows, in all three of the passages under discussion in the present chapter, some but not all of the subjects refer to what the Bristol group perceived to be the discourse topic of the passages: "courses," "modules," "types of courses and modules" (see section 5.2.1). In some cases, then, "topical" meanings have been mapped onto the experiential participant A meanings.

Columns 1 and 3 are not as easy to relate to experiential meaning. Column 3 is rather difficult to make generalizations about, since there are only two items in it and one of these is only rather tentatively assigned. It *could* be argued that each of these two items could be interpreted as realizing a circumstance, in which case column 3, like columns 2 and 4, could be regarded as representing an experientially derived constituent. There is nothing here which incontrovertibly goes against the hypothesis.

However column 1 is a problem. Some of the items in this column can be regarded as referring to circumstances—for example, *in the third year*—but not all. As indicated in section 5.4.3.2, items such as *Additionally* and *In addition* would be regarded by Halliday as having no experiential meaning. This means that the column as a whole cannot be related to any experiential constituent. And even if it were decided that it was wrong to group these items together in the table, separating out the items that *were* regarded as having experiential meaning would still leave a number of items apparently floating in space without any experiential anchor. Does this mean that the hypothesis needs to be modified, that it is not just experiential meaning that is responsible for the segmentation of a clause into constituents? This will be discussed further below.

I have not attempted to divide the righthand side of Table 1.1 into columns since I have not been discussing matters relevant to the later parts of clauses.[19]

5.6.2. The realization of interpersonal meaning

Halliday hypothesizes (e.g. IFG 1994: 36) that interpersonal meaning will be prosodically realized; that is, it will be mapped on to

---

[19]I have assumed that the material following the colons in passage 3 is, in each case, in apposition to material that precedes the colon and that it should therefore be regarded as part of the same clause.

the segments arising from the experiential dimension, probably cutting across those segments in the sense that a particular meaning will be mapped on to more than one segment. How far can this hypothesis account for the distribution of the types of interpersonal meaning I have been discussing in this chapter?

A glance at Table 1.1 suggests that the main location for the realization of interactional meaning is represented by column 2. It is true that only three of the five instances of interactional meaning occur in this column, but also in this column appear the most frequent instances of the items whose meanings were thought by the Bristol group to contrast with the interactional meanings: *student* and *candidate* (see section 5.4.2.1). These items were regarded as indirectly referring to the reader in that they were referring to roles into which readers might be expected to project themselves. The contrast between the direct and indirect references to reader seemed to be largely responsible for the differences in (im)personality that the Bristol group perceived between the passages. It would appear then that column 2 represents the main site for the realization of the relevant meaning *contrast*. (It could also be said that *In your third year* of passage 2 contrasts with *In the third year* of passage 1. However this would seem to have to do with the structure of a group, and I am at present discussing the structure of the clause. More accurately, I am only discussing the structure of main clauses (see sections 5.4.3.9 and 5.4.4 regarding the remaining instance of *you*).)

The items in column 2 that realize interactional meaning and its contrast are also realizing participant A in their respective clauses. In other words, interactional meaning and its contrasting meaning have been mapped onto a segment generated by the experiential component, just as Halliday's hypothesis would predict. Indeed it could be said that more than one experiential segment is affected. Although column 2 contains the overt, noticeable realizations of interactional meaning, it could be argued that there are repercussions also in column 4. This does not show up in the examples from the passages here owing to the prevalence of modal auxiliaries that do not inflect for number and person. But elsewhere, and certainly in languages that preserve more of their verb inflections than English, interactional meaning would have to be regarded as prosodically realized, because it would be mapped onto both the participant A segment and also the segment that realizes the process.

Obligation/prohibition meaning is mainly realized by items that occur in column 4, auxiliaries and lexical verbs, as too are most of the meanings thought to contrast with this type of meaning (see section 5.4.2.2). Obligation/prohibition meaning was regarded as one type of regulatory meaning. Other items considered relevant to regulatory meaning or its contrast are again *candidate* and *student*, which as noted earlier occur in column 2. (*No student*, relevant to prohibition meaning, also occurs in column 2 but, as in the case of *your*, the precise contribution of *No* would have to be accounted for in terms of group structure rather than clause structure.)

The distribution of obligation/prohibition meaning and the other meanings with which it is associated can, like interactional meaning and its associates, be regarded as following the predictions of Halliday's hypothesis. Again the interpersonal meanings can be said to be mapped on to segments derived from the experiential component. Again one particular segment seems to be the main location of realization, but again there are repercussions affecting another segment. It is interesting that, in the case of both interactional meaning and obligation/prohibition meaning, the segments most concerned are the segments that realize participant A and process, because these are the segments onto which the mood marking functions are assumed to be mapped, mood marking usually being regarded in SFL as the quintessential type of interpersonal meaning.

The prosodic realization of interpersonal meaning hypothesis is looking very promising. The only relevant items not yet accounted for are *your*, the *you* that occurs in a subordinate clause, and the two instances of *With the consent of the Head of Department*. As already indicated, the instances of *your* and *you* would be expected to be accounted for elsewhere in the grammar, under the headings of nominal group structure and subordinate clause structure respectively. It could be argued that the two instances of *With the consent of the Head of Department*, as well as having interpersonal implications, represent experiential circumstances. These too would then be in accordance with the hypothesis. However, since these items appear in the table in the problematic column 1, they will be discussed further below.

5.6.3. The realization of textual meaning

Halliday's hypothesis for textual meaning (e.g. IFG 1994: 36) is that it is realized culminatively (i.e. by positioning at beginnings and ends of units). This is, of course, what I have mainly been discussing in this chapter. How does it relate to the interpersonal meanings that I have also been discussing?

The problem with textual meaning is that the term seems to be used in IFG in two different senses: a broad sense and a narrow sense. It is defined (IFG 1994: 36) as "creating relevance to context."

This seems to be a very broad sense indeed. Assuming that "context" here includes both "cotext" and "context of situation," textual meaning would seem to *include* interpersonal meaning. It is surely the interactional meanings and the obligation/prohibition meanings I have been discussing that do most to create relevance to their respective contexts of situation. How can these meanings be interpersonal and textual at the same time? Interpersonal and textual meaning are usually regarded in SFL as distinct. This question is answered when Halliday (1978: 145) emphasizes that textual meaning categories are second order categories, that textual meaning has an "enabling" function with regard to the other types of meaning. Presumably what it enables, through its culminative positioning, is the giving of prominence to the other types of meaning. The interpersonal meanings are distinct types of meaning, defined in their own terms, but when one begins, as I have done, to discuss *prioritization* of these types of meaning, then presumably I am discussing the textual enabling of interpersonal meaning. The meanings, regarded as first order meanings, are interpersonal, but they also have a second order meaning, a degree of prominence, and that, according to Halliday's distinction, is textual.

That seems to clarify the broad sense of "textual meaning." What of the narrow sense? When Halliday (IFG 1985: 54; 1994: 53–4) comes to classify particular types of Theme as "Textual Themes," the term *textual* seems to have a very narrow meaning indeed. The only types of item that are permitted to qualify are: "continuatives," for instance, discourse markers such as *yes, no, well;* "structural Themes," such as conjunctions; and "conjunctive Themes," such as *however, in addition.* These items do not seem to me to be enabling the prioritization of interpersonal meanings or experiential meanings. They seem to have a type of meaning of their own. The textual metafunction is supposed to be non-representational (Matthiessen 1992: 76); it is not supposed to have anything to do with construing reality. But items such as *however* and *in addition* surely do represent construals of reality, though construals of relationships between events rather than construals of relationships within events. The meanings of the so-called "Textual Themes" would seem to me to be first order meanings, ones that themselves need to be enabled. Maybe there is a branch of textual meaning concerned with enabling them, but first they need to be recognized as meanings in their own right. They would appear not to be either experiential meanings, or interpersonal meanings. I have not yet discussed logical meanings. Could the meanings of the so-called "Textual Themes" be accounted for under this heading? I will return to the discussion of textual meaning after logical meaning has been considered.

5.6.4. The realization of logical meaning

Halliday (IFG 1994: 36) defined logical meaning as "constructing logical relations." It is said to be realized by "iterative structures." When logical relations come to be discussed in detail (IFG: chapter 7), they seem to be realized by some of the items earlier said to be realizing "Textual Themes." Is it possible that "Textual Themes" are not actually either textual or Themes, but instead have more in common with logical meaning? If so, this would solve the problem of the previous subsection, of finding a way of representing them as first order meanings before discussing how they are enabled by the second order textual metafunction. As first order meanings, they would be logical meanings, which would then receive a particular degree of prominence through the second order textual metafunction.

If, at the same time, it were possible to solve another problem, this would be even better. There is another problem, one that I left unsolved in section 5.6.1: there seemed to be no experientially derived segment to which it was possible to relate the meanings realized by the items in column 1 of Table 1.1. There may well be a connection with the problem currently under consideration, since some of the items in column 1 are items that Halliday would regard as "Textual Themes."

As indicated above, logical meaning is regarded by Halliday as a subtype of ideational meaning, the other subtype of ideational meaning being experiential meaning. Presumably both subtypes can be regarded as representational, as having to do with construing experience, the difference between them being that experiential meaning has to do with construing the internal relations of events, while logical meaning has to do with construing relations between events. (This may be stretching the meaning of the term *logical*. Halliday [IFG 1985: 193; 1994: 216] puts "logical" in quotation marks, to indicate that he too is stretching it. For the moment I will do the same. Hopefully, it will some day be possible to agree on a more suitable term.[20]) Since "logical" meaning is so like experiential mean-

---

[20]Matthiessen (1992) used the term *transitional relations* in this connection. This would seem to be a very suitable term. It is true that there may be confusion with the Prague School use of the term *transition* (see note 18), but there is probably going to be confusion with something, no matter what term is chosen. The best that can be hoped for is that the term will be reasonably transparent. The Fries (1983) term *method of development* is probably better kept for a particular kind of transitional relation. Fries himself uses it to describe the transitional relations of texts that show consistency in their principle of organization, such that particular methods of development can be recognized (e.g. relative location method, component parts method).

ing, it would not be departing very far from Halliday's original hypothesis about constituent structure to permit "logical" meaning, like experiential meaning, to generate constituents.[21] If we assume that typically the "logical" component will generate for each clause at least one constituent whose function is to relate the meaning of that clause to the meaning of other clauses, this would give us an ideationally, though not experientially, derived constituent that could form the basis for the meanings in column 1. This is surely preferable to allowing the textual component to generate constituents, which is what the term *Textual Theme* seems to imply. A second order metafunction surely by definition cannot generate constituents.

All this of course needs to be argued in much greater detail than is possible here. A discussion of constituency in an SFL framework needs an article to itself. All that is possible here is a few brief preliminary observations (see Berry, forthcoming for further discussion).

5.6.5. The realization of textual meaning (revisited)

If "textual" meaning in the narrow sense can be subsumed under "logical" meaning, and if "logical" meaning can be regarded as realized through the generation of a (particular type of) constituent, as just suggested, this leaves "textual" meaning in the broad sense to be realized according to Halliday's hypothesis (i.e. culminatively). It would seem reasonable to expect that first order "logical" meanings will usually have as their second order meaning a high degree of prominence, which would explain why they usually occur at the beginnings of clauses.

However, another possibility needs to be considered at least briefly. This is where the unusual position hypothesis becomes relevant (see section 5.4.1). Is it that high degree of prominence is realized by positioning at beginning or end of unit? Or is it that high degree of prominence is realized through placing in an *unusual* position, wherever that may be?

According to my own intuitions, in the first two of the following pairs of clauses, the (a) clause is more marked than the (b) clause, but in the case of the third pair, the (b) clause is more marked than the (a). In other words, the meaning(s) of *With the consent of the Head of Department* receive a greater degree of prominence in (a) than in (b), the meaning(s) of *always* receive a greater degree of

---

[21]Bateman (1989) permitted the logical metafunction to generate microfunctions.

prominence in (a) than in (b), but the meaning(s) of *then* receive a greater degree of prominence in (b) than in (a). (It is important to note that the statements I am making here are *relative* statements. I perceive all these meanings as having a high degree of prominence, but some as having a higher degree than others.)

With the consent of the Head of Department, a candidate may substitute a dissertation for twenty credits worth of Level B or Level 3 modules. (1a)

A candidate may, with the consent of the Head of Department, substitute a dissertation for twenty credits worth of Level B or Level 3 modules. (1b)

But always the special subjects include modules focusing on specialist areas in modern English language and in medieval and modern literature. (2a)

But the special subjects always include modules focusing on specialist areas in modern English language and in medieval and modern literature. (2b)

Then they choose a further six modules. (3a)

They then choose a further six modules. (3b)

I have no idea as yet if other language users share these intuitions. If it turns out that they do, it would presumably be necessary to account for these intuitions by hypotheses along the following lines: that the usual position for a constituent that realizes experiential circumstance meaning and that has interpersonal meaning mapped onto it will be in the region of the constituents that have mood marking functions; that the usual position for a constituent that realizes "logical" meaning, with or without experiential circumstance meaning, will be at the beginning of the clause; when the combination circumstance + interpersonal is to receive special prominence, it will be moved into the position normally occupied by "logical" meaning; when "logical" meaning is to receive special prominence, it will be moved into the position normally occupied by circumstance + interpersonal meaning. (It should perhaps be explained here that Halliday (IFG 1985: 50; 1994: 49) assumed that *always* has interpersonal meaning.)[22]

If it *is* necessary to set up hypotheses along these lines, unusual positioning would have to be regarded as at least an alternative, if not a rival, to culminative positioning as the realization for textual meaning. One possibility might be that textual meaning *is* realized culminatively, in the sense that prioritized interpersonal and "logical" meanings are positioned in the first part of the clause (i.e. in the part up to and including the constituent that realizes the process), but that within this area it is possible to detect *degrees* of prominence and that these are accounted for by unusual positioning. Further discussion must await further evidence.

5.6.6. A tentative answer to the sixth question

If the reasoning in the previous subsections can be accepted, the answer to Huddleston's sixth question would be: the constituent structure of a clause "with multiple Theme$_F$" would be whatever was jointly determined by the ideational—experiential and "logical"—metafunctions.

However, it would also be possible to group the ideationally de-rived constituents in terms of their status with regard to the mo-bility of interpersonal meanings. Constituents in the area of partici-pant A and process (i.e. the mood marking area) would be the most likely locations for the realization of interpersonal meaning (cf Rav-elli in press). But interpersonal meanings *could* occur earlier than the participant A constituent. This gives rise to a second grouping, consisting of all the constituents up to and including the process constituent. The hypothesis is that the process constituent acts as a cut-off point for interpersonal meaning, that very few interpersonal meanings will occur after the process constituent, and such that do will be perceived to have a low degree of prominence.

The process constituent is similarly hypothesized to be a cut-off point with regard to the mobility of "logical" meanings. (Hypothesis 8b, in section 5.4.3.8, now needs to be reworded, since the term *textual* was there being used in the narrow sense that I am here attempting to subsume under "logical.") The hypothesis is that very few "logical" meanings will occur after the process constituent and such that do will be perceived to have a low degree of prominence.[23]

---

[22]Certain types of item realizing "logical" meaning, of course, cannot move (e.g. conjunctions).

[23]I would hope not only that "logical" meaning might be renamed *transitional*

It is this second grouping of constituents, the constituents up to and including the process constituent, that was regarded in section 5.4.4 as the most likely candidate for the status of Theme$_F$. Certainly, all but one of the prioritized meanings discussed in this chapter occurred in the area of this second group of constituents (the one exception being in a subordinate clause). This will be particularly interesting if further evidence supports the hypotheses discussed in section 5.4.3.8 and in the present section, if it can be shown that the area of this second grouping of constituents is regularly the domain for the realization of prioritized interpersonal and "logical" meanings.

As a final note in this section, it is perhaps necessary to comment on the use of the phrase *with multiple Theme$_F$*, because there is an apparent contradiction. The hypothesis I am arguing for is that each clause would have *one* Theme$_F$, this extending up to and including the constituent that realizes the process. *With multiple Theme$_F$* would then have to be regarded as merely a shorthand way of saying with reference to a particular clause *either* that more than one ideationally derived constituent was to be found in the thematic area *or* that meanings from more than one metafunction were being prioritized in the thematic area. I would probably myself choose not to use the phrase at all.

This discussion of constituency was necessarily brief, since the issue represents just one question in a list of seven. The discussion will be continued in Berry (forthcoming).

5.7. What is the Nature of the Empirical Evidence Supporting the Analysis?

Hopefully, it will be recognized that the whole of this chapter has been an attempt to answer this seventh question. All that will be offered here, therefore, is a brief summary of what has been said.

A distinction was drawn between discourse Theme$_M$, a priority set of meanings reflecting the writer's main concerns for a text as a whole or for a large section of a text such as a paragraph, and clause Theme$_M$, a priority set of meanings reflecting the writer's main concerns for a particular clause. The empirical evidence for the components of discourse Theme$_M$ consists in the first instance of observations by writers as to their own priorities and observations by

meaning (see note 20), but that it might be broadened to include "topical" meaning (see section 5.6.1). This would bring together all types of meaning that have to do with making connections between the meanings of different parts of the text.

readers as to general types of meanings that have been given prominence. These are the intuitions to be accounted for in a Theme–Rheme analysis rather than intuitions about grammaticality. In order to account for such intuitions, hypotheses were set up as to the specific types of meaning prioritized. The next step was to see whether the meanings hypothesized to be priority meanings had in fact been given priority. The evidence here was distributional: whether the meanings occurred more frequently in texts hypothesized to be prioritizing the meanings than in texts not so hypothesized.

Clause $Theme_M$ was not discussed in detail. However it was assumed that, in order to justify recognition of clause $Theme_M$, it would first be necessary to establish a connection between discourse $Theme_M$ and a particular part of a clause or other grammatical feature to be known as $Theme_F$. Justification for recognition of clause $Theme_M$ would then depend on evidence that readers associated $Theme_F$ with the realization of important meanings, either the priority meanings that formed the components of discourse $Theme_M$s or meanings that had a purely local importance.

The evidence for $Theme_F$ was assumed to be distributional: whether the priority meanings of discourse $Theme_M$s were regularly associated with a particular section of a clause or other grammatical feature.

Distribution was again assumed to be the criterion when discussing issues of constituency, in particular distribution of meanings associated with the various metafunctions. It was hypothesized that the basic constituents of a clause were derived from the ideational metafunctions, the experiential and the "logical," but that it was also possible to recognize types of organization superimposed on the basic constituents. In particular it was hypothesized that it is possible to identify a section of the clause, in fact the section of the clause already hypothesized to be $Theme_F$, which was the main location for the realization of interpersonal and "logical" meanings. It may be that $Theme_F$ is the location, not for priority meanings in general, but for priority meanings of the types that are communicatively important: meanings that have to do with establishing tone of voice, social relations, type of interaction—i.e., interpersonal meanings; and meanings that have to do with making connections between the meanings of different parts of a text—i.e., "logical" meanings. If further distributional evidence supports the view that priority meanings of these types occur in the early parts of clauses, while priority meanings of an experiential nature occur in the later parts of clauses, this would indeed be good reason for dividing clauses into two parts after the manner of a Theme–Rheme analysis.[24]

6. CONCLUSION

It has been repeatedly emphasized that it is not the purpose of the present chapter to draw conclusions, but rather to develop a line of argument. This line of argument was ideationally summarized in section 5.7. In this concluding section, therefore, I will return to the interpersonal purpose of this volume.

What Halliday has achieved is to overturn the usual assumptions of linguistics about where one starts and what is important. In SFL, meaning is given priority over form and texts over sentences. Intuitions about degrees of prominence and the appropriateness of such degrees of prominence to particular readerships and particular purposes are given priority over intuitions about grammaticality. Interpersonal meaning, "logical" meaning and textual meaning are given parity of treatment with experiential meaning. All this offers opportunities to applied text linguists such as myself to explain differences between texts and text types and to account for evaluations of texts in ways that make sense to ordinary language users.

REFERENCES

Bateman, J. (1989) Dynamic systemic-functional grammar: A new frontier, *Word* 40, 1–2: 263–286.

de Beaugrande, R. and Dressler, W. (1981) *Introduction to Text Linguistics*. London: Longman.

Berry, M. (1975) *An Introduction to Systemic Linguistics: I. Structures and Systems*. London: Batsford. Reprinted by Dept of English Studies, University of Nottingham 1989.

---

[24]An interesting hypothesis to investigate would be that experiential meanings only occur before the process constituent when accompanied by interpersonal or "logical" (transitional) meanings. The circumstance constituents that occur before the process constituent in the passages I have been discussing here all seem to have interpersonal or "logical" implications, as do the constituents realizing participant A. In fact one might expect that the selection of which participant to represent as participant A would be made, not on experiential grounds, even though the participant is an experiential function, but on interpersonal/"logical" (transitional) grounds; on grounds, that is, of which participant could best be seen as combining with an interpersonal/transitional meaning.

Berry, M. (1987) The functions of place names, in T. Turville-Petre and M. Gelling (eds.) *Studies in Honour of Kenneth Cameron (Leeds Studies in English New Series XVIII)*. Leeds School of English, University of Leeds, 71–88.

Berry, M. (1989) Thematic options and success in writing, in C.S. Butler, R.A. Cardwell and J. Channell (eds.) *Language and Literature—Theory and Practice: A Tribute to Walter Grauberg (University of Nottingham Monographs in the Humanities VI)*. Nottingham: University of Nottingham, 62–80.

Berry, M. (1995) Thematic options and success in writing. In M. Ghadessy (ed.), *Thematic Development in English Texts*. London: Pinter, 55–84. [Revised version of Berry (1989)].

Berry, M. (in press) Theme and the enacting of social relationships.

Berry, M. (forthcoming) Theme and the creating of relevance to context.

Brown, G. and Yule, G. (1983) *Discourse Analysis*. Cambridge: Cambridge University Press.

Christie, F. (1985) Language and schooling, in S. Tchudi (ed.) *Language, Schooling and Society*. New Jersey: Boynton/Cook.

Davies, F. (1988) Reading between the lines: thematic choice as a device for presenting writer viewpoint in academic Discourse, *Especialist*, 9, 1(2): 173–200.

Davies, F. (1991) Writing across text-types and genres; the potential of marked Theme as a device for structuring text. University of Liverpool, English Language Unit.

Dixon, J. (1967) *Growth through English*. Reading: National Association for the Teaching of English.

Dixon, J. (1987) The question of genres, in I. Reid (ed.) 1987, 9–21.

Downing, A. (1991) An alternative approach to theme: a systemic-functional perspective, *Word*, 42(2): 119–143.

Enkvist, N.E. (1973) Theme dynamics and style: an experiment, *Studia Anglica Posnaniensia*, 5: 127–35.

Firbas, J. (1986) On the dynamics of written communication in the light of the theory of functional sentence perspective, in C.R. Cooper and S. Greenbaum (eds.) *Studying Writing: Linguistic Approaches*. Beverly Hills, California: Sage, 40–71.

Fries, P.H. (1983) On the status of theme in English: arguments from discourse, in J.S. Petofi and E. Sozer (eds.) *Micro and Macro Connexity of Texts*. Hamburg: Buske Verlag, 116–152.

Fries, P.H. (1995) Introduction: A personal view of Theme. In M. Ghadessy (ed.), *Thematic Development in English Texts*. London: Pinter, 1–19.

Gibson, T.R. (1993) *Towards a Discourse Theory of Abstracts and Abstracting (Monographs in Systemic Linguistics 5)*. Nottingham: Dept of English Studies, University of Nottingham.

Halliday, M.A.K. (1964) Syntax and the consumer, in R. O'Brien (1968) *Georgetown University Round Table Selected Papers in Linguistics*

1961–1965, Washington, D.C.: Georgetown University Press, 189–202.

Halliday, M.A.K. (1967) Notes on transitivity and theme in English, Parts 1 and 2. *Journal of Linguistics* 3, 1: 37–81 and 3, 2: 199–244.

Halliday, M.A.K. (1968) Notes on transitivity and theme in English, Part 3, *Journal of Linguistics*, 4, 2: 179–215.

Halliday, M.A.K. (1969) Relevant models of language, in M.A.K. Halliday (1973) *Explorations in the Functions of Language*. London: Edward Arnold, 9–21.

Halliday, M.A.K. (1975) Language as social semiotic, in M.A.K. Halliday (1978), 108–126.

Halliday, M.A.K. (1977) Text as semantic choice in social contexts, in M.A.K. Halliday (1978), 128–151.

Halliday, M.A.K. (1978) *Language as Social Semiotic*. London: Edward Arnold.

Halliday, M.A.K. (1985, 2nd edn. 1994) *An Introduction to Functional Grammar*. London: Edward Arnold.

Halliday, M.A.K. and Hasan, R. (1976) *Cohesion in English*. London: Longman.

Halliday, M.A.K. and Hasan, R. (1985/1989) *Language, Context and Text: Aspects of Language in a Social-Semiotic Perspective*. Victoria: Deakin University Press (1985)/Reissued by Oxford University Press (1989).

Hasan, R. (1978) Text in the systemic-functional model, in W.U. Dressler (ed.) *Current Trends in Textlinguistics*. Berlin: de Gruyter.

Hasan, R. (1995) The conception of context in texts, in P.H. Fries and M. Gregory (eds.) *Discourse in Society: Functional Perspectives*. Norwood, NJ: Ablex.

Huddleston, R. (1988) Constituency, multi-functionality and grammaticalisation in Halliday's Functional Grammar. *Journal of Linguistics* 24, 1: 137–174.

Huddleston, R. (1991) Further remarks on Halliday's Functional Grammar: a reply to Matthiessen and Martin. *Occasional Papers in Systemic Linguistics* 5: 75–129.

Hudson, R. (1986) Systemic grammar, *Linguistics* 24: 791–815.

Keenan, E.O. and Schieffelin, B. (1976) Topic as a discourse notion, in C.N. Li (ed.) *Subject and Topic*. New York: Academic Press.

Matthiessen, C. (1992) Interpreting the textual metafunction, in M. Davies and L. Ravelli (eds.) *Advances in Systemic Linguistics: Recent Theory and Practice*. London: Pinter.

Matthiessen, C. and Martin, J.R. (1991) A response to Huddleston's review of Halliday's *Introduction to Functional Grammar, Occasional Papers in Systemic Linguistics*, 5: 5–74.

Morgan, J.L. (1975) Some remarks on the nature of sentences, in *Papers from the Parasession on Functionalism*. Chicago Linguistic Society.

Quirk, R., Greenbaum, S., Leech, G. and Svartvik, J. (1985) *A Comprehensive Grammar of the English Language.* London: Longman.

Ravelli, L.J. (in press) Metafunctional interaction from a dynamic perspective: implications for the description of Theme. To appear in R. Hasan and P.H. Fries (eds.) *On Subject and Theme: From the Perspective of Functions in Discourse.* Amsterdam: John Benjamins.

Reid, I. (ed.) (1987) *The Place of Genre in Learning: Current Debates.* Victoria, Australia: Deakin University Press.

Stainton, C. (1993) *Metadiscourse and the Analytical Text: A Genre-Based Approach to Children's Written Discourse.* PhD Thesis, University of Manchester.

Stainton, C. (in press a) What is this thing called Genre? To be published in *Nottingham Working Papers.*

Stainton, C. (in press b) So why do I state "In this paper I will discuss"? To be published in *Nottingham Working Papers.*

Stainton, C. (in press c) Theme: comparisons and contrasts. To be published in *Nottingham Working Papers.*

Stainton, C. (in press d e f) Reports on three specific genres of business and industry. To be published in *Nottingham Working Papers.*

Vande Kopple, W.J. (1991) Themes, thematic progressions and some implications for understanding discourse, *Written Communication,* 8, 3: 311–347.

Widdowson, H.G. (1984) *Explorations in Applied Linguistics 2.* Oxford: Oxford University Press.

2

Experiential Enhanced Theme in English*

Guowen Huang

Computational Linguistics Unit
University of Wales, Cardiff

1. INTRODUCTION

I have been interested in Systemic Functional Linguistics since I was an undergraduate, but it was only when I met Professor Michael Halliday in 1985 at the International Symposium on Teaching English in the Chinese Context in my home university in Guangzhou that I began to take the Hallidayan theory seriously. I was doing my MA course in linguistics and applied linguistics at that time, and in my MA dissertation I applied some of Halliday's ideas about the Experiential Function (e.g., TRANSITIVITY) to the analysis of "The Killers," a short story by Ernest Hemingway (Huang 1986). My interest in Systemic Functional Linguistics continued and was further strengthened when, in 1993, Dr. Robin Fawcett, Director of the Computational Linguistics Unit at the University of Wales, Cardiff,

---

*I am extremely grateful to Dr. Robin Fawcett—Director of the Computational Linguistics Unit, University of Wales, Cardiff—not only for his warm encouragement and insightful comments on the first version of this chapter, but also for his generosity in sharing his ideas with me with regard to the Cardiff Model of Systemic Functional Grammar. Needless to say, all the errors that remain are mine. I would also like to express my sincere thanks for the financial support from the School of English Studies, Communication and Philosophy, University of Wales, Cardiff.

offered me the chance to work with him on Systemic Functional Grammar. Here I would like to express my sincere thanks to both Michael and Robin for their influences on my understanding of language and linguistics.

This chapter is concerned with the experiential enhanced theme construction in English (known as "predicated theme" in the Hallidayan Model of Systemic Functional Linguistics, and "it-cleft" or "cleft sentence" in formal grammars).[1] I will explain the reasons for preferring the term "enhanced theme" in Section 3. In this chapter I will begin with a brief discussion of Halliday's treatment of predicated theme and Fawcett's syntactic and semantic analysis of the construction. Although it can be argued that there is a single predicated theme construction at the level of syntax, at the level of "meaning potential"—for instance, semantics—there are two main types. Halliday (1994: 58–61, 98) offered an account of the better known type, which may be termed the "contrastive" type. In this chapter, I will comment on the differences between the two types in terms of their information structures and discourse functions.

2. HALLIDAY'S TREATMENT OF "PREDICATED THEME"

Halliday was the first systemic functional linguist to offer a comprehensive study of the predicated theme construction in English. In this section, I shall briefly review his studies of the construction.

2.1. The "Agnate" Assumption

It was more than 30 years ago, in his "Syntax and the consumer" (1964/1981), that Halliday first drew attention to one of the impor-

---

[1]There are in fact three types of "Enhanced Theme" in English: (a) the experiential Enhanced Theme, (b) the evaluative Enhanced Theme, and (c) the existential Enhanced Theme. The first is the type that is being discussed in this chapter. An example of the second type is *It is possible that Helen is Henry's girlfriend.* This construction is "evaluative" in that the Attribute (e.g., *possible* here) expresses the Performer's "evaluation" of the proposition in the Carrier (e.g., *that Helen is Henry's girlfriend* here). This construction is usually called the "extraposed construction" (or "extraposition") in formal grammars (Huang and Fawcett 1994). An example of the existential type is *There is a young man in your office.* This construction is termed "existential sentence" in formal grammars. When I use the term "Enhanced Theme" in this chapter it will always be an abbreviation for "experiential Enhanced Theme."

tant ways of selecting and highlighting a theme, which he termed "theme predication" or "predicated theme." In this publication Halliday argued that "theme predication" and "theme selection" are simultaneous in the choice in a system network. This is intended to reflect the fact that we can have a clause with both a predicated theme and what was said to be a "subject theme," as in Example (1)· below; alternatively we can have a clause with a predicated theme and a supposedly "complement theme," as in (2) below:

It was the queen who sent my uncle that hatstand.   (1)

It was that hatstand that the queen sent my uncle.   (2)

There is a "predicated" theme in both (1) and (2), in that both *the queen* and *that hatstand* are placed after *it is*. According to Halliday, (1) and (2) are incongruent versions of Example (3) below:

The queen sent my uncle that hatstand   (3).

Since *the queen* and *that hatstand* in (3) are Subject and Complement respectively, in terms of syntax, Halliday assumed that the predicated theme in (1) (i.e., *the queen*) is Subject with regard to theme selection. By contrast, the predicated theme in (2) (i.e., *that hatstand*) is a Complement.

The idea of theme selection discussed here is closely related to Halliday's understanding of the "source" of the predicated theme construction. Halliday (1994: 98) pointed out that "a clause with predicated theme always . . . has a NON-PREDICATED AGNATE CLAUSE: *it was last year that he fell ill: he fell ill last year*" (my emphasis). Clearly, Halliday's perception of the nature of the predicated theme construction is more acceptable than that of the many scholars in both the traditional school and the generative school (e.g., Jespersen 1937/1969; Fichtner 1993), who argued that the predicated theme construction is the result of "cleaving" a "non-cleft" clause. In this chapter I will, following Fawcett (in preparation c), believe that the predicated theme construction and its corresponding "non-predicated agnate clause" are related at the level of logical form, and not at the level of language. Like Halliday, I will assume that Examples (1) and (2) above are the incongruent versions of the congruent form in (3), but like Fawcett, I shall assume that, in the overall model, this "agnation" occurs at the "pre-linguistic" level of logical form.

2.2. Thematic Structure

Halliday (e.g., 1985, 1994) treated theme predication as a way of organizing thematic structure. He claimed that "any element having a representational function in the clause can be marked off by predication" (Halliday 1994: 58). While this may be true, I feel that some acknowledgement should be made of the fact that examples such as (4c) strike many native speakers as being even more heavily marked than usual—even though *the head* has a "representational function" in the clause:

He is the head.   (4a)

It is he that is the head.   (4b)

?It is the head that he is.   (4c)

Clearly, what is needed here is a model of grammar that includes probabilities, as is increasingly the case in the Cardiff Grammar.

Figure 2.1 below is Halliday's analysis of the theme–rheme structure.

From this figure we can see that Halliday proposed a dual thematic analysis. That is, the whole construction is first broken down into two parts, the theme and the rheme (i.e., Halliday's "Version (b)"), and then each is further divided into thematic patterns (i.e., Halliday's "Version (a)"). According to Halliday (1994): "Version (a) shows the local thematic structure; here both Themes are unmarked (*it* and *who* are both Subjects). Version (b) shows the thematic structure of the whole clause as predicated Theme" (Halliday 1994: 60). In the present study, I will only regard *his teacher* in Figure 2.1 as the theme, rather than the words *it was his teacher*, for two reasons. First, the words *it was his teacher* DO NOT constitute a clause-as-theme (Halliday 1994: 54–58), as I will shortly show, and, secondly, only *his teacher* is highlighted or enhanced (*it was* being the "thematic build-up," see Fawcett and Huang 1995, and Fawcett in preparation a). As rheme is not identified in the Cardiff Grammar, the analysis of the thematic structure of the predicated theme construction in the present study will only be concerned with theme. This is because we believe that it is sufficient to identify the theme: Once the theme is identified, what is left is the rheme, but it has no meaning other than "that which is not theme."

it	was	his teacher	who	persuaded him to continue

(a)	Theme	Rheme	Theme	Rheme

(b)	Theme		Rheme	

Figure 2.1. Thematic structure of clause with predicated theme (Halliday 1994: 60)

2.3. Syntactic Analysis and the Identified-Identifier Classification

There are three aspects of Halliday's analysis of this construction I wish to query. Firstly, in making a syntactic analysis of the predicated theme construction, Halliday (e.g., 1994) assumed that the Subject consists of both the item *it* and the embedded clause. Thus, according to Halliday (1994: 60, 98), in *it was his teacher who persuaded him to continue*, the Subject is *it . . . who persuaded him to continue*, *was* is the Predicator (and Finite) and *his teacher* is the Complement, as in Figure 2.2 below.

As Figure 2.2 shows, there is for Halliday "a discontinuous Subject" (Halliday 1994: 98) in the clause with predicated theme, because the Subject is separated into two by the Predicator and the Complement. I will shortly present an alternative analysis.

Secondly, Halliday (1967, 1994) treated the predicated theme construction as an equative structure. He argued that:

> Predication may involve any cognitive theme [. . .] and is exemplified by *it was John who broke the window*; it is thus realized as an equative structure, with *it . . . who broke the window* as identified, *John* as identifier, the relator being [. . .] the class 2 *be*.
> (Halliday 1967: 236)

Clearly Halliday is at this point treating the predicated theme construction as an equative structure with an Identified and an Identifier. However, Halliday also observed that examples such as (5) are not equative structures. As he pointed out, Example (5) "has no identifying equivalent," adding: "It does not make sense to highlight *in spite of the cold* in a coding relation, though it makes perfectly good sense to highlight it as a theme" (Halliday 1967: 236).

It was in spite of the cold that he went swimming. (Halliday 1967: 236)   (5)

It is therefore clear from Halliday's own writings that there can be a predicated theme even in a non-equative structure. This suggests

It	was	his teacher	who	persuaded him to continue
Sub-	"(past) Finite	be" Predicator	Complement	-ject
Mood		Residue		

Figure 2.2. Syntactic and mood analyses (after Halliday 1994: 98)

that it is not desirable to associate the predicated theme construction with the Identified–Identifier structure, because there are predicated theme constructions that do not show such a relationship.

Thirdly, the assumption that *it* and *who sent my uncle that hatstand* in (1) together are said to function as the Subject suggests that *it* is a referring expression rather than a semantically empty item. This analysis is similar to the approach adopted by Jespersen, who argued that in examples such as *it is the wife that decides*

> the relative clause [the "embedded clause" in our terminology] . . . might be said to belong rather to "it" than to the predicative following after "it is." (Jespersen 1928/1965: 89)

The idea that *it* in (1) is a referring expression is adopted by other systemicists. For example, Martin (1992: 130) regarded this *it* as "structurally cataphoric."

In this chapter I will assume, following Fawcett (in preparation a) and others, that the Subject of the clause is only filled by *it* in order to express the MOOD of "information giver" (or "declarative"). It is experientially empty, and is therefore not "structurally cataphoric." Moreover, the embedded clause (such as *who sent my uncle that hatstand* in Example (1) above) is not part of the Subject of the clause as a whole, because the Mood element only consists of *it* (Subject) and *was* (Operator and Main Verb), as can be seen in (6) below, which is an information seeker:

<u>Was</u> it the queen who sent my uncle that hatstand? (6)

2.4. Information Structure

The information patterns of the enhanced theme construction are a complex matter, as we will see in Section 4.5 below. Here I will simply summarize what Halliday (1994: 59) had to say about the matter. Halliday (1985, 1994) pointed out that predication is an effective way of telling the Addressee how to interpret the information conveyed by a predicated theme construction. In this structure:

> One part is the news: what the listener is being invited to attend to as new, or unexpected, or important. The other part is the old stuff: what is presented as being already known to the listener, that which he can take as "given." The "new" is signalled by the tonic accent, a clear fall or rise (or more complex movement) in pitch. (Halliday 1994: 59)

Thus, in the predicated theme construction in (7) below, the "new" element is mapped onto the predicated theme, because: "the tonic accent [. . .] falls on *teacher;* the fact that John continued is taken as given, and the contrast is between his teacher's attitude and that of his father" (Halliday 1994: 60). Halliday's thematic analysis of the clause with predicated theme in (7) is as in Figure 2.1 above.

> John's father wanted him to give up the violin. It was his teach-
> er who persuaded him to continue. (Halliday 1994: 60) (7)

Example (7) illustrates the fact that one of the major functions of predicated theme constructions is to be "contrastive," in the sense that one element is being contrasted with something external, either explicitly or implicitly. In (7) above, the contrast is explicit, because *John's father* and *his teacher* are the two entities in contrast at the level of semantics.

Let us look next at the discussion of the information pattern of the predicated theme construction by Downing and Locke (1992: 247–249). Following Halliday (e.g., 1985), they stated that typically the predicated theme represents new information and that the embedded clause provides given information. However, they also observed that "the New information may fall in the second part, the relative construction [the embedded clause]" (p. 247). The following is their illustration (Downing and Locke 1992: 248).

Figure 2.3 indicates that the "main focus" in B's answer is on *Rome* (i.e., on an element of the embedded clause) rather than on the predicated theme. The construction clearly serves a rather similar discourse function as Example (7). (In terms of the taxonomy offered in Section 5, Example (7) is a "counter-expectation" and the example in Figure 2.3 is a "correction.") I will return in Section 4.5.2 to consider the problem of the internal structure of the example in Figure 2.3.

A. We flew to Paris on a Jumbo JET.	
B. No, it was `on a Jumbo secondary focus Given Predicated Theme	that we flew to RÒME. main focus New

Figure 2.3. The Information structure of a Theme predication (Downing and Locke 1992: 248)

2.5. Concluding Remarks

Halliday's (e.g., 1967, 1985, 1994) study of the predicated theme construction appears to be only concerned with the contrastive type of Theme predication. On this basis, one might think that Halliday's generalization holds for all cases except those in which there is a contrastive item in the embedded clause. But this is not so, as this chapter will show. Indeed, it has long been observed that there are different types of the predicated theme construction in English (e.g., Collins 1991, Declerck 1988, Delin 1989, Hedberg 1990, Prince 1978).

In this chapter, then, I will discuss both the contrastive and the non-contrastive types of enhanced theme construction. The structural analysis that I will use for all enhanced theme constructions, whether or not they are contrastive, is in fact different from Halliday's, while being equally "systemic functional." It has a number of features that help to clarify the status of both the units and the elements of the structure. The model is essentially that of Fawcett (e.g., 1973-4/1981, 1980, 1987, 1990, in preparation a, in preparation b). In the rest of this chapter I will therefore use the terminology of the Cardiff Model of Systemic Functional Grammar. I will begin by summarizing Fawcett's approach to this construction, which provides the basis for this chapter. Then I will discuss the two main types of construction with regard to their information patterns and discourse functions.

3. FAWCETT'S ANALYSIS

Fawcett and Huang (1995), following Fawcett (in preparation a, in preparation b), proposed the term "enhanced theme" as a more appropriate term than Halliday's "predicated theme." The reasons are as follows: First, Fawcett suggested that the item *it* and the form *be* in examples such as (1) above are combined to create a "thematic build-up." Here *be* is not "semantically empty," as many scholars have assumed in the past. The effect of using *it be* is to enhance the theme, hence the term "enhanced theme." Second, the term "predicated" is clearly derived from the term "Predicator," with the initial form of *be* being said to be the Predicator. The problem here is that for many linguists, including those who use the Cardiff Grammar, elements such as Operator, Auxiliary and Main Verb are treated as direct elements of the clause—so that there is no "verbal group" and so no clause element such as Predicator. And, in any case, it seems desirable in a functional model to use an explicitly functional label.

Perhaps the main innovation in Fawcett's approach (Fawcett 1980, 1987, in preparation a, in preparation b) is to treat examples such as (1) above as a clause in which the Main Verb of the matrix clause represents a relational process. In other words, the verb *be* after *it* is in fact the Main Verb of the matrix clause. As with Halliday's earlier writings (1967: 236), Fawcett held the view that, in a functional approach to such clauses, we should assign Participant Roles to the process of "being." However, he proposed different Participant Roles from "Identified" and "Identifier," for the reasons I gave in Section 2.3 above. To illustrate the analysis to be used here, let us look at Figure 2.4.

Here the symbols "At," "Ca," "Ag" and "Af" are Participant Roles, which are semantic in nature. From Figure 2.4 we can see that examples such as (8) have a matrix clause with a relational process of "being," and that it is composed of five clause elements: S^{it}, O/M, C, C. In terms of Participant Roles, the first Complement (C) is an Attribute and the second Complement (C) a Carrier. The Attribute is said to be conflated with the first Complement, and the Carrier with

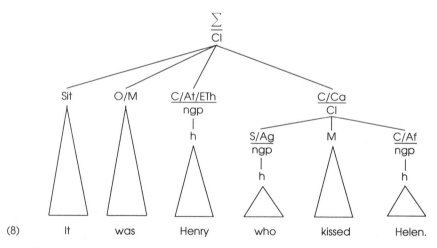

Keys: Σ = Sentence, Cl = Clause, S^{it} = the empty Subject *it*, O = Operator, M = Main verb, C = Complement, / = conflated with, At = Attribute, ETh = Enhanced Theme, Ca = Carrier, S = Subject, Ag = Agent, Af = Affected, ngp = nominal group, h = head (of a nominal group)

Figure 2.4. A syntactico–semantic analysis of the enhanced theme construction

the second Complement. The Carrier is filled by an embedded clause whose Main Verb represents a material process that expects, in terms of Participant Roles, an Agent (Ag) and an Affected (Af). The analysis of Example (8) in Figure 2.4 above is incomplete in that only the TRANSITIVITY, the MOOD and the ENHANCED THEME are indicated. There are other strands of meaning that can be illustrated in a full semantic representation of the example, and these include the following: (a) Interactional, (b) Logical, (c) Polarity, (d) Validity, (e) Affective (see Fawcett in preparation b, Fawcett and Huang in preparation, Huang 1995). For a full discussion of the various analyses proposed in the past and a fuller explanation of why we have adopted the analysis presented here, see Fawcett and Huang (1995).

4. TYPES OF ENHANCED THEME CONSTRUCTION

In the literature to date, there are various classifications of the types of enhanced theme construction in English (e.g., Collins 1991; Declerck 1988; Delin 1989; Geluykens 1988; Hedberg 1990, Prince 1978). In this section, I will briefly discuss the most influential of these, namely Prince's study and then present my own related distinction. Mine, however, is at the level of meaning, and it is supplemented by a taxonomy in terms of discourse functions to be presented in Section 5.

4.1. Prince's (1978) Distinction

Prince (1978) was the first scholar to clearly identify two different types of enhanced theme constructions,[2] and she did this on the

---

[2]In fact, as early as in 1962, Erades (1962: 137–39) pointed out that there is another type of enhanced-theme construction in English:

It is not to say that all sentences opening with *It is*, etc. belong to this type [i.e., the type in which the Enhanced Theme receives "extra-strong stress and extra-high intonation"—GWH]. The case quoted, *It was in 1886 that . . . Lewin published the first systematic study of the cactus* is a case in point. For one thing *It was in 1886* is not strongly emphatic, nor does [siks] [i.e., '6' of '1886'—GWH] bear the extra high intonation . . . There is, that we can see, no reason why the adverbial adjunct should be given emphatic front-position . . . All this points to only one conclusion: this is a different type of sentence.   (Erades 1962: 137–8)

It is a pity that Erades did not discuss the issue in detail. To the best of my knowledge, the first most serious attempt to recognize another type of the enhanced theme construction is in Prince (1978).

basis of information distribution. She proposed a distinction between (a) the "stressed-focus *it*-cleft" and (b) the "informative-presupposition *it*-cleft."

4.1.1. Prince's "stressed-focus" type

In the "stressed-focus" type, the Enhanced Theme represents new
information, whereas the embedded clause represents what she
called "given" information. For example:

"We can't ignore what's going on," he said, getting straight to it.
"We're going to have to face it."
"It's you who have to face it," Deena said, trying to keep her fury
under control. (Collins 1990: 449)   (9)

Here *you* represents information that is not only "new" but, as I shall
term it here, "contrastively new." But the embedded clause *who
have to face it* conveys presupposed information. This is typically
realized by a Tone 3, in Halliday's terms, but it is also regularly
presented as the "tail" that follows the Tonic on the Enhanced
Theme when it is deemed to be recoverable. (Halliday (1994: 60)
seemed to imply that it is always "given," but this is not so. I will give
a fuller specification of the possible patterns in Section 4.5 below.)
   The reason for Prince (1978) to call the enhanced theme construction in examples such as (9) "stressed-focus *it*-clefts" is that the
element serving as theme (i.e., "focus" in Prince's terminology) is
always "stressed" phonologically. The type of enhanced theme construction discussed by Halliday (1985, 1994) belongs to this type.

4.1.2. Prince's "informative-presupposition" type

In the "informative-presupposition" type, the information in the
embedded clause is "a known fact, unknown only to the readership"
(Prince 1978: 898). The Performer uses the enhanced theme construction to inform the Addressee of the information in the embedded clause, which is "a known fact—or simply KNOWN" (Prince 1978:
904, original emphasis). It is for this reason that Prince gave the
name "informative-presupposition" to the construction in question.
In this type of enhanced theme construction, the Enhanced Theme
represents EITHER new OR given information, whereas the embedded
clause always contains new information. For example:

It was on a cool, showery day in mid-April that Ronald dropped
his bombshell. He had called to see me at my flat in the Barbi-
can, on a day when I was looking forward to hearing progress

reports from a committee meeting I had called for that evening. (Player 1993: 142)   (10)

I sat numbly behind the wheel as Big Ben chimed the single stroke of 1 a.m., the sound carrying clearly across the river. My dressing-gown was soaked in dark blood, my hands were sticky, and my feet felt slippery by the pedals.
It was then that I heard the voice. It came from both outside and within me, deep and gentle, with a calm, almost hypnotic quality that transfixed me in my seat. (Player 1993: 32)
(11)

In Example (10), the Enhanced Theme (the prepositional group *on a cool, showery day in mid-April*) conveys new information—as the embedded clause (*that Ronald dropped his bombshell*) does also. But in (11), the item *then* signals "recoverability" (for which Prince used mistakenly Halliday's term "given"). In Halliday's terms, "givenness" is realized intonationally, and it would indeed be possible to read this sentence, in a natural manner, with a single Tonic on *voice,* so that in Halliday's terms, too, only the embedded clause contains new information. Essentially, Prince's distinction is based on the Performer's estimate of the types and strengths of "novelty" and "recoverability" in the belief system of the Addressee (see Fawcett and Huang (1995) and (in preparation)).

4.2. The "Contrastive" Versus "Non-contrastive" Distinction

Although there are justifications for classifying types of enhanced theme construction according to the "recoverability strength" of the element in the Addressee's belief system, I want to argue here that in a fully functional approach it is helpful first to distinguish the constructions according to their semantic functions and, second, to categorize them according to their functions in the discourse. First, then, I want to classify them at the semantic level into two types: (a) the contrastive type and (b) the non-contrastive type. As the terms imply, the contrastive type is used to express "contrast," whereas the non-contrastive is used to express any meaning except "contrast." An element that is "contrastive" is also, of course, "new," so I will express this fact here by calling such an element "contrastively new." This follows the practice in the Cardiff Grammar (e.g., Fawcett 1990). For example, in Example (7) above, *his teacher* is "contrastively new" in relation to *John's father* in the preceding clause.

Similarly, in (9), *you* in the enhanced theme construction is in contrast with *we* in the preceding utterance. By contrast, the themes of both (10) and (11) are not being contrasted with anything, as far as we can see from the co-text.

4.3. Some Differences from Prince's Distinction

The distinction discussed in the previous section is not the same as that proposed by Prince (1978), even though judgements based on the two classifications typically overlap. There are cases where application of the different criteria has resulted in different classifications. Since Prince's distinction is based on the Performer's estimate of the "recoverability strength" of the event or object in the Addressee's belief system, and on what seems to us an over-simple set of information patterns, there is no direct relationship between Prince's (1978) distinction and the one proposed here. Specifically, some examples classified by scholars as Prince's "informative–presupposition" type would in our classification be the "contrastive" type.

I will illustrate this point by looking at an example. Following Prince's distinction, Delin (1989: 5) treated Example (12) (her (13)) below as belonging to Prince's "informative–presupposition" type.

A. (seeing a mistake in a transcript of some elicited linguistic data in B's thesis) Did the subject really make this error?
B. No it's *me* that can't TYPE properly. (12)

Delin (1989: 5) pointed out that "the accent on the head of the cleft [i.e., *me*] [in (12)] is considerably stronger (although still weaker than the nuclear accent in the complement)." It seems that the main reason why Delin regarded her example as belonging to the "informative–presupposition" type is that the embedded clause (*that can't type properly*) conveys presupposed or new rather than "given" information.

If we look at the semantic function of the enhanced theme construction in (12), we can see that a major purpose of the construction is to present a referent—a person in this case—who is both the Enhanced Theme and contrastively new. In this case, the discourse function is, as we shall see, "correction." Thus, *me* is contrasted with *the subject* in A's question, and at the same time, *type properly* is in contrast with *make this error*. Thus, this construction is "contrastive" in terms of our classification, where the pattern in the embedded clause is not criterial, as we will see in Section 4.5 below. It would therefore seem that our classification is not the same as that of Prince (1978).

The discussion in this section suggests that Prince's distinction of enhanced theme constructions was based on the types of information in the belief systems of the Performer and Addressee, whereas our semantic classification is based on the semantics of the information structure, at the intra-linguistic level of semantics. Thus the two classifications are partially overlapping but are significantly different.

4.4. Some Problems with Prince's Criteria

In this section I will briefly discuss two problems with Prince's (1978) identification of the "informative–presupposition" enhanced theme construction. The first problem is concerned with the nature of the construction, and the second problem is concerned with the characteristics of the construction.

4.4.1. To "inform" or to "remind"?

The main reason that Prince (1978) called examples such as (10) and (11) "informative–presupposition *it*-clefts" is that the information in the embedded clause is "a known fact, unknown only to the readership." Thus, the Performer uses the construction to inform the Addressee of the information in the embedded clause. Prince pointed out that with the "informative–presupposition" enhanced theme constructions:

> Not only is the hearer not expected to be thinking about the information in the *that*-clause, but s/he is not expected even to KNOW it. In fact, the whole point of these sentences is to INFORM the hearer of that very information. (Prince 1978: 898) (original emphasis)

Clearly, Prince assumed that the "information–presupposition" constructions are used to "inform" the Addressee of the information in the embedded clause. However, as Hedberg (1990: 188–189) observed, these constructions can also be used to REMIND the Addressee of some familiar information. This is because "clefts whose clauses carry accent can also contain information which is familiar" (Hedberg 1990: 188). In my data, there are examples (which belong to Prince's "informative–presupposition" type) that are not used to inform, but to remind. The following is such an example:

Love is in the air in Summer Bay. After months of ups and downs, this week Shane and Angel get engaged. It wasn't long ago, of course, that they split up. "Though Angel fell for Shane at first sight, she hasn't made it easy for him," says 17-year old Melissa George, who plays her. "She has a need for constant reassurance." (*What's on TV*, 10–16 December 1994, p. 9)   (13)

Example (13) is the beginning of an article in a TV magazine published in Britain. This article is to tell the Addressee what is going to happen in the week's episodes of the soap opera *Home and Away*. Interestingly, the enhanced theme construction is not used to inform the Addressee of the fact that it was not long ago that Shane and Angel split up. It instead serves as a reminder of what happened before because readers of this text should have known the information in the embedded clause. The use of *of course* helps to make this point, indicating that the information in the embedded clause is not really new to the Addressee. This may suggest that the term "informative–presupposition" is not adequate in capturing the features of this type of enhanced theme construction.

4.4.2. Structural characteristics

Prince (1978) tried to identify formal characteristics of her two types of enhanced theme construction. Prince stated that her "informative–presupposition" type has the following three characteristics, which distinguish this type from the "stressed–focus" type:

Informative–presupposition *it*-clefts are formally and unambiguously identifiable. First, unlike stressed-focus *it*-clefts, they have normally (vs. weak) stressed *that*-clauses. Second, they generally have a short and anaphoric focus, which, in my data, is either a (subject) NP or an adverbial, generally of time, place, or reason—Kuno's "thematic scene-setting" adverbials (1975, 1978). Third, in such sentences, *that/wh-* is not deletable. . . . But it is often possible to delete *that* after a focused adverbial, so long as the construction is of the stressed-focus type.
(Prince 1978: 899)

Our study of the enhanced theme construction confirms only the first of these three specifications. From the examples in our data we can see that the enhanced theme in Prince's "informative–presupposition" type is very frequently NOT a "short and anaphoric" expression and that it may also be a long group (as in (10) above). We can also see that this element is not necessarily a "subject" or an "adverbial" in the congruent version. For example:

Objection is sometimes made to the habit . . . of using the cleft sentence structure with an item that might be less obtrusive with simple fronting. . . . The habit can be defended in that an adjunct (especially of time or place) is a fitting scene-setting and that it is **this function** that the cleft structure empha-sizes. (Quirk *et al* 1985:1384)   (14)

We also want to show how the meanings relate to the most surface aspects of the grammar; we therefore select a method of codification which will enable us to do this. ·
   It is **this method of codification** that we have been consid-ering in Chapters 8 and 9. (Berry 1975: 193)   (15)

In these two examples, the Enhanced Theme (*this function, this method of codification*) is clearly not a Subject or an "adverbial" in the congruent version, but a Complement (or "Object" in the termi-nology of Quirk *et al* 1985).
   When the element serving as Enhanced Theme is an adverbial, it is not necessarily an adverbial of time, place, or reason; other types of "adverbial" also frequently occur. For example, in (16), *through this concept of "first inherent role"* is an Adjunct ("adverbial") of Means in the congruent version; the prepositional group *with great sadness* in (17) is an Adjunct of Manner.

It is through this concept of "first inherent role" that we can, in the thematic component, make generalising statements that can refer in the same rule to different types of inherent role, generated in different parts of the network. (Fawcett 1980:150)
                                                       (16)

IN MEMORIAM SIMON C. DIK (1940–1995)
   It is with great sadness that we inform you of the death, on March 1, 1995, of Simon C. Dik, one of the world's lead-ing theoreticians in functional linguistics. Simon had occu-pied the chair of General Linguistics at the University of Amsterdam for 25 years when in 1994 his illness, which had manifested itself two years earlier, forced him to resign. (FUNKNET@OREGON.UOREGON.EDU.06 Mar 1995 10:28)
                                                       (17)

In the following three examples, the element as theme is an Adjunct of Direction, Purpose or Relation in the congruent version:

It is syntax that receives most attention in the systemic literature, since it was from the study of syntax that the theory
developed. (Fawcett 1980: 47)   (18)

This feature is not to be interpreted as something negative or
deviant; it is partly in order to avoid any such connotations
that we have used the term "metaphorical" rather than "incongruent." (Halliday 1985: 345)   (19)

It is the use of language in "non-predictive" situations, I suggest, that should be the central object of study as we seek to
discover the nature of the linguistic code, and it is in relation to
this that we should expect to explain the use of language in
specialised contexts. (Fawcett 1980: 250)   (20)

In our data the element as Enhanced Theme can be other types of
Adjunct in the congruent version. Examples of (14)–(20) show clearly that Prince's second specification quoted above is not valid.

Prince (1978: 899) is right in saying that "it is often possible to
delete *that* after a focused adverbial" in her "stressed-focus" enhanced theme construction, as in (21) below:

[cupping cheeks] "It's HERE I look like Mina Davis." (Prince
1978: 899)   (21)

In our data there are a number of examples such as (21), whose *that*
at the beginning of the embedded clause is also not realized lexically.
However, this is only half of the picture because in informal style
that can be deleted even if the "focused" element is Subject or Complement (or "Object"). For example, in (22) below *me* is the Subject in
the congruent version, but *that* or *who* is not realized lexically.

"By the way—you hear Magno Records all set to sign us to a
fantastic contract? New Billing—"Rosa and the Promises."
Next year it will be *me* can use a bodyguard." (Collins 1977:
143) (original italics)   (22)

The following are examples given by Quirk *et al* (1985), whose Enhanced Theme would be the Subject in the congruent version. In
these two examples, *that* or *who* is not realized in the sentence:

It's Simon did it. (Quirk *et al* 1985: 1250)   (23)

It was the President himself spoke to me. (Quirk *et al* 1985:
1387)   (24)

In Example (25) below, the Enhanced Theme *Dallas* is the Complement of the Main Verb ("see") in the congruent version, while in (26) *poor old George* is a Complement (if "worry about" is treated as a prepositional verb) or a completive (if *about poor old George* is regarded as a prepositional group). In both cases, *that* (or *who*) is not realized lexically.

"I mean this is the *first* interview Al King has given in *six* months. The first since his *crash.*"
"Who cares about Al King," sniffed the woman reporter, "<u>it's Dallas *I'm* here to see</u>. *She's* the star as far as *I'm* concerned."
(Collins 1977: 590) (original italics)   (25)

"But I feel good. In fact I never really felt anything except a diabolical headache when I woke up. <u>It's poor old George I'm worried about</u>. He's broken about everything there is to break."
(Collins 1971: 218)   (26)

Examples (22)–(26) help us to complete the picture: If the enhanced theme construction belongs to Prince's "stressed–focus" type, the "relative element" such as *that* and *who* can be absent in informal style, no matter whether the element as theme is Adjunct, Subject or Complement in the congruent version.

Now let us return to the question of whether *that/wh-* can be deleted if the enhanced theme construction belongs to Prince's "information–presupposition" type. In my data, I came across a number of examples (which are Prince's "informative–presupposition *it*-clefts") whose *that* (or *who*) is not realized lexically. The following are two examples:

When they saw that we were interested, the caterpillars made room for us, <u>and it was at these times we managed our earliest successful communications</u>. (Mitchison 1976: 89–90)
                                                                           (27)

I missed you two, but Dad was different. I couldn't say I missed being with him, because I couldn't remember the last time we'd been together as a couple.
We were always there for you, and we loved you very much. But suddenly I wasn't sure we'd ever loved each other. <u>It was then I realised how hollow my marriage had been</u>. ("Don't blame me for your dad leaving home." *Woman's Own.* [Magazine] Summer 1995, p. 90)   (28)

Downing and Locke (1992: 249) pointed out that the "relative pronoun" can be zero. They give an example (taken from Somerset
Maugham's short story "The Happy Couple"), which happens to be
an "informative–presupposition" enhanced theme construction:

> I don't know if I very much liked Landon. He was a member of a
> club I belonged to, and I had often sat next to him at lunch. He
> was a judge at the Old Bailey, <u>and it was through him I was able
> to get a privileged seat in court when there was an interesting
> trial that I wanted to attend.</u>   (29)

Note that in Examples (27), (28) and (29), the element as theme is an
Adjunct (of either Time or Means) in the congruent version. However, this does not mean that only when the element as theme is an
Adjunct can *that* be "deleted." In the following example, the element
as theme is a Complement (the Main Verb being "call") in the congruent version, but *that* (or *who*) is not realized lexically:

> One thing struck me as unusual, and it happened every time
> we were together. Shortly after midnight Steven would leave the
> bed with an apologetic "Don't be angry —I've just got to make a
> quick phone call."
> Sometimes the quick phone call would last close to half an
> hour, but I was too drowsy to care. <u>Eventually I would come to
> realize it had to be Sarah he was calling with such regularity,
> always around the same time.</u> (Player 1993: 115)   (30)

In formal style there should be a *that* or *who* after *Sarah*, which is
absent in the clause. Examples (27)–(30) clearly indicate that
Prince's claim that in the "informative-presupposition" type "*that/
wh-* is not deletable" is not correct. But it must be pointed out that
in our data "*that/wh-* deletion" is more frequent in Prince's
"stressed–focus" type than in the "informative-presupposition"
type.

4.5. Criteria at the Semantic Level (Informational Meaning)

Let me now state the criteria followed here. The two main types of
enhanced theme constructions have quite different information patterns. In the literature to date, there are several fairly similar proposals for the information patterns of the construction (e.g., Collins
1991; Declerck 1988; Delin 1989; Geluykens 1988; Prince 1978). In
the following, I will discuss the basic information patterns found in

our data in explicitly systemic functional terms, paying careful attention to realizations in actual (or inferable) intonation. The result is that our classification yields a more complete set of alternatives.

4.5.1. Information patterns associated with the contrastive type

The contrastive type has one basic information pattern associated with it, together with three variants internal to the embedded clause. The basic pattern is that the Attribute/Enhanced Theme represents contrastively new information, as is shown in Figure 2.5 below. It must be emphasized that the new information within the Attribute is not just "new" but contrastively new (Fawcett 1990, in preparation a, in preparation b). Notice that, in both Pattern A1 and Pattern A2, the information in the embedded clause is "presupposed," in terms of the "belief system." Here "presupposed" information refers to the information presented by the Performer as a belief that is shared by both the Performer himself/herself and the Addressee. Note also that information that is presupposed (in this sense) must then be processed by the Performer at the level of meaning for presentation to the Addressee as either "new" or "given" information. If it is "new" it can be presented as "new but supplementary" by giving it a rising tone, and thus it is in fact a typical pattern for the construction.

Example (9) above is an interesting example because it could be Pattern A1 or Pattern A2. It is clearly Pattern A because *you* is clearly the Enhanced Theme, and it is "contrastively new" information expressed in a Contrastive Tonic—rather than being simple new information expressed by a Nuclear Tonic (these terms being taken from Fawcett 1990).

But how is it that Example (9) can exemplify both Pattern A1 and A2? Because of the repetition of *who have to face it*, it is natural to read (9) in such a way that everything after *you* is in the "tail" of the Tonic, and so marked as "given," as in (9a):

It's 'YOU who have to face it.   (9a)

	Sit (it)	O/M (be)	C/At/ETh (element as Theme)	C/Ca (embedded clause)
Pattern A1			CONTRASTIVELY NEW	GIVEN
Pattern A2			CONTRASTIVELY NEW	NEW
Pattern A3 (rare)			CONTRASTIVELY NEW	CONTRASTIVELY NEW

Figure 2.5. Information patterns associated with the contrastive type

But it would also be possible to read the construction in (9) with a rise on *face*, indicating that *who have to face it* is being presented as "new but supplementary" information, as in (9b):

It's 'YOU who have to 'FACE it.   (9b)

As we shall see, one major discourse function of the enhanced theme construction regularly involves the use of Pattern A2 (i.e., the "reactivating" function, see Section 5.3.5 below).

Examples (12) above illustrates the information distribution in Pattern A3—a relatively rare type. In this example there are two separate information units; *me* is in contrast with *the subject* and *type properly* with *make this error*. Here both *me* and *type* receive a Contrastive Tonic:

it's 'ME that can't 'TYPE properly.   (12a)

While the salience of the first Tonic is, as Delin (1989: 5) pointed out, less than that of the second, thus it follows naturally from the fact that it is the second that is the main Tonic (i.e., the one that carries a MOOD meaning).

Thus, the main characteristic of the information pattern in the contrastive type is that the Enhanced Theme always receives a Contrastive Tonic.

4.5.2. Information patterns associated with the non-contrastive type

The information patterns of the non-contrastive type are significantly different from those associated with the contrastive type, in that they do not inherently contain Contrastively New information. The key feature of the non-contrastive type is that the Enhanced Theme does not represent contrastively new information. The Enhanced Theme can carry either given or non-contrastively new information, depending on the context and the structure of the element. Thus, there are two basic patterns of information structure for the non-contrastive type, as shown in Pattern B1 and Pattern B2 in Figure 2.6.

In Pattern B1, there is typically only one information unit. Example (11) could be read in a natural way to illustrate this pattern, as in (11a) below:

It was then that I heard the 'VOICE.   (11a)

In this example, there is only one information unit and the last lexical item *voice* receives a Nuclear Tonic. The enhanced theme

Sit (it)	O/M (be)	C/At/ETh (element as Theme)	C/Ca (embedded clause)
Pattern B1		GIVEN	NEW
Pattern B2		NEW	NEW
Pattern B3 (rare)		GIVEN	CONTRASTIVELY NEW
Pattern B4 (rare)		NEW	CONTRASTIVELY NEW

Figure 2.6. Information patterns associated with the non-contrastive type

construction in Example (31) below seems to have this information pattern.

Conversation was stilted, to put it kindly—frequently punctuated by those awful silences in which you can hear yourself chewing your own food, and in which the clink of knife and fork on a plate sounds as long as Big Ben. When someone did venture a remark, it took its usual course—veering towards the Press, and how rotten the tabloids were to the Royal Family. It was Sarah who dominated the discussion. "Isn't it terrible what they write about Diana?" she said—and this was eight weeks before the Andrew Morton book was published. (Player 1993: 272–273)   (31)

In Pattern B2, there are normally two separate information units, each with its own Tonic. The information distribution in Example (10) above belongs to this type.

It was on a cool, showery day in mid-'APRil that Ronald dropped his 'BOMbshell.   (10a)

In this example both information units have their own Tonics, falling on *April* and *bombshell* respectively. Notice that Example (11) could also be read in this way—even though *then* is, in terms of the Performer's estimate of its recoverability strength in the Addressee's belief system, recoverable—as in (11b):

It was 'THEN that I heard the 'VOICE.   (11b)

Thus the final test depends on how a text would be spoken, so that there is inevitably an element of guesswork when interpreting written texts.

In Section 2.4 above, I pointed out that Downing and Locke (1992: 248) suggested a second information pattern for the unusual type of case in which the Contrastive Tonic falls not on the Enhanced Theme but on the last lexical item in the embedded clause. Consider Example (32), which first appeared in Figure 2.3.[3]

A: We flew to Paris on a Jumbo `JET.
B: No, it was on a 'JUMBO that we flew to `ROME. (Pattern B4)

(32)

Note that B's reply in (32) could also have been spoken as in (32a):

It was on a Jumbo that we flew to `ROME. (Pattern B3)

(32a)

What we have here is essentially the same phenomenon that we noted in Pattern A. That is, it is possible, if unusual, to present the "new" information in the embedded clause as "contrastively new." In other words, in Pattern B the Enhanced Theme may or may not be presented as "new," this being the "internal" variable within Pattern B that we have just noted, and the embedded clause may be New or, in rare cases, just as with Pattern A, Contrastively New. In our corpus of well over a thousand examples there is only one case of either of Pattern B3 or Pattern B4, and like Downing and Locke's (1992: 248) example it is Pattern B4. But (32a) shows clearly that Pattern B3 can occur too.

4.5.3. Summary

I will now summarize the information patterns associated with the enhanced theme construction as follows. I have set out all of the possible (basic) patterns of information structure associated with the enhanced theme construction, and I have examined each to see whether it represents a genuine sub-category of the construction or whether it arises as a result of an independent variable. The conclusion is that there are essentially only the two patterns that we have named Pattern A and Pattern B (i.e., the contrastive type and the non-contrastive type). The identifying characteristic of Pattern A is that the Enhanced Theme represents contrastively new informa-

---

[3]However, this example seems a little unnatural; the example provided by Downing and Locke (1992: 248) before the present one is certainly more natural:

A: We flew to Paris on a Jumbo JET.
B: No, it was to RÒME that we `flew on a jumbo.

tion, and the identifying characteristic of Pattern B is that it is not—and that the content of the embedded clause is presented as New. The fact that the meaning of New in the embedded clause, whether in Pattern A or Pattern B, can occasionally be presented as Contrastively New does not affect this basic pattern. Thus in Pattern A the embedded clause can be Given, New or, rarely, Contrastively New, while in Pattern B the embedded clause can be only New or, rarely, Contrastively New. All this shows that Pattern A is significantly different from Pattern B.

But note that it follows from this that a sentence of Pattern B (the "non-contrastive" type) may, if only on rare occasions, serve one of the discourse functions that are typically associated with the "contrastive" type (i.e., with Type A). These discourse functions are those of "correction" and "counter-expectation." So a sentence that is the "non-contrastive" type of enhanced theme construction may, apparently anomalously, serve what may loosely be termed a "contrastive" discourse function. This is because it is the presence in the sentence of "contrastiveness," whether it is located on the Enhanced Theme or elsewhere, that enables the sentence to serve these discourse functions. Indeed, any sentence that includes an element that is Contrastively New, whether or not it is an enhanced theme construction, serves one of these discourse functions. It is, of course, only an apparent anomaly, because in our definition of the two types, it is the Enhanced Theme—and not the sentence as a whole—that is said to be either "contrastive'" or "non-contrastive." Thus, Example (32) above, whose embedded clause conveys contrastively new information but whose Enhanced Theme represents non-contrastively new or given information, is said to belong to Pattern B.

I turn now to the discourse functions that are served by the two basic semantic types of enhanced theme construction.

5. THE DISCOURSE FUNCTIONS OF THE ENHANCED THEME CONSTRUCTION

While there have been several studies of the information patterns of the enhanced theme construction, there are relatively few discussions of the discourse functions that it serves. In this section I will first distinguish the "functions" discussed by Prince (1978), Delin (1991) and others. Then I will propose my own classification. I should make it clear that this will not be a system network of options between which one chooses when constructing discourse, but simply a classification of the functions served by the enhanced theme construction, which might be drawn on in attempting the complex task of building a discourse planner.

5.1. Recent Proposals

Although most descriptive and pedagogical grammars to date (e.g., Downing and Locke 1992; Quirk *et al* 1985) recognized only one type of enhanced theme construction (i.e., the contrastive type), a number of scholars have observed that there is, fundamentally, more than one type. As we have seen, Prince (1978) identified two main types, based on the distribution of information, and I will shortly refer to certain sub-types of her "informative–presupposition" type. Her work has been widely adopted, adapted or modified in the period since it was published (e.g., by Collins 1991; Declerck 1984, 1988, Delin 1989; Geluykens 1988; Hedberg 1990), and it is in the writings of Prince and those who have been influenced by her that we will find ideas about the discourse functions of the enhanced theme construction.

Thus, although the main focus of Prince's (1978) paper was on the characteristics of "*it*-clefts" and "*wh*-clefts," she also identified a few sub-functions of her "informative–presupposition" type in terms of their uses in discourse. Among these are (a) cause-effect marking and (b) scene-setting. Jones and Jones (1985) observed that the enhanced theme construction is often used to mark the topic of a text, while Delin (1991) suggested three other functions: (a) correction (i.e., correcting some previous claim by challenging it), (b) continuation (i.e., continuing the discourse by asserting more information), and (c) filling (i.e., filling a variable in a salient proposition in the discourse). I will find a place for all of those functions in the taxonomy that I will shortly propose, with the exception of Delin's (1991) "filling" function. To explain why I will omit this candidate function, I must examine first her "correction" function because I will argue that Delin's "filling" function is of this type. Thus, in the light of this, I will then consider her "filling" function.

5.2. The "Correction" Function

Delin (1991) used Example (33) below to illustrate the "correction" function of the enhanced theme construction:

A: Jane bought the stamps
B: No, it was the envelopes that Jane bought (Delin 1991: 123)

(33)

Delin regarded the function of the enhanced theme construction in (33) as a direct correction. But I would say that "correction" is a discourse function and that it is expressed in language, at the level of meaning, by the use of "contrastive newness." In other words, I would add a semantic level to the explanation, between the levels of discourse and form. Thus, in B's belief system there are two propositions that are set in contrast with each other:

Jane bought **the stamps** ↔ Jane bought **the envelopes.**

From (33) one could say that A believes the proposition that "Jane bought the stamps," but that B wishes A to believe the proposition that "it was the envelopes that Jane bought" (typically because B believes that A's belief is untrue). The main reason for B to make *the envelopes* the Enhanced Theme in (33) is that, by so doing, B can give it "double highlighting," (i.e., by making it the Enhanced Theme as well as the Contrastively New element).

Similarly, in Example (9) above, Martin [*he*] believes that "both he and his wife Deena [*we*] are going to have to face it" (a very embarrassing situation of extra-marital affairs). But Deena believes Martin's belief is untrue or unacceptable. Therefore, she corrects him (his idea) by highlighting *you* in "it's you who have to face it."

As for Delin's (1991) "filling" function, she unfortunately did not discuss it in any detail. Essentially, it seems that the type of enhanced theme construction that performs this function is one that is used to answer a "new content seeker" ("*wh*-interrogative" question). Since Delin (1991) did not give any example to illustrate the "filling" function, I will have to use an example from our data. According to Delin (1991), the following enhanced theme construction is used to instantiate the variable "what" to *your spit:*

"How can they make it [a Gobstopper] keep changing colour?"
"It's your spit that does it," young Thwaites proclaimed. (Dahl 1984:
32)   (34)

In this example, the question *How can they make it keep changing colour?* is more or less the same in meaning as *What makes it keep changing colour?* So Delin would say that, in the answer, *your spit* is the value assigned to the variable "what." But this does not explain why it is not the case that all new content seekers expect the enhanced theme construction as the answer. Probably this example is in fact a correction, with the difference that here the correction is not to the proposition itself but to a PRESUPPOSITION. The mistaken presupposition is that the area in which one should seek an explanation of what causes a Gobstopper to change color is in the manufacturing process, rather than in the consumption process.

Thus, a "correction" may be either to something explicit in the text, or to something implicit, such as a presupposition. Any "correction" of the Addressee in interactive discourse constitutes a "challenge," in terms of the discourse flowchart model of Fawcett, van der Mije and van Wissen (1988).

5.3. Towards a Taxonomy of Discourse Functions

Here I would like to set out an exploratory taxonomy of discourse functions. Figure 2.7 below shows a primary distinction between functions that contribute to the "development" of a discourse and that serve to "repair" it. I have already discussed the "repair" function of "correction," so this and the following sections will be concerned with the variety of ways in which the enhanced theme construction is used to "develop" a discourse. The functions that are concerned with the development of discourse fall naturally into those that serve to initiate a stretch of discourse ("initiation"), those that develop it further ("continuation"), and those that help in concluding it ("concluding").

As I pointed out in the previous section, earlier scholars suggest a number of different discourse functions. In the taxonomy proposed here, Prince's (1978) "scene-setting" is seen as a sub-type of the function of "initiation," while Jones and Jones' (1985) "topic-marking" is another type. I have suggested a third, "ritual genre-marking," to which I shall return shortly. Prince's "cause–effect marking" is treated as an instance of "highlighting rhetorical relationships," and one of the two typical uses of the "contrastive" type is introduced here as "counter-expectation." These two appear to correspond to two of the more frequent "rhetorical structure" relations recognized by Mann and Thompson (1987), and indeed by many previous and subsequent researchers. And there are other rhetorical relations that are expressed through the enhanced theme construction (as well as those shown under "concluding") such as "purpose" in Example (35) below:

As was shown in 2.1.2 systemic linguistics is also concerned with questions of usualness or likeliness. . . . It is in order to verify hypotheses about the relative likelihood of linguistic options that systemic linguists make use of statistical techniques. (Berry 1975: 31)   (35)

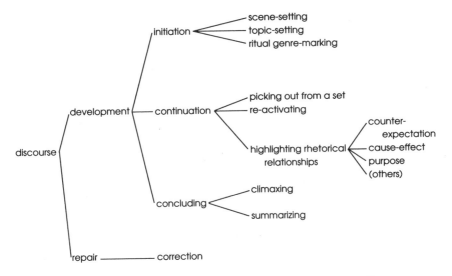

Figure 2.7. Discourse functions of enhanced theme constructions

The primary distinction in the taxonomy, however, is that between those functions that contribute to the "development" of the discourse, and the one that contributes to the "repair" of discourse. There are, of course, many types of repair, but only one that we have identified so far that uses the enhanced theme construction, namely "correction." This fact illustrates clearly the nature of this taxonomy. It is not a decision tree, but merely a way of classifying the various functions of this particular construction. It should therefore be emphasized that, when the Performer is planning a text, he or she will select from these discourse functions AND MANY OTHERS when making decisions about discourse structure.

It must be pointed out that there are, of course, functions other than those presented in Figure 2.7 above, and that it simply reports our thinking at this stage of our research.

5.3.1. The "initiation" function of "scene-setting"

In this section and the following two I shall look at the three subfunctions of "initiation." I shall begin with the "scene-setting" function.

The discourse function of Example (10) above and (36) below is that of "scene-setting." Example (10) is the first clause in a chapter of a book about personal stories. In (36) below, it is the first clause in the introduction of a collection of papers.

It was three centuries ago that the philosopher John Locke proposed that we should recognize, as one of the three major sub-divisions of science, semiotic, "the business whereof is to consider the nature of signs, the mind makes use for the understanding of things or conveying the knowledge to others." (Fawcett *et al* 1984: xv)   (36)

It was after a separation of some ten years that a happy accident enabled me to catch up with Henry Miller, my old friend. (Durrell 1983: 9)   (37)

Example (37) is the first clause in a preface of a collection of letters. And Example (38) is the beginning of a note in an academic paper:

It was back in 1972–3 that I first established the main framework for the proposals to be presented here; though detailed modification has continued since then. (Fawcett 1987: 179)   (38)

All these examples have two points in common: (a) they all occur at the beginning of a discourse (or a section of a discourse), and (b) they are all used to set the scene in terms of the position in time of the event.

While the most frequent type presents the time as the Enhanced Theme, place also occurs regularly. For example:

Within a month Steven found himself in a pleasant Queens church acting out the role of best man. It was **there** he met Sue-Ann's cousin, Aileen. He noticed her at once. (Collins 1981: 499)   (39)

Note that Example (11) above (i.e., . . . *It was then that I heard the voice.* . . .) is also "scene-setting," but that it does so by reference to a time—and typically an event—that has just been referred to, so that it is referred to anaphorically. This construction is frequent with *then, now, there* and *here* as the Enhanced Theme. In some cases, of course, the scene-setting is not initial in the discourse as a whole; it simply sets the scene for the next section of the discourse. Note that the referring expression may be complete, as in (10), or recoverable, as in (11) and (39).

To summarize so far, any scene-setting use of the enhanced theme construction involves ensuring that the Addressee knows the time and place of the event, and scene-setting uses of the construction may refer to either time or place or, occasionally, to both, as in

(40) below:

> So as soon as her fifth child (another daughter) was born, she
> sold the big house and moved to a smaller one a few miles away
> in Llandaff. It was called Cumberland Lodge and it was nothing
> more than a pleasant medium-sized suburban villa. <u>So it was
> in Llandaff two years later, when I was six years old, that I went
> to my first school.</u>
> The school was a kindergarten run by two sisters, Mrs Cor-
> field and Miss Tucker, and it was call Elmtree House. (Dahl
> 1984: 22)   (40)

Although the enhanced theme construction in Example (40) occurs
in the end of a paragraph, it in fact serves the function of "scene-
setting" for the narration that is to come in the next paragraph. In
this construction, there are three elements that function as the Enhanced Theme. The first element (*in Llandaff*) refers to place, and
the second and third (*two years later, when I was six years old*)
refer to time.

We come now to a potential problem example. It illustrates the fact
that an enhanced theme construction, which may at first appear to
"set the scene" for the next stage of the discourse, in fact primarily
serves a different function. Consider (41):

> Her first face-lift, seven years ago, was straightforward. . . .
> Two years later, Maureen had an operation to tighten the skin
> around her eyes. But <u>it was in May 1993 that she took the
> biggest plunge, when she agreed to be a guinea pig for a cos-
> metic operation called a composite face-lift.</u>
> Widely available in the States, it was the first time the
> £13,000 operation had been performed at the Bromsgrove Hos-
> pital. "It's a more serious operation than my first face-lift," ex-
> plains Maureen, who received the pioneering treatment for
> free. (*What's on TV,* 15–21 October 1994, p. 7)   (41)

In this example, the prepositional group *in May 1993* certainly tells
us when the event took place. But notice that it is the third of three
closely related events—a typical pattern. In this case, the function of
the enhanced theme construction seems to be that of announcing
that the third event constitutes the climax of this stage of discourse,
which is the most newsworthy "event," as shown below:

1. **In 1987,** Maureen had her first face-lift, and it was
   straightforward.

2. **In 1989,** Maureen had an operation to tighten the skin around her eyes.

3. **In May 1993,** Maureen took the plunge to have her second face-lift.

Note that the description (narration) that follows the enhanced theme construction gives further details of the event in the enhanced theme construction. As to its discourse function, in my view the enhanced theme construction in (41) is serving the "climaxing" function, and it is coincidental that the set of roles to which *in May 1993* is the climax is a "time position"; it can as well be an agent in the event. For example:

> But by far the most loathsome thing about Mrs. Pratchett was the filth that clung around her. Her apron was grey and greasy. Her blouse had bits of breakfast all over it, toast-crumbs and tea stains and splotches of dried egg-yolk. <u>It was her hands, however, that disturbed us most</u>. They were disgusting. They were black with dirt and grime. They looked as though they had been putting lumps of coal on the fire all day long. (Dahl 1984: 33–34)   (42)

In this example, the first sentence serves as a "topic sentence." This is followed by three sentences describing "Mrs Pratchett," the last of which is the "climax," which is an enhanced theme construction.

1. **Her apron** was grey and greasy.
2. **Her blouse** had bits of breakfast all over it, . . .
3. **It was her hands,** however, that disturbed us most.

The climax here is followed by detailed descriptions of the agent (*her hands*) in the event in the enhanced theme construction:

1. They were disgusting.
2. They were black with dirt and grime.
3. They looked as though they had been putting lumps of coal on the fire . . .

Note that in both Example (41) and (42) there is a Conjunctive element (*but, however*) in the enhanced theme construction, which helps the construction to express the "climax" meaning. Therefore (41) and (42) belong logically in Section 5.3.7 below.

5.3.2. The "initiation" function of "topic-setting"

The "topic-setting" function is discussed in detail in Jones and Jones (1985). They went so far as to claim that the majority of cases of the enhanced theme construction serve the function of marking the topic for discussion. However, in our data there are rather few examples of this kind. The following is one of them:

> In the experiential structure, therefore, <u>it is the Numerative that is embedded</u>; and since it is embedded, it comes to the front and may be followed by a fully structured nominal even beginning with a Deictic, as in *a cup of that good strong tea*. This is the same pattern that we get with *three of those enormous spiders*, where the Numerative is made the Head of the logical structure. Analysis in Figure 6–13. (Halliday 1994:195) (original italics) (43)

In this example, the element that serves as Enhanced Theme is the topic of the whole paragraph and it is the point of departure for the development of the whole paragraph:

1. The Numerative is embedded
2. The Numerative comes to the front and may be followed by . . .
3. The Numerative is made the Head of the logical structure
4. The analysis of the Numerative is provided in Figure 6–13

Thus we can say that the use of the enhanced theme construction in Example (43) is to "enhance" the referent of *the Numerative* as the topic of the rest of the paragraph.

Our data suggest that the enhanced theme construction can be used to highlight the topic of a paragraph, but not the topic of a whole, independent discourse (e.g., an article). Jones and Jones (1985: 6) used the following example in attempting to show that the enhanced theme construction can be used to announce the topic of an article:

> <u>It is evidently a universal of narrative discourse that in any extended text an overt distinction is made between the language of the actual story line and the language of supportive material which does not itself narrate the main events</u>. I refer to the former—the parts of the narrative which relate events belonging to the skeletal structure of the discourse—as FOREGROUND and the latter as BACKGROUND. Swahili provides a

typical and relatively uncomplicated example of the distinction. (Hopper 1979: 213, cited in Jones and Jones 1985: 6)   (44)

However, careful analyses of this example will show us that the underlined clause in this example is NOT an enhanced theme construction at all. The clause type is the same as Example (45) below:

It is a common observation that there are no two objects in nature that are exactly alike.   (45)

In formal grammars, the construction used in Example (45) is called an "extraposed" construction (or "extraposition"), because it is believed that *it* is (the head of) the "formal Subject" and the *that*-clause is the "real Subject"—the "'real Subject" is said to have been "extraposed." In our terminology, both (44) and (45) are evaluative enhanced theme constructions (Huang and Fawcett 1994, Fawcett in preparation a). I conclude, therefore, that the use of the enhanced theme construction to "set the topic" is limited to the "paragraph" level in writing, and to some equivalent unit such as the "transaction" (Sinclair and Coulthard 1975) in conversation.

5.3.3. The "initiation" function of "ritual genre-marking"

The enhanced theme construction can be used to express "formulaic" meanings where the main function appears to be to establish or to confirm the particular type of genre in which the interactants are involved (for a discussion of the "ritual" function of language, see Fawcett 1984). I have observed this formulaic use of the construction in both obituaries and acknowledgements. Let us look at the latter first.

1. In acknowledgements
In our data there are a number of examples of non-contrastive enhanced theme constructions appearing as the first clause in acknowledgements. It seems that this use of the construction is formulaic. Here are two examples:

It is with mixed feelings of gratification and regret that I have put the last touches to this portion of my work. It is, of course, highly gratifying to . . . (Poutsma 1916: iii)   (46)

It is with great pleasure and gratitude that I dedicate this paper to Michael Halliday, whose description of English relational clauses in "Notes on transitivity and theme in English," and an

early draft of *Introduction to Functional Grammar* first stimulated and informed my interest in this area of grammar.
(McGregor: "Attribution and identification in Gooniyandi" in
this volume)   (47)

Note that the element as Enhanced Theme in these two examples is
an Adjunct of Manner in the congruent version. In our data, if the
construction is used in a formulaic way, the element as theme is
always a prepositional group that would be an Adjunct of Manner in
the congruent version.

Before leaving "acknowledgements," I should point out that we
shall meet, in Section 5.3.7, examples (i.e., (60) & (61)) where the
enhanced theme construction is used as the final clause in an acknowledgement. There it appears to be performing a "climaxing"
function, but it may well at the same time also serve as a final
reminder of the ritual genre nature of the text as a whole.

2.   Obituaries
During the past year I was very sad to learn from the LINGUIST
and FUNKNET (both are Internets) of the deaths of three linguists,
each from a different country. Interestingly, each of the three obituary notices contains an enhanced theme construction to introduce the sad news. The following are two of them (both are from
LINGUIST):

Date: Fri, 07 Oct 1994 23:43
Subject: John Hinds

Since many readers of this list knew John Hinds, I am posting
this message because you may not have heard the same news:
John returned home to Amherst last May knowing that he had
advanced pancreatic cancer. Although he was planning to go
back to Nagoya to teach this Fall, that was not possible. His
health deteriorated over the summer. It is with deep sadness
that I let you know that John died on Sept 27th, 1994 in Amherst. In keeping with John's wishes, there was no public fu-
neral. Those of us who were his students, colleagues, friends,
and admirers will miss him.

Gene Halleck
Oklahoma State University   (48)

Note that, although the enhanced theme construction comes late in
the text, it marks the beginning of the obituary itself. Here the informal register of electronic mail may have blurred the boundary between personal views and a formal obituary nature.

Date: Thu, 2 Feb 95 00:57
Subject: S. Hattori dies

<u>It is with great sorrow and regret that, on behalf of his family,
we have to inform you that our respected teacher, the linguist
Dr. Shiro Hattori, member of the Japan Academy, passed away,
at the age of eighty-six at 0:03 o'clock, January 29th, 1995,
after a long illness.</u>
We would like to inform his friends that . . .   (49)

Example (17) above is also an obituary, which I read in FUNKNET.
The enhanced theme construction in this example, like that in (48)
and (49), is also the first clause in the text.

Recently, I came across another obituary notice. This time it was
in the Newsletter *BETWEEN OURSELVES*—News from the UWCC
[University of Wales College of Cardiff] Branch of UNISON (No. 8, May
1995, p. 1):

Deaths
<u>It is with great sadness that we announce the deaths in
March of Mrs. Maureen Hocking and Mrs. Jeanette Thomas
who both worked in the Estates Section.</u>

Also with regret we record the death, also in March, of Mr.
Roger Warren who was Branch Secretary of the UNISON Cardiff
Institute of HE and a member of the UNISON HE Service Group
Executive representing Cymru Wales region.

They will be sadly missed. Our sincere condolences are extended to all families and friends.   (50)

Note that (48) is not an official obituary notice and its tenor is informal. However (49), (17) and (50) are official (or semi-official) obituary
notices and their tenor is formal. The three formal notices all begin
with an enhanced theme construction. There are many similarities
between the four enhanced theme constructions in the obituaries:

It is with deep sadness that I let you know . . .   (48a)

It is with great sorrow and regret that . . . we have to inform
you . . .   (49a)

It is with great sadness that we inform you . . .   (17a)

It is with great sadness that we announce . . .   (50a)

The similarities include: (a) all of the Main Verbs are in the present
simple tense (*It is . . .*); (b) the Enhanced Theme is realized by a

prepositional group expressing Manner (*with deep sadness, with great sorrow and regret, with great sadness*) in the congruent version; (c) the Subject of the embedded clause is the Performer (or the Performer as a spokesperson for a group) (*I, we*); (d) the Addressee is an interactant/Addressee (*you*); and (e) the Main Verb in the embedded clause is an "informing" one (*let you know, inform, announce*) (because (48) is informal in tenor, *let you know* is used instead of the formal item *inform* or *announce*).

It is because of these similarities that I would say that the enhanced theme construction is used in these cases as a formulaic expression that makes the ritual function of texts that are obituaries and acknowledgements, and no doubt of other such genres too. This would be an interesting field for future sociolinguistic research.

5.3.4. The "continuation" function of "picking out from a set" (and an exceptional case)

As was pointed out in Section 5.1 above, Delin (1991) identified a "continuation" function of the enhanced theme construction. Our data suggest the value of recognizing that there are at least three main functions under the broad function of "continuation," two with possible subdivisions. The first is the function of "picking out" an entity that has recently been introduced as one of a set, and establishing it as a significant entity for the current section of the discussion. Such entities may be "objects" or "persons."

1. Picking out an object
There are a number of examples in our data that illustrate the function of picking out an object. The following is an example where the referent is an object:

She was blonde and pretty, with slightly pointed features, fashionably thin in all the right places, with a reasonable-sized bosom, and **long dancer's legs.** It was **her legs** that had first attracted Paul's attention. It was **her legs** that first attracted *everyone's* attention. (Collins 1977: 24) (original italics)

(51)

In this example, there are in fact two enhanced theme constructions, and the theme of each is *her legs*. The question is: "What discourse function(s) do the two constructions serve?" Let us take the first example first. The nominal group *her legs* is among the things described in the first clause of Example (51), and we can see that the discourse function of the first construction is "picking out an object." This is because any other of the objects available in the discourse could have been be picked out in the same way. For example, (51) could be changed into (52) below:

> She was blonde and pretty, with slightly pointed features, fashionably thin in all the right places, with a reasonable-sized bosom, and long dancer's legs. It was **her bosom** that had first attracted Paul's attention. It was **her bosom** that first attracted *everyone's* attention. (52)

In fact, this "picking out" function serves both to select one thing from the available set of things, and to make it the topic of the discussion that follows, thus contributing to the immediate next step in the development of the discourse. Syntactically, such Enhanced Themes are typically filled by a short nominal group, and the embedded clause expresses the main information. Semantically, the Enhanced Theme in (51) (*her legs*) is presented as contrastively new.

Thus, in the first enhanced theme construction in (51), *Paul* is simply presented as new information, along with the rest of the embedded clause. But in the second construction, to which we now turn, *everyone* is contrastively new, because it is in contrast with *Paul* in the previous clause. While the information pattern of the first enhanced theme construction in (51) belongs to Pattern A2, that in the second construction belongs to Pattern B3 or B4 (see Section 4.5 above). This is because it is a direct copy of the preceding text. In principle, it should be read as Pattern B3, with the first part presented as "given" information; in practice, however, native speakers typically read it with an intonation that is copied from the previous construction, so resulting in the unusual Pattern A3. Semantically, therefore, it is like Pattern B3, with the "copied" element functioning as "given," but formally it is Pattern A3, with the "copied" pattern containing a copied Contrastive Tonic. And what is its discourse function? The answer is similar: It is a pseudo-repeat of the previous "picking out" construction, but in fact it advances the discourse as the rhetorical relation of counter-expectation—but one that functions like a tired cliché.

2.   Picking out a person

Like "picking out an object," the "picking out a person" function selects one person from the set that is relevant in the present discourse. Here is an example:

> I am greatly indebted to Susumu Kuno, Margaret Thomas, Karen Courtenay and Kenichi Takami for reading an earlier ver-

sion of this paper and giving many important comments on both content and style. It was **Kuno** who suggested to me territory of information as a gradable, continuous notion in a specific form. (Kamio 1994: 67)   (53)

In this example, the person that has been picked out is *Kuno*, who is among the people who had read "an early version of this paper and given [giving] many important comments on both content and style." As with the case of the object, another person could have been picked out:

I am greatly indebted to Susumu Kuno, Margaret Thomas, Karen Courtenay and Kenichi Takami for reading an earlier version of this paper and giving many important comments on both content and style. It was **Thomas/Courtenay/Takami** who suggested to me territory of information as a gradable, continuous notion in a specific form.   (54)

Thus, in order for the Performer to pick out a person or object, the candidate should be recoverable in the co-text by repetition, or semantic equivalence (Halliday and Hasan 1976). In both (53) and (54) the Enhanced Themes are recoverable by repetition.

5.3.5. The "continuation" function of "re-activating"
In contrast with "picking out from a set," the present function "picks up" a referent from earlier in the discourse. This re-activating function involves the use of the "contrastive" type, as identified at the semantic level in Section 4.2 above. Thus, this is one of the functions served by the contrastive version of the construction in those cases when its purpose is NOT to try to repair damage to the flow of information in the discourse by issuing a correction. As an example, consider (55) below, where *my mother* was mentioned two pages before in the narration.

[p. 31: One terrible night, the fragile shell finally cracked. **My mother** had come to stay for the weekend . . .]
    Jim was waiting for me in the hall, his face registering shock at the apparition stumbling in through the porch. All I wanted was for him to gather me into his arms and say: "It'll be all right." Instead, he uttered just three words: "Oh my God!"
    And he walked out into the night and got into his own car and drove away from me.

It was **my mother** who ran downstairs to help me. She grabbed hold of me to stop me fainting, took me into the kitchen, put my dressing-gown into the washing machine, mopped the blood off the floor of the Jeep, and managed to contact my brother to tell him to clean up the mess outside his front door before anyone saw it and started asking questions. (Player 1993: 33)   (55)

In this example, the element *my mother* is being re-activated by being the Enhanced Theme. The function is regularly used to re-introduce to a narrative or a description a person or object that has been mentioned earlier, but which the Performer presents as surprising to or unexpected by the Addressee in the present context. Typically, the re-activated entity is a person, as here, rather than an object, and typically this person (*he, she, they,* etc.) plays a significant role in what follows in the discourse. Here in (55), for example, *my mother,* after being introduced (re-activated) in the enhanced theme construction, is the Agent of no less than six subsequent processes in the following narration.

5.3.6. The "continuation" function of "highlighting rhetorical relationships"

Sometimes the enhanced theme construction is used to reinforce a rhetorical relationship of the type found in rhetorical structure relations (Mann and Thompson 1987).

In highlighting a rhetorical relationship between the current proposition and an earlier one, the Enhanced Theme often contains a preposition expressing a rhetorical relationship followed by an anaphoric referring expression, such as *because of this, for this reason, in relation to this, in spite of this, in order to achieve this,* etc. The construction is often introduced by semantically compatible Linkers such as *and, for, so, and so, then, yet* or *so that.*

The principle of central importance is that the language, whether syntax, lexis or semantics, is stored as PROCEDURES, a point which I shall return to in Chapter 2. It is because of this that the language can be integrated with other parts of the mentality. (Fawcett 1980: 13) (original emphasis)   (56)

Now, it is clearly the SF *it*-cleft which is most amenable to simple generalizations about form/function relationships, **and** it is perhaps for this reason that many analysts have viewed the SF *it*-cleft as basic, and have treated the IP *it*-cleft (if at all) as exceptional. (Ball 1994: 609)   (57)

The third observation that helps to explain the acceptability of sentences such as (33, a–d) is that the variable NP is special in that it is not wholly old (or inferrable) information. . . . This observation is important, **for** it is precisely because of this that the opposition between an indefinite noun head and a definite one becomes possible. (Declerck 1988: 20)   (58)

There are a number of rhetorical structure relations in English. The enhanced theme construction can certainly highlight many of the relations. In Example (35) above, the construction has *in order to verify hypotheses about the relative likelihood of linguistic options* as its Enhanced Theme, so that the "purpose" meaning is highlighted. In the following example, the enhanced theme construction expresses something that may not be expected by the Addressee before he or she reads it. The use of the Linker *but* at the beginning of the clause helps to highlight this "counter-expectation:"

The origin of the present book was in a short paper presented to a psycholinguistic seminar organised by David Bennett in London in 1971–2. But it was the more explicit version prepared for the 1972 Sheffield meeting of the LAGB that gave these ideas their first public exposure, and that led to the expansion of the paper into two (1973a and b). (Fawcett 1980: 267)   (59)

Apart from those discussed here, there are certainly many other rhetorical relations that can be highlighted by the enhanced theme construction.

5.3.7. The "concluding" function of "climaxing"
I turn finally to the two functions that mark the "conclusion" of a stretch of discourse. Here I regard "climaxing" and "summarizing" as sub-types of "concluding." It must be pointed out that the construction having this function must occur at the end of a stretch of discourse (e.g., a section or a chapter in a book).

I already gave two examples of the climaxing function. One in Example (41) (. . . *it was in May 1993 that she took the biggest plunge . . .*) and the other in (42) (*It was her hands, however, that disturbed us most.*). Here I will present some other examples to broaden the picture.

In some types of discourse, the Performer uses the enhanced theme construction as the clause that ends the text. This clause often expresses a proposition that is presented as more important than any of the others in the preceding text. I find that in many paragraphs expressing "acknowledgement," this is the case—often the last person to be thanked being the one who deserves most thanks from the Performer. I have come across three acknowledgements in academic books, each of which has the enhanced theme constructions as the final clause. Here are two of them:

I am also indebted to Mr. and Mrs. G.R. Furse who have faithfully supported me throughout my studies. I thank them for their generosity and understanding. Finally no amount of thanks would be enough for my parents and for my wife. Without their love and encouragement my work could never have begun. So it is to them that the finished product is dedicated. (Taylor 1980: vi)   (60)

Our son David has also contributed in immeasurable ways by giving me good reasons to take time off and for making that time off so much fun: it is to him that I dedicate this book. (Schiffrin 1994: x)   (61)

Each of these is an example of the "climaxing" function of the construction. Note that in (60) the enhanced theme construction is introduced by a Conjunctive Adjunct *so* and that in (61) it is preceded by a colon (:). These two grammatical items help to mark the coming of the climax.

We should note, however, that the first clause in acknowledgements can also have this function. Here is an example:

It is, of course, Jeanette Gundel to whom I owe the greatest debt for inspiring and supporting this dissertation. I would also like to thank the other final and former members of my committee—Michael Kac, Jerry Sanders, Betsy Bernes, Randy Fletcher, Larry Hutchinson, and Jim Morgan—for stimulating questions and useful comments on my prospectus and on the version of the thesis that I defended. (Hedberg 1990: i)

(62)

From this example, it is shown that the person who Hedberg owes the greatest debt is Jeanette Gundel. Thus, it is natural that *Jeanette Gundel* is used as the Enhanced Theme. Perhaps we should add "climaxing" to the "initiation" function to accommodate such examples.

5.3.8. The "concluding" function of "summarizing"

When the Performer uses an enhanced theme construction as the last clause of a discourse or of an independent section of a discourse, he or she may use it to summarize what has been discussed. The following is a typical example:

> The main thesis of this book is that an act of ostension carries a guarantee of relevance, and that this fact—which we will call the *principle of relevance*—makes manifest the intention behind the ostension. We believe that it is this principle of relevance that is needed to make the inferential model of communication explanatory. (Sperber and Wilson 1986: 50) (original italics)　　　　　　　　　　　　　　　　　　　　(63)

This example is the end of Section 9 ('Relevance and ostension') in Chapter 2 of *Relevance* (Sperber and Wilson 1986). Clearly, the enhanced theme construction summarizes one of the authors' main arguments in the chapter.

5.4. Summary

This section discusses some discourse functions of the enhanced theme construction. I first looked at proposals made by researchers such as Prince (1978), Delin (1991) and others. Then I examined Delin's (1991) identification of the "correction" function and "filling" function. This was followed by my proposal of a taxonomy of discourse function served by the enhanced theme construction. I suggested that there are two broad categories of discourse functions: (a) those used in the development of discourse, and (b) that used as "repair." Then each of the functions was illustrated by examples.

The discussion in this section has focused on the functions served by the enhanced theme construction in discourse, and the categories introduced here can be related—at least in their typical manifestations, to the "contrastive" versus "non-contrastive" distinction at the level of semantics. Table 2.1 below summarizes the relationships.

From Table 2.1 we can see that discourse functions are closely related to typical semantic types. It is clear that "re-activating," "counter-expectation" and "correction" functions inherently express "contrastive" meaning, while "scene-setting," "topic-setting" and "ritual genre-marking" usually express "non-contrastive" meanings.

TABLE 2.1
Relationships Between Discourse Functions and Semantic Types
(HRR = highlighting rhetorical relationship)

Discourse function	Typical semantic type
scene-setting	non-contrastive
topic-setting	non-contrastive
ritual genre-marking	non-contrastive
picking out from a set	contrastive/non-contrastive
re-activating	contrastive
HRR: counter-expectation	contrastive
HRR: cause-effect, purpose	non-contrastive
climaxing	non-contrastive
summarizing	non-contrastive
correction	contrastive

6. SUMMARY AND CONCLUDING REMARKS

In this chapter, I have summarized Halliday's treatment of the enhanced theme construction in English. His proposal that our purpose in using this construction is to highlight the news value of the element that is thematized has been very insightful. However, Halliday's account of the construction describes only the "contrastive" type, where the Enhanced Theme always carries contrastively new information. This chapter has shown the importance of the non-contrastive type, using the Cardiff Model of Systemic Functional Grammar. Fawcett's analysis and analytical framework (in preparation a, in preparation b) has been adopted both here and in Fawcett and Huang (1995), showing the value of using Participant Roles in the analysis.

I have identified two basic information patterns with regard to the information structure of the enhanced theme construction. Patterns A has three variants, as shown in Figure 2.5 (i.e., Pattern A1: contrastively new + given; Pattern A2: contrastively new + new; Pattern A3: contrastively new + contrastively new), while Pattern B consists of four sub-patterns, as in Figure 2.6 (Pattern B1: given + new; Pattern B2: new + new; Pattern B3: given + contrastively new; Pattern B4: new + contrastively new). Pattern A3, Pattern B3 and Pattern B4 are rare types. Pattern A3 is rare in that both the Enhanced Theme and the embedded clause express contrastively new information. Pattern B3 and Pattern B4 are rare is that the embedded clause expresses contrastively new information while the Enhanced Theme conveys either given or new information.

Finally, I have proposed a tentative taxonomy of the discourse functions that are served by the enhanced theme construction. This represents ongoing research, and there may, of course, be other functions than those discussed here. But the functions identified in this chapter are certainly some of the more important ones, and they represent the fullest attempt to identify the complete range of the functions in discourse served by the enhanced theme construction.

It must be emphasized that the taxonomy of discourse functions is a first attempt to identify the uses of the enhanced theme construction in discourse. Very often the construction plays more than one role at a time. For example, the discourse function of the enhanced theme construction in Example (13) in Section 4.4 (*It wasn't long ago, of course, that they split up.*) can be regarded as "reminding." However, if we take the whole text as a narrative discourse, we may say that the enhanced theme construction serves as "orientation" of the narration (Labov 1972, Labov and Waletsky 1967, Quirk *et al* 1985: 1432–1433). Similarly, in the following example:

> Dominique sighed. ". . . Shep forced me to . . . He took advantage of me. If you had stayed and not run out on me . . ."
> "Let me remind you, it was *you* invited him to join us."
> "I thought he was your friend."
> "If I had wanted him to join us I would have been quite capable of asking him myself. . . ." (Collins 1975: 92) (original italics)   (64)

The enhanced theme construction in this example belongs to my contrastive type. Here *you* conveys contrastively new information, and we can say that the discourse function is "correction": "It was you who wanted to be with him." But the discourse function may be "reminding," because the enhanced theme construction is preceded by *let me remind you.*

As we saw in Sections 5.3.1, Examples (41) and (42) play two different functions at the same time. On the one hand, the enhanced theme construction help to "set the scene." On the other hand, they express the "climaxing" function.

All this shows that it is often possible for one construction to serve more than one discourse function at the same time, depending on the context and the analyst's point of view and research interest.

REFERENCES

Ball, C.N. (1994) "The origins of the informative-presupposition *it*-cleft." *Journal of Pragmatics* 22: 603–628.

Berry, M. (1975) *Introduction to Systemic Linguistics, Vol 1: Structures and Systems.* London: Batsford.

Collins, J. (1971) *Sinners.* London: Pan Books.

Collins, J. (1975) *The World Is Full of Divorced Women.* London: Allen and Co.

Collins, J. (1977) *Lovers and Gamblers.* London: Pan Books.

Collins, J. (1981) *Chances.* London: Pan Books.

Collins, J. (1990) *Lady Boss.* London: Pan Books.

Collins, P.C. (1991) *Cleft and Pseudo-cleft Constructions in English.* London: Routledge.

Dahl, R. (1984) *Boy —Tales of Childhood.* Harmondsworth: Puffin Books.

Declerck, R. (1984) "The pragmatics of *it*-clefts and WH-clefts." *Lingua* 64: 251–289.

Declerck, R. (1988) *Studies on Copular Sentences, Clefts and Pseudo-clefts.* Leuven, Belgium: Leuven University Press.

Delin, J. (1989) *The focus structure of it-clefts.* Research Paper EUCCS/RP-25. Centre for Cognitive Science, University of Edinburgh, UK.

Delin, J. (1991) "Towards a model for generating cleft sentences." In Verschueren, J. (ed.) *Pragmatics at Issue.* Amsterdam: John Benjamins, pp. 113–132.

Downing, A., and Locke, P. (1992) *A University Course in English Grammar.* New York: Prentice Hall.

Durrell, L. (1983) "Preface." In Sindel, G.S. (ed.) (1986) *Dear, Dear Brenda.* New York: Knightsbridge, pp. 9–10.

Erades, P.A. (1962) "Points of modern English syntax XLIII." *English Studies* 43:13641.

Fawcett, R.P. (1980) *Cognitive Linguistics and Social Interaction: Towards an Integrated Model of a Systemic Functional Grammar and the Other Components of an Interacting Mind.* Heidelberg, Germany: Julius Groos.

Fawcett, R.P. (1973-74/1981) *Some Proposals for Systemic Syntax.* Cardiff, UK: Polytechnic of Wales.

Fawcett, R.P. (1984) "Language as a resource." *Australian Review of Applied Linguistics* 7(1): 17–56.

Fawcett, R.P. (1987) "The semantics of clause and verb for relational processes in English." In Halliday and Fawcett (eds.), pp. 130–183.

Fawcett, R.P. (1990) "The computer generation of speech with semantically and discoursally motivated intonation." In *Proceedings of 5th International Workshop on Natural Language Generation*, Pittsburgh, PA, pp. 164–73a.

Fawcett, R.P. (in preparation a) *Handbook for the Analysis of Sentences in English Text. Volume 1: How to Analyse Syntax.* Cardiff: Computational Linguistics Unit, University of Wales, Cardiff CF1 3EU, UK.

Fawcett, R.P. (in preparation b) *Handbook for the Analysis of Sentences in English Text. Volume 2: How to Analyse Meaning.* Cardiff: Computational Linguistics Unit, University of Wales, Cardiff CF1 3EU, UK.

Fawcett, R.P. (in preparation c) "Equivalence rules in the generation of various types of Theme constructions in English." Cardiff: Computational Linguistics Unit, University of Wales, Cardiff CF1 3EU, UK.

Fawcett, R.P., Halliday, M.A.K., Lamb, S.M. and Makkai, A. (eds.) (1984) *The Semiotics of Culture and Language.* (Vol. 1). London: Pinter.

Fawcett, R.P. and Huang, G.W. (1995) "A functional analysis of the enhanced theme construction in English." *Interface* 10/1: 117–148.

Fawcett, R.P. and Huang, G.W. (in preparation b) *Enhanced Theme in English.*

Fawcett, R.P., van der Mije, A. and van Wissen, C. (1988) "Towards a systemic flowchart model for discourse structure." In Fawcett and Young (eds.), pp. 116–143.

Fawcett, R.P. and Young, D.J. (eds.) (1988) *New Developments in Systemic Linguistics, Vol. 2: Theory and Application.* London, UK: Pinter.

Fichtner, E.G. (1993) "Cleft sentences in English: A comprehensive view." *Word* 44(1): 130.

Geluykens, R. (1988) "Five types of clefting in English discourse." *Linguistics* 26: 823–841.

Halliday, M.A.K. (1964/1981) "Syntax and the consumer." In Stuart, C.I.J.M. (ed.) *Report of the Fifteenth Annual (First International) Round Table Meeting on Linguistics and Language Study.* Washington, D.C.: Georgetown University Press, 1964, pp. 11–24; reprinted in Halliday, M.A.K. and Martin, J.R. (eds.) (1981) *Readings in Systemic Linguistics.* London: Batsford, pp. 21–28.

Halliday, M.A.K. (1967) "Notes on transitivity and theme in English, Part 2." *Journal of Linguistics* 3(2): 199–244.

Halliday, M.A.K. (1985) *An Introduction to Functional Grammar.* London: Arnold.

Halliday, M.A.K. (1994) *An Introduction to Functional Grammar* (2nd edition) London: Arnold.

Halliday, M.A.K. and Fawcett, R.P. (eds.) (1987) *New Developments in Systemic Linguistics, Vol. 1: Theory and description.* London: Pinter.

Halliday, M.A.K. and Hasan, R. (1976) *Cohesion in English.* London: Longman.

Hedberg, N.A. (1990) *Discourse Pragmatics and Cleft Sentences in English.* PhD thesis, University of Minnesota, UMI order number 9109340.

Hopper, P.J. (1979) "Aspects and foregrounding in discourse." In Givón, T. (ed.) *Syntax and Semantics.* Vol. 12. New York: Academic Press, pp. 213–241.

Huang, G.W. (1986) *A Stylistic Analysis of Hemingway's "The Killers."* MA dissertation, Guangzhou Institute of Foreign Languages, China.

Huang, G.W. (1995) "A multi-strand analysis of the experiential enhanced theme construction in English." Paper presented at the 22nd International Systemic Functional Congress. Beijing, China.

Huang, G.W. and Fawcett, R.P. (1994) "A systemic functional approach to the evaluative *it*-construction." Paper presented at the 21st International Systemic Functional Congress. Gent, Belgium.

Huang, G.W., and Fawcett, R.P. (in press) "A functional approach to two 'focussing' constructions in English and Chinese." In Turner, K., and Jaszczolt, K. (eds.) *Proceedings of the First International Conference in Contrastive Semantics and Pragmatics.* Amsterdam: Elsevier.

Jespersen, O. (1928/1965) *A Modern English Grammar on Historical Principles III*. London: George Allen and Unwin.

Jespersen, O. (1937/1969) *Analytic Syntax*. New York: Holt, Rinehart and Winston, Inc.

Jones, L.B. and Jones, L.K. (1985) "Discourse functions of five English sentence types." *Word* 36(1): 121.

Kamio, A. (1994) "The theory of territory of information: The case of Japanese." *Journal of Pragmatics*, 21: 67–100.

Kuno, S. (1975) "Conditions for verb phrase deletion." *Foundations of Language*, 13: 161–175.

Kuno, S. (1978) "Two topics on discourse principles." *Bulletin of the ICU Summer Institute in Linguistics*. 2.

Labov, W. (1972) *The Language in the Inner City*. Philadelphia: University of Pennsylvania.

Labov, W. and Waletsky, J. (1967) "Narrative analysis: Oral versions of personal experience." In Helm, J. (ed.) *Essays on the Verbal and Visual Arts*. Seattle: University of Washington Press, pp. 12–44.

Mann, W.C. and Thompson, S.A. (1987) *Rhetorical Structure Theory: A Theory of Text Organization*. USC Information Sciences Institute, Technical Report ISI/RS-87-185.

Martin, J.R. (1992) *English Text*. Amsterdam: John Benjamins.

Mitchison, N. (1976) *Memoirs of a Spacewoman*. London: The Women's Press.

Player, L. (1993) *My Story—The Duchess of York, Her Father and Me*. London: Grafton.

Poutsma, H. (1916) *A Grammar of Late Modern English* (Part II). Groningen, the Netherlands: Noordhoff.

Prince, E.F. (1978) "A comparison of WH-clefts and *it*-clefts in discourse." *Language* 54: 883–906.

Quirk, R., Greenbaum, S., Leech, G., and Svartvik, J. (1985) *A Comprehensive Grammar of the English Language*. London: Longman.

Schiffrin, D. (1994) *Approaches to Discourse*. Oxford, UK: Blackwell.

Sinclair, J.McH. and Coulthard, R.M. (1975) *Towards an Analysis of Discourse*. Oxford, UK: Oxford University Press.

Sperber, D. and Wilson, D. (1986) *Relevance—Communication and Cognition*. Oxford, UK: Blackwell.

Taylor, T.J. (1980) *Linguistic Theory & Structural Stylistics*. Oxford, UK: Pergamon.

3
Theme and Information until Shakespeare*

Martin Davies

Department of English Studies
Stirling University

1. INTRODUCTION

In both editions of *An Introduction to Functional Grammar* (1985, 1994), in addition to writing about his primary concerns, Michael Halliday writes many tantalizing paragraphs in which he opens up inviting vistas for exploration, with no necessary implication that he's been down them but nevertheless with a note of confidence that makes it seem unlikely that he hasn't. In fact, his interests have always been wider than those of many linguists and, for example, he has written notably both on literary and historical themes, and this paper draws on his work both in these and in other areas throughout.

One of the vistas concerns the historical development of English (1994: 163):

> The coming of this pattern (*sc.* of ergativity) to prominence in the system of modern English is one of a number of related developments

---

*I am very grateful to those both at the Helsinki Systemic Congress in 1989 and also at the subsequent Nottingham Mini-International Systemic Conference devoted especially to Theme in the same year, who gave me helpful comments, encouragement and criticism of this paper, especially to Jim Benson, Margaret Berry and Michael Cummings.

that have been taking place in the language over the past five hundred years or more, together amounting to a far-reaching and complex process of semantic change. *These changes have tended, as a whole, to emphasize the textual function in the organization of English discourse*, by comparison with the experiential function; and, within the experiential function, to emphasize the cause-and-effect aspect of processes by comparison with the 'deed-and-extension' one. There is no such thing, of course, as 'completed' change in language; waves of change are passing through the system all the time. But this aspect of English—its transitivity system—is particularly unstable in the contemporary language, having been put under great pressure by the need for the language continually to adapt itself to a rapidly changing environment, and by the increasing functional demands that have been made upon it ever since Chaucer's time.

[My emphasis. M.D.]

This is fascinating! One wonders: have all these changes been charted? Over so great a period of time? If so, over how many texts? During most of this period, what evidence we have about the spoken language before the invention of the tape-recorder is the testimony of only very few reliable reporters, such as Steele (Abercrombie 1965, Ch. 5) or the only indirect evidence of written forms, so what can we know of those elements of the textual function that are realized prosodically? But then, three years later, in "On the language of physical science," in Ghadesy (1988), he gives us an account outlining some major aspects of these changes, from Chaucer onward, showing that he has indeed been down that vista, and giving us major insights into what is to be seen there.

Then, again, one wonders what things were like earlier still, in the 800 years or so before Chaucer, in our earliest extant Old English texts? Since the textual function is what enables us to construct our rhetorics, specifically we may ask how far a conscious rhetorician like Chaucer, in his complex and subtle exploitation of the resources available to him, was ahead of his time, even though in *A Treatise of the Astrolabe* he was not advancing science and the language of science in the way Halliday has shown us Newton and his successors were to do later? Was Chaucer merely exploiting to the full what was available to everyone else, or was he perhaps developing new uses for the system and thus developing the system itself? (The answer to the latter questions is, "Not discernibly.") And for how long before him had the language displayed a range of options broadly approximating to the range Chaucer used? These questions could not be fully answered in such a short study as this, but some approach to them might be made.

Such questions could be answered adequately only by an Anglo-Saxonist; however, in the context of teaching a very short undergraduate course on the history of English, it did seem at least possible to look in the texts used to illustrate the main changes in English, to see what sort of variety of thematic patterns had been used by the writers we examined. Verse was at first excluded on the grounds that versification introduced—and by convention admitted—a greater range of variation in word order than would be found in prose texts, but eventually it had to come in, from Chaucer's time onward. Also, the question had to be decided whether to go back before Chaucer, as far back as Old English, and it was decided to do this, the main source used being the text-book for the period (Quirk *et al.*, 1975); but verse was excluded in the Old English period because versification in Old English encouraged too much variation in word order. The other texts used were standard collections: Davis (1953), Dickins and Wilson (1951), Hayward (1949), Onions (1946), and Robinson (1957).

The main interest was in Chaucer himself, to see in what ways he might either lack the resources of modern English and have developed them for himself or, on the other hand, might have been original in developing new uses of resources that were available to his contemporaries. At the same time, since English changed so rapidly in the hundred years after his death (because of the Great Vowel Shift and other processes), it seemed worth looking to see whether English had changed as much in Theme during that century as it had in phonology and morphology, so Shakespeare and Donne came into the picture. At the same time, it seemed possible that certain kinds of thematic patterns that are register-specific might be found. (Papers by Cummings (1991a, b) show this very convincingly in Old English.) In the event, less than a quarter of all this was examined at all closely, and this is therefore very much only an initial exploration.

However, before going further, it is important to note that it is unreasonable to assume that analysis of texts from earlier periods in terms of the present-day system of Theme can yield valid accounts of the language of their times: because the whole point of the investigation was to see how it had changed, the system could not reasonably be investigated as though it had not changed. However, not thinking to set up systems of Theme for earlier periods *de novo*, I followed this unreasonable procedure; and I was comforted in my insecurity in so doing by finding Quirk *et al.* (1975, 1986) appearing to do much the same, at a place to be cited below (p. 127). And perhaps it is not so unreasonable because doing this can be used as a way in to the problem, throwing up instances that prove the need for different accounts of Theme at earlier periods, so that these can be considered and the different patterns identified.

Four main variables were considered: Clause Themes, clause-complexes, Marked and Unmarked Themes, and Method of Development (Fries, 1981), the last only in Chaucer's portrait of his knight. And since the effects of choices of these kinds were to be examined, some of the implications of such choices for Tonality and Tonicity (and sometimes Tone) were also touched on, so that in consequence it was occasionally useful to consider instances of Predicated Theme, where it occurred. Chaucer's portrait of his knight is what had first prompted the idea of looking at the implications of Halliday's paragraph more closely, when a particular feature of Chaucer's Marked Themes in the "General Prologue" to *The Canterbury Tales* was observed, this then leading to noticing a feature of the opening lines of the Prologue.

But taking history backwards (cf. Strang, 1970), in order to proceed from the known to the unknown, and assuming that the twentieth century system is "known," the first stage of this account takes a step backwards to about 1600, examining some features in the writing of Shakespeare's contemporary, John Donne.

2. JOHN DONNE

In his prose letters, Donne regularly uses both Marked Theme and Clause Themes:

TO SIR. H. GOODERE [Mitcham, Sept. 1608]

Sir, Every tuesday I make account that I turn a great hourglass, and consider that a weeks life is run out since I writ. But *if I ask myself what I have done in the last watch, or would do in the next,* I can say nothing; *if I say that I have passed it without hurting any,* so may the Spider in my window. The primitive Monks were excusable in their retirings and enclosures of themselves; for even of them every one of them cultivated his own garden and orchard, that is, his soul and body, by meditation, and manufactures; and they ought [i.e. 'owed'] the world no more since they consumed none of her sweetnesse, nor begot others to burden her. But for me, *if I were able to husband all my time so thriftily, as not onely not to wound my soul in any minute by actuall sinne, but not to rob and cousen her by giving any part to businesse, but bestow it all upon her in meditation,* yet even in that I should wound her more, and contract another guiltinesse (p. 454).

[Marked Themes are underlined; Clause Themes are italicized. All quotations from Donne are from Hayward (1949).]

This is highly wrought, of course, not a personal letter in any everyday modern sense; not far from the quieter passages in his sermons, in fact. But the uses of the Themes, both marked and unmarked, are strikingly similar to those normal today: as in Modern English, Marked and Unmarked Themes regularly set contexts for the processes that follow, as with <u>Every tuesday</u>, setting a frequency, or (as a special case of this, and apart from the balanced antithesis he is creating) shift the flow of information on to a new setting, the conditions under which certain behaviours will happen, as with:

βα, ββ1, ββ2 . . .   if I ask myself ‖ what I have done in the last
                                    watch, ‖ or would do in the next . . .

βα, ββα, βββ . . .   if I say ‖ that I have passed it ‖ without hurt-
                                    ing any . . .
                                    [‖ marks clause boundaries]

or, more simply,

The primitive Monks . . .
for me . . .

(the last having the antecedent of the modern "as for" introduction to a Theme). And a Clause Theme can be complex—

βα   *if I were able to husband all my time so thriftily,*
ββ1   *as not onely not to wound my soul in any minute by*
            actuall sinne,
ββ21   *but not to rob and cousen her by giving any part*
                to businesse,
ββ22   *but bestow it all upon her in meditation,*

α   *yet . . .*

—so it is not surprising that he turns Theme patterns to account in his verse as well, especially in the use of Marked Theme to create a striking beginning:

<u>For every houre that thou wilt spare mee now,</u>
I will allow,
Usurious God of Love, twenty to thee,
When with my browne, my gray haires equall bee . . .

LOVES USURY [p. 8].

Of course, the Marked Theme does not create the entire effect of itself: there is much else going on, as in the mapping of the first line on to the Marked Theme, and the late placing of the vocative together-er with the surprising (even after the title) epithet "Usurious;" but these do not diminish the effect of the Marked Theme but rather combine with it, and reinforce and are reinforced by it. Similarly, in the verses of LOVES DIET beginning

v. 1   *To what a combersome unwieldinesse*
              And burdenous corpulence my love had growne,
              But that I did . . . / . . . Give it a diet . . .
              ["had" = 'would have;' "but that" = 'except that;' "did . . . give" = 'gave']

v. 2   <u>Above one sigh a day</u> I'allow'd him not . . .
              ["Above = 'more than,' him" = '(personified) love']

and

v. 3   *If he wroung from mee'a teare,* I brin'd it so
              With scorne or shame, that him it nourish'd not . . .

                               LOVES DIET [p. 41].

there are two coordinated constituents (*a combersome unwieldiness, burdenous corpulence*) in the initial Clause Theme of verse 1, there is a Marked Theme (*Above one sigh a day*) in the first clause of verse 2, a Clause Theme in the first line of verse 3—together with a Marked Theme ("him") in the third clause of that verse, and so on, all working as in the modern system. On the other hand, in:

Before I sigh my last gaspe, let me breathe,
Great love, some Legacies . . .   THE WILL [p. 42]

the Clause Theme does not get the initial line to itself, the end of the line being marked by the syntactic break required by the late placing of the vocative initiating the next line. And finally, as an example of the subtlety with which Donne can counterpoint a complex Clause Theme against verse lineation, there is no better example than:

                 A VALEDICTION: FORBIDDING MOURNING
β1   *As virtuous men passe mildly away,* ‖
β2α, β2β   *And whisper to their friends,* ‖ *to goe,* ‖
γ1α   *Whilst some of their sad friends doe say,* ‖
γ1β, γ2α, γ2β   *The breath goes now,* ‖ *and some say,* ‖ *noe:* ‖
α   So let us melt . . .   [p. 36].

where the clause boundaries within the Clause Theme are indicated by ||, showing how they both do and do not coincide with the line-ends, and how a line may consist of one, two or three clauses within the Clause Theme. It is often remarked in literary contexts that in such poems of Donne's as this the reader can hear "the speaking voice"; but many different kinds of pattern in literature can give rise to the same comment, for example Pepys' Diary, which is quite unlike this but nevertheless gives rise to the same comment. On the other hand, it is not often pointed out that the kind of complexity in the clause-complex here is of very much the same kind as is noted as typical of conversation in Halliday (1985: 85).

To return to Donne's prose, and searching for other kinds of Theme in THAT WOMEN OUGHT TO PAINT, which is one of his Paradoxes: in one place Donne wants to specify as part of his point the kind of exclusivity expressible by means of a Thematic Equative, in this case with the nominalization as Theme, and he writes:

What thou lovest in her face is colour, (and painting gives that.)
[p. 338]

i.e. 'what thou lovest in her face is colour and nothing else (and painting gives that)'.

And in the letters, there are Predicated Themes, as in:

But it is the other capacity which must make mine acceptable
[p. 228]

rather than "But the other capacity must make mine acceptable;" and, though they seem to be uncommon elsewhere, in THAT VIRGINITY IS A VERTUE there is:

All other Vertues lodge in the Will (*it is the Will* that makes them vertues). But *it is the unwillingness to keep it, the desire to forsake it,* that makes this a vertue.   [p. 348].

Here, it is the predications that are italicized; and here—as they do today—they serve to put the Focus on what would be Given in the unpredicated form (i.e. on "keep" and "forsake") by suggesting that they should be New.

3. SHAKESPEARE

Turning now to Shakespeare himself, we have much less of his prose than of his verse, and what we have is in his plays, often for conversation, usually of a less than elevated kind, especially in comedy. But, for example, in *Antony and Cleopatra*, we have a correlative Clause Theme in:

> *Iras:* Dear goddess, hear that prayer of the people! for, *as* **it** *is a heart-breaking to see a handsome man loose-wived*, so **it** is deadly sorrow to behold a foul knave uncuckolded.

(I.ii.68–71) [cited from Houghton, 1962]

together with Themes consisting of a postposed embedded Subject using anticipatory **it** in both Clause Theme and Clause Rheme. And a (perhaps rare) Marked Theme with an imperative is:

> *Enobarbus: Under a compelling occasion* let women die.

(*ibid,* I.ii.137)

There is nothing surprising about these, not even, let us hope, in the sentiment in the latter, since the Marked Theme strongly suggests that "compelling" is part of the New, implying "only," possibly even with a primary focus, perhaps even contrastive Tone 53—

//53 Under a com/<u>pell</u>ing oc/casion let /women /<u>die</u> . . . //

or perhaps just Tone 5—

//5 Under a com/<u>pell</u>ing oc/casion let /women /die . . . //.

There are other possibilities, of course, but there is nothing about any of them that suggests that the Theme pattern is not part of the normal system at this date.

Turning to verse, it is not difficult to illustrate his uses of types of Themes, which are in the modern mold. He uses Marked Themes regularly, and this can be economically illustrated from the Sonnets, where he uses them very carefully in a variety of ways. A Marked Theme, for example, begins the first one:

[1]   <u>From fairest creatures</u> we desire increase . . .

and takes up a whole initial line in:

[20] <u>A woman's face, with nature's own hand painted,</u>
Hast thou, the master mistress of my passion . . .

(The sonnets are quoted from Booth (1977).)

Here, in addition to the Marked Theme suggesting Marked Tonality, the conceit suggests that "woman's" should carry a Marked Tone, probably Tone 1+ or, less probably, Tone 5,

//1+ a /<u>wo</u>man's /face //

rather than

//5 a /<u>wo</u>man's /<u>face</u> //

[The "addressee" of the sonnets may sometimes be a man, but whether or not this is so, the text is ambivalent.]

Clause Themes of very varied lengths are used in the Sonnets, sometimes becoming the organizing principle of the whole poem, successive quatrains being individual clause-complexes within the Theme, occasionally incorporating a Marked Theme within the Clause Theme as well. They range in length from half a line:

[113] *Since I left you,* mine eye is in my mind

through whole lines

[138] *When my love swears that she is made of truth*
I do believe her . . .

to two lines

[2] *When forty winters shall besiege thy brow,*
And dig deep trenches in thy beauty's field,
Thy youth's proud livery, so gazed on now,
Will be a tottered weed of small worth held . . .

four lines

[32] *If thou survive my well-contented day,*
When that churl death my bones with dust shall cover,
And shalt by fortune once more re-survey
These poor rude lines of thy deceased lover,
Compare them with the bett'ring of the time . . .

and eight lines

[12] *When I do count the clock that tells the time,*
And see the brave day sunk in hideous night,
When I behold the violet past prime,
And sable curls all silvered o'er with white,
When lofty trees I see barren of leaves,
Which erst from heat did canopy the herd,
And summer's green all girded up in sheaves
Borne on the bier with white and bristly beard,
Then of thy beauty do I question make . . .

to ten;

[64] *When I have seen by time's fell hand defaced*
The rich proud cost of outworn buried age;
When sometime lofty towers I see down razed,
And brass eternal slave to mortal rage,
When I have seen the hungry ocean gain
Advantage on the kingdom of the shore,
And the firm soil win of the wat'ry main,
Increasing store with loss, and loss with store,
When I have seen such interchange of state,
Or state itself confounded to decay,
Ruin hath taught me thus to ruminate.

In the Sonnets we can also find Theme Predications, both of an Unmarked Theme, "my love"—

[61] It is my love that keeps mine eye awake . . .

and a Marked one ("thee, myself"[1])—

[62] 'Tis thee, myself, that for myself I praise . . .

—both fulfilling their modern function in writing of ensuring that the predicated elements, "my love" and "thee," are New—and probably "myself" as well, since it probably carries tone concord in apposition with "thee," and this is the point of the poem; and in all three cases—"love," "thee" and "my/self"—Shakespeare also takes advantage for metrical purposes of the salience this requires.

Thematic Equatives are rare (although this may be because I have not found examples of the kind of context in which they are at all common), and in fact in the sonnets there seem to be only approximations to them rather than genuine examples:

[74] The worth of that is that which it contains . . .

---

[1]There is an oddity here, but it is the oddity of the conceit that equates "thee" and "myself," not in making them Thematic.

But though this is Identifying and involves some rankshift, it does not have the true Equative form and hence does not have the "excluding"meaning characteristic of a Thematic Equative. Compare also, in prose:

> *Clown:* Who you are and what you would are out of my welkin
>
> (*Twelfth Night,* III.i.56–7, in Dent, 1938)

where again it is not a true Equative but there are simply two coordinated nominalizations as Carrier in an Attributive rather than an Identifying Relational Clause, and again there is no trace of the excluding meaning.

Continuing now with prose, here—as we would expect—Shakespeare uses the basic patterns of Unmarked Theme, Marked Theme and Clause Theme as in modern English, but with some uses that are now archaic. The Unmarked Themes in the following are normal:

> *Prince:*   Why thou owest God a death.
> *Falstaff:* 'Tis not due yet: I would be loath to pay him before his day.
>
> (*I Henry IV,* V.i.126–8) [Quoted from Newman (1952).]

But, a few lines later, the following would be abnormal in the modern system:

> *Falstaff:* Yea, but how if honour prick me off when I come on?
>
> (*1 Henry IV,* V.i.130–1)

(though we can imagine "What about if . . . ?" in modern English, and it may be the elliptical use of "How" rather than anything else about the Theme which makes this archaic to our ears); and, earlier in the scene, we have a type of interrogative, with a verb as Theme, which—quite apart from its suffix and the form of the second person pronoun—is no longer available:

> *Prince:* Swearest thou ungracious boy?
>
> (*op.cit.,* II.iv.436);

while in

> *Falstaff:* But to say I know more harm in him than in myself were to
> say more than I know.
>
> (*op.cit.,* II.iv.457–8),

the more likely modern pattern (even if all other archaisms, such as *were,* were left unchanged) would be:

But it were to say more than I know, to say I know more harm in him than in myself.

In any case, Falstaff uses very complex rhetoric, Shakespeare sometimes using him incongruously to parody Lyly; for example,

Falstaff: For *though the camomile, the more it is trodden on the faster it grows,* yet youth, the more it is wasted the sooner it wears.

(*op.cit.*, II.iv.393–5),

where, in order to make both "camomile" and "youth" New so that he can point up the balanced antithesis he is building between them, he indicates Marked Tonality in both cases by commas (if the punctuation is to be trusted, though the structure would indicate such Tonality anyway, without the commas); and also he uses not a cataphoric **it**, which is common elsewhere [e.g. in *Hamlet* (see below)], but an anaphoric one. If, in each half, the first of the two occurrences of **it** is removed, and their referents are put into the places they vacate, we get:

For though the more the camomile is trodden on the faster it grows, yet the more youth is wasted the sooner it wears.

retaining the parallel and part of the contrast but losing the combination of contrast and New on "camomile" and "youth."

As mentioned above, Horatio uses an anticipatory **it** in *Hamlet:*

Hamlet: Why may not imagination trace the noble dust of Alexander, till he find it stopping a bung-hole?
Horatio: 'Twere to consider too curiously, to consider so.

Hamlet (V.i.196–199)

And, Claudius had used a recapitulatory **it**:

Claudius: *For your intent*
In going back to school in Wittenberg,
It is most retrograde to our desire;

(*Hamlet*, I.ii.112–4)

where "It" is there for metrical as well as rhetorical reasons, but at the same time—while pointing up the Marked Theme—shows the availability of the pattern within the system. [We may note, too, the introductory "For . . . ," announcing the Theme, rather than "As for . . . ." *Cf.* Halliday (1994), p.39.]

To conclude this purely illustrative account of the period, however, we may cite one Clause Theme, not by Shakespeare but by his editors Heminge and Condell, in the dedication of the First Folio edition of his works:

Whilst we study to be thankful in our particular, the many favours we have received from your Lordships, we are fallen upon the ill fortune, to mingle two the most diverse things that can be, fear and rashness; rashness in the enterprize, fear of the success.

Although this is elaborate, there appears to be nothing grammatically forced or unusual in the opening Clause Theme itself, *Whilst we study . . . from your Lordships,* the more strange patterns to modern ears being the apposition within it between <u>our particular</u> and <u>the many favours we have received from your Lordships</u> (together with the archaic use of <u>particular</u>), and the now very archaic group "two the most diverse things . . . " that follows. Today this would more probably be something like "the two most diverse things" or "the most diverse two things," although the use of "diverse" in these structures would still be uncommon. But the Clause Theme seems comfortable and well established, as indeed it is, because it had been in use since the Old English period.

What have been found only rarely in this very sketchy survey of this period are the kind of Identifying forms, such as Thematic Equatives, the growth and development of the functions of which Halliday explores in Ghadesy (1988) (and which this sentence exemplifies). It is possible that instances might be found, and certainly instances of Identifying Clauses involving rankshift at Head can be found, as in the *Twelfth Night* example cited above; but the total syndrome of features Halliday described had not—although this may be because, to find any precursors of the syndrome, we should look in scientific prose, perhaps Bacon's *Advancement of Learning or Novum Organum* (though Bacon is a complex stylist anyway, and perhaps not easy to fit in). Certainly, if they can be found, they are not very frequent, and not in any very wide range of functions. Going back 200 years to Chaucer's time, the picture is less clear. Both Marked Themes and Clause Themes are common, and in functions that they serve today, but Predicated Themes do not seem to appear, and there were various other patterns then (though they can be shown only cursorily) that no longer occur. We will return to these, but first we will go back even earlier to the Old English period, the picture there being (as we would expect) rather different, although the main outlines of today's system are already clear.

4. OLD ENGLISH

The textbook by Quirk *et al.* (1975), gives an excerpt from the Old English Chronicle, and the entry for the year 991 (probably written in the form in which we now have it not very long afterwards) begins:

	Here	was Ipswich	plundered
991	Her	wæs Gypeswic	gehergod
	In this year	Ipswich was	sacked.

[The Old English text is given in the middle line, the words above it give a literal translation of the individual words, and the bottom line gives a more idiomatic translation.]

Here the Subject, "Gypeswic," follows the verb "wæs." This would be unlikely to happen in Modern English: *In this year was Ipswich sacked* is not to be expected.

Then, the entry for the next year begins:

	Here	Oswald	the blessed	archbishop,	left	this life
992	Her	Oswald, se	eadiga	arcebiscop,	forlet	þis lif
	In this year,	Oswald,	the saintly	archbishop,		died

and went	to that	heavenly (one)
ond ġeferde	þæt	heofonlice
and went	to	heaven.

In both years, the first word "Her" (usually translated "In this year") is the standard form used initially in most sentences beginning an entry for a year in the Old English Chronicle, and it is not the Subject of the clause, functioning in fact just like a Marked Theme in Modern English and introducing a shift in the Development, to a new year. Also, in the first clause of the entry for 992, the Subject, "Oswald, se eadiga arcebiscop," precedes the verb, "forlet;" while in the second the Subject does not appear because the clause is branched.

Moreover the entry for the earlier year, 991, continues:

and after that very early	was Brihtnoth ealdorman slain	at Maldon.
ond æfter þam swiðe raðe	wæs Brihtnoð ealdorman ofslægen	æt Mældune.
and very soon after that	ealdorman Brihtnoth was slain	at Maldon.

And on that year	man	counselled
Ond on þam geare	man	ġerædde
And in that year	it was first	decided

that man   paid first tribute to Danish men
þæt man   geald ærest gafol   Deniscan mannum
that we should pay   tribute to the Danes.

Here, the Marked Themes are underlined, and Textual Themes—whether before Marked or Unmarked Topical Themes—are in bold. The pattern is as in modern English: whether a Theme is Marked or not, any textual element in the Theme normally precedes the Topical element. And while the Subject in the first clause, "Brihtnoð ealdorman," lies after the Finite within the verbal group "wæs . . . ofslaægen," in both the next two clauses the impersonal Subject "man" precedes the verbs, "geraædde" and "geald." However, two lines lower, we get:

That advice counselled Siric archbishop.
Þæne ræd   ġerædde   Siric arcebiscop.
Archbishop Siric made that suggestion.

where the Marked Theme is followed immediately by the verb "geraædde," and the Subject, "Siric arcebiscop", comes at the end. The literal translation in the top line follows a very unlikely if not impossible sequence in modern English. (Interestingly, it might be taken to suggest that a better translation in modern English might have been a Predicated Theme—"It was Archbishop Siric who made that suggestion." In this, by being final in the predication, "Archbishop Siric" retains in Modern English the status as New that it probably had in Old English.) As the editors say (*op.cit.*, p.73):

As well as arrangements like "Oswald forlet þis lif", 'Oswald gave up this life', normal in Modern English, we find considerable variety of order in Old English. Indeed, the exact reverse of the type just illustrated occurs in the preceding line: "Þæne ræd ġerædde Siric", 'Siric decided on the plan', where we recognize that the writer has chosen to mention the object first, because it is already known about, but to delay revealing the subject until, in end position, it can have the greatest impact."

It is not difficult to recognize here what in Systemic terms would be termed "Given" ("because it is already known about") and "New" ("in end position, it can have the greatest impact"), whether or not the system of Information was exactly the same in Old English as today. And similarly, "the writer has chosen to mention the object first" clearly refers to a Thematic choice, in this instance a marked one.

The editors continue with a reference to another passage given in their book, an episode from a longer work, not dated but probably from the late tenth or early eleventh century, to which they give the title "Apollonius and Arcestrates." They refer to the final clause in the following section:

β	- α1
‖ When the king that saw	‖ then took he Apollonius's hand, ‖
‖ Ða se cyngc þæt ġeseah,	‖ þa nam he Apollonies hand, ‖
‖ When the king saw this,	‖ then he took Apollonius's hand, ‖

α2	- α21 -
‖ and himself hence from the knights turned	‖ and quoth: ‖
‖ ond hine hwon fram þam cnihtum ġewænde,	‖ ond cwæð: ‖
‖ and went a little distance from the young men,	‖ and said: ‖

α22	‖‖ 1 -
‖ 'Knowest thou the shipwrecked man?'	Apollonius quoth: ‖
‖ 'Wast þu þone forlidenan man?'	Apollonius cwæð: ‖
‖ 'Do you know who is the shipwrecked man?'	Apollonius said: ‖

‖ 2β	- 2α
‖ 'Thou good king, if thy will be,	‖ I him know.'
‖ 'Ðu goda cyning, gif þin willa bið,	‖ ic hine wat.'
‖ 'Thou good king, if it please you,	‖ I know him.'

[In this quotation only, the underlined Themes are not necessarily marked. Note, also, the Interpersonal Theme, Ðu goda cyning, preceding the Topical Theme in the last clause.]

The editors say:

> similarly, where the object is a pronoun (and hence obviously known about), the verb frequently takes up the climactic end-position: "ic hine wat . . . ", 'I know him' (loc. cit.)

in other words, both pronouns are part of the Given and the verb becomes New. However, to do this is to miss an opportunity—for which there is textual motivation—to make "ic" New (leaving both "hine" and "wat" as Given), which would enable Apollonius to contrast himself with everyone else as being the only person who knows the identity of the "shipwrecked man," because it is he who had been shipwrecked, and the reader already knows this. We cannot tell, though, whether this Tonicity would be contrastive, which would be possible only if the unmarked case was defined differently from the case today. Similarly, we can not tell if the Tone was contrastive in some way (for example contrasting his state of knowledge with the ignorance of the rest of the court), though difficulty with this is frequently the case in Modern English writing, too. (But it is the case here, as normally elsewhere, that there are several other possible intonations, which would give different Information Structures, dependent upon giving the clause different Marked Tonalities.)

In this passage we also get, in "Wast," an antecedent of the interrogative lexical verb as Theme "Swearest thou, ungracious boy," quoted from *I Henry IV* above (p. 9). (Shakespeare could and did use "do," e.g. he could have said "Dost thou swear at me . . . ?", but by choosing not to do so he can make the lexical verb Theme, whereas it was not possible to use **do** as an operator in this way in the Old English period.) And we also get a Clause Theme, "Ða se cyngc pæt ġeseah" at the beginning, linked by the correlative to the next clause, "Ða . . . ‖ Þæ . . . , a special instance of a very frequent Textual Theme in narrative in Old English as in Modern English (i.e. "then"). (The spelling variant Ð/Þ, is not significant, both letters being equivalent to modern "th," in this instance representing [θ].) And in this passage we also get the verb ("nam") immediately following "þa," which is here the second part of the correlative. The verb therefore takes on a Thematic flavor, which it also has in non-correlative contexts (as in the next example below: "Ða ġerædde se cyng"). When independent in this latter way, "þa" is usually both internally and externally conjunctive, and "þa + verb" with "þa" in this double sense is a very common sequence in which the verb gains prominence from its Thematic position in a way that is not now possible (because "Then sank the ship to the bottom" no longer occurs except archaically).

Elsewhere in the extract from the Chronicle, we get:

Then decided the king
Ða   ġerædde se cyng
Then the king decided

with the Subject, ("se cyng") in final position after the verb, and:

Then sent   the ealdorman Elfric
Ða   sende se ealdorman Elfric
Then   ealdorman Elfric sent out orders,

with the Subject again in final position after the verb, and:

And then   met   the   army   the ships of East Anglia and of London
Ond þa   ġemette se   here   ða scipu of Eastenglum ond of Lundene
And then   the   Danish army met the ships from East Anglia and London.

again with the Subject after the verb but not in final position. (The spellings, "cyning," "cyng" and "cyngc" for "king," are dialect variants from different MSS.)

Similarly, in "Apollonius and Arcestrates" we get a Clause Theme introduced by "ða," but doubled to act as an introductory correlative:

β
When Arcestrates the king   had   that letter over-read
Ða ða Arcestrates se   cyningc hæfde þæt ġewrit ofer-ræd,
When Arcestrates the king   had read through the letter,

α
then ne wist he which shipwrecked   his daughter named
þa   niste   he hwilcne forlidenne   his dohtor   nemde
he didn't know   which shipwrecked man his daughter meant

and

1α   - 1β
Then quoth of them one   that (one) called Ardalius:
Ða   cwæð heora   an   ‖ se   hatte Ardalius:
Then   one of them,   called   Ardalius, said:

in this case, the Subject, "heora an," following the verb, "cwæð", together with a slightly rearranged initial sequence "then quoth one of them," being still just possible in Modern English, though strongly (and usually consciously) archaic—even if "said" or "saith" is used instead of "quoth"—and rarely used, if at all, outside religious and literary contexts (e.g. "Thus said the prophet"). We also get:

2
With me thou book-craft learnedst
Mid me þu   boccræft   leornodest . . .
You've been studying with me,

where the point of the Marked Theme most probably is to give it not only prominence in itself but also its own Tone Group, so that "With me" is New as well, pointing up the impossibility in the story of the addressee being anywhere else—certainly not being shipwrecked. We also get another example of Clause Theme:

βα   -   ββ
When   that   king not might find   which of them shipwrecked were
Mid ði þe se   cyngc ne mihte findan   hwilc heora   forliden   wære,
When   the   king could not find out   which of them had been the
                                                          shipwrecked one,

(where a perhaps better translation might use an Equative (not apparently available at the time): "when the king could not find out *which of them was the one who had been shipwrecked"*)

α1	- α2	- 2β
he be-saw to Apollonius	and quoth:	'Take thou, Apollonius, this letter
he beseah to Apollonius	ond cwæð:	'Nim ðu, Apolloni, þis ġewrit
he looked at Apollonius	and said:	'Take this letter, Apollonius, . . .

Then the penny drops and the king sees what has happened, which we are told in a clause which provides an example of "Ða" followed by the verb, with the Subject afterwards, in:

Then understood he the   words,
Þa   ongeat   he þone cwyde,
Then he understood the meaning of the speech

[i.e., what Apollonius has just said],

the passage ending with a sentence that contains an emphatic Clause Theme, together with a prominent Marked Theme in the Clause Rheme, that brings the story—or at least this extract—to a conclusion:

‖‖ -	‖‖ β	-
‖‖ 'Rejoice, rejoice, Apollonius:	because my daughter wills that,	‖
'Blissa, blissa, Apolloni:	*for ðam þe min dohtor ġewilnað þæs*	‖
'Good for you, Apollonius:	If my daughter wants it,	‖

α	‖‖
thee my will is.'	
ðe min willa is.'	
you're my choice!'	

It would be interesting to know whether "ðe" is in any sense marked here, in addition to being Marked Theme (because it is initial but not the Subject), perhaps in getting its own Tonic (with Marked Tonality), as would be quite likely if this structure were possible in Modern English; but there seems to be no way of discerning any such markedness in writing. And also it would be interesting to know whether "min" got some kind of antithetical markedness as well, as its contrast with "min dohtor gewilnað þæs" and the lexical repetition "gewilnað . . . willa" suggest.

// 4 ð̠e   //1+ m̠in /willa   /is //
‖   New ‖   New —Given → ‖

In that case, there could be a neat sequence of two combinations of kinds of prominence: the combination of Marked Tonality and Marked Theme for "ðe," and the combination of Marked Tonicity and Marked Tone ("1 +" rather than "1," though Marked Tone would have been an extra) on "min."

The final example in the Old English period was suggested by Margaret Berry (personal communication). It provides an excellent illustration, from the old English period, of the use of Clause Themes and Marked Themes to shift the topic and give a text a clearly structured Development. The text is a "Medicinal Recipe" in Davis (1953: 30), detailing the medicinal uses of a herb, a kind of wort called "betony." After describing the herb, and where and how it should be gathered, the recipe goes on to describe its specific uses. This new topic—the first of its uses—is introduced by means of a Clause Theme:

```
|||  β                                           -
     If (a)   man's    head    broken    be
|||  Gif      mannes heafod tobrocen    sy,  ||
     If a     man's    head    is        hurt,
```

```
     α1                                          -
     take        of that same wort   betony
||   genim      þa      ylcan wyrte betonican,  ||
     take some of that same wort,  betony,
```

```
     α2                  -  α3                                            |||
     shred   it then      and pound (it)    very    small to dust
||   scearfa hy þonne ||  and gnid           swyþe smale to duste.  |||
     then shred it,       and pound it to a very    fine    powder.
```

```
     1                                           -
     Take    then    two    drachms weight,
|||  Genim þonne twega trymessa wæge,  ||
     Then    take    two drachms weight,
```

```
     2                                                        |||
            take it   then    in  hot       beer
||          Þige hit þonne on hatum beore.  |||
     and    then    drink   some  in  hot   beer.
```

```
     Then    healeth that head    very    readily after that drink.
|||  Þonne halað   þæt heafod swyðe hraðe æfter þam drince.  |||
     The     head    heals    very    quickly after  that    drink.
```

"Ðonne" is a form which replaced "Þa," in very similar functions. In the last clause, where it is immediately followed by the verb (as in the examples with "þa" given above, with the Subject subsequently following on afterward), it marks out a move from description of the treatment to prediction of a satisfactory prognosis. But in the previous sentences, where it marks out only the sub-stages of the preparation, it always follows the imperatives, as in "Genim þonne" (twice), and sometimes the Complements as well (as in "Scearfa hy þonne" and "Þige hit þonne"). In this respect it differs from the translation given, which had been provided before this point was noticed. In that translation, "Then" had always been initial (though this is not obligatory in modern English).[2] It looks as though a further degree of Thematic emphasis might have been provided by the initial position, though to establish whether or not this was general in the system at that time would require extensive further investigation.

Then:

1   -
Against eyes ∶ sore, take   of that same wort (the) wort-roots
||| Wið   eagena sar, ġenim þære   ylcan wyrte   wyrttruman, ||
to treat sore   eyes, take   (some) of the root of the same wort,

Here, the Marked Theme, "Wið eagena sar," marks the move to the next condition whose treatment is to be described.

2   -
seethe in water   to third   part,
|| seoð   on wætere to þriddan dæle, ||
seethe (it) in three parts of water,

3   -
and of that water   bathe the eyes
|| and of þam wætere beþa þa eagan ||
and with the water bathe the eyes:

Here, the Marked Theme "and of þam wætere," although not in a clause that is initial in the clause-complex, moves the topic on from the particular kind of preparation suggested to the treatment for which it is to be used.

---

[2]*Cf.* Malcolm Coulthard's discussion of the use of "then" non-initially in police reports, in *Questioning Statements,* English Language Research, Birmingham, 1995.

42   - 41

and take   of that selfsame wort (the) leaf   and crush it

‖ and ġenim þære   sylfan   wyrte   leaf   ‖ and bryt hy, ‖

and take   some of the leaf of the wort,   and crush it,

5   ‖‖

and lay   over the eye   on the   face.

‖ and lege ofer þa eagan on þone andwlitan. ‖‖

and lay it over the eye   on the   face.

1α   -

‖‖ Against ears   sore,   take   of that same wort (the) leaf

<u>Wið   earena sar</u>   ġenim þære   ylcan wyrte   leaf ‖

For   sore   ears,   take   some of the leaf of that wort . . .

Again, as with start of the account of eye treatment, the Marked Theme "Wið earena sar," after discussing the next method of preparation, moves the discourse on to discussing the next condition, earache, that can be treated.

1β

when   it   greenest   be,

‖ þonne heo grenost   beo,   ‖

when it is at its most   green,

21   - 22   ⸗

boil (it) in water   and wring   that   juice,

‖ wyl   on wætere ‖ and wring   þæt   wos,   ‖

boil it in water   and squeeze out its juice,

3β   - 3α   ‖‖

and after   it   has been   stood,   make it   again warm

‖ *and siþþan hyt ġestanden beo,*   ‖ do   hit   eft   wearm ‖‖

and after   it   has   stood for a little while, warm   it   again

Again, although the clause "*and siþþan hyt ġestanden beo*" is not Thematic in the whole clause-complex, it is Clause Theme within the sub-clause-complex that it initiates—the third element in the larger parataxis ("*siþþan hyt ġestanden beo,* ‖ do hit eft wearm"); and its function here is to be Sub-Clause Theme within this sub-clause-complex, again moving the development on from the description of one stage of the preparation of the herb to the next:

1α   - 1β   -
||| Wið earena sar, ǧenim þære ylcan wyrte leaf || þonne heo grenost beo, ||

21   - 22   -
|| wyl on wætere || and wring þæt wos, ||

3β   - 3α |||
|| and siþþan hyt ǧestanden beo, || do hit eft wearm . . . |||

An interesting point arises here about the relationship between
the Marked Themes and the Clause Themes. Both "Wið eagena sar"
and "wið earena sar" look very much like grammatical metaphors for
what congruently would be Clause Themes (i.e. something like "If you
want to treat sore eyes/ears," paralleling "Ġif mannes heafod tobrocen
sy" earlier). Something similar may occur in the final clause, in which
a more congruent Clause Theme is offered in the translation,

4 |||
and   through   wool drip (it) in that ear.
|| and   þurh   wulle drype   on þæt eare. |||
and using a thread of wool, drip   it   into the ear.

in which "and þurh wulle" moves the development on from the final
stage of making the preparation to the application of the preparation.

5. CHAUCER

Moving forward now to Chaucer, whose "Treatise on the Astrolabe" is
the earliest text discussed in Halliday (1988), the treatise itself has
examples of nearly all the varieties that have been discussed. The
second sentence, for example, is:

> Than for as mochel as a philosofre saith, "he wrappith him in his
> frend, that condescendith to the rightfull praiers of his frend", there-
> fore have I yeven the a suffisant Astrolabie.

> [All Chaucer quotations are from Robinson (1957)]

in which the correlative structure, "for as much as . . . (therefore . . .)" forms a Clause Theme.

Also, it is noticeable that, although the opening 109 lines constitute a sort of "prospectus," outlining what he is going to say, and
this is in part made up of an outline of what each of the five sections
of the Treatise are going to be about, Chaucer does not use Marked

Themes to introduce each section as he easily might have done (and did do elsewhere, as will be shown later), but labels them with headings in Latin—*Prima pars, Secunda pars,* etc. However, Marked Themes (though not Predicated[3] or Equative ones), are used strikingly in a number of cases within each of the Parts, to move on from one numbered subsection to the next. So, in Part I we have twenty-one numbered sections, among which are:

5. <u>Overthwart this foreseide long lyne</u> there crossith him another lyne;

7. <u>Fro this litel cros</u> (+) up to the ende of the lyne meridionall, under the ryng, shalt thou fynden the bordure divided with 90 degrees;

9. <u>Next this</u> folewith ("followeth") the cercle of the daies;

10. <u>Next the cercle of the daies</u> folewith the cercle of the names of the monethes;

12. <u>Next the foreseide cercle of the A B C</u>, under the cross lyne, is marked the skale;

19. <u>From this cenyth</u> ("zenith"), . . . there comen a maner croked strikes;

20. <u>Next these azymutz</u>, under the cercle of Cancer, ben there 12 divisiouns embelif (Robinson, pp.547–9),

showing that the use of Marked Theme for topic shifting is working normally in prose at this date.

But some of those make one a little uneasy, and they do not seem to fit comfortably into modern categories. Some are of kinds that are archaic for non-Thematic reasons, for instance,

<u>Of the whiche lyne</u>, from a litel cros (+) in the bordure unto the centre of the large hool, is clepid the est lyne . . .

(Robinson, p. 547, subsection 5)

<u>over the whiche degrees</u> ther ben noumbres of augrym . . .

(*loc. cit.*, subsection 7)

---

[3]It is said that the first known instance of a Predicated Theme occurs in the second quarter of the fifteenth century, perhaps 35 years after Chaucer's death, in *Sir Gawain and the Green Knight* (ll.5–6). But it is also said that the example is suspect, not being a true Predicated Theme. The disputed sentence is: "Hit wat3—Ennias þe athel, and his highe kynde, / Þat siþen depreced provinces . . . ", (i.e., "It was Aeneas the noble, and his great race, that afterwards subdued provinces").

in both of which (not "in both of the which") it is the presence and position of the article that are intrusive and archaic.

> Tho lokid I doun upon myn est (*sc.* "east") orisounte, and fond there 10 degrees of Scorpius ascending, whom I tok for myn ascendent. And thus lerned I to know onys for ever in which manere I shuld com to the houre of the nyght.   (*op.cit.*, p. 550, right hand column)

Here, in the second sentence, if "thus" is behaving as a kind of Clause Substitute, it is presumably the Topical Theme. But if (as seems better) it is to be taken as a reference item (*i.e.* as a Textual Theme) then the Middle English "Predicator–Subject" declarative sequence "lerned I" that follows forces us to recognize the Predicator as Topical Theme. This is now an uncommon option in Modern English, except in stage directions such as "Enter Hamlet" which is itself an archaism. (But this may be an imperative—see Halliday (1994), p. 47, though the types exemplified there are not like this.) Whatever it is, it is a common type in this text and elsewhere—both in Chaucer and in other Middle English texts—whereas other types are not found here, in "A Treatise on the Astrolabe," so commonly as in the verse. (It is worth pointing out, however, that if "thus" is interpreted as a Clause Substitute, the meaning will be:

> And by loking down upon myn est orisounte, and fonding there 10 degrees of Scorpius ascending, and taking this as myn ascendant, lerned I to know.

and this might be an antecedent of the procedures developed by Newton by means of which he was able to nominalize clauses to act as Theme.)

Fiona McDonald, a student at Stirling, wrote a detailed Thematic analysis of *The Canterbury Tales'* entire Prologue and first tale—that of the Knight. Here, first of all the contribution made by the Clause Theme to the opening sentence of "The Prologue" was noted:

β11
Whan that Aprill with his shoures soote The droghte of March
                                        hath perced to the roote,
Clause Theme ————————————————————————————→
Theme————→ - Rheme ———————————————————————→
Struct. - Topical |

Here, within the clause it is open to question whether "with his shoures soote" is embedded as Qualifier to "Aprill," in which case it

is part of the Theme, or is a Means—or possibly Accompaniment—
in Transitivity, in which case it is not part of the Theme. It seems to
be ambiguous, as both Means and Accompaniment, so it has been
left out of the Theme.

β12
And   'Aprill hath' bathed every veyne in swich licour [Of which
                              vertu engendred is the flour[4]]
Clause Theme (continued) ——————————————————→
Theme   - Rheme ——————————————————————→
Struc - 'Top' |

β21
Whan   Zephirus eek with his sweete breeth Inspired hath in every
                              holt and heeth The tendre croppes,
Clause Theme (continued) ——————————————————→
Theme ————→ - Rheme ——————————————————————→
Struc - Topical |

β22
and   the yonge sonne   Hath in the Ram his halve cours yronne,
Clause Theme (continued) ——————————————————→
Theme ————————→ - Rheme ——————————————————→
Struc - Topical ————→ |

β23α
And   smale foweles   maken melodye,
Clause Theme (continued) ——————————→
Theme ————————→ - Rheme ————→
Struc - Topical ——→ |

β23βα
That   slepen al the nyght with open yë
Clause Theme (continued) ——————————————→
Theme → - Rheme ——————————————————————→
Struc/Top |

---

[4]Perhaps this is a ranking clause elaborating the previous one, rather than a
Modifier, but there are doubts about this, because it seems possible that the force
of the "swich" indicates defining, i.e., 'in that kind of liquor by whose power the
flower is engendered'.

β23ββ
(*So   priketh hem nature in hir corages*)
Clause Theme (continued) ────────────→
Theme - Rheme ──────────────────────→
Textual |

α1
Thanne   longen folk to goon on pilgrimages . . .
Clause Rheme ────────────────────────→
MTh → - Rheme ──────────────────────→
Topical |

This wonderful opening, which for many is the first sentence of Chaucer's they read, is not an easy one for a beginner, largely because of the delay in resolution created by the complexity of the Clause Theme, but it grows on us as it becomes more familiar. Its particular kind of complexity anticipates Shakespeare's 64th Sonnet—whose Clause Theme has one less iambic pentameter but twelve rather than six clauses (quoted above, p. 7)—by some 200 years, during which time there was the rapid change in the language already mentioned, which meant that Chaucer could not be read by the Elizabethans and was dismissed as unreadable and not worth reading, since they could not scan him. Yet throughout the changes of the fifteenth century—the Great Vowel Shift, the loss of many of the remaining inflections, and so on—the pattern that enabled Chaucer to create this sentence persisted, to make possible also the equally well-managed opening sentence of "A Valediction: Forbidding Mourning" (quoted above, p. 118), with the same number of clauses (seven) as Chaucer's, though much shorter, less spacious and more concentrated ones.

After noting this, a number of related but quite distinct phenomena were found. First there were a set that did not easily fall into the modern categories. For example:

[19] Bifil that in that seson on a day

where "Bifil," the past form of "bifallen," "to befall, or happen," in the formulaic "Bifil that" (somewhat equivalent to "once upon a time," is an initial verb, lacking (and not needing) an "it" to precede it, so it is therefore Theme in a way that is now impossibly archaic. Again,

[37] Me thinketh it accordaunt to resoun

which is presumably an antecedent of the modern metaphorical Interpersonal Theme, for example,

I	- think	‖ it		is only reasonable
Theme[1]	⟶		- Rheme[1] ⟶	
Interpersonal	- Topical			
Theme[2]	- Rheme[2]	‖ Theme[3]	- Rheme[3] ⟶	
Topical		‖ Topical		

looks distinctly odd if analyzed in the same way—

me	- thinketh	‖ it	accordaunt to resoun
Theme[1]	⟶		- Rheme[1] ⟶
Interpersonal	- Topical		
Theme[2]	- Rheme[2]	‖ Theme[3]	- Rheme[3] ⟶
Topical		‖ Topical	

—not only because of the uncomfortable initial "me" but also because it is unlikely that it is meant metaphorically.

Another (and a favorite) type is

[94] Wel koude he sitte on hors and faire ride

where an Old English pattern, not previously cited, persists:

Easily may (it) happen
Eaðe mæg ġewurðan . . .
It may easily happen (that you know something I don't know).

> *Apollonius & Arcestrates,* in Quirk *et al.* (1975: 14)

In this, the Finite, "mæg," precedes the Subject in a declarative (rather than in a polar interrogative) and in a position where we can no longer retain the Interpersonal Theme without sounding forced in modern English: "Easily may it happen" or "Easily it may happen." Other examples of this pattern—which is most common with "Wel"—are:

[130] Wel koude she carie a morsel
[130] and wel ('koude she') kepe / (That no drope ne fille upon hire brest.
[236] Wel koude he singe
[278] Wel koude he in eschaunge sheeldes (i.e. coins) selle

(We cannot now say "Well could I do with a beer after that lecture," even if it is true, whether we have given or listened to it.)

Despite these patterns, which are anomalous in twentieth century terms, the basic patterns and functions are familiar. For example, in the first 15 lines of the portrait of the knight, Marked Themes regularly move the description on a stage, for instance:

A KNYGHT   ther was,
Marked Theme   - Rheme →
Topical |

and   that   a worthy man,
Theme ———→   - Rheme ———→
Struc   - Top |

That | fro the tyme [[that he first bigan To riden out]] , | he loved chival-
                                                                   | rie, Trouthe and
                                                                   | honour, Fredom
                                                                   | and curtesie.
Marked Theme ————————————————→   - | Rheme ———→
Struc - | Topical |

Ful worthy   was he in his lordes werre,
Marked Theme   - Rheme ————————→
Topical |

And therto   hadde he riden, «¹   » As well in cristendom
                                                          as in hethenesse,
Marked Theme   - Rheme ————————————→
Struc - Topical |

«¹ no man   'had ridden' ferre,»
   Theme   - Rheme ———→
   Topical |

And evere honoured for his worthynesse.
Rheme ————————————→

At Alisaundre   he was
Marked Theme   - Rheme
Topical |

whan   it   was wonne.
Theme   - Rheme ——→
Struc - Top |

Ful ofte tyme   he hadde the bord bigonne Aboven alle nacions in
                                                          Pruce
Marked Theme   - Rheme ————————————→
Topical |

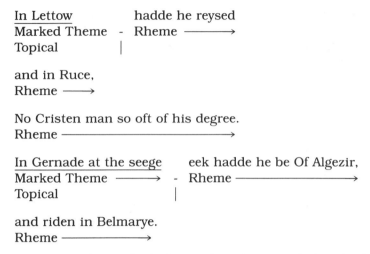

In Lettow   hadde he reysed
Marked Theme - Rheme ⟶
Topical |

and in Ruce,
Rheme ⟶

No Cristen man so oft of his degree.
Rheme ⟶

In Gernade at the seege   eek hadde he be Of Algezir,
Marked Theme ⟶ - Rheme ⟶
Topical |

and riden in Belmarye.
Rheme ⟶

[Only the Marked Themes have been underlined. There are no
Clause Themes in these examples.]

In the 15 clauses here, one—"no man ferre"—is both an included one and elliptical (we must supply "had ridden" from the previous clause to make sense of it, in the way it is done today); one—"and in Ruce"—if taken (as here) as a separate clause, is elliptical in the same (i.e. the "modern") way, needing the meaning 'hadde he reysed' to be supplied; one—no Cristen man so oft of his degree" is similar, needing at least 'hadde he reysed' to be supplied, to enable us to make sense of it; and two clauses—"and that a worthy man" and "And even honoured for his worthynesse"—are elliptical in ways not likely to occur in modern English, lacking verbs (perhaps some form of be) but seeming to consist wholly of Rhemes. This leaves 10 full clauses, of which eight have Marked Themes. Yet this plethora of Marked Themes creates no feeling of excess. Rather, in constantly moving the topics on, as happens in both the Prologue and the more vivid tales, it contributes to the feeling of bubbling liveliness that animates Chaucer's descriptions—in "The Prologue," for example, helping to give the illusion, so often remarked, that Chaucer-in-the-character-of-one-of-the-pilgrims' eye is constantly moving, noting details which Chaucer-as-writer is using to reveal the character of the figures he is creating.

However that may be, the use of Marked Theme to move the topic on in this way is even more striking if we look only at the first line of each portrait in "The Prologue."

A Knyght   ther was . . .
Marked Theme - Rheme →

With hym   there was his sone (A yong Squier) . . .
Marked Theme - Rheme ————————————————→

A Yeman · hadde he . . .
Marked Theme - Rheme →
(but note the Subject after the verb, as in several other instances here)

Ther   was also a Nonne, a Prioresse . . .
Theme - Rheme ————————————→

Another Nonne with hire hadde she . . .
Marked Theme - Rheme ————————→

A Monk   ther was . . .
Marked Theme - Rheme →

A Frere   ther was . . .
Marked Theme - Rheme →

A Marchant was ther . . .
Marked Theme - Rheme →

A Clerk   ther was . . .
Marked Theme - Rheme →

A Sergeaunt of the Lawe, war and wys,
[That often hadde been at the Parvys], Ther was also . . .
Marked Theme ————————————————→ - Rheme ————→

A Frankeleyne was in his compaignye . . .
Theme ————→ - Rheme ————————→

An Haberdashere and a Carpenter . . . A Webbe, a Dyere, and a Tapycer . . .
Rheme ——————————————————————————————→

A Cook   they hadde with hem . . .
Marked Theme - Rheme ————————→

A Shipman was ther . . .
Marked Theme - Rheme →

With us   ther was a Doctour of Phisik . . .
Marked Theme - Rheme ————————————→

A good Wif was ther of biside Bath . . .
Marked Theme - Rheme ————————→

A good man   was ther of religioun . . .
<u>Marked Theme</u>   -   Rheme ————→

With hym   ther was a Ploughman . . .
<u>Marked Theme</u>   -   Rheme ————→

Ther ·   was also a Reve, and a Miller . . . A Somnour, and a
    Pardoner also, A Maunciple, and myself . . .
Theme   -   Rheme ————————————————→

The Miller   was a stout carl for the nones . . .
Theme →   -   Rheme ————————→

A gentil Maunciple   was ther of a temple . . .
<u>Marked Theme</u> →   · -   Rheme ————→

The Reve   was a sclendre colerik man . . .
Theme   -   Rheme ————→

A Somnour   was ther with us . . .
<u>Marked Theme</u>   -   Rheme ———→

With hym   ther rood a gentil Pardoner . . . ·
<u>Marked Theme</u>   -   Rheme ————→

Of these 23 clauses, 19 have a Marked Theme. One feature of the marked instances, when they are followed by *was* + *ther*, is that for metrical reasons these two words may come in that order or in the reverse order (*ther* + *was*), depending on whether the character being introduced has one syllable—"knyght," "clerk"—or two— "merchaunt," "somnour"—in their name. This is in order to keep "ther" non-salient, not only for metrical reasons but also to distinguish it from the adverb of the same form; but the choice is made possible also because of the pattern still available to Chaucer from Old English of having the verb before the Subject—"was ther"— without any interrogative sense, whereas we cannot now say, "A pub was there, at the corner of the road" (at least, not if "there" is non-salient as a variant of "There was a pub . . . "). More importantly, in these 24 instances (omitting the five Guildsmen—the haberdasher and the rest—because they are mentioned in a clause consisting of Rheme only), 17 of the remaining 23 portraits begin with Marked Theme; in other words, when he wants to move on to describe another pilgrim in a new section, the way in which Chaucer most frequently signals the move is by the use of a Marked Theme, usually including the name of the character whose portrait is beginning.

    Chaucer was a conscious and skilled rhetorician, in an age when sophisticated rhetoric was very highly valued, and when audiences, too, were sophisticated, discerning and appreciative of rhetoric. In "The Franklin's Tale," he makes the Franklin poke ironic fun at the tradition, pretending to be "a burel man" (i.e. a plain, unsophisticated, rhetorically incompetent story-teller) a ploy that is itself an instance of a rhetorical trope called *diminutio* i.e. "self-deprecation" (a device from which—much weakened—derives the dismal modern phrase "Unaccustomed as I am to public speaking"). He then gives a dazzling display of rhetorical expertise that both subverts and gives point to his *diminutio* by demonstrating his virtuosity. Because it would have made no sense to combine the initial trope with the subsequent disproof of what it said if he had not been able to assume his audience would get the point, so in "The General Prologue" there can be no doubt that in Marking his Themes he knows very well what he is doing and why he is doing it: he is giving prominence to some element of clause structure, both for its own sake and to indicate a shift in topic. He is also choosing the element he needs as Theme to further his Method of Development. For the purposes of the Prologue, at least, Chaucer uses this device very systematically, in part thereby creating the larger structure of the portraits collectively, as well as using the pattern to move things on within individual portraits.

However, we have to set this in perspective. Themes in "The Prologue" are not marked only in the initial clauses. I have no figures for modern texts generally, but the numbers of Marked Themes in the portraits seem to be high, ranging from 67% of the Cook's 6 Themes to 20% of the Maunciple's 15 clauses, with the median percentage being 37%, and the average 35%. Perhaps this may contribute to the sense of narrative speed (of the story constantly moving rapidly on) mentioned earlier. However, whether or not this is so, it is notable that Nevil Coghill's version of "The Prologue" in the Penguin series—whatever its virtues—does not use Marked Themes to anything like the same extent to mark the transition from one portrait to the next, retaining the pattern in the initial clauses of only three of the 23 portraits. And in Mayhew's nineteenth century prose work, *London Labour and the London Poor* (Bradley, 1965), which like "The Prologue" consists of a series of portraits (though very different from Chaucer's), only one out of a series of six portraits marks the shift from one to the next in this way.[5]

Finally, Chaucer uses his Themes, whether marked or not, to create a Method of Development as described in the work of Peter

---

[5]I am grateful to Martin Gray for suggesting I should make this comparison.

Fries (1981) within individual portraits. So, for example, in the portrait of the knight already quoted, the knight himself is established as the starting-off point of the description, being the referent of the Head noun in the Theme of the first clause, and also in the second, and being referred to pronominally as Theme in five more clauses at the end of his portrait (lines 70–78); and semantically he is Theme also in the last clause, although this is not made explicit because the clause is branched:

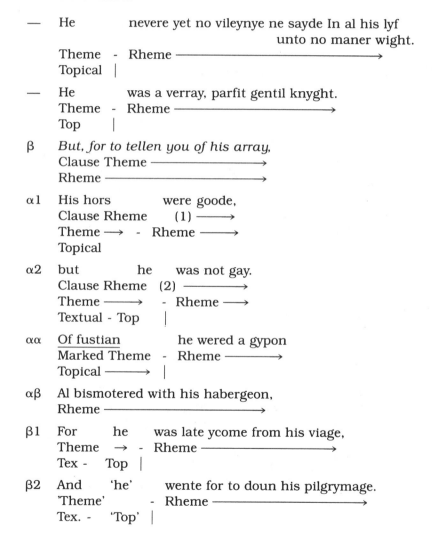

— He   nevere yet no vileynye ne sayde In al his lyf
                                 unto no maner wight.
   Theme - Rheme ——————————————→
   Topical |

— He   was a verray, parfit gentil knyght.
   Theme - Rheme ————————————→
   Top |

β   *But, for to tellen you of his array,*
   Clause Theme ———————————→
   Rheme ———————————————→

α1 His hors   were goode,
   Clause Rheme   (1) ——→
   Theme —→ - Rheme ——→
   Topical

α2 but   he   was not gay.
   Clause Rheme (2) ——————→
   Theme ———→ - Rheme ——→
   Textual - Top |

αα <u>Of fustian</u>   he wered a gypon
   Marked Theme - Rheme ——————→
   Topical ——→ |

αβ Al bismotered with his habergeon,
   Rheme ————————————→

β1 For   he   was late ycome from his viage,
   Theme   → - Rheme ———————————→
   Tex -   Top |

β2 And   'he'   wente for to doun his pilgrymage.
   'Theme'   - Rheme ——————————————→
   Tex. - 'Top' |

Further, one of his prominent characteristics—"worthiness"—had been given emphasis as Marked Theme in the fourth clause (line 47), and he himself is Theme again in "This ilke worthy knyght" (line 64). Moreover he[6] is present as a possessive pronoun in the Marked Theme of the clause in line 69, as the basis for the identification of another of his virtues:

Of his port ['he was'] as meek as is a mayde,

and again possessively in the Theme in the clause on line [74],

His hors were goode.

He had also been the implied Theme (though not expressed in form, because the clause is branched) in line [50], where the Rheme also tells us that he "was ever honòured for his worthynesse." And the knight also forms the basis of another Thematic motif in the listing of the number of places to which he has been to fight for Christendom: Chaucer makes the list Thematic to make it the basis of his Method of Development at that point, the list seeking to impress by its range and by the importance of the battles and campaigns at the places mentioned. It thereby gives a particular kind of emphasis to his "worthinesse," a worthiness that had been recognized in "ever honòured," and had there received Marked Focus because the immediately subsequent "for his worthiness" contains lexical reiteration. Alexandria, Lettow, Russia, Gernade, Lyeys, and possibly Satalye are thus all made Theme (although perhaps Satalye has to be taken just as Rheme). So Thematically the picture is one of a consistent Method of Development, with variation but nevertheless centering on the knight, his worthiness, his constancy, his travels in defence of Christianity and his exploits, in a way that shows the system being used as it can be today.

6. CONCLUSION

I have not wished to controvert any of the suggestions in Halliday (1988), and if I had wished to do so I have found nothing that would enable me to do so. Rather, I have tried to indicate somethiang of the background against which the developments he described took

---

[6]I am indebted to Mrs. Jackie Tasioulas for the information that there is controversy over whether or not "he" refers to the knight or to the horse, the balance of opinion being in favor of the horse.

place, and which continues as part of the system today. At most, I have only been able to show some of the origins of those features. It is clear that what the new developments had to start from was a system for creating text which—as we would expect—goes back a long way, not just before Newton but before Chaucer, its leading features being discernible in 991 or thereabouts, more than 700 years before Newton's Opticks (1704), and in fact earlier still. During that time the system had changed, as we would expect, but the range of functions to which the system was put was well-established in the Old English period, the potential for future development was there then, and could be used with sophistication by the fourteenth century.

REFERENCES

Abercrombie, D. (1965) *Studies in phonetics and linguistics*. London: Oxford University Press.

Abercrombie, D. (1951) "Steele, Monboddo and Garrick" in Abercrombie (1965).

Booth, S. (1977) *Shakespeare's Sonnets*. New Haven & London: Yale University Press.

Bradley, J.L. (ed.) (1965) *London Labour and the London Poor by H. Mayhew Selections and an Introduction*. London: Oxford University Press.

Cummings, M.J. (1991a) "An Approach to the Analysis of Theme/Rheme in the Historical Dialects of English." 2nd National Systemic Functional Seminar, University of Suzhou, Suzhou, People's Republic of China, July 16th.

Cummings, M.J (1991b) "Theme and Rheme in Old English Narrative." 18th International Systemic Congress, International Christian University, Tokyo, Japan, July 30th.

Davis, N. (1953) *Sweet's Anglo-Saxon Primer*, revised by Norman Davis. Oxford: Clarendon Press.

Dent, J.C. (1938) *Twelfth Night*. The New Clarendon Shakespeare. Oxford: The Clarendon Press.

Dickins, B., and Wilson, R.M. (1951) *Early Middle English Texts*. London: Bowes and Bowes.

Fries, P. (1981) "On the status of Theme in English: arguments from discourse." *Forum Linguisticum* 6: 1, 1–38.

Ghadesy, M. (1988) *Registers of Written English: Situational Factors and Linguistic Features*. London: Pinter Publishers.

Halliday, M.A.K. (1985a) *Spoken and written language*. Melbourne: Deakin University Press.

Halliday, M.A.K. (1985b, 1994) *A Short Introduction to Functional Grammar* (2nd edition). London: Edward Arnold.

Halliday, M.A.K. (1988) "On the language of physical science." in Ghadesy (1988).

Hayward, J. (1949) *Donne: Complete Poetry and Selected Prose*. London: The Nonesuch Press.

Houghton, R.E.C. (1962) *Antony and Cleopatra*. The New Clarendon Shakespeare. Oxford: The Clarendon Press.

Newman, B. (1952) *Henry the Fourth, Part I*. Oxford: Clarendon Press.

Onions, C.T. (1946) *Sweet's "ANGLO-SAXON READER, in Prose and Verse,"* Tenth Edition. Oxford: Clarendon Press.

Quirk, R., Adams, V., and Davy, D. (1975) *Old English Literature, A Practical Introduction*. London: Edward Arnold.

Robinson, F.N., (1957) *The Works of Geoffrey Chaucer*, Second Edition. Boston: Houghton Mifflin.

Strang, B.M.H. (1970) *A History of English*. London: Methuen.

B:
Interpersonal
Meaning
and Form

4

On the Concept
of an Interpersonal
Metafunction
in English*

Christopher S. Butler

Linguistics and Modern Languages
University College of Ripon and York St John

It is not only the most obviously ritualized utterances—greetings, apologies, toasts, etc.—that have as their primary function that of oiling the wheels of social intercourse. Looked at from one point of view, this might be correctly identified as the most basic function of language, to which all others—including its descriptive function—are subordinate [. . .] Languages vary as to the degree in which social meaning can or must be conveyed in sentences of various kinds. It must not be thought, therefore, that social meaning can be left to the sociolinguist and is of no concern to the microlinguist. —(Lyons 1981:143)

1. INTRODUCTION

One of the most influential features of the work of Michael Halliday is undoubtedly his insistence that "non-cognitive" aspects of meaning are just as worthy of the linguist's serious attention as the "cog-

---

*I am grateful to Robin Fawcett for comments on earlier drafts of this article.

nitive" aspects, which have formed the core of most modern work in semantics. Others, of course, have also emphasized the social function of language seen as so important by Lyons, as well as (in the work of Prague school linguists in particular) aspects of message organization. Halliday's unique contribution was to suggest that the non-cognitive (or, as he would put it, non-ideational) functions are not extrinsic to language, but that they, just as much as ideational functioning, are built into the linguistic system itself, in the form of "functional components," later renamed "metafunctions," representing relatively discrete areas of "meaning potential" within the system networks of a language (see, for instance, Halliday 1979). It was this claim and others closely related to it that were responsible for the name by which Halliday's model is now generally known—Systemic Functional Grammar.

Halliday's model has been adopted as a starting point for a large number of projects in both descriptive and applied linguistics. Although most descriptive work has been on English (with important effects on the model as a whole—for discussion, see Butler 1992), some has also been carried out on other languages, including Yoruba, Arabic, Hindi, also Philippine and Australian aboriginal languages. Applications of systemic theory in stylistics, educational linguistics and artificial intelligence have met with considerable success (for a review, see Butler 1993). For many linguists, especially in applied fields, who see transformational generative linguistics as less than fruitful for their purposes, the semantic functional orientation of Halliday's model, together with its emphasis on text, make it very attractive. However, with this well-deserved success comes the possibility of danger. Users of grammatical models, engaged in such endeavors as stylistic analysis or the construction of language teaching courses, are understandably often unwilling to spend the considerable time and effort necessary to examine critically and in detail the theoretical proposals that appear so attractive to them. The more the systemic model is used for such applications, the greater the danger that certain key features of the model will be assumed to be "correct." This danger is all the greater in view of the tendency, commented on recently by Asp (1992: 2) with respect to the metafunctional hypothesis, for some publications in systemic linguistics to "seem to have more to do with legitimizing a theoretical position than they do with examining it critically for strengths and weaknesses."

Michael Halliday, I am sure, never wanted to be a linguistic guru. He believes that others can make, and have indeed made, worthwhile contributions to systemic theory, and would certainly agree that the theory should be constantly scrutinized and subjected to constructive criticism, so that it may be refined and extended to yield further insights about language. It is in this spirit that I should like to offer my contribution to this celebration of Michael Halliday's work. If many of my comments seem somewhat critical, it is because I believe in the inherent value of Halliday's achievement, and should like to make some small contribution towards the further development of systemic theory. I have written elsewhere (Butler 1985a) about the several concepts of "function" that are central to systemic views of language. Here, I shall focus on the concept of metafunction, and more specifically on the interpersonal metafunction, not only because I find this area of particular interest, but because I believe it is a crucial testing area for the theory as a whole.

2. CRITERIA FOR RECOGNIZING
THE INTERPERSONAL METAFUNCTION

2.1. Level-Internal Criteria

Halliday's claim that the linguistic system is functionally organized dates back to the late 1960s:

> If we represent the set of options available to the speaker in the grammar of the English clause, these options group themselves into a small number of subsets, distinct from one another in that, while within each group of options there is a very high degree of interdependence, between any two groups the amount of interdependence, though by no means negligible, is very much less.   (Halliday 1968: 207)

These subsets of the clause options were: transitivity, representing the ideational ("content") function; mood and modality, representing the interpersonal (social and expressive) function; and theme, representing the textual (text-forming) function.

Let us now examine Halliday's claim with reference to the interpersonal metafunction. Various versions of the mood network are available in Halliday's writings (see Halliday 1969: 84, 1973: 40, 56, also in Kress 1976: 104–9): an amalgamated network incorporating the major options is shown in Fig. 4.1.

The inclusion of the terms [modal/non-modal] bears on Halliday's (1970) discussion of the two basic uses of modal verbs in English: as "modalities" (corresponding to what most linguists have called "epistemic" use) and as "modulations" ("root" uses, including, for exam-

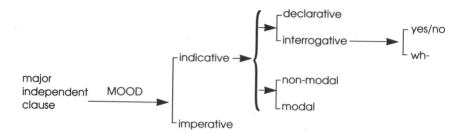

Figure 4.1 A basic mood network

ple, Palmer's (1979) "deontic" and "dynamic" categories). As realizations of modalities, Halliday related modal verbs to adverbs such as *possibly, probably, certainly, presumably, surely,* etc., as well as to the associated adjectives and nouns (*possible, possibility,* etc.). As realizations of modulations, he related modals to periphrastic forms such as *be able to, be willing to, be obliged to,* etc. The distinction between modality and modulation is presented in the context of a discussion of functional diversity in language. Modalities are said to be basically interpersonal, in that they represent the participation of the speaker in the speech event and, not being subject to distinctions of tense or polarity, are not part of the ideational content of the clause. Modulations, on the other hand, are said to be basically part of the ideational content of the clause, as they are subject to tense and polarity distinctions. The arguments from tense and polarity are, I believe, suspect (see Butler 1985b: 175). Here, however, I want to focus on these areas in relation to the claim of relative independence of choices in different metafunctional components.

If Halliday's claim is correct, we should expect:

1. that choices in modality should be dependent on choices of mood, but that options from modulation should be relatively independent of mood selection;
2. that choices in mood and modality should be relatively independent of choices of process type, though modulation might interact with transitivity options;
3. that choices in mood, modality and modulation, and choices of theme, would be relatively independent.

As far as expectation 1 is concerned, there is certainly an interaction between mood and modality, in that modalities, whether realized by a modal verb or by some other means, are confined to indicative clauses. That this is not wholly due to the lack of non-finite forms for modal verbs is shown by examples such as (4)

I might (possibly) go to London on Friday. (1)

Might you (possibly) go to London on Friday? (2)

*Might go to London on Friday. (asterisk imperative) (3)

*Possibly go to London on Friday. (4)

However, this restriction applies equally to modulations:

I can go to London on Friday. (5)

I am able to go to London on Friday. (6)

Can you go to London on Friday? (7)

Are you able to go to London on Friday? (8)

*Can go to London on Friday. (asterisk imperative) (9)

?Be able to go to London on Friday. (10)

Thus it seems that modal meanings in general, rather than just modality meanings, are incompatible with imperative mood. A plausible explanation for this (developed in detail in Butler 1982: 269–73) is that by their inherent nature modals, however used, express stative semantic predicates, and imperative mood is normally compatible only with dynamic predicates. Whatever the correct explanation may be, these observations show clear links between choices allocated by Halliday to different metafunctions. Choices in modulation depend on a prior choice in the interpersonal metafunction and not, as predicted by Hypothesis 1, in the ideational. It is worth noting that this dependency is built into the very large systemic functional grammar, called GENESYS, which lies at the heart of the COMMUNAL text generation system (for descriptions of GENESYS, see e.g. Fawcett, Tucker and Lin (1992, 1993)).

   Let us turn now to our second prediction from Halliday's claim. This is concerned with the relationship between mood, modality and modulation, on the one hand, and transitivity on the other. As I mentioned above, there is dependence between mood and process type in that normally only dynamic (non-stative) processes can occur in the imperative. Where verbs that are normally stative occur in the imperative, this forces a dynamic interpretation, as in (13) and (14):

Go to London on Friday. (11)

*Resemble your father. (12)

Be good. (= "behave well") (13)

Be like your father. (= "act in such a way as to be or become like him") (14)

As Berry (1982: 77) pointed out, this weakens the claim that choices in different functional components are largely independent.

We can, however, adduce some evidence for Halliday's position if we look at the relationship between modally realizable meanings and process types. There is an interaction between process type and modulation, in that modulations only occur comfortably with dynamic processes, whereas modalities are unrestricted in this respect, so providing evidence for Hypothesis 2. Note, for instance, that (15) can only be interpreted naturally as a modality, whereas (16) could receive either a modality or a modulation interpretation:

You must resemble your father. (15)

You must travel a lot. (16)

I turn now to Hypothesis 3, which concerns the relationship between mood/modality/modulation and thematization. We may note that Halliday's own stated view (1994: 42–8) is that what counts as unmarked and marked theme will vary according to the mood of the clause: for a declarative clause the unmarked theme is the subject, for a polar interrogative it is the finite verb, and for a wh-interrogative it is the wh-word, while in imperative clauses such as *Sit down*, there is an implicit "I want you to" thematic element, but the lack of realization of this element in any clause constituent gives the initial constituent, the verb, thematic character. Nevertheless, it could be argued that the systemic distinction between marked and unmarked still applies because there is still a choice of what to put first. This is indeed a defensible position, but it is also true that there are differences in the degree of markedness of marked themes in association with the different moods. Consider the following examples:

On Friday I am going to London.   (17)

On Friday are you going to London?   (18)

On Friday go to London.   (19)

My intuitions are that whereas (17) is quite normal, (18) and (19) are rather less usual, though still grammatical and capable of contextualization. This may be because (18) and (19) would most probably have the function of setting the scene for the following stretch of discourse, while (17) could be either a scene-setter or simply a time position indicator thematized for, for example, contrastive reasons[1]. Differences in the probability of particular combinations of systemic options are being explicitly recognized in much current work in SFG (see, for example, the work of Fawcett *et al* on GENESYS referred to earlier, also Halliday (1991, 1993), Nesbitt and Plum (1988)).

Similar dependencies between modality and theme also exist, but reside in the nature of the possible realizations of modalities in combination with marked theme, in that if the speaker wishes to thematize the modality element, s/he must choose an option whose realization does not involve the use of a modal verb:

Jim possibly went to London on Friday.   (20)

Possibly Jim went to London on Friday.   (21)

*May Jim have gone to London on Friday. (asterisk marked
theme variant)   (22)

Since Halliday believes that almost all syntactic differences reflect semantic differences, he would probably want to see the distinction between verbal and adverbial realizations as reflecting a delicate semantic difference (as would Fawcett (personal communication)), and if this is so, then we have here a clear case of a relationship of systemic dependence between modality and theme.

---

[1]For a discussion of "spatial frameworks" of this type, see Downing (1991: 132–3) who, however, suggested that all initial spatial adjuncts "mark a temporal discourse span which holds until a new span is introduced."

It is clear, then, that there are various pieces of evidence that contradict any strong claim that choices in different metafunctions are independent. It might be objected, however, that Halliday has not made such a strong claim: he hypothesizes merely that there will be relative independence between choices in different metafunctions. But just what does "relative" mean here? In order to make it mean something useful, we should have to develop statistical measures of dependence between systems or subnetworks of systems, and to show that there was a statistically significant difference between the degree of dependence of options within and between metafunctions. Unfortunately, no such measures have as yet been discussed in the systemic literature, although current work on the formalization of systemic functional grammars for use in computationally based projects such as COMMUNAL is now providing information that is potentially relevant to such discussion.

In discussing the problem of "relative independence" I have focused specifically on matters relating to interpersonal choices. Others, however, have addressed the problem in wider terms, with equally uncomfortable conclusions. Fawcett (1980: 34–8) observed that if networks are drawn not just for the "central" areas of transitivity, mood and theme, but for other areas of English too, it turns out that a fair number of networks seem to be almost completely independent of others. Should these therefore be allocated to their own separate metafunctions? Fawcett himself, having rejected the independence criterion as inadequate to determine partitioning into components, suggested that options in the same component relate to the same kind of knowledge about the world. In this approach, which is consistent with Fawcett's primarily cognitive viewpoint on language, one important criterion for grouping networks into functional components is thus no longer internal to the language system itself. He in fact postulates as many as eight different components. For instance, Halliday's interpersonal component is split into "interactional," "modality" and "affective" functions, the first being concerned with speech roles, the second with epistemic modality, and the third with the expression of emotional attitude. Martin (1984) reviewed the criteria that appear to have been adopted by Halliday, Fawcett and others in assigning networks to metafunctions, and concluded that "internal" criteria: "do not always uniquely determine the functional address of systems, and some method of ranking and weighting the criteria will have to be devised whenever function rank matrices are drawn up" (p. 65). A useful review of the various positions on metafunction can be found in Gregory (1987).

So far, I have discussed only Halliday's original motivation. More recently Halliday (1978, 1979) has proposed two other kinds of motivation concerned with relationships between options in the functional component networks and (a) the contextual categories of field, tenor and mode, and (b) modes of realization. I shall look at each of these in turn, in relation to the interpersonal metafunction.

2.2. Criteria "From Above"

The categories of field, tenor and mode, initially developed by Halliday and his colleagues in the 1960s, have more recently been integrated in an interesting way into the systemic functional model. The suggestion is that the values of these social contextual variables control, in a selective manner, the ranges of meanings which can be chosen to create a text in a particular type of context:

> The type of symbolic activity (field) tends to determine the range of meaning as content, language in the observer function (ideational); the role relationships (tenor) tend to determine the range of meaning as participation, language in the intruder function (interpersonal); and the rhetorical channel (mode) tends to determine the range of meaning as texture, language in its relevance to the environment (textual). (Halliday 1978: 117)

In relation to the interpersonal metafunction, then, this claim would predict that the selection of particular types of interpersonal meaning should depend principally on the tenor of discourse, rather than on either field or mode. It should be noted that there are somewhat divergent views among systemicists as to exactly what comes under the heading of "tenor:" indeed, as Martin (1984) remarked, the situational categories are just as problematic to define as the functional components themselves. As indicated by the above quotation, Halliday himself included under tenor only the personal and institutional role relationships of the participants, involving such dimensions as degree of familiarity and authority status, giving rise to varying degrees of formality or informality. Gregory (Gregory 1967: 184ff, 1987: 102–3; Gregory and Carroll 1978: 53ff.), on the other hand, also included distinctions of what we might call rhetorical genre (informative, didactic, instructional, persuasive, etc.), which Halliday (1965) once regarded as part of field but now places under mode. These additional factors were labelled "functional tenor," as opposed to "personal tenor" relationships.

Let us first look at possible relationships between personal tenor and interpersonal meanings. Although there is an unfortunate lack of detailed and comprehensive textual study in this area, it is intuitively reasonable to claim that mood, modality and intonationally conveyed attitudinal meanings do vary with personal tenor. For instance, speakers are likely to use different formulations for certain types of speech act according to their relationship with their hearers. Consider the following excerpts from one speaker's contribution to a dialogue recorded as part of the Survey of English Usage (see Svartvik and Quirk 1980: 408–35). The prosodic annotations in the original are omitted here. Brackets « » enclose incomprehensible material.

... good now then I I wonder while I've got you here whether you could give me a little bit of biographic«al» oh «1 syll» you want another glass of sherry my dear chap you can't sit there (23)

may I ask what you've done since nineteen fifty-one (24)

The conversation is between two academics of age 48 and 50 respectively, and the content of the whole text shows clearly that the two participants do not know each other well, if at all. This lack of familiarity is clearly reflected in the use of particular types of formal realization for speech acts. In (23), a directive is issued by means of a declarative containing the hedging verb *wonder* and the modal *could*, rather than by means of the imperative mood. In (24), a question is asked in the congruent interrogative form, but in an indirect way that involves a modal of permission and an embedded "performative" verb. Clearly, the choices made in (23) and (24) would be inappropriate in a context where participants of similar status knew each other very well. In support of this, consider (25), again from a conversation recorded by the Survey of English Usage (Svartvik and Quirk 1980: 302–28), in which a female academic addresses a question to a female housewife of about the same age, which is very similar to that in (24), in that it asks for personal details about the addressee:

but how did you come to be sent to Farnborough Elsie (25)

Here, in a conversation where there is presumably a greater degree of familiarity (as suggested by the use of the addressee's first name), the complex modal hedge is not appropriate. Other intuitively plausible claims would be that participants who are socially distant, because of status differences, lack of familiarity or both, might opt for more modalities, as qualifications to their assertions, and might show more intonationally realized tentativeness, than participants with minimal social distance, other things being equal. Plausible as such suggestions may be, we shall not know whether they are correct until a great deal of painstaking textual analysis has been carried out.

Now consider the following subtexts:

GENERAL DESCRIPTION

The Drayton TRV2 is a self-operated thermostatic valve for controlling the temperature in a space by regulating the flow of hot water to a radiator. It also has locking and range-limiting facilities which allow the valve to be either locked at a given setting or allowed to be operated over a restricted temperature range. A frost protection setting marked * is additionally provided.

(26)

INSTALLATION

Fit manual operating cap provided to the valve body and then fit the body at the radiator inlet as a normal radiator valve. The valve may be mounted in either a vertical or horizontal attitude. Horizontal mounting is preferred if flow temperatures are likely to exceed 82°C (180°F) or if there are high convection temperatures around the head. If mounted in this attitude, however, the pump head should not exceed 25ft.   (27)

These form part of a leaflet enclosed with the appliance concerned. As indicated by the headings, (26) is a description, the functional tenor of which can be taken as informative, while (27) is clearly instructional. This is reflected in an obvious way in the mood choices of the texts, in that all the clauses in (26) are declarative, while those two clauses that give direct instructions in (27) are imperative. So far, then, the very small amount of evidence from these texts bears out the claim that functional tenor affects the mood choices made in a text.

But what of the remaining clauses in (27)? They are declarative, but it is noteworthy that two of them contain modals, and the third an item (*preferred*) that in context is perhaps distantly related to modal meaning in that the import seems to be "the valve should be mounted horizontally if." Note, however, that the modals are being used as modulations (*may be mounted, should not exceed*), not as modalities. Indeed, in general it is modulation that is involved in those declaratives that are communicatively quite close to imperatives. Other frequent examples are *ought to, must* (as in one sense of

(16)). Here, then, we have an effect of functional tenor on what Halliday claimed to be ideational choice.

Further examination of (26) and (27) reveals another problem. It is characteristic of instructional material that compression is often achieved by the omission of grammatical words such as determiners: The first clause of (27) affords an example, although the writer chooses the non-ellipted form in subsequent clauses. Here, we appear to have an effect of functional tenor on choices concerned with particularization or definiteness, which arise from the textual metafunction. This fits in with Halliday's allocation of rhetorical genre to mode rather than to tenor. And yet, as we have seen, it is Gregory's scheme that correctly predicts the effects of rhetorical genre on mood choices. The situation is further complicated by the fact that in recent work, Gregory (1988: 315) rejected his earlier category of functional tenor, precisely on the grounds that unlike personal tenor, field and mode, it has no clear corresponding metafunctional realization! A similar position is taken by Martin (1992 : 501), who concluded that "'rhetorical purpose' is the wild card in contextual description," and is better seen in terms of the concept of genre, which deals with "the integration of meanings engendered by field, tenor and mode as systemically related social processes" (Martin 1992: 495).

Martin (1992) presented a much more detailed description of the possible values of the variables of field, tenor and mode than was available hitherto. These variables themselves, however, are still seen as systematically related to ideational, interpersonal and textual meaning respectively, each contextual variable being seen as the projection of the relevant range of metafunctional meanings on to context (Martin 1992: 494).

The overall conclusion from this discussion must surely be that further work in the area of the relationship between register and metafunction is required in order that the various (sometimes mutually exclusive) claims can be evaluated.

2.3. Criteria "From Below"

I turn now to Halliday's third type of evidence for metafunctional organization: the types of structure that are claimed to realize options within different functional areas. The claim (Halliday 1979) is that ideational choices tend to be realized by configurations of discrete constituents, while interpersonal choices tend to be realized through prosodic structures distributed throughout the clause, and textual choices by "culminative" structures involving the association of peaks of prominence with unit boundaries. Example (23), discussed earlier, provides one example of the kind of prosodic realization that Halliday pointed to as being typical of interpersonal choices: the notion of "tentativeness' is realized twice in the lexicogrammatical structure—as I *wonder* and as the tentative or hypothetical modal form *could*. A further example is provided by (28), taken from the same conversation as (25):

$$\searrow \quad \vee^{\nearrow} \quad \searrow$$
+ ‖ but + − ‖ and I . !really THINK#   ‖ YOU know#   it ‖ must be ˮ!TERRIBLE#.

$$\rightarrow \quad \searrow \quad \vee^{\nearrow}$$
‖ WHEN# . she ‖ says NONE of us# .   sort of ‖ go to   :SEE her or ˋanything# .

$$\searrow$$
‖ but . and my ‖ brother !never rings :UP

The prosodic transcription is modelled on Crystal's (1969) system, the conventions employed above being as follows:

‖	Onset of tone unit
#	End of tone unit
↘	Fall
→	Level
	(Rise)-fall-rise
:	Booster: higher than preceding syllable
!	Booster: higher than preceding pitch-prominent syllable
ˋ	Stress: normal
ˮ	Stress: heavy
.	Brief pause (of one light syllable)

A variety of the range of meanings treated by Halliday as interpersonal are realized in (28), in I *think*, the modality modal *must*, the attitudinal loading of the lexical item *terrible*, together with the associated heavy stress, the addressee-oriented phrase *you know*, perhaps also the items *sort of* and *or anything*, and the intonation choices. This observation supports Halliday's view. And yet note that the main device for the realization of mood here, as in most finite clauses in English, is the ordering of two discrete constituents, the subject nominal group and finite verb as in *it must be*. . . . As with the "relative independence of networks" argument discussed earlier, defenders of Halliday's position on this issue could answer that the correlation between "metafunctional address" and mode of realization is only probabilistic. Again, however, we are faced with the problem of how many exceptions we can allow before we consider Halliday's claim to be refuted: The realization of mood as an ordering of discrete elements is absolutely central to this area, and the claim is virtually untestable unless it can be made in stronger and more precise terms.

Further problems with the postulated association between interpersonal meaning and prosodic realization are discussed by Asp (1992) and Matthiessen (1991). Matthiessen argued, following Halliday, that interpersonal phenomena such as concord between the Subject and Finite element are specifically amenable to description in prosodic terms. Asp observed, however, that the argument rests on the incorrect assumption that whereas constituency is inherently segmental in nature, prosody is inherently non-segmental. Asp pointed out that prosodies involve the layering of segments and their features, and that prosodic features are thus not, in principle, different from others in this respect. To demonstrate the point, Asp showed that transitivity analyses, which are absolutely central to the concept of ideational functioning, can be reinterpreted prosodically, since a role such as Agent can only be allocated on the basis of the relationship between a particular constituent and other constituents with which it is syntagmatically associated in the clause. Asp also argued against Matthiessen's view that the mobility of attitudinal adjuncts such as *hopefully* within the clause correlates with the interpersonal functioning of this element. As Asp observes, certain conjunctions (*however, nevertheless,* etc.) are also to some extent mobile, but fulfill a textual function.

An additional problem with the evidence "from below" is that the proposed correlations between metafunction and realization type may not be universally applicable, and so cannot form a central part of any grammar that takes typological adequacy seriously (see also Butler 1992): "the structural tendencies, though clearly non-arbitrary—we can see why it is that each should take this form—may differ very considerably from one language to another" (Halliday 1979:70).

Finally, we should note a point made by Fawcett (personal communication), namely that even if there is some significant degree of association between interpersonal meaning and realization at various points in the clause, this may reflect the very broad nature of Halliday's interpersonal category, which covers sets of choices that, according to Fawcett, are in principle independent.

3. METAFUNCTION IN RELATION TO THE MODEL AS A WHOLE

I want to turn now to a rather different, but to my mind extremely important, kind of question: Where exactly does, and should, the concept of metafunction fit into a systemic model as a whole? Putting this in a slightly different way, what is the interpersonal component meant to be a component of?

3.1. The Problem

I have so far assumed that the functional component networks are semantic, but we shall now see that this is only one of a rather confusing range of positions that Halliday appears to have taken. In an early account (1967a: 199) he wrote of transitivity, mood and theme as "three main areas of syntactic choices in the English clause," which "relate to" cognitive content, speech roles and the presentation of information, referred to as "areas of meaning." The view that the functional components are themselves lexicogrammatical, though reflecting the semantics, is also expressed in the comment (Halliday 1968: 207) that the falling of English system networks into three major blocks with a high degree of independence, "provides a syntactic basis for the concept of language functions, and suggests how the diversity of functions recognizable at the semantic levels may be organized in the course of realization."

Slightly later writings present a less clear picture. In the same article it is claimed both that the functional components (called "macrofunctions" at this stage) "take the form of 'grammar'" (Halliday 1973: 356)—it being made quite clear that "grammar" here means the lexicogrammatical level—and that 'the ideational function [. . .] is a major component of meaning in the language system" (Halliday 1973: 358). A potentially fruitful hint (Halliday 1973: 100) that the concept of "functional component" applies to the lexicogrammar, while "macrofunctions" are different, being "extralinguistic in origin and orientation," is negated by a diagram (p. 101) in the same article, in which the two are equated, and placed in limbo between semantic and lexicogrammatical networks.

By the mid-1970s the confusion seems to be clearing a little. In a paper first published in 1975, but reprinted in Halliday's 1978 book, the components, now called "metafunctions," are seen as "functional components of the semantic system," but are "reflected in the lexicogrammatical system in the form of discrete networks of options" (Halliday 1978: 112–113), these options being those of transitivity, mood and theme. By 1977, however, we appear to have a further shift: the transitivity, mood and theme networks are now considered as themselves constituting the main semantic options relevant to the clause. This position is confirmed in certain other papers of this period (Halliday 1979, 1980).

And yet, in a paper written in the early 1970s but published much later (Halliday 1984), and also in the *Introduction to Functional Grammar* (Halliday 1994: 68–105), the area of mood is given a rather different treatment that is in some ways more like that found in Halliday's earlier work. Mood choices themselves are again regarded as grammatical, but there is now a layer of choices in "speech function," viewed as part of the semantic stratum, combinations from which are realized by the mood options. Furthermore, the speech function options are themselves claimed, in the 1984 paper, to realize options at a "social contextual" level that is "above" the linguistic system. At this social contextual level, a "move in dialogue" (a unit that is left undefined by Halliday) is categorized along two dimensions: whether the speaker is "giving" or "demanding" something; and whether what s/he is giving or demanding is "information" or "goods-and-services." The combination [giving, information] is "congruently" realized as a "statement;" [giving, goods-and-services] as an "offer;" [demanding, information] as a "question;" [demanding, goods-and-services] as a "command." To each of these initiating speech functions there is an expected response (acknowledgment of a statement, acceptance of an offer, answer to a question, undertaking to carry out the action commanded), and also a discretionary alternative (contradiction, rejection, disclaimer and refusal, respectively). Halliday (1984) postulated that statements, questions and commands each have a "congruent" realization at the grammatical level: Statements are congruently [declarative], questions [interrogative] and commands [imperative]. He also mentioned the existence of other, non-congruent realizations for each speech function, and, in Halliday (1994: 363) the possibility of specifying more delicate classes of function (e.g. "threat" vs. "promise") by the introduction of further features into the networks. I have discussed elsewhere (Butler 1985b: 150–51, 1986, 1987) various problems with this model and its refinement by Martin (1981). Here, I want to concentrate on just two interrelated issues.

The first problem is which of the three levels of networks is/are to be seen as organized into functional components. Halliday presents no clear answers to this question, though I suspect that he would regard all three levels of systemic choice as being functionally organized: that is, the semiotics of verbal exchange, the semantics of speech function and the grammar of mood all represent interpersonal, as opposed to ideational or textual, aspects of language functioning. There is, however, a second problem that is fundamental for the model as a whole, and it is to this that we now turn.

3.2. Where, if Anywhere, Do the "Speech Function" Networks Belong?

The question that now poses itself is whether Halliday is justified in allocating the speech function networks to the semantic level. He himself commented that "There is no clear line between semantics and grammar, and a functional grammar is one that is pushed in the direction of the semantics" (Halliday 1994: xix). I would go further: he is also pushing the semantics, this time in the direction of what I would want to call pragmatics.

The distinction between semantics and pragmatics, like that between competence and performance, or between the linguistic code and its use, is one I believe Halliday (and probably many, though not all, other systemicists) would regard as misleading, or at least irrelevant. And yet I believe that a close look at the area of speech function reveals that there is a clear need for systemic linguists to be concerned with the kinds of argument entered into by pragmaticians (for more detailed discussion see Butler 1988a, b). Consider Halliday's four main speech functions: statement, question, command and offer. As Halliday (1994: 363) pointed out, these are merely the most general categories; for instance, under the general specification of "offers" as (giving, goods-and-services) he recognized threats, promises, vows and undertakings as more delicate categories, and noted that "the speech act itself carries no explicit signal of being an instance of this or that specific category." Which specific act is being performed is, according to Halliday, signalled by five kinds of factor: (a) simultaneously present lexicogrammatical features; (b) syntagmatically associated lexicogrammatical features; (c) paralinguistic and behavioral features such as voice quality, gesture, etc.; (d) features of the context of situation; and (e) features of the context of culture. The last two of these are particularly significant for our discussion: What Halliday is saying is that the full speech act force of an utterance can only be worked out in detail if the social and cultural context is taken into account. Utterances whose speech act force is not expressed congruently in the lexicogrammar are regarded by Halliday as an interpersonal type of "grammatical metaphor," explained as follows (1994: 366).

In all the instances that we are treating as grammatical metaphor, some aspect of the structural configuration of the clause, whether in its ideational function or in its interpersonal function or in both, is in some way different from that which would be arrived at by the shortest route—it is not, or was not originally, the most straightforward coding of the meanings selected.

Halliday does, then, have something in his latest model that is very like the concept of indirect speech act that has been so extensively discussed in the pragmatics literature. There are, however, two major differences between Halliday's account and a more typically "pragmatic" approach.

Firstly, note that the more delicate speech act categories, to which utterances can be assigned only via consideration of context, are regarded by Halliday as semantic. And yet, as Leech (1983:23) pointed out, even detailed contextual knowledge will often not allow us to determine that an utterance counts as, say, just a promise and nothing else. An utterance can perform more than one speech act at once, and one of the main sources of flexibility in language is the very negotiability of speech act force. Any attempt to categorize the speech act force of an utterance in terms of semantic features of a yes-or-no kind thus runs into considerable difficulty, and Leech (1983: 57–8, 75) rightly saw Halliday's account of this area as an example of "overgrammaticalization" of an inherently pragmatic phenomenon.[2]

Secondly, Halliday has rather little to say about *why* speakers use indirect means of achieving their goals, or *how* speakers arrive at certain kinds of realization rather than others, and how hearers can work out the communicative significance of indirect speech acts. Indeed, he seems rather skeptical about the possibility of explaining such things, when he writes that "there is no way of tracking the process whereby a speaker or writer has arrived at a particular mode of expression in the discourse" (Halliday 1994: 366). But of course there is now a considerable body of literature dealing with questions of just this kind. Grice's (1975, 1978) Co-operative Principle and its associated maxims are intended to show how very general and powerful principles of human behavior can account for the conveying of more than is obvious from the literal propositional content of what

---

[2]Note that this is *not* the same thing as saying that we cannot, or should not, analyze the meanings of speech act verbs such as *promise, vow, undertake*. These do have specifiable meanings (insofar as the meaning of any lexical item is specifiable): Indeed, Leech's book attempts an account of this kind.

is said. The work of Searle (1975) and later writers has demonstrated that these principles can be extended to cover the inference of one speech act force from another. The work of Brown and Levinson (1978/1987), Butler (1982, 1988c) and Leech (1983) has shown that in the area of interpersonal aspects of language the selection of one form of communicative strategy rather than another can often be motivated by considerations of politeness. All of these studies, and many more deriving from them, are directly relevant to any program whose aim is to answer the following question posed by Halliday (1978: 108): "How do people decode the highly condensed utterances of everyday speech, and how do they use the social system for doing so?"

It seems to me extremely unfortunate that certain systemicists, prominent among whom are Halliday and Gregory, have insisted that the aims of systemic linguistics are so different from those of linguists espousing the more "philosophical" approaches that work in such frameworks is largely irrelevant to our endeavors. The concerns of many pragmaticians are in many ways very similar to those of systemic linguists: to explain the ways in which speakers and hearers interact in contexts. It is true that the currently influential "relevance theory" approach (see Sperber and Wilson (1986) or, for a more accessible treatment, Blakemore (1992)) made a rigid distinction between the study of "communication" and that of "social institutions," which most systemicists, including myself, would want to reject.[3] Even relevance theory, however, has many valuable insights to offer if, with Halliday, we seriously wish to address the question of how people understand the full import of the highly condensed utterances of everyday speech. One of the most important areas discussed in the pragmatics literature during recent years is the interpersonal functioning of language, especially questions relating to how we should handle the discrepancies between what is actually said and what is conveyed, and why speakers often choose to convey messages in indirect ways. Too little attention has been given, within systemic linguistics, to arguing for and against different ways of accounting for particular types of linguistic phenomena, and nowhere is this better illustrated than in the area of speech function. I hope I have shown in this chapter that there are some serious argu-

---

[3] For criticisms of Sperber and Wilson's theory, see, for example, Levinson (1989), Mey and Talbot (1988), Nemo (1988), Seuren (1988), Ziv (1988) and the various contributions to the debate in *Behavioural and Brain Sciences* 10, 697–754, 1987.

ments to be countered by defenders of Hallidayan views on speech function, and on metafunctional organization in general.

I have suggested that systemicists need to take careful account of recent work in pragmatics. I am also convinced, however, that pragmaticians could benefit greatly from a serious look at systemic models. Pragmatics is largely about the speaker's choice of one way of putting something rather than another and the hearer's interpretation of such choices. It therefore seems reasonable that a model based on paradigmatic organization will stand a better chance of hooking up with pragmatics than one, such as transformational generative grammar, which is essentially syntagmatic in its orientation. A second advantage of systemic models is the importance they accord to the semantic organization of language, since, as Leech (1983: 12) pointed out, the "grammar" (in his wide sense of the term, to include semantics, syntax and phonology) interacts with pragmatics largely via the semantics.

4. SO WHITHER THE INTERPERSONAL METAFUNCTION?

Are we, then, to conclude from the foregoing that Halliday's concept of metafunction, and in particular the concept of an interpersonal metafunction, should be totally scrapped? To this, I think we must answer an unequivocal "No." Recent work, in other functionally oriented theories as well as in SFG, has demonstrated convincingly not only that interpersonal meanings can indeed be coded in specific ways in the grammars of languages, but also that the distinction between ideational (or "representational") and interpersonal meanings has important effects on the ways in which those grammars are organized. To my mind, the most interesting and thought-provoking of this work is within the framework of the Functional Grammar theory first propounded by Simon Dik. Like other theories, Dik's is not without its problems (see Butler (1991) for a review of Dik (1989)). In the past few years, however, important advances in FG have been made by Hengeveld (1988, 1989, 1990), building on ideas previously put forward not only by Dik, but also by Halliday, and by Foley and Van Valin (1984), Bybee (1985) and others.

Hengeveld proposed that the semantic structure of clauses should be seen as organized into two major levels, labelled the *interpersonal* (following Halliday) and the *representational* (following Bühler, 1934). Each of these levels consists of two layers. The interpersonal level consists of (a) the clause layer, representing a speech act, which can be evaluated in terms of its felicity, and (b) the proposition, representing a propositional content, evaluated in terms of its truth. The representational level consists of (a) the predication layer, representing a State of Affairs, evaluated in terms of its reality, and (b) the layer of terms (arguments and "satellites" (see below)), representing entities, evaluated in terms of their existence. Each of the four layers has associated with it a set of *operators*, specifying those properties, at the given layer, which are realized grammatically, and a set of *satellites*, specifying similar properties lexically. More recently, it has been suggested that there may be operators and satellites at an even higher level, specifying properties that relate a clause to the surrounding discourse.

Operators and satellites are the nearest equivalents, in FG, to the systemic features of SFG, in that they represent the contrasting values that are possible for features such as tense and time specification, aspect, modality, definiteness, number, and so on. It is therefore of considerable interest to note that one of the several strands of evidence adduced by Hengeveld (1989: 141–4) for his layering proposals is concerned with the scope of operators at the various layers. He proposed, with evidence from several unrelated languages, that operators at level n influence the choices available to operators of level $n-1$. Particularly important from the point of view of the present article is the suggestion that operators at the propositional layer, within the interpersonal level, influence the selection of operators from the predicational layer, within the representational level. Hengeveld also demonstrated that the preferred order of realization of operators, in a number of languages, can be represented as $\pi_4\ \pi_3\ \pi_2\ \pi_1$ Pred <u>or</u> Pred $\pi_1\ \pi_2\ \pi_3\ \pi_4$ (where π is an operator, Pred = predicate, and the subscript numbers represent layers, 4 being the outermost, speech act, layer). Hengeveld's own work on mood and modality in Spanish (Hengeveld 1987a, 1987b, 1988) also provided evidence for layering that is not in parallel strands, as in SFG, but hierarchical. Recent work by Nuyts (1992) and Bolkestein (1992) suggested that Hengeveld's proposals may be somewhat too simple, because there is evidence that a greater number of layers, or at least a more gradual progression of layers, may be needed to account for a number of phenomena in English and Latin. Nevertheless, there appears to be good evidence for a hierarchical arrangement rather than a parallel one.

My conclusion, then, is that to deny interpersonal meaning its importance within the linguistic system would be to throw a healthy baby out with its somewhat suspect bath water. The ideational/interpersonal distinction is indeed fundamental to the organization of grammars, and it is to Halliday that the credit must go for the original insight. Where (on the strength of the present evidence) we need to part company with Halliday is in the claim that the two kinds of meaning (and also the textual) are (relatively) independent; on the contrary, there appear to be significant unidirectional (scoping) effects involved. It would also be wise not to place too much reliance on the purported evidence for metafunctional organization from patterns of realization.

5. SKETCH OF AN ALTERNATIVE MODEL

To conclude, I will present a sketch of a model of language that is strongly influenced by Leech's model, but differs from it in two important ways. Firstly, its central component is a paradigmatically based systemic semantics. Secondly, it takes greater account of situational factors than Leech's model. Leech (1983: 10) restricted himself to the study of "general pragmatics," by which term he meant, "to distinguish the study of the general conditions of the communicative use of language, and to exclude more specific 'local' conditions on language use."

The study of how language is affected by different social situations, as well as different cultures or language communities, is separated off as "socio-pragmatics," and Leech had nothing to say about it. For instance, when dealing with politeness phenomena, he discussed only the "inherent politeness" of particular forms, purposely excluding their relative politeness in particular types of context. But this means that he could give no account of the systematic relations between, for instance, politeness and personal tenor. His scheme did not, for example, provide any way of explaining why, in certain kinds of situation, a form with high inherent politeness might be too polite for the context, and so interpreted as ironic or impolite. This is where systemic linguistics may be able to help—but *only* if future research can provide adequate definitions of the contextual categories of field, tenor and mode.

My tentative model is shown diagrammatically in Fig. 4.2. As in Leech's model, the speaker has certain communicative goals that s/he wishes to fulfill linguistically. It is important to recognize that these goals will arise partly from the content and structure of the preceding discourse. In order to realize the goals, the speaker must select, from the semantic resources of the language, an appropriate propositional content for the utterance (ideational/representational),

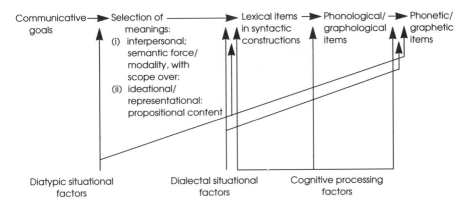

Figure 4.2   A tentative model

and also an appropriate "semantic force"[4] with which to present that content, perhaps modified by a modality (interpersonal). Note that following the work in FG reviewed briefly in Section 4 above, I assume that the interpersonal will have hierarchical dominance over the ideational/representational.

What counts as an appropriate choice is determined by a complex set of situational factors, which we may hope to be able to describe in terms of more rigorously defined categories of field, tenor and mode. For instance, personal tenor is involved in the speaker's selection of an appropriate propositional content and semantic force for conveying a request for a particular action. Compare (29)–(31) below:

You will put the electric fire on.   (29)

Will you put the electric fire on?   (30)

I'm awfully cold.   (31)

In my approach I would claim that (29) and (30) have the same propositional content (which we may gloss as "addressee—put on—electric fire"), but different semantic forces. On the other hand, (31)

---

[4]I have discussed the concept of semantic force elsewhere (Butler 1982, 1987); it is based on the work of Hudson (1975) and is concerned with truly semantic properties of sentences that have definable relations with the syntax.

has the same semantic force as (29), but different propositional content. All could be used in an attempt to achieve the goal of getting the hearer to put the fire on. The selection of one rather than another is conditioned largely by the personal tenor relations of the participants. Now consider (32) and (33):

Lend me your pen. (32)

Lend me $10,000. (33)

Whereas (32) would be quite normal between participants separated by a rather small social distance, it is unlikely that anyone would seriously attempt to secure a large loan using (33), however small the social distance. Appropriateness in the selection of ways of requesting depends not only on the relationships between participants, but also on the content of the request; that is, the field of interaction ("negotiating a substantial loan") also has an effect. It could also be argued that mode is involved: (33) is even less likely to be used if the request is being made in writing rather than in speech.

Having selected, from the semantic networks, a propositional content and a semantic force that are appropriate in the respects outlined above, the speaker then has to select an appropriate way of realizing the semantic content as lexical items linked in syntactic constructions (and ultimately, of course, as sequences of sound events or marks on paper).

One important type of factor involved in the selection of appropriate coding is concerned with the facilitation of the addressee's processing of the text, "a textually 'well-behaved' utterance being one which anticipates and facilitates h's [the hearer's: CSB] task in decoding, or making sense of, the text" (Leech 1983: 60).

Consider (34) and (35):

That Mary can't come to the party at Jim's on Friday night is a pity. (34)

It's a pity that Mary can't come to the party at Jim's on Friday night. (35)

(34) and (35) have the same propositional content and semantic force, but vary in syntactic structure. What reasons are there for preferring the more normal (35) over (34)? The answer is at least partly to be found in the well-known principle of "end-weight," whereby larger, "heavier" constituents are usually placed toward the

end of a sentence of English[5]. But, as Leech (1983: 64–5) pointed out, the principle seems to be rather more general than this, because it also applies to the phonological level: as Halliday (1967b) and others have observed, the unmarked position for the tonic element of a tone group is on the last fully lexical item, and this "end-focus" principle appears to be very widespread in languages (see Clark and Clark 1977: 548). What we are dealing with here is presumably a general principle of human cognitive processing: Putting the weightiest or most important item last helps the hearer to process the utterance, and so conforms to what Leech calls the "processibility principle," which enjoins the speaker to present the text in a way that makes it as easy as possible for the hearer to interpret in ongoing time. Like all pragmatic principles, however, the processibility principle can be overridden by more pressing considerations; for instance, tonic prominence can be given to an item that is not final in the tone group, if, for example, that item is contrastive as in (36):

Mary can't come to the party. (though Bill can, etc.)   (36)

In such cases, the processing cost occasioned by violation of the end-focus maxim of the processibility principle is outweighed by the value of the extra information that can be inferred.

The processibility principle is just one of several falling under Leech's "textual rhetoric." The "economy principle" says that simplifying processes are favored at all levels, because they, like end-weight and end-focus, help the addressee to process the text efficiently. Compare (37) with (38):

Mary will be coming to the party, Bill will be coming to the party, and Sue will be coming to the party.   (37)

Mary, Bill, and Sue will be coming to the party.   (38)

The more concise (38) would normally be preferred over the repetitive (37), though the principle of economy, like all other rhetorical principles, can be overruled by even stronger principles. For instance, as Leech (1983: 68) observed, an "expressivity principle," concerned with expressive and aesthetic effects of language, may

---

[5]It may also have something to do with the fact that the thematized element contains an evaluative item *pity* (cf. *It's nice to see you*, etc).

favor repetition. A well-known example is the following, from Churchill's speech to the House of Commons on June 4, 1940:

We shall defend our island, whatever the cost may be; we shall fight on the beaches, we shall fight on the landing grounds, we shall fight in the fields and in the streets, we shall fight in the hills; we shall never surrender.   (39)

A fourth textual principle proposed by Leech (and clearly related to Grice's submaxim of manner, "Be perspicuous") is the "clarity principle," which enjoins the speaker or writer to maintain a transparent relationship between the message to be conveyed and the text by means of which it is conveyed. This will include the use of unmarked constituent ordering so the principle can be invoked to deal with theme–rheme relations.

The textual rhetoric is much less well worked out than the interpersonal rhetoric in Leech's account, but it already gives a good idea of how studies of human cognitive processes can help to explain a variety of phenomena that appear in Halliday's textual component in a way that does not require the over-neat categorization of choices forced on us by a system network.

Cognitive processing factors are not, however, the only ones to be taken into consideration in discussing what is an appropriate form of lexicosyntactic coding for semantic feature complexes. Here, as in the selection of semantic features, the situation type, defined by values of field, tenor and mode, also has a part to play. Consider (40) and (41):

Someone titrated the solution with 0.1N hydrochloric acid.
(40)

The solution was titrated with 0.1N hydrochloric acid.
(41)

Examples (40) and (41) have the same propositional content, but differ in that in (40) the "agent" is actualized in the syntactic structure, whereas in (41) the selection of the passive form allows non-actualization of the agent in the syntax. Example (41) is, of course, much more likely in an report of a chemistry experiment than (40). Probably field, tenor and mode are all involved here. It is the activity of technical reporting (field), which makes the use of the passive more likely, but (41) is also more likely in a written report than in a spoken account (mode), and written reports tend to be more formal than spoken ones (tenor).

As a second and final example of the effects of situational factors on the receding of semantic options, compare (42)–(44):

The Lake District is very beautiful.   (42)

The Lake District, it's very beautiful.   (43)

It's very beautiful, the Lake District.   (44)

All of these have the same propositional content. However, most native English speakers would probably agree that although (42) could equally well appear in either speech or writing, (43) and (44) are characteristic of spoken language. Mode therefore has an effect on syntactic coding here.

Finally, compare (44) with (45):

It's very beautiful, is the Lake District.   (45)

Example (45) is restricted to certain Northern varieties of British English, and this reminds us that dialectal factors also have to be taken into account when specifying appropriate lexicosyntactic realizations of meanings. Systemic linguists have barely begun to attend to the question of what effects dialect might have on the choice of meanings from semantic networks.

6. CONCLUSION

It will be obvious, from the skeletal nature of this account, that much descriptive work needs to be done before we can judge the merits and demerits of the model I am advocating. I hope that even at this early stage, it is clear that there are considerable advantages to be gained from a marriage of systemic linguistics and pragmatics (and also from at least a flirtation between SFG and Dik's FG) and that these advantages are highly visible in the area of the interpersonal functioning of language. But without the seminal work of Michael Halliday, to whom this chapter is dedicated, this hoped for coming together would never have been possible.

REFERENCES

Asp, E. (1992) "On some natural and unnatural grammatical relations: a critique of a current trend in systemic-functional linguistics." *Network*. 18, 54–60.

Benson, J.D., Cummings, M., and Greaves, W.S., eds., (1988) *Linguistics in a Systemic Perspective.* (Current issues in Linguistic Theory, 39) Amsterdam: John Benjamins.

Berry, M. (1982) Review of Halliday 1978. *Nottingham Linguistic Circular* 11, 64–94.

Blakemore, D. (1992) *Understanding Utterances: An Introduction to Pragmatics.* Oxford and Cambridge, MA: Blackwell.

Bolkestein, A.M. (1992) Limits to layering: locatability and other problems. In Fortescue, Harder and Kristoffersen, 282–403.

Brown, P. and Levinson, S. (1978/1987) Universals in language usage: politeness phenomena. In E. Goody, ed., (1978) *Questions and Politeness: Strategies in Social Interaction.* Cambridge: Cambridge University Press, 56–311. Revised version (1987) published as *Politeness: Some Universals in Language Usage.* Cambridge: Cambridge University Press.

Bühler, K. (1934) *Sprachtheorie.* Jena: Fischer.

Butler, C.S. (1982) *The Directive Function of the English Modals.* Unpublished PhD thesis, University of Nottingham.

Butler, C.S. (1985a) Function in systemic linguistics. *Linguistic Journal of Korea.* 10/1, 23–57.

Butler, C.S. (1985b) *Systemic Linguistics: Theory and Applications.* London: Batsford.

Butler, C.S. (1986) What has systemic functional linguistics contributed to our understanding of spoken text? *Proceedings of the 1984 Working Conference on Language in Education.* Brisbane: Brisbane College of Advanced Education.

Butler, C.S. (1987) Communicative function and semantics. In Halliday and Fawcett, 212–29.

Butler, C.S. (1988a) Pragmatics and systemic linguistics. *Journal of Pragmatics.* 12, 83–102.

Butler, C.S. (1988b) Systemic linguistics, semantics and pragmatics. In E. H. Steiner and R. Veltman, eds., *Pragmatics, Discourse and Text: Some Systemically Inspired Approaches.* London: Frances Pinter, 13–27.

Butler, C.S. (1988c) Politeness and the semantics of modalised directives in English. In Benson, Cummings and Greaves, 119–53.

Butler, C.S. (1991) Standards of adequacy in Functional Grammar. (Review article on Dik 1989) *Journal of Linguistics.* 27, 499–515.

Butler, C.S. (1992) Criteria of adequacy in functional grammars, with particular reference to Systemic Functional Grammar. *Network.* 17, 61–9.

Butler, C.S. (1993) Systemic Grammar in applied language studies. In R.E. Asher and J.M.Y. Simpson (eds.) *The Encyclopedia of Language and Linguistics.* Pergamon Press, 4500–4504.

Bybee, J.L. (1985) *Morphology: A study of the relation between meaning and form.* Amsterdam: John Benjamins.

Clark, H.H. and Clark, E.V. (1977) *Psychology and Language: An Introduction to Psycholinguistics.* New York: Harcourt Brace Jovanovitch.

Cole, P., and Morgan, J.L., eds., (1975) *Syntax and Semantics 3: Speech Acts.* New York: Academic Press.

Crystal, D. (1969) *Prosodic Systems and Intonation in English.* Cambridge: Cambridge University Press.

Dik, S.C. (1989) *The Theory of Functional Grammar. Part 1: The Structure of the Clause.* Functional Grammar Series, 9. Dordrecht: Foris Publications.

Downing, A. (1991) An alternative approach to theme: a systemic-functional perspective. *Word.* 42,2: 119–43.

Fawcett, R.P. (1980) *Cognitive Linguistics and Social Interaction: Towards an Integrated Model of a Systemic Functional Grammar and the other Components of a Communicating Mind.* Heidelberg: Julius Groos Verlag and Exeter: University of Exeter.

Fawcett, R.P., Tucker, G.H. and Lin, Y. (1992) The COMMUNAL project: how to get from semantics to syntax. In *Proceedings of COLING92: 14th International Conference on Computational Linguistics (Nantes) 1992.* Morristown, NJ: Bell Communications Research, 1315a–f.

Fawcett, R.P., Tucker, G.H. and Lin, Y. (1993) How a Systemic Functional Grammar works: the role of realization in realization. In H. Horacek and M. Zock, eds., *From Planning to Realization in Natural Language Generation.* London: Pinter, 114–86.

Foley, W.A. and Van Valin, R.D., Jr. (1984) *Functional Syntax and Universal Grammar.* Cambridge: Cambridge University Press.

Fortescue, M., Harder, P. and Kristoffersen, L., eds., (1992) *Layering and Reference in a Functional Perspective.* Amsterdam/Philadelphia: John Benjamins.

Gregory, M. (1967) Aspects of varieties differentiation. *Journal of Linguistics.* 3, 177–98.

Gregory, M. (1987) Meta-functions: aspects of their development, status and use in systemic linguistics. In Halliday and Fawcett, 94–106.

Gregory, M. (1988) Generic situation and register: a functional view of communication. In Benson, Cummings and Greaves, 301–29.

Gregory, M. and Carroll, S. (1978) *Language and Situation: Language Varieties and their Social Contexts.* London: Routledge and Kegan Paul.

Grice, H.P. (1975) Logic and conversation. Harvard William Jones Lectures, 1967. In Cole and Morgan, 41–58.

Grice, H.P. (1978) Further notes on logic and conversation. In P. Cole, ed., *Syntax and Semantics 9: Pragmatics.* New York: Academic Press, 113–28.

Halliday, M.A.K. (1965) Speech and situation. *Bulletin of the National Association for the Teaching of English: Some Aspects of Oracy.* 2, 2.

Halliday, M.A.K. (1967a) Notes on transitivity and theme in English, Part 2. *Journal of Linguistics.* 3, 199–244.

Halliday, M.A.K. (1967b) *Intonation and Grammar in British English.* Janua Linguarum Series Practica 48. The Hague: Mouton.

Halliday, M.A.K. (1968) Notes on transitivity and theme in English, Part 3. *Journal of Linguistics.* 4, 179–215.

Halliday, M.A.K. (1969) Options and functions in the English clause. *Brno Studies in English*. 8, 81–8. Reprinted in F.W. Householder, ed., (1972) *Syntactic Theory 1: Structuralist*. Harmondsworth: Penguin, 248–57. Also reprinted in M.A.K. Halliday and J.R. Martin, eds., (1981) *Readings in Systemic Linguistics*. London: Batsford, 138–45.

Halliday, M.A.K. (1970) Functional diversity in language, as seen from a consideration of modality and mood in English. *Foundations of Language*. 6, 322–61. Reprinted in part in Kress, 189–213.

Halliday, M.A.K. (1973) *Explorations in the Functions of Language*. London: Edward Arnold.

Halliday, M.A.K. (1978) *Language as Social Semiotic*. London: Edward Arnold.

Halliday, M.A.K. (1979) Modes of meaning and modes of expression: types of grammatical structure and their determination by different semantic functions. In D.J. Allerton, E. Carney and D. Holdcroft, eds., *Function and Context in Linguistic Analysis: Essays Offered to William Haas*. Cambridge: Cambridge University Press, 57–79.

Halliday, M.A.K. (with R. Hasan) (1980) Text and context: aspects of language in a social-semiotic perspective. *Sofia Linguistica* 6, 4–91. (Later published in revised form as Halliday, M.A.K. and Hasan, R. (1985) *Language, Context and Text: Aspects of Language in a Social-Semiotic Perspective*. Geelong: Deakin University Press. Republished in 2nd ed. (1989) by Oxford University Press.)

Halliday, M.A.K. (1984) Language as code and language as bahaviour: a systemic-functional interpretation of the nature and ontogenesis of dialogue. In R.P. Fawcett, M.A.K. Halliday, S.M. Lamb and A. Makkai, eds., *The Semiotics of Culture and Language, Vol 1: Language as Social Semiotic*. London: Frances Pinter, 3–35.

Halliday, M.A.K. (1991) Corpus studies and probabilistic grammar. In K. Aijmer and B. Altenberg, eds., *English Corpus Linguistics: Studies in Honour of Jan Svartvik*. London and New York: Longman, 30–43.

Halliday, M.A.K. (1993) Quantitative studies and probabilities in grammar. In M. Hoey (ed.), *Data, Description, Discourse*. London: HarperCollins, 1–25.

Halliday, M.A.K. (1994) *Introduction to Functional Grammar*. 2nd ed. London: Edward Arnold.

Halliday, M.A.K. and Fawcett, R.P. eds., (1987) *New Developments in Systemic Linguistics. Vol. 1: Theory and Description*. London: Frances Pinter.

Hengeveld, K. (1987a) Clause structure and modality in Functional Grammar. In J. van der Auwera and L. Goossens, eds., *Ins and Outs of the Predication*, Functional Grammar Series 6, Dordrecht: Foris Publications, 53–66.

Hengeveld, K. (1987b) The Spanish mood system. *Working Papers in Functional Grammar*, 22. Amsterdam: University of Amsterdam.

Hengeveld, K. (1988) Illocution, mood and modality in a Funcional Grammar of Spanish. *Journal of Semantics*. 6, 227–69.

Hengeveld, K. (1989) Layers and operators in Functional Grammar. *Journal of Linguistics*, 25, 127–57.

Hengeveld, K. (1990) The hierarchical structure of utterances. In J. Nuyts, A.M. Bolkestein and C. Vet, eds., *Layers and Levels of Representation in Language Theory*, Amsterdam/Philadelphia: John Benjamins, 1–23.

Hudson, R.A. (1975) The meaning of questions. *Language*. 51, 1–31.

Kress, G., ed., (1976) *Halliday: System and Function in Language*. London: Oxford University Press.

Leech, G.N. (1983) *Principles of Pragmatics*. London: Longman.

Levinson, S.C. (1989) Review of Sperber and Wilson (1986). *Journal of Linguistics*. 25, 455–72.

Lyons, J. (1981) *Language and Linguistics*. Cambridge: Cambridge University Press.

Martin, J.R. (1981) How many speech acts? *UEA Papers in Linguistics*. 14/15, 52–77.

Martin, J.R. (1984) Functional components in a grammar: a review of deployable recognition criteria. *Nottingham Linguistic Circular*. 13, 35–70.

Martin, J.R. (1992) *English Text: System and Structure*. Philadelphia/Amsterdam: John Benjamins.

Matthiessen, C.M.I.M. (1991) Metafunctional complementarity and resonance in syntagmatic organization. Paper presented at ALS 90. Sydney: Department of Linguistics, University of Sydney.

Mey, J.L. and Talbot, M. (1988) Computation and the soul. Review article on Sperber and Wilson (1986). *Journal of Pragmatics*. 12, 743–89.

Nemo, F. (1988) Review of Sperber and Wilson (1986). *Journal of Pragmatics*. 12, 791–5.

Nesbitt, C. and Plum, G. (1988) Probabilities in a systemic-functional grammar: the clause complex in English. In R.P. Fawcett and D.J. Young, eds., *New Developments in Systemic Lingusitics. Volume 2: Theory and Application*. London and New York: Pinter, 6–38.

Nuyts, J. (1992) Subjective vs. objective modality: what is the difference? In Fortescue, Harder and Kristoffersen, 73–97.

Palmer, F.R. (1979) *Modality and the English Modals*. London: Longman.

Searle, J.R. (1975) Indirect speech acts. In Cole and Morgan, 59–82.

Seuren, P.A.M. (1988) The self-styling of relevance theory. *Journal of Semantics*. 5, 123–43.

Sperber, D. and Wilson, D. (1986) *Relevance: Communication and Cognition*. Cambridge, Mass.: Harvard University Press and Oxford: Blackwell.

Svartvik, J. and Quirk, R. (1980) *A Corpus of English Conversation*. Lund Studies in English 56. Lund: CWK Gleerup.

Ziv, Y. (1988) On the rationality of "relevance" and the relevance of "rationality." *Journal of Pragmatics*. 12, 543–5.

5
Modality and Modulation in Chinese

Yongsheng Zhu

*Department of Foreign Languages
and Literature
Fudan University
Shanghai 200433
China*

1. PREFACE

My interest in linguistics began when I was a university student more than 20 years ago. However, it was not until I got the opportunity to study under Professor Halliday's supervision for two years from 1983 to 1985 at the Linguistics Department of Sydney University did I really come to understand what linguistics is, what it does and what we can achieve through linguistic studies.

I still remember the first day when I saw Professor Halliday after I got transferred to Sydney University (with Halliday's help) from another university in Australia, which was extremely glad to have students from China but, much to my disappointment, offered no linguistics courses. Professor Halliday was going to give a lecture in the Quad that day and said "Right now!" when I anxiously asked him, "When can I start?" There and then I became his student!

Throughout the two years of my stay in Sydney, Professor Halliday helped me in many ways. Whenever I met with problems I could not solve alone in my studies, he would give me detailed explanation; whenever I was lacking in confidence, he would give me timely encouragement; and whenever there were muddled views in my course papers and MA thesis, he would give me valuable guidance. Being his student was really a happy and memorable experience.

In the past 10 years since my return to China in February 1985, I have received further help from Professor Halliday, who found time to answer my questions about linguistics, sent me materials for my research work and accepted my invitation to attend the Second National Workshop of Systemic-Functional Grammar, which was held at Suzhou University in China in July 1991, which was not a good time for a large-scale meeting because Suzhou was then suffering from a very big flood!

For a long time I have been longing for an opportunity to express my gratitude to Professor Halliday and now the opportunity has come: I can make a contribution to a festschrift for this great linguist. The topic of my paper is modality and modulation in Chinese. Professor Halliday showed much interest in this topic when I chose it for my MA thesis at Sydney University and gave me all the help a supervisor could give. So before the discussion of this topic here, I would like to thank Professor Halliday for his instructions. At the same time, I would like to thank the four editors as well for giving valuable suggestions about the revision of my paper and including the paper in this book.

2. INTRODUCTION

According to Halliday (1985: 69–71), in verbal interaction, the participants may make statements, ask questions, give commands or make offers. In statements and questions, certain information is given or asked for; in commands and offers, goods and services are exchanged. In the information exchange, the speaker makes a proposition; in the goods and services exchange, the speaker makes a proposal. Propositions and proposals may appear in polar forms. In propositions, the positive pole is "it is so" and the negative pole is "it isn't so." In proposals, the positive pole is "do it" and the negative pole is "don't do it." Between the two categories of polarity there are intermediate values. The intermediate values in propositions are degrees of probability (i.e. maybe yes and maybe no) and degrees of frequency (i.e. sometimes yes and sometimes no). The intermediate values in proposals are degrees of obligation in a command (i.e. be required, supposed or allowed to do something) and degrees of inclination in an offer (i.e. be determined, anxious or willing to do something). The degrees of probability and frequency form the realm of modality and the degrees of obligation and inclination form the realm of modulation.

The distinction between proposition and proposal made by Halliday is significant in that it tells us that there is more than one way of getting from the positive pole to the negative pole in English and that the intermediate values, like the polar ones, fall into the category of information or goods and services type.

In the literature of Chinese linguistics, modality has also been a topic of interest for a long time. Many books and articles have been written on this subject but few have taken a systemic–functional approach. The distinction between information and goods and services has never been explicitly made. The study of modality has been confined to syntactic properties and meanings of modal verbs. Realization forms such as adverbs, full verbs, nouns and mood particles have been either ignored or treated in an unsystematic way. In this paper, however, efforts will be made to examine modality and modulation in the Chinese language from the systemic–functional approach of Michael Halliday. Modal verbs will be reclassified and various realization forms of modality and modulation will be discussed. Comparisons between Chinese and English will be made in a tentative manner.

2.1. A Brief Survey of Modal Verbs

In English there is a distinction between modal and non-modal auxiliary verbs. In Chinese, however, there is no such thing as non-modal auxiliaries corresponding to "be" (as in "He is reading a book") and "have" as in "We have met each other before") in English. The terms modal verbs, auxiliary verbs and nengyuan ("ability–wish") verbs can be used interchangeably.

Modal verbs have long been recognized as a special category by Chinese grammarians and linguists such as Chao Yuan Ren, Wang Li and Lu Shuxiang. These verbs possess grammatical properties that make them distinguishable from full verbs and other word classes such as adverbs. It is necessary to take a brief look at their syntactic features and the meanings they express because they are of great importance to the study of the realization of modality and modulation in the Chinese language.

2.1.1. Grammatical properties

2.1.1.1. Profile by Chao. In the study of modal verbs, Chao (1968) took a structural approach while Wang (1959; 1984) and Lu

(1980; 1982) paid more attention to the meanings these modal verbs express.

Chao (1968: 731–733) furnished the syntactic profile of Chinese modal verbs, or auxiliary verbs as he called them. This profile succeeds in giving all the grammatical features of Chinese modal verbs. What follows are their most important features:

1. An auxiliary verb, like full verbs, takes <u>bu</u> for a negative (e.g. <u>bu neng</u> "cannot");
2. The negative word <u>mei</u> "not" applies in a restricted way to auxiliary verbs;
3. The adverb of degree <u>hen</u> "very" applies to most but not all auxiliary verbs;
4. Auxiliary verbs can occur in succession (e.g. <u>huiyao</u> "may want to");
5. There is no tentative reduplicate like <u>nengneng</u> "can can";
6. Auxiliary verbs do not take the progressive marker <u>zhe</u> or the perfective marker <u>le</u> (e.g. *<u>nengzhe</u> "can-ing," *<u>bixu le</u> "must-en");
7. Auxiliary verbs do not occur singly in imperatives (i.e. there is no one-word imperative (e.g. *<u>Neng</u>! "Can!");
8. The V–not–V form of questions is applicable to all auxiliary verbs (e.g. <u>neng bu neng</u> "can or cannot").

2.1.1.2. Modal verbs versus full verbs.   Modal verbs resemble full verbs in the following ways (Zhu 1984: 48–49):

1. Both modal verbs and full verbs can be negated syntactically by <u>bu</u>;
2. Both can form V–not–V questions;
3. Both can be used alone to answer yes/no questions.

They differ from full verbs chiefly in that:

1. They, unlike full verbs, cannot take aspectual markers such as <u>zhe</u> and <u>le</u>;
2. They, unlike full verbs, cannot appear in one-word imperatives; and
3. They, unlike full verbs again, cannot form a predicator by themselves in the transitivity system except in elliptical sentences.

It is not difficult to see that although modal verbs and full verbs share some features, they do not belong to the same category. Modal verbs have their own properties that full verbs do not possess.

2.1.1.3. Modal verbs versus adverbs. Modal verbs differ from adverbs syntactically in the following ways (Zhu 1984: 49–50):

1. They can be negated by bu whereas most adverbs cannot undergo such a negation (e.g. *bu yexu "not perhaps," *bu dagai "not probably");
2. They can occur in V–not–V construction but adverbs cannot (e.g. *yexu bu yexu "perhaps and not perhaps," *dagai bu dagai "probably and not probably");
3. They can be used alone to answer yes/no questions, whereas only two- and polysyllabic adverbs can be used alone as a response to yes/no questions, as in:

—Ni   mingtian yiding lai   ma[1]?
you tomorrow sure   come m-p
Are you sure to come tomorrow?
—Yiding.
sure
Sure.   (1)

Monosyllabic adverbs cannot be used in the same way:

—Ni   mingtian hai lai   ma?
you tomorrow again come m-p
Will you come again tomorrow?
—*Hai.
again
Again.   (2)

2.1.2. Classification of modal verbs

2.1.2.1. Wang's classification.   Wang (1959: 130) divided modal verbs into two groups: keneng "possibility" and yizhi "inclination." The first group covers the meanings of (a) ability (i.e. one's capability to do something as in Ta hui youyong "He can swim;" (b) permission from an authority or social conventions, or consent from circum-

---

[1]In this paper "m-p," "a-p" and "cl." are used as short forms of mood particle, aspectual particle and classifier respectively.

stances as in <u>Zheli bu xu chouyan</u> "No smoking is allowed here;" (c) probability (i.e. the likelihood of certain occurrences as in <u>Ta gai shuizhao le ba</u> "He should be asleep by now;" and (d) necessity (i.e. something must or should be done because of the need of the circumstance as in <u>Xia lou dei dangxin</u> "You must be careful when you go downstairs.") The second group, on the other hand, refers to one's desire and inclination to do something as in <u>Wo yao qu</u> "I want to go." This classification can be shown in Figure 5.1:

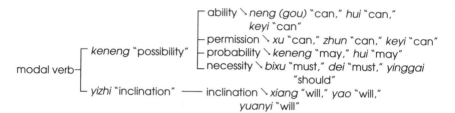

Figure 5.1. Wang's classification of modal verbs

2.1.2.2. Lu's classification. Lu (1982: 246) also divided modal verbs into two groups, but in a different way. Instead of classifying them as <u>keneng</u>-group and <u>yizhi</u>-group, he categories them as <u>keneng</u> "possibility" and <u>biyao</u> "necessity." Within each group there are three basic notions. The first group covers ability, permission and probability. The second group encompasses subjective necessity (i.e. one's inclination to do something), objective necessity (i.e. something should or must be done to satisfy the need of a certain situation or to be compatible to the accepted code of human conduct), and finally certainty. This classification can be illustrated in Figure 5.2:

Figure 5.2. Lu's classification of modal verbs

2.1.2.3. A new classification. Chao (1968: 731–733) and Li and Thompson (1981: 172–183), whose study of modal verbs is structure-based, and Wang (1959: 130) and Lu (1982: 246), whose study of modal verbs is meaning-based, succeeded in helping me get a good understanding of the Chinese modals. However, they did not fully realize that the speaker, by employing modal verbs, can do two things—make a proposition and make a proposal. Although I do not expect all linguists to follow Halliday in language studies, it is my belief that a reclassification of modal verbs will shed some new light on modality and modulation in Chinese:

```
                  ┌ modality ───────── probability ＼ keneng "can," hui "can," gai "should"
modal verb ┤                        ┌ ability ＼ neng (gou) "can," hui "can," keyi "can"
                  └ modulation ──┤ inclination ＼ xiang "will," yao "will,"
                                            │                yuanyi "will"
                                            └ obligation ＼ bixu "must," dei "must," yinggai
                                                              "should," xu "can," zhun "can,"
                                                              keyi "can"
```

Figure 5.3.   A new classification of modal verbs

This classification, like those made by Wang (1959: 130) and Lu (1982: 246), is also meaning-based. The difference lies in the fact that this classification recognizes the distinction between modality and modulation and therefore recognizes the distinctions between the two major functions that can be performed by Chinese modal verbs. Here the term *modality* covers the meanings of probability and certainty in Lu's classification, and the term *obligation* encompasses the meanings of permission and necessity in Wang's classification and the meanings of permission and obligation in Lu's classification.

3. MODALITY IN CHINESE

The term *modality* used by Halliday (1985: 335) refers to both probability and frequency (or usuality). As far as I understand it, frequency and probability are considered under the same heading because (a) they are both intermediate values between yes and no and (b) they are overlapping in their realization forms in English (i.e. modal verbs). In Chinese, however, frequency is not expressed by modal verbs or any other forms that indicate probability (cf. Figure 5.6). Therefore, frequency is not part of Chinese modality, to use the word *modality* in its strict Hallidayan sense. In what follows, I will examine probability and its realization forms only.

3.1. Continuum of Probability

In language interaction we often pass our judgments and make our assessments. These judgments and assessments may alter according to the degree of probability of the occurrence in question. Broadly speaking, there are three degrees of probability in Chinese: high, median and low, or certain, probable and possible as shown in Figure 5.4:

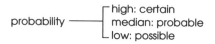

$$
\text{probability} \longrightarrow \begin{cases} \text{high: certain} \\ \text{median: probable} \\ \text{low: possible} \end{cases}
$$

Figure 5.4. Continuum of probability

3.1.2. Realization of probability

The notion of probability can be realized by modal verbs, other word classes or by modal verbs plus some other word classes.

3.1.2.1. Modal verbs. The modal verbs that can express probability are keneng, hui and gai. Keneng and hui indicate a low degree of probability, as in:

Ta mingtian keneng lai   kan ni.
he tomorrow   may   come see you
Perhaps he'll come to see you tomorrow.   (3)

Ta bu hui bu zhidao zhe jian shi.
he not can not   know this cl. thing
It is impossible that he does not know about it.   (4)

Note that hui is a full verb in:

Wo hui   yingyu.
I   know English
I can speak English.   (5)

Women yiqian meiyou   hui guo.
we   before not   meet a-p
We haven't met each other before.   (6)

Gai indicates a high degree of probability, as in:

Ta shangchuang ban xiaoshi le, gai   shuizhao   le.
he go-to-bed   half hour m-p should asleep   m-p
He went to bed half an hour ago and should be asleep by now.
                                                           (7)

Shi   dian   le. Ta <u>gai</u>   dao   Beijing le.
ten o'clock m-p he should arrive Beijing m-p
It's ten o'clock. He should have arrived in Beijing by now.

(8)

<u>Gai</u> has a negative form: <u>bu gai</u>. But this negative form never ex-
presses the meaning of probability. It is used only in the sense of
modulation, meaning "shouldn't" or "not supposed to." To express
what is not likely to happen or something seems not to be the case,
<u>bu hui</u> or <u>bu keneng</u> is used, as in:

—Ta gai   dao   Beijing le.
  he should arrive Beijing m-p
  He should have arrived in Beijing by now.
—<u>Bu hui</u> ba/<u>Bu keneng</u> ba.
  not can m-p/not   can m-p
  That's impossible, isn't it.   (9)

<u>Gai</u> can also be used as a transitive verb, meaning 'owe' as in:

Ta <u>gai</u> wo shi kuai qian.
he owe me ten yuan money
He owes me ten yuan.   (10)

Chao (1968: 741) treated this use of <u>gai</u> as a combination of "ought
to" and "owe." He was right to say so if he looked at it from the point
of view of its semantic features. But he labeled this <u>gai</u> as an auxiliary verb. It is true that <u>gai</u> can be a transitive verb and an auxiliary
verb. But it does not perform both functions at the same time. In the
above example, <u>gai</u> functions as a transitive verb taking <u>wo</u> "me" as
its Goal and <u>shi kuai qian</u> "ten yuan" as its Range. I can see no way
to treat this <u>gai</u> as an auxiliary verb, which cannot immediately
precede a nominal group. In <u>Ta gai huan wo shi kuai qian</u> "He
should pay ten yuan back to me," however, <u>gai</u> is an auxiliary verb
because it comes before a full verb and does not take a nominal
group as its Goal. The meaning expressed by <u>gai</u> here is not modality
but modulation (i.e. obligation).

The median degree of probability is not expressed by modal verbs
but by adverbs and full verbs.

3.1.2.2. Adverbs.   Adverbs play an important role in the realization of the three degrees of probability.

The four adverbs <u>yiding</u>, <u>kending</u>, <u>biding</u> and <u>zhun</u> all express a
high degree of probability, as in:

Ta hai mei lai,   yiding/kending/biding shi wu che   le.
he still not come   must/must/must   be miss train m-p
He hasn't come yet. He must have missed the train.   (11)

Mei   cuo.   Zhun/Yiding/Kending shi ta.
no   mistake   must/must/must   be him
It must be him.   (12)

These two sentences indicate a high degree of probability but they
are less certain than 13 and 14, which take the form of polarity:

Ta wu che   le.
he miss train m-p
He missed the train.   (13)

Mei   cuo.   Shi ta.
no   mistake be him
It's him.   (14)

The words dagai and duoban express a median degree of probability,
as in:

Ta dagai/duoban   shi wu che   le.
he probably/probably be miss train m-p
Probably he missed the train.   (15)

Huiyi   dagai   yanqi   le.
meeting probably postpone m-p
The meeting has probably been postponed.   (16)

A low degree of probability can be realized by the adverbs yexu and
huoxu, as in:

Ta   yexu/huoxu   shi bing le.
she perhaps/perhaps be ill   m-p
Perhaps she is ill.   (17)

Ta   yexu/huoxu   bu neng lai.
she perhaps/perhaps not can   come
Perhaps she can't come.   (18)

The adverbs in (17) and (18) can be replaced by the modal verb
keneng, which also expresses the low degree of probability.

From the discussion above, we can say that the modal verb gai
and the adverb yiding both express certainty. But a closer examination will show that the degree of probability expressed by yiding is
higher than that expressed by gai. Yiding corresponds to the English modal "must;" gai is equivalent to the English modal "should."

Another difference between yiding and gai is that the former is more subjective than the latter. Gai is used when the speaker makes his judgment entirely on the basis of the situation. It carries some objective flavor that is not found in other modal verbs such as hui. In other words, it is the circumstances that lead to the speaker's assessment. Yiding, on the other hand, can express one's judgment on the basis of a certain situation or as a result of one's imagination as in Ta yiding dao Bejing le "He must have arrived in Beijing now" and Ta yiding shuo guo zhe zhong hua "He must have said that."

3.1.2.3. Modal verbs plus adverbs. Adverbs and modal verbs of probability do not co-occur (possibly to avoid redundancy), with zhun gai "certainly should" as an exception:

Shi dian le, ta   zhun   gai   dao   Beijing le.
ten o'clock m-p he certainly should arrive Beijing m-p
It's ten o'clock now. He certainly should have arrived in Beijing.
(19)

Note that adverbs of probability precede the word hui in (20), (21) and (22). This hui, however, is not a modal verb denoting probability, but a marker of future time:

Ta yiding hui lai   de.
he certainly will come m-p
He'll certainly come.   (20)

Ta   dagai hui lai   de.
he probably will come m-p
He'll probably come.   (21)

Ta   yexu hui lai   de.
he perhaps will come m-p
He'll come perhaps.   (22)

3.1.2.4. Full verbs. Full verbs such as xiangxin "believe," guji "estimate," kan "think" and xiang "reckon" express a median degree of probability, as in:

Wo kan   na tian shi xingqiwu
I   think that day be Friday
I think it was Friday that day.   (23)

Wo xiang ta yiding zhidao le.
I   reckon he certainly know m-p
He already knows it, I reckon.   (24)

When these verbs co-occur with modal verbs or adverbs expressing probability, the degree of probability is mainly indicated by the modal verbs or adverbs with these full verbs adding tentativeness to the whole utterance, as in:

Wo <u>kan</u>   na tian <u>yiding</u> shi xingqiwu.
I   think that day certainly be   Friday
In my opinion it must be Friday that day.   (25)

Wo <u>xiang</u>   ta <u>keneng</u> yijing   dao Beijing le.
I   reckon he   may   already arrive Beijing m-p
He may have arrived in Beijing already, I reckon.   (26)

High degree of probability can also be realized by the expressions <u>bu yong shuo</u> "needless to say" and <u>haowu yiwen</u> "no doubt," as in:

<u>Bu yong shuo</u>, zhun shi ta.
not need say   must be him.
Needless to say, it must be him.   (27)

<u>Haowu yiwen</u>, ta xianzai bu   zai jia.
no   doubt he' now   not at home
No doubt, he's not at home now.   (28)

These expressions can combine with adverbs or modal verbs that indicate high degree of probability (as in 27). They do not, however, co-occur with those expressing median or low degree of probability, for the resulting sentence would make the speaker sound self-contradictory by saying "he's sure" and then "he's not sure." The following sentences, though grammatically correct, are not acceptable to a native speaker of Chinese:

*<u>Bu yong shuo</u>,   <u>dagai</u>   shi ta.
not need say   probably be him
Needless to say, it is him probably.   (29)

*<u>Haowu yiwen</u>, ta <u>keneng</u> yijing   dao Beijing le.
no   doubt he   may   already arrive Beijing m-p
No doubt that he may have arrived in Beijing already.   (30)

3.1.2.5. Mood particle: ba.   Probability can also be expressed by the mood particle <u>ba</u>, which occurs at the end of a clause and makes the speaker's judgment tentative:

Ta dao Beijing le   <u>ba</u>.
he arrive Beijing m-p m-p
He has arrived in Beijing now, hasn't he.   (31)

<u>Ba</u> often co-occurs with modal verbs, adverbs or full verbs denoting probability. The degree of probability is then mainly expressed by the modal verbs, adverbs or full verbs:

Ta <u>keneng</u> shengbing le   <u>ba</u>.
he   may   ill   m-p m-p
Maybe he is ill, isn't he.   (32)

Ta <u>yiding</u>   dao le   <u>ba</u>.
he certainly   arrive m-p m-p
He has certainly arrived, hasn't he.   (33)

Wo <u>kan</u> ta you wushi   sui   le   <u>ba</u>.
I   think he have fifty   years old m-p m-p
I think he is about fifty, isn't he.   (34)

In an interrogative sentence ending with the mood particle <u>ba</u>, the speaker expresses his own speculation rather than asking a real question; in this case, the answer expected from the addressee is normally "yes" (cf. Lu 1982: 297–298), as in:

Ni   mingtian keyi kan   wan   le   <u>ba</u>?
you tomorrow can   read finish m-p m-p
You can finish reading it tomorrow, can't you?   (35)

To ask a real yes/no question, another mood particle <u>ma</u> is used, as in:

Ni   mingtian keyi kan   wan   <u>ma</u>?
you tomorrow can   read finish m-p?
Can you finish reading it tomorrow?   (36)

Here there is no implication of the speaker's judgment. The answer he will get from the addressee can be "yes" and can be "no."

3.1.3. Probability and negation

All the modal verbs expressing probability can be negated by the negative marker <u>bu</u>: <u>bu gai</u> "shouldn't," <u>bu keneng</u> "can't," <u>bu hui</u> "can't." <u>Bu keneng</u> and <u>bu hui</u> can still indicate probability. <u>Bu gai</u>, however, as was already mentioned in 3.1.2.1, does not express probability but modulation.

The inverseness or complementarity of possibility and necessity (i.e. not (POSSIBLE p) = NECESSARY (not p); POSSIBLE (not p) = not (NECESSARY p)) discussed by Lyons (1977: 787), Leech & Coates (1979: 80) and Halliday (1970: 333) and other linguists of the

English language also works for Chinese. This can be illustrated by the following examples:

Ta bu yiding shi yingguo ren = Ta keneng bu shi yingguo ren.
he not certain be English man = he may not be English man
It is not certain whether he is an Englishman =
It is possible that he is not an Englishman. (37)

Ta bu keneng shi yingguo ren = Ta yiding bu shi yingguo ren.
he not may be English man = he certain not be English man
It is not possible that he is an Englishman =
It is certain that he is not an Englishman. (38)

Halliday's approach to modality has so far provided a sound guide to my study of this area of meaning in Chinese. But I come now to a point where I have to part company with Halliday. The points to be made here are relevant to both English and Chinese. Halliday (1970: 333), in his discussion of English modality and modulation, considered it "surely wrong" to assume that there is negative modality. He argued that a thesis can be negative but "the modality itself is not subject to negation," "since the total number of negative modalities is no greater than the total number of positive modalities." I find, however, this argument is not very convincing. It is absolutely true that all "modality negative" forms can be paraphrased as "thesis negative," but this does not give me enough reason to say that there is no such thing as negative modality in semantics. Furthermore, Halliday recognized the distinction between "modulation negative" and "process negative" as in his example "he is not allowed not to tell." I know that "he is not allowed not to tell" can be paraphrased as "he is required not to tell." Can I say then, by analogy, that "modulation negative" can be paraphrased as "process negative" and that there is no such thing as negative modulation? In my opinion, modality can be negated just as modulation can. The distinction between "modality negative" and "thesis negative" is parallel to that between "modulation negative" and "process negative."

3.1.4. Probability and time reference

Modal verbs and full verbs of probability, like all the other modal verbs and full verbs, do not have tense forms. However, they have a time reference. The time they indicate is the time when the speaker makes his judgment. The acts of assessing the probability of occurrence of situation signalled by them are simultaneous to the utterance of the speaker, because what is assessed is what he has to say at the time of his utterance.

Chinese verbs do not have tense but they have aspects: progressive and perfective, which are typically indicated by the aspectual markers zhe "–ing" and guo "–en" respectively. In Chinese, probability may combine with propositions in these aspects, as in:

Ta keneng hai zai mang zhe ne.
he may still now busy a-p m-p
He may be still busy.   (39)

Wo xiang ta yijing   dao guo Beijing le.
I   think he already go   a-p Beijing m-p
I think he has been to Beijing already.   (40)

4. MODULATION IN CHINESE

4.1. Ability

4.1.1. Realization
The meaning of ability can be realized by the four modals: neng, nenggou, keyi and hui. When the Actor is animate, these words are interchangeable as in:

Ta neng/nenggou/keyi/hui shuo si zhong waiguo   yu.
he can/can/can/can   speak four cl. foreign language
He can speak four foreign languages.   (41)

When the Actor is inanimate, hui cannot be used:

*Zhe jian wu hui zhu san ge   ren.
 this cl.   room can live three cl. person
 This room can hold three people.   (42)

In sentences such as (42), the other three modals can be used instead.
Hui differs from neng, nenggou and keyi also in that it not only means that one has the ability to do something but he can do it well. For example:

Ni zhen hui shuohua.
you really can   talk
You really know how to talk.   (43)

Here hui does not mean that "he" can produce meaningful sounds but that "he" is good at expressing himself or has a glib tongue.

4.1.2. Permanent ability versus single achievement

The four modal verbs we have just studied can all indicate permanent ability or habitual ability. But when a single achievement in the past is under consideration, they are not used, for they would only mean that you had the ability to do something without the implication that you really did it. Therefore, to express the idea that "He passed the exam," I can say Ta kaoshi tongguo le, in which the past achievement is indicated by the full verb tongguo "pass" plus the perfective marker le. A modal verb cannot be used here.

However, when a failure in the past is under discussion, modal verbs can be used, as in:

Ta mei neng tongguo kaoshi.
he not could pass   exam
He couldn't pass the exam.   (44)

In this respect, these modal verbs are similar to the English modal "could." To quote Palmer (1979: 92), the rules for "could" are:

1. Positive could is not used to refer to a single action;
2. there is no similar restriction on negative couldn't;
3. could may be used if there is reference to habitual or repeated actions;
4. there is no restriction similar to (1) on the forms of BE ABLE TO.

He gives the following paradigm examples:

1. *I ran fast and could catch the bus.
2. I ran fast but couldn't catch the bus.
3. I used to run fast and could always catch the bus.
4. I ran fast and was able to catch the bus.

Leech & Svartvik (1975: 129–130) made similar distinction between "could" and "be able to." They said that a permanent or habitual ability is expressed by "could" and the ideas of "ability" and "achievement" are not conveyed by "could" but by "was/were able to." To explain this point, they gave the following examples:

1. He could play the piano when he was five.
2. By acting quickly, we were able to save him from drowning (i.e. "We could, and did, save him").

4.1.3. Co-occurrence with verbs of perception
Modal verbs of ability can co-occur with verbs of perception such as kanjian "see" and tingdao "hear." This is again similar to the English language. Look at the following examples (cf. Leech & Svartvik 1975: 70; Palmer 1974: 193; Quirk et al. 1985: 203):

I can see someone through the window, but I can't hear what they're saying. (45)

I could feel vibrations. (46)

Can you smell the soap? (47)

In Chinese, when modal verbs are used, the ability of seeing or hearing is emphasized; when a verb of perception occurs alone, the result of seeing or hearing is stressed.

4.2. Inclination

Three degrees of inclination can be recognized in inclination: high, median and low, or insistence, intention and willingness, although the distinction here is not as sharp as that between the degrees of probability.
Inclination can be realized by modal verbs and adverbs.

4.2.1. Modal verbs
The four modal verbs yao, xiang, yuanyi and ken can indicate inclination.
Yao expresses insistence and is usually stressed, as in:

Ta yao qu.
he will go
He WILL go. (48)

Xiang indicates intention, as in:

Wo xiang shi yi   shi.
I   wish try one try
I'd like to have a try. (49)

Yuanyi and ken denote willingness, as in:

Ta yuanyi/ken bangzhu   ren.
he will/will   help   people
He is willing to help others. (50)

Ken is much more common than yuanyi when we express one's consent to do something at the request of someone else, as in:

Women qing ta   lai,   ta que bu ken lai.
we   invite him come he but not will come
We invited him, but he wouldn't come.   (51)

4.2.2. Adverbs

The adverbs yiding, pian and fei all indicate a high degree of inclination, as in:

Bu   gai   ta qu, ta que yiding/pian/fei   yao   qu.
not should he go   he but must/must/must want go
He was not supposed to go there but he insisted on going.
                                                         (52)

These adverbs often co-occur with the modal verb yao, as in (52), in the case of which the adverbs and the modal verb reinforce each other.

A perverse behavior can be expressed by these adverbs, too, as in:

Waimian xia   yu, ni   weishenme yiding/pian/fei yao   wang   wai   pao?
outside   drop rain you   why   must/must/must want   to   outside run
It's raining. Why must you go out now?   (53)

Yiding has a negative form: bu yiding, which can express inclination, too, as in:

Tamen yao   wo qu, wo ziji dao bu   yiding xiang qu.
they   want me go I   self but not   must want go
They want me to go there but I am not really keen on it.   (54)

Pian and fei have no negative forms: *bu pian, *bu fei. To indicate that one insists on not doing something, the form yiding/pian/fei + bu + V can be used, as in:

Wo yiding/pian/fei   bu   qu.
I   must/must/must   not go
I won't go there.   (55)

4.3. Obligation

Three degrees of value can also be distinguished in the notion of obligation: high, median and low, or compulsion, expectation and permission. All these meanings are typically realized by modal verbs. Sometimes they are expressed by other word classes.

4.3.1. Modal verbs

Compulsion is often expressed by the modals yao, bixu and dei, as in:

Women yao/bixu/dei   huxiang   bangzhu.
we   must/must/must   each-other   help
We must help each other.   (56)

Of the three modals, dei is the most colloquial form.

Expectation can be indicated by the modal verbs yinggai, yingdang and gai, as in:

Ta bing le,   women yinggai/yingdang/gai   qu kankan.
he ill   m-p   we   should/should/should   go   see
He's ill. We should go and see him.   (57)

Permission can be realized by keyi, xu, zhun and de. With keyi, it is always the Actor who is given the permission, as in:

Ni   yi   ci   keyi   jie   liang ben shu.
you one time may borrow two cl. book
You can borrow two books each time.   (58)

When xu is used, as in (59) there can be ambiguities in terms of the giver and receiver of the permission:

Ta   xu   bu   xu   qu?
he allow not allow go
Can he go? or
Does he allow (us or someone else) to go?   (59)

In the second interpretation, xu should be analyzed as a full verb and the omitted receiver of the permission is understood from the context.

De is always used in its negative form to indicate prohibition, as in:

Bu   de   suidi   tutan.
not can everywhere spit
No spitting.   (60)

Here de can be replaced by xu or zhun.

4.3.2. Alternative forms

Full verbs, such as yaoqiu "require," qiangpo "compel," rang "let" and yunxu "permit," and nouns such as yiwu "duty," zeren "responsibility" and xuke "permission" can also convey obligation, as in:

Ta yaoqiu women jintian wancheng renwu.
he require us   today   finish   task
He requires us to finish the task today.   (61)

Shui rang ni   jinlai de?
who let   you enter m-p
Who let you in?   (62)

Zhichi   disan shijie shi womende yiwu.
support third world be   our   duty
It is our duty to support the third world.   (63)

Weijing   xuke,   bu de   runei.
without permission not can enter
No admission without permission.   (64)

4.3.3. Co-occurrence of modal verbs and alternative forms

Modal verbs and alternative forms that also denote obligation can co-occur:

Ni dei   rang wo kan yi   kan.
you must let   me see one see
You must let me have a look.   (65)

Ni bu yinggai qiangpo ta   zheyang zuo.
you not should compel him   this   do
You shouldn't force him to do it.   (66)

4.4. Modulation and Negation

Negative modulation is typically realized by the negative marker bu plus modal verbs (e.g. bu hui "cannot, be unable to" as in (67), bu ken "won't, be unwilling to" as in (68) and bu yinggai "shouldn't, be not supposed to" as in (69):

Wo bu hui kaiche.
I   not can drive
I can't drive.   (67)

Ta <u>bu ken</u> lai.
he not will come
He won't come. (68)

Ni <u>bu yinggai</u> zai zher chouyan.
you not should in here smoke
You shouldn't smoke in here. (69)

Example (70) below is an example of negative modulation followed by a negative process:

Ni <u>bu yinggai</u> <u>bu lai</u> kai hui.
you not should not come hold meeting
You shouldn't have failed to attend the meeting. (70)

Note that the negative form of <u>bixu</u> "must" is <u>bubi</u> "needn't," not
*<u>bu bixu</u>. When <u>bixu</u> is negated, <u>xu</u> is dropped out. To avoid confusion and misunderstanding, it might be necessary here to point out that the <u>xu</u> in <u>bixu</u> and the <u>xu</u> that expresses permission are two different Chinese characters with different meanings.

4.5. Modulation and Time Reference

Modal verbs of inclination and obligation are inherently future oriented. There is no point of saying that one is willing, allowed or required to do what has already been done.

Modal verbs of ability, however, may refer to the past and the present as well as the future, although they do not have tense forms:

Wo nashihou yi tian <u>neng</u> zou liushi li.
I then one day can walk sixty li
At that time I could walk twenty miles a day. (71)

Ni <u>hui</u> shuo eyu ma?
you can speak Russian m-p
Can you speak Russian? (72)

Dao nashi ni jiu <u>keyi</u> zhaodao gongzuo le.
to then you then can find job m-p
By then you'll be able to find a job. (73)

As we can see from these examples, times of past, present and future are often expressed by adverbs (e.g. <u>nashihou</u> "then") and by prepositional phrases (e.g. <u>dao nashi</u> "by then").

4.6. Modulation and Voice

Only compulsion and permission can be expressed by a passive structure. For example:

Ta beipo likai le jia.
he compelled leave a-p home
He was forced to leave home.   (74)

Ta bei pizhun chuguo le.
he m-p permitted go-abroad m-p
He is permitted to go abroad.   (75)

The fact that only compulsion and permission can be expressed by means of a passive is again similar to English. Halliday (1970: 339–340, 345, 351) made the distinction between "active" and "passive" modulation. By "active" modulation, he meant ability and inclination, in which the modulation "relates to and is intrinsic to the actor." By "passive" modulation, he meant compulsion and permission, in which the modulation "likewise relates to the actor, but is extrinsic." The following examples are all taken from him (1970: 339, 341):

Active type:
    Jones will/is willing to tell you
    Jones can/is able to tell you
Passive type:
    you may/can/are allowed to tell
    you should/ought to/are supposed to tell
    you must/are required to tell

The distinction between intrinsic and extrinsic as well as that between active type and passive type made by Halliday is applicable in the analysis of the Chinese modulation.

4.7. Networks of Modality and Modulation

From my discussion above, the networks of modality and modulation in Chinese can be presented in Figure 5.5:

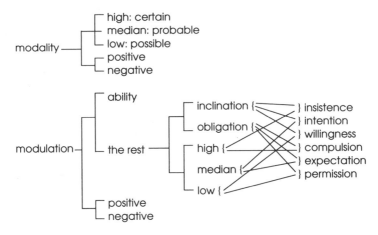

Figure 5.5.   Networks of modality and modulation

5. COMPARISONS BETWEEN CHINESE
AND ENGLISH

5.1. Similarities

The notions of modality and modulation are present in both Chinese and English. Verbal interaction in the two languages falls into two major categories: exchange of information and exchange of goods and services. In a clause of each of these exchanges, Chinese and English speakers alike may select one of the categories of polarity (i.e. "it is so/it isn't so" in the information type (proposition) or "do it/don't do it" in the goods and services type (proposal)). They may also select an intermediate degree (i.e. probability "maybe yes/maybe no" in the information type, and inclination "want to do it" or obligation "is wanted to do it" in the goods and services type).

The system networks of modality and modulation in Chinese and in English share the following features:

1. There is a continuum of value in the notions of probability, inclination and obligation in both languages;
2. Ability has no such continuum in either language;

The realization of modality and modulation also have something in common:

1. The meanings of "virtually certain" and "possible" under modality and all the meanings under modulation can be realized by modal verbs in both languages;
2. The meanings of "certain," "virtually certain" and "probable" under modality can be expressed by full verbs and adverbs in both languages;
3. The meanings of ability, inclination, obligation and probability can be realized by full verbs in both languages;
4. Modal verbs of ability do not co-occur with alternative forms in either language;
5. The elements of modulation can co-occur, in which case these elements are cumulative in meaning (e.g. the co-occurrence of compulsion and permission in the Chinese sentence Yiding dei rang ta chuqu and its English translation "He must be allowed to go out");
6. Proposals to be carried out can be realized by the structure "modal verb + V" in both languages (e.g. the Chinese sentence Ni yinggai xia gongfu and its English translation "You should work hard").

Some of the similarities mentioned above is shown in Figure 5.6.

Similarities can also be found between English and Chinese in terms of time reference:

1. Modal verbs of modality all refer to the speaker-now. The thesis with which they combine, however, can refer to any time;
2. When modulation is conveyed by modal verbs, the time to which the modulation is assigned is normally simultaneous to the time the speaker makes his comment on one's ability or obligation. The oblique English modals "would," "could," etc. can also function as sequent or tentative, but they do occasionally refer to earlier time.

5.2. Differences

The differences between English and Chinese can be summarized as follows:

1. All English modal verbs except "shall" can express both modality and modulation. Among the Chinese modal

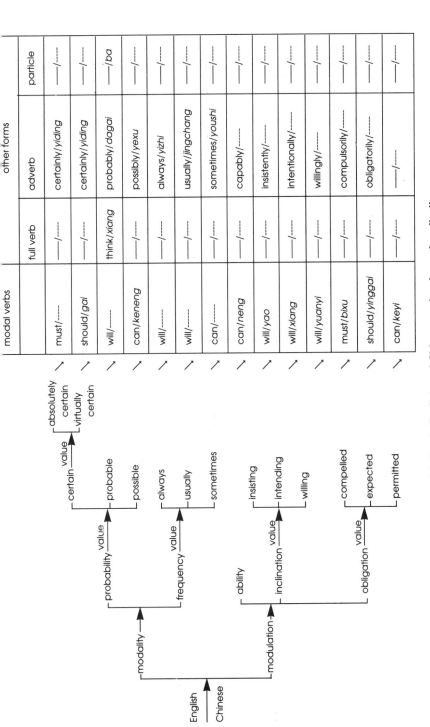

Figure 5.6. Comparisons of modality and modulation in English and Chinese: networks and realization

(Note: it can be seen from Figure 5.6 that the notion of frequency is not realized by modal verbs but by adverbs: yizhi "always," jingchang "usually" and youshi "sometimes." This can help to explain why frequency is not considered part of modality in Chinese.)

verbs, however, there are only a few that can be used for both modality and modulation. The following figure will illustrate the correspondence between English modals and Chinese modals, which, I hope, will be of some help to those who are interested in contrastive linguistics.

Figure 5.7. Correspondence between English and Chinese modals

2. Modal verbs in English, unlike those in Chinese, cannot occur in succession: *should can, *may must;

3. Modal verbs in English, unlike those in Chinese, can co-occur with adverbs of probability as in "Perhaps that might have been my wife" and "Probably that will be my wife";

4. In English the negative marker "not" always come after modal verbs: can't or cannot, but not *not can; in Chinese the negative marker bu normally precedes modal verbs (e.g. bu hui, bu yinggai);

5. In Chinese, probability can be expressed by the mood particle ba. In English, there is no such thing as mood particles.

The meaning indicated by b̲a̲ in Chinese can be expressed by tags in English, as in "You will do it, won't you" and "He can't come, can he."

6. Frequency can be considered part of English modality but not part of Chinese modality.

REFERENCES

Chao, Y.R. (1968) *A Grammar of Spoken Chinese.* Berkeley: University of California Press.

Halliday, M.A.K. (1970) Functional Diversity in Language, as seen from a consideration of modality and mood in English, in *Foundations of Language* 6(3), 322–361.

Halliday, M.A.K. (1985) *An Introduction to Functional Grammar.* London: Edward Arnold.

Leech, G. & Svartvik, J. (1975) *A Communicative Grammar of English.* London: Longman.

Leech, G. & Coates, J. (1979) Semantic Indeterminacy and the Modals, in *Studies in English Linguistics* (edited by Sidney Greenbaum et al.), London: Longman.

Li, C.N. & Thompson, S.A. (1981) *Mandarin Chinese,* Berkeley, CA: University of California Press.

Lu Shuxiang (1980) *Xiandai Hanyu Babai Ci,* Beijing: Commercial Press.

Lu Shuxiang (1982) *Zhongguo Wenfa Yaolue,* Beijing: Commercial Press.

Lyons, J. (1977) *Semantics,* 2, London: Cambridge University Press.

Palmer, F.R. (1974) *The English Verb,* London: Longman.

Palmer, F.R. (1979) Can, Will and Actuality, in *Studies in English Linguistics* (edited by Sidney Greenbaum et al.), London: Longman.

Quirk, R., Greenbaum, S., Leech, G. & Svartvik, J. (1985) *A Comprehensive Grammar of the English Language,* London: Longman.

Wang Li (1959) *Zhongguo Yufa Lilun,* Shanghai: Commercial Press, China.

Zhu Yongsheng (1984) *Modality and Modulation in English and Chinese* (unpublished MA(Hons) thesis), Fisher Library: University of Sydney.

6

Amplification as a Grammatical Prosody: Attitudinal Modification in the Nominal Group

Cate Poynton

Faculty of Humanities & Social Sciences
University of Western Sydney, Nepean

> 'That,' said her spouse, 'is a lie.'
> 'It's the truth,' said she.
> 'It's a dirty rotten stinking lousy bloody low filthy two-faced lie,' he amplified.
>
> —Criena Rohan (1963), *Down by the Dockside.*

1. INTRODUCTION

This paper is concerned with attitudinal nominal groups, that is, nominals that are strongly 'expressive' rather than referential in orientation. The data from which the detailed descriptions are drawn were collected for a study of grammatical resources for vocation in Australian English (Poynton 1990a, forthcoming). Much of this material came from spoken sources, with a certain amount being drawn from contemporary Australian literary material (fiction and drama) employing colloquial spoken English. The data are therefore very much spoken in orientation and strongly "expressive" or attitudinal in character, these two features together perhaps explaining the absence of previous detailed description of the phenomena under discussion. Although the bulk of the data is attested only in Australian English, some examples are drawn from British data (such as Mühlhäusler 1983) and a range of evidence exists to suggest that the resources described below are not peculiar to Australian English, though some aspects of their usage may be.

Many vocatives are realized as first names or as other simple nominals consisting of head only, such as family titles (*Mum, Granpa. . .*), occupational categories (*nurse, driver. . .*), endearments (*dear, love, sweetheart. . .*) or insults (*idiot, wog, dickhead. . .*). More elaborated forms of both endearment/compliment and insult are common, however, and it is these that form the basis for this paper. Vocatives such as *you stupid bloody idiot* and *you precious itsy-bitsy little darling thing* display iterative (and other) features that need to be accounted for in the structure potential of the nominal group. The extent to which one can simply extrapolate from this data to attitudinal nominal groups in general is unclear, however. There are preliminary indications that attitudinal vocatives might be more elaborate, employing more iteration, than other attitudinal nominals. A separate study would need to be undertaken to clarify this and to explore the frequency of variously iterated structures in different contexts. A study of the material explored here has considerable value in itself, however, in providing an insight into a kind of meaning, and the resources available for realizing it, that has rarely been touched on in the grammatical literature (but see Roger Wescott's work on slang (e.g. Wescott 1976) for a notable exception).

The paper is both descriptive and theoretical, as it explores the implications of the iterative structures described at nominal group rank for an understanding of the register category tenor and ultimately for an understanding of the interrelations of the three generalized functions of language, or metafunctions, which underpin Halliday's grammatical work on English (Halliday & Hasan 1985, Halliday 1994). The paper speaks from both 'inside' systemic linguistics, especially as it has been articulated by Michael Halliday and elaborated by J.R. Martin and his students (of whom I was one) at the University of Sydney in the 1980s, but also takes up a position of interrogation with respect to aspects of that framework. In particular, the paper problematizes aspects of Halliday's account of the interpersonal, both its earlier characterization as the "intruder" function (1979: 60) and its more recent focus on social relations (the 'inter-'), with its relative inattention to the self or subject (the '-personal'). Current feminist/poststructuralist work on 'positioning'—the inevitable nexus of power/knowledge (Foucault 1980)—renders both such conceptions problematic.

Vocation is a site that forces attention to speaking subjects, to their respective positionings (including ways of representing each other) and to their investments in those positionings. The existence, and to some degree the extent, of those investments is manifested most clearly through the phenomenon of amplification as an expressive resource—ways of 'speaking louder,' which include a range of phonological features, together with forms of iteration and intensification at all grammatical ranks from morpheme to clause. Amplification was identified as the mode of realization of the affect dimension of the register or contextual category tenor (Poynton 1985, 1990a, forthcoming), the dimension concerned with the articulation of what is variously referred to as attitude, expression, feeling or emotion. This kind of meaning is conceived of here as both personal (experienced, often with considerable intensity, by the individual) but also as necessarily social (articulable as meaning because of shared systems of meanings and values).

Amplified nominal group structures as non-name terms of address seem to work by backgrounding representational issues and foregrounding attitudinal ones. Issues of representation are never entirely nullified, however, by the force of the attitudinal component. As Mary Douglas (1975) pointed out with respect to insults, their representational focus is profoundly revealing of cultural values. To take one example from the English of current address, the vocabulary of abuse among men that derogates other males by identifying them with either women (*you girl*) or with female sexual parts (*you cunt*) has to be read not simply as insult but as a signifier of the widespread misogyny of English-speaking cultures that has been the focus of feminist critique from the 1970s onward (see Greer 1970, Stanley 1977, Summers 1994).

The paper will proceed with, first, a more elaborated account of amplification at both phonological and lexico-grammatical strata, then with the specific data for attitudinal nominal group vocatives. The conclusion will return to Halliday's work on the structural differentiation of grammatical systems realizing the experiential, interpersonal and textual metafunctions, to (briefly) problematize their conventional structuralist conceptualization.

2. AMPLIFICATION AS A MODE OF REALIZATION OF ATTITUDE

The preliminary identification of the phenomenon of amplification emerged from the analysis of address forms involving iteration at two ranks: at word rank, iteration of diminutive suffixes in names (producing iterated forms such as *Suzikins* and *Mikeypoodles*, using the suffixes [y], [kin], [poo], [Dle] and [s] in predictable combinations and ordering (Poynton 1990a, forthcoming)); at nominal group rank, iteration of Epithet (as in the example cited above: *you precious itsy-bitsy little darling thing* and the Criena Rohan prefatory quote).

The phenomenon also occurs at clause rank in clause sequences such as:

We won, we won!
We won! We beat them! We thrashed them!

In the first example, the amplification involves iteration of the same item—the whole clause. In the second example, the lexical verb is amplified by what I have called reiteration: the use of a formally distinct but functionally equivalent item, in this case increasingly amplified forms of the lexical verb. It is this form of iteration that is used in multiply suffixed diminutive forms of names.

As the Criena Rohan quote indicates, some speakers are aware of the amplificatory effect of iterated Epithet, the issue that will be pursued in the next section. The linguistic forms of amplification of which speakers tend to be most aware, however, are lexical and phonological. Lexical manifestations include:

- swearwords, which function as intensifiers either of Epithet or of Thing and have varying taboo weightings (Taylor 1976): compare the weight of *damn, bloody* and *fucking*. There is some evidence of restrictions of distribution of swearwords related to the positive or negative orientation of the nominal group. (One should not assume, however, that the use of negatively oriented lexis always means negative attitude. The most commonly noted use of apparently negative forms to convey positive attitude is among males, where *you bloody mongrel* can be a term of affection in the right context and said in the right way. This inversion phenomenon is widely found within marginalized groups with some analysis of their marginality, where the use of what, by an outsider, would be a derogatory term of reference, functions as a solidary marker.

Thus some teenage groups of girls (and some feminists) address each other as *bitch*, blacks in the U.S. can address each other as *nigger*, gays can address each other as *poof* or *fag*);
- various other forms of overt intensification, including *very, really, total(ly), utter(ly), absolute(ly), complete(ly)*. These can be attached (in appropriate form) to either Epithet or Thing (*really nice, utterly charming, complete idiot*), and can occur iteratively (*really really great, completely and totally devastating*);
- purely attitudinal Epithets, such as *fantastic* and *awful*, which are understood to speak with various degrees of "loudness" of attitudinal or expressive meaning; and
- lexical items combining varying degrees of attitudinal meaning with experiential meaning, typically nouns or lexical verbs (*mob* compared with *crowd*, *adore* compared with *love*). Speakers are often less aware of the attitudinal loading of these, reading them as statements of fact rather than attitudinal representations.

Phonological manifestations of amplification include amplified forms of speech rate, pitch range and amplitude, together with manipulations of speech sounds including flattening-out usual stress and rhythm patterns, lengthening of speech sounds (especially vowels) and repetitions such as alliteration and assonance. Behind these phonological realizations lie the bodily forms of amplification that commonly accompany the linguistic realizations, involving a range of kinds of physical behavior including facial expression, gesture, body stance, proxemic behavior, rate of movement.

The 'reading' of such phenomena is complex, bedevilled by assumptions about both 'naturalness' and 'normativity.' This is especially true of gendered readings, where what may be read as 'natural' for women (such as the extent of pitch range) is also read as non-normative, as involving an inbuilt amplification (see Sally McConnell-Ginet's 1983 paper on gender and intonation, which suggests that the greater pitch variability of women's speech is often read in terms of emotional volatility and instability). The problem is that all meaningful options involving phonological and bodily amplification are culturally produced, are learned—though this is by no means generally recognized. In particular, such learnings are profoundly gendered. In what follows, no attempt has been made to explore who is understood to be using what forms of amplification, but such empirical work clearly needs to be done in order to understand amplification as a socio-cultural, not simply a linguistic, phenomenon.

3. ATTITUDINAL MODIFICATION: PROSODIC SCOPE AND REALIZATION AS STRUCTURE

This section presents a descriptive account of the resources for amplification available in the English nominal group. In dealing with this terrain, attention needs to be drawn to two interconnected issues: the prosodic way in which attitudinal meaning actually works and the structural (i.e. syntagmatic) aspects of the realization of amplification that is realized at specific points in the structure of the nominal group. This is precisely parallel to the way in which modality, an interpersonal phenomenon at clause rank, is realized through both local amplification and discontinuous iterative realization throughout the clause, with the locations of individual realizations structurally identifiable: Not all places are equally available for insertion of a modal. Attitude in the nominal group functions prosodically, as Halliday claimed for all interpersonal systems (Halliday 1979, 1994), but its realizations must be located discontinuously, however cumulative their effects may be.

With respect to the scope of attitudinal prosody, attitudinal meanings are extraordinarily powerful, constituting force fields, which in effect run over the top of experiential meanings. I have previously commented on this phenomenon in relation to gender, in terms of the particular example of a film review's characterization of the two central characters in the film *Cal* as *the unemployed 19-year-old Cal* and *a pretty Catholic librarian:*

> There is a curious effect in the second [nominal] group whereby the very presence of the word *pretty* leaches out some of the experiential force of *Catholic* (important in that the film in which these two are characters is set in contemporary Northern Ireland) and *librarian* (a job for which a relatively high level of education is required and which consequently has a certain amount of prestige attached to it). It is hard to take seriously a *Catholic librarian* who is *pretty*—a *19-year-old Catholic librarian* would be someone a little more substantial. Age is a significant diminisher of potency but gender is more powerful, it would seem.

The linguistic status of *pretty* in the example cited would seem to be the key to understanding what is going on: it is attitudinal as well as referential but probably more strongly the former, i.e. it is interpersonal. Interpersonal meanings habitually spread themselves through linguistic structures, and what seems to be happening here is that the

interpersonal force of the word, bolstered by ideological considerations, is spreading into the more experientially oriented part of the
group.   (Poynton 1985: 61–2)

Part of my purpose in quoting this is to make the point that in
talking about attitude, one is not simply talking about the transient
and purely personal, as is implied by both Halliday's term "speaker's
subjective attitude" concerning attitudinal Epithets (1994: 184) and
Quirk et al's reference to "emotive, evaluative, or subjective adjectives" (1985: 1339). Even when representing events such as hitting
your thumb instead of the nail or missing the bus when it's raining
and you haven't got an umbrella, the attitude that may be manifested and amplified is not merely personal because the meanings
being activated are not (and cannot be) purely personal. Structures
of feeling are just as much culturally produced as are linguistic
structures.

Nevertheless, there are (linguistic) structural regularities to be
observed. Halliday (1994) observes that attitudinal Epithets (e.g.
splendid, silly, fantastic) tend to precede non-attitudinal (experiential) ones within nominal groups (e.g. *splendid old, nasty green*).
(Halliday 1994: 184. Cf. Quirk et al. 1985: 1339 for the same observation cast in slightly different terms). It may be that the first realization of attitude as initial Epithet has particular significance (it is
commonly, after all, the first lexical item of the structure), functioning rather like a key signature announcing the tonality of the music
it precedes. An initial attitudinal Epithet could be seen as announcing the relevant attitudinal 'key' whose scope is, initially, the whole
nominal group, spreading it over the rest of the group (and ultimately the utterance), having the effect of foregrounding the attitu-
dinally salient information and 'backgrounding' experiential content.

Beyond this initial observation about Epithet sequence, Halliday
does not address the question of further sub-categories of Epithet.
There are various accounts of this issue, in the form of discussions
of adjective sequence in nominal groups (e.g. Fries 1970, Sussex
1974, Dixon 1977, Bache 1978), but almost all of them concentrate
exclusively on experientially oriented meanings and, even when potentially attitudinal items are included, their iterative potential and
its amplificatory effect are not discussed. Quirk et al. (1985: 1337–
41) provide the most satisfactory account: their grammar is eclectic, they are aware of attitude, they take it seriously in relation
to modifier sequencing and, perhaps most importantly, their work
is corpus-based. Their schema for the sub-classification of mod-

ifiers in nominal groups certainly recognizes that iteration of the function Epithet occurs, but does not allow for the potential for iteration of certain sub-categories of Epithet involving particular kinds of lexical choices: their description will not adequately account for a moderately amplified vocative such as *you filthy lousy rotten bastard.*

The following section will detail an amount of the vocative data, identifying both possible sequences of Epithet sub-categories and lexical sets of varying sizes which can iterate within sub-categories, as a first step toward a formal statement of the structure potential of attitudinal nominal groups.

4. EPITHET SUB-CATEGORIES AND ITERATION

The basic structure of the attitudinal nominal group can be specified as:

$$D \wedge N \wedge E[a \wedge ex] \wedge C \wedge T \wedge Q$$

where a = attitudinal Epithet, and ex = experiential or non-attitudinal Epithet. The attitudinal prosody does seem to spread out to encompass non-attitudinals (as discussed above), so that once Ea has been chosen all subsequent Epithets, Thing (and probably also Classifier and Qualifier) come within the scope of that attitudinal prosody, making the structure in effect:

$$D \wedge N \wedge Ea \wedge Ca \wedge Ta \wedge Qa \text{ (where a = attitudinal).}$$

Before embarking on the substance of this section, a detailed description of Epithet sub-categories distinguished in the corpus of vocatives, I will comment briefly on the functional category Qualifier, which will not be further examined in this paper. Qualifiers are rare in vocative nominal groups, though not necessarily in other attitudinal nominals.

The potential for Classifier, as for Epithet, would seem to differ somewhat depending on whether the orientation of the group as a whole is positive or negative, negative structures having a slightly larger set of categories. For positive vocatives, there seems to be a small set of items realizing Classifier function, including *darling, angel, baby,* and selection is potentially iterative. Thus a form like *Mummy's precious darling angel baby boy* is possible though not attested. There seem to be two categories of Classifier in negative vocatives: a provenance category (after Quirk et al.), which includes usually derogatory terms referring to an addressee's race or place of origin (e.g. *wog* (person of Mediterranean origin), *abo* or *boong* (Aboriginal Australian), *Pom* (person of English origin)), and a small more general abusive set, selection within which is iterative, including such items as *mug, mongrel, scumbag. Mug copper* is attested and forms like *mongrel scumbag lowlife* seem feasible.

Returning to the major focus on Epithet, a number of sub-categories utilized in attitudinal nominal groups will be identified. Within each sub-category, a number of potentially iterable lexical sets are identifiable. For example, SIZE is an identifiable Epithet sub-category used iteratively in attitudinal nominal groups such as *you darling itsy-bitsy little thing* and *you great big silly.* The categories and their deployment (as positively or negatively oriented) will be identified and commented on below, and the section will conclude with a more detailed re-statement of structure potential for attitudinal nominal groups. The major Epithet sub-categories utilized in attitudinal nominal groups, in the order in which they may appear, are as follows:

- evaluative
- experiential/attitudinal (=exp/att)
- size
- age
- color
- participial

A number of specific observations will be made about each of these Epithet sub-categories.

4.1. Evaluative Epithet

Lexical realizations tend to occur in sets belonging to a small range of semantic domains with strong evaluative loading in English-speaking cultures. These include ethical/moral value, attractiveness, stupidity. Relevant lexis includes:

- *good*
- *dear/darling/sweet/cute*
- *pretty/lovely/handsome/beautiful/gorgeous*
- *precious/wonderful/scrumptious*
- *naughty/bad/wicked*

- *dirty/filthy/rotten/lousy/stinking*
- *horrible/nasty/awful/revolting*
- *silly/dumb/stupid*

Selection within this category is iterative, two or three choices constituting a moderate degree of amplification and four or five a high degree. There are three kinds of iteration:

- repetition of the same item (e.g. *you pretty pretty/silly silly thing*);
- iteration within a semantic field (e.g. *you dear darling/ handsome gorgeous/bad wicked/nasty horrible thing*);
- iteration across semantic fields (e.g. *you gorgeous darling cute little thing, you rotten horrible thing*).

There seem to be some limits on iterative combinations across domains, but there is insufficient data to be able to specify these adequately at the moment.

Many of the items listed here can be used in other contexts/structures with predominantly experiential meaning, though words like *beautiful* may be regarded as involving a degree of speaker judgment even when a claim is being made for the 'truth' of that judgment. When used as evaluative Epithets, especially if iterated, such items retain little or no experiential force.

4.2. Experiential/Attitudinal Epithet

This sub-category is realized in a small set of negatively oriented lexical items apparently referring to negatively valued aspects of experience or behavior: *ugly, lazy, selfish, fat, messy.* Note that participial forms such as *whinging* and *snivelling* (which otherwise occur as the final Participial Epithet sub-category) can occur in this position.

Items realizing this sub-category clearly have attitudinal force but are much more overtly experiential in meaning than items in the evaluative sub-category. Particular choices made generally have some relation to features of the appearance or behavior of the addressee: *ugly* to anyone not stunningly beautiful, *skinny* to the slim or even average-sized, *fat* to anyone not slim, *messy* to anyone not maintaining the speaker's standards of tidiness, *selfish* to anyone not doing what the speaker wants.

4.3. Size Epithet

This sub-category consists of two iterable lexical sets: *little/tiny/ weeny/itty-bitty (itsy-bitsy)/teensy-(weensy)* and *big/great*. Items within either sub-set are iterative (e.g. *you little tiny itty-bitty thing, you great big lump*) but there is no iteration across sub-sets.

The *little* set consists effectively of lexicalized diminutives, with an inherently positive orientation, and the *big* set lexicalized augmentatives, usually with some degree of negative orientation, at least in my data (e.g. *great lump, big boofhead*). Note, however, that 'bigness' is highly valued for boys, and to a considerable extent for all children (*When I'm big . . .* being the fervent aspiration of most children), so that positively oriented uses of *big/great* almost certainly occur in vocatives.

Big words, despite their overt meaning of largeness, do not necessarily amplify to a greater extent than other attitudinal items, though one might have expected some semantic consonance between experiential largeness and attitudinal amplification. They can have a mitigating effect: compare *big boofhead* or *great big silly* with *stupid fool*, where the selection of Epithet and Thing from the same semantic field has a stronger amplifying effect than the use of even iterated *big* words.

The word *little* itself can be used in negatively loaded vocatives, but not any of the more overtly diminutive alternatives that are available in positively oriented attitudinal vocatives. This seems consistent with a reading of *little* forms as diminutives (i.e. inherently positively oriented). *Great* and *big* are both available for negatively loaded vocatives and can be used iteratively, which is what one would expect from their basically augmentative function.

4.4. Age Epithet

This sub-category is realized basically in two lexical items: *young* and *old*. In negatively loaded vocatives, (re)iterated sequences such as *geriatric old fool* can occur. No instance of such an amplified choice as *infantile* with *young* (parallelling *geriatric* with *old*) is attested and seems unlikely, since *young* does not seem to be used as negatively as *old*.

Young seems to occur more frequently as sole Epithet (e.g. *you young idiot*) than as part of an Epithet sequence (e.g. *you dear sweet young thing*, though *you stupid young fool* from an older to a younger driver certainly occurs), while *old* appears regularly in Epithet sequences (e.g. *you lousy old Pommy bastard*).

4.5. Color Epithet

The vocative examples in my data all have racial connotations (*black, brown, yellow*) so could be regarded as Classifiers, except that further Epithets can follow them (e.g. *you black bludging bastard* (*bludging black bastard* is also possible)). Dabke (1977: 82) notes the use of *white* in pejorative address to a football umpire (*you white mongrel*), the reference being not to skin color but to identifying clothing. While it may be the case that the racially pejorative use of *white* by non-white speakers was not available in the 1970s in Australia, it is certainly not the case now, particularly among politicized Aboriginal people for whom *whitey* is a readily available pejorative term of both address and reference for Australians of European origin.

4.6. Participial Epithet

Most of the realizations attested are present participles: positively oriented realizations include *smiling, laughing, bouncing, smooching* and negatively oriented ones *bludging, whinging, whining, snivelling, loafing, sticky-beaking*. Note the use in affectionate vocatives of items such as *blue-eyed* and *curly-headed*, items analogous in form to past participles. Realizations are clearly experiential but the meanings involved are those that have positive value in English-speaking cultures (i.e. are also attitudinal). The positively oriented items included in the list above would mostly be used in address to babies or small children.

Returning finally to the question of specification of the structure potential for attitudinal nominal groups, a double description is required because the potential differs for negatively oriented compared with positively oriented structures. The specific structure potentials for positively and negatively oriented attitudinal nominal groups can then be characterized separately as:

+ve	D N Eα	Cα	T	Qα
	eval^size^age^participial			
−ve	D N Eα	Cα	T	Qα
	eval^exp/att^size^age^color^participial	prov(a)^eval		

Key:

eval(uative): inherently attitudinal (e.g. *good, bad, sweet, horrible*);

exp/att: some experiential meaning retained, but strongly attitudinal (e.g. *filthy, miserable*);

size (small or large): implicitly attitudinal—effectively lexicalized diminutive or augmentative;

age (young or old): implicitly attitudinal;

color: used to people, refers to race (i.e. attitudinal);

participial: commonly combining attitudinal and experiential meanings.

Two questions remain to be asked: first, why these, and not other, particular Epithet sub-categories; second, why the potential for negatively oriented attitudinal nominal groups is more extensive than that for positively oriented structures (paralleled by the more extensive range of negative compared with positive lexis, which can function as head). In both cases, the answer would seem to revolve around subject positioning.

Beyond the entirely or largely evaluative categories, Epithet sub-categories would appear to draw on a set of fundamental categories for positioning people. Positively oriented vocatives are mostly addressed to children, particularly small children. Their function can be understood as primarily pedagogical: teaching a positive sense of identity for the child and teaching it cultural values and appropriate forms of behavior. It is not surprising, then, that size (small) and age (young) feature along with strongly attitudinal lexis, as ways of signalling the child's status in relation to the adult. This can be seen as a form of 'othering,' of putting the child in a separate (and subordinate) category to the one which the speaker sees themself as belonging. The cultural and psychic operation of diminutives is complex, however, particularly taking into account intimate adult usage of some of the same kinds of vocatives as are used to small children, including diminutives.

Negatively oriented vocatives are addressed to both children and others, who may or may not be intimates. They function to position others as impinging (by making demands, by their very presence) or as transgressing. The more extensive set of Epithet sub-categories would appear to extend the resources not only for identifying the source of the transgression (if there is one) but especially for othering the addressee, signalling impingement. The inclusion of the color Epithet sub-category is unsurprising, then, because race is one of the most fundamental othering systems in Western cultures. The Classifier category provenance, allowing othering in terms of ethnicity, is likewise unsurprising.

5. ATTITUDE AND THE MULTIPLE PRESENCE
OF THE SPEAKER

This detailed description of the structure potential of the attitudinal nominal group clearly bears out the relevance of the distinction Halliday (1979) makes between the characteristic prosodic or wave structure of clause rank realizations of the interpersonal metafunction, the compositional or particle structure characteristic of experiential meanings and the culminative or field structure associated with the textual metafunction. In addressing the structure of the nominal group, however, he does not see it as appropriate or necessary to differentiate structural strands as for the clause: "Although we can still recognize the same three components [ideational, interpersonal, textual], they are not represented in the form of separate whole structures, but rather as partial contributions to a single structural line" (Halliday 1994: 179).

The concluding section of the discussion of the nominal group makes it clear that "single structural line" is defined in terms of particulate (experiential) structure:

> The kind of meaning that is expressed in a particle-like manner is the experiential; it is this that gives us our sense of the building blocks of language. Since we are using particle theory (constituency) as the foundation of the present analysis—it tends to be conceptually and operationally simpler than models of wave or field—it is natural to represent the structure of the nominal group, in which the functional components are (in English) rather clearly defined, in straightforwardly experiential terms. (Halliday 1994: 190)

The greater conceptual and operational simplicity of constituency structure of which Halliday speaks has, of course, led in other models of language to a degree of privileging of the referential (or experiential) that has effectively obscured other structural principles simultaneously operative within language. I have argued elsewhere (Poynton 1990b) that such privileging is not, in fact, motivated simply by organizational features of language itself, but by a variety of factors, linguistic and ideological, which have as much to do with Western epistemology and political practice as with structural features of language. Two factors of particular importance have been the privileging of written at the expense of spoken language, and the privileging of rationality, the realm of reason and judgment, at the expense of the realm of feeling and emotion (Lloyd 1984).

There is a considerable degree of irony in the very body of work which, uniquely in linguistic theory, gives such a central place to the interpersonal in structural as well as semantic terms, orienting its description of the nominal group to experiential meaning and thus appearing to background the particular kinds of interpersonal meaning operative at this structural level. Issues around the status of the apparently emotional and even irrational would, on the face of it, seem relevant. The absence of overt attitude in discourse is widely taken to be an indication of 'objectivity' (i.e. the use of language to represent things as they are rather than how we see them). And note that it is the presence not the absence of attitude that is usually commented on: its absence is seen as the 'natural' state of language, the attitudinal constituting an added (unnatural?) feature.

But language does not function unproblematically to represent things as they are. The resources of all three metafunctions operate to construct representations (through the resources of transitivity), to order attention in relation to the elements of those constructions (through the resources of Theme/Rheme) and to articulate investments in those ordered representations (through the resources of modality/modulation and amplified structures of various kinds). Speakers, in other words, always articulate positions that are grounded in structures of feeling as well as institutional norms of representation—Foucault's power/knowledge nexus again.

The lines between the metafunctions, then, are not as clearcut as is implied in Halliday's account:

> If the ideational component is language as reflection (the speaker as observer of reality), and the interpersonal component is language as action (the speaker as intruder in reality), the textual component is language as relevance (the speaker as relating to the portion of reality that constitutes the speech situation, the context within which meanings are being exchanged).   (Halliday 1979: 60)

The same issue—the blurring of the lines between the metafunctions—is raised by pursuing the basic opposition, in the mood system, of indicative and imperative. Indicative clauses, realizing propositions, are by virtue of that fact fundamentally concerned with the question of (though not the content of) representations. The functional element Subject, part of the mood structure of the clause distinguishing indicative from imperative, can therefore be seen as functioning to insert the speaker, not into the speech situation itself (s/he is already there, of course), but into the representation being constructed, given that the grammatical Subject in everyday conversation is highly likely to be first person *I* (Halliday 1994: 44). Where it is not, in speech and particularly in writing, third person subjects create the illusion of objectivity about linguistic representations because of the absence of the representation of (not, of course, the absence of the actual speaking) *I*. The use of attitude, then, is only one kind of overt "intrusion" of the speaker into the speech event: s/he has always been there, constructing the representation in the first place and ordering attention with respect to its elements, thereby positioning the addressee very precisely in terms of how they should know, simultaneously with their interpersonal positioning with respect to how they should feel and act.

REFERENCES

Bache, C. (1978) *The Order of Premodifying Adjectives in Present-Day English.* (Odense University Studies in English, 3). Odense: University Press.

Dabke, R. (1977) Swearing and abusive language of Australian Rules Football spectators. *Talanya* 4: 76–90.

Dixon, R.M.W. (1977) Where have all the adjectives gone? *Studies in Language* 1: 19–80.

Douglas, M. (1975) Social and religious symbolism of the Lele. In *Implicit Meanings: essays in anthropology,* ed. Mary Douglas. London: Routledge & Kegan Paul. 9–25.

Fries, P.H. (1970) *Tagmeme Sequences in the English Noun Phrase.* Norman, Oklahoma: Summer Institute of Linguistics.

Foucault, M. (1980) *Power/Knowledge: selected interviews and other writings 1972–1977,* ed. Colin Gordon. Brighton: Harvester Press.

Greer, G. (1970) *The Female Eunuch.* London: Paladin.

Halliday, M.A.K. (1979) Modes of meaning and modes of expression: Types of grammatical structure, and their determination by different semantic functions. In *Function and Context in Linguistic Analysis,* ed. D.J. Allerton, Edward Carney & David Holdcroft. Cambridge: Cambridge University Press, 57–79.

Halliday, M.A.K. (1994) *An Introduction to Functional Grammar.* Second edition. London: Edward Arnold.

Halliday, M.A.K. & R. Hasan (1985) *Language, Context and Text: Aspects of language in a social-semiotic perspective.* Geelong, Victoria: Deakin University Press.

Lloyd, G. (1984) *The Man of Reason: "Male" and "female" in Western philosophy.* Minneapolis: University of Minnesota Press.

McConnell-Ginet, S. (1983) Intonation in a man's world. Revised version in *Language, Gender and Society,* eds. Barrie Thorne, Cheris Kramarae & Nancy Henley. Rowley, MA: Newbury House. 69–88. Originally published in *Signs: Journal of Women in Culture and Society* 3 (Spring 1978): 541–59.

Mühlhäusler, P. (1983) *Stinkiepoos, cuddles* and related matters. *Australian Journal of Linguistics* 3, 1: 75–91.

Poynton, C. (1985) *Language and Gender: making the difference.* Geelong, Victoria: Deakin University Press.

Poynton, C. (1990a) *Address and the Semiotics of Social Relations: A systemic–functional account of address forms and practices in Australian English.* PhD thesis, Linguistics Department, University of Sydney.

Poynton, C. (1990b) The privileging of representation and the marginalising of the interpersonal: A metaphor (and more) of contemporary gender relations. In *Feminine/Masculine and Representation,* eds. Terry Threadgold & Anne Cranny-Francis. Sydney: Allen & Unwin. 231–55.

Poynton, C. (forthcoming) *Language and Social Relations: A social semiotic model of tenor and its realization in address forms and practices.* Amsterdam: Benjamins. (Pragmatics and Beyond).

Quirk, R., S. Greenbaum, G. Leech & J. Svartvik (1985) *A Comprehensive Grammar of the English Language.* London: Longman.

Rohan, C. (1963/1984) *Down by the Dockside.* Ringwood, Victoria: Penguin Australia.

Stanley, J.P. (1977) Paradigmatic woman: The prostitute. In *Papers in Language Variation,* eds. David L. Shores & Carole P. Hines. Birmingham, Alabama: University of Alabama Press. 303–321.

Summers, A. (1994) *Damned Whores and God's Police.* Revised edition. Ringwood, Victoria: Penguin Australia.

Sussex, R. (1974) The deep structure of adjectives in noun phrases. *Journal of Linguistics* 10: 111–131.

Taylor, B. (1976) Towards a sociolinguistic analysis of 'swearing' and the language of abuse in Australian English. In *Australia Talks: Essays on the sociology of Australian immigrant and Aboriginal languages,* ed. Michael Clyne. Canberra: Australian National University. (Department of Linguistics, Research School of Pacific Studies). (Pacific Linguistics Series D–No. 23), 43–62.

Wescott, R. (1976) The phonology and morphology of American English slang. In *The Third LACUS Forum,* eds. Robert J. di Pietro & Edward L. Blansitt, Jr. Columbia, South Carolina: Hornbeam Press. 108–119.

C:
Experiential Meaning and Form

7

Transitivity in Tagalog: A Functional Interpretation of Case

JR Martin

Department of Linguistics
University of Sydney

1. INTRODUCTION

In this paper the idea that what are generally known as case relations (Halliday's participant roles) can be usefully approached from the point of view of clause rather than verb classes will be explored with respect to one major Philippine language: Tagalog. In addition, the paper will adopt Halliday's (1976; 1985) strategy of dividing clauses into three major classes (doing, sensing and being) and setting up case relations peculiar to each, rather than building up a general inventory of cases for the language as a whole. In these two respects, the model pursued differs from that assumed in case grammar (Fillmore 1968) and lexicase (Starosta 1988) and provides a complementary perspective to the work done within these frameworks by Ramos (1974) and De Guzman (1978) respectively.

The paper will begin with a discussion of cryptotypes and the role they play in transitivity analysis, focusing on the work of Whorf, Fillmore and Halliday. Then, in section 3, a number of issues arising from Ramos and De Guzman's work will be considered by way of introduction to the analysis undertaken here. Subsequently, a grammar of doing, sensing and being processes from a systemic functional perspective will be presented, drawing on Halliday's notions of process types and participant roles. (For further discussion of the relation between Hallidayan and other approaches to case relations see Martin (in press a). (For related work from a Hallidayan perspective on interpersonal and logical meaning in Tagalog, see Martin 1990, 1995.)

2. COVERT CATEGORIES

Tagalog, like other Philippine languages, is rather extravagant in terms of the amount of explicit morphology it devotes to signalling experiential and textual relationships among processes, participants and circumstances in clause structure. In (1) for example, the verbal prefix *na-* indicates experientially that the Topic[1] of the sentence is the participant being observed; at the same time the marker *ang* identifies this participant textually as Topic. The other two markers in the clause, *ng* and *sa* distinguish between the woman and the street as additional participant and circumstance respectively.

na-halata ng babae   ang boyfriend niya sa kalsada[2]
noticed   woman TM   her   street
"The woman noticed her boyfriend in the street."   (1)

This complex interaction of verbal affixes and markers is complicated by two factors. First, almost all of the participants and circumstances in a Tagalog clause are candidates for Topic (see Cena 1979 for a full review); and verbal affixes are used to distinguish among the different kinds of participant and circumstance that function as Topic. If we take the experiential structure of (1) for example, and vary it textually by making the woman rather than her boyfriend Topic, then the verbal affix has to change; in (2) *naka-* shows that the Topic is the observer, not the observed:

---

[1]Philippinists generally use the term *Topic* to refer to what systemicists would call Theme (following Schachter & Otanes 1972) and the term *focus* to refer to the THEME system organizing Topic choice (following Kerr 196). Throughout this paper the term Topic will be used in this way, and verbal affixes described as *focussing* on the Topic.

[2]The affixes that focus on the Topic will be underlined in all examples, and the *ang* marker will be labelled TM (Topic Marker). To simplify the presentation, all verbs will be presented in completed aspect, only common nouns will be used as participants and circumstances, and textual and interpersonal variations on clause structure will be avoided.

naka-halata[3] ang babae ng boyfriend niya sa kalsada
noticed   TM woman   her   street
"The woman noticed a boyfriend of hers[4] in the street."   (2)

The second complication is that the affixes used to identify the experiential role of the Topic differ from one clause class to another. If we switch from processes of perception as in (1) and (2) to processes of cognition as in (3) or processes of reaction as in (4), new types of affixation appear. In (3) the discontinuous *na-* . . . *-an* marks the Topic as the phenomenon understood; in (4) the discontinuous *ka.* . . . *-an*[5] signals that the Topic is the object of the woman's anger.

na-unawa-an ng babae   ang boyfriend niya
understood   woman TM   her
"The woman understood her boyfriend."   (3)

k-in-a-galit-an ng babae   ang boyfriend niya
was angry at   woman TM   her   (4)
"The woman was angry at her boyfriend."

To complete the picture, note what happens to the affixes if we focus on the woman instead of the boyfriend; *naka-* in (5) marks the Topic as the participant who understands, while *na-* in (6) shows that the Topic is the participant who reacts.

naka-unawa   ang babae ng boyfriend niya
was able to understand TM woman   her
"The woman was able to understand a boyfriend of hers."   (5)

na-galit   ang babae sa boyfriend niya
was angry at TM woman   her
"The woman was angry at her boyfriend."   (6)

Examples 1–6 illustrate the kind of problem analysts have faced when trying to sort out the interaction of affixes and markers in Philippine languages. If provisionally we refer to the role played by the woman in 1–6 as senser and the role of the boyfriend as phenomenon, then it would appear that:

---

[3]Along with the change in focus, the prefix *naka-* also introduces an abilitative/involuntary action meaning, which will be passed over here; see section 4.1 for discussion.

[4]The change in Topic also leads to a change in definiteness here; see Martin (1983) for discussion.

[5]*Ka-* itself surrounds the aspectual infix *-in-*.

1. both *naka-* and *na-* identify the Topic as senser.[6]
2. all of *na-, na-* . . . *-an* and *ka-* . . . *-an* identify the Topic as phenomenon.
3. both *ang* and *ng* are used to mark the senser.
4. all of *ang, ng* and *sa* are used to mark the phenomenon.[7]

In the face of these difficulties, linguists have in general adopted two sorts of descriptive strategy. One is to stick closely to the affixes and markers themselves, and list the different ways in which they are used. Bloomfield for example treats each of (7), (8) and (9) as *instrumental passives* with *i-* denoting "an object given forth, parted from, or used as an instrument or the person for whom" (1917: 248).

i-t-in-apon ng babae   ang basura
threw out   woman TM rubbish
"The woman threw out the rubbish."   (7)

i-p-in-utol ng babae   ang gunting
cut with   woman TM scissors
"The woman cut with the scissors."   (8)

i-b-in-ili ng beer ang lalaki
bought   TM man
"The man was bought some beer."   (9)

This approach contrasts with that of the cases grammarians who instead of listing the uses of affixes and markers set up cases and verb classes on a different level of abstraction from the affixes and markers themselves (eg. Ramos 1974). Ramos stressed the importance of identifying case "without regard to its means of expression. The reason for emphasis upon the relationship without regard to its means of expression comes from the fact that for Philippine lan-

---

[6]As noted, all examples are in completed aspect; prefixes beginning with *m-* in their aspectless form change *m-* to *n-* to mark completed aspect. These affixes will be cited in their aspectless forms except where specific examples are being discussed.

[7]As noted, only common nouns will be used as participants and circumstances in this paper. Human names have different markers: *si, ni* and *kay* corresponding to *ang, ng* and *sa* respectively; pronouns, which only refer to humans, come in *ang/ng/sa* forms, taking a marker only if circumstantial—for example, first person singular *ako, ko, sa akin* ("I/me/to me"); demonstratives also have distinct forms and do not appear with markers—for example, singular proximate *ito, nito, dito* ("this/this/this here").

guages, surface forms do not always reveal easily underlying case relations" (1974:19). And similarly for verb classes: "It is of interest as an aside to note that when the investigator initially posited semantic features for the verb, no thought was given to a one-to-one correspondence with surface representations" (1974:11).

Cases and verb features are then used to try and generalize across some of the interactions between affixes and markers. Ramos for example treats the rubbish as the Objective case in (7), the scissors as Instrumental in (8) and the man as Benefactive in (9). And the verbs themselves fall into different classes according to their effect on what is thrown out, cut or bought.

Case grammarians pursue their study within a general framework of universal grammar, as part of the search for a set of substantive universals (i.e. cases). Ramos, following Fillmore, treated cases as "universal, presumably innate concepts which identify certain types of judgements human beings are capable of making about events that are going on around them" (1974:7). Within this framework, the purpose of investigating case relations in Tagalog is apparently to test, and if necessary modify, proposals for the neurologically programmed set of cases underlying all human languages. De Guzman (1978:25) summed up this orientation as follows:

> Working on Fillmore's hypothesis that there exists a finite and universal set of case relations and Starosta's claim to a corresponding universal set of case forms and, consequently, to the necessity of accounting for the system of case expression to achieve explanatory adequacy (Starosta 1973b), we will identify the case relations which Tagalog distinguishes and, concomitantly, the system it adopts in expressing them.

In the event, both Ramos and De Guzman found Fillmore's proposals wanting as far as transitivity in Tagalog is concerned. Ramos (1974:23) for example adjusted Fillmore's objective case for Tagalog as follows:

> The objective case (O) is the most neutral case semantically. According to Fillmore (1968a:25) it is the case of anything representable by a noun whose role in the action or state is identified by the semantic interpretation of the verb, limited probably to things affected by the action or state identified by the verb. Where Fillmore limits the concept to inanimate objects, the objective case in Tagalog includes experiencer animate entities too.

But she stopped short of renovating the relevant set of substantive universals on the basis of Tagalog. De Guzman disagreed with

Ramos's interpretation at several points, again usually without taking the step of adjusting the finite and universal set of case relations. Her treatment of Locative was exceptional in this respect. She treated Ramos's Directional and Locative cases as indistinct because "it has been found that there are no discernible syntactic or semantic differences between the supposed [+DAT] and the [+LOC] actant" (De Guzman 1978:52). She cited as evidence the following factors:

1. The [+DAT] and [+LOC] are both marked by *sa*.
2. When Topic, the [+DAT] and [+LOC] are so signalled with the affix *-an*.

This she then pursued as a general claim about Directional and Locative cases in universal grammar (see also Starosta 1978; 1988).

Regardless, both Ramos and De Guzman concentrated on working out a set of case relations for Tagalog, leaving the implications of this language-specific set of cases for universal grammar unclear. This is hardly surprising given the difficulties inherent in motivating case relations at the degree of abstraction necessary for them to be considered universal. Ramos and De Guzman's proposals for Tagalog are themselves abstract enough that what counts as evidence is less than clear. Before proceeding further it is thus appropriate to look more closely at Fillmore's own argumentation as far as motivating cases is concerned.

Fillmore (1968:3), in introducing case grammar, made explicit reference to the work of Whorf, who was the first to stress the importance of categories lacking obvious morphemic realizations. Fillmore treated cases as *covert* categories (following Whorf; see especially 1956:89, 92, 165) with syntactic significance, which helps make it possible "to believe that at bottom all languages are essentially alike" (1968:3); and he is somewhat surprised that they led Whorf to the opposing relativistic position (see Martin (1988) for a Whorfian perspective on Tagalog grammar). But this is hardly surprising when one looks at the nature of Whorf's covert categories and the way in which he motivated them in terms of their grammatical significance (their *reactances*). Whorf was what we would now call a functional grammarian: Covert categories were conceived as part of the grammar of a language and justified in terms of as many reactances as possible. And Whorf considered linguistics as essentially a quest for meaning, with the analysis of covert categories playing a key role in this endeavor (1956:73).

Whorf characterized covert categories and their realization as follows:

A covert category is marked, whether morphemically or by sentence pattern, only in certain types of sentence and not in every sentence in which a word or element belonging to the category occurs. The class membership of the word is not apparent until there is a question of using it or referring to it in one of these special types of sentence, and then we find that the word belongs to a class requiring some sort of distinctive treatment, which may even be the negative treatment of excluding that type of sentence. This distinctive treatment we may call the reactance of the category. In English, intransitive verbs form a covert class marked by the lack of a passive participle and the passive and causative voices; we cannot substitute a verb of this class (eg. "go, lie, sit, rise, gleam, sleep, arrive, appear, rejoice") into such sentences as "It was cooked, It was being cooked, I had it cooked to order."   *(Whorf 1956:89; first published 1945)*

Fillmore's approach is precisely parallel: "*The second assumption I wish to make is the importance of covert categories*" (1968:3).

One example of a 'covert' grammatical distinction is the one to which traditional grammarians have attached the labels 'affectum' and 'effectum'. . . . The distinction, which is reportedly made overt in some languages, can be seen in Sentences 1 and 2.

1. *John ruined the table.*
2. *John built the table.*

. . . The distinction does have syntactic relevance, however. The effectum object, for example, does not permit interrogation of the verb with do to, while the affectum object does.   *(1968:4)*

I am going to suggest below that there are many semantically relevant syntactic relationships involving nouns and the structures that contain them, that these relationships—like those seen in 1 and 2— are in large part covert but are nevertheless empirically discoverable, that they form a specific finite set, and that observations made about them will turn out to have considerable cross-linguistic validity. I shall refer to these as 'case' relationships.   *(1968:5)*

Work on covert categories (or cryptotypes as Whorf also referred to them) was developed further by Halliday, whose 1985 functional grammar of English deploys them in large numbers. Like Whorf and Fillmore, Halliday was concerned with the way in which a cryptogrammar is motivated and commented as follows:

The grammar needs to be explicit, if it is to go on being useful: it must generate wordings from the most abstract grammatical categories by some explicit set of intermediate steps . . . the requirement that this should be possible leads to an important principle, namely that all categories employed must be clearly 'there' in the grammar of the language. They are not set up simply to label differences in meaning. On other words, we do not argue: "these two sets of examples differ in meaning; therefore they must be systematically distinct in the grammar." They may be; but if there is no lexicogrammatical reflex of the distinction they are not. (1985:xx)

This principle he takes as a fundamental characterization of functional grammar:

If we simply took account of differences in meaning, then any set of clauses or phrases could be classified in all kinds of different ways; there would be no way of preferring one scheme over another. The fact that this is a 'functional' grammar means that it is based on meaning; but the fact that it is a 'grammar' means that it is an interpretation of linguistic forms. Every distinction that is recognized in the grammar—every set of options, or 'system' in systemic terms— makes some contribution to the form of the wording. Often it will be a very indirect one, but it will be somewhere in the picture.

(1985:xx)

In this paper an attempt will be made to develop a systemic functional interpretation of case in Tagalog following on from Whorf, Fillmore and Halliday's remarks on covert categories and reactances. Unlike Ramos and De Guzman, this study will not be pursued within the framework of universal grammar. However, based on previous systemic studies of transitivity, the analyst assumed that:

1. The grammar of the Tagalog clause would be organized with respect to experiential, interpersonal and textual meaning.

2. From the point of view of experiential meaning, processes would fall into distinct sets (involving at least doing, sensing and being) with distinctive case relations for each.

3. Again, from the perspective of experiential meaning, the clause would be made up of some combination of process, participant(s) and circumstance(s).

4. Transitive and ergative models of voice might both be relevant, perhaps depending on process type (or possible person and mood).

5. The grammar would be functionally organized in the sense that patterns of affixes and markers would be neither random nor arbitrary.

Of these, the major challenge in Tagalog had to do with 4; accordingly, a different model of voice based on the notion of centrifugality will be proposed below.

In contrast to Bloomfield (who began with markers and affixes) and to Ramos and De Guzman (who began with verb classes), the point of departure for the analysis will be the clause. This reflects the semantic and contextual orientation of systemic functional grammars that try to interface with considerations of meaning and use as sensitively as possible. It also facilitates the integration of experiential structures with interpersonal and textual ones, whose domain is clearly that of the clause and not of the morpheme, word, group or phrase.

3. ISSUES ARISING FROM RAMOS AND DE GUZMAN

It is beyond the scope of this paper to review all of the relevant literature on Tagalog case (for an effective summary see De Guzman 1978:106–128). Instead, five key issues will be highlighted, as they bear critically on the analysis to follow:

3.1. Transitive or Ergative

The issue here has to do with whether Tagalog is basically a transitive or ergative language, or possibly something else altogether. Ramos and De Guzman defined their Agentive and Objective cases in such a way as to disagree fundamentally on this point. Ramos identified the doer in (10) and (11) as realizing the same case, the Agentive, treating the done-to as Objective.[8] De Guzman, on the other hand, required that every clause contain at least an Objective case, and so treated the doer in (10) as realizing the same case, the Objective, as the done-to in (11).

t-um-akbo   ang babae
ran   TM woman
            Agentive   (Ramos)
            Objective (De Guzman)
"The woman ran."   (10)

---

[8]Ramos does treat certain inanimate unintentiional doers as Objective—for example, the water in k-um-ulo ang tubig "The water boiled"—so her analysis is really of a mixed transitive and eregative type.

b-u͟m-ili ang babae   ng beer
bought   TM woman
         Agentive   Objective (Ramos & De Guzman)
"The woman bought some beer."   (11)

Thus Ramos treated Tagalog as basically transitive, identifying the intransitive and transitive doer as the same role, while De Guzman treated it as basically ergative, identifying the intransitive doer with the transitive done-to. The distinction between agentive and nonagentive clauses is the primary distinction as far as verb subclassification is concerned for both Ramos and De Guzman and so the treatment of Tagalog as transitive or ergative is at the heart of their analysis. Notably however, neither raised this aspect of their interpretation when defining Agentive and Objective cases (indeed De Guzman 1978:199 used the term *ergative*, somewhat oddly, to refer to verbs that prefer the done-to as Topic when a doer is present).

As far as the affixes and markers are concerned, the affixes support the transitive analysis while the typical pattern of use of markers points to the ergative. Note that in (10) and (11) for example, the same affix *-um-* identifies the Topic as a doer; and a different affix *-in-* would have been used to focus on the done-to in (11) (as in (12)): The affix pattern in other words looks transitive. As far as markers are concerned, however, (11) is in fact less common than (12):

b-i͟n-ili ng babae   ang beer
bought   woman TM
"The woman bought the beer."   (12)

Done-tos must be Topic in Tagalog when definite and in general Tagalog is a "patient-prominent" language (see Cena 1978 for a next to exhaustive discussion of this point). Thus the markers tend to identify the doer of the intransitive with the done-to of the transitive, reflecting an ergative pattern[9] (for further, albeit rather indirect and analogous, arguments from syntactic patterning that Tagalog is ergative, see Payne (1982).

---

[9]It can also be noted that in action processes the typical pattern is for infixes to focus on the doer (*-um-*) and the done-to (*-in-*), prefixes on agents (*mag-*), extra agents (*magpa-*) and beneficiaries (*i-/ipag-*), and suffixes (*-an*) on circumstances; this differential function of infixes, prefixes and suffixes appears to symbolize the ergative interpretation.

So, it would appear, with evidence pointing in both directions, that Tagalog is a mixed transitive/ergative language—or perhaps something else as will be suggested below.

3.2. Types of Process

The question here has to do with to what extent one can base one's analysis on action clauses. Almost all of Bloomfield's (1917) examples consisted of doing clauses; what little he had to say about mental processes, for example, is scattered through his discussion of secondary as opposed to primary formations. Schachter and Otanes, in their outline of affix correspondence classes, commented that Tagalog has very few bases in the classes realizing perception and cognition (1972:295–296). Ramos recognized 15 major classes of verb, only one of which is non-action. And finally De Guzman, while redressing this imbalance somewhat by taking mental and verbal processes into account, still devoted five out of seven primary verb subcategories to doing clauses (1978:102). And none of these authors treat being clauses as relevant to a discussion of case because in Tagalog relational processes for the most part do not contain verbs.

To begin, it needs to be granted that Tagalog has more action verbs than verbs of any other kind, that these appear with a higher frequency than other verbs averaging across contexts (McFarland 1976) and that they are learned before other verbs by children (Gonzales 1984). However, none of these factors dictates that the grammar of action clauses will be the same as that of other processes nor that they will serve as a useful model. To pursue this point, consider Ramos's and De Guzman's analysis of (13):

na-gulat	ang babae	sa ingay	
was surprised	TM woman	noise	
	Objective	Instrumental	(Ramos)
	Dative	Objective	(De Guzman)
"The woman was surprised at the noise."			(13)

Ramos treated the senser here as Objective, identifying it with the done-to of an action clause, apparently on the grounds that it is affected by the process but does not initiate it. De Guzman, on the other hand, introduced a Dative role for the senser in mental processes (1978:55–56), arguing that the noise should be treated as Objective and that because only one instance of each case is allowed per clause, a new case is needed for the senser. Ramos treated the noise as Instrumental (but, because Instrumentals must be inanimate, would have to analyse (6) above differently; there the phenomenon reacted to was conscious—the boyfriend).

As far as Ramos's analysis is concerned, no insights are gained as far as affixation is concerned: *Ma-* identifies the Topic as Objective only when abilitative in meaning (normally *i-*, *-in-*, or *-an* focus on the Objective case); and the *ka-* . . . *-an*, which would focus on her Instrumental in (13) (cf. (4) above) is unrelated to the *i(pang)-* affixes used to focus on other Instrumentals (see (18) below). The markers as well would mark the Instrumental in (13) differently from other Instrumentals, which are normally marked with *ng* or *sa pamamagitan ng*, not *sa*.

De Guzman treated the phenomenon not as Instrumental but as Objective. Once again it is unusual to have an Objective case focused on with *ka-* . . . *-an* and marked with *sa*. Moreover, De Guzman's analysis of (14) leads to further problems:

g-<u>in</u>-ulat   ng ingay ang babae
surprised   noise TM woman
           Agentive   Objective   (De Guzman)
"The noise surprised the woman."   (14)

In this example De Guzman (1978:300) treated the noise as Agentive and the woman as Objective. This fits what might be expected for markers and affixes on the basis of patterns in action clauses. But while bringing out the difference between (13) and (14), it fails to note the similarity; the senser and phenomenon are given quite different analyses in the two clauses (De Guzman does derive the verb in (14) from that in (13), showing a lexical relationship, but this does not bring out the fact that the role of the woman in the two clauses is in some respect the same).

These examples illustrate the difficulty of taking cases such as the Objective and Instrumental, which have been defined primarily with action clauses in mind and applying them directly to processes of other kinds. In the analysis presented below, doing clauses will be treated differently from clauses of sensing and being.

3.3. Types of Participant

Following Fillmore, Ramos and De Guzman distinguished between doer Agentives and Instrumentals on the basis of animacy. Thus, the doer in (15) is taken as Agentive, while that in (16) is Instrumental.

b-in-asa   ng babae   ang boyfriend niya
wet   woman TM   her
     Agentive   Objective   (Ramos & De Guzman)
"The woman wet her boyfriend"   (15)

b-in-asa ng ulan   ang boyfriend niya
wet   rain   TM   her
     Instrumental Objective   (Ramos & De Guzman)
"The rain wet her boyfriend."   (16)

As far as the affixes and markers are concerned, Tagalog treats (15) and (16) as identical, so the semantic distinctions being made here appear to be grammatically vacuous (nor are there any reactances to bring into play). And, as with the problems raised with respect to Ramos's analysis of the phenomenon in reaction clauses like (13), the distinction weakens any predictions about affixes and markers that could be made from the Instrumental case, because the rain in (16) is not at all like the tool in (17) and (18) (note in passing that if Topic, both the woman in (15) and the rain in (16) would be focused on with the prefix *nag-*; cf. *ipang-* for the tool Topic in (18)).

g-in-upit ng babae   ang tela   sa pamamagitan ng gunting
cut   woman TM   cloth with   scissors
"The woman cut the cloth with some scissors."   (17)

ip-in-ang-gupit ng babae   ng tela   ang gunting
cut with   ng   cloth TM scissors
                woman
"The woman cut the cloth with the scissors."   (18)

Somewhat ironically, while making use of animacy as the basis for distinguishing Agentive from Instrumental buys nothing and simply creates problems here, Ramos made no use of it where it might help. For example, the senser in a mental process clause must be conscious (animacy is not really the relevant grammatical variable for Tagalog; "endowed with human consciousness" is closer to the mark). This means that personal pronouns, which only refer to "human" participants in Tagalog, and proper names for "human" participants, which take distinctive markers (*si, ni, kay*), are much more strongly associated with the senser than with any other case. By collapsing Dative with Objective, Ramos lost the apparatus to focus on this association. De Guzman did not appeal to consciousness when arguing for Dative against Ramos, but it is part of her definition of this case relation.

Pursuing this point, there is also the question of what types of phenomena (people, places and things) and metaphenomena (ideas, locutions and facts) might fit into case frames with Dative. In distinguishing mental and verbal processes from processes of other kinds, De Guzman never appealed to the fact that they can be used to report and quote other clauses (see (34) to (36) below). But reported and quoted clauses are linked to their projecting clause (see Halliday 1985:248–251 for a summary of projection) by the hypotactic linkers η/na, not by the markers *ang*, *ng* and *sa*, and so an important observation about markers is being set aside. In the analysis developed below, both the consciousness and phenomenality of participants will be taken into account.

3.4. Participants and Circumstances

Ramos and De Guzman also disagreed on where to draw the line between participants and circumstances. Their treatment of the ambiguity in (19) illustrates this point.

t-<u>um</u>-akbo ang babae   sa Roxas Boulevard
ran   TM woman
                Direction or Location (Ramos)
                Locative   (De Guzman)
    "The woman ran to/on Roxas Boulevard."   (19)

Ramos treated the *sa* phrase as realizing either Direction or Location; for De Guzman only a Locative case is recognized, with verbs subclassified to capture the different interpretations of (19). In other words, Ramos divided De Guzman's Locative case into a Direction, which is more participant-like, and a Location, which is more circumstantial. What, in general, do Tagalog's affixes and markers have to say about the distinction between participants and circumstances?

As noted in section 2, Tagalog's markers draw an apparent distinction between participants and circumstances in that participants are marked with *ng* when Topic and circumstances with *sa*.[10] This is easiest to see when clauses are nominalized or in recently completed aspect and so have no Topic:

magaling ang pagka-intindi ng babae ng wika
clever   TM understanding woman   language

---

[10]Note that with pronouns, only circumstantial roles in fact take a marker; for example, *siya, niya, sa kaniya* "he/him/to him."

sa biyahe niya
   trip   her
"The woman's understanding of languages on her
trip was clever." (20)

ka-ra-rating   ng babae sa probinsiya dahil sa   Pasko
has just arrived   woman prinvince because of Xmas
"The woman has just arrived from the province
for Christmas." (21)

As (21) illustrates, certain of these *sa* markers can be expanded to
give more specific meanings. Using an ad hoc semantic classification of circumstances, these can be listed as follows:

Matter	*tungkol sa, ukol sa* "about"
Accompaniment	*kasama ng* "with," *sa halip na* "in place of," *bukod sa* "besides," *maliban sa* "except"
Cause	*dahil sa* "because of"
Benefactive ，	*para sa* "on behalf of"
Instrument	*sa pamamagitan ng* "with"
Location	*galing sa* "from," *patungo sa* "to," *sa gitna ng* "in the middle of," *sa harap ng* "in front of," etc.

Actually the picture is not quite as neat as the *ng/sa* opposition in
(20) and (21) would imply. Not all circumstances are in fact marked
with *sa:* eg. *kasama ng* "with" listed under Accompaniment above.
In addition, Manner and Extent are marked with *nang*, distinguished orthographically from *ng*, but phonologically identical; and
Role is marked with *bilang* "as." What characterizes all circumstances is their inability to be marked simply with orthographic *ng*.
More problematic, as far as distinguishing participants and circumstances is concerned, are *sa* phrases that cannot be expanded
to make the nature of their relation to the process more specific.
These can be listed as follows:

1.   the receiver of goods in an action clause

i-b-in-igay ng boyfriend niya ang pera   sa babae
gave   her TM monay   woman
"Her boyfriend gave the woman some money." (22)

2. the receiver of information in a saying clause

s-in-abi ng boyfriend sa babae na[11] uuwi siya
said woman LK go home he
"The boyfriend told the woman he'd go home." (23)

3. the phenomenon in a mental process of reaction clause

na-inis ang babae sa boyfriend niya
was irritated with TM woman her
"The woman was irritated with her boyfriend." (24)

4. the secondary actor in a causative construction

i-p-in-a-bigay ng babae sa boyfriend niya ang pera
made give woman her TM money
"The woman made her boyfriend give her the
money." (25)

5. the joint actor with a social verb

naki-inom ang babae sa boyfriend niya
joined to drink with TM woman her
"The woman joined her boyfriend for a drink." (26)

6. the definite object of an actor focus verb in an embedded clause[12]

p-um-asok ang lalaki-ng naka-halata sa babae
came in TM man LK happened to notice woman
"The man who happened to notice the
woman came in." (27)

Ramos dealt only with type 1, treating the receiver of goods in (22) as Direction. De Guzman proceeded as follows (the affixes used to focus on each case are shown except for Comitative where topicalization is not possible):

Locative [-an]—receiver of goods in (22)

Dative [-an]—receiver of information in (23)

Objective [-an]—phenomenon reacted to in (24)

---

[11]Na/ŋ realize the hypotactic relation between a locution and its projecting process; they will be referred to as linkers, and labelled LK in examples.

[12]As McFarland (1976:25) pointed out, these definite sa phrases are not supposed to occur outside embedded clauses, but do so and are accepted by many speakers when drawn to their attention; in (27) sa babae "the woman" contrasts with ng babae "a woman."

Dative [-*in*-]—secondary actor in (25)
Comitative—joint actor in (26)
Objective [*na*-]—phenomenon perceived in (27)

As is typical with borderline categories, the evidence is mixed. The last three examples, secondary actor, joint actors and definite embedded *sa* phrases, could perhaps be regarded as "demoted" participants; certainly in directly related non-causative (see Starosta 1978), non-social (see Martin 1988:253–254) and unembedded constructions (see McFarland 1976:25) the roles in question pattern like other participants in every way. This leaves the *sa* phrases in 1, 2 and 3, along with the locations associated with verbs of motion (as in (19) above).

One strategy for handling the problem is to make use of delicacy, subclassifying process first with respect to clear participants, then at a second stage with respect to borderline cases, and finally with respect to clear circumstantial roles. This is, in effect, the strategy adopted by Ramos and De Guzman, who subclassified verbs first on the basis of potential *ng* phrases (contrast Schachter and Otanes 1972:71, whose primary classification of verbs according to complement classes includes direction). De Guzman, for example, treated verbs first as agentive or not (i.e. Agentive plus Objective or Objective only), then as dative or not (i.e. Agentive plus Objective plus Dative addressee or Objective plus Dative experiencer) and then as locative or not. This is the basic strategy that will be adopted in this paper; the dispute over Direction and Location thus resolves itself into a question of delicacy, with Direction (De Guzman's inner locatives) brought into the subclassification of processes earlier than Location (De Guzman's outer locatives).

3.5. Unmotivated Categories

In section 3.1 through 3.4, various aspects of the case inventories of Ramos and De Guzman were criticized because they led to analyses that are unrevealing with respect to affix and marker patterns. Similar problems arise with respect to their verb subclassifications.

Schachter, for example, in his 1977 review of Ramos, noted that while many of Ramos's categories are both semantically and grammatically motivated, a number are largely intuitive and at times conflict with grammatical evidence. If we look at affixation for example, (28) and (29) (focus affix -*in*-) would appear to fall into the same class as opposed to (30) (focus affix -*an*).

in-ipon ng babae   ang pera
saved   woman TM money
"The woman saved the money."   (28)

s-in-unog ng babae   ang pera
burned   woman TM money
"The woman burned the money."   (29)

p-in-unas-an[13] ng babae   ang pera
wiped   woman TM money
"The woman wiped the money."   (30)

And one might posit some semantic feature such as [+/− surface action] to explain the pattern. Ramos, however, distinguished (28) from (29) and (30) on the grounds that the done-to in (28) does not undergo a change of state, and then distinguishes (29) and (30) in terms of whether the change of state is total or partial. This shows something of the possible danger of placing too much emphasis on giving no thought to a one-to-one relationship between verb features and surface representations (Ramos 1974:11).

4. TRANSITIVITY IN TAGALOG

Unlike case grammar, which attempts to associate a universal inventory of case relations with subclasses of verbs, systemic grammar begins with a subclassification of clause types and attempts to associate with each of these distinctive case frames. As noted above, it was expected following on from previous systemic studies of transitivity (especially Halliday 1985) that an initial division of clauses into action, sensing and being would prove fruitful. Any overt or covert evidence that could be uncovered was taken into account; for the most part this involved:

1.   the affixes used to identify the role of Topic
2.   the markers used for non-Topic participants and circumstances
3.   the number and nature of the participants associated with the process
4.   the form of the relevant nominalization

---

[13]The -in- infix here is signalling completed aspect, not focus; it contrasts with the -in- in (28) and (29), which is a portmanteau realization of both aspect and focus.

5. the type of general verb used to refer to the process
6. the presence or absence of a process
7. the bidirectionality of the process
8. marked patterns in the process's abilitative, social or causative paradigms

4.1. Mental Processes (De Guzman's 1978:192 Psych Verbs)

In Tagalog, sensing clauses deal with reaction, perception and cognition. They involve two key participants, one endowed with human consciousness and the other admitting a wide range of phenomena, including those realised by clauses. They distinguish themselves from other process types with respect to the following features (cf. Halliday 1985:108–111 on criteria for distinguishing mental and material processes in English):

1. their processes are realized by *ma-* class verbs (eg. (31)–(33))
2. one key participant may be introduced with a linker (η/*na*) instead of a marker; where the verb focuses on the participant introduced in this way, the mental process clause will thus lack a Topic marker (eg. (35) below)
3. one key participant must be endowed with human consciousness; the other need not be and may be realized by a clause (coding an act, idea or fact—see Halliday 1985:227–251 for a discussion of macro- and meta-phenomena)
4. they are nominalized with the prefix *pagka-* (eg. (20))
5. they cannot be questioned with a general doing verb (*gawa/ mangyari*) or with a wh verb (*ano*)
6. a process is always present and realized by a verb
7. they have defective ability/involuntary action paradigms because their *ma-* prefix is identical to the object focus ability/involuntary action prefix used in action clauses.

Except for De Guzman, analysts have almost completely ignored this process type. Examples of mental process verbs are given below, provisionally grouped into reaction, perception and cognition classes. Grammatical criteria for distinguishing these subclasses will be presented as the analysis unfolds. One example of each subclass is provided to show something of the affix/marker interaction differentiating subclasses.

1. REACTION

na-awa ang babae sa boyfriend niya
pitied   TM women   her
"The woman pitied her boyfriend." (31)

galit "be angry at," *gulat* "be surprised at," *inggit* "envy," *hiya* "be ashamed of," *tuwa* "be happy about," *inis* "be irritated with," *takot* "be afraid of," *lungkot* "be sad about," *awa* "pity," *lita* "be confused about," *inip* "be bored with," *balisa* "be anxious about," *suklam* "be disgusted with," *sabik* "be eager for," *yamot* "be annoyed with," *galak* "be glad about" ("deep"[14] Tagalog), *poot* "hate" (deep Tagalog), *sawa* "be fed up with"

2. PERCEPTION

na-dama ng babae   ang kamay niya
felt   woman TM hand   his
"The woman felt his hand." (32)

kita "see," *dinig* "hear," *puna* "notice," *amoy* "smell," *tikim* "taste," *pansin* "notice," *masdan* "observe," *tanaw* "view," *batid* "be aware of," *aninaw* "see through a haze," *aninag* "see through a transparency," *darama* "feel," *dama* "feel," *halata* "notice," *hipo* "feel by touch," *reparo* "notice," *alala* "to have return to the mind"

3. COGNITION

na-limut-an ng babae   ang payong
forgot   woman TM umbrella
"The woman forgot her umbrella." (33)

limot "forget," *tanda* "remember," *intindi* "understand," *tuto* "learn," *alam* "know," *isip* "think," *unawa* "understand (be in sympathy with); *tuklas* "discover," *danas* "experience," *balita* "receive news," *tagpo* "find out," *gusto* "wish," *usisa* "investigate," *wawa* "get the drift of," *kutob* "have a premonition of," *watas* "understand," *tulos* "catch the point of," *damdam* "feel," *asa* "hope," *mata* "realise," *hula* "guess"

One of the chief differences between mental processes and process of acting and being has to do with the phenomenality of the two

---

[14]The term *deep* is used by Tagalog speakers to refer to words still used in some Tagalog speaking provinces, but not current in Manila.

central participants. To explore this further, consider (34) to (36) below; in each the participant endowed with consciousness is sensing a different order of phenomena from that exemplified in (31) to (33) above—an act (34), an idea (35) and a fact (36):

ACT
na-masdan ng babae   ANG ISDA L-UM-ANGOY[15] SA TUBIG
observed   woman TM fish swimming   water
"The woman observed the fish swimming in the water." (34)

IDEA
na-kutob-an   ng pangulo NA TA-TAKAS   SIYA
had a premonition   head   LK will escape he
"The president had a premonition he'd escape."   (35)

FACT
na-suklam   ang tao   SA BAGAY NA NAG-DAYA ANG PANGULO
were disgusted TM people   think LK cheated TM head
"The people were disgusted with the fact that the president cheated."   (36)

Example (34) illustrates what Halliday (1985:225–227) refered to as an *act*—a type of nominalized clause: *ang isda l-um-angoy sa tubig* "the fish swimming in the water." The process in acts is aspectless in Tagalog, reflecting the act's downgrading from "clausehood"; and because it is a macro- rather than a meta-phenomenon, it is not linked to *na-masdan ng babae* "the woman observed" with a linker (that is, it is not projected by the process *masdan*)—it functions simply as an embedded clause participant.

In (35), *na ta-takas siya* is linked to *na-kutob-an ng pangulo* (by *na*)—it is projected by the mental process; unlike the act in (34) it selects for aspect (in this case [not begun]). Clauses projected by mental processes in this way are referred to by Halliday (1985:233) as *ideas*. These are characterized as metaphenomena and described as dependent on their projecting clause but not embedded in it.

In (35), a second type of metaphenomenon is illustrated, a *fact* (Halliday 1985:243–248). These he described as embedded clauses that have the feature projected, but are not projected by the mental process in which they may be embedded. In Tagalog, these can all be introduced with (*ang/sa bagay na*) ("the fact that"), although the optionality of *ang/sa bagay* means that in many cases the distinc-

---

[15]Note that *ang isda* is not linked to *lumangoy sa tubig* and so the latter cannot be read as a relative clause. Compare: *na-kita ng babae bilh-in ng lalaki ang gulay* "The woman saw the man buying vegetables"; *bilhin* is clearly aspectless here, and the absence of a linker between *na-kita ng babae* and *bilh-in ng lalaki ang gulay* along with the position of *ng lalaki* following *bilhin* point clearly to an act.

TABLE 7.1
Mental Processes and Orders of Phenomena

Mental Subclass	Unmarked Order of Phenomena
perception:	phenomena & macro-phenomena (acts)
cognition:	phenomena & meta-phenomena (ideas)
reaction:	phenomena & meta-phenomena (facts)

tion between ideas and facts is not formally marked. It is only by testing the metaphenomenon with the preface *ang/sa bagay* (the relevant reactance) that the distinction can be uncovered.

Only mental processes accept all orders of phenomena as participants, and ideas are peculiar to this process type (acts are found as well in doing and being clauses, and facts as well in being ones). Within mental processes, some orders of phenomena appear more closely associated with one process type than another. Quantitative studies are required to explore this point, but the predictions in Table 7.1 are worth testing.

Turning now to point 5 in the list of criteria for distinguishing mental processes from other process types, the absence of a general verb should be noted. This means that the identifying clause in (37) is unacceptable—*tuto* "learn" is not a kind of *gawa* "do" (the English gloss constructs *learn* as a kind of action process [behavioral; see Halliday 1985:128–129], an interpretation the morphology blocks in the Tagalog version).

*ang g-<u>in</u>-awa niya ay   na-tutuh-<u>an</u> ang Cebuano
    did   she IM[16] learn   TM
"What he did was learn Cebuano."   (37)

Similarly, mental processes cannot be queried with a wh verb; the response in the following adjacency pair is thus inappropriate (the natural query for a mental process of reaction is in fact *bakit* "why," which follows from the causative-like affixes used to focus on the phenomenon; see (40) below:

<u>um</u>-ano ang babae
whatted TM woman
"What did the woman do?"   (38)

---

[16]The particle *ay* signals that the Topic is being realized in first position in the clause (it signals in other words a marked Theme; see Martin 1983); it is labelled IM (= "inversion marker").

* -na-lungkot siya
was sad   she
"She was sad."

Finally, with respect to criteria 7 above, note that the pairs *na-rinig/naka-rinig* and *na-gawa/naka-gawa* are not proportional. With doing processes both *na-gawa* ("was able/happened to"; done-to focus) and *naka-gawa* ("was able/happened to"; doer focus) involve an abilitative/involuntary action meaning. On the other hand, with the mentals, only *naka-rinig* ("was able/happened to hear"—senser focus) is associated with the abilitative/involuntary action paradigm. With the phenomenon in focus, *na-rinig* means simply "heard," not "was able/happened to hear" (see Rafael 1978 for discussion).

As far as case is concerned then, two basic roles will be recognized: A participant endowed with human consciousness, which following Halliday (1985) will be referred to as a Senser, and a participant realized by all orders of phenomena, which following Halliday (1985) will be referred to as a Phenomenon. In order to explore the realization of these roles in more detail, subclassification of mental processes into reaction, perception and cognition will have to be considered.

Within mental processes, the basic distinction is between reaction clauses on the one hand, and perception and cognition on the other. Reaction clauses have the following distinctive features:

1. the prefix *ma-* focuses on the Senser, not the Phenomenon.

2. causative-like focus affixes are used to focus on the Phenomenon (*ika-* and *ka-* . . . *-an*)

3. when not in focus the Phenomenon is marked with *sa-*.

4. they are two-way (*ma-takot*—Senser fearing Phenomenon vs *t-in-akot*—Phenomenon frightening Senser)

5. they do not allow social (*maki-takot) or causative (*mag-pa-takot) affixes

6. their unmarked metaphenomenon is a fact.

These distinctive features are summarized in Table 7.2, which will also be drawn on in contrasting perception with cognition.

Semantically, the features that distinguish reaction processes from the others reflect the fact that a reacting Senser is responding to rather than exploring the world. The *ma-* prefix in Tagalog typically focuses on participants undergoing an experience, rather than

TABLE 7.2
Mental Processes Reactances

	Reaction	Perception	Cognition
Senser focus affix	ma-	maka-	maka-
Phenomenon focus affix	ika-/ ka-...-an	ma-	ma-...-an
Phenomenon marker (non-Topic)	sa	ng	ng
directionality	two-way	one-way	one-way
causative affixes	no	yes	yes
social affixes	no	yes	(if reciprocal)
unmarked clause Phenomenon	fact	act	idea
Senser marker (non-Topic)	ng	ng	ng

undertaking one. The Senser's response is triggered in one of two ways: (a) by a Phenomenon in a "causal" circumstantial relation to the process as in (39) and (40); or (b) by a Phenomenon in an agentive role as in (41).

na-gulat   ang babae   (dahil) sa   boyfriend niya
was surprised at TM   woman   because of   her
"The woman was surprised at her boyfriend."   (39)

k-in-a-gulat-an[17]   ng babae   ang boyfriend niya
was surprised because of   woman TM   her
"The woman was surprised at her boyfriend."   (40)

Note that when the Senser is Topic, the Phenomenon is realized through a *sa* phrase, which can be optionally expanded to *dahil sa*, meaning "because of." This means that Phenomena in this process type are closely related to circumstances of cause and that the distinction between "The woman was surprised at her boyfriend" and "The woman was surprised because of her boyfriend" is grammatically slight. The *ka-* prefix used as part of the affixation to focus on the Phenomenon is also part of the morphology (*ika-*) used in general to focus on circumstances of cause across process types (see Schachter and Otanes 1972:313–314; eg. *ik-in-a-luha ng babae ang boyfriend niya* "Her boyfriend made the woman cry").

---

[17]Nominalized Phenomena tend to be focused on with *ika-* rather than *ka- . . . -an*: *ik-in-a-gulat ng babae ang g-in-awa niya* "The woman was surprised at what he did."

Causality of the agentive kind is illustrated in ((41) below. Here the Senser is being affected (*provoked* is De Guzman's 1978:299 apt characterization) by an agentive *ng* phrase and focused on with *-in-* as a kind of done-to (cf. the use of *-in-* to focus on done-tos in the discussion of action clauses below). This *ng* phrase cannot itself be made Topic; there is thus a restricted focus potential in provocation reaction clauses.

g-in-ulat ng boyfriend ang babae
surprised   TM woman
"The boyfriend surprised the woman."   (41)

The fact that the Phenomenon can trigger a reaction in either way gives rise to the bidirectionality of this process type.

Because the Senser in a reaction clause is responding to rather than exploring the world, reaction clauses are more naturally associated with facts than ideas. Facts are fait accompli—the Senser is not involved in constructing them; whereas with ideas, the Senser is projecting meanings into existence. What is being suggested here as the marked pattern, pending quantitative studies to confirm the point, is illustrated in (42), which on one reading has the reaction process projecting an idea.

na-takot ang babae   na da-rating ang boyfriend niya
feared   TM woman LK will come TM   her
"The woman was afraid her boyfriend would come."   (42)

It is presumably this passive role of the Senser that lies behind the unacceptability of social and causative affixes with reaction processes. It is possible to frighten the Senser (41) above) but not to make or let the Senser fear (*p-in-a-takot ng boyfriend niya ang babae* "Her boyfriend made/let the woman fear"); neither is it possible to join in with the Senser in fear (*naki-takot ang boyfriend sa babae sa kidlat.* "The boyfriend joined with the woman in fearing the lightning"). Both the causative and social affixes would involve the Senser in deliberate action that contradicts the responsive role of the Senser in reaction clauses (contrast the more active role of the Senser in (45)–(47) below).

With perception and cognition the Senser is more active—exploring rather than responding to the world (though still not acting in or on it). The *ma-* prefix focuses on the Phenomenon as undergoer, not the Senser; and when not in focus the Phenomenon is marked with *ng* as a participant, not with *sa; ng* is associated in general with circumstances.

These perception and cognition processes are essentially one way. The effect of the -in- affix is to introduce intentionality, not to reverse the process; it maps agentive meaning in other words onto the Senser, not onto the Phenomenon as with reaction processes. Compare (43) and (44) below with (41) above ((43) cannot be glossed as "The mountain made the woman observe it").

t-in-anaw	ng babae	ang bundok
tried to observe	woman TM	mountain

"The woman tried to observe the mountain." (43)

in-alam	ng babae	ang sagot
tried to find out	woman TM	answer

"The woman tried to find out the answer." (44)

Exploring the world through perception and cognition processes is active enough for causative affixes to be possible:

i-p-in-a-rinig ng babae sa boyfriend niya ang tugtog
let hear woman her TM music

"The woman let her boyfriend hear the music." (45)

i-p-in-a-tuto ng babae sa boyfriend niya ang sagot
made learn woman her TM answer

"The woman made her boyfriend learn the answer." (46)

Again, unlike reaction processes, perception processes allow an extra participant to join in:

naki-rinig	ang lalaki sa babae ng tugtog
join in hearing TM man	woman music

"The man joined the woman in hearing some music." (47)

Cognition processes are also open to joint action, provided they are reciprocal as well: _naki-pag-unawa ang mga babae_ "The women joined together in understanding each other."

In addition to this restriction on the use of social affixes, perception processes can also be distinguished from cognitive ones in terms of the affixes used to focus on the Phenomenon (perception _ma-_ vs cognition _ma-_ . . . _-an_) and by their proposed unmarked association with acts rather than ideas. This latter point follows from the fact that in general the Senser in a perception process is perceiving phenomena (i.e. people, places, things, things happening and people doing things) while in cognitive processes the Senser is

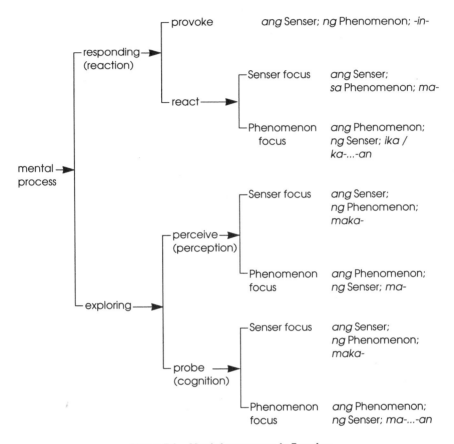

Figure 7.1. Mental processes in Tagalog

constructing (with the mind's eye) meanings. Interestingly the *-an* suffix used in part to focus on the Phenomenon in cognitive processes is the affix used by action processes to focus on objects that are only marginally affected rather than created or disposed. So there is a sense in which cognitive processes in Tagalog "probe" phenomena while perception processes "act" on them.

The distinctions outlined above are reformulated systemically in Figure 7.1. As far as mental processes are concerned, a basic distinction is drawn between responding (reaction) and exploring (perception and cognition). Then [responding] is divided into reaction and provocation according to whether the Phenomenon is "circumstantial" (eg. (39) and (40) above) or "agentive" (eg. (41) above). Exploring processes, on the other hand, are divided into those that probe (cognition) and those that perceive (perception). The markers and affixes associated with the Senser and Phenomenon are displayed following the relevant subclass of mental process. (For a summary of the other relevant reactances see Table 7.2 above.)

Before turning to a consideration of action processes, it should be stressed again that networks such as that in Figure 7.1 classify clauses, not verbs. This point is important because many verbs in Tagalog can be used to realize more than one process type or subtype (as a glance through Panganiban 1973 reveals). *Isip* "think," for example, was listed among cognitive processes above, but it is more commonly treated as if it were a process of saying by Tagalog speakers, affixed with *mag-* and *-in-* rather than *ma-* . . . *-an* and *maka-* (which are also possible). It is as if Tagalog prefers to treat thinking as "saying to oneself" rather than as "constructing an idea," but allows both interpretations. There is nothing surprising in this. The verb *feel*, for example, is used in English across action, sensing and being clauses: *She felt along the shelf/She feels it must be there/She feels tired.* One advantage of subclassifying clauses into process types is thus to allow verbs to operate in different case frames; marker and affix patterns make it clear which meaning is being meant (cf. De Guzman, whose lexicase framework would involve deriving one *isip* from the other—vacuously as far as any derivational morphology is concerned).

It should also be noted by way of reservation that processes of desire (eg. hoping, wishing, wanting, liking, desiring, etc.) have not been included here (cf. Halliday 1985:111 who groups reaction and desire processes together under the heading affection for English). These meanings are normally realized in Tagalog through productive optative constructions (generally including the particle *sana*) or through modal-like unaffixed verbs (eg. *gusto* "like," *ayaw* "not like," *nais* "wish," *ibig* "love"). For further discussion see 5.2 below.

4.2. Material Processes

Material process are processes of doing and may involve up to three key participants. Naming these participants involves decisions about whether a language is to be treated as transitive, ergative, a mixture of the two or something else. So to begin traditional labels will be avoided (eg. Medium or Patient or Object plus or minus Agent or Causer from the ergative perspective, and Actor plus or minus Goal or Object from the transitive viewpoint). The terms doer and done-to will be used as neutrally as possible to begin with respect to decisions of this kind.

As noted above, action clauses have been extensively investigated in Tagalog. They can be distinguished from other processes with respect to the following features:

1. their processes are realized by -*um*- or *mag*- doer focus verbs[18]; and the affixes -*in*-, *i*- or -*an* are used to focus on the done-to ((54))–(56) below)
2. they may include one, two or three key participants, up to two marked by *ng* when not in focus and one by *sa*
3. the participants may or may not be endowed with human consciousness with no consequences for affixes and markers; but they cannot be metaphenomena (facts, ideas or locutions)
4. they are nominalized through the prefix *pag*- (without reduplication for -*um*- verbs: *pag-sulat* "writing"; with reduplication for *mag*- verbs: *pag-bi-bigay* "giving")
5. they can be questioned with the general verbs *gawa* "do" or *mang-yari* "happen" or a wh verb (eg. *in-ano* "whatted to")
6. they have fully productive abilitative/involuntary action paradigms

The differences between material and mental processes are summarized in the following table:

TABLE 7.3
Differences Between Material and Mental Processes

	Material	Mental
verb class	-um-, mag-	ma-
"undergoer" focus affix	-in-, i-, -an	ma, ma-...-an, ika-, ka-...-an
# key participants	1, 2 or 3	2
metaphenomenon	not possible	possible
participant consciousness	+/– conscious	one conscious participant
general verb	ano/gawa/ mangyari	—
nominalizing affix	pag-	pagka-
abilitative/involuntary action paradigm	full	defective

---

[18]To simplify the presentation *mang*- and *ma*- action processes will be set aside; *mang*- verbs are essentially distributive -*um*- type verbs; and the *ma*- class is very small. See section 7 below.

The basic questions that need to be examined are far as material processes are concerned are:

1. what is the difference between -um- and mag- processes?
2. when are -in-, i- and -an used to focus on the done-to?
3. where does one draw the line between participant and circumstantial sa phrases?

The mag-/-um- problem will be treated first because it is central to the treatment of material processes developed here.

Ramos (1974:46) made an important distinction between what she referred to as *centrifugal* verbs, which "portray an action which moves in a direction away from the agentive source," and *non-centrifugal* verbs, which "specify a type of action which goes back towards its source." To illustrate this she contrasted (48) with (49):

1. CENTRIFUGAL

   nag-bili ang babae ng gulay
   sold   TM woman   vegetables
   "The woman sold some vegetables."   (48)

2. CENTRIPETAL (i.e., non-centrifugal)

   b-um-ili ang babae ng gulay
   bought   TM woman   vegetables
   "The woman bought some vegetables."   (49)

Ramos noted as well that i- is used to focus on a done-to "transported away from an agent to a directional goal" (1974:125) but that -in- focuses on done-tos gathered in from a directional source. This contrast is illustrated in (50) and (51):

1. CENTRIFUGAL

   i-p-in-ag-bili ng babae   ang gulay   sa lalaki
   sold   woman TM vegetables   man
   "The woman sold the vegetables to the man."   (50)

2. CENTRIPETAL

   b-in-ili ng babae   ang gulay   sa lalaki
   bought   woman TM vegetables   man
   "The woman bought the vegetables from the man."   (51)

Very few verb stems take both mag-/i- and -um-/-in- affixes to display this opposition (as does for example abot: um-abot "reach for" vs. *mag-abot* "hand to"). However there are large numbers of verbs that pattern like one or the other.

mag-/i- CENTRIFUGAL PATTERN (Ramos 1974:84–86 class 4):
abuloy "contribute," *bagsak* "drop," *bigay* "give," *bayad* "pay," *sabit* "hand," *hulog* "drop," *akyat* "carry up," *tali* "tie," etc.

-um-/-in- CENTRIPETAL PATTERN (Ramos 1974:87–88 class 6):
hingi "ask for," *dukot* "draw out," *tanggap* "receive," *agaw* "snatch," *abot* "reach for," *hila* "pull horizontally," *hanap* "search for," etc.

The idea of importing or exporting done-tos can be related to another of Ramos's distinctions. Following Lopez (1941), she distinguished between *external* verbs, which "express an activity or verbal action which occurs outside of the agent" (1974:45) and *internal* verbs, which express "inner motion or an internally induced action by an agent" (1974:45). Lopez himself contrasted (52) with (53) to illustrate this opposition (cf. Ramos's *t-um-ayo* "stand up" vs. *mag-tayo* "build"):

Ako   'y b-um-angon
I (Topic) IM got up
"I got up."   (52)

Ang pari 'y nag-bangon ng bago -ng bahay
TM priest IM erected   new LK house
"The priest built a new house."   (53)

Schachter and Otanes gave the following examples to illustrate this opposition (1972:293):

INTERNAL:		EXTERNAL:	
1-um-abas	"come out"	mag-labas	"take out"
p-um-asok	"enter"	mag-pasok	"take in"
um-akyat	"climb"	mag-akyat	"carry up"
um-alis	"leave"	mag-alis	"remove"
um-uwi	"go home"	mag-uwi	"take home"

Again, there is a large class of verbs corresponding to each of these series. The external class is the same as the *mag-/i-* class noted above; and corresponding to the *-um-* internal pattern is Ramos's class 7 (1974:88–89):

-um- INTERNAL PATTERN
dapo "alight," *kapit* "hold," *pasok* "enter," *luhod* "kneel," *upo* "sit," *higa* "lie down," *tayo* "stand up," *lakad* "walk," *langoy* "swim"

The challenge appears to be to integrate these two apparently distinct types of opposition (i.e. centrifugal *mag-* vs. centripetal *-um-* and external *mag-* vs. internal *-um-*) into a single model that would explain the *mag-/-um-* opposition and something more besides. The traditional transitive/intrasitive model will not do since both *b-um-ili* and *mag-bili* involve a doer and a done-to. Neither is the ergative middle/effective (see Halliday 1985:151) appropriate since (54) can be related to "middle" (i.e. one key participant as in (55) and (56); Medium without Agent in Halliday's terms) clauses via either participant.

nag-labas ang babae ng dugo
took out   TM woman   blood
"The woman took out some blood."   (54)

1-um-abas ang babae
went out   TM woman
"The woman went out."   (55)

1-um-abas ang dugo
went out   TM blood
"The blood went out."   (56)

Yet there is some sense in which the *-um-* processes "feel" intransitive and middle while the *mag-* processes "feel" transitive and effective.

Pursuing this problem, Ramos noted as well the following opposition between stems allowing both affixes:

p-um-utol ang babae ng kahoy
cut   TM woman   wood
"The woman cut off a piece of wood."   (57)

nag-putol ang babae ng kahoy
cut   TM woman   wood
"The woman cut some wood."   (58)

Ramos (1974:139) noted futher examples as follows:

h-um-iaw	"slice off"	mag-hiwa	"slice"
p-um-unit	"tear off"	mag-punit	"tear"
b-um-ali	"break off"	mag-bali	"break"
t-um-aga	"hack off"	mag-taga	"hack"
g-um-upit	"scissor off"	mag-gupit	"cut with scissors"

This distinction resembles the b-um-ili/mag-bili "buy/sell" opposition in that the -um- processes refer to actions designed to provide done-tos for the doer; the proportionality is not perfect, however, because done-tos in mag- processes are not in motion away from the doer to someone or somewhere else.

One way to generalize these three oppositions is to argue that action clauses in Tagalog are based on two different types of clause nucleus, where the nucleus consists of a Process and a Medium through which that Process is actualized. One of these, the -um- type, is basically implosive (or centripetal): It involves events in which the Medium either simply acts, or acts on done-tos in such a way as to draw them into the nucleus. The other, the mag- type, is basically explosive (or centrifugal to use Ramos's term): It involves more volatile events in which the Medium acts in a way that has repercussions for other participants—the done-to (Goods) must undergo a change of state or position, and if it undergoes a change of position then a third participant (Direction), who receives the done-to, is implicated.

Given this implosive/explosive distinction, Ramos's action verb classes can be reorganized as follows; the process types are graded from most centripetal to most centrifugal, beginning with meteorological processes where one might argue that the Medium and Process themselves have collapsed into a single constituent nucleus:

IMPLOSIVE CLASSES

• meterological—Process only; class 13

um-ulan
rained
"It rained."   (59)

• intransitives not implying direction—Process + Medium (+/− conscious); classes 9 and 14

g-um-ising ang babae
woke up   TM woman
"The woman woke up."   (60)

b-<u>um</u>-ukas ang pinto
opened   TM door
"The door opened."   (61)

- intransitives implying direction—Process + Medium (+/−
  conscious) + Direction (to or fro); classes 8, 9 and 15

p-<u>um</u>-asok ang babae sa disco
entered   TM woman
"The woman entered the disco."   (62)

t-<u>um</u>-akas ang babae sa boyfriend niya
escaped   TM woman   her
"The woman escaped from her boyfriend."   (63)

b-<u>um</u>-aon ang kotse sa putik
sank   TM car   mud
"The car sank in the mud."   (64)

b-<u>um</u>-agsak ang libro sa mesa
fell   TM book   table
"The book fell from the table."   (65)

- transitives of acquisition—Process + Medium + Goods acquired + Direction source (+/− conscious); class 6

h-<u>um</u>-ingi ang babae ng pera   sa boyfriend niya
asked for TM woman   money   her
"The woman asked for some money from
her boyfriend."   (66)

- transitives of ingestion—Process + Medium; class 5

<u>um</u>-inom ang babae ng beer
drank   TM woman
"The woman drank some beer."   (67)

EXPLOSIVE CLASSES

- transitives in which goods are thoroughly affected (created,
  disposed of or arranged)—Process + Medium; classes 1 and 3

<u>ni</u>-luto[19] ng babae   ang pagkain
cooked   woman TM food
"The woman cooked the food."   (68)

---

[19]*ni*- is a morphological variant of infix -*in*-.

w-<u>in</u>-asak ng pangulo   ang kaliban   niya
destroyed   president TM opponent his
"The president destroyed his opponent."   (69)

<u>in</u>-ayos   ng babae   ang kaniyang damit
arranged   woman TM   her   clothes
"The woman arranged her clothes."   (70)

- transitives in which the goods are superficially affected—
  Process + Medium + Goods; class 2

h-in-alik-<u>an</u> ng babae   ang boyfriend niya
kissed   woman TM   her
"The woman kissed her boyfriend."   (71)

- transitives implying moving goods—Process + Medium +
  Goods + Direction towards (+/− conscious); class 4

<u>i</u>-t-in-apon ng babae   ang basura sa kalsada
threw out   woman TM   garbage   street
"The woman threw the garbage out into the street."   (72)

<u>i</u>-b-in-igay ng babae   ang pera   sa nanay niya
gave   woman TM   money   mother her
"The woman gave the money to her mother."   (73)

The distinction between implosive and explosive processes is
hardest to predict, at least for non-native speakers, when the Goods
participant is not in motion (as in (67) through (70) above). The -*in*-
Goods focus affix effectively neutralizes the distinction; comparing
(74) and (75) for example, it is not easy to see where Tagalog will
draw the line between -*um*- and *mag*- Medium focus verbs:

h-<u>in</u>-uli ng babae   ang manok
caught   woman TM chicken
"The woman caught the chicken."   (74)

p-<u>in</u>-atay ng babae   ang manok
killed   woman TM chicken
"The woman killed the chicken."   (75)

In fact (74) belongs to the -*um*- series and (75) to the *mag*-; but the
processes are borderline. Had people rather than animals been involved as Goods in (75), the appropriate Medium focus affix would
have been -*um*-, not *mag*-.

Right on the borderline are what Ramos (1974:139) referred to as
destructive processes that take both -*um*- and *mag*- affixes (eg.

basag "break," *durog* "pulverize," *tunaw* "melt," *bayo* "pound"). Semantically these can be read as either providing Goods for the Medium (i.e. implosive) or as completely changing the condition of the Goods (explosive). Tagalog seems to favor the explosive interpretation, because the *-um-* forms are regularly used only in embedded clauses where grammatical downgrading can perhaps be seen as weakening the volatility of the nucleus. Ramos also noted that the *mag-* forms are preferred in imperatives; this follows from the implosive/explosive opposition developed above because imperative clauses act on the world, whereas declaratives and interrogatives simply observe.

The second question raised in the introduction to material processes above had to do with the affixes used to focus on the Goods (*-in-*, *i-* and *-an*). These oppositions are relevant to explosive processes and have to do with the ways in which the Goods are affected by the nucleus. The basic distinctions have to do with Goods that are thoroughly affected by the nucleus (*-in-*), Goods that are only superficially affected (*-an*) and Goods that are being expelled (*i-*). This can be interpreted in terms of degrees of volatility: With the *i-* affix, the nucleus is getting rid of Goods; with *-an* it is affecting them without really getting hold of them; and with *-in-* it has them by the throat, as it were (which in turn borders on consuming them—the general meaning of *-in-* in implosive processes). This scaling is illustrated in (76) through (79) (compare as well: *i-lura* "spit out," *halik-an* "kiss," *sipsip-in* "sip," or *i-tapon* "throw out," *hawak-an* "hold," *yakap-in* "hug"[20]):

EXPLOSIVE (*mag-* Medium focus):

i-b-in-ayad ng babae   ang 200 pesos
paid   woman TM
"The woman paid the 200 pesos."   (76)

b-in-ayar-an ng babae   ang kuwenta
paid   woman TM bill
"The woman paid the bill."   (77)

t-in-ipon ng babae   ang mga   kuwenta
gathered   woman TM many bill
"The woman gathered together the bills."   (78)

---

[20]Aspectless forms have been used in these series.

IMPLOSIVE (-um- Medium focus):

k-in-uha ng babae   ang pera
took   woman TM money
"The woman took the money."   (79)

The way in which this i-/-an/-in- gradation codes the Goods participant is consonant with the more general use of -in- to focus on
clear participants ("direct objects"), -an to focus on borderline participants ("indirect objects") and i- to focus on circumstances (eg.
beneficiaries, instruments and causes), which was what gave rise to
Bloomfield's three types of passive.

The third question raised above had to do with the distinction
between participants and circumstances. As noted, Tagalog transitivity patterns are sensitive to the ways in which Goods are affected by the nucleus, especially where the Goods are in motion.
This implicates a third key function for material processes, which
will be referred to as Direction. With implosive processes, this represents the source of the Goods acquired (eg. (66)) or the direction in
which or from which the Medium is moving (eg. (62) and (63)). With
explosive processes it represents the direction in which the Goods
are moved—to some location or human recipient. As far as markers
and affixes are concerned Tagalog does not distinguish among these
types of Direction. All are focused on with -an and marked by sa
when not in focus:

ni-lapit-an ng babae   ang boyfriend niya
approached   woman TM   her
"The woman approached her boyfriend."   (80)

ni-layas-an   ng babae   ang boyfriend niya
ran away from   woman TM   her
"The woman ran away from her boyfriend."   (81)

h-in-ing-an ng babae ng pera   ang boyfriend niya
asked for   woman   money TM   her
"The woman asked her boyfriend for some money."   (82)

b-in-igy-an ng boyfriend niya ng pera   ang babae
gave   her   money TM woman
"Her boyfriend gave the woman some money."   (83)

Proceeding along these lines means that the Direction function is
being set up as an intermediate category, on the border between

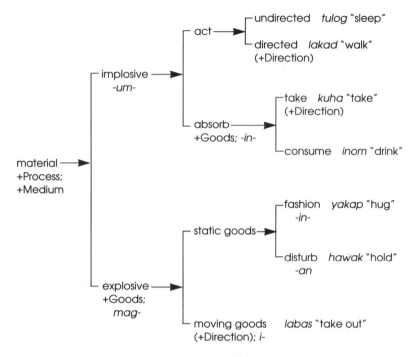

Figure 7.2.   Basic material processes

participants and circumstances. Its focus affix and marker, along with the fact that it is optional in (80) through (83), code it as circumstantial. However, whether explicitly realized or not, it is clearly implicated by the meaning of the nucleus in (80) through (83) and is criterial as far as subclassifying implosive and explosive processes beyond primary delicacy. Its "circumstance as participant" status will be reflected through the scale of delicacy in the network for material processes (Figure 7.2).

The line between Direction and Location can be drawn on the basis of the affix used to focus on Location as opposed to Direction; note the contrast between (84) and (85) (from Ramos 1974:127):

DIRECTION

s-in-ulat-<u>an</u> niya ang mesa
wrote   he   TM table
"He wrote (directly) on the table."   (84)

LOCATION

p-in-ag-sulat-an niya ang mesa
wrote   he TM table
"He wrote (something—eg. a letter) on the table."   (85)

In addition, it is important to note following McFarland (1976:18) that Location focus clauses are generally restricted to embeddings, whereas Direction focus is fully productive.

Setting aside meteorological processes for the moment, the oppositions discussed to this point can be formalized systemically as in Figure 7.2. Realization rules for the basic functions Process, Medium, Goods and Direction are provided along with the affixes relevant to focusing on Medium and Goods; note that the Direction function is generated later in delicacy than Process, Medium or Goods. An example process is provided for each terminal feature.

Before expanding this network slightly to handle meteorological processes, one further class of implosive processes needs to be considered. This class is illustrated in (86) and referred to by De Guzman (1978:189) as involving verbs of *affliction*.

in-ulan ang babae
rained TM woman
"The woman got rained on."   (86)

Affliction processes use -*in*- and less commonly -*an* to focus on the Medium as a done-to rather than a doer. The main sources of affliction are weather (as in (86)), times of the day (87), pests (88) and bodily discomforts (normally physiological as in (89) but also psychological as in (90)):

g-in-abi   ang babae
benighted TM woman
"The woman was overtaken by night."   (87)

ni-lamok   ang babae
mosquitoed TM woman
"The woman was attacked by mosquitos."   (88)

p-in-awis-an ang babae
sweated   TM woman
"The woman sweated."   (89)

s-in-ipag   ang babae
industriousized TM woman
"The woman got industrious."   (90)

As with the -*um-/mag-* oppositions discussed above, affliction processes have no natural analysis from either the transitive or ergative perspective. From the transitive point of view they look like transitive clauses with missing doers; however, it makes no sense to ask about the identity of the actor in these clauses. From the ergative standpoint they look middle, but the focus affix is not that used for intransitive doers. The way out seems to be to argue that for imploding processes Tagalog is drawing a distinction between Mediums that undertake a Process and Mediums that are being undertaken by one. Instead of the Medium simply acting or acting to gather Goods, the world closes in on the Medium itself.

Cena (1977:8) argued that affliction clauses should be viewed as having an underlying agent and modelled on (91) (cf. i̲n-*ubo ang babae* "The woman had a cough"):

in-atake ng ubo   ang babae
attacked   cough TM woman
"The woman came down with a cough."   (91)

There is no grammatical trace of this agent in affliction clauses and so this suggestion will not be pursued here. It does, however, raise the question of how to classify De Guzman's *calamity* processes, which resemble (91). Calamity processes have explicit doers afflicting the Medium, but these doers cannot become Topic (cf. Schachter & Otanes's 1972:306 pseudo-transitives). De Guzman (1978:224–225) treated the doer in clauses such as (92), (93) and 94 as an Instrument.

s-in-unog ng apoy ang babae
burned   fire TM woman
"The fire burned the woman."   (92)

b-in-uhus-an ng ulan ang babae
drenched   rain TM woman
"The rain drenched the woman."   (93)

i-ni-lubog ng bagyo ang barko
sank   storm TM ship
"The storm sank the ship."   (94)

The problem here lies in whether to treat the doer as a kind of elaboration of the process (cf. Schachter & Otanes's 1972:306 actor adjuncts) and include calamity processes in the implosive class; or whether to treat them as explosive clauses with a defective focus paradigm. This brings us once again to the borderline between implosive and explosive processes; and once again it is processes of destruction that are at issue.[21]

Calamity processes will be grouped with explosive processes here for three reasons: First, their focus affixes -*in*-, -*an* and *i*- pattern as they do in the explosive processes reviewed above (92–94); they are sensitive to how thoroughly the participant on which the calamity falls is affected by it. Second, if calamity processes were treated as implosive, a special class would have to be set up in which only non-conscious doers could act; this would mean making human consciousness criterial for the first time as far as material processes was concerned. And third, if implosive, the doer would have to be treated as an elaboration of the Process, similar to Halliday's Range function in English (1985:134–137). However, this would mean setting up a Range for just this one subclass of material processes; Tagalog does not systematically elaborate processes into verb plus noun realizations the way English does: *walk/take a walk* for example, corresponds simply to the Tagalog process *l-um-akad* "walk." For these reasons calamity processes will be treated as explosive processes with a defective Topic focus paradigm here (as noted above, their doer cannot be topicalized; calamity processes always focus on the done-to).

Before incorporating meteorological processes and processes of affliction into our material process network, let us review the cases, or to put it systemically, the transitivity functions suggested for material processes:

PROCESS

MEDIUM (including the undertaker/undergoer in implosive processes and the actor in explosive ones)

GOODS (including goods received in implosive processes and those affected in explosive ones)

---

[21]Because of its borderline nature, the hitting/killing clause type, which often acts as point of departure in case grammar (eg. Fillmore 1968, examples 1, 4, 18–25), would thus be an unfortunate place to start an analysis of Tagalog transitivity.

DIRECTION (including human and non-human directions, with the latter including both source and destination depending on the direction of the moving participant)

Four types of evidence were presented as pointing in the direction of interpreting the *mag/-um-* opposition as an implosive/explosive one:

1. the opposition of centrifugal *mag-/i-* and non-centrifugal *-um-/-in-* verbs; eg. *mag-bili* "sell" versus *b-um-ili* "buy"
2. the opposition of external *mag-* and internal *-um-* verbs; eg. *mag-labas* "take out" versus *l-um-abas* "go out"
3. the opposition of affecting *mag-* and taking away from *-um-* verbs; eg. *mag-taga* "hack" versus *t-um-aga* "hack off"
4. the association between *mag-* and imperative for destruction verbs otherwise affixed with either *mag-* or *-um-*

Aside from affixes and markers it can be noted that the *-um-* class includes verbs that do not implicate Goods and that may not even implicate a Medium (meteorological processes), whereas explosive processes always implicate both Medium and Goods. In addition, *-um-* verbs are nominalized through the prefix *pag-*, whereas explosive processes require reduplication of the first syllable of the stem in addition to *pag-*: *pag-inom* "drinking" versus *pag-bi-bigay* "giving." Reduplication is associated aspectually with processes that are not completed, and so can be interpreted as rendering *mag-* class nominalizations more active than *-um-* ones. Further evidence could certainly be uncovered if the material process network were extended in delicacy so as to account for the types of circumstantial relation associated with implosive and explosive classes (for example the relationship between implosive processes and circumstances of extent and location, or explosive processes and instruments and beneficiaries). This interaction between basic process types and circumstantial relations is unfortunately beyond the scope of this paper.

The expanded network for material processes is presented in Figure 7.3. One subclass of action clause that has not been incorporated is that of "intransitive" *mag-* verbalizations. To illustrate this class, compare (95) and (96).

nag-beer muna ang babae
beered first TM woman
"The woman had a beer first."   (95)

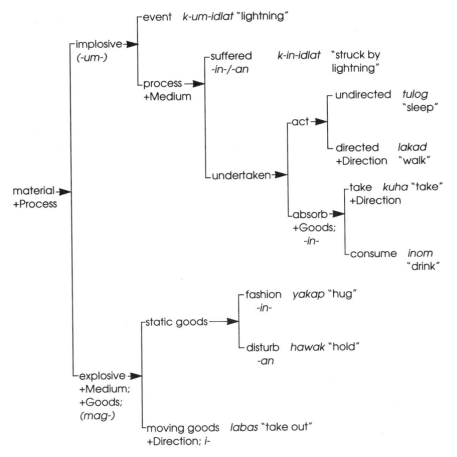

Figure 7.3. Material processes in Tagalog

nag-hintay muna ang babae
waited   first TM woman
"The woman waited first."   (96)

The second of these, (96), clearly implicates two participants, even though only the Medium is expressed; it is understood that the woman is waiting for someone. This follows as noted above from the basic meaning of explosive processes: a nucleus impinging on the world. The *mag-* in (95) on the other hand is not volatile; it simply represents Tagalog's productive verbalizing affix. As such it is commonly used with borrowings: for example, *mag-tennis* "play tennis," *mag-jogging* "jog," *mag-DunkinDonuts* "go to Dunkin Donuts." The *mag-* verbalizations may correspond to either explosive or implosive processes:

implosive: *mag-beer/um-inom ng beer*
explosive: *mag-tennis/mag-laro ng tennis*

These *mag-* verbalizations will not be further discussed here; from a historical point of view it would be useful to investigate just what impact they may have had on the uncertainty surrounding the *mag-/-um-* opposition under focus in Figure 7.3 below.

The network in Figure 7.3 distinguishes first between implosive and explosive processes (the basic *-um-* vs. *mag-* opposition). Implosive processes are then subclassified as involving only a Process (meteorological) or involving both Process and Medium. If both Medium and Process are involved, then a distinction is made between Mediums that undergo a Process (affliction clauses) and those that undertake it. Where the Process is undertaken, then the question arises as to whether a further participant, the Goods, is introduced. Simple acts not involving Goods can then be directed or not; where Goods are involved, these may be drawn from some source, or simply consumed.

With explosive processes the basic distinction is between static and moving Goods; if static Goods, then these may be fashioned (covering the senses "created," "disposed of" and "arranged") on the one hand or disturbed on the other. The options for implicit or explicit realization of Goods have not been included (cf. (96) above where the Goods were implicated, but implicit). The features have been arranged from the most centripetal at the top of the network to the most centrifugal at the bottom, with the classes of consuming and fashioning Goods next to each other in the middle reflecting this area of uncertainty with respect to affixation with *-um-* or *mag-*.

As stressed by Ramos and De Guzman, the realization relationship between process type features and markers and affixes is by no means biunique. Nevertheless, the network represents an attempt to generalize the semantics of the *-um-/mag-* opposition and to scale the *-in-, -an, i-* affixes with respect to centrifugality. In addition, by considering material processes separately from mental ones (itself admittedly a complication in the analysis) the amount of non-biuniqueness between cases, features, markers and affixes has been considerably reduced.

4.3. Congruence between Mental and Material Processes

Halliday (1985:144–145), reflecting on his presentation of English case relations broken down into six process types, commented as follows:

> It is true that, from one point of view, all these types of process are different. Material, behavioural, mental, verbal, relational and existential processes each has a grammar of its own. At the same time, looked at from another point of view they are all alike. At another level of interpretation, they all have the same grammar: there is just one generalised representational structure common to every English clause.

This raises the point that having distinguished mental from material processes in Tagalog, it is important to look back and see whether or not there are generalizations that cut across both sensing and doing. These will inevitably be more abstract and harder to motivate than those discussed so far (see Halliday (1984/1988) for a discussion of ineffability and linguistic categories), simply because the grammar is so sensitive to differences between the two kinds of process. Nevertheless, there are systemic parallels that are worth noting.

First, the mental responding/exploring system that opposed reaction processes to perception and cognition is not unlike the implosive/explosive one that separates -um- from mag- classes. The Senser in reaction clauses is like the Medium in implosive ones: It undergoes feelings much as the Medium undertakes action:

RESPONDING: IMPLOSIVE (undergoing feelings: undertaking action)

na-galit   ang babae
was angry TM woman
"The woman was angry."   (97)

1-um-akad ang babae
walked   TM woman.
"The woman walked."   (98)

And at the same time both the Senser and the Medium may be overtaken by events:

RESPONDING: IMPLOSIVE (being made to feel: being made to suffer)

g-in-alit ng pangulo   ang babae
angered   president TM woman
"The president angered the woman."   (99)

s-in-ipon ang babae   (cf. in-atake ng sipon ang babae)
colded   TM woman   attacked   cold TM woman
"The woman had a cold."   ("The cold attacked the woman.")
                                                          (100)

In (97) through (100), then, it is the woman who acts and feels without repercussions for her environment; and in both sensing and doing clauses, she may either be herself responsible for the doing or feeling ((97) and (98)) or the initiative may lie elsewhere, beyond her control ((99) and (100)).

The Senser in processes of perception and cognition, on the other hand, is more like the Medium of explosive processes. It acts on experience, either directly by perceiving it or indirectly by thinking about it, much as explosive clauses act on or simply disturb Goods. Compare the following:

EXPLORING: EXPLODING (acting mentally or physically on the world)

na-kita ng babae   ang bahay
saw   woman TM house
"The woman saw the house."   (101)

ni-linis ng babae   ang bahay
cleaned   woman TM house
"The woman cleaned the house."   (102)

PROBING: DISTURBING (approaching mentally or physically)

na-isip-an   ng babae   ang sagot
thought over   woman TM answer
"The woman thought over the answer."   (103)

p-in-unas-an ng babae   ang mesa
wiped   woman TM table
"The woman wiped the table."   (104)

There is nothing in mental process clauses corresponding to the ejected Goods (i- affix) of the most volatile of explosive action clauses,

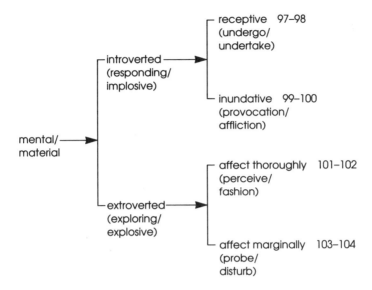

Figure 7.4. Generalized network for material and mental processes

but there is a parallel between -*an* (affecting indirectly) and *na*- or -*in*- (affecting directly) affixes. A generalized network along the lines of Figure 7.4 could be used to further explore these parallels.

4.4. Relational Processes

Relational processes are processes of being. These processes are generally verbless in Tagalog, and so are omitted from case grammarians' analyses. Once clauses rather than verbs are taken as point of departure however, they can be addressed in the same terms as action and sensing clauses. Halliday's 1985 interpretation of relational process in English shows them to be as complex, if not more so, than other process types as far as case relations are concerned. So it is worth considering to what extent Tagalog provides distinctive case relations for being clauses.

Relational processes can be distinguished from material and mental ones with respect to the following features:

1. they typically do not contain a process
2. one of their two key transitivity functions may not be realizing a participant.

Halliday's (1985:112) categories of intensive, possessive and circumstantial provide a useful point of departure for Tagalog as well as English. These are illustrated in (105) to (107) respectively:

INTENSIVE

titser   ang babae
teacher TM woman
"The woman is a teacher."   (105)

POSSESSIVE

sa kaniya ang babae
   him   TM woman
"The woman is his (with him)."   (106)

CIRCUMSTANTIAL

nasa bar ang babae
in   TM woman
"The woman is in the bar."   (107)

Each of these examples contains two transitivity roles realizing phenomena on the same level of abstraction, but differing in generality. None contain a Process. One participant, the woman, is being assigned to a general class of phenomena: to the class of teachers (105), to belongings (106) and to things in the bar (107).

In the intensive type (105), the general class may be realized by either a noun (as with *titser* "teacher" in (105) above) or an adjective as in (108):

maganda ang babae
beautiful TM woman
"The woman is beautiful."   (108)

This realization of the general class to which one participant is assigned distinguishes intensive from other relational clauses. The general class in (106) and (107) is realized by a *sa* phrase; in order to distinguish possessive from circumstantial clauses it is necessary to follow up their distinctive reactances in existential clauses. This reactance reflects the fact that the possessive type contains two participants while the circumstantial is made up of a participant and a circumstance (the existential clause type also underscores the fact that the intensive contains just one participant function). Consider (109) through (111) below (the existential structure is marked by the particle *may*):

EXISTENTIAL INTENSIVE

may titser   na babae
   teacher LK woman
"There is a woman teacher."   (109)

EXISTENTIAL POSSESSIVE

may babae   siya
   woman he
"He has a woman."   (110)

EXISTENTIAL CIRCUMSTANTIAL

may babae   sa bar
   woman
"There's a woman in the bar."   (111)

The effect of the existential structure in (109) is simply to posit the existence of a general class; *titser* does not function as a distinct transitivity role once the particular participant to which it is ascribed is existentialized. In (111), on the other hand, the bar does maintain its status as a clause constituent, circumstantially locating the existentialized participant. Note that neither of these types of existentialized relational clause has a Topic.

The possessive type does, however, have a Topic, reflecting the fact that there is still a participant around to topicalize once what is possessed is made existential. In summary, intensive, possessive and circumstantial relationals can be distinguished as follows:

intensive: one participant only (participant plus quality)

possessive: two participants (possessor plus possessed)

circumstantial: participant and circumstance

(cf. Ramos and Cena 1980 who derive (110) from (106) and (111) from (107), though not (109) from (105)).

The transitivity roles in relational clauses may differ in abstraction ((112)–(114) below) rather than generality ((105)–(107) above):

ang titser   ang babae
   teacher   woman
"The woman is the teacher."   (112)

ang mayroon[22] niya ang babae
            he   woman
"The woman is what he has." (113)

ang pupuntahan niya ang babae
   will go to   he   woman
"The woman is where he is going." (114)

Whereas existential constructions in a sense "weaken" a predication by positing someone rather than someone in particular as a member of a general class, these identifying constructions strengthen it by asserting that someone in particular and no one else represents that class. In (112) to (114) it is the woman (not someone else) who fills the role of the teacher, what the man has and where the man is going respectively. Identifying structures differ from those in (105)–(107) and (112)–(114) in that they are reversible without special intonation (eg. *ang titser ang babae* or *ang babae ang titser*) and consist of two *ang* phrases.

The role of the central participant, the woman, in each of these three types of structure ((105)–(107), (109)–(111) and (112)–(114)) will be designated as follows:

Specifier (105)–(107)
Existent (109)–(111)
Isolator (112)–(114)

These labels are oriented to the different functions of this role in making the three types of predication arguable. Specifiers provide a candidate to ground the generality; existents simply propose the existence of a class of candidates without selecting from it; and Isolators suggest one candidate to the exclusion of others.

Further roles are need to distinguish between intensive, possessive and circumstantial clauses. The *titser* in (105) and *maganda* in (108) will be referred to as **Attributes,** whose function is to note the general class to which the Specifier belongs. The *sa kanya* phrase in (106) will be termed **Possessor** and the *nasa bar* in (107) a **Circumstance.** Structural analyses for (105)–(107), (109)–(111) and (112)–(114) are presented below:

titser   ang babae
Attribute Specifier (105)

---

[22]*Mayroon* is an alternative existential marker to *may*, required in this construction, though a variant in 109–111.

sa kaniya ang babae
Possessor Specifier   (106)

nasa bar   ang babae
Circumstance Specifier   (107)

may titser na babae
Existent   (109)

may babae siya
Existent   Possessor   (110)

may babae sa bar
Existent   Circumstance   (111)

ang titser ang babae
Attribute Isolator   (112)

ang mayroon niya ang babae
Possessor   Isolator   (113)

ang pupuntahan niya ang babae
Circumstance   Isolator   (114)

The network formalizing these oppositions is outlined in Fig 7.5; the first class of relational clause considered (105)–(109) is referred to as ascriptive.

Note that the network in Fig. 7.5 treats the answer to the question of whether what are traditionally referred to as possessive *may* constructions (eg. (110)) and existential *may* constructions (eg. (109) and (111)) are the same or different as both yes and no (cf. McFarland 1978). All of (109)–(111) realize the feature [existential], meaning that they provide a class of candidates to make their predications arguable, but they differ in that (109) is intensive, (110) possessive and (111) circumstantial.

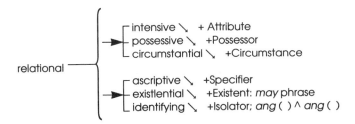

relational

intensive \   + Attribute
possessive \   +Possessor
circumstantial \   +Circumstance

ascriptive \   +Specifier
existlential \   +Existent: *may* phrase
identifying \   +Isolator; *ang* ( ) ∧ *ang* ( )

Figure 7.5. Relational processes in Tagalog

4.5. Congruence between Relational, Material and Mental Processes

As Ramos and Cena (1980) pointed out, the existential option provided in Fig. 7.5 is not limited to relational clauses but applies productively to all types of process. The main difference and complicating factor is that while relational clauses contain just one participant that can be existentialized (i.e. the Specifier if existential clauses are interpreted as deriving from ascriptive ones), material and mental processes allow any participant or circumstance focused on by the verb to be turned into an indefinite class. The Senser for example is existentialized in (115) and the Medium in (116):

may na-galit   sa babae
     was angry   woman
"Someone was angry at the woman."   (115)

may d-um-ating
     came
"Someone came."   (116)

Note that these examples are Topicless, like (109) and (111) above.
When the Phenomenon or Goods are existentialized however, the Senser and Medium take over as Topic, producing the apparently anomolous structures in (117) and (118):

may k-in-a-galit-an ang babae
     was angry at   TM woman
"The woman was angry at someone."   (117)

may in-inom ang babae
     drank   TM woman
"The woman drank something."   (118)

The verbs in (117) and (118) focus on the missing class of existentialized participant while the Topic marker falls on the out of focus Senser or Medium. Contrast (119) and (120) with focus affixes and Topic markers in step:

k-in-a-galit-an ng babae   ang tao
was angry at   woman TM   man
"The woman was angry at the person."   (119)

Checklist for words-links

$$\frac{n \times (n-1)}{2} = \lambda$$

1-10		11-20		21-30		31-40	
1.	0	11.	55	21.	210	31.	465
2.	1	12.	66	22.	231	32.	496
3.	3	13.	78	23.	253	33.	528
4.	6	14.	91	24.	276	34.	561
5.	10	15.	105	25.	300	35.	595
6.	15	16.	120	26.	325	36.	630
7.	21	17.	136	27.	351	37.	666
8.	28	18.	153	28.	378	38.	703
9.	36	19.	171	29.	406	39.	741
10.	45	20.	190	30.	435	40.	780

Handwritten annotations (11-20 column): 5, 5.5, 6, 6.5, 7, 7.5, 8, 8.5, 9, 9.5
Handwritten annotations (21-30 column): 10, 10.5, 11, 11.5, 12, 12.5, 13, 13.5, 14, 14.5
Handwritten left margin: 1:½, 1:1, 1:1.5, 1:1.5, 2, 2.5, 3, 3.5, 4, 4.5

in-inom ng babae   ang inumin
drank   woman TM drink
"The woman drank the drink."   (120)

What seems to be going on here is that Tagalog clauses prefer to have Topics and if there are inherent participants in the clause that are more agentive than the existentialized participant, then these are selected as Topic in spite of the verbal focus affixes. This appears to be what was going on in the existential possessive relational clauses reviewed above, which unlike the intensive or circumstantial type did turn out to have a Topic in their existential form.

Like existential constructions, identifying structures also apply productively to mental and material processes:

ang babae ang na-galit   sa tao
        woman   was angry   person
"The woman was the one who was angry at the person."   (121)

ang babae ang um-inom ng beer
        woman   drank
"The woman was the one who drank the beer"   (122)

Identifying clauses are in fact preferred for information questions about participants:

sino ang um-inom ng beer
who   drank
"Who (was the one who) drank the beer?"   (123)

sino ang k-in-a-galit-an ng babae
who   was angry at   woman
"Who was the one the woman was angry at?"   (124)

And identifying structures are the normal way of quoting speech:

"Sino ang um-inom ng beer?" ang tanong   niya
who   drank   question his
"Who (was the one who) drank the beer? (was the question)
he asked."   (125)

In general these structures are more frequently used than in English, and occur in Filipino English in situations where they sound odd to a native speaker. The following, for example, is common when two friends are about to go out:

Let's go now. I will be the one to accompany you.   (126)

Apparently simply making *I* the Subject does not sound exclusive enough to Filipino ears.

The productivity of both existential and identifying structures, as far as mental and material processes are concerned, raises the question of whether non-existential non-identifying structures, such as those in (119) and (120), are basically ascriptive. This has in fact been suggested by Naylor (1980) and is clearly implied in the work of Bloomfield (1917), Lopez (1941) and McFarland (1978). The main point these authors make is that non-focus participants in clause structure are related to verbs by the same morphology that structures partitive and possessive constructions in the nominal group. In (127)–(129), for example, the morpheme /naŋ/ (orthographically ng and nang) relates babae to the nominal groups ang damit and titser and to the verb na-kita.

```
ang damit   ng babae
     clothes      woman
"the woman's clothes"                              (127)

titser    nang babae    iyon
teacher          woman    that
"that teacher of women"                            (128)

na-kita ng babae    ang titser
saw          woman TM  teacher
"The woman saw the teacher."                       (129)
```

Similarly, in (130)–(132), kaniya "her/his" is linked in the same way to both nominal groups and verbs.

```
ang kaniya-ng damit
     her    lk  clothes
"her clothes"                                      (130)

kaniya-ng titser    iyon
her    lk  teacher  that
"That's a teacher of hers."                        (131)
```

kaniya-ng na-kita ang titser (cf. Naylor 1980:41)
her   lk saw   TM teacher
"She saw the teacher."   (132)

Bloomfield (1917:170ff) referred to the *ng/nang* phrases in all these examples as expressing disjunctive attribution; similarly, Lopez (1941:271–273) talked of enlarging both Subject and Predicates by attribution in these structures. As far as markers are concerned, they would argue, Tagalog makes no distinction between nominal and verbal predicates as far as their internal structure or relation to the Topic is concerned. Using the terms of reference of this paper, this is to argue that the relationship between the Topic and the rest of the sentence in relational, mental and material processes is identical, with the implication that it is relational ascriptive clauses that provide the clearest model of the relationship between Topic and predicate.

In short then, like relational processes, material and mental processes can be treated as having ascriptive, existential and identifying variants. Let us try to develop this argument once again for non-relational processes, beginning with the nominalization in (133):

ang pag-inom ng babae ng beer
    drinking   woman
"the drinking by a woman of some beer"   (133)

How does one argue with something like this? The necessary step is to pin down the predication, by de-nominalizing and adding focus:

um-inom ang babae ng beer
drank   TM woman
"The woman drank some beer."   (134)

in-inom ng babae   ang beer
drank   woman TM
"The woman drank the beer."   (135)

But note that this is just one way of tying down the predication. One might want to argue that it was the woman and no one else who drank, or the beer and nothing else that was drunk:

ang babae ang um-inom ng beer
    woman   drank
"The woman was the one who drank some beer."   (136)

ang beer ang <u>in</u>-inom ng babae
          drank   woman
"The beer was what the woman drank."   (137)

Or, alternatively, one might wish simply to state that someone, or some woman, drank some beer—or that something, or some beer, was drunk:

may <u>um</u>-inom ng beer
    drank
"Someone drank some beer."   (138)

may babae- ng <u>um</u>-inom ng beer
    woman lk drank
"There was some woman drank some beer."   (139)

may <u>in</u>-inom ang babae
    drank   TM woman
"The woman had something to drink."   (140)

may beer na <u>in</u>-inom ang babae
        lk drank   TM woman
"There was some beer the woman drank."   (141)

Unfortunately this brings us to the problem of Subject and Topic in Tagalog—whether or not these two functions are distinct, and if so, what the special meaning of each is. Having set aside interpersonal meaning, in other words, in order to concentrate on experiential transitivity structures, one finds that the metafunctions are not water-tight. Like strata, they leak—and there is no way of pursuing the discussion here without taking interpersonal meaning into account. Such an extension is beyond the scope of this paper.

It should be noted in passing, however, that both existential and identifying clauses contain two Topic or Subject-like constituents: the two *ang* phrases of the identifying clause and the Topic and missing focused participant of the existential.[23] The interpretation of existential and identifying options in terms of arguability sketched out here may provide some basis for a distinctive characterization of Subject and Topic (or perhaps better Theme) in Tagalog.[24]

---

[23]Two such constituents are also found in marked theme constructions, such as *ang babae ay dumating ang nanay niya* "The woman, her mother came."

[24]Ramos and Cena (1980) also used existential constructions as the basis for distinguishing deep and surface Subjects; see also Cena (1978) on patient primacy.

To this point only verbless relational processes have been considered. Tagalog cannot in fact verbalize circumstantial relationals; but it can verbalize both the intensive and possessive types:

p-um-ula ang bulaklak
went red TM flower
"The flower turned red."   (142)

nagka-pera ang babae
got money TM woman
"The woman got/came to have some money."   (143)

With the intensive type (142) the Process conflates with the Attribute, and inflected with -um-;[25] with the possessive type the Process conflates with the possession and is inflected with magka-.

As noted above, intensive processes contain just one participant, and so the use of -um- once again as an intransitive middling affix is predictable.[26] The use of mag- with possessives is much less clear, since the Possessor is obtaining goods, and gathering is an implosive meaning. Taken within the context of relational processes themselves, however, the possessive type is certainly more extroverted than the intensive: One participant is affecting another and the goods are in motion.

The meaning of causative-like affixation with the intensive type is also revealing. The magpa- prefix, which normally introduces an extra agent who then makes or lets the Medium or Senser do something, takes on a purely "reflexive" meaning. Thus nagpa-ganda ang babae means "The woman made herself beautiful"; only the woman is involved. These reflexive causatives look like the relational process counterpart of mental processes of provocation and material processes of affliction in that the Topic is affected by the Process.

Pushing a point then, relational, material and mental processes are generalized in Fig. 7.5.[27]

---

[25]Mang- is also used where the change in intensives is more transient; here again, the mang- affixes will be set aside as variants on -um-.

[26]Ramos treats the flowers in (142) as Objective case; note that this fails to bring out the relationship between pula ang bulaklak "The flowers are red" and p-um-ula ang bulaklak "The flowers turned red"; the flowers would both be treated as Specifier in the analysis developed here.

[27]Clauses containing verbalized adjectives, such as ni-laks-an ng babae ang tugtog "The woman turned up the music" are on the borderline between relational and material processes; predictably they focus with -an since they affect the quali-

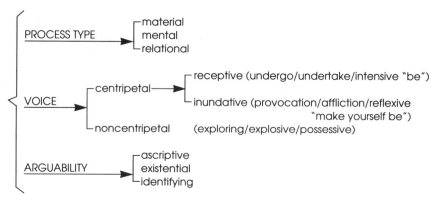

Figure 7.6. Generalized network for Tagalog transitivity

Note in passing that the basic centripetal or not opposition in Tagalog is consonant with the parallel ambiguities in causative, abilitative and acquisitive processes: The causative affixes mean either to make or to let something happen (*magpa-, pa-* . . . *-in-, ipa-*); the abilitative affixes mean either that someone was able to or happened to do something (*maka-, ma-*); and the acquisitive *magka-* ((143) above) means either that someone got deliberately or simply came to have something. It would be interesting to follow this up with distributional studies focusing on correlations between centripetality and letting, happening to and coming to have on the one hand and noncentripetality and making, being able to and deliberately getting on the other.

5. A NOTE ON VERBAL AND AFFECTIVE PROCESSES

5.1. Verbal Processes

Verbal processes are processes of communication that have the ability to project (to quote or report). In Tagalog these are identical to explosive material processes as far as affixes and markers are concerned. Their only distinctive feature as far as action clauses are concerned is their ability to accept a metaphenomenon as complement (eg. (145) below).

---

ty of the Topic, not its basic structure. Such clauses will be treated at this stage as material, involving a Medium (which cannot become topic) and Goods.

As noted above, when quoting, they typically appear in identifying structures:

"Huwag um-uwi,   ang sigaw niya sa kaniya-ng boyfriend."
don't go home   shout her   her   lk
"Don't go home" (was what) she shouted to her boyfriend."   (144)

When reporting, the metaphenomenon is usually in focus, but linked to the rest of the clause with a linker (signalling hypotaxis) rather than marked with *ang*. Thus, the apparently Topic-less (145):

s-in-abi ng boyfriend niya sa babae   na u-uwi   siya
said   her   woman lk will go home he
"Her boyfriend told the woman he would go home."   (145)

Answers are often treated as ejected, and focused on with *i-:*

i-s-in-agot ng boyfriend niya na wala[28] siya-ng ga-gaw-in
answered   her   lk   he   will do
"Her boyfriend answered there was nothing he would do."   (146)

5.2. Desire Processes

Desire processes are processes of wishing, wanting, hoping and the like. These resemble verbal and mental processes in that they can project, usually reporting rather than quoting:

gusto ng babae   na huwag um-alis ang boyfriend niya
want   woman lk don't   leave   TM   her
"The woman wished her boyfriend wouldn't go."   (147)

As the negative proposal particle *huwag* in (147) indicates, desire processes typically project in the imperative mode (commands and offers rather than statements and questions as with other mental processes).
     Desire processes are distinctive in Tagalog because of their lack of affix marking and lack of choice of Topic as far as markers are concerned. They are closely related to optative constructions like (148):

huwag sana   siya-ng um-alis
don't   optative he   lk leave
"Let him not leave/I don't want him to go."   (148)

---

[28]*Wala* is the negative counterpart of existential *may*.

They can often simply be treated as modulations in a verbal group complex:

ayaw niya-ng um-alis
not want he lk leave
"He doesn't want to leave." (149)

6. A NOTE ON -AN AND I-

6.1. -an

The interpretation of transitivity developed to this point has suggested four different roles for the suffix -an:

1. focus on superficially affected Goods in material processes
2. focus on the Direction in material processes
3. focus on Location
4. focus on the Phenomenon in mental process clauses of cognition and reaction

When not in focus, the participant in question is marked with sa if Direction, Location or the Phenomenon in reaction clauses; otherwise, the participant is marked with ng.

Functionally, it would appear then that -an is generally used to focus on participants that are circumstance-like in some respect and that some kind of generalized meaning of "place" is involved.

6.2. i-

A number of different roles have also been noted for -i-:

1. focus on Goods in explosive material processes
2. focus on Instrument
3. focus on Beneficiary
4. focus on Goods of all kinds in causative material processes and the Phenomenon in causative mental processes

When not in focus, Goods and Phenomena are marked with ng, Instruments with sa pamamagitan ng and Beneficiaries with para sa.

The meaning of this affix is very diverse experientially. However, from the perspective of interpersonal meaning, it seems to be associated with the idea of a service—an action undertaken by someone for someone else, possibly in response to a request. This is clearly the case in the causative constructions, where *i-* neutralizes the *-in-/-an/i-* opposition discussed above. In (150), the woman is making or letting her boyfriend act on her behalf:

i̱-p-in-a-sulat ng babae sa boyfriend niya ang bilin
made write   woman   her TM message
"The woman made her boyfriend write the message."   (150)

Beneficiaries are explicit clients for a service; and moving Goods are offered to conscious Direction participants. It remains to be argued that Instruments are typically focused on in a serving context (for which unfortunately there is as yet no distributional evidence).

The general meaning suggested for *i-* here then is an interpersonal, rather than an experiential one: It focuses on a range of participants and circumstances involved in the general meaning of "doing for."

7. LIMITATIONS OF THIS STUDY

Before summing up it is important to note that at least three major affix classes in Tagalog have not been functionally interpreted in this paper.[29] These are:

1. *ma-/p-in-a* verbs

na̱-nood ang babae ng sine
watched TM woman   film
"The woman watched some movies."   (151)

p̱-in-a̱-nood ng babae   ang sine
watched   woman TM film
"The woman watched the movie."   (152)

paniwala "believe," paligo "bathe," pakinig "listen," panood "watch," pangako "promise," panaginip "dream in sleep,"

---

[29]I am indebted to Wilfredo Muyargas and Frank Flores of the Inter-Church Language School for drawing these classes to my attention.

pangarap "day-dream," pangaral "teach," panganak "give birth," pakiramdam "feel out," pakisama "get on with," pakialam "meddle," panalangin "pray"

2. *mag-/i-pa* verbs

nag-dala ang babae ng sulat
sent   TM woman   letter
"The woman sent some letters."   (153)

i-p-in-a-dala ng babae   ang sulat
sent   woman TM letter
"The woman sent the letter."   (154)

ipaliwanag "explain," ipahinga "rest," ipatawad "forgive," ipalabas "show," ipaalam "say good-bye," ipadala "send," ipangalan "name," ipakilala "introduce," ipahayag "reveal," ipakita "make known"

3. *mag-/i-pag-/pag-* . . . *-an* verbs

nag-bawal ang pangulo   ng welga
forbad   TM president   strikes
"The president forbad strikes."   (155)

i-p-in-ag-bawal ng pangulo   ang welga
forbad   president TM strike
"The president forbad the strike."   (156)

p-in-ag-bawal-an ng pangulo   ang manggagawa sa pagtitipon
forbad   president TM workers   assembling
"The president forbad the workers from assembling."   (157)

magmalaki "be proud of," magkaloob "offer," magkatiwala "trust," magbawal "forbid," magbilin "give orders," magtapat "confide," maglihim "keep secret," maglingkod "serve," magkanulo "betray," magkaila "deny," magdiwang "celebrate," magtanggol "defend"

As well, circumstances have not been discussed in a principled way. Because most circumstances can in fact be made Topic of a sentence, and so are critically involved in a description of marker and affix interaction, this is a serious shortcoming.

8. SUMMARY AND CONCLUSION

In this paper a reinterpretation of Tagalog case relations within the framework of systemic functional linguistics has been proposed. The interpretation is functional in that it starts with the notion of process type (sensing, doing and being) and establishes distinct case frames for each of these different types of experiential meaning. At the same time the interpretation is grammatical in that no semantically oriented categories have been established unless clearly implicated in the grammar. These case frames are reviewed in (158)–(162).

mental—Process + Senser + Phenomenon

na-hiya	ang babae	sa bahay niya
was ashamed	TM woman	house her
Process	Senser	Phenomenon

"The woman was ashamed of her house."   (158)

material—Process + Medium (+ Goods) (+ Direction)

k-um-uha	ang babae	ng pera	sa bangko
took	TM woman	money	bank
Process	Medium	Goods	Direction

"The woman took some money from the bank."   (159)

relational—Specifier + Attribute or Possessor or Circumstance

ma-bait	ang babae
nice	TM woman
Attribute	Specifier

"The woman is nice."   (160)

sa kaibigan ko	ang babae
friend my	TM woman
Possessor	Specifier

"The woman belongs to (is with) my friend."   (161)

nasa bahay	ang babae
in house	TM woman
Circumstance	Specifier

"The woman is in the house."   (162)

In addition it has been suggested that voice in Tagalog functions not in terms of a transitive or ergative model but is organized around centrifugality. Thus, each process type has both introverted and extroverted nuclei depending on whether the nucleus is a kind of "super nova" or "black hole." These oppositions are outlined in (163)–(168).

centripetal

na-inip   ang babae
was bored TM woman
"The woman was bored."   (163)

t-um-ulog ang babae
slept   TM woman
"The woman slept."   (164)

p-um-uti   ang babae
whitened   TM woman
"The woman turned pale."   (165)

noncentripetal

i-ni-hulog ng babae   ang damit   niya sa sahig
let fall   woman TM clothes her   floor
"The woman let her clothes fall to the floor."   (166)

na-tanda-an ng babae   ang g-in-awa niya
remembered   woman TM did   he
"The woman remembered what he did."   (167)

nagka-sakit ang babae (cf. nagkaroon ng sakit ang babae)
got sick   TM woman
"The woman got sick."   (168)

Further, it was noted that within the centripetal type, a distinction could be drawn between nuclei that are simply receptive and those that are actually inundated by the environment. Thus, the oppositions in (169) to (174).

receptive

k-um-ain ang babae ng isda
ate   TM woman   fish
"The woman ate some fish."   (169)

na-inis   ang babae sa kapatid niya
got irritated TM woman   sibling her
"The woman got irritated with her sister."   (170)

g-um-anda   ang babae
grew beautiful TM woman
"The woman grew beautiful."   (171)

inundative

g-in-utom ang babae
hungried TM woman
"The woman got hungry."   (172)

in-inis   ng kapatid niya ang babae
irritated   sibling her TM woman
"Her sister irritated the woman."   (173)

nagpa-ganda   ang babae
made herself beautiful TM woman
"The woman made herself beautiful (put on her
make-up)."   (174)

Finally it was argued that the ascriptive/identifying/existential oppositions that display themselves most clearly in relational clauses are in fact fully productive in Tagalog throughout the process type paradigm; further, these options are interpretable in terms of the way in which predications are made arguable. The ascriptive type presents one of a number of candidates as Topic to specify the argument; the identifying type presents this candidate to the exclusion of others; and the existential type simply posits the existence of a set of candidates.

ascriptive

na-tanaw ng babae   ang anak niya
observed   woman TM child her
"The woman observed her child."   (175)

identifying

ang anak ang na-tanaw ng babae
     child   observed   woman
"The child was the one the woman observed."   (176)

existential

may <u>na</u>-tanaw ang babae
observed   woman
"The woman observed someone."[30]   (177)

In his Introduction to *An Introduction to Functional Grammar*
Halliday comments on 20th century linguistics as follows:

> Twentieth-century linguistics has produced an abundance of new the-
> ories, but it has tended to wrap old descriptions up inside them; what
> are needed now are new descriptions. Tasks have changed, ideas have
> changed, and languages have changed. . . . The old interpretations
> were good, but not good enough to last for all time, even when dressed
> up in new theoretical clothes.   (xxxiv)

While the description presented here does Tagalog up in new (systemic functional) theoretical clothes, it is hoped as well that it has
provided some new descriptions of transitivity patterns. Specifically,
it has been suggested that:

1. by first dividing clauses into process types a better motivated and more revealing set of cases can be proposed;
2. the central notion as far as voice is concerned is that of
   centrifugality;
3. ascriptive, identifying and existential options cross-classify process types with respect to arguability.

Finally it may be observed that a functional grammar whose
terms are carefully motivated with as many reactances as possible
does in fact lead, as Whorf initially suggested, to an interpretation of
languages as individuals. Instead of beginning boldly with a comprehensive set of universal categories and testing languages against
them, a functional grammar postpones the issue of universals until
more languages have been described on their own (not someone
else's) terms. It is in this sense that Halliday's systemic functional
grammar can be seen to be most clearly Whorfian in design.

---

[30]Note that in circumstantial relational processes, either the Specifier or the
Circumstance can be existentialized; thus related to *nasa bar ang babae* "The
woman is in the bar" one finds both *may babae sa bar* "There is a woman in the
bar" and *mayroon ang babae* "The woman is there" (cf. *wala siya* "She not
there"; *wala si Ruby* "Ruby's not there"); in the latter a definite Specifier is quite
natural.

REFERENCES

Bloomfield, L. (1917) *Tagalog Texts with Grammatical Analysis. Part 1: Texts and translation. Part 2: Grammatical analysis.* (University of Illinois Studies in Language and Literature 2 & 3) Urbana, Ill.: University of Illinois.

Cena, R. (1977) On resurrecting buried agents in certain Tagalog verbs. Mimeo.

Cena, R. (1978) Patient primacy in Tagalog. Paper presented at 1978 LSA Winter Meeting.

Cena R. (1979) Tagalog countererxamples to the accessability hierarchy. *Studies in Philippine Linguistics 3.* 119–124.

De Guzman, V. (1978) *Syntactic Derivation of Tagalog Verbs.* (Oceanic Linguistics Special Publication 16) Honolulu: University of Hawaii Press.

Fillmore, C. (1968) The case for case. E. Bach & T. Harms [Eds.] *Universals in Linguistics Theory.* New York: Holt, Rinehart & Winston. 1–88.

Fillmore, C. (1977) The case for case reopened. P. Cole & J.M. Saddock [Eds.] *Grammatical Relations (Syntax and Semantics B)* New York: Academic Press. 59–82.

Gonzales, A. (1984) *Acquiring Pilipino as a First Language.* Manila: Linguistic Society of the Philippines.

Halliday, M.A.K. (1976) Types of process. G. Kress [Ed.] *Halliday: system and function in language.* London: Oxford University Press. 159–173.

Halliday, M.A.K. (1984) On the ineffability of grammatical categories. A. Manning, P. Martin & K. McCalla [Eds.] *The Tenth LACUS Forum 1983.* Columbia, S.C.: Hornbeam Press. 3–18 [reprinted in J.D. Benson, M.J. Cummings & W.S. Greaves [Eds.] (1988) *Linguistics in a Systemic Perspective.* Amsterdam: John Benjamins (Current Issues in Linguistic Theory 39). 27–52.

Halliday, M.A.K. (1985) *An Introduction to Functional Grammar.* London: Edward Arnold.

Huddleston, R.D. (1970) Some remarks on case grammar. *Linguistic Inquiry,* 1(4) 501–511.

Lopez, C. (1941) *A Manual of the Philippine National Language.* Manila, Philippines: Institute of National Language.

Martin, J.R. (1983) Participant identification in English, Tagalog and Kâte. *Australian Journal of Linguistics* 3(1) 45–74.

Martin, J.R. (1988) Grammatical conspiracies in Tagalog: Family, face and fate—with regard to Benjamin Lee Whorf. J.D. Benson, M.J. Cummings & W.S. Greaves [Eds.] *Linguistics in a Systemic Perspective.* Amsterdam: Benjamins. 243–300.

Martin, J.R. (1990) Interpersonal grammatization: mood and modality in Tagalog. *Philippine Journal of Linguistics* 21(1) (Special Issue on the Silver Anniversary of the Language Study Centre of Philippine Normal College 1964–1989—Part 2). 2–51.

Martin, J.R. (in press a) Metalinguistic diversity: The case from case.

R. Hasan, C. Cloran, & D. Butt [Eds.] *Functional Descriptions: Theory in practice.* Amsterdam: Benjamins (Current Issues in Linguistic Theory) 1996. 323–372.

Martin, J.R. (1995) Logical meaning, interdependency and the linking particle {-ng/na} in Tagalog. *Functions of Language.* 2(2), 189–228.

McFarland, C.D. (1976) *A Provisional Classification of Tagalog Verbs.* (Studies of Languages and Cultures of Asia and Africa Monograph Series 8) Tokyo: Institute for the Study of Languages and Cultures of Asia and Africa.

McFarland, C.D. (1978) Tagalog existentials. *Philippine Journal of Linguistics* 9. 1–2. 1–13.

McFarland, C.D. (1984) Computers and Tagalog grammar. A. Gonzales [Ed.] *Language Planning, Implementation and Evaluation: Essays in honour of Bonifacio P Sibayan on his sixty-seventh birthday.* Manila: Linguistic Society of the Philippines. 230–245.

Naylor, P.B. (1980) Linking, relation marking and Tagalog syntax. P.B. Naylor [Ed.] *Austronesian Studies: Papers from the second Eastern conference on Austronesian languages (Michigan papers on South and Southeast Asia)* Ann Arbor, MI: Centre for South and Southeast Asian Studies. 33–50.

Panganiban, J.Y. (1973) *Diksyuunaryo—Tesauro Pilipino—Ingles.* Manila, Philippines: Manlapaz.

Payne, T.E. (1982) Role and reference related subject properties and ergativity in Yup'ik Eskimo and Tagalog. *Studies in Language* VI(1) 75–106.

Rafael, T. (1978) Topic in Tagalog revisited. *Studies in Philippine Linguistics* 2. 36–48.

Ramos, T. (1974) *The Case System of Tagalog Verbs.* (Pacific Linguistics Series B 27) Canberra, Australia: The Linguistic Circle of Canberra.

Ramos, T. & Cena, R. (1980) Existential, locative and possessive in Tagalog. *Philippine Journal of Linguistics* 11 (2) 15–26.

Schachter, P. (1977) Review of T. Ramos The Case System of Tagalog Verbs. *Language* 53(3) 707–711.

Schachter, P. & Otanes F. (1972). *Tagalog Reference Grammar.* Berkeley, CA: University of California Press.

Starosta, S. (1973) The faces of case. *Language Sciences* 25. 1–14.

Starosta, S. (1978) The one per Sent solution. W. Abrahamn [Ed.] *Valence, Semantic Case and Grammatical Relations.* Amsterdam: John Benjamins. 459–576.

Starosta, S. (1988) *The Case for Lexicase.* London: Pinter.

Whorf, B.L. (1956) *Language, Thought and Reality: selected papers of Benjamin Lee Whorf.* J.B. Carroll [Ed.] Cambridge, MA: MIT Press.

8

A Systemic Functional Approach to Complementation in English

Robin P. Fawcett

Computational Linguistics Unit
University of Wales, Cardiff

1. THE PURPOSE OF THIS CHAPTER

A festschrift is a compliment to a significant figure in some field of study. This chapter is offered as a compliment to the person to whom I owe the most—by far—in developing the understanding of language I now possess. But this chapter is not simply a compliment; it is also offered as a complement: a complement to Halliday's own work in a particular area of the lexicogrammar. It is moreover a complement that concerns complements—or rather, because it is the tradition in Systemic Functional Grammar (SFG) to use a capital letter for elements of clause structure, it is a compliment that concerns Complements.[1]

As with so much of Michael Halliday's writing, his *Introduction to Functional Grammar* (1985/94) (henceforth IFG) is full of mar-

---

[1]The work reported here was supported by grants from The Speech Research Unit at DRA Malvern as part of Assignment No. ASO4BP44, on Spoken Language Understanding and Dialogue (SLUD), and by The University of Wales, Cardiff. I am grateful to my fellow members of the COMMUNAL team, who have helped de-

velous insights that refresh traditional grammar and challenge the syntax-bound assumptions of the formalist tradition.[2] However, while it covers a great deal of the grammar of English, it cannot cover every aspect of both meaning and form for the whole of the language. And when it is looked at as a systemic functional grammar of English, it has two major lacks that must be made up in order to produce a satisfactory account of our topic.

The first, which seems at first sight a surprising one in a volume that is the first book-length description of English by the major architect of SFG, is that IFG contains hardly any *system networks*. In other words, there are virtually no diagrams that set out the sometimes complex relations between choices of meaning that lie at the heart of the systemic view of language. However, as Halliday himself says (1994: xvii):

> This book is not an account of systemic theory, nor does it present the system networks for English grammar. . . . It presents the structures that are the "outputs" of the networks—which realize collectively the sets of features that can be chosen.

At this point I should perhaps remind you of Halliday's purpose in writing IFG. As he emphasizes in the *Introduction*, IFG is, as its title states, an "introduction" to understanding the nature of language. His strategy in this difficult task is to approach the phenomenon of language by starting from the relatively observable and then to move on to the relatively more abstract. So here he starts from text—or, more specifically, examples of *text-sentences*—and moves to their multi-functional structure. No doubt he will in due course give us a further volume that describes his vision of the even less directly

---

velop the ideas presented here—especially Gordon Tucker, with whom I have shared the gradual discovery that lexis is, in a sense, less like "most delicate grammar," as originally proposed by Halliday (1961), and more like "fairly delicate grammar"—as exemplified here for lexical verbs. I am also grateful to Yuen Lin, for many good talks on many aspects of the model, for help in implementing it, and for developing further DEFREL (the implementation language for GENESYS, first developed by Joan Wright). I would like to express my thanks to Chris Butler for his comments on an earlier version of this paper—and in particular for prompting me to make explicit in this chapter my view (a) that syntax and the corresponding parts of semantics are mutually defining, rather than one determining the other, and (b) that I assume, as a working hypothesis, that differences of form typically reflect differences of meaning.

[2] I shall normally refer to the 1994 Edition, since there are a number of changes from the 1985 version.

observable aspect of language—the system networks for the meaning potential itself. In the metaphor of computing, this is the core of the program of which the text-sentences are the outputs (Fawcett 1993).

However, in many cases the major outlines of the system networks are there in IFG—if only implicitly. Despite the lack of explicit system network diagrams, the systemically minded reader can to some extent infer from Halliday's verbal descriptions—and even more clearly from many of the matrix-type diagrams—at least the broad-brush patterns of the system networks that underlie the functional analyses of sentences that he offers. (We shall shortly come to two examples of such "inferred networks.")

From the viewpoint of a reader who wants a full overview of what a SFG of English is like, there is a second and equally serious lack—though it is perhaps less obvious. It is one that was inevitable once the decision was taken to omit the system networks. It is the lack of the *realization rules* (or "realization statements," to use Halliday's term for them). It is these vital little components of the grammar that convert the relatively abstract set of *semantic choices* in the system network into *forms*—the relatively concrete *structures* consisting of multiple elements (or "functions," in one sense of that overworked term) and *items*—words and morphemes. Yet such realization rules are essential, as will be seen, if we are to gain a satisfactory understanding of the relationship between the system networks of semantic features and their realization in items, syntax and intonation—or in the preference of features to be selected on later passes through the network.[3] (The overall approach to modelling language used here is set out most fully in Fawcett 1980, and subsequent publications with a special bearing on the nature of the lexicogrammar include Fawcett 1983, 1987, 1988b and c, 1990, 1993, and 1995. The fullest current statement is in Fawcett, Tucker and Lin's "How a Systemic Functional Grammar Works" (1993).) The particular problem addressed in this chapter requires that the rules that realize the choices in the networks be spelled out very clearly.

---

[3]Although Halliday does not foreground the term "semantics" in his writings, no doubt because of the conceptual baggage that it carries with it, he uses the term "semantic" throughout IFG to describe the types of meanings with which he is concerned. It seems to me that systemic linguistics, with its "pluri-functional" approach to meaning, can legitimately claim to offer a broader approach to meaning than other theories. I therefore feel happy to use the term "semantics" to refer to the level of choices in the "meaning potential" of clauses and their component units.

What precisely is the problem to be addressed here? In the terms of traditional grammar, it can be expressed as the problem of how best to handle the way in which lexical verbs appear to determine the structure of the clauses that are, in some sense yet to be defined here, "dependent" on them. In the literature of transformational generative grammar and its successors, and in most current descriptive grammars, this phenomenon is known as "complementation" (and sometimes as "complementization"). It is widely regarded—and with some justification—as a fairly complex problem for the grammarian, and so as something of a test for a theory of grammar. It may therefore be useful to outline how a SFG can handle this phenomenon—this being the first such account to be published, as far as I am aware. (Hudson 1971 describes an approach to the problem that is "systemic," but it is set in a syntactic rather than a semantic framework, so that it fails to capture the concern with meaning that is a dominant characteristic of SFG; some further comments on the differences follow shortly.)[4]

In an SFG, however, we would wish to redefine the problem. As we shall see in due course, this relationship between the formal phenomenon of a lexical verb and the associated "complement structure" is expressed via the system networks that define the *meaning potential* of the language—and this "semanticization" of our view of language somewhat changes the picture.

Specifically, I shall examine some typical cases of *mental Processes*, these being the type where this phenomenon most typically occurs. Thus, this chapter describes a SFG approach to a small but significant portion of a major area of the syntax and semantics of English. Here I assume that, while there is very often NOT a one-to-one relationship between syntax and semantics, the two levels of form and meaning in language are MUTUALLY DEFINING. In other words, the range of what one can "mean" through language is restricted by what one can "say," and one cannot "say" (except by talking nonsense) things that are not built into the meaning system of the language (see Fawcett 1980 and especially Fawcett 1983).

---

[4]Moreover, if a Subject is regarded as a special type of Complement—as a Participant Role—that has been given the additional task of marking the MOOD, then I can say that I am using the term in a sense that brings the Hallidayan and the Chomskyan schools closer (at least in this regard). In a full treatment of complementation, then, we would also need to handle clauses that fill a Subject, such as *For Ike to become a vegetarian will create problems for Ivy,* as well as those that fill Complements, as in *Ivy would prefer Ike not to become one.* However, we shall not be involved with the first type here.

I should make it clear at this point that the model of language drawn on here is the one that is currently being developed in a computer implementation of a SFG in the COMMUNAL Project (COnvivial Man-Machine Understanding through NAtural Language) at the University of Wales, Cardiff, in an integrated text production and text understanding system.)[5] The challenge of Computational Linguistics (CL) to the linguist is to make one's model explicit enough to be expressed as a computer program. This is a demanding discipline, and it is the need to meet that requirement that has led to the formulation of the grammar to be described here—and specifically to the innovations to be described in Section 5. The Cardiff Grammar, as it is coming to be known, has been developed by Fawcett, Tucker, and other colleagues, both for the analysis of text and as a component in an overall computer model of natural language generation. It is, in a sense, a "sister" grammar to that described in IFG, in that it has grown out of the general framework of SFG that has been developing since around 1970. The two approaches are compatible, in the sense that one can often import insights from one to the other, with certain adaptations. In what follows I will make clear where the Cardiff Grammar differs from IFG—but here, in this festschrift for Michael Halliday, I will concentrate less upon the differences between my model and his than on an aspect of lexicogrammar that is needed in BOTH frameworks. The essential point is that, whichever way one decides on the matters of difference, the phenomenon of "complementation" requires some such procedure as that to be described here.

Let us now specify "complementation" as precisely as possible in terms that are more explicitly *systemic functional*. The task is to specify the various types of internal structure found in the clauses that may occur as the Complements of clauses in which the Main

---

[5]COMMUNAL stands for COnvivial Man-Machine Understanding through NAtural Language, and it is a long-term project in building a system for communication with computers that draws on systemic functional linguistics (supplemented by other concepts when they are found useful). At its heart lies the GENESYS sentence generator, so called because it GENErates SYStemically (i.e. using a SFG). . See Fawcett (1988a) for an account of the founding assumptions of the project, which began in 1987. See Fawcett and Tucker (1990) for a "mid-term" report, and for the fullest account yet published of how a SFG works (specifically when functioning as the sentence generator in a computer model of natural language generation, see Fawcett, Tucker and Lin (1993). (Other relevant papers include Fawcett 1990, 1994a and 1994b.) The grammar used in GENESYS—and also for related work in textual description—is sometimes referred to as "the Cardiff Grammar"; see Fawcett (in preparation a) and (in preparation b) for the fullest descriptive account of the latter.

Verb is one that expresses certain types of mental Process. More precisely, I shall suggest here that such a clause fills the Phenomenon of the "mother" clause—and that in some cases that Phenomenon may become the Subject, so that we must interpret "Complement" in the sense of "a Participant Role that is expected by the Main Verb." I will not have space to present more than a "narrow slice" of the full picture of the proposed solution to this complex problem area, a full treatment of which would require a whole book. But I believe it will be sufficient for our present purposes, and that it will demonstrate how the much fuller model implemented in COMMUNAL works. I will exemplify the problem and the proposed solution by referring to some central senses of the two verb forms *know* and *remember*.

One of the odd facts about the systemic literature of this area is how little is said about *know*—despite the fact that it is the realization of one of the most frequent of all cognitive Processes. It is simply not mentioned at all in the only serious attempt so far in a systemic framework at handling the syntax of complementation generatively. This is Hudson's *English Complex Sentences* (1971), a work that offers very full lists of the verbs covered. Nor, in fact, does Halliday have much to say in IFG about the Process of "knowing." We do at least know from its inclusion in Table 7(14) on p. 270 that Halliday would not regard the clause dependent on it as a Participant Role in the Process; see the discussion of this matter in Section 3. Here I will provide a fairly full—but still incomplete—picture of the complementation of "knowing." We shall find that, by working in a combination of the two paradigms of systemic functional grammar and computational linguistics, it is possible to develop an overall model that has the attraction of being relatively simple to understand (without oversimplifying matters) and sufficiently flexible to handle the rich variety of data that are relevant to the topic.

The specific questions addressed here are as follows:

1. What types of choice in meaning cause the type of re-entry to the overall network that generates dependent clauses? (The answer given here is exemplified through mental Processes of "cognition," but similar questions and answers can be provided for each other type.)

2. What are the types of semantic choice relevant to determining the internal structure of such clauses? (The answer is exemplified here by a wide range of types.)

3. How can we most completely and yet economically provide for the fact that different Process-types (sometimes consisting of a class with only one member) require different ar-

rays of such structures? (Answers considered here include repeating the relevant features in many sub-networks, having one large system for complementation, having very complex "wiring" to single features, and/or by various types of "preference re-setting rules" that change the probabilities in systems.)

2. PAST SYSTEMIC APPROACHES TO "COMPLEMENTATION": AN OVERVIEW

The term "complementation" is one that has long been associated with a Chomskyan approach to language—Transformational Generative Grammar (TG) and its descendants such as Government and Binding (GB), Generalized Phrase Structure Grammar (GPSG) and Lexical Functional Grammar (LFG)—with their emphasis on syntagmatic relations at the level of form ("syntax"). However, the term has found its way into the systemic literature through the work of Hudson (see especially 1971 and 1976) and Butler 1985. This Chomskyan emphasis on *syntagmatic* relations at the level of *form* is in clear contrast with the Hallidayan emphasis in SFG on *paradigmatic* relations between *meanings*. However, because of the long-established use of the term "Complement" in systemic linguistics, the term "complementation" in fact lends itself fairly happily, with some minor adaptations, to use in systemic grammar too. Indeed, the fact that systemic grammar uses the traditional term "Complement" in a sense that includes the term "Object" means that the systemic usage is quite close to the sense of the term "complementation" in Chomskyan syntax.[6]

"How well," it may be asked, "has SFG coped with this challenge?" Butler (1985: 96f), in his chapter "Systemic syntax," offered a useful summary of recent systemic work in syntax. However, it is important to distinguish between two types of description of complementation. The first type simply specifies the descriptive apparatus needed to describe text-sentences (i.e. the syntactic *outputs* of a generative grammar). The second type describes the generative grammar itself.

---

[6]However, in Young's (1980) systemically based account of English clause structure, "complementation" is used in a much broader sense (i.e. as a cover term for a discussion of the number and type of Complements). Following Halliday's earlier approach, Young handles the problems discussed here in terms of "phase"—for which see the next section.

Butler (1985: 102) offers a rather stark evaluation of systemic work in this area up to 1985. He states that "clausal complementation . . . . has received scant attention in Halliday's publications," and later (p. 230) he adds my name to Halliday's, saying, "syntactic phenomena such as complementation have been neglected by Halliday and Fawcett." This criticism (which could in fact be levelled at all systemic linguists except Hudson) is certainly true of Halliday's and my provision in PUBLISHED WORK for complementation in terms of the system networks and realization rules. However, it seems to ignore the fact that both Halliday and I have provided frameworks for describing the *syntactic structures* of complementation found in sentences in texts. Thus, I would claim to have provided at least a descriptive framework for these cases as early as 1974 (see Fawcett 1974, 1975, 1976, 1981), and I would point out that Butler himself provides a summary of these proposals (1985: 94–102). Similarly, Halliday could justifiably claim that IFG outlines an innovative functional approach to the structure of many aspects of this area (see the next section)—though IFG had of course not been published at the time that Butler was writing.

As Butler rightly points out, it is Hudson (1971: 102–114) who has made the most detailed systemic proposals for complementation published so far—but he did so in a framework that is rather different from what is needed in a SFG approach. His work was oriented to syntax at the level of *form,* and he made no claim to handle the equivalent phenomena at the *semantic* level. The question then becomes: "How far would complementation in a semantically motivated systemic grammar differ from Hudson's proposals?" The answer, based on a comparison between Hudson's network and the system networks for the meaning potential of this area in the Cardiff Grammar (excerpts of which are published here for the first time) is that the semantic system networks are significantly different. It is not simply a question of "semanticizing" the labels on Hudson's networks, but of re-thinking, from basic principles, the nature of semantically motivated system networks. But at the same time there is a considerable debt to Hudson's pioneering systemic work, especially in relation to realization rules.

3. HALLIDAY'S TWO APPROACHES TO COMPLEMENTATION

Let us now look briefly at how Halliday has approached the phenomenon of "complementation." He has in fact taken two quite different approaches to the problems of this area, and both have found their way into IFG.

In his early "Scale and Category" work (deriving from Halliday 1961), Halliday made extensive use of the concept of "phase" to describe examples such as (1a) & (1b) and (2a) & (2b) below. Here the two Main Verbs in each pair (*want* and *go* and *promise* and *go*) were both regarded as elements of a single clause. Thus the clause structure analysis of (1a) & (2a) was said to be S P P (where S = Subject; P = Predicator; and C = Complement). And that of (1b & 2b) would be S P C P (or S P C/S P or S P Z P, where Z = C/S). The distinction between (1b) and (2b) to be made below in Section 4 would therefore not be made.

Ike wanted to go. (1a)

Ike wanted Ivy to go. (1b)

Ike promised to go. (2a)

Ike promised Ivy to go. (2b)

In Halliday (1994: 259), on the other hand, there are not one but two clauses in such cases. The second is in a "hypotactic" relationship to the first (i.e. one of dependency without embedding).

We will now taker a closer look at Halliday's current proposals for mental Processes and the dependent clauses associated with them. There are in fact TWO parts of IFG that refer to the area of grammar that we are considering. In "Mental processes: processes of sensing" (1994: 112–119) Halliday outlines his approach to *mental Processes* in English. Specifically, he proposes that there are three types: *perception* (for Processes of "seeing," "hearing," etc.), *affection* ("liking," "fearing," etc.), and *cognition* ("thinking," "knowing," "understanding," etc.). In the other major Process types—material and relational Processes—he distinguishes the major sub-categories by having different configurations of *Participant Roles* (Halliday 1970: 146, Fawcett 1980: 135–6). It is therefore a little surprising to find that his Participant Role analysis for mental Processes is that all three types have the same two PRs (i.e. what Halliday termed in IFG the *Senser* and the *Phenomenon*).

One difference between Halliday's approach and mine is that, in my own fuller network for mental Processes (which, as almost always, owes a great deal to Halliday's pioneering work) I do not use the term "Senser." I distinguish instead three different Participant

Roles, the *Perceiver* (in *perception* Processes), the *Emoter* (in *emotion* Processes) and the *Cognizant* (in *cognition* Processes).[7] One might predict that there would be some such differentiation, simply on the grounds that mental Processes are a major area of variation in type of Process, and the variation within each type is quite marked. Cognition and perception Processes, for example, can have a "third party" who "causes" a Cognizant or Perceiver to "know" or "see" something, but one can't cause someone to "love" or to "hate" something. Support for recognizing these three PRs also comes from the fact that there is a usable "re-expression test" for identifying each (Fawcett in preparation b)—whereas it would be hard to devise a test broad enough to handle the more general notion of "Senser." For our present purposes it does not matter which way one decides on this issue, because the need here is simply to have a second Participant Role to put with the role of Phenomenon.

A second difference between Halliday and myself concerns the question of what may "fill" the Phenomenon. This is more serious. In looking for common ground, I might point out that Halliday says of the Phenomenon at one point (1994: 115): "it may not only be a 'thing' but also a 'fact'." It seems that Halliday does not really intend this sense of "fact" to include all representations of "facts" in clauses, because his analyzed examples handle such clauses as "projections" (with the exception discussed below). As IFG makes very clear at many points, the hypotactic relation of "projection" is ABOVE the clause rather than WITHIN the clause (unlike the relation of a Participant Role to the Process). So there is perhaps less common ground here than might at first appear. I will shortly suggest (in contrast with what is clearly Halliday's position in IFG) that a Phenomenon may be filled by a wide variety of complementation types of both "thing" and "situation"—the latter corresponding roughly to what Halliday at times terms a "meta-Phenomenon." Some of these have

---

[7]My terminology for this area was fixed long before the publication of IFG, so it is particularly pleasing to note the parallels with the framework in IFG. My general policy on terminology is to adopt Halliday's terms, now that they have the stability of the publication of IFG. Halliday's "affection" is certainly preferable to his earlier "reaction," but I need to retain the term that I introduced in preference to "reaction" (i.e. "emotion") as a parallel to the associated Participant Role of "Emoter." This is because of my decision to retain Halliday's earlier term "Affected" (which I find preferable on grounds explained in Fawcett 1987: 180–1 to his later term "Medium"). The problem is that if "emotion" Processes are called "affection" Processes, what is the associated role to be called, other than "Affected"? In any case, the term "emotion" is preferable to "affection" because, unlike "affection," it has both positive and negative connotations.

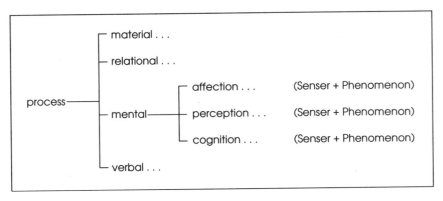

Figure 8.1.   A Hallidayan view of mental Processes in English

labels that are fairly close to Halliday's "proposition" and "proposal," but none of them—perhaps surprisingly—is a "fact."

A third difference is that I treat Halliday's "verbal" Processes as a sub-category of cognition Processes, where a "third party" Agent comes in to "cause someone to know something," (i.e. to "tell" them something). But none of these differences materially affect the framework to be proposed in Section 5.

The picture of Halliday's model as it has emerged so far can be summarized in Figure 8.1.

Later in IFG, in a much longer section on "Reports, ideas, facts: three kinds of projection" (1994: 250–273), Halliday describes the various types of clause associated with mental Processes (and with some other types). I have tried several times over the past two decades to reconsider these proposals positively, but I have to say that I still do not find Halliday's account of mental Processes in terms of "hypotaxis" (dependency without embedding) persuasive.[8] Perhaps the fact is that I am simply being slow to see the light—or perhaps it is hard for anyone to have the "right" insight about everything, when one is being as innovative as Halliday has been in relation to the grammar of English. Here I will simply indicate the main differences between Halliday's approach and how I model these areas of the grammar, and pass on to my main proposals.

Halliday introduces the concept of "projection" to handle many of

---

[8]Nor, in fact, do I find some aspects of his account of parataxis persuasive. There are many jewels of insights in this, the longest chapter of IFG, but I would offer a rather different overall framework for these phenomena, highlighting different "proportionalities." (For a comparison of the two positions, see Fawcett 1994c, and for a fuller explanation of the position adopted here see Fawcett (in preparation a).

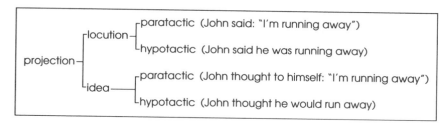

Figure 8.2. Halliday's four types of "projection"

the phenomena to which the term "complementation" refers. From the diagrams on page 220 of IFG we can infer the system network shown in Figure 8.2.

It is the "idea" type of "projection" with which we are concerned here, as we focus on the "cognition" Processes of "knowing" and "remembering." Halliday then goes on to make a further interesting distinction within "hypotactic ideas" (which is paralleled for the other features). It is a distinction between "propositions," exemplified in (3), and "proposals," exemplified in (4).

He thought that he could. ("proposition")   (3)

She wanted him to do. ("proposal")   (4)

Halliday suggests (1994: 259) that "whereas propositions . . . are projected mentally by Processes of cognition—thinking, knowing, understanding, wondering, etc.—proposals . . . are projected by affective Processes . . . : wishing, liking, hoping, fearing and so on." Here, then, Halliday offers an interesting generalization about the semantics of what are traditionally described as "finite clauses" and "non-finite" clauses, in relation to two major types of Process. His insight here is helpful, and it corresponds to part—though only to part—of what I shall say in Section 5 about the complementation patterns of certain cognition Processes.

Two questions that arise at this point therefore are:

1. How are the two Hallidayan networks inferred from IFG shown in Figures 8.1 and 8.2 related to each other?
2. Does Halliday's framework of "proposal" vs. "proposition" provide for all of the semantic options realized in dependent clauses—and so, through them, for their realizations in syntax?

There is not a clear answer to (1) in IFG—perhaps because the focus is on the functional structure of clauses rather than on the networks from which they are generated. In the major section of this chapter (i.e. Section 5), I will show the way in which, in the Cardiff Grammar, the equivalents of Figures 1 and 2 relate to each other— and to certain other networks that are a necessary part of the explanation, and to the lexicogrammar as a whole. In answer to (2), I will suggest that we need to provide for quite a number of additional choices in meaning.

To complete the picture, I must mention a proposal of Halliday's that I do not accept. Because it does not materially affect the framework that I wish to propose here, I will discuss it only briefly. Halliday suggests that in cases such as (5), taken from p. 270 of IFG, *that it was so* is not a Participant Role in the Process of "knowing," and so not a Phenomenon, but is "projected by" the Process of "knowing." (See pp. 250f of IFG for Halliday's reasons for taking this position.) However, Halliday would not analyze *the answer* in (6) as a projection, but as a Phenomenon.

She knew that it was so.   (5)

She knew the answer.   (6)

As we shall see in Section 5, I would treat *that it was so* and *the answer* as equally predicted by *know*, so that each would be seen as a PR in the Process of "knowing."

There is a very fine distinction in Halliday's approach between "facts" and other types of "complementation." Consider his analysis on p. 267 of IFG of *the fact that Caesar was dead* in (7a) as a Phenomenon, and, because he treated *the fact* as optional, *that Caesar was dead* in (7b) as a Phenomenon also. However, he analysed *that Caesar was dead* in (8) not as a phenomenon, but as a "projected" clause.

Mark Anthony regretted the fact that Caesar was dead. ("fact" as Phenomenon)   (7a)

Mark Anthony regretted that Caesar was dead. ("fact" as Phenomenon)   (7b)

Mark Anthony thought that Caesar was dead. ("projection")
                                                            (7c)

I accept, as every grammarian must, that there is a different array of possible patterns of complementation for *regret* and *think*, but I do not think that the difference between them is as great as it is made in Halliday's treatment of the two. So, while I gladly acknowledge that Halliday's analysis of these phenomena casts a novel and sometimes insightful light on them, it does not seem necessary to suggest that a clause such as *that Caesar was dead* cannot be a Participant Role that is "expected" by a Process of "thinking" or "knowing" (or even, to borrow Halliday's term for a moment, "projected" by the Process). Whether or not one accepts Halliday's proposals for this area (and one should make a full study of the relevant sections of IFG before deciding), it is still necessary to find a way of making the connection between (a) the type of Process (including cases of one-member classes) and (b) the internal structure of the dependent clause. Section 5 shows what I consider to be the most insightful way of doing this, in EITHER type of SFG.

4. SOME CRUCIAL ELEMENTS OF THE MODEL ASSUMED HERE

At this point, in preparation for Section 5, it is necessary to establish certain concepts that will be central to the components of the lexicogrammar introduced there. I will introduce three such concepts, each of which requires a modification of the viewpoint presented in IFG. The first is that the Cardiff Grammar recognizes as a basic organizing principle that:

Principle 1a: Each clause expresses one and only one Process,

and therefore that:

Principle 1b: Each clause can have only one Main Verb.

The concept of "phase," then, which I introduced briefly at the beginning of the last section, will have no place in the model assumed here. With this in mind, I will return to the example sentences from Section 3 (which I reproduce here for convenience):

Ike wanted to go.   (1a)

Ike wanted Ivy to go.   (1b)

Ike promised to go. (2a)

Ike promised Ivy to go. (2b)

It will now be clear that I regard *to go* in (1a), (2a) and (2b) as a Participant Role (i.e. as a Phenomenon) in the Processes of "wanting" and "promising," and I would consequently treat them syntactically as Complements. That is what a Complement is: an element of clause structure that, as the Subject typically is also, is demanded by the Process (whether or not it is actually realized in any given clause output). Thus in (1b) *Ivy to go* is the Complement (compare *What Ike wanted was for Ivy to go*). However, in (2b) the Process of "promising" predicts three Participant Roles, so that *Ivy* is the first Complement and *to go* is the second.

Secondly, I showed in Fawcett 1980 (pp. 131–8) how to integrate lexical verbs into the lexicogrammar as "most delicate grammar" (cf. Halliday 1961). The proposal was that such lexical verbs functioned directly as the exponents of the Main Verb, this being a direct element of the clause (rather than as a constituent of the "verbal group" that fills a "Predicator" (Fawcett 1980: 48, 1987: 134). There are many convincing reasons, both formal and functional, for treating all of the elements that some linguists would assign to the "verbal group" as direct elements of the clause, and this chapter provides further evidence for taking this view with regard to the Main Verb. Hence:

Principle 2: The Main Verb is a direct element of the clause in which it occurs.

We now turn to the relation between a lexical verb and its "complementation." I assume that there is essentially the same relationship between (a) a lexical verb (realizing a Process type) and a nominal group that "complements" it as there is between (b) a lexical verb and a clause that "complements" it. They are BOTH Participant Roles in the Process expressed in the matrix clause, and it is natural to reflect this in the grammar. We handle nominal groups that fill Participant Roles as "one layer down the tree diagram" (and, in the case of a nominal group, one step down the rank scale), and we similarly handle clauses that realize Participant Roles as "one layer down the tree diagram" (i.e. as a case of embedding). Where the two cases differ is in the nature of the unit at this next layer down—and IT IS AT THAT POINT THAT IT IS APPROPRIATE FOR THE ANALYSIS TO SHOW THE DIF-

FERENCE. Thus the relationship with which I am concerned here is a kind in which there is not merely the "sister dependency" of dependency grammar, but instead the part–whole "daughter dependency" of constituency. I therefore assume:

Principle 3: A clause that is "dependent" on a verb in another clause is modeled as **filling** a **Participant Role** in the situation expressed in the higher clause, and so as **embedded** in it.

How does the adoption of these three principles help in understanding the concept of "complementation" in a systemic functional description of English? The SFG approach has always included a specification of the configurations of Participant Roles in clauses, in the TRANSITIVITY network. And the integration of lexical verbs into these networks is demonstrated in Fawcett 1980. So the answer to the question is that it provides a way for the grammarian to make explicit the fact that different classes of mental Process accept different arrays of types of Complement—or, strictly speaking, different systems of types of situation filling their Phenomenon.

It may be that you prefer Halliday's position on some of these matters to mine. If so, it does not affect the essential thesis of this chapter. This is because, one way or another, the relationships accounted for here must be expressed in the lexicogrammar.[9]

5. THE FRAMEWORK FOR COMPLEMENTATION

5.1. Introduction to the Framework

This section introduces the components of the lexicogrammar that are necessary in an explicit systemic functional grammar of complementation. It outlines a "generative" grammar of the semantics and forms of the internal structures that are "demanded" by Process

---

[9]I have to say that, although the remainder of this chapter demonstrates how this can be done in the framework presented here, it is not immediately clear to me how these procedures could be adapted to a version of SFG in which the Main Verb (realizing all or part of the Process) was NOT a direct element of the clause structure. And, although I can imagine ways of generating the "complement" clause without its filling a Participant Role of the mother clause, I can see no reasons for doing so in the case of "projection" clauses and many reasons for adopting the view proposed here. ("Raising" phenomena, as exemplified in *He is considered by many people to be quite bright* and *Who did she claim had eaten it?* are not, so far as I can see, argurments for the "projection" approach.)

types. (In an oversimplified view, a "Process type" is a "verb sense," but we must also include here Processes that are realized in phrasal, prepositional, and phrasal–prepositional verbs, as well as simple lexical verbs.)

We will need to consider three separate but related portions of the overall system network for the semantics of English, and also a fourth component of the overall system that lies, strictly speaking, outside language. For each of the three components of the lexicogrammar we will look first at the network itself and then at the realization rules associated with it. The three are as follows:

1.   A portion of the TRANSITIVITY network that covers (a) *situations* (realized in *clauses*), and (b) their *Processes*, realized in *Main Verbs* (and in other elements, in cases of phrasal, prepositional and phrasal–prepositional verbs). Here I will concentrate on a couple of small portions of the *system network* for the COGNITION part of the MENTAL PROCESS sub-network, together with their associated *realization rules.* These generate (a) configurations of Participant Roles and (b) Main Verbs and their lexical exponents.

2.   The dependent "complementation" parts of the network, the semantic labels for which are ROLE AS THING and ROLE AS SITUATION, and their associated realization rules. Although we will take note of cases where the Phenomenon is filled by a nominal group, we will focus in particular on two cases where the Process type demands that its Phenomenon be filled by one of a wide range of types of embedded situation— and so, ultimately (see (3) below), a wide range of types of embedded clause. In doing so, we will meet many (but not all) of the wide range of types of "complementation" that are recognized by formal syntacticians (and a few new ones). The realization rules on the features in these systems then specify the features to be chosen on re-entry to the total network. This brings me to the third component of the explanation.

3.   The DEPENDENCE network. This is the network in which the features chosen on re-entry are to be found. Thus it is these features whose realization rules specify precisely the potential and constraints of the *embedded clauses* that fill the Phenomenon (or, in Halliday's terms, the clauses that are "projected" by the Process type).[10]

---

[10]An interesting aspect of the DEPENDENCE sub-network is that it does not

The realization rules in (2) map the relatively many "complementation" types that are specified in the ROLE IN SITUATION systems (around two dozen, the number depending on the criteria used for distinguishing different types) onto the relatively fewer features in the DEPENDENCE network (around ten). The former specify the "external" semantics and syntax of the embedded clause, and the latter specify its "internal" semantics and syntax.

Some types of dependent clause are "full" dependent clauses that are typically marked by an introductory Binder such as *that*, which specifies the relationship to the matrix clause. Others are "full," but are introduced by a *wh*-item. Such items are limited to a particular set, such that the *wh*-items that introduce the dependent clause in *I know who/what she saw* are different from those in a relative

---

fall self-evidently into any one of the functional components, or "meta-functions," of the lexicogrammar. This is the case with either of the two sets proposed by Halliday—whether in his earlier model (e.g. 1970) or his later model (e.g. 1985), where the "logical" component is "above the clause"—or the larger "subdivided" set later proposed by myself (Fawcett 1980). For a discussion of the two frameworks see Gregory 1987: 97–100). If one wished to, one could argue that the DEPENDENCE network has affinities of one sort or another with several different meta-functions: (a) with what I term the "informational" component (Fawcett 1980; which is the "information structure" part of Halliday's "textual"), (b) with the "logical relationships" component (originally part of Halliday's "ideational," but in IFG a completely separate component that is "above the clause"), and (c) with the MOOD network in the "interpersonal." In fact it is in the latter that the equivalent system is usually placed by systemic grammarians (though without any explanation as to why this system is "interpersonal"). I would now take the view that such arguments are beside the point. The work done by my colleagues and myself in the COMMUNAL Project on developing various aspects of a very large lexicogrammar of English and smaller lexicogrammars for Chinese and Japanese suggests—as does the work reported here—that the main value of the concept of "functional components" or "meta-functions" is as a REMINDER OF THE VARIOUS SORTS OF MEANING THAT THERE ARE IN LANGUAGE (e.g. to the working linguist who is describing a text, building a grammar or planning a language teaching course). Although there are, of course, large and central system networks such as TRANSITIVITY and MOOD that fall squarely into one meta-function or another, my many years of experience in grammar-writing and textual analysis suggests that it is a pretty pointless exercise to agonize over whether a given bit of the overall network for language should be located in one component or another. What matters in grammar-writing is what features in what other systems the system is dependent on, and what features in what other systems are dependent on it. And what matters in the analysis of texts is that this aspect of meaning should be described somewhere in the analysis. I myself analyze it in the "strand" of analysis used for "interpersonal" meaning, because it is complementary to reported MOOD meanings, and, as I will show, inclusive of them when they are "reported." (See Fawcett (in preparation b).) In analysis I would use the features in the ROLE AS SITUATION systems from which the DEPENDENCE features are predicted, because these are more semantically revealing.

clause as the qualifier in a nominal group, as in *the person who/that I saw* and *the thing which/that I saw*. Moreover, we will find features that specify both types in the DEPENDENCE system, but only the first in the "complementation" systems. (This is because relative clauses within nominal groups are generated from the "thing" portion of the overall network.[11]) The second major type of "dependent" clause is the set of types that are quite severely limited in the semantic options that can be chosen, especially in meanings realized in modal verbs and in auxiliary verbs. Because such clauses are in direct contrast with "full" clauses, they are termed "partial" clauses in the present grammar, on the grounds that they only express "part" of the full range of meanings that are characteristically available for situations.[12]

The fourth component of the overall model is the part of the *belief system* in which certain aspects of the "meaning" of lexical verbs is spelled out. Although this is not, strictly speaking, part of the grammar of complementation, it is part of the specification of the verbs concerned, and I will therefore add a brief section on this topic after the discussion of the first of the above components.

The three fragments of the lexicogrammar of English are parts of a very large computer implementation of a generative grammar. This is the core component of a major project in computational linguistics—specifically in natural language generation, and the fragment of the belief system mentioned above is another part of that overall system. As Halliday said (1994: xii), in referring to the Penman Project at the University of Southern California and the COMMUNAL Project at The University of Wales, Cardiff, "These two are among the largest grammars existing anywhere in computational form." As this chapter will show, the COMMUNAL lexicogrammar has been able to accept the challenge set by Halliday's goal of building lexis into the lexicogrammar, unlike Penman. This was partly because there were fewer restrictions on the project and partly be-

---

[11]This does not prevent the lexicogrammar from generating "pseudo-relative" clauses, such as the underlined portion of *It was Ike that saw her first*, for which see Huang's chapter in this volume, Fawcett and Huang (in press a) and Fawcett and Huang (in press b).

[12]In traditional grammar, "partial" clauses are termed "non-finite" clauses. The term "partial" is preferred here for two reasons. First, the term "non-finite" is clearly in contrast with "finite"—but in the present grammar the term "finite" would describe a clause that was EITHER [independent] OR [dependent] and [full]. Second, the meanings of the terms "finite" and "non-finite" are by no means transparent (especially to students).

cause it has developed more recently. It is currently undergoing a major revision and further expansion.[13]

5.2. Relevant Aspects of the TRANSITIVITY Network

I begin with the network for TRANSITIVITY, as in Figure 8.3.

Before you try to read it, let me remind you of some widely used conventions for representing system networks. First, one works through a network from left to right, collecting a bundle of features on the way. Square brackets represent "or" and curly brackets represent "and." (For a fuller treatment of the conventions, see almost any introduction to SFG; for this and a discussion of the concepts involved see Fawcett, Tucker and Lin 1993.) The semantic features between which a user of a language chooses are written in lower case letters, and the names of systems are written in capitals. It is only the features that are part of the generative grammar, and not the names on the systems. (The names on the systems are simply there to help the human user to find her/his way around the network, whether in a diagram representation or a computer implementation.) A row of dots after either a feature or the name of a system indicates that in a fuller grammar there would be more "delicate" choices at this point. Important parts of the network have in fact been cut out, in order to allow us to concentrate on the matters with which we are concerned here. (I will mention these briefly when we come to them.) Finally, note that the features from networks are, by convention, shown in running text by square brackets, as in the case of [independent] in the following paragraph.

Not surprisingly, this network has quite a lot in common with the diagram summarizing the main features of Halliday's system network for this area of meaning given in Figure 8.1. Figure 8.3 additionally shows the other systems that are entered in parallel with TRANSITIVITY. (For any reader who is wondering where the MOOD system is, it is entered from within the DEPENDENCE system, when [independent] is chosen, as we will see in Figure 8.10.) Here, however, we will not be concerned with these other systems.

As I pointed out in Section 3, one characteristic of this grammar is that the significant differences that exist between the three major types of mental Process are reflected here in the fact that each has associated with it a different Participant Role: Cognizant for cogni-

---

[13]In addition to lexis (for which see Fawcett (1994b), Tucker (1995) and in this volume) the COMMUNAL lexicogrammar also includes intonation and punctuation. For a description of the latter in COMMUNAL, see Fawcett (1990).

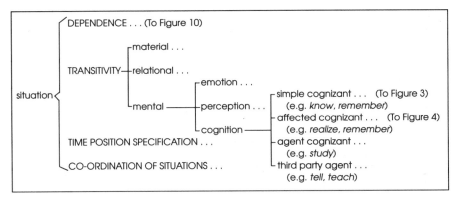

Figure 8.3. A highly simplified system network for "situation" in English

tion, Perceiver for perception and Emoter for emotion. (Thus there is not just a Senser for all three types, as in IFG.) There are "Re-expression Tests," for which see Fawcett (in preparation b), and these distinguish both between these three and between the further types of Participant Role found within "cognition" that are to be described now (and which are also found in Processes of "perception.")

As Figure 8.3 shows, I distinguish here between (a) those cognition Processes that have a simple Cognizant, (b) those where the Cognizant is also an Affected (as in typical uses of the lexical verb *realize*), (c) those with an Agent-Cognizant (as with *study*), and (d) those with a Third Party Agent. In this last type a "third party" enters the Process, and causes (or "tries to cause") someone to "know" something—as in the Processes of "telling," "teaching," etc. Here we must unfortunately skip the interesting discussions that we could have on each of these topics, and move on to the question of how these options are realized in structure.[14]

When you are reading a system network, it is always helpful to know what the typical realizations are.[15] Oversimplifying (as we

---

[14]Processes such as "telling" would be dealt with in IFG as "verbal" Processes. Here we treat all such Processes as "causing someone to know something," thus simplifying the already complex picture of Participant Roles.

[15]There is a general point that might well be made here—though it applies in fact to ALL features in system networks (except those that are pre-selected by a previous realization rule). This is that the name of a feature is essentially a mnemonic for the felicity condition (or "inquiry"; cp. Mann and Matthiessen 1983/85: 52f.) that must be satisfied if that feature is to be chosen. This involves relating the features in the system networks to higher components in the overall model of a communicating mind. I will return to this concept shortly.

must, in order to make progress) the realization rules for the features in Figure 8.3 are essentially as set out below. They are expressed informally, in order to minimize the interpretation necessary for readers not used to systemic conventions. (Notice that the names of some of the *features* consist simply of the names of the *Participant Role* that is introduced to the structure if that feature is chosen. Once the difference between a feature and the PR that it generates is grasped, this causes no problems. This is helped by the fact that the names of clause elements and PRs are written, as you will recall, with an initial capital letter. In this way, the number of technical terms required is significantly reduced.)

1. The choice of [mental] is realized by the presence of a Phenomenon
   ("what is known or not known"—in a "cognition" process);

2. The choice of [simple cognizant] is realized by the presence of a Cognizant
   ("the one who does or does not know");

3. The choice of [affected-cognizant] is realized by the presence of an Affected-Cognizant
   ("one who comes to know");

4. The choice of [agent-cognizant] is realized by the presence of an Agent-Cognizant
   ("one who causes her/himself to come to know");

5. The choice of [third party agent] is realized by the presence of an Agent who is a "third party" (rather as in car insurance), in addition to the presence of an Affected-Cognizant and a Phenomenon
   ("one who causes someone to come to know").

The purpose of this chapter is to show how complementation works in a SFG. To achieve this purpose, I have chosen to concentrate on two high frequency VERB FORMS, *know* and *remember*, each of which has a variety of associated VERB SENSES and COMPLEMENTATION PATTERNS. By examining these in some detail, we will get a clear picture of the principles that operate for the whole range of such verb senses and their complementation. We will find that these two verb forms involve us in TWO of the possible configurations of participant roles listed above: (a) a simple Cognizant and a Phenomenon and (b) an Affected-Cognizant and a Phenomenon. It is the features

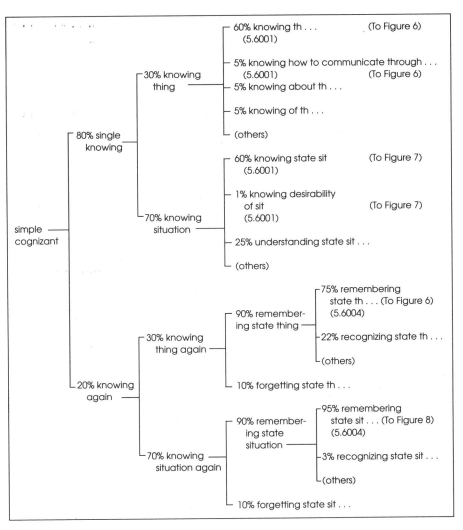

Figure 8.4. Part of the TRANSITIVITY network for lexical meaning (simple cognizant)

dependent on [simple cognizant] and [affected-cognizant] in Figure 8.3 that specify the actual *lexical items* (i.e. the lexical verbs that will expound the clause element *Main Verb*).

These two features are the entry conditions to the parts of the network shown in Figures 8.4 and 8.5. And here again we will limit ourselves, as I have said, to just the two verb-forms of *know* and *remember.* However these two forms express, as we will see, a great many meanings.[16]

Figure 8.4 shows part of the network that is dependent on [simple cognizant]. This network provides more detail than Figure 8.3. First, percentages precede each feature, and I will comment on these shortly. Second, the different senses of a word are indicated by adding suffixes to the main part of the name of each feature—such as "state" (indicating that this is the sense of *understand* that refers to a "state" rather than the sense that refers to a "change of state"), "th" (for "thing"), and "sit" for "situation"). Third, the numbers of the realization rules for the Process types are given—but only for those features in which we are interested. These also have an indication of which dependent system they lead on to, such as "To Figure 8.6."

There are two important systems in the full TRANSITIVITY network for cognition that are dependent on the features [knowing thing] and [knowing situation] (and on their equivalents lower in the network), but which are not shown in Figures 8.4 and 8.5. These include systems offering choices in whether a role (e.g. Cognizant) is to be "overt" or "covert," and, if "overt," whether it is to be "presented," "sought" or "relating out"—and, for each, whether it is to be conflated with the Subject ('voice'), and, if not, whether or not it is to be made a "marked" Theme.[17] Note, then, that the possibility of making a role "covert" means that a semantic role may be present in the structure, but not expounded in the output text-sentence. Essentially, there are TWO such system networks for the portions of the cognition network presented here, depending on whether the Phenomenon is a "thing" or a "situation." (I will return briefly to this difference shortly.) Here, however, I will for simplicity's sake assume that the PRs are all to be overt and unmarked (i.e. "presented" rather than "sought" where "sought" involves a *wh*-form).

As you will see, the network in Figure 8.4 recognizes four senses of *know* and two of *remember*—and there are three more senses of *remember* to come in Figure 8.5. (We will unfortunately have to ignore here the senses of *know about, know of* and *remember about.*)[18]

---

[16]I will cover a good many of the variations here, but not, for example, *He has known great poverty,* or *you know* in *Ivy's pretty clever, you know.*

[17]This part of the network makes several innovations, which I consider to be significant for systemic functional theory, and which are not found in the networks for TRANSITIVITY of linguists other than those working in the framework of the Cardiff Grammar. I hope to write an account of these at some point in the not too distant future.

[18]A meaning of *know* that has been omitted here is the case where the Phe-

While there are clear differences between the four senses of *know* included here, they also have a great deal in common. The first is the FORM of their realization, and this is expressed neatly in the grammar through their sharing a common realization rule (Rule 5.6001). Thus, once the level of FORM is reached, all four senses of *know* are treated in exactly the same way, so that all of the complexity deriving from the fact that *know* is an "irregular verb" is expressed just once. The second type of common ground between the four senses of *know* is the partial overlap in the "dictionary definition" part of their MEANING, and I will come to this in the next section. Precisely the same points hold for the different senses of *remember*, as you will see if you compare Figures 8.4 and 8.5 (with the second point holding more strongly).

The realization rules for the features that we are looking at are as follows:

5.6001 : knowing_th or knowing_how_to_communicate_through or knowing_sit or knowing_desirability_of_sit :
'irr'(knowing).
5.6004 : remembering_state_th or remembering_state_sit or remembering_cos_sth or remembering_cos_sit or remembering_and_executing_intended_situation :
'r', M < "remember".

The first of these means: "Whichever of the four named features is chosen, the realization is that the grammar will apply the special sub-rule for "irregular" ("irr") verbs, which includes the realizations of "knowing." (I will return shortly to the question of where all the named features occur in the network.) This sub-rule lists the various forms of *know*, for instance, *know*, *knew* and *known*, in a table,

---

nomenon is a type of "message," such as *the question, the news* and *all the answers*. In such cases the "thing" is not something that one can "know" in the same sense as that in which one can know a person, a place or a work of art, etc. One possible solution to how best to model these is to introduce another sense of *know*, with the meaning "know the contents of." This would then select for its Phenomenon the feature [phenomenon_thing_as_message], in the same way that I model the feature [know how to communicate through] as selecting [phenomenon thing as semiotic system]. Other Process types such as "remembering" and "forgetting" would use the feature also. "Knowing the name of someone or something" can be seen as a special case of this. There is also the unusual case of *She knows her Geography*, typically with a possessive, as here, where "knowing" has the "being familiar with" meaning. These cases are omitted from the discussion, both here and in subsequent sections, but this slight simplification does not affect the validity of the general framework being described here.

along with the rest of the irregular verbs of English, and this ensures that the grammar always generates the correct forms (using
simple rules that we do not need to go into here). The lexical verb
remember, on the other hand, is "regular" ("r"), so that in this case
the rules for regular verbs apply. So Rule 5.6004 means "The verb
realizing this meaning is "regular" ('r'), and the Main Verb of the
clause ('M') is expounded by *remember*." (This is written as "remember" in the computer program, from which these rules are taken,
because computer programs do not operate with the linguistic convention that a word in italics is a FORM. The origin of these rules in
the computer also explains the presence of the underscore between
the parts of the feature name.)

The most important difference among the various types of "knowing" is that between "knowing things" and "knowing situations."[19]
As it happens, there are different lexical items for these two types of
"knowing" in many other languages (e.g. *connâitre*, and *savoir* in
French, and *kennen* and *wissen* in German). However, the main
reason for distinguishing the two in a lexicogrammar of English is
that they have significantly different probabilities in their associated syntax—and therefore in the meanings realized in this syntax.
This affects both the clause in which they occur and the internal
structure of the associated Phenomenon. For example, "passive"
constructions—constructions in which the Phenomenon becomes
the Subject-Theme—are far more frequent when the Phenomenon is
a "thing." The fact that such clauses are rare (or odd or even ungrammatical in some cases) in cognition Processes is covered in part
by having a different TRANSITIVITY sub-network for "thing" and
"situation," and partly by the grammar's ability to re-set probabilities in specific cases. This is a complex topic and, because it is
not the focus of this chapter, I will avoid getting into an explanation
of it any more than is needed.

A second general source of differences between similar verb forms
can be illustrated from the case of *remember*. This is the difference
between a "state" and a "change of state." (This difference doesn't
apply to *know*, which always refers to a "state." The "change of state"
equivalent to "knowing" is "coming to know," and the prototypical
verb for expressing this—but only in relation to situations—is *realize*.) Thus simple Cognizants, as in Figure 8.4, are associated with
'state' Processes of cognition, and Affected-Cognizants, as in Figure

---

[19]Some grammarians would bring in the term "facts" here, or "propositions"—
but, as we shall see, here "propositions" are just one type of "situation" that may
be "known."

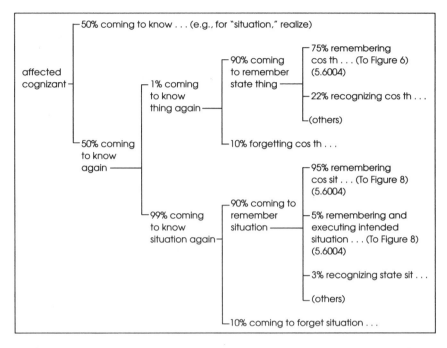

Figure 8.5.   Part of the TRANSITIVITY network for lexical meaning (affected cognizant)

8.5, are associated with the simplest form of "change of state" Processes of cognition. (The suffix "cos" on some features in Figure 8.5 is an abbreviation for "change of state.")

If you inspect Figures 8.4 and 8.5 carefully, you will notice that there is some repetition of items that function as the "base" of the features in these diagrams, especially between the features dependent on "coming to know again" as a "state" and "coming to know again" as a "change of state." In terms of Fawcett (1988b), this represents a decision to present the network as a "displayed" network rather than as a "consolidated" network. I could have reduced the number of "repeated systems" by introducing *same pass preference re-setting rules* (as I did in an earlier version of this network), but this does not reduce the complexity of the overall lexicogrammar. (We will come to examples of these later in this chapter.) The present networks are in fact more "robust" (e.g. it is easier to make changes in one part of the lexicogrammar without this affecting another part adversely).

A final point to note about Figures 8.4 and 8.5 is that they illustrate certain regularly occurring but idiosyncratic senses of *know* and *remember*. The meaning of [knowing how to communicate through] in Figure 8.4 is the meaning that occurs in *He knows French* and *He knows semaphore*—the Phenomenon can be any semiotic system (and not just a language), and the meaning is equivalent to "be able to communicate through." The meaning of [knowing desirability of sit] in Figure 8.4 is the meaning found in *He knew to use a fork* and *She knows to keep quiet.*[20] And there is a "change of state" meaning of *remember* in Figure 8.5 that is exemplified in *Ivy remembered to buy the cabbage.* Such cases provide a special challenge to the lexicogrammarian, and you will see in what follows the solutions proposed for these two problem cases in the present framework. (I will come to the "dictionary definition" aspect of their meanings in the next section.)

Here, then, we find the aspects of the semantics of the Process type, which will be expressed, at the level of form, in the Main Verb— and also sometimes in other elements that I will ignore here, as in the case of [knowing about], which is realized in the prepositional verb *know about.*[21]

We are now in a position to consider a major theoretical issue that is illustrated in these networks: the relationship between syntax and lexis. It was an act of remarkable foresight, long before the time when Chomskyan grammarians became pre-occupied with lexis, when Halliday proposed the concept of "lexis as most delicate grammar" (Halliday 1961). In the COMMUNAL Project, my fellow members and I are implementing this concept for the first time in a major SFG model of language—but we are finding, as is to be expected, that there is a need for modifications to the original concepts.

There is no need for any caveat at all, of course, if those meanings that are realized by lexical items are, by definition, the "most deli-

---

[20]A search of the COBUILD (Bank of English) corpus (for whose cooperation we give grateful thanks) has produced just one example of *know/knew to*, where the meaning is clearly not one that can be glossed by "knowing desirability of sit," (i.e. *We knew to expect a single digit briefing).* Because all of the other examples confirm the appropriateness of the present feature name, there is no incentive to change it to include this "expectation" sense. We should therefore make special arrangements for this case. There is already a complementation feature [potential situation] that is realized by the *to*-form with a suitable meaning, and because it is not otherwise used by [knowing sit], we could allow it into the system in Figure 8.7—but with a very low probability. Notice that this sense of *know to* requires that the Main Verb of the embedded clause be *expect* (or a lexical verb that is semantically close), so it is indeed a special case. This can be handled by a realization rule that re-sets the preferences on re-entry to generate that clause.

[21]However, I should point out that we provide, in full detail, for "prepositional verbs" and "phrasal verbs" in the source grammar implemented in the computer.

cate." In systemic functional theory, the term "most delicate" would normally also be taken to mean that no further systems are dependent on that feature—and it is here that a modification is needed. In the networks shown in Figures 8.4 and 8.5—as in all of the networks for mental Processes—the early choices are realized structurally, and I will come later to others that are realized lexically (i.e. as verb forms—typically expounding the Main Verb). So far this is just as the "lexis as most delicate grammar" hypothesis would predict. However, in the lexicogrammar for complementation presented here, it often happens that these features lead on to further systems of FEATURES WHOSE REALIZATIONS ARE IN SYNTAX—and in standard systemic functional theory this runs counter to the assumed view of the relationship between grammatically realized meanings and lexically realized meanings. Thus, if one were to insist on the view that systems that are dependent on other features are necessarily "more delicate" than those features, then the lexically realized features in the networks presented here are NOT of the "most delicate" type. In Section 5.4 I will show how those dependent networks for "complementation" relate to the present one. (So one might wish to modify the characterization of lexis as "most delicate grammar" to that of "fairly delicate grammar"—unless one simply changes the definition of "most delicate" so that it allows dependent systems.)

This concept of an integrated network for meanings that are realized in either syntax or grammatical items or lexical items (and indeed in intonation or punctuation), is the broad framework in which SFG accommodates the awareness that syntax needs to be sensitive to lexis. This awareness has been growing among linguists working in all theories from the 1970s onward, and it has even been evident in the names of several models of language that have appeared in recent decades—such as Lexical Functional Grammar, Lexicase Grammar and Word Grammar. However, the problem with these other grammars is that they accept uncritically the concept of "the lexicon" as a component that is separate from "the grammar." Such grammars then have to repeat, for each individual verb (or verb-sense), all of the relevant information about its complementation patterns, etc. Halliday's innovative proposal was to suggest that a "grammar" should not be just a grammar, but a "lexicogrammar"—just as the proposals outlined here are. (For a much fuller discussion of this question, see Tucker's chapter in this volume.)

It is the fact that syntactic structures are generated from the same overall network as lexical items that gives SFG its great advantage when modelling relations between grammar and lexis. More precisely, it is the general relationship of dependency between the features in a system network that allows the grammarian to bring together larger or smaller sets of semantic features as the entry condition to a dependent system. The great problem about the complementation patterns of English Processes is that sometimes they apply to a large group of Process types that can be captured by a superordinate feature well to the right in the lexically realized part of the network, sometimes to a smaller group, and sometimes to a set of just one Process type. In the SFG approach there are essentially two ways of capturing the relevant generalizations.

In the first method, the system networks for complementation can be entered from features that are prior to—i.e. "superordinate to"—the feature that specifies the Main Verb itself (to slightly oversimplify). In other words, when the complementation patterns of a set of Process types are the same, the feature that shows that "sameness" can lead directly into the relevant system, so capturing the generalization. (I should point out, however, that this is not in fact a possibility with the Process types that we are considering here.) When this is done it allows for SETS of terminal features, each of which specifies a different Process type, to be brought together when it is appropriate to do so, and for each to be treated INDIVIDUALLY when that is appropriate.

But it often happens, as in the cases we are considering here, that the features about which some generalization is to be made are NOT covered by a non-terminal feature. For example, several of the verb-senses that are in the same system, such as [remembering state sit] and [recognizing state sit], require a slightly different array of complementation patterns, so that the relevant system cannot be entered from the superordinate feature (i.e. [remembering state situation]). However, the system network concepts of SFG can handle this situation too. This is done by bringing together the relevant features from the different parts of the network by a *disjunctive entry condition*, and then entering the relevant complementation system network. Thus if either of features a, b, c or d is chosen, then the system is entered. As I will show in Section 5.5, this is the pattern that is needed in the cases of the meanings realized in *know* and *remember* that we are considering here.

Let me now comment briefly on the percentages that precede the features in Figures 8.4 and 8.5. Their purpose is to give an indication of the general likelihood that this feature will be chosen. The network shows, for example, that it is more common to use the word *remember* than *recognize* when the Phenomenon is a "situation," but that when it is a "thing" the likelihood of using *recognize* increases considerably.

When members of the COMMUNAL team give demonstrations of the COMMUNAL generator, we are often asked where our probabilities come from. The answer is that the probabilities given here are based, wherever we can find relevant studies, on data from corpora—but that when these are not available we make informed guesses. We consider that this is preferable to delaying the exploration of the value of probabilities as an addition to the grammarian's toolkit of concepts, and that it would be foolish to suspend all further research in this area until we had fully accurate data (which will probably never happen). In any case, the probabilities can always be adjusted as data become available.

In fact, there are some quite serious problems in obtaining accurate data for the PARADIGMATIC probabilities that are needed for the features in system networks, when one draws on the SYNTAGMATIC evidence available through using current techniques in corpus linguistics. Moreover, the data available in corpora are at the level of FORM, but for the networks of the meaning potential of a language, we require data at the level of SEMANTICS. So the data obtainable from computer corpora are at TWO removes from what we require; they are syntagmatic and formal, rather than—as is required in a model of a language's "meaning potential"—paradigmatic and semantic. We therefore have to take these problems into account in making our estimates, even when corpus data are available. And we expect to have to revise these estimates, possibly quite drastically in some cases, when more relevant evidence becomes available. Even if all these problems were solved, however, there could be no ultimate "final" set of probabilities, because they vary with changes in register, as is shown by Nesbitt and Plum (1988), and also over time.

Let me summarize so far. I have shown that the system networks tell us a considerable amount about the "meaning" of a lexical verb. If you work LEFTWARD through the system network from the feature that specifies any given sense, you find the features that specify what Participant Roles are associated with it. If you look at the features IN THE SAME SYSTEM, you may find ones with a very similar meaning, and by exploring the NETWORK AROUND THE SYSTEM you can find other Process types with fairly similar or contrasting meanings. The DEPENDENT SYSTEMS for complementation, to which I will come in the section after next, provide a specification, in terms of semantic features, of the internal characteristics of the Phenomenon associated with the Process type. These include cases where the Phenomenon is a "thing," realized in a nominal group, as well as cases where it is a "situation," realized in a clause. The REALIZATION RULES, as we have seen, give the relevant information about the realization of a Process type at the level of form, and the network also carries information on the PROBABILITIES of many of these phenomena. So the system network and its associated realization rules, taken together, carry a considerable amount of vital information about the meanings and forms of lexical verbs.

What is missing here is the equivalent of the "dictionary definition" of each Process type, and in the next section we shall take a brief look at where this is located in the overall model.

5.3 Specifying the Meaning of Verbs: The Contribution from the Belief System

In the overall model of how a text is generated, we need to take account of a number of procedures that are logically prior to the choices in the semantics of the lexicogrammar. Specifically, there is a "network-like" set of relations between *predicates* in a higher component of the overall model, among which the Performer of a text decides. As you might guess, the relations between these predicates have some striking parallels to the relations within the network being considered here. The crucial difference is that the present network is at the INTRA-LINGUISTIC level of *semantics* (where "semantics" is a level of language), while the higher network is part of the language user's *belief system.* So, just as there is an "ontology" of types of "object" that corresponds in many respects to the system network for "noun senses" (Fawcett 1994b), so too there is an ontology of "predicate-types" that corresponds in certain ways to the system network of lexical verb senses that are being considered here. Each has, for example, its associated Participant Roles, and these correspond precisely with those specified in the lexicogrammar. (However, the network in the lexicogrammar specifies various intra-linguistic choices that are not present in the belief system, so the two are not isomorphic.) It is in this higher component—in one that is at TWO removes from the word-form—that the "dictionary meaning" of, say, [knowing sit] is spelled out.

These specifications of "meaning" are attached to the equivalent of the semantic feature in the ontology of predicates, and they are expressed in the same "logical form" in which the rest of the belief system is represented.[22] Thus, if the conditions that the "definition" specifies are met, the predicate type is deemed to be appropriate for use. These conditions, perhaps not surprisingly, have a lot in common

---

[22]This is work currently in progress. A specially adapted type of logical form is currently under development by Yuen Lin and myself, called Systemic Functional Logical Form. It is a specially adapted Davidsonian logical form that can, we think, represent the types of meaning found in natural languages rather more naturally than can many existing logical forms, most of which tend to over-emphasize experiential meaning at the expense of most other types, or to add on just one type, such as quantification or speech act theory.

with good dictionary definitions, so that in constructing them one can get significant help from dictionaries. Indeed, the following informal examples of the specifications given in the ontology of predicates take account of—but do not directly reflect—two of the most linguistically oriented recent dictionaries, the *Longman Dictionary of Contemporary English (New Edition)* (LDOCE) (Summers 1987) and the *COBUILD English Language Dictionary* (Sinclair 1987). Specifically, the general principle is followed of restricting the lexis and syntax for representing the "conditions" to something close to that of the defining vocabulary and syntax of LDOCE. Here are some sample specifications (represented in English rather than the logical form). Notice that they may include supplementary notes, as in the first example.

know th: to have in one's memory a visual representation of an object and sufficient facts about that object for one's present purpose. Such objects are prototypically (a) a person or persons, typically known because one has talked with them; (b) a place, typically known because one has visited it; (c) any other "nameable" object, such as an animal with which one has a relationship similar to a relationship with a person, or a work of art. Such objects are typically nameable by proper names, such as *Fred, Iceland, Lassie* and *Treasure Island*. Less typically, any object can be said to be "known" in the way that, for example, a work of art is known. (cp. French *connâitre*, German *kennen*.)
(e.g. *Ike knows Mrs. Cadwallader/Iceland/my cat/my car /Beethoven's Ninth*)

Note that "facts," in the sense of the term "fact" assumed here, are not necessarily "true"; they are beliefs that the Performer believes the Cognizant to believe to be valid as a basis for action or reasoning (and the Performer may or may not be the Cognizant).

know sit: to have in one's memory a representation of an event and to feel certain that it is correct (cp. French *savoir*), German *wissen*)
(e.g. *Ike knows that Mrs. Cadwallader is rich*)

remember th: to have in one's conscious memory a representation of an object that one first knew in the past
(e.g. *I remember the first banana that I ever ate*)

remember sit: to have in one's conscious memory a representation of an event that one first knew in the past
(e.g. *I remember seeing her last week*)

coming to remember th: to come to have in one's conscious memory a representation of an object that one first knew in the past

(e.g. *I suddenly remembered the first banana that I ever ate*)

coming to remember sit: to come to have in one's conscious memory a representation of an event that one first knew in the past

(e.g. *I suddenly remembered that she was rich; I remembered how to open it; etc.*)

Notice that it is not just the existence of different verbs for *know th* and *know sit* in other languages that motivates the setting up of these two senses of *know* in English; there is a sense of "being familiar with" about the first and a belief about the "correctness" of the second that distinguish them from the apparently equivalent senses of [remember]. Indeed, in the Cardiff Grammar we are now proposing to treat expressions such as *be familiar with* as phrasal-prepositional verbs, such that *be familiar with* would be located semantically in the network shown in Figure 8.4, close to [knowing th] and [knowing sit]—while allowing *familiar* to have all the potential semantics and syntax of an adjective (e.g. as described in Tucker 1992, 1995 and especially (in press)).

Before we move on, we should note the following three special cases, each of which has a clear correlate in the networks in Figures 8.4 and 8.5. Notice that the first and third use a common form of clausal complementation—a "partial" clause with the *to*-form of the lexical verb (which typically realizes the meaning of "potential situation," as in *He wants to stroke the cat*. However, this form is not used with *know* or *remember*, except in the cases below, so that no ambiguity occurs.

know desirability of situation: to know that an authority (typically a social group) considers the situation to be desirable.

(e.g. *She knew to leave at four o'clock precisely*)

know how to communicate through: to know how to produce and understand a semiotic system. Prototypically the Phenomenon is a natural language.

(e.g. *She knows Chinese / semaphore really well*)

remember and execute intended situation: to come to have in one's conscious memory a representation of an event that one first knew in the past and that one had decided to cause, and then to cause that event to occur.

(e.g. *Ike remembered to take her a bunch of flowers*).

The odd thing in the last case is that, while the "remembering" is something that "happened to" Ike (i.e. he is an Affected-Cognizant) the use of this verb IMPLIES that Ike actually did carry out the intended action (and so functioned in an Agent-like manner).[23]

5.4. The "Complementation" Part of the Network: "Knowing Things"

The problem that this section and the next address is: "How can we most adequately and economically provide for the fact that different Process-types (sometimes consisting of a class with only one member) require different arrays of internal structures in the units that fill the phenomenon?"

In principle there are at least four ways in which this Phenomenon could be modelled in a SFG, and these will be compared in Section 5.7. Here I shall present the solution to the problem preferred in the COMMUNAL Project. I will begin with the case where a "thing" fills the Phenomenon, and then move quickly on to the case where a "situation"—and so a clause—is generated.

Consider (9a) and (9b):

I know Fred/London/Beethoven's Pastoral Symphony/that pencil well.   (9a)

I remember Fred/London/Beethoven's Pastoral Symphony/that pencil well.   (9b)

These two examples illustrate most of the range of types of "thing" that can fill the Phenomenon of a Process of "knowing" and "remembering." They are not the focus of this chapter, but it is important to show the parallels—as well as the differences—between a "thing" as Phenomenon and a "situation" as Phenomenon. Thus, just as there

---

[23]Examples such as this do not sound persuasive when given the test for an Agent (i.e. *What Ike did was to remember to take her a bunch of flowers* sounds extremely odd, as does *What happened to Ike was that he remembered to take her a bunch of flowers*). However, it seems sensible to treat the "remembering" as the dominant aspect of this compound predicate, and to treat the action as something that follows logically from it. Thus we would treat the Participant Role as an Affected-Cognizant.

are "preferred" features that are more likely to be selected in generating a clause that fills the Phenomenon in a Process of "knowing," so too there are preferred features when a nominal group fills the Phenomenon.

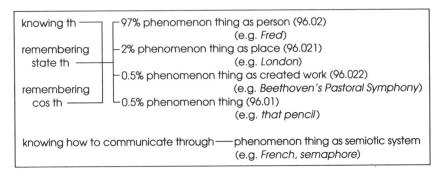

Figure 8.6. Some "thing" options in complementation for Process of cognition

Figure 8.6 shows the system that offers choices in generalized types of "thing" that is entered from either [knowing th], [remembering state th] or [remembering cos th], together with their estimated general probabilities. The choice of any one of these entry conditions means that, when the network is re-entered to generate the nominal group to fill the Phenomenon, its pathways through the network for "thing" will be constrained to those that will generate an appropriate nominal group. As you will see, these relate directly to the types of object listed in the note on the "dictionary definition" in the belief system, as outlined in the last section.

Here is a sample realization rule:

```
96.02 : phenomenon_thing_as_person :
     for "Ph" re_enter_at entity,
     for "Ph" prefer [thing, stereotypical_thing,
         10% interactant / 90% outsider,
         concrete_c,
         99.9% living / 0.1% non_living,
         0.01% plant / 99.99% creature,
         99.5% human_cr / 0.5% non_human_cr,
         whole_hum].
```

It is of course not easy to interpret this rule, partly because it is written in the form used by a computer program, and partly because it refers to features in the "thing" network, which we do not have here. However, I expect that you will be able to recognize enough of the meanings to get the flavor of what the effect of these preference rules is. (The rule in fact needs some minor additions, to enable it to prefer animals, vehicles, etc., when these are treated as quasi-persons and so are "nameable," as in *I know the S.S.Waverley well; she's a very fine old ship.*) Similar rules express the preferences to ensure that a "place" or "created work" get generated. "Created works" include books, plays, films, pieces of music, pictures, sculptures, and so forth.[24] Thus these are the "things" that are "knowable," in the sense of the French verb *connâitre* and the German verb *kennen*, and the objects are ones that can typically be referred to by a "proper name." Part of what is known about the "meaning" of this sense of *know* is knowing what types of "thing" are prototypically "knowable," and what the probabilities are for these and the less typical types.

Figure 8.6 also shows the "one-term system" for [knowing how to communicate through], and this obligatorily chooses as its type of Phenomenon a "semiotic system." This is prototypically a natural language, such as *French* or *Chinese,* but it may be a secondary semiotic system such as *semaphore* or *morse.* It is an interesting fact that, while one may regularly talk of *knowing French,* in the sense of "knowing how to communicate through French," one does not talk of *remembering French,* in the sense of "remembering how to communicate through French."[25]

5.5. The "Complementation" Part of the Network: "Knowing Situations"

I come now to the primary focus of this chapter: complementation in clauses. To put it in these terms is to adopt a syntactic viewpoint, but from now on, because I am here modelling the meaning potential of the language, I shall give priority to the semantic viewpoint— while always paying attention to how the meanings are realized.

---

[24]Such preference rules must allow for the generation of pronouns and proper names as well as "full" nominal groups, so they can become a little more complicated than the example given. However, they always turn out to be surprisingly short and easy to state, considering the depth and complexity of the full "thing" network.

[25]On the other hand, I can say *During the second week of her visit she gradually began to remember her French* (where the possessive is virtually obligatory). Such cases show why it may be of value to recognize as a distinct type of Phenomenon a [phenomenon thing as semiotic system]. People do, of course, talk of *remembering French,* in the same way that we can talk of "remembering" ANY object. I will not pursue these matters further here, because our focus is on cases where the phenomenon is filled by a "situation," not a "thing."

In a moment I will ask you to examine Examples (10a) to (23b). These are intended to illustrate the wide range of choices in meaning that are relevant when it is a "situation" that fills the Phenomenon, and when the Process is one of "knowing" or "remembering." (Here I illustrate just the "state" sense of *remember*, but the complementation patterns for the "change of state" sense are the same.) As you peruse these examples, you will see that this is a fairly full treatment of the complementation of these two Process types. It is considerably fuller than any dictionary or grammar that I know of, and it even includes some types that, as far as I am aware, have not been distinguished before.

As you will see, I have included some examples of relative unacceptability. The asterisk is used here in the traditional way, (i.e. to indicate a case where the example is completely unacceptable grammatically when used in the sense intended). The single and double question marks indicate two degrees of doubt about the example, but an unwillingness to treat it as "ungrammatical." As we shall see, the probabilities introduced to the lexicogrammar to be presented here offer a far more delicate tool for handling such matters.

The crucial point that this set of examples illustrates is that, although the meaning potentials for the Phenomenon in these two Process types have quite a lot in common, there are certain semantic patterns that occur with only one or other of them. Indeed, experience suggests that the only safe approach to this area of grammar is to take as one's initial working assumption that each Process type may in principle have a different pattern of complementation, if only in probabilistic terms, and then to work cautiously from the individual cases to those generalizations across sub-networks that so delight the hearts of systemic functional linguists. Our experience in COMMUNAL is that when we come to try to write a fairly detailed lexicogrammar for mental Processes that will generate what should be generated and rule out what should not—and which will also show as borderline what should be so shown—then we find that there are fewer and fewer cases of "complementation classes" that cover more than one Process type.[26] (This was also one of the findings of my

---

[26]For example, one might suppose that the two Processes of "liking" and "disliking" would share the same pattern. Although we can say both *I like reading* and *I like to read*, the pattern is different with "disliking." *I dislike reading* is fine, but *I dislike to read* is very unlikely to occur—although perhaps not totally impossible. In the approach to modelling grammar advocated here, we avoid having to make gross judgements of whether or not such cases are "grammatical." We simply show them as "very unlikely indeed," by giving them a probability of 0.001%.

earlier detailed study of a very different area of TRANSITIVITY, i.e. relational Processes (Fawcett 1987).)

The features to the right of the examples are those that have been chosen in the ROLE AS SITUATION systems—"ROLE AS SITUATION" simply being "clausal complementation" looked at as a type of meaning. These features are therefore the ones that will be encountered shortly in the networks in Figures 8.7 and 8.8. For two types of complementation, I give examples of cases where the *wh*-element may be either a Participant Role (indicated by "PR") or a Circumstantial Role (indicated by "CR"). Now please consider the following examples, noting the similarities and differences between the complementation of "knowing" and "remembering":

I know (that) Ivy ate the caviar.	[proposition ph]	(10a)
I remember (that) Ivy ate the caviar.		(10b)
* I know eating the caviar.	[performance of situation,	(11a)
I remember eating the caviar.	with S-theme recoverable]	(11b)
* I know Ivy greedily eating the caviar.	[performance of situation,	(12a)
I remember Ivy greedily eating the caviar.	with S-theme not recoverable]	(12b)
I know who ate the caviar.	[report of quasi-reply to new	(13a)
I remember who ate the caviar.	content seeker, full report] (PR)	(13b)
I know when/where/why/how Ivy ate it.	[report of quasi-reply to new	(14a)
I remember when/where/why/how Ivy ate it.	content seeker, full report] (CR)	(14b)
I don't know whether/if Ivy ate it.	[report of quasi-reply to polarity	(15a)
I don't remember whether/if Ivy ate it.	seeker, full report]	(15b)
Ivy knew what to eat first.	[report of quasi-reply to new content seeker,	(16a)
Ivy remembered what to eat first.	with S-theme recoverable] (PR)	(16b)
Ivy knew when/how/etc to eat it.	[report of quasi-reply to new content seeker,	(17a)
Ivy remembered when/how/etc to eat it.	with S-theme recoverable] CR)	(17b)
Ivy doesn't know whether/*if to eat it.	[report of quasi-reply to polarity	(18a)
? Ivy doesn't remember whether/*if to eat it.	seeker, with S-theme recoverable]	(18b)
Ivy knows how to eat the caviar.	[skill ph]	(19a)
Ivy remembers how to eat the caviar.		(19b)
I know Ivy to have eaten it.	[quasi-archaic partial situation with S-theme]	(20a)
?? I remember Ivy to have eaten it.		(20b)
* I forget Ivy to have eaten it.		(20c)
* I know Ivy's greedily eating the caviar.	[reification]	(21a)
I remember Ivy's greedily eating the caviar.		(21b)
* I know Ivy's greedy eating of the caviar.	[reification]	(22a)

I remember Ivy's greedy eating of the caviar.   (22b)

Ivy knew to eat the caviar first.   [knowing desirability of sit] +
                                                              [potential sit]   (23a)
Ivy remembered to eat the caviar first.   [remembering and executing
                                            intended sit] + [potential sit]   (23b)

As you can see, this set of examples shows clearly the very considerable overlap in the complementation patterns of *know* and *remember*, when used in their "knowing a situation" senses—but also some important differences. The first of these differences is the fact that we do not speak of "knowing" the "performance of a situation," in the sense realized by the *ing*-form, as (11a) and (12a) clearly show—although we speak regularly of "remembering doing things." The second difference is that we cannot 'reify' the Phenomenon of a Process of "knowing" (i.e. we cannot, when the Process is one of "knowing," re-package an "event" as an "object" as one of the various types of "nominalization." This is shown in Examples (21a) and (22a).[27] Thirdly, note the oddness of (18b) in contrast with (18a)—and the even greater oddness of (20b) as compared with (20a). And, finally, there is the complete difference of the semantics of the pair of examples in (23a) and (23b)—despite their similarity at the level of form.

Examples (10a) to (23b) also illustrate a good number of the full set of complementation types in English—although by no means all of them. We shall meet the features shown to the right of the above examples in the ROLE AS SITUATION systems to be examined shortly, and we will examine them in their role as terms of a system at that point in the discussion.

But first we shall consider briefly three points of interest—and perhaps controversy—in the grammar proposed here. All three points are relevant to both "knowing" and "remembering." The first is that I make a distinction here between two types of complementation that other grammars such as Quirk *et al.* (1985) treat as one type (perhaps because those grammars give less weight to semantic criteria than is given here—while giving functional criteria some weight). Consider (13c and d) below, and compare them with (13a), which is repeated below for convenience:

Ike asked me who ate the caviar.   (13c)

Ike told me who ate the caviar.   (13d)

I know who ate the caviar.   (13a)

---

[27]In the COMMUNAL model, the decision to "reify" or "nominalize" occurs in the "pre-linguistic" planning.

All three have the same wording of *who ate the caviar* as their Phenomenon. Let us begin with (13c). It reports the content—as opposed to the wording—of a "new content seeking" question such as *Who ate the caviar?* It therefore seems reasonable to characterize its Phenomenon as a [report of new content seeker]—as we do in this grammar. This is the equivalent, in explicitly semantic terms, of what most current grammars would say. However, although the FORM of the Phenomenon in (13c) is the same as in (13a and d), the MEANING is different. This is because, in these last two examples, it is NOT necessarily the case that a question has been asked—although it is, of course, quite possible that the clauses could be uttered in a context where one had. It is "as if" a question had been asked. All we can legitimately infer, therefore, is that each such case is a "quasi-reply to a new content seeker"—and [quasi-reply to new content seeker] is the name for this feature in this grammar. So in (13a) and (13d) we do not know for certain that a question was asked; all that is known is that the Phenomenon gives material that could be the answer to such a question. The advantage of introducing this new feature is that it enables us to show what the two types of complement have in common, semantically, while recognizing that they are NOT, as most current grammars that refer to this phenomenon suggest, the same. Thus you will not find, in the ROLE AS SITUATION systems for "knowing" and "remembering," the feature [report of new content seeker], but instead [quasi-reply to new content seeker]. The same distinction also applies to the "partial report" type of [quasi-reply to new content seeker] exemplified in (17a and b), and also for the "full" and "partial" "polarity seekers," as exemplified in (15a and b) and (18a and b).

The second point is that the present lexicogrammar does not, as one might at first think it might, treat "knowing how to do something" as similar to "knowing the method by which something is done." (Precisely the same points hold for "remembering.") In other words, I suggest that, in English at least, *Ike knows how to open a beer bottle with his teeth* is ambiguous between (a) "his having the knowledge of the method of doing it," as in Examples (17a and b), and "his having the skill or ability to do it," as in Examples (19a and b). (Note that here "Method" is a Circumstantial Role, somewhat similar to Halliday's "Means."[28]) My assumption that one should

---

[28]I originally used Halliday's term "Means" for what I now call "Method," following the principle of conforming to Halliday's IFG terminology whenever possible. I have found that the difference between the range of phenomena for which Halliday uses this term and what I need to cover is too great. I find the term "Method" preferable for the sense intended here, because it implies a Process through which

distinguish these two senses is supported by the fact that there is a systematic equivalence between "being able to do something" (e.g. *Ike can/is able to open a beer bottle with his teeth*) and the "skill" sense of "knowing how to do something," although there is no such equivalence with the "knowledge" sense.[29] (As a supplementary point, notice that it is the "knowledge of method" sense that is sought when someone asks *How did you do that?* The standard punning answer *With difficulty!* is clearly a play on the ambiguity between the Manner and the Method senses of *how*. In other words, Method is one of a set of Circumstantial Roles, along with Time Position, Place, Manner, etc., which can be the "sought" role in a [report of new content seeker] or a [quasi-reply to new content seeker], as suggested by Examples (14a and b) and (17a and b).)

The third common point of interest is the use of the feature [quasi-archaic partial situation with S-theme], for cases such as (20a and b). This construction is the equivalent in English of the Latin "accusative plus infinitive" construction, and it has an old-fashioned, outdated ring to it. However, it is clearly still present in modern English, and the expression "quasi-archaic" in the name for the feature tries to capture something of this. (It may be useful to add, at this point, that this type of complementation is formally rather similar to a combination of features that I will mention when we come to the ROLE AS SITUATION system for "remembering" (i.e. the combination of [potential situation] and [with S-theme recoverable], as found in *I wish Ivy to eat it.*) However, semantically the two are different; in the present case, the situation is not "potential" but "actual"—or one might even say "factual"—in that *I know Ivy to have eaten it* is very close in meaning to *I know that Ivy ate it*.)

Finally, note (23c). Here I have allowed in a third verb form (i.e. *forget*) in order to give yet another illustration of the difference in complementation between Process types that one might at first assume to share the same patterns: "remembering" and "forgetting." *Remember* may be odd with this construction, but *forget* is probably unacceptable. The safest procedure, as I have suggested earlier, is for the grammarian to begin by treating each Process type in its own right, and then later to make the generalizations across verb-

---

something is done, and so a "situation." Halliday's "Means" includes "Instrument" (which I take to be a separate CR, because it can co-occur with a Method Adjunct) and appears to exclude clauses such as *by opening the window* in *Ivy got some fresh air into the room by opening the window*. See Fawcett (in preparation b).

[29]The "equivalences" are modelled in the COMMUNAL framework at the level of "logical form"—a topic that I will set aside here.

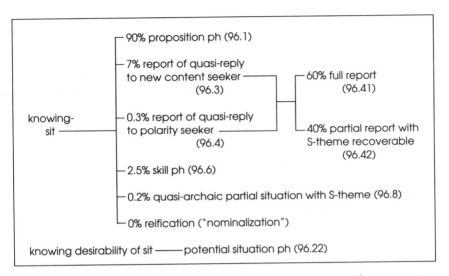

Figure 8.7. The ROLE AS SITUATION ("complementation") system for [knowing sit]

senses—as is done in Figure 8.8 below (and as is also done, for example, with certain "emotion" Processes).

Now I come to the central theoretical issue of this chapter. The question is: "What do the *semantic system networks* that will generate these patterns of complementation look like?" The answer comes in two stages: first in the networks presented below, and then in the DEPENDENCE network to be introduced in Section 5.6. The present networks provide a semantic specification of the type of Phenomenon IN RELATION TO THE PROCESS TYPE, and the task of the DEPENDENCE network is to specify the INTERNAL STRUCTURE of the embedded clause that fills the Phenomenon. Then, in Section 5.7, I shall discuss and evaluate four possible alternatives to modelling complementation in SFG.

Figure 8.7 illustrates three general properties of all the ROLE AS SITUATION (or "complementation") systems for Process types in a SFG. First, the semantic features that make up the initial system are selected from a larger set, the full complement of which (no pun intended) is designed to be sufficient to capture the semantics of all the possible types of complementation of Processes—and, where possible, sets of Process types). Thus the features that appear in this system appear also in the ROLE AS SITUATION systems for other process types. Second, features typically have significantly different probabilities when they appear in the systems for different Process types, including very low probabilities indeed, signalling "very unlikely but just possible." (The theoretical issues involved in (a) repeating features and (b) having the same feature with differing probabilities will be discussed in Section 5.7.) Third, the dependent system in Figure 8.7 is not specific to the complementation system for [knowing sit], it is shared by many of the other complementation systems. So if either of the features in its entry condition occur in any complementation system, the system is entered. I will introduce this system again in Figure 8.8, where you will also meet another one that operates in the same way. Thus these two dependent ROLES AS SITUATION systems are picked up by many different features. In sum, then, there is not a single ROLE AS SITUATION network, but instead (a) a set of systems for each Process type, and (b) a couple of dependent systems that are entered from one or two of a small sub-set of the features that occur in those initial systems.

I shall now look at some of the specific characteristics of Figure 8.7. First, notice the probabilities in this ROLE AS SITUATION system for [knowing sit]. The most probable feature by far is [proposition ph] (which I take to be very similar to Halliday's IFG sense of "proposition"). It is realized in examples such as (10a).[30] The position taken here is that probabilities are an important part of one's "knowledge" of a language, so that it is a significant part of one's knowledge of English, for example, that *I know Ivy to have eaten it* (20a) is quite rare by comparison with *I know that Ivy ate it* (10a). And, as I will show in Figure 8.8, the probability of having a proposition as the Phenomenon is very much lower in a Process of "remembering."

If the Performer chooses [proposition ph], he/she will be able to generate a "full" dependent situation (i.e. one with a full range of choices in "time" meanings and the various types of meaning realized in modal verbs). You can see much of this by examining its realization rule. (You may notice that the same realization rule is used for two other types of situation that can fill a Phenomenon. This is often the case at the semantics-form interface, and we shall find other examples below. In particular, one is a "report of content of information seeker"—but I will not discuss these other cases further here.)

96.1 : proposition_ph or
(e.g. *I knew that he was there*)
situation_perceived_as_fact or
(e.g. *I saw that he was there*)

---

[30]The suffix "ph" is there to differentiate this type of "proposition" from other types (e.g. a proposition that fills the PR of Carrier) as in *That Ivy ate the caviar is known to everyone in the Embassy.*

report_of_content_of_information_giver:
    (e.g. *I told her that he was there*)
for "Ph" prefer
[situation, congruent_situation,
dependent, full_dependent_sit,
proposition_sit],
for "Ph" re_enter_at entity.

Another rule (in the part of the TRANSITIVITY network that I am omitting here) will have already located a Complement (C2) at a place in the structure of the clause currently being generated, typically at Place 120. (The atypical case would be if the Phenomenon were the Subject, as in *That he was there was known by almost everybody.*) That rule then puts the Phenomenon (Ph) by the Complement—it conflates the two. The crucial task of the present rule is to state WHAT IS TO BE CHOSEN WHEN THE OVERALL SYSTEM NETWORK IS RE-ENTERED, when generating a unit to fill that Phenomenon. The rule states that a number of features are to be preferred, and these are listed in the rule in square brackets. As you can see, the first two are [situation] and [congruent situation], and the fact that it chooses these ensures that the unit generated will be a clause—and not a nominal group (as it would be if [reification] were chosen). (This is a semantic label for the phenomenon known in the more syntax-oriented terminologies as "nominalization." It is a large topic with relevance in other areas of the lexicogrammar besides complementation, and it must therefore await another occasion.) As I will show in the next section, when I look at the DEPENDENCE system, the other features provide that the grammar will enter all the relevant system networks on re-entry—and that it will NOT enter those that do not apply to it.[31] The significance for the internal structure of the embedded clause of these preferences will be clearer when we come to look at the realization rules for that network.

What is the status of the Binder *that?* As Example (10a) shows, it is not always obligatory. However, it sometimes is, and other rules (omitted here because they are not part of the complementation of Processes) provide for cases such as when a Phenomenon is conflated with the Subject, as in *That he was there was known by almost everybody.* The cases when it is optional are handled, as

---

[31]Further rules located elsewhere in the grammar ensure that dependent clauses of this type are severely limited in other respects too (e.g. that they will be less likely to have a marked theme than an independent clause). But we do not have time to explore that interesting aspect of the Cardiff Grammar here.

we shall see, at the point when it is about to be generated (i.e. on the pass through the network to generate the embedded clause). That decision will be guided by considerations of register (specifically features in the system for TENOR of discourse). All of these factors are already built into the computer implementation of the Cardiff Grammar.

Now we shall look at the other features in the system. The feature [report of quasi-reply to new content seeker] generates examples such as (13a), (14a), (16a) and (17a). Similarly, [report of quasi-reply to polarity seeker] produces examples such as (15a) and (18a). And, as Figure 8.7 shows, whichever of these features is chosen, it leads to a further system. One of the features, [full report], generates a clause that is "full" in the sense described above for [proposition ph], as in (13a), (14a) and (15a), and the other generates a "partial" clause, as in (16a), (17a) and (18a). In the second trio of possibilities the Subject-Theme is always recoverable from the matrix situation— so that, for example, in (16a) *Ivy knew what to eat first*, the Subject-Theme of the embedded clause *what to eat first* has the same referent as the Subject-Theme of the matrix clause (i.e. "Ivy"). This, then, is the condition for selecting this feature. I should note that, although it is a NECESSARY condition, it is not a SUFFICIENT condition— because one can say both *Ivy knew what to eat first* and *Ivy knew what she should eat first*.

The four realization rules for these four features are set out below. You will notice that these rules, like the one for [proposition ph], serve other features than the ones in which I am interested. The way in which each rule functions is, as for [proposition ph], to state preferences for when the network is re-entered to generate the embedded clause. Again, these rules are not easy to read without detailed study, and you may prefer to move directly to the next part of the exposition. However, it is important, as evidence in support of the proposals made in this chapter, that I should demonstrate that the lexicogrammar presented here is not simply a piece of descriptive apparatus, but a fully operational working model.

96.3 : report_of_content_of_new_content_seeker or
      e.g. (*He asked me where Ivy was.*)
      e.g. (*He asked me where to sit.*)
   report_of_quasi_reply_to_new_content_seeker :
      e.g. (*He told me where Ivy was.*)
      e.g. (*He told me where to sit.*)
      e.g. (*He knew where Ivy was.*)
      e.g. (*He knew where to sit.*)

for "Ph" prefer
[situation, congruent_situation, dependent,
situation_with_role_sought],
for "Ph" re_enter_at entity.

96.4 : report_of_content_of_polarity_seeker or
e.g. (*He asked me if/whether Ivy was there.*)
report_of_quasi_reply_to_polarity_seeker :
e.g. (*Tell me if/whether Ivy is there.*)
e.g. (*He knew if/whether Ivy was there.*)
for "Ph" prefer
[situation, congruent_situation, dependent,
situation_with_polarity_sought, positive],
for "Ph" re_enter_at entity.

96.41 : full_report :
for "Ph" prefer [full_dependent_sit],
for "Ph" re_enter_at entity.

96.42 : partial_report_with_S_theme_recoverable :
for "Ph" prefer
[partial_dependent_sit, potential_process, partial_report],
for "Ph" re_enter_at entity.

In relation to Rule 96.4, I should explain that the constraints on using *if* signalled in Examples (18a and b) are handled at the time when the embedded clause itself is being generated (i.e. in the next section).

I have already discussed the two features [skill ph] and [quasi-archaic partial situation with S-Theme], and their two realization rules are given below.[32]

96.6 : skill_ph :
(e.g. *Ivy knows how to ride a monocycle/speak Chinese.*)
for "Ph" prefer
[situation, congruent_situation,
dependent, partial_dependent_sit,
potential_process, method, method_sought],
for "Ph" re_enter_at entity.

---

[32]In Rule 96.6 we use the wording for asking about the Method of doing something to generate the item *how*—as provided for in the last two preferred features in the rule above.

96.8 : quasi_archaic_partial_situation_with_S_theme :
       (e.g. *I consider him to be a fool.*)
   for "Ph" prefer
     [situation, congruent_situation, dependent,
      partial_dependent_sit, potential_process,
      with_overt_S_theme],
   for "Ph" re_enter_at entity.

As stated earlier, I will have to omit here any discussion of the feature [reification], and the fact that it is given a probability of 0% simply signifies that it is not being covered here.

Finally, we should note the feature [knowing desirability of sit], and the specification of its Phenomenon as [potential situation ph]. This is one of the "problem cases." The solution adopted here is to recognize this as a separate sense of "knowing," and to let it lead, by what is in effect a "one-feature system," to a semantically appropriate feature that is in any case required for many other Process types. (I will return to this case after considering the next network.)

Now let us look at the system for "remembering." As Figure 8.8 shows, the entry condition is disjunctive, so that the claim implicit

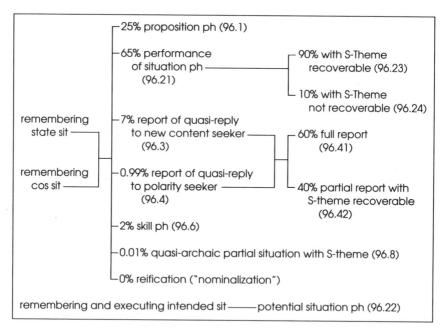

Figure 8.8. The ROLE AS SITUATION ("complementation") system for [remembering sit]

in the grammar is that the same options in ROLE AS SITUATION are required, whether "remembering" is being used in its "stative" or its "change of state" sense.

A quick comparison of Figures 8.7 and 8.8 will show that all of the features available for [knowing sit] are also available for "remembering sit"—together with an important addition, [performance of sit]. This leads in turn to two different complementation types, and I will return to these in a moment. There are a number of points on which to comment.

First, consider the initial system in Figure 8.8 as a whole. As you will notice, some of the probabilities on some of the features in Figure 8.8 are rather different from those in Figure 8.7. In particular, the 90% predominance of [proposition-ph] for "knowing sit" is reduced here to a mere 25%, and the most likely type of complementation is now [performance of situation]. Note too that the probability of [quasi-archaic partial situation with S_theme] is very low indeed, reflecting the "??" with which it is marked in Example (18b).

We look next at the feature [performance of situation]—and so at the dependent system. (Recall from the earlier discussion of the dependent system in Figure 8.7 that such dependent systems function as "free-floating" parts of the ROLE AS SITUATION networks, and that they can be entered by any relevant input feature.) The feature [performance of situation], which is realized by the -ing form of a verb, is best considered at the same time as the feature [potential situation], which is realized by a to-form. These terms are adopted from Quirk et al. (1985), as the most functionally transparent of the various alternative terms found in the literature, and they capture neatly the semantics of these two features. The feature [potential situation] is needed for many other Process types (e.g. as in *Ivy wants to wake up at 7 a.m.*) and for the two "special case" features [knowing desirability of sit] and [remembering and executing intended sit] shown at the foot of Figures 8.7 and 8.8 respectively.

Each of [performance of situation] and [potential situation] leads on to the system shown in Figure 8.8 as dependent on [performance of situation]. As you see, this offers the choice of whether or not to have the Subject-Theme of the embedded clause (here "S-theme") realized overtly. Therefore, it is like the second dependent system (which is immediately below it and which I introduced in Figure 8.7), in that both systems allow the Performer to have a *covert Subject Theme*. But it is unlike the lower system in that it is not at the same time choosing between having a "full" clause (with choices in "tense" and "modality," etc.) and a "partial" ("non-finite") clause.) The most frequent pattern, as the system shows, is that the Participant Role that is conflated with the Subject Theme is recoverable.

Now consider the case when the dependent system is NOT open—as when the entry condition is [knowing desirability of sit] or [remembering and executing intended sit]. In such cases [with S-theme recoverable] must be selected, in order to generate a simple *to*-form, with no overt Subject, and to achieve this a *same pass preference re-setting rule* ensures that the probabilities change so that [with S-theme recoverable] is preferred 100%. This example illustrates nicely the "absolute" use of a same pass preference re-setting rules (i.e. to state a 100% preference). Note too that the rule is attached to the feature, which specifies the "special case" lexical item, so that a "special case" feature and its associated rules are all found at the same point in the lexicogrammar—thus aiding both robustness and economy.)

The types of clause that get generated are as in Examples (11b) and (12b). And, as (11a) and (12a) show, we do not want to generate them if the Process is one of "knowing." Here, then, is a clear example of the need for different ROLE AS SITUATION networks for different Process types.

Now consider the problem of (18b), *Ivy doesn't remember whether/if to eat it*. This was marked with a single query ("?"), indicating doubt as to its acceptability. This type of "borderline acceptability" can be accommodated within the present framework by a second type of *same pass preference re-setting rule*. In the current system the probability of selecting [report of quasi-reply to polarity seeker] is 40%, but the rule changes this to 0.01%. It covers both [remembering state sit] and [remembering cos sit], and it directs that the probabilities be re-set to 99.9% [full report] and 0.01% [partial report with S-theme recoverable].

I give below the essential parts of the realization rules required for Figure 8.8 that have not been introduced already for Figure 8.7—and I include also the rule for [potential situation]. (There is a similar rule for [bare situation], as found in *Ivy made/helped Ike open the door*, but I will omit that here.) Notice the feature [not_period_marked] in Rule 96.21. The realization of "period marking" is the *ing*-form, so that this preference prevents the generation of *I remember Ivy being telling me that*. (A few other rules, which we shall omit here, provide further constraints on what "tenses" (in the broadest sense of the term) can be chosen when these features are selected.)

96.21 : performance_of_situation_ph :
for "Ph" prefer [situation, congruent_situation, dependent,
partial_dependent_sit, performance_of_process,
not_period_marked],
for "Ph" re_enter_at entity.

96.22 : potential_situation_ph or
report_of_content_of_directive :
for "Ph" prefer
[situation, congruent_situation, dependent,
partial_dependent_sit, potential_process],
for "Ph" re_enter_at entity.

96.23 : with_S_theme_recoverable : for "Ph" prefer
[with_covert_S_theme].

96.24 : with_S_theme_not_recoverable : for "Ph"
prefer[with_overt_S_theme].

Finally, I should add that there are several more "complementation types" that are required in a full system. As it happens, the realization rules presented here include all four of the main types of complementation that report the "content" of a clause realizing MOOD option, because these use similar internal structures to some of the complementation types with which I am concerned here— [report of content of information giver], [report of content of new content seeker], [report of content of polarity seeker], and [report of content of directive].[33] As well as "proposition ph," there is a "delayed proposition," as in *I like it that she's coming.* There are a few other types of complementation, including most importantly the case where the Phenomenon is NOT filled by a clause but by a *text*— as in "direct speech" such as *She said "I don't like him"* and "direct thought" as in *She thought: "I don't like him."* However, in considering *know* and *remember* I have covered most types (other than "reification," realized as "nominalization"), and I will leave a discussion of how the others would be most appropriately modelled for another occasion.[34]

---

[33]The term "directive," which is one type of "proposal" in the MOOD network, is fairly close to the sense of Halliday's "proposal" in IFG, though I think his use of the term would include my [potential situation].

[34]Such cases have already been implemented in the COMMUNAL Project, and are covered fully in Fawcett (in preparation a and b).

So far, all the examples considered here have come from the network for mental Processes of *cognition*. However, almost all mental Processes enter such systems, whether they are Processes of *emotion, perception* or *cognition*—including Processes of "causing someone to know something," such as "telling" or "asking" (each in two senses), as we have just seen for the various "report" types of complementation. Indeed, dependent clauses—and so the features in this system through which they are pre-selected—can be the result of choices in many different parts of the overall grammar. Examples of such cases include having a proposition or a partial situation as the Carrier in an *attributive* Process of "being," as in the underlined portions of (24) to (26); or the use of a "report of a quasi-reply to a new content seeker or a polarity seeker," as in (27) and (28)—and many others. As it happens, each of the examples given below can occur in the equivalent "evaluative enhanced theme construction" (to use a functional term for what formal grammarians call "extraposition"). For further discussion of this construction see Fawcett (in preparation a).

That Ike loves Ivy is obvious.   (24a)

It is obvious that Ike loves Ivy.   (24b)

To err is human.   (25a)

It is only human to make mistakes now and then.   (25b)

Seeing you again has been really nice.   (26a)

It has been really nice seeing you again.   (26b)

Where he went is a mystery.   (27a)

It is a mystery where he went.   (27b)

Whether he died immediately is doubtful.   (28a)

It is doubtful whether he died immediately.   (27b)

What all the underlined clauses in these examples have in common is that they play a role in another clause—or, in semantic terms, each is a situation that plays a role in another situation—so that they are all the result of choices in a ROLE AS SITUATION system.

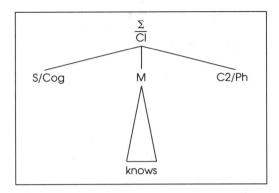

Figure 8.9. A typical structure generated after the first pass through the overall network

(In the next section, I will show where "relative clauses" enter the picture.)

Perhaps the best way to summarize what we have seen of the lexicogrammar so far is to show a typical structure that might be generated when the parts of the lexicogrammar introduced are used. Figure 8.9 presents one such case.

At this point in the generation of this one-clause sentence, the Subject and Complement have been inserted, the Participant Roles have been conflated with them appropriately, and the item *knows* has been generated as the exponent of the Main Verb. Further decisions have been made in the relevant ROLE AS SITUATION systems. But so far we cannot see the effect of those choices, because these only occur when the overall system network for the meaning potential of English is re-entered, in order to build the embedded clause that will fill the Phenomenon. You will see what this looks like when we reach Figure 8.11.[35]

---

[35]In this section I have also introduced—but only as a side issue—the important new concept of *same pass preference re-setting rules*. These are a device for modifying a system network as one works one's way through it. This type of rule is being increasingly widely used in the COMMUNAL lexicogrammar, in a spirit of exploration and experiment. One major aim of the current work in COMMUNAL is to discover what such rules can and cannot do for the lexicogrammarian who is trying to escape two long-recognized but ultimately misleading dichotomies in linguistics. The first is between "grammar" and "lexis," and the second is between "grammaticality" and "ungrammaticality." Here, in the area of "complementation" we have a fine test-bed to evaluate and refine this powerful yet delicate new concept in systemic functional linguistics.

5.6. Realizing Semantic Features in ROLE AS SITUATION: Re-entry and Pre-selected Features in the DEPENDENCE Network

As we have seen, the procedure through which the realization rules for the features in the ROLE AS SITUATION system operate is that those rules CONTROL what options may be selected in certain parts of the network on the re-entry to generate the dependent clause. It will by now be clear that the use of this procedure depends on one's acceptance of the set of assumptions about how language works that I set out in Section 8.4. (Indeed, the fact that this procedure works so naturally is one of the arguments in favor of accepting those assumptions.) Clearly, the present procedure is only possible because (a) the Process type is generated here as part of the situation (so that the Main Verb is generated as a direct element of the structure of the clause) and (b) that the unit whose internal structure we wish to control is one that is generated when the overall system network is re-entered. In IFG, where the dependent clause is related "hypotactically" to the main clause (i.e., it is said to be dependent but not embedded, as it is here), it must be possible to use some such procedure as this, but I leave it to others to explain how these dependencies may be handled in a framework in which these two conditions specified above are not met.[36]

My final task is therefore to specify what the part of the "situation" network that is re-entered is like. In early, syntax-oriented systemic grammars, of which the most complete is the one presented in Hudson (1971), one often finds a simple system with a choice between [main] and [subordinate]. However, what is needed in a sys-

---

[36]After the presentation of a very much earlier version of the material in this chapter (at the 13th International Systemic Workshop at Canterbury in 1986), Christian Matthiessen commented that a fairly similar overall strategy was being used in the Nigel grammar then being developed at the Information Sciences Institute of the University of Southern California (private communication). It is encouraging, but not surprising, to discover that two independent lines of research, working on the same broad principles, have come to similar conclusions. Nonetheless it is hard to reconcile this statement with the grammar as presented in IFG. I await with interest the publication of a detailed description of this aspect of the Nigel system, so that more detailed comparisons can be made. Thus it would appear that the clause relations described as "hypotactic" (rather than "embedded") in IFG are handled, in the Nigel grammar in Penman, in a fashion that is essentially the same as that used here (i.e. by treating the dependent clause as embedded) and then pre-selecting the relevant features. That this is the case in the Nigel grammar has recently been confirmed to me by John Bateman (personal communication, 1995).

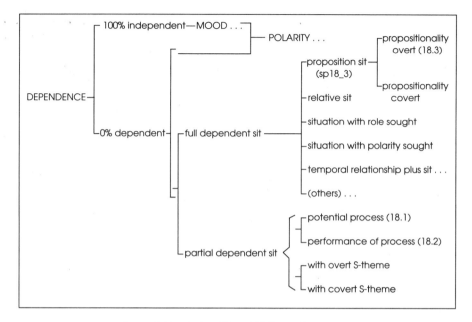

Figure 8.10. A simplified DEPENDENCE network

temic functional lexicogrammar—in one that seeks to model the full meaning potential of a language—is something more like the network in Figure 8.10.

As will be clear, the realization rules attached to the features in the ROLE AS SITUATION system pre-select features in the DEPENDENCE system network shown in Figure 8.10. In this way a semantic choice in one layer of the semantic structure—and so the syntactic structure—is passed down to a lower layer of the developing tree diagram. Indeed, virtually all of the features in this network are preselected, as we will see. This explains why there are no probabilities on the systems—with the exception of the first, to which I will come in a moment.

As you can see, the many types of complementation that I have recognized at the level of semantics are reduced here to a relatively small number of features. Yet this little set of features has the ability to show the different realizations of around a couple of dozen semantically differentiated types of complement. Indeed, some of the features in the DEPENDENCE network in Figure 8.10 serve the needs of other types of dependent situation, and so other types of dependent clause. Thus [relative sit] provides for "relative clauses," (i.e. clauses embedded as the qualifier of a nominal group) of both the "identifying" and the "supplementary" types ("restrictive" and "non-restrictive," in the terms of traditional grammar). The clauses that fill various types of "temporal" Adjunct introduced by a Binder such as *while, after, when, before,* and *since* are also located here; they are found in systems dependent on the feature [temporal relationship plus sit]. The same is true of a number of other types of clause that are dependent but that do not fill a Phenomenon, so that here we are only interested in three of the first four features for "full" dependent situations, and in the "partial" ones.

The first system in the network may strike you as odd. It illustrates a different use of probabilities from the uses that I noted earlier, where they were intended to represent a general probability. Clearly, it is not the case in the present system that one feature is chosen 100% of the time, or there would be no need to have a system. Here, then, we are using the probability re-setting procedure for an absolute rather than a relative preference. So the feature [independent] is the default option, in the sense that it will be chosen unless a rule from an earlier pass has changed the probabilities. Thus this option is always chosen on the first pass through the network, and for any clauses that are coordinated with it. However, as I demonstrated in the last section, the realization rules for complementation regularly state that [dependent] is to be chosen, and the effect of this is to over-rule the default probabilities.

I now turn to the rules that actually implement higher choices about complementation in terms of the internal structure of the embedded clause currently being generated. First, notice that the MOOD network is not entered for dependent clauses. This is because MOOD can only be selected for the topmost clause (or set of coordinated clauses) in a sentence. Essentially the same structures are generated for [full dependent sit] as for "information givers"— but they are not necessarily, even informally, "information givers." (Recall that the complementation types include "report of new content seeker," etc.) On the other hand, "dependent" situations do choose in the POLARITY system, because dependent clauses can be "negative" as well as "positive"—though the grammar specifies that they do so with a greatly reduced chance of choosing [negative]. (This is provided for by preference rules not shown here.)

I come now to the more delicate features. There is no realization rule for [proposition sit], because the internal structure of a clause that realizes a "proposition" is the unmarked structure for a clause. What is more interesting is the same pass preference resetting rule on [proposition sit]. This states:

sp18_3 : proposition_sit :
  if formal then for same_unit prefer
    [99# propositionality_overt / 1# propositionality_covert],
  if casual then for same_unit prefer
    [1# propositionality_overt / 99# propositionality_covert].

In other words, features in the TENOR of discourse system (which are available to choices such as these) are invoked as conditions for resetting the probabilities in this system. Now consider the rule for [propositionality overt]. It simply places a Binder in the clause (at Place 8) and expounds it by *that.*

18.3 : propositionality_overt : "B" @ 8, "B" < "that."

As you will notice, there is no realization rule for [relative sit]—with which I am not concerned here—or for [situation with role sought]—with which I AM concerned here. The reason is that these features are referred to as conditional features in rules that are located elsewhere in the lexicogrammar. This is just as important a function for a feature to serve as to have a realization rule of its own attached to it. In this case there are rules at the relevant stage of each major network for TRANSITIVITY that set preferences within that network—and some of the features in those networks specify that a given Participant Role should be what we here term "sought"—an element that is "sought" being typically realized by an "interrogative pronoun." (I cannot go into the reasons why such features must be included in the TRANSITIVITY networks in this chapter, except to say that in a fully generative lexico-grammar it is necessary to introduce them, because they drastically affect the availability of certain dependent systems in the network, e.g. those to do with thematizing a Participant Role.) The effect of selecting [situation with role sought], then, is to ensure that the grammar generates *who ate the caviar* in *I know who ate the caviar* and *I remember who ate the caviar,* as in (13a and b) in the last section, and *I know/remember where/when/why/how Ivy ate it,* as in (14a and b). Thus it is the "interrogative pronouns" that must be generated in this construction, not the "relative pronouns."[37]

---

[37]Thus, in the matrix clause, the feature chosen to generate examples such as (13a) *(I know she ate the caviar)* is [report of quasi-reply to new content seeker], while in the embedded clause the fact that a "sought role" semantic feature is chosen in the relevant TRANSITIVITY network—so generating an "interrogative"

On the other hand, the choice of [situation with polarity sought] is realized directly. It has the following relatively simple realization rule:

18.4 : situation_with_polarity_sought :
    "B" @ 8,
    if partial_dependent_sit or (full_dependent_sit and formal)
    then "B" < "whether,"
    if full_dependent_sit and (consultative or casual)
    then "B" < "if").

This rule provides neatly for the fact that *if* is not found in partial dependent clauses (i.e. **He knows/is wondering if to come*). It says that the Binder will be expounded by *whether* in all cases of a "partial dependent" clause and if a "full dependent" clause is "formal," and that otherwise it will be expounded by *if*—if the "full dependent" clause is "consultative" or "casual."

However, that is all that is necessary for the many different types of complementation that are realized in "full" dependent clauses. I turn now to those realized in "partial" clauses, and here too there is a pleasing economy. Consider first Rule 18.1:

18.1 : potential_process : "I1" @ 52, "I1" < "to".

This simply states that the first Infinitive Element (I) is to be located at Place 52, and that it will be expounded by the item *to*. (Further conditions will provide a *for* when necessary, as in *For Ivy to say that would be surprising* and *It would be surprising for Ivy to say that*.) The rule for [performance of situation] is more complex, because it must provide for adding +*ing* to any of a number of Auxiliary Verbs or the Main Verb. (The features referred to in the following rule are the semantic features corresponding to "perfect(ive)" and "passive," etc., but this is not the place to describe this part of the grammar further.)

18.2 : performance_of_process :
    if (retrospective_from_trp or past_from_trp)
    then "Xr" <+ "+ing,"
    if unmarked_passive and not
        (retrospective_from_trp or past_from_trp)

---

item—is reflected by pre-selecting the feature [situation with role sought]. In other words, we have here a neutralization of the matrix clause distinction between [new content seeker] and [report of quasi-reply to new content seeker].

then "Xp" <+ "+ing,"
if not (retrospective_from_trp or
    past_from_trp or
    unmarked_passive)
then "M" <+ "+ing."

Finally, there is the question of how the meanings of [with overt S-theme] and [with covert S-theme] are realized—because these too have no realization rules. The answer is as for [situation with role sought]. In other words, the importance of these features lies in the fact that one of them, [with covert S-theme], is a vital *conditional feature* in the realization rules for certain features in the TRANSITIVITY network. That is, for any Participant Role that is to serve also as Subject-Theme—and that will therefore be conflated with the Subject—the question must be asked: "Is it or is it not to be expounded by actual words?" The answer is that this depends on whether it is (a) the Subject of a "proposal for action" (such as *Eat it now!*) or (b) the Subject of a "partial dependent" clause with a "covert Subject" (such as *what to eat first* in (16a and b) in the last section, or *to eat the caviar first* in (23a or b)). If it is either of these there will be no re-entry to the network. The actual form of the condition in such rules is:

if not (proposal_for_action or with_covert_S_theme)
then. . . . .

and there then follows the specification for re-entering the network.

Probably the clearest way to illustrate how such rules work is to show the effect of the realization rule attached to the relevant features in the DEPENDENCE network on the example shown in Figure 8.9. We will assume that the network has been re-entered for the Cognizant, and that *the chairman* has been generated, as shown in Figure 8.11, as the exponent of the Subject/Cognizant. (To simplify the diagram, I will not show the internal structure of the nominal groups.) The effect of the choice of [proposition ph] is to pre-select the features [full dependent sit] and [proposition sit]. Thus a clause is added to the structure, as in Figure 8.11. In this case, the further feature [propositionality overt] has been chosen, because of the "formal" tenor of the discourse. The realization of this is that there will be a Binder expounded by *that*. After this, portions of the lexicogrammar that are not discussed here will generate, say, *we ate all the ice cream.*

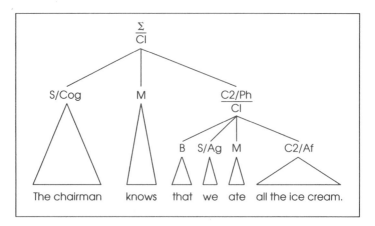

Figure 8.11.   A typical structure generated after the second pass through the "situation" network

5.7. Alternative Ways of Modelling Complementation

In the preceding sections I have described the way of modelling complementation which, to those of us working on the lexicogrammar of English in the COMMUNAL Project, seems to be the best. It is "best" in that it gives the strongest combination of (a) providing a clear model with clear categories, (b) having the ability to handle the differences of detail of individual Process types, including differences in probabilities, and (c) being explicit enough to be computationally implementable. However, there are at least three other possible ways in which we might have modelled complementation, and I will now briefly summarize and compare the solution to the problem described in this chapter and the other three. The first three share the same basic assumptions, and the fourth is more radical.

Le me restate the task. This is to specify, by using system networks that model the meaning potential of the language, which Process types are open to which choices of semantic patterning in their Phenomenon—and so which are open to which types of internal syntactic patterning in the clauses that fill the Phenomenon. Furthermore, I want to do this in a way that allows me to state that some of these complementation patterns are very frequent, that some are much less frequent but fully regular, and that some are so unusual as to be barely acceptable—and all possible variations between these, as the data become available from corpus studies. I shall evaluate each possible solution to the problem in terms of (a) the visual clarity of the resulting network (and other rules) to the "reader," and

(b) its suitability as an explicit lexicogrammar that is usable for a computer implementation—especially in terms of its robustness when the lexicogrammar is altered (e.g. to add further Process types). Indeed, I shall not regard these considerations as peculiar to a computer implementation, but as general characteristics to be looked for in any large generative grammar.

The first three possible solutions to the problem to be outlined here all make the assumption that there should be a set of "semantic complementation" features—features such as those that I have placed in the ROLE AS SITUATION systems.

In *Solution 1* (i.e. the solution to the problem advocated in this chapter) there is (a) a very large set of features that are Process types, typically realized as Process types (a, b, c, d, e, f, g, etc.) and (b) a finite set of about two dozen features specifying types of ROLE AS SITUATION, or "complementation types," (v, w, x, y, z), such that each Process type (or set of Process types) enters its own INDIVIDUALLY TAILORED SYSTEM of complementation types. (The fact that there are also two further systems that are dependent on some of these features, as shown in Figure 8.8, doesn't significantly affect the comparisons that will be based on this summary.) It is an important advantage of this approach that it allows us to state in a simple manner the probabilities among the complementation types for each Process type. The range of possible relations can be modelled as in Figure 8.12. This approach is efficient both as a visual representation and as an explicit grammar that is well-suited to implementation in a computer.[38]

How could this solution be improved on? Some systemic grammarians might criticize the fact that Figure 8.12 allows the REPETITION OF FEATURES. (Another criticism might be that there should not be a "one-feature system" (the bottom "x"), and the only way to address this would be as suggested in Solution 3, to which I will come in a moment.) There are two ways to avoid repeating features, and

---

[38]Its only disadvantage is that it is dangerous, when drawing system networks, to repeat a feature that is NOT a terminal feature in a network. This is because any system that is dependent on a given feature will automatically be entered from ANY instance of that feature, wherever it occurs in the overall network. (Hence the use of suffixes, to prevent the inadvertent repetition of features that it might be tempting to use in more than one context, such as "neutral" or "unmarked," etc.) The potential problem in our case is that some of the complementation features are NOT terminal—as Figure 8.8 illustrates. However, in practice this isn't a problem, because the network has been built with this potential problem in mind—and it is extremely unlikely that new instances of the relevant features will ever be added to the lexicogrammar.

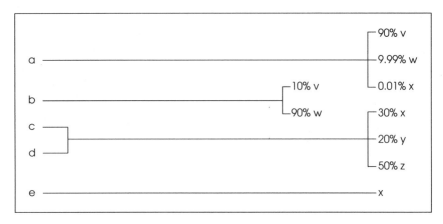

Figure 8.12. A schematic representation of Process types and complementation types

these are the basis of each of the next two possible solutions to the problem. So the question becomes: "What is the effect, judged by each of the two criteria, of drawing the network in such a way as to avoid repeating features?" Consider *Solution 2.* In this solution we would simply have a single, full set of complementation features on the right hand side of the diagram, with a "disjunctive" ("or") entry condition to each, and with lines coming from each of the relevant Process types (from a systemic "or" after each). The two sides of the diagram would be related by some extremely complex wiring (a point that we shall return to shortly). To implement this solution would require us either to abandon the use of probabilities (together with their ability to model very unusual cases), or to have a very large set of same pass preference re-setting rules that spelled out the PROBABILITIES FOR EVERY PROCESS TYPE. Thus, while the network representation would certainly do the work of specifying which complementation features were to be available, preference rules would still be required to handle the probabilities.[39] In computational terms this would all be completely feasible (and this was in fact the model used when I first developed this area of the lexicogrammar). However, in terms of trying to provide a helpful visual network representation of the choices available, the result is chaos. To see why this is so, consider the complexity of the complementation patterns re-

---

[39]The only alternative, which I cannot imagine anyone seriously advocating, would be to label each feature that had a different probability from any others with a different label, such as "50% x" and "0.1% x."

quired by just the TWO verb forms seen earlier in this chapter, and then try to imagine the enormous complexity of the interwoven lines that would result if we tried to draw a network, for example, for ALL of the "cognition" Processes! As a simple exercise, may I invite you to draw a network based on these principles for the "grammar" shown in Figure 8.12? This particular task is in fact not too hard—but imagine it magnified by having five times as many complementation types and perhaps a hundred times as many Process types. Finally, note that you will also need to provide preference re-setting rules for each Process type. So this solution has no advantage over Solution 1, and some clear disadvantages.

The problem of the enormous amount of work that this last consideration involves brings us to *Solution 3*. This too was explored in a trial model. Here the right side of the diagram is occupied by ONE LARGE ROLE AS SITUATION SYSTEM that contains all of the two dozen or so possible complementation types. These would never, of course, all be available at the same time, so that it is not a genuine system—and so is no solution to the supposed "problem" that Solution 1 allows "one-feature" systems. (In fact I do not see this as a "problem," but as part of the data, i.e. as one of the relatively rare "non-systemic" features in the network.) In Solution 3, then, there would be a separate line from each Process type leading to the unified complementation system—and in that sense the network representation could be said to be quite simple. However, the consequence is that it would be necessary for each feature specifying a Process type to have a same pass preferrence re-setting rule attached to it, and for this rule to state (a) which features in the system were to be activated, and (b) the probability of each. In other words, the preference rule for each Process type would have to spell out explicitly all of the features in the complementation system network relevant to itself, with the probabilities of each. So it would have the same degree of complexity as Solution 1, with the addition of a spurious and unnecessary system. Also, from the viewpoint of a visual display, it would have the disadvantage, in comparison with Solution 1, that the choices open to each Process type would not be presented as a single system. Finally, the "single system" cannot even be defended on the grounds that it alone provides an opportunity to see all of the complementation types together. This is because, by referring to the realization rules whose numbers begin with 96, you can find precisely this: the set of ROLE AS SITUATION features and their associated realization rules (as well as the ROLE AS THING features introduced in Section 5.3).

So far, then, there seems to be no advantage in adopting either of Solutions 2 or 3. *Solution 4* is an even more drastic alternative. It would completely omit from the lexicogrammar any concept of a set of features specifying the complementation types. In other words, it would imply that there are NO general abstractions concerning the meanings of what types of "situation" occur as the Phenomenon in mental Processes available at the level of the "mother" clause. So all of the categories listed in the ROLE AS SITUATION systems in Figures 8.7 and 8.8 would disappear. How could this be achieved? It would be done by having, as part of the realization rule attached to each Process type, a specification of what features are to be preferred on re-entry to generate the unit to fill the Phenomenon of the clause currently being generated. This would avoid the similarities found in the current grammar between some of the features in the ROLE AS SITUATION and DEPENDENCE networks, but the cost would far outweigh any apparent advantage. This is because the preferences would have to be stated afresh for each Process type—rather than, as is done here, stating the preferences just once for each complementation type. So Solution 4 would involve an enormous number of missed generalizations, and so repetition. It would also leave a yawning gap in the systemic functional account of the meaning potential for this area of language.

We have experimented with implementations of each of the first three of these possible solutions, and the clear conclusion is that Solution 1 offers the best combination of characteristics—for all the reasons given at the start of this section.

6. CONCLUSIONS

As I hope I have shown, a systemic functional model for this area approaches the problem from an angle that is rather different from the line adopted by syntax-oriented grammarians—even though we are all ultimately dealing with the same complex phenomena. The present approach, using an explicitly systemic functional framework, is also markedly different from the one previous substantial systemic effort in this area: that of Hudson 1971 and 1976. This is because a systemic FUNCTIONAL approach must be from the SEMANTIC end of language—while paying due attention, as one always must, to the syntax in which these various types of meaning are realized.

Let me return briefly to the theme of the first paragraph of this chapter—that this is a "complement" as well as a "compliment." It will be clear that the debt to Halliday's ideas throughout this chapter, as throughout all my work on language, is beyond measure. Consider only (a) the concept of modelling language as, essentially, a "meaning potential," (b) the fact that we do this through the conventions of system networks and their realizations, (c) the acceptance of Halliday's broad divisions of the lexicogrammar, right down to the relative detail of including "cognition" as a sub-type of "mental Process," (d) the concept that TRANSITIVITY is realized in the clause (and not just the Main Verb), and (e) the categories and relations assumed here in the output structures (which go back, with a few modifications, to Halliday 1961)—and many more such foundational concepts. Against this background the differences that I find it necessary to make from what is proposed in IFG are relatively small. In this chapter, I have given further reasons (adding to those given in many of my other writings over the last couple of decades) for treating the meanings realized in the Main Verb as being generated AT THE SAME TIME that the rest of the clause is generated—on the same pass through the network. This follows naturally from the Hallidayan concepts that (a) TRANSITIVITY is realized in the clause, and (b) that lexical verbs, like other lexical items, realize choices in "most delicate grammar." And the area of the grammar in which they offer the "most delicate" choices cannot be anything other than TRANSITIVITY.[40] Finally, I have greatly expanded the number of complementation types (implicit in IFG in labels such as "proposition" and "proposal") to around two dozen, most of which have been introduced here.

Despite these differences, then, the portions of lexicogrammar offered here are complementary to Halliday's own writings about these topics—in the sense that he does not propose explicit system networks and realization rules for this (or any other area of the grammar). The bits of lexicogrammar offered here are also complementary in that IFG is essentially—and necessarily—a grammar rather than a lexicogrammar. However, the fact is that, in trying to provide this "complement" to Halliday's proposals for this area (which were outlined in Section 3), I have found that I have had to work with a model that has some significant differences from that implied in IFG. So it is, to that extent, an alternative as well as a complementary portion of the lexicogrammar of English.

My usual experience in reading Halliday's writings is to recognize the insights and to incorporate them gratefully into my model. However, occasionally I feel that he may be pushing an idea too far (as

---

[40]Furthermore, it is hard to see how a model in which the lexical verb is tucked away lower down the "rank scale" as an element of a verbal group, can handle the dependencies that so clearly exist between a Process type and its patterns of complementation, because the verb expresses the Process type.

here, in proposing that the "hypotactic" relation of "projection" is "above the clause") or that he does not give sufficient weight to criteria that I take to be important (as when he retains the Main Verb as an element of the verbal group rather than allowing it to be an element of the clause).[41] On such occasions I have to find my own solutions—although I always find it useful to ensure that they fit within the overall framework of a systemic functional approach to understanding language.

Whatever one's judgement on any particular matter, all functionally oriented grammarians owe a great debt to Halliday for his wonderful cornucopia of stimulating and insightful ideas—and the debt extends, moreover, over several decades of some of the most exciting developments in linguistics. It was Michael Halliday, essentially, who set up the broad, systemic functional approach to language, which provides the structure within which we other systemic functionalists can explore the data and find and develop our own insights. Even though no linguist can expect to be judged to be "right" (whatever that means) about everything, it is still the case that, if one is seeking a source of new insights into what language is like and why it is as it is, the most insightful single source of challenging ideas today is Halliday's IFG.

---

[41]On the other hand, some of his diagrams in IFG (e.g. pp. 74 and 79) imply an analysis that is much more like that proposed here. That is, there is a "Finite" (which is in many ways equivalent to my "Operator") and a "Predicator" (which in some of these diagrams looks deceptively equivalent to my "Main Verb"), and both are presented is if they were direct elements of the clause—along with the Subject. However, the similarities are not in fact as great as this, especially with regard to the Predictor. Halliday states clearly (p. 79) that it "is realized by a verbal group minus the temporal or modal operator" (so that it is clearly NOT equivalent to my "Main Verb"), and Figure 4-8 on p. 81 corroborates this. However, he also writes (p. 74) that "the presence of the Mood element, consisting of Subject plus Finite, realizes the feature 'indicative'"—"indicative" being, of course, a feature of the clause, so implying that the Finite is an element of clause structure. This is essentially the position proposed here, with the principle being extended so that the Main Verb too is treated as an element of clause structure (as also are the Auxiliaries). Halliday's summarized his position on p. 196, when he says "the verbal group is the constituent that functions as Finite plus Predicate . . . in the mood structure . . . . and as Process in the transitivity structure." Thus in his model the elements of the verbal group "realize" (his term) two different elements of the clause, rather than one, so that the element "Finite" in the verbal group functions as the element "Finite" in the clause. It will be clear that I think the grammar operates in a manner that is simpler—but just as richly insightful in terms of the strands of meaning interwoven into the structure—if one treats all the elements of the "verbal group" as direct elements of the clause.

The final compliment to Michael Halliday must be to express gratitude, on behalf of all who work in the theory, for the way he has handled his undisputed leadership of this theory. He has manfully resisted the temptation—which no doubt at times must have been overwhelming—to try to curb the explorations of his fellow systemic functionalists. In this he has shown a greater tolerance and—as I believe it will ultimately be shown to be—a greater wisdom than that of some other linguists who have had the power to influence the development of our subject in the second half of the twentieth century.

This chapter has spelled out, in quite precise terms, a framework for handling the relationship between (a) the "most delicate grammar" of *Process types* realized as Main Verbs and (b) their *complementation* in the ROLE AS SITUATION systems (whether this is handled as "projection," as in IFG, or as the "embedding" of a clause as the Phenomenon, as here). My claim is that this framework, or something closely related to it, is what is needed in a SFG—whatever the "dialect" of the theory in which one is working.

Finally, it must also be said that another set of concepts that is in principle a separate matter has intruded regularly into the discussion—despite my best efforts to sideline it for the purposes of this chapter. This is the use of (a) *probabilities* on features and (b) *same pass preference re-setting rules.* It is this combination that permits the lexicogrammarian to introduce a delicacy in expressing probabilities that is light years away from the gross distinctions of formalist grammarians into the "grammatical" and the "ungrammatical."[42] This too is an aspect of modelling language advocated by Halliday, so in this respect this chapter is both a "complement" to his work and a "compliment" to him. The need is to develop ways of modelling degrees of probability, and especially of very low probability, in specific lexicogrammatical contexts—and beyond that in specific social contexts. As we have seen in this chapter, complementation is an area of lexicogrammar that provides a rigorous challenge to the researcher who is trying to implement such concepts.

---

[42]The lexicogrammarian also, of course, has to face the challenge of how to avoid generating text-sentences that contain various types of complete ungrammaticality. Although it is the primary task of the system networks and realization rules to specify a language's meaning potential, the corollary is that at the same time they ensure that such types of "ungrammaticality" are not generated. But that is not the issue here.

REFERENCES

Butler, C.S. (1985) *Systemic Linguistics: Theory and Application.* London: Batsford.

Fawcett, R.P. (1974) "Some proposals for systemic syntax: Part 1." In *MALS Journal 1(2):* 1–15.

Fawcett, R.P. (1975) "Some Proposals for systemic syntax: Part 2." In *MALS Journal 2(1):* 43–68.

Fawcett, R.P. (1976) "Some proposals for systemic syntax: Part 3." In *MALS Journal 2(2):* 36–68.

Fawcett, R.P. (1980) *Cognitive Linguistics and Social Interaction: Towards an Integrated Model of a Systemic Functional Grammar and the Other Components of an Interacting Mind.* Heidelberg: Julius Groos and Exeter University.

Fawcett, R.P. (1981) *Some Proposals for Systemic Syntax* (revised version of 1974, 1975 and 1976). Cardiff: Polytechnic of Wales (now University of Glamorgan).

Fawcett, R.P. (1983) "Language as a semiological system: A re-interpretation of Saussure." Invited Lecture to the Linguistics Association of Canada and the United States 1982. In Morreall, J., (ed.) 1983, *The Ninth LACUS Forum 1982,* Columbia: Hornbeam Press, pp. 59–125.

Fawcett, R.P. (1987) "The semantics of clause and verb for relational processes in English." In Halliday and Fawcett 1987: 130–83.

Fawcett, R.P. (1988a) "Language generation as choice in social interaction." In Zock, M., and Sabah, G., (eds.), *Advances in Natural Language Generation Vol 1.* London: Pinter, pp. 27–49.

Fawcett, R.P. (1988b) "What makes a good system network good?—four pairs of concepts for such evaluations." In Benson, J.D., and Greaves, W.S., (eds.) (1988) *Systemic Functional Approaches to Discourse: Selected Papers from the 12th International Systemic Workshop,* Norwood, N.J.: Ablex, pp. 1–28.

Fawcett, R.P. (1988c) "The English personal pronouns: An exercise in linguistic theory." In Benson, J.D., Cummings, M., and Greaves, W.S., (eds.) (1988) *Linguistics in a Systemic Perspective,* Amsterdam: Benjamin, pp. 185–220.

. Fawcett, R.P. (1990) "The computer generation of speech with semantically and discoursally motivated intonation." In *Procs of 5th International Workshop on Natural Language Generation,* Pittsburgh, pp. 164–73a.

Fawcett, R.P. (1993) "Language as program: A reassessment of the nature of descriptive linguistics." In *Language Sciences* 14(4): pp. 623–57.

Fawcett, R.P. (1994a) "A generationist approach to grammar reversibility in natural language processing." In Strzalkowski, T., (ed.), *Reversible Grammar in Natural Language Generation,* Dordrecht: Kluwer, pp. 365–413.

Fawcett, R.P. (1994b) "On moving on on ontologies: mass, count and long thing things." In McDonald, D. (ed), *Proceedings of the Seventh Inter-*

national *Workshop on Natural Language Generation*, pp. 71–80. Association for Computational Linguistics, available through Computer Science, Brandeis University, Waltham MA.

Fawcett, R.P. (1995) "Some complexities in the semantics and syntax of the grammar of the English cardinal numbers." In de Smedt, K., Mellish, C., and Novak, H-J., (eds.) (1995) *Proceedings of the Fifth European Workshop on Natural Language Generation*, pp. 223–7.

Fawcett, R.P. (in preparation a) *Handbook for the Analysis of Sentences in English Text. Volume 1 Syntax: A Systemic Functional Approach.* Cardiff: Computational Linguistics Unit, University of Wales, Cardiff CF1 3EU.

Fawcett, R.P. (in preparation b) *Handbook for the Analysis of Sentences in English Text. Volume 2 Meaning: A Systemic Functional Approach.* Cardiff: Computational Linguistics Unit, University of Wales, Cardiff CF1 3EU.

Fawcett, R.P., and Huang, G.W. (1995) "A functional analysis of the enhanced theme construction in English." *Interface: Journal of Applied Linguistics*, 10.1:113–44.

Fawcett, R.P., and Huang, G.W. (in preparation) *Enhanced Theme in English.*

Fawcett, R.P., and Tucker, G.H. (1990) "Demonstration of GENESYS: A very large, semantically based systemic functional grammar." In *Procs of COLING 90*, Vol 1 pp. 47–49.

Fawcett, R.P., Tucker, G.H., and Lin, Y.Q. (1993) "How a systemic functional grammar works: The role of realization in realization." In Horacek, H., and Zock, M., (eds.) (1993) *New Concepts in Natural Language Generation*, London: Pinter, pp. 114–86.

Gregory, M. (1987) "Meta-functions: Aspects of their development, status and use in systemic linguistics." In Halliday and Fawcett (1987): 94–106.

Halliday, M.A.K. (1961) "Categories of the theory of grammar." In *Word* 17: 241–92.

Halliday, M.A.K. (1970) "Language structure and language function." In Lyons, J. (ed.) 1970, *New Horizons in Linguistics*, Harmondsworth: Penguin, pp. 140–65.

Halliday, M.A.K. (1985) *An Introduction to Functional Grammar.* London: Arnold.

Halliday, M.A.K. (1994) *An Introduction to Functional Grammar (Second Edition).* London: Arnold.

Halliday, M.A.K., and Fawcett, R.P. (eds.) (1987) *New Developments in Systemic Linguistics, Vol 1: Theory and Description.* London: Pinter.

Huang, G.W. (this volume) "Experiential Enhanced Theme in English."

Hudson, R.A. (1971) *English Complex Sentences: An Introduction to Systemic Grammar.* Amsterdam: North Holland.

Hudson, R.A. (1976) *Arguments for a Non-transformational Grammar.* Chicago: Chicago University Press.

Mann, W.C., and Matthiessen, C.M.I.M. (1983/85) "A demonstration of the Nigel text generation computer program." In Mann, W.C., and Matthiessen, C.M.I.M., *Nigel: a Systemic Grammar for Text Generation.* Marina del Rey, CA: ISI/USC, and in Benson, J.D., and Greaves, W.S., (eds.), *Systemic Perspectives on Discourse, Vol 1: Selected Theoretical Papers from the Ninth International Systemic Workshop,* Norwood, N.J.: Ablex, pp. 50–83.

Nesbitt, C., and Plum, G. (1988) "Probabilities in a systemic-functional grammar: The clause complex in English." In Fawcett, R.P., and Young, D.J., eds. (1988) *New Developments in Systemic Linguistics, Vol 2: Theory and Application.,* London: Pinter, pp. 6–38.

Quirk, R., Greenbaum, S., Leech, G., and Svartvik, J. (1985) *A Comprehensive Grammar of the English Language.* London: Longman.

Sinclair, John (ed.) (1987) *Collins COBUILD English Language Dictionary.* London: Collins.

Summers, D. (ed.) (1987) *Longman Dictionary of Contemporary English (New Edition).* London: Longman.

Tucker, G.H. (1992) "An initial approach to comparatives in a systemic functional grammar." In Davies, M. and Ravelli, L., (eds.) (1992) *Advances in Systemic Linguistics: Recent Theory and Practice.* London: Pinter, pp. 150–65.

Tucker, G.H. (1995) *The Treatment of Lexis in a Systemic Functional Model of English with special reference to Adjectives and their Structure.* PhD Thesis. Cardiff: University of Wales, Cardiff, School of English Studies, Communication and Philosophy.

Tucker, G.H. (this volume) "Cultural classification and system networks: A systemic functional approach to lexis."

Tucker, G.H. (in press) "So grammarians haven't the faintest idea: reconciling lexis-oriented and grammar-oriented approaches to language." In Hasan, R., Butt, D., and Cloran, C., (eds.) *Functional Descriptions: Language Form and Linguistic Theory.* Amsterdam: Benjamin.

Young, D.J. (1980) *The Structure of English Clauses.* London: Hutchinson.

9
Turning Grammar On Itself: Identifying Clauses in Linguistic Discourse

Kristin Davidse

University of Leuven
Belgium

1. INTRODUCTION

One of M.A.K. Halliday's most original contributions to linguistics has been to reveal the dialectic between grammar and grammatics, the theory of grammar. Nowhere is this clearer than in Halliday's analysis of identifying clauses and his concomitant view on the definition of linguistic categories. First, he found in his grammatics a semantic model to shed light on identifying clauses, which he interpreted as the grammaticalization of the semiotic concept of "realization" (Halliday 1967b:228; 1985:115). In identifying clauses, Halliday argued, the correlation between both participants, allowing for identification, is one of symbolic representation or coding: One participant is construed as "representans" or Token, and the other is construed as "represented" or Value. (Hence, this type of clause can also be referred to more precisely as "coding-identifying.") In a second movement, Halliday used the grammatical analysis of coding-identifying clauses to clarify central issues of linguistic categorization and definition. In particular, he (1988:29) pointed out that one should carefully distinguish between two fundamentally different kinds of linguistic definition. The *encoding* definition identifies a grammatical category in terms of its formal realization, or Token. It specifies how the category can be recognized, as in the following encoding definition of the category "finiteness:"

> *Finiteness (Value/Identified) is expressed by means of a*
> *verbal operator which is either temporal or modal (Token/*
> *Identifier). (Halliday 1985:75)*   (1)

The *decoding* definition identifies the grammatical category in terms of its meaning, or Value. It glosses what the category means, as in this definition of "primary tense:"

> *Primary tense (Token/Identified) means past, present or fu-*
> *ture at the moment of speaking (Value/Identifier); it (To-*
> *ken/Identified) is time relative to "now" (Value/Identifier).*
> *(Halliday 1985:75)*   (2)

In this chapter, I will further pursue this dialectic between grammatics and grammar in the area of relational grammar. More specifically, I will look at some pending questions associated with the lexicogrammar of coding-identifying clauses, by investigating these in a corpus of linguistics texts. This data base consists of Halliday's (1991) paper "Towards probabilistic interpretations" (21 pages of text; 113 instances of coding-identifying clauses) and the first 23 pages (92 instances of coding-identifying clauses) of Wierzbicka's *The Semantics of Grammar*, excluding the Introduction (1988:23–43). Naturally, I expected this small corpus to be both very privileged and very restricted for a pilot-study of this kind. As pointed out by Halliday (1994:xx), it can be advantageous to break into the semantics of a grammatical system in "a fairly restricted register." So why not start close to home? The hypothesis is that coding-identifying construals grammaticalize "symbolic correlation." Surely, the register of linguistic argumentation and reflection is the one whose intricately varying semiotic perspectives we are most likely to be able to interpret. At the same time, of course, any descriptive results will be intrinsically limited and register-specific and can only provide hypotheses for further research encompassing other registers.

2. CODING-IDENTIFYING CLAUSES: THE GRAMMAR OF METAREDUNDANCY

2.1. The Grammatico-semantic Paradigm of Coding-identifying Clauses

Working toward insight into the grammar of identifying clauses has involved for me a rediscovery of Halliday's earlier treatment of them in "Notes on Transitivity and Theme" (henceforth "Notes"), which, I argued in Davidse (1992) and Davidse (in press) truly captures the central parameters in the grammaticalization of "symbolic correlation." Some of these central vectors were lost in the later treatment in the first edition of Halliday's *Introduction to Functional Grammar* (1985).

There are two crucial differences between these two treatments. The most striking difference is that *Introduction to Functional Grammar* (1985:126–127; 1994:136–137) attributes a *four*-cell grammatical paradigm to identifying clauses, whereas in "Notes" Halliday (1967a:68–69; 1967b:277; 1968:190–192) had set out the grammatical vectors of identifying construals in terms of an *eight*-cell paradigm[1]. Concretely, this difference is due to the following. The paradigm in *Introduction to Functional Grammar* allows for only *one* possible assignment of the functions Token (Tk) and Value (Vl) to the two terms of the identification. For instance, for the identification "Mr. Garrick is Hamlet," it brings into the picture only the assignment of Token to Mr. Garret and of Value to Hamlet:

Mr Garrick is/plays Hamlet.   Hamlet is/is played by Mr Garrick.
Tk   *Vl*   *Vl*   *Tk*

(3)

This Token-Value assignment imposes on the identification the semantics of play-acting, in which the symbolic directionality goes from the "first-order" term (the real-life actor Mr. Garrick) to the "second-order" term (the fictional character Hamlet). Or, in general terms, the Token is situated at a less abstract symbolic stratum and the Value at a more abstract symbolic stratum.

The paradigm in "Notes," however, allows for *redistribution* of the functions Token and Value[2] to the two terms of the identification: Not only

John is the leader.   The leader is John.   (4)
Tk   Vl   Vl   Tk

---

[1]Comparison and discussion of these two paradigms can be found in Davidse (1992; in press). However, the analysis presented here makes corrections to these earlier discussions in that it brings out the distinct semantics of the "expression" and "motivation" subparadigms as a cross-classificatory system simultaneous with the decoding-encoding option.

[2]In "Notes" Halliday used the labels of *Variable* and *Value* but he later replaced *Variable* by *Token*. For simplicity's sake, I will use *Token-Value* throughout the article, also when representing the position of "Notes."

but also

The leader is John. John is the leader.　　　　　(5)
Tk　　　*Vl*　　*Vl*　　*Tk*

This paradigm thus stipulates that there is not only a Token–Value relation going from the "less abstract" to the "more abstract" symbolic stratum, or from the person John to his role the leader; there is also a Token–Value relation, which goes from the "more abstract" to the "less abstract" symbolic stratum, or from the role the leader to the role holder John. In other words, the "Notes" paradigm posits, semantically, that a symbolic relation is intrinsically invertible— that it goes both "upward" and "downward" between its two symbolic interfaces. Being a grammatico-semantic paradigm, it posits that this invertibility of symbolic directionality is grammaticalized, that it is part and parcel of the *system* of the lexicogrammar of English.

The second central vector of coding-identifying grammar is the *decoding-encoding* contrast (Halliday 1967a:67–69; 1967b:227–231; 1968:190–193; 1994:124–125,129,167). The systemic option of decoding versus encoding construal is realized by specific *mappings of Identified–Identifier onto Token–Value*. After Token and Value have been assigned to the two terms of the identification in either of the two possible directions discussed above, Identified (Id) and Identifier (Ir) can, in their turn, be distributed in either direction over the Token-Value configurations. This gives the grammatical paradigm represented in Figure 9.1.[3]

The "coding" configuration Token–Value and the "identifying" configuration Identifier–Identified are two independently variable experiential structures (Halliday 1967b:228; 1968:191). Hence their combination leads to eight distinct structure types, with differential mappings of "coding" and "identifying" roles assigned to each term of the identification (Halliday 1967b:228; 1968:191).

What is the semantic import of the grammatical vectors of this

---

[3]I should point out that I have changed the *topology* of the paradigm in comparison with "Notes." More specifically, the order of the horizontal decoding-encoding bars (1 to 4) corresponds, in the numerical terms of Figure 9.1, to the order 1-4-3–2 in "Notes." This is because the "Notes" paradigm foregrounds the "identifying" dimension (which is John? which is the leader?), whereas I am foregrounding here the "representing" or "coding" dimension, stressing the *inversion* of the "represent" relation in subparadigm II. However, where the grammatical analysis of the individual clause types is concerned, there is no difference between the "Notes" paradigm and that used here.

Subparadigm I: John "represents" the leader

1. decoding: which is John?

1a.	John is the **lead-**	1b.	The **leader**	John.
	Tk/Id **er.**		is	Tk/Id
	Vl/Ir		Vl/Ir	

2. encoding: which is the leader?

| 2a. | **John** is the leader. | 2b. | The leader is | **John.** |
| | Tk/Ir   Vl/Id | | Vl/Id | Tk/Ir |

Subparadigm II: The leader "represents" John

3. decoding: which is the leader?

| 3a. | The leader is | **John.** | 3b. | **John** is the leader. |
| | Tk/Id | Vl/Ir | | Vl/Ir   Tk/Id |

4. encoding: which is John?

| 4a. | The **leader** is | John. | 4b. | John is the **leader.** |
| | Tk/Ir | Vl/Id | | Vl/Id   Tk/Ir |

Figure 9.1. The paradigm of coding-identifying grammar.

paradigm? As shown above, Token–Value assignment fixes the "symbolic directionality": "upward" from the less to the more abstract symbolic stratum as in John (Tk) is the leader (Vl); "downward" from the more to the less abstract symbolic stratum as in The leader (Tk) is John (Vl).

On each symbolic directionality, two different "identifying" perspectives can be construed. On the one hand, one may take the Token side of the symbolic correlation for granted and use a *Value*/Identifier to bring about identification. In this case, we take the *decoding* perspective: into what Value can the Token be decoded? For instance, the addressee knows John but does not know his function: (which is John?)—John (Tk/Id) is the **leader** (Vl/Ir). John (construed as Tk) is identified in terms of the social role the leader (construed as Vl), which he plays. On the other hand, we may take the Value side of the symbolic correlation as known and look for the *Token*/Identifier which will bring about identification. This is the *encoding* perspective: By what Token is the Value realized? For instance, the addressee knows that there is a leader but not who it is: (which is the leader?)—**John** (Tk/Ir) is the leader (Vl/Id). Here, the role of the leader (construed as Vl) is correlated with the role filler John (construed as Tk). So, the general grammatical principle is that encoding identifying clauses have Token/Identifiers, whereas decoding identifying clauses have Value/Identifiers (Halliday 1967b:229).

What about the semantic import of the decoding–encoding contrast? If the paradigm represented in Figure 9.1 is correct, then the systemic literature has provided only *half* an answer to that question. Indeed, all the semantic glosses given so far of decoding-encoding have tended to restrict themselves to the paradigm with "upward" symbolic directionality (subparadigm I of Figure 9.1). Consider, for instance, Halliday's well-known glosses (1988:28; 1994:138), according to which the decoding construal answers the question "what does the Identified mean?" and the encoding "how can the Identified be recognized?" These two meanings can be illustrated with the traditional (6) and Halliday's functional (7) definition of Subject respectively:

encoding: *Subject (Vl/Id) is that noun or pronoun that is in person and number concord with the verb (Tk/Ir) (Halliday 1994:73)* (i.e. "how can the category Subject be recognized?")

(6)

decoding: *Subject [. . .] (Tk/Id) specifies the entity in respect of which the assertion is claimed to have validity (Vl/Ir) (Halliday 1994:76)* (i.e. "what does the category Subject mean?")

(7)

Both these glosses clearly focus on the "upward" symbolic directionality: They take the grammar, or the less abstract semiotic interface, as Token and the semantics, or the more abstract semiotic interface, as Value. What the decoding–encoding contrast means when applied to the "downward" symbolic perspective has not been systematically investigated so far.

With all these unresolved questions in mind, I set about analyzing all the coding–identifying clauses in the corpus of linguistic texts described above (section 1). The two main goals guiding the investigation were:

1. to find more semantic and lexicogrammatical arguments with regard to the necessity of positing *two* subparadigms, one with "upward" and one with "downward" directionality, for the grammar of coding–identifying clauses (section 2.2);

2. to clarify the semantic value of the decoding-encoding contrast in the subparadigm with "downward" symbolic directionality (section 2.3).

2.2. The "Expression" Versus the "Motivation" Subparadigm

If we are to investigate the argumentation for positing an eight-cell paradigm for coding–identifying clauses, we should begin by recapitulating Halliday's original grammatical argumentation in "Notes." His main argument was that coding–identifying clauses with <u>be</u> in written discourse (i.e. without indication of tonic prominence) can display four-way ambiguity (1967a:68; 1967b:228), which can only be accounted for by the eight-cell paradigm. Thus, Halliday (1967b:228) pointed out, a clause like <u>John is the leader</u> allows for four different readings:

1. decoding of John: <u>John</u> (Tk/Id) <u>is the leader</u> (Vl/Ir) (decoding:active)
2. encoding of the leader: <u>John</u> (Tk/Ir) <u>is the leader</u> (Vl/Id) (encoding:active)
3. decoding of the leader: <u>John</u> (Vl/Ir) <u>is the leader</u> (Tk/Id) (decoding:passive)
4. encoding of John: <u>John</u> (Vl/Id) <u>is the leader</u> (TK/Ir) (encoding:passive)

Following on from this position, I subsequently argued (Davidse in press) that, if we consider examples marked for tonic prominence, we are left with a potential *two*-way ambiguity for coding–identifying construals with <u>be</u>. I illustrated this ambiguity with the example (8) **Smiley** is Alec Guinness, which can, according to the eight-cell paradigm (Figure 9.1), instantiate either structure type 1b (decoding:passive) of subparadigm I or 4a (encoding:active) of subparadigm II. In subparadigm I, we are construing the symbolic directionality of Alec Guinness "representing" Smiley, or of the actor playing the role. For instance, in a discussion of the distribution of roles, a construal is imaginable such as (8a) **Smiley** (Vl/Ir) <u>is Alec Guinness</u> (Tk/Id) (**Smiley** should be played by Alec Guinness, i.e. decoding:passive). In subparadigm II, in contrast, we are construing the symbolic directionality from fictional character to real-life actor—a directionality that is perfectly conceivable in a case like this where the role has become strongly identified with the actor. Thus, construals can be contextualized such as (8b) **Smiley** (Tk/Ir) <u>was Alec Guinness at his best</u> (Vl/Id) (**Smiley** featured Alec Guinness at his best, i.e. encoding:active). This ambiguity is missed, I pointed out, by Halliday's four-cell paradigm in *Introduction to Functional Grammar* (1985:126–127; 1994:136–137), according to which

Smiley is Alec Guinness can only be analyzed as passive: **Smiley** (Vl/Ir) is/is represented by/is played by Alec Guinness (Tk/Id). However, the passive analysis is clearly impossible for **Smiley** (Tk/Ir) is/represents/features Alec Guinness at his best.

The "Notes" position on the potential ambiguity of coding–identifying clauses with be thus boils down to this: the eight-cell paradigm contains four sets of two be-structures whose instantiations seem, in terms of word order and tonic prominence, like identical syntagms (the structure types are referred to with the numbers of Figure 9.1): 1a and 4b, 1b and 4a—the structures illustrated by examples (8a) and (8b)—2a and 3b, 2b and 3a. However, as is so often the case in language, these "apparently" identical syntagms turn out to be structurally ambiguous when analyzed in terms of their agnates (Gleason 1965), or systematically related paradigmatic variants, such as the corresponding wh-interrogatives, and agnates with represent or other verbs displaying voice. The sets of structures involved in potential ambiguity all comprise one structure from subparadigm I and one from subparadigm II. Hence, the ambiguity at stake is one of Token–Value assignment, as in example (8) Smiley is Alec Guinness: Is Alec Guinness Token or Value and is Smiley Value or Token?

What is needed now, to shed more light on the possibility of redistributing Token and Value to the two terms of an identification, is more actual data. Systematic examples with verbs other than be are needed, because for these, there is no possible ambiguity of Token–Value assignment. What is more, we need data whose semantic "purport"[4] with regard to symbolic strata and symbolic directionality can be interpreted reasonably well. We should, indeed, be able to give a reasonably confident answer to the question whether the Token in a specific construal is situated at a less or more abstract symbolic stratum vis-à-vis the Value. The sample from Halliday's and Wierzbicka's linguistic discourses described above should provide such data.

As could be expected of "semantic grammarians" or "semanticians of grammar," both Halliday and Wierzbicka look at the relation between *grammar* and *semantics*, construing it frequently in terms of coding–identifying clauses. In this specific paper of Halliday's, this relation is construed exclusively with the symbolic directionality going from grammar to semantics. As the semantic inter-

---

[4]"Purport" is used here in the Hjelmslevian (1969:50) sense of the hypothetical "semantic substance" translatable between languages, the "thought itself," as it were, considered apart from language-specific codings.

pretation of forms is not the main concern of this article, it contains only 11 construals relating grammar to semantics, for instance:

that this is possible is because the lexicogrammatical fea-
tures that (Tk/Ir) carry these features (Vl/Id) are quantita-
tively foregrounded ((Halliday 1991:48) (9)

the semantic features involved in this variation (Vl/Id)
are realized, non arbitrarily, through grammatical systems
to which probabilities can be assigned (Tk/Ir) (Halliday
1991:48) (10)

The lexical verbs used in these construals are: construe, constitute, carry, realize and be.

In contrast, in the present sample of Wierzbicka's descriptive work, the symbolic relation between grammar and semantics is construed *both* in terms of the "upward" relation going from grammar to semantics (56 instances) and in terms of the "downward" relation going from semantics to grammar (15 instances). Clear examples of the "upward," or form-to-meaning, directionality are:

Bolinger takes a bolder stand and formulates his theoretical
credo without any such hedges "a difference in syntactic form
(Tk/Id) always spells a difference in meaning (Vl/Ir)"
(1988:127) (Wierzbicka 1988:25) (11a)

decide ON (Tk/Id) doesn't mean the same (Vl/Ir) as decide TO
(Wierzbicka 1988:25) (11b)

speech act verbs which (Tk/Id) express intention (Vl/Ir)
(Wierzbicka 1988:37) (12)

the intention ("X thought this: I want this: I will do this")
(Vl/Id) is conveyed by the TO complement (Tk/Ir), not by the
ING. (Wierzbicka 1988:31) (13)

The same semantic elements (Vl/Id) are of course implied by
the "allative" TO (Tk/Ir). (Wierzbicka 1988:28) (14)

In the piece of discourse analyzed, the following set of lexical verbs is used: mean, spell, denote, refer to, fit, describe, imply, suggest, indicate, presuppose, appeal to, convey, express, present, offer, constitute, be. If this list is combined with that gleaned from Halliday's paper, there begins to emerge a specific paragraph from a grammatically motivated lexical thesaurus (the lexical verbs usable in coding–identifying construals with "upward" symbolic directionality).

Examples in Wierzbicka's discourse of construals with "downward" symbolic directionality include:

> *they (Tk/Id) [general semantic rules] explain some of the most recalcitrant cases of apparent arbitrariness (Vl/Ir) (Wierzbicka 1988:26)* (15)

> *The semantic structure postulated above (Tk/Id) explains immediately why verbs of intention take TO complements (Vl/Ir) (Wierzbicka 1988:31)* (16)

The lexical verbs used here by Wierzbicka are: explain, account for, affect, and be. One verb that should also be mentioned in relation to this list is motivate. In this specific sample it does not occur in a congruent two-participant structure, but:

> *the choice of complements is semantically motivated (Wierzbicka 1988:25)* (17a)

can certainly be related to the agnate construal

> *the choice of complements (Vl/Id) is motivated by semantics (Tk/Ir)* (17b)

"Motivation" is a central term here, because linguists will immediately recognize that examples (9)–(14) versus (15)–(17) illustrate the contrast between two different methodological perspectives, which are, in essence, inverse construals of the symbolic relation between grammar and semantics:

1. how do forms express meanings?
2. how does meaning motivate form?

Question 1 instantiates the "upward" symbolic directionality from less to more abstract symbolic stratum and question 2 the "downward" symbolic directionality from more to less abstract symbolic stratum. To denote these two symbolic directionalities of the coding–identifying paradigm in general, I propose to use, from now on, the labels of "expression" versus "motivation" construals, whose mnemonic force will be immediately clear to linguists.

Linguists exploring the semiotic interface between grammar and semantics continually formulate their specific descriptive hypotheses in terms of either "expression" or "motivation" construals, mostly using a mix of both, even though the mixture may vary and one type may be more predominant. Wierzbicka's programmatic goal, for instance, is to reveal the "semantic foundations" (Wierzbicka 1988:23), or the semantic motivation, of syntax. That is, she takes the semantics as Token and syntax as Value. In accordance with this program, she tends to use "motivation" construals at the beginnings and conclusions of sections. However, the main thrust of her actual descriptive reasoning is predominantly in terms of "expression" construals: "What meanings are expressed by certain forms?" (Of the 71 coding–identifying construals pertaining to the semantics of grammar in the sample, 56 instances are "expression" construals, of which 51 are decoding).

Halliday (1994:xx), on the other hand, situates his descriptive work mainly as "functional grammar," or "an interpretation of linguistic forms," rather than as "functional semantics," because, he (1985:xxxv) says, "The face of the grammar that is turned to the semantics is hardly illuminated at all." In "Towards probabilistic interpretations" he uses exclusively "expression" construals for whatever descriptive points have to be dealt with. Taking the grammar as Token and the semantics as Value is doubtless the main heuristic perspective in his descriptive work. However, in accordance with specific linguistic goals, such as the description of semantic systems in the context of code or register variation, or in the context of text generation, he also adopts the "motivation" perspective, as evidenced by the following reflection from his grammatics:

> When we describe semantic systems, we are saying what (Tk/Ir) it is that "preselects" the grammatical categories (Vl/Id): what choices in meaning (Tk/Id) call on what features in the grammar (Vl/Ir) for their realization. (Halliday 1987:46)   (18)

In "Towards probabilistic interpretations," Halliday also focuses on the relation between social context and grammar, defined here not in the narrow sense of "form," but in the broader sense of "form and meaning." Between these two strata he also construes a symbolic relation, which he interprets in coding–identifying clauses with both "upward" and "downward" directionality. The following examples illustrate the "upward" relation, in which aspects of the linguistic system are viewed as the expression of social factors.

If the linguistic system was not inherently of a probabilistic kind, it (Tk/Id) could not display these sociolinguistic effects (Vl/Ir) (Halliday 1991:46)   (19)

It [register variation] is variation in the tendency to select certain meanings rather than others (Tk/Id) realizing variation in the situation type (Vl/Ir) (Halliday 1991:57)   (20)

"Downward" directionality, in which the social order is depicted as "conditioning" linguistic variation, is construed in the following examples:

So while the overall probability of past/present was fairly even (57%/43%) the conditioning effect of social class (Tk/Id) skewed this (Vl/Ir) in opposite directions (Halliday 1991:46)
                                                                                                (21)

the options (Vl/Id) differentially favored by one or other social group (Tk/Ir) (Halliday 1991:46)   (22)

The sets of lexical verbs used here for the "upward"–"downward" contrast clearly continue and extend the semantic motifs of those used for the relation between grammar and semantics. For this reason, we can keep "expression" and "motivation" as mnemonic cover terms for the two symbolic directionalities:

expression: display, reveal, represent, realize, express, be
motivation: account for, favor, skew, condition, distribute, shape, affect, be.

Now, as pointed out by Halliday (1992:20), linguists also tend to code certain redundancy relations that are intra-stratal *as if* they were inter-stratal. The interpreting statements used to capture the regularities on one semiotic stratum, split it up, as it were, into another Token–Value system. In Halliday's article, a splitting up of the grammatical stratum is found, whereas in Wierzbicka's article, it is the semantic stratum that tends to be coded as a symbolic system in its own right. Let us see, then, whether such generalizations about either the grammatical stratum or the semantic stratum in their own right are expressed by the same lexicogrammar as that used to construe the inter-stratal relations between grammar and semantics, and between the linguistic system and the social context.

In Halliday's discussion (1991:51) of Nesbitt & Plum's quantitative research into tactic and logico-semantic relations in the clause
complex, we find, for instance, an explanatory definition of "coordination," which states the meaning of the grammatical category
"coordination" in terms of two other grammatical categories:

> "coordination," which (Tk/Id) is a complex of hypotaxis and
> extending (Vl/Ir) (Halliday 1991:51)   (22)

This is an "expression" identifying clause. In the same discussion,
there also are numerous "motivation" construals, which are statements of, as Halliday (1991:48) puts it, "conditioning *within the
grammar itself*," as in:

> elaborating (Tk/Id) favours parataxis (Vl/Ir) (Halliday 1991:
> 52)   (23)

> parataxis (Tk/Id) favours extending (Vl/Ir) (Halliday 1991:
> 52)   (24)

If there is "partial association" (Halliday 1991:53) between systems,
such as between the tactic and logico-semantic relations in the
clause complex, then each term of one system can be studied in
terms of its "effect on," that is, "as conditioning environment for"
(Halliday 1991:52) a term from the other system. Or, to sum up in
the "expression" mode:

> either system (Tk/Id) can take either role (Vl/Ir) (Halliday
> 1991:52) [i.e. that of either "conditioned" or "conditioning"]
>   (25)

Clearly, Halliday is exploiting here the complementarity between the
"expression" and the "motivation" perspectives to arrive at a diver-
sified interpretation of purely grammatical phenomena, such as the
intersecting grammatical systems referred to in examples (22)–(25).
The verbs used in these construals are either the same or clearly
related to the lexical selections noted earlier for "expression" and
"motivation" construals:

expression: represent, model, reflect, show up, take (a role)
motivation: (dis)favor, condition, determine, govern, affect.

For Wierzbicka (1988:25), the ultimate goal of her descriptive
work is to set up rigorous and intersubjectively testable hypothe-

ses. Not surprisingly, she evaluates semantic hypotheses in terms of both expression (26) and motivation (27) construals:

The following semantic formulae (Tk/Ir) portray this [semantic] relationship (Vl/Id) (Wierzbicka (1988:43)   (26)

the analysis offered by the Kiparskys (Tk/Id) fails to account for the differences in meaning between the infinitival and the gerundive versions (Vl/Ir) (Wierzbicka (1988:42)   (27)

We can conclude that, in the texts analyzed, the lexicosemantics of "upward" and "downward" symbolic directionality are remarkably consistent for all the relations construed between semiotic interfaces. For the "upward" directionality, we find the common semantic component of the more concrete stratum "manifesting" the more abstract one symbolically. Particularly with regard to the grammar-semantics interface, a number of linguists tend to use verbs such as construct and construe, which emphasize the active part of the grammar in the symbolization process more. However, as a cover term for *all* the relations from less to more abstract semiotic stratum, including, for instance, that from phonology to lexicogrammar, "expression" remains arguably the more generally applicable term. In the "downward" directionality, the more abstract semiotic stratum is typically construed as making clear the reasons, or determining factors, of specific forms of behavior on the more concrete stratum. This is meant to be captured by the term "motivation." So, as expected, this text analysis has uncovered specific semantic instantiations (viz. "expression" versus "motivation") of the two possible symbolic directionalities between semiotic interfaces.

It will be interesting, now, to return with the expression–motivation contrast as a starting hypothesis, to the question of grammatical ambiguity, as displayed by the following example with lexical verb be, whose "purport" with regard to symbolic strata is not, in contrast with the linguistics examples, immediately clear.

Here the organizing concept is not the object that is being investigated—the "field" of study—but the kinds of questions that are being asked. (Halliday 1991:39)   (28)

This sentence, which deals with the structure of scientific knowledge, is ambiguous in the following way. One possible reading is the one in which the semantic content or the significance of "the organizing concept" is described. This is the reading construed by the decoding:active from the "expression" subparadigm (28a).

the organizing concept (Tk/Id) is (i.e. presupposes, refers to) not the object that is being investigated—the "field" of study— but the kinds of questions that are being asked (Vl/Ir)
(28a)

Another possible reading interprets "the object investigated" and "the questions asked" as determining factors of the organizing concept. This reading corresponds to the encoding passive from the "motivation" paradigm (28b).

the organizing concept (Vl/Id) is not (determined by) the object that is being investigated—the "field" of study—but the kinds of questions that are being asked (Tk/Ir)
(28b)

This specific structural ambiguity is an instance of one of the four types of ambiguity predicted by the eight-cell paradigm of coding-identifying grammar (see above, section 2.1 and Figure 9.1), namely, that between structure types 1a and 4b. Note that this ambiguity hinges on the question whether the object [. . .] investigated and the questions [. . .] asked are construed as Value (in an "expression" construal) or as Token (in a "motivation" construal).

Here we are up against the profound semantic motivation of the intrinsic possibility of re-assignment of Token and Value to the two terms of the identification. Quite simply, the semantic model of "symbolic relationship" being grammaticalized by the coding–identifying grammatical pardigm *is* intrinsically invertible. As stressed by Halliday (1991:59; 1992:24), the concept of "symbolic relation," or "realization," should not be confused with that of "causation" in this respect. Realization is a symmetrical relation, whose direction can be reversed (Halliday 1992:24). Causation, in contrast, is strictly a uni-directional, non-invertible relation. Whether we say the organizing concept is/refers to the questions being asked or the questions being asked are/determine the organizing concept, we are construing different experiential perspectives on the *same* semiotic inter-relation. This is what enables the ambiguity of The organizing concept is the **questions referred to**. But when we say The vicar hit the burglar and The burglar hit the vicar, we are not representing the same causal interaction, we are representing two different causal processes. This is why The vicar hit **the burglar** is not ambiguous. So, ultimately it is the intrinsic invertibility of the concept of "symbolic correlation" that motivates the redistribution of Token and Value in the coding–identifying grammatical paradigm.

An important consequence of all this is that the grammar can "mean" a far more abstract and illuminating grammatics model (namely, symbolization as a symmetric relation) than most everyday lexical terms can name. As shown in this section, apart from the very general verb be, the "expression" and "motivation" construals tend to take distinct and contrastive sets of lexical verbs, so one cannot easily lexicalize the full abstract concept of "symbolic correlation" *in* its invertibility, except perhaps as a symbolic mode of "being." The meanings of words from everyday use are typically somewhere in the middle between general and specific—or "basic-level" (Lakoff 1987:15). The semantic models encoded by grammar, in contrast, involve highly general and abstract categories and this is, presumably, why linguists find it so hard to get a grasp of grammatical meaning and describe it accurately.

Interestingly, semiotic thinkers also do battle with the limitations of everyday lexical usage when they reflect on the invertibility of the sign relation. Thus, Peirce (1982:332) stretches the everyday use of the verb represent in a remarkable passage on a typical example of representation (viz. portrait painting). He observes that, evidently, "the portrait represents the sitter" but then goes on to assert that "the sitter also represents the portrait." In other words, he uses represent to name both the symbolic direction from less abstract to more abstract order and that from more abstract to less abstract order. In a similar vein, Hjelmslev (1969:58) explicitly discusses how the meaning of the word sign should be generalized way beyond its common usage to name the two inverted directions that are involved in a semiotically consistent concept of it: "The sign is then—paradoxical as it may seem—a sign for a content–substance and a sign for an expression–substance" (Hjelmslev 1969:58). Reflecting about "realization," Halliday (1991:59) writes:

> In order to avoid a crude cause-and-effect interpretation, we have tried to remove all directionality from the system, using constructivist metaphors that are made to face both ways: the context constructs the grammar, and the grammar constructs the context.
>
> (Halliday 1991:59)

However, he (1991:59) concludes, extending construct to both symbolic directionalities leads to the "constructivist trap, which seems to force an unreal choice between 'language expresses reality' and 'language creates reality'."

Thus, Halliday has more recently been using Lemke's term "metaredundancy" (in preference to Hjelmslev's "realization") to refer to "the purely symbolic relation between two semiotic interfaces" (Halliday 1992:25) such that if an element **a** from interface **A** "redounds with" **p** from interface **P, p** also "redounds with" **a** (Halliday 1992:24). It takes a verb rather far removed from everyday use and with a very general meaning such as <u>redound with</u> to express the symmetry of the "realization" relation satisfactorily. Moreover, Halliday (1992: 24–25) explicitly points out that the concept of metaredundancy does not refer to separate "dyadic" relationships. The semiotic space is at least three-dimensional (phonology—lexicogrammar—semantics) and potentially n-dimensional, extending also into, for instance, the social order as semiotic. "Metaredundancy" is thus meant to capture the symbolic mode of being at its most general level, with its intrinsic reversibility of symbolic direction and applying to an n-dimensional semiotic space. As shown in this section, this is exactly the "content-substance" construed by coding-identifying grammar. Thus, the coding-identifying system can also be thought of as the grammaticalization of meta-redundancy.

2.3. The Decoding–Encoding Contrast

2.3.1. Realization and quantitative instantiation of decoding and encoding construals

As shown in section 2.1, the contrast between decoding and encoding construals is realized by how Identified and Identifier are mapped onto Token and Value. Decoding construals have a Value/Identifier, encoding construals have a Token/Identifier. Just as with the contrast between expression and motivation construals, it is instructive to begin by looking at a text example of ambiguity. Consider:

> From the point of view of European structuralism, a human system was a nexus of paradigmatic and syntagmatic relations that could be construed from the way they were manifested in patterns of behaviour. Saussure's langue/parole was one of the first formulations of this view. (Halliday 1991:40)
>
> (29)

The identifying clause in (29) is ambiguous between the following two readings:

decoding: *Saussure's langue/parole (Tk/Id) was* **one of the first formulations of this view** *(Vl/Ir).*   (29a)

encoding: **Saussure's langue/parole** *(Tk/Ir) was one of the first formulations of this view (Vl/Id).*   (29b)

To appreciate the ambiguity involved in (29a) and (29b), we should first be clear about the experiential semantics of Identified and Identifier. "Identified" has the following twofold meaning. On the one hand, it is the element whose value is represented as fixed, like a "constant" in an algebraic equation. By the same token, it is the element that needs further "identification" by being correlated with a second element that stands in a symbolic[5] relation to it. The Identifier is defined in terms of the same two semantic vectors: It is the element for whose value there are, potentially, several candidates under consideration, like the "variable" in an algebraic equation. Specification of its value brings about identification. As stressed by Halliday (1967b:231–233), the only test with 100% validity for structurally identifying the Identifier is that of the wh-interrogative corresponding to the coding–identifying construal. However, this criterial agnate also indicates the semantic contribution of the Identifier: The Identifier is the side of the symbolic correlation we are looking for. For instance, in (29a), Saussure's langue/parole is taken as "constant" and its significance is being looked for: What (Ir) was Saussure's langue/parole? The decoding construal (29a) identifies the historical significance of Saussure's conceptual pair. In (29b), in contrast, one of the first formulations of this view is the side of the correlation taken for granted and the search is for the more concrete entity corresponding to this value: What (Ir) was one of the first formulations of this view (Id)?

The semantic motivation of the "identifying" configuration is, ultimately, the *correlativeness*, or the relation of potential *co-definition*, between the two terms of the identification. As in (29), one of the first formulations of this view can define Saussure's langue/parole and, vice versa, Saussure's langue/parole can define one of the first formulations of this view. The semantic criterion of "co-definition" is rather useful when it comes to drawing a line between identifying and verbal or material clauses. Consider the following examples:

---

[5]In possessive:identifying clauses, which are not being considered here, the Identifier stands in a *possessive* correlation with the Identified (Davidse in press).

verbal: *Dixon, despite his own successes in explaining many cases of apparent arbitrariness, (Wierzbicka 1988:25)*

(30)

coding–identifying: *Furthermore, the semantic difference between the two complement types seems to explain why some verbs can only take ING whereas some others can only take TO (Wierzbicka 1988:24)*

(31)

material: *when I was constructing my original system networks for English in the early sixties (Halliday 1991:43)*

(32)

coding–identifying: *the grammar constructs the context (Halliday 1991:59)*

(33)

Apart from the fact that the participants in relational clauses are mostly inanimate, whereas the Sayer, for instance, is typically conscious, the Actor in material and the Sayer in verbal clauses do not stand in a relation of symbolic correlation and mutual co-definition to the Goal or Range. This is, of course, why there is no "identifying" dimension to material and verbal clauses.

Identified–Identifier are experiential roles but they have associated with them default correlations with textual factors. More specifically, the Identifier carries, in the unmarked case, the information focus and thus conveys the most salient part of the New information (Halliday 1994:124). With regard to (29), for instance, the Identifier carries the information focus in both readings: in (29a) the information focus comes in its unmarked place at the end of the information unit, whereas in (29b) it is in marked clause initial position.

The issue of the textual defaults of Identified–Identifier is naturally tied up with the question of the relative quantitative instantiation of the eight structure types distinguished by the paradigm of coding–identifying grammar. To get a first impression of the sorts of frequencies involved, I counted the occurrence of these structure types in Halliday's and Wierzbicka's texts. The result of these counts is given in Table 9.1.

Thus, for both the expression and motivation subparadigms, the most frequent structure types are those with typically *unmarked information focus* (i.e. with focus on postverbal Identifier). The structure types with unmarked information distribution are the decoding:active and the encoding:passive.

The less frequent structure types are those where we expect *marked initial information focus;* that is to say, when their clause

TABLE 9.1
Quantitative Instantiation of the Types
of Coding–Identifying Structures in the Data Base.

		Halliday	Wierzbicka	Total
expr:	1a dec:act	38	57	95
	1b dec:pas	0	0	0
	2a enc:act	6	9	15
	2b enc:pas	27	10	37
motiv:	3a dec:act	28	14	42
	3b dec:pas	0	0	0
	4a enc:act	3	2	5
	4b enc:pas	11	0	11
total		113	92	205[6]

initial Identifiers are lexically full items they will carry the information focus, as in:

Cladistics *(Tk/Ir) is one such theme (Vl/Id). (Halliday 1991: 39)*   (34)

The structure types concerned here are the decoding:passive and the encoding:active.

The decoding:passive is non-occurrent in this specific data-base. Its extreme infrequency is predicted by a combination of markedness factors, namely, its marked information focus as well as its voice status as marked Range-passive (Halliday 1994:167).

The encoding:active is relatively more frequent. Roughly, it occurs half as frequently as the encoding:passive, which has typically unmarked information focus. Closer study of the encoding:active construals in the corpus strongly suggests that marked information focus is one of the most important factors limiting their use. Indeed, of all the attested examples, only two or three actually have the initial information focus, namely, examples (26), (29b) and (34) quoted above.

Configurations of factors that can lead to non-tonic Identifiers in encoding:actives include the following:

---

[6]For the relatively rare cases of decoding-encoding ambiguity only one reading was counted for simplicity"s sake.

1. The Identifier is a non-contrastive anaphoric pronoun, for instance:

   This being so, we seem to have reached a stage when anybody wishing to seriously advance the view that syntax has semantic foundations simply must meet the challenge of English complementation. This (Tk/Ir) is precisely the goal of the present chapter (Vl/Id). (Wierzbicka 1988:23) (35)

   To be or not to be—that (Tk/Ir) is the question (Vl/Id) (Wierzbicka 1988:27) (36)

   In these examples, the Identifiers are clearly <u>this</u> (which refers to the last clause of the preceding sentence) and <u>that</u> (referring to the preceding non-finite clause). They are the constituents whose value is under question and which bring about identification, as evidenced by the corresponding wh-interrogatives:

   'What is the goal of this chapter? (35)

   'What is the question? (36)

   However, because non-contrastive, anaphoric pronouns can never be intonationally focal (Halliday 1967b:231–233), they do not carry the information focus.

2. The Identifier is the wh-element in an interrogative, for example:

   What (Tk/Ir) WAS Hamlet's question (Vl/Id)? (Wierzbicka 1988:27) (37)

   Line (37) is, of course, agnate to (36). It is, moreover, the agnate type systematically used to identify the Identifier in the corresponding sentence. Naturally, it is the wh-element itself that is the Identifier in such interrrogatives. Typically, it will be non-focal, as it is in (37), even though in marked cases it could receive the tonic: WHAT was Hamlet's question?

3. The Identifier is a relative pronoun, for instance:

   that this is possible is because the lexicogrammatical features that (Tk/Ir) carry these semantic patterns (Vl/Id) are quantitatively foregrounded (Halliday 1991:48) (38)

   The identifying clause in (38) is an encoding active, which identifies the formal means by which the <u>semantic pat-</u>

terns mentioned earlier in the discourse are encoded. The constituent <u>that</u> is thus the Identifier, but as a relative pronoun, it is, like an anaphoric pronoun, non-focal.

Furthermore, predicated theme structures (Halliday 1994:58–61), or it-clefts, which are also encoding actives, do have the tonic accent on the Identifier, but avoid putting the Identifier in clause initial position. For instance:

> *it is the ING clause, not the TO clause (Tk/Ir), which implies possibility (Vl/Id) (Wierzbicka 1988:31)* (39)

The motivation of the internal predication is, precisely, to create a local textual structure with unmarked tonic accent (Halliday 1994:59), as in it is **the ING clause, not the TO clause**. By contrast, the non-cleft agnate of (39) would have marked initial focus: **The ING clause, not the TO clause,** (Tk/Ir) implies possibility (Vl/Id).

We can conclude that, at least in this data base, encoding:actives are mostly used, when, by some grammatical resource, marked initial information focus can be avoided.

2.3.2. The semantics of "decoding"–"encoding" in the "expression" and "motivation" subparadigms

In this last section, some reflections are in order about the distinct meanings of the decoding–encoding contrast in the "expression" and "motivation" subparadigms. Let us now home in on the issue at the *grammar–semantics* interface. The vectors of "expression"–"motivation" and "decoding–encoding" allow us to identify four distinct semiotic perspectives, or four distinct trajectories along the symbolic relationship between grammar and semantics. Voice reversal (i.e. the alternation between the a and b structure types of the paradigm in Figure 9.1) does not construe different kinds of inter-stratal relation. As we saw in section 2.3.1, the choice of either the active or passive variant is to a large extent determined by textual factors, most importantly, that of placing the tonic in its unmarked position at the end of the information unit.

The distinct meanings of the four possible inter-stratal trajectories between grammar and semantics can then be glossed as follows:

expression:decoding: this grammatical category (Tk/Id) fulfills the following semantic function (Vl/Ir) *expression:encoding:* this semantic function (Vl/Id) is encoded by the following formal characteristics (Tk/Ir)

motivation:decoding: this semantic hypothesis (Tk/Id) explains the following grammatical facts (Vl/Ir)

motivation:encoding: this grammatical phenomenon (Vl/Id) is motivated by the following semantic factor (Tk/Ir)

(In each case, I have glossed the construal types in their textually unmarked voice variant, that is, the decoding ones in the active and the encoding ones in the passive.) Linguists will, I suspect, readily recognize all four of these "tracks" leading into the purely symbolic space between grammar and semantics. All of these methodological perspectives tend to be taken by linguists, at one stage or other, in the formulation of their descriptive hypotheses.

However, because the use of coding–identifying construals is not restricted to linguistic description, we should also look for semantic glosses with more general applicability. Here, of course, we need further studies of coding–identifying lexicogrammar in the registers of other disciplines. However, even at this stage, an exploratory start can be made to give more general glosses for each of the four symbolic interpretative modes.

Regarding the expression:decoding mode, I find it helpful to think of it as the *diagnostic* mode. Whether used in linguistics, medicine, sociology, or economy[7], this is the interpretative mode that diagnoses the (more abstract) significance of more concrete phenomena.

Frequency in text (Tk/Id) is the instantiation of probability in the system (Vl/Ir). (Halliday 1991:42) (40)

The sequence of the simple bead-like molecules along a stretch of DNA (Tk/Id) constitute a "message" that dictates the production by the cell of a protein (Vl/Ir). (WSJ) (41)

The decline in education (Tk/Id) reflects a society lacking a commitment to future generations (Vl/Ir). (WSJ) (42)

---

[7]The non-linguistic examples are taken from the Wall Street Journal Corpus, compiled and edited by the Association of Computational Linguistics and made available by the Berkeley Artificial Intelligence Research Group.

A reading below 50% (Tk/Id) generally indicates a slowing in
the industrial sector of the economy (Vl/Ir). (WSJ)   (43)

Its complementary mode, the expression:encoding, appears to me
to have, as one of its core meanings, *symptomatic* interpretation.
Here, it is indicated by which more concrete symptoms a more abstract "entity" is externalized or embodied. Once again, the symptomatic interpretative mode extends over various disciplines.

the end of the New element (Vl/Id) is marked by tonic promi-
nence (Tk/Ir) (Halliday 1994:296)   (44)

Cystic fibrosis (Vl/Id) is marked by faulty digestion, difficulty
breathing and excessive loss of salt through the sweat glands
(Tk/Ir) (WSJ)   (45)

Surprisingly, it [this attitude] (Vl/Id) is manifested by female
colleagues nearly as often as by males (Tk/Ir) (WSJ)   (46)

The unrecognized culprit (Vl/Id) is the budget surplus (Tk/Ir)
(WSJ)   (47)

Note that in both these "expression" modes, the Tokens are more
concrete and the Values more abstract.

In the two "motivation" modes, in contrast, the Tokens are located
at the more abstract stratum of symbolic interpretation and the
Values at the more concrete one. As seen in section 2.2, the general
meaning of the "motivation" perspective is that of the more abstract
stratum revealing the reasons, or the determining factors, of certain forms of behavior on the less abstract stratum. The motiva-
tion:decoding mode, then, identifies the concrete results of, or the
reactions to, these determining factors. Therefore, we could refer to
it as the *reactive* mode. With cross-disciplinary examples:

Such systems (Tk/Id) could generate indefinitely long strings
(Vl/Ir) (Halliday 1991:43)   (48)

the semantic choices made by the mother (Tk/Id) affect the
child's ways of reasoning and of learning (Vl/Ir) (Halliday
1991:48)   (49)

The restructuring (Tk/Id) will involve the transfer and lay-off
of employees in U.S. operations (Vl/Ir). (WSJ)   (50)

The motivation:encoding mode, on the other hand, answers the question: What are the more abstract determining factors, or the catalytic factors, of specific more concrete phenomena? Hence, we can think of it as the *catalytic* mode, for example:

how the choice of a/b (Vl/Id) is affected by the choice made in the same system in the preceding clause (Tk/Ir) (Halliday 1991:57)   (51)

Outcomes (Vl/Id) often are determined by the policy preferences of judges and ideological litigants rather than by those of Congress and the President (Tk/Ir) (WSJ)   (52)

Rates (Vl/Id) are determined by the difference between the purchase price and face value (Tk/Ir) (WSJ)   (53)

3. CONCLUSION

In this article, I have, on the basis of a corpus study of linguistic texts, proposed semantic clarifications for the grammatical vectors of coding-identifying clauses as originally set out by Halliday in "Notes on Transitivity and Theme." I have advanced the view that the redistribution of Token and Value in the identifying paradigm of "Notes" realizes, at least in the register studied, the semantic contrast of "expression" versus "motivation" construals. The specific mappings of Identified and Identifier onto these Token–Value configurations further yield four distinct "trajectories" between the symbolic strata involved: diagnostic versus symptomatic in the "expression" mode, and reactive versus catalytic in the "motivation" mode.

There is, however, a second theme running through this article, namely, that of the dialectic between grammatics and grammar—that of using grammatics as meta-language for grammar and grammar as meta-language for grammatics. The very corpus studied, linguistic reflection and argumentation, drives home that our grammatics is construed by the categories of our grammar. In doing linguistics, we are using language as its own meta-language. As Halliday (1992:32) pointedly observes, there is nothing else we can do! Where people go wrong, in my opinion, is to view this as a limitation. Or rather, because of the polysemous and basic-level nature of lexical items, metalinguistic *vocabulary* does tend to lead to reification and simplification of concepts, and to residues of unintended associations. However, using categories of the *grammar* to generally "think with" about the grammar avoids most of these problems and brings with it considerable bonuses in terms of the required abstraction and univocality of concepts, as well as in terms of the privileged fit between the material and formal object of linguistics. In particular, the relational—or semiotic—grammar of linguistic discourse reveals the true semiotic contours of the linguistic model construed and the descriptive methodology used. And "turning grammar on itself" is what we have learned from and owe to M.A.K. Halliday.

REFERENCES

Davidse, K. (1992) "A semiotic approach to relational clauses," *Occasional Papers in Systemic Linguistics*. 6, 99–131.

Davidse, K. (in press) "Ditransitivity and Possession," *Functional Descriptions: Linguistic Form and Linguistic Theory*. R. Hasan, D. Butt and C. Cloran (eds). Amsterdam: Benjamins.

Gleason, H.A. (1965) *Linguistics and English Grammar*. New York: Holt.

Halliday, M.A.K. (1967a) "Notes on transitivity and theme in English 1," *Journal of Linguistics*. 3, 37–81.

Halliday, M.A.K. (1967b) "Notes on transitivity and theme in English 2," *Journal of Linguistics*. 3, 199–244.

Halliday, M.A.K. (1968) "Notes on transitivity and theme in English 3," *Journal of Linguistics*. 4, 179–215.

Halliday, M.A.K. (1985) *An Introduction to Functional Grammar*. London: Arnold.

Halliday, M.A.K. (1988) "On the ineffability of grammatical categories," *Linguistics in a systemic perspective*. J.D. Benson, M.J. Cummings and W.S. Greaves (eds.) Amsterdam: Benjamins, 27–51.

Halliday, M.A.K. (1991) "Towards probabilistic interpretations," *Functional and Systemic Linguistics: Approaches and Uses*. Ventola, E. (ed.). Berlin, Germany: Mouton de Gruyter, 39–61.

Halliday, M.A.K. (1992) "How do you mean?" *Advances in Systemic Linguistics: Recent Theory and Practice*. M. Davies and L. Ravelli (eds). London: Pinter, 20–35.

Halliday, M.A.K. (1994) *An Introduction to Functional Grammar* (Second Edition). London: Arnold

Hjelmslev, L. (1969) *Prolegomena to a Theory of Language* (revised English translation by F.J. Whitfield of *Omkring sprogteoriens grundloeggelse* (1943)). Madison, WI: University of Wisconsin Press.

Lakoff, G. (1987) *Women, Fire and Dangerous Things*. Chicago: University of Chicago Press.

Peirce, C.S. (1982) *Writings of Charles S. Peirce. Volume I.* Bloomington, IN: Indiana University Press.

Wierzbicka, A. (1988) *The Semantics of Grammar.* Studies in Language Companion Series 18. Amsterdam: Benjamins.

10

Attribution and Identification in Gooniyandi*

William B. McGregor

University of Melbourne
Parkville, Victoria 3052, Australia

1. INTRODUCTION

In this contribution I discuss the ways in which attribution (expression of quality) and identification (expression of equality or identity) are expressed in Gooniyandi, an Australian language spoken by approximately 100 Aborigines in the Fitzroy Crossing region of the southern Kimberley, Western Australia. Gooniyandi is a prefixing, non-Pama-Nyungan language, a member of the Bunuban family,

*It is with great pleasure and gratitude that I dedicate this paper to Michael Halliday, whose descriptions of English relational clauses in "Notes on transitivity and theme in English," and an early draft of *Introduction to functional grammar* first stimulated and informed my interest in this area of grammar. I am grateful to the editors of this festschrift, Margaret Berry, Chris Butler, Robin Fawcett and Guowen Huang for their helpful comments on an earlier draft of this paper. The bulk of the fieldwork on which this paper is based was conducted in 1980 and 1982, under grants from the then Australian Institute of Aboriginal Studies. An ARC Research Fellowship (A9324000) and Grants (A58930745 and A59332055) held at University of Melbourne have provided me the opportunity to gather further data, and complete the final revision of the present paper. My greatest debt is of course to my Gooniyandi teachers, especially Jack Bohemia and Dave Lamey, for imparting the information to me in the first place.

which consists of just two languages, Gooniyandi and Bunuba (McGregor 1990a:1).

Gooniyandi has a class of verbless clauses that express attribution and identification. It is, however, usually possible to add one of the three verbs of stance—*bagi-*"lie,"[1] *warang-*"sit" and *wara-*"stand"—and still express a meaning that would translate into English as a "be" relational clause. In both of these respects Gooniyandi is a typical Australian language. These facts are generally accounted for under the assumption that the verb is optional, and that the two modes of expression differ only slightly, if at all, in meaning (see e.g. Dixon 1977:271–272, Heath 1984:516, Tsunoda 1981:123), or that the verb is a type of auxiliary or copula, used principally as a locus for tense and mood inflection (e.g. Austin 1981:104; and cf. Huddleston 1984:183–184, and Lyons 1968:322, 388).

My primary objective in this paper is to argue against these suggestions as adequate descriptions of the Gooniyandi facts. Instead, I will argue that there is a primary grammatical opposition between verbless relational clauses and verbal situation clauses, and that this grammatical contrast is not a mere formal contrast, but is also a semantic one. An attempt will be made to specify this semantic contrast. Roughly, clauses of the former type assert logical type relations imputed by the speaker, but clauses of the latter type refer to real or imaginary situations or goings-on. As I will show, this contrast coincides with Halliday's distinction between the logical and experiential components of the ideational metafunction (Halliday 1973:106; cf. Fawcett 1980:31): Verbless clauses express meaning from the logical metafunction, and verbal clauses express meaning from the experiential metafunction.

My second aim, which is closely connected with my first, is to provide a descriptively adequate account of attribution and identification in Gooniyandi clauses. It is here that the systemic approach shows most clearly its advantages over other approaches. As I have pointed out elsewhere (McGregor 1990a:291), it is impossible to give a general description of Gooniyandi clauses as syntagms of units of particular classes. It is only when, as in systemic theory, class is distinguished from function that significant general patterns are discernible. Furthermore, more specifically, Halliday's work on English (especially 1994:119–138) provides what seems to me to be the most insightful approach to attribution and identification available.

---

[1]For transcribing Gooniyandi words I employ the practical orthography currently in use by literate Gooniyandi speakers. It should be noted that in this system *oo* represents the high back vowel (IPA *u*).

Section 3 will describe Gooniyandi attributive and identifying relational clauses using Halliday's insights. Of course, Halliday's description of English does not carry over in all its details to Gooniyandi. There are a number of interesting points of agreement and difference, which I will comment on as they arise. However, there will be no attempt to systematically compare English (as described by Halliday 1994) and Gooniyandi. I will also be dealing (section 4), albeit briefly, with a topic dealt with in some detail in Halliday's seminal article "Notes on transitivity and theme in English" (Halliday 1967/8), but unfortunately omitted from Halliday (1994): attribution and identification in non-relational clauses. It is my hope that this article will demonstrate some advantages of systemic functional theory, not by explicit comparison with other theories—which in any case have not been applied to Gooniyandi—but rather by example of the range of phenomena it brings to light and the ways it can account for them.

2. OUTLINE OF GOONIYANDI GRAMMAR

To orientate the reader, this section provides some brief remarks on Gooniyandi grammar. It is convenient to recognize a rank scale of grammatical units, distinguishing clause, phrase, word and morpheme. Although systemic grammar recognizes a further rank for English—namely the group (see e.g. Halliday 1961)—there is no reason to distinguish two ranks between word and clause in Gooniyandi. I use the term "phrase" in preference to "group" for the single rank between word and clause, partly because it is more in keeping with general (non-systemic) linguistic usage, and partly because the term "group" does not seem suitable for one of the major subtypes at this rank. I will first describe phrases, then clauses; discussion of the other units is not necessary here. (See McGregor 1990a for further details.)

2.1. The Rank of Phrase

There are two principal phrase types in Gooniyandi, nominal phrases and verbal phrases (VPs).

2.1.1. Nominal phrases

These are either noun phrases (NPs) or postpositional phrases (PPs). NPs typically consist of nominals or pronominals, which may occur in almost any order. However, different word orders *do* convey different meanings, and the structure of the NP may be described functionally in terms of the roles that its constituents realize, and their order:

(Deictic)^(Quantifier)^(Classifier)^Entity^(Qualifier)   (1)

As (1) indicates, the Entity—"Thing" in Halliday's (1994:180) terminology—is the only inherent role. The Deictic element contextualizes the phrase by relating it to the context of speech, usually in terms of proximity to the speaker. The Quantifier indicates the quantity or number of items referred to. The Classifier indicates the type of thing the Entity nominal refers to, while the Qualifier indicates a quality or property of the referent. (For detailed discussion of these roles, and justification of the analysis, see McGregor (1990a:253–276).) Some examples are:

Deictic	Quantifier	Classifier	Entity	Qualifier
ngirndaji			*yoowooloo*	*nyamani*
this			man	big
"this big man"				

(2)

Deictic	Quantifier	Classifier	Entity	Qualifier
	garndiwirri	*gardiya*	*goornboo*	
	two	white:person	woman	
"two white women"				

(3)

PPs consist of NPs in constituency with postpositions. These occur one per phrase and are distributionally bound to the word they follow, which may be any word of the phrase, regardless of its position. Postpositions mark number—*-yoorroo* DU(al) and *-yarndi* PL(ural); and "case"—the main ones being *-ngga* ERG(ative), *-yoo* DAT(ive), *-ya* LOC(ative), *-nhingi* ABL(ative), *-yirra* ALL(ative), and *-ngarri* COMIT(ative). (4) is an example of an ergative PP.

ŋgoorroo -ŋgga yoowooloo
that   -ERG man
"by that man"   (4)

2.1.2. Verbal phrases

These are units of phrase rank, but constitute single distributional words (no subpart has the potential of independent occurrence). Their structure may be described as follows:

Process—(Aspect)—(mood)—Classifier Complex—(mode)—
(Oblique pronominal)—(number)   (5)

The Process refers to an action, state, happening, occurrence, and so forth and is normally realized by a verbal lexeme. The other inherent role, the Classifier Complex, consists of morphemes indicating tense, person and number of the Actor and Goal (if the clause is transitive), and the type of process referred to. Oblique pronominals cross-reference the Affected participant (see below). The remaining labels do not require explanation here (but see McGregor 1990a:190–227). Because of its internal complexity, and because morphemic divisions are obscured by morphophonemic alternations, whole VPs will in this paper be given interlinear glosses appropriate to the intended sense in the particular instance; no attempt will be made to provide morpheme by morpheme glosses.

2.2. The Rank of Clause

The unit next up on the rank scale is the clause. There are two primary clause types in Gooniyandi, distinguished on both formal and functional grounds: RELATIONAL clauses and SITUATION clauses. The body of this paper is devoted to explicating the semantic difference between these two clause types; the following paragraphs provide a brief orientating summary.

1. Relational clauses are verbless, and assert "logical" relationships of existence, identity, and quality. They refer to entities, qualities and/or circumstances, not to situations. It should be noted that this usage of the term "relational" is somewhat different to Halliday's (e.g. 1994:119). In my usage it refers to a "connection," and has nothing to do with "being" (cf. Benveniste 1960/71:164). In section 5 I attempt to make the difference clear.

2.   Situation clauses refer to situations[2], which involve an inherent[3] Process (realized by a VP), together with at least one actant, referred to by an NP or PP and simultaneously cross-referenced by a bound pronominal in the VP. Such actants are by definition PARTICIPANTS (McGregor 1990a:293; cf. Halliday 1970:146, 149, 1994:107–109, Fawcett 1980:135ff). Four transitivity types may be identified in terms of the configuration of inherent participant roles:

i.   *Intransitive*, with an inherent Medium realized by an NP;

ii.   *Transitive*, with an inherent Medium realized by an NP, and an inherent Agent realized by an ERG PP;

iii.   *Middle*, with an inherent Agent realized by an ERG PP, and an inherent Affected realized by a DAT PP; and

iv.   *Reflexive/Reciprocal*, with an inherent Agent realized by an ERG PP.

Briefly, a Medium is something through which the situation is enacted (Halliday 1994:163–164, McGregor 1985:258); an Agent is something engaged in directed action (McGregor 1985:258–9); and an Affected[4] is something affected or changed by the situation (McGregor 1985:215, 1990a:330ff).

---

[2]In reference to clauses I use the term "situation" similarly to the way Halliday uses "process" (1970:146,1994:106), to refer to any sort of occurrence. However, my term is intended to reflect the crucial presence of actants, circumstances and so on, in these occurrences, and to maintain a clear terminological distinction from occurrences in the abstract, for which I employ Halliday"s term "process." (In effect, I use "situation" for clauses, and "process" for words and phrases.) Note that unlike Fawcett (1980:88–89), from whom the term "situation" was borrowed, I do not use it to refer to the actual referent situation itself, except when the term referent is prefixed.

[3]I use the term "inherent" in the sense it customarily has in systemic grammar, in reference to roles that necessarily occur in structures of particular types. That is, the particular role must be realized by a linguistic expression, unless it has been ellipsed—the absence of a realizing expression indicates that it is taken to be understood what thing fulfills that role. However, as I use the term, it does not necessarily refer to participants, as systemic usage usually has it (e.g. Fawcett 1980:135–136).

[4]This role corresponds to Halliday's term Beneficiary (1994:144ff), NOT to his earlier (1967/8:185, 1970:157) Affected, now Medium (1994:163ff). I prefer Affected because something in this role does not always benefit from the situation (cf. Fawcett 1987:146–150).

3. RELATIONAL CLAUSES

As mentioned in the previous section, relational clauses are verbless clauses that assert logical relations of existence, attribution (subclass membership in logical terminology) and identity (logical equality). The clauses themselves refer to *entities*, not to situations, and either: present them to the hearer's attention—existential clauses; characterize them in terms of a quality or property they exhibit—characterizing clauses (attributive clauses in Halliday's terminology (1994:119)); or equate them with something else—identifying clauses. This defines three types of relational clauses, which I will show to be grammatically distinct in Gooniyandi:

i.   existential   "here is *x*"
ii. characterizing "*x* has the attribute *a*"
iii. identifying   "*x* has the identity *a*"

Existential clauses have just one inherent role, whereas characterizing and identifying clauses each have two; this justifies grammatically separating (i) from (ii) and (iii). Examples (6)–(8) below illustrate the three types in order:

yoowarni boolga/   marlami boolga/   yanoonggoonyali
one   old:man   not   old:man   young
yoowooloo/
man
"There was an old man; not really an old man, [he was] still a young man."   (6)

ngirndaji maa thoowoorndoo
this   meat rotten
"This meat is rotten."   (7)

nganyi nyibayarri
I   [name]
"I'm Nyibayarri."   (8)

The first clause/phrase of (6), *yoowarni boolga* "one old man," introduced that person for the first time into the text, and thus to the hearer's attention. This phrase fulfills the role EXISTENT in the clause in which it appears. In (7), a quality, rottenness, is attributed to an entity, the meat. There are thus two roles in characterizing clauses, the ATTRIBUTE and the CARRIER (in Halliday's 1994:120 terminology).

And in (8) one designation is used to identify the thing referred to by the other phrase. Identifying clauses therefore have the roles IDENTIFIED and IDENTIFIER. I will describe identifying clauses in section 3.1, and characterizing clauses in 3.2. I have discussed existential clause elsewhere (McGregor 1988), and mention them only in passing.

There are a number of grammatical differences between identifying and characterizing clauses in Gooniyandi; they are not just logically distinguishable types, as Fawcett (1987) suggested is the case in English. Firstly, and most importantly, the Attribute is invariably realized by an NP WITH A QUALIFIER and an optional head Entity, but no pre-Entity roles, or by a PP. Examples in section 3.2 support this claim, as does (7) above, in which the Attribute NP consists of just the Qualifier *thoowoorndoo* "rotten." On the other hand, both the Identifier and the Identified are always realized by NPs with overt Entity or pre-Entity roles, but NO post-Entity Qualifier; nor may they be realized by PPs. Supporting evidence will be found in the examples provided in section 3.1; in (10), for instance, the Identifier NP consists of just the Entity nominal Gooniyandi, and the Identified NP consists of a Deictic *ngarragi* "my," and an entity *thangarndi* "word." This difference in FORM justifies distinguishing the Attribute from the Identifier and Identified (cf. Halliday 1994:xix–xx, Fawcett 1987:178, Martin 1986:46, 1987:16), and ultimately the contrast between identifying and characterizing clauses.

A second, derivative difference (cf. Halliday 1994:120–121, 123) is that constituent order in identifying clauses is usually free, and with certain qualifications relating to ellipsis of the Entity nominal, either NP may occur first. In other words, the Identifier may precede or follow the Identified. However, in characterizing clauses constituent order is relatively rigid: The Carrier usually comes first. The reader is referred again to the following sections for supporting evidence.

An explanation of these generalizations is not hard to find (cf. Halliday 1994:121). In Gooniyandi, as in English, Theme is realized by initial position in the clause (Halliday 1970:161,1994:37ff, McGregor 1990a:371ff). Identifying clauses—at least intensive ones (see below)—make reference to two entities, and either may be made Theme. On the other hand, characterizing clauses refer to a single entity, the Carrier (Attributes are not entities). There is in Gooniyandi a definite preference for thematizing entities over qualities or processes (cf. McGregor 1990a:378). So the Carrier is the natural choice of Theme. In the few examples available of the reverse order, the Carrier and the Attribute NPs come on distinct intonation contours, typically with a pause between them, and a rise on the first. I have shown elsewhere (McGregor 1990a:376) that this is a tagged Theme construction in which the Theme is added in as a type of afterthought; thus the Carrier remains Theme. One such example is:

joodoo/ ngarragi garingi/
straight my   wife
"My wife is straight (i.e. of the correct marriage class) for me?"   (9)

(Further, the preference for thematizing entities also explains why exemplifying and naming identifying clauses (see below) are irreversible.)

Thirdly, only to (some) characterizing clauses, but to NO identifying clauses, do there correspond situation clause agnates with an inherent Process referring to the mode of "being" of the Carrier (see section 4). To put things more simply, and somewhat imprecisely, it is only when one nominal phrase is related to the other as an attribute that a verb of stance can occur in the clause. An explanation for this will emerge subsequently.

Finally, the two clause types have distinct, non-parallel subtypes. Whereas identifying clauses are intensive ("equals"), exemplifying ("be exemplified by"), or naming ("be named"), characterizing clauses are either intensive ("be"), circumstantial ("be at, for, with, etc."), or possessive ("be someone's"). In Gooniyandi there are no parallels to the English circumstantial identifying clauses *tomorrow is the tenth, the best way to get there is by car* (Halliday 1994:131). The subtypes, as far as I have been able to determine them, are:

identifying		characterising	
(I)	intensive	(I)	intensive
(II)	exemplifying	(II)	circumstantial
(III)	naming	(a)	locative
		(b)	purposive
		(c)	associative
		(d)	comparative
		(e)	source
		(III)	possessive

Figure 10.1. Clause subtypes.

3.1. Identifying Clauses

In identifying clauses, an equation is set up between the two terms, the Identified and the Identifier. The three subtypes differ in terms of the exact nature this relation of equality takes. There are in each case also grammatical differences supporting the distinction; these will be commented on as the discussion unfolds.

3.1.1. Intensive identifying clauses

In intensive identifying clauses a relation of identity is set up between the referents of two distinct phrases, as a means of identifying one of them.

$$_{NP1}[ngarragi\ thangarndi]_{NP1}\ _{NP2}[Gooniyandi]_{NP2}$$
  my   language   Gooniyandi
"My language is Gooniyandi."   (10)

This clause asserts that the expression [*ngarragi thangarndi*] "my language" and the name [*Gooniyandi*] are identical in reference, although different in sense. The phrases are, that is, co-referential, and provide alternative designations of a single entity.

In (10), Gooniyandi identifies the speaker's language: In the context of its utterance the speaker knew that I had been learning the language for a few months, and so identified his own language by this designation. Clearly, he was not using the clause to identify the language Gooniyandi. Thus, [*ngarragi thangarndi*] "my language" is the Identified, and [*Gooniyandi*] the Identifier. However, the same clause might also be used to identify Gooniyandi: Had I been requesting information about the language, the speaker could have identified it as his language.

The two NPs provide alternate designations of a single entity, but differ in their "mode" of referring: One NP specifies the form—how the item is to be recognized; the other specifies the function—how the item is valued (cf. Halliday 1994:124). For example, in (10) the speaker's language is being identified by its name, thus indicating how it is to be recognized. Following Halliday (1994:124) I will use the terms TOKEN and VALUE for these two different modes of referring, respectively. Unlike Identifier and Identified, Token and Value are usually uniquely assigned to the constituents of an Identifying clause. The Token normally corresponds to the nominal constituent, which is most lexically specific; the Value usually corresponds with the nominal constituent, which is least lexically specific. In terms of my example above, *Gooniyandi* is more specific than *thangarndi* "language."

The NPs in an identifying clause simultaneously realize one of the roles Identifier/Identified, and one of the roles Token/Value. The choices are independent, thus giving rise to two distinct types of identifying clause: DECODING identifying clause, in which the Identified is associated with the Value, Identifier with the Token; and ENCODING, in which the Identified is associated with the Token, the Identifier with the Value (Halliday 1967/8:202). Each of the four feature combinations occurs initially—each may realize the textual function of Theme. The following are some examples:

Identified/Value	Identifier/Token
ngarragi thangarndi	*Gooniyandi*
my language	Gooniyandi
"My language is Gooniyandi."	

(10)

Identified/Token	Identifier/Value
ngirndaji riwi	*ngirrangi*
this camp	ours
"This place is ours."	

(11)

Identifier/Value	Identified/Token
ngoorndoo	*niyaji yoowooloo*
someone	this man
"Who is this man?"	

(12)

Identifier/Token	Identified/Value
ngoonyoo	*ngaanggi jiginya*
which	your child
"Which (one) is your child?"	

(13)

The first two orders, in which the Identified occurs first, are the most frequent (cf. Kuno & Wongkhomthong 1981:79–80). The reverse order occurs mainly in examples such as the two shown above, in which the Identifier is an indefinite determiner that is being used interrogatively, in a request for information as to the identity of some entity. There is an unmarked association between the role of Identifier and the textual role of New (cf. Halliday 1967/ 8:226,1994:124): The Identifier is normally singled out by tonic prominence. However, there is reason to doubt that the association is perfect (cf. Halliday 1967/8:227), although it is much better than the association between Identified and Theme and between Token and information Focus, proposed by Fawcett (1987:176–177), as an examination of the examples in this section will reveal. Partly for this reason, and partly because, although an identifying clause need not contain a Given NP, it always contains an Identified, the distinct *ideational* roles of Identifier and Identified must be set up and distinguished from the *textual* roles of New and Given.

Halliday (1994:132ff) distinguished a subtype of possessive identifying clauses in English that identify an item as someone's possession. In Gooniyandi, however, the corresponding clauses appear to be intensive: They instantiate the relation equals (cf. Fawcett 1987:152). The two NPs provide alternative designations for a single entity, the possession; they do not relate an entity and its owner by the relationship of possession. Consider example (11), the English translation of which is a possessive identifying clause. Gooniyandi does not have a distinct set of possessive pronouns occurring as heads of NPs. Thus (11) is elliptical, with the Entity nominal ellipsed from the second NP, being given: *ngirrangi* "our" realizes the Diectic role in NP2. Compare what happens when the NPs occur in the reverse order. There are two possibilities:

$_{NP2}[$ *ngirrangi riwi*$]_{NP2}$ $_{NP1}[$ *ngirndaji*$]_{NP1}$
our   camp   this
"Our place is this (one)."   (14)

$_{NP2}[$ *ngirrangi*$]_{NP2}/$ $_{NP1}[$ *ngirndaji riwi*$]_{NP1}$
our   this   camp
"Ours is this place."   (15)

The unmarked pattern is illustrated by (14), where in addition to the change of word order vis-à-vis (11), the phrase with Deictic *ngirrangi* "our" has the Enitiy nominal *riwi* "camp," and the *following* phrase is elliptical. With the reversal of the phrases, of course, it is now NP2 in which *riwi* is New; it is then Given in NP1. The less common pattern represented by (15), in which the order of the two NPs has been simply reversed, does not contradict this claim. The clause is uttered in two tone units, the second being secondary (see McGregor 1986a:139), an "afterthought" to the first. (15) is thus a marked construction with an afterthought Theme.

3.1.2. Exemplifying clauses

Exemplifying clauses establish a particular entity or class of entities as an instance or subset of a generic type. They are characterized by an initial Identified/Value referring to a generic or indefinite class of entities of which the Identifier/Token is a member. There are no examples available in which the reverse order occurs. Examples are:

[*yaanya gawi*] [*gooloomangarri*]
other   fish   catfish
"Another fish is the catfish." (16)

[*yaanya gambangarna -nyali*] [*diwiwi*]
other   water:dweller   -REP   short-necked:turtle
"Yet another water dweller is the short-necked turtle." (17)

The Token and Value are related as subordinate to superordinate in a hierarchy of (cultural) classification: A catfish is subordinate to fish, a short-necked turtle to water creatures.

Halliday (1994) does not distinguish a corresponding relational clause type in English, and he would presumably treat the English translations of examples such as (16) and (17) as a subtype of intensive identifying relational clauses. For this reason it may be useful to lay out my reasons for distinguishing them as a separate type. Exemplifying clauses differ from intensive clauses in that (a) they have indefinite Identifieds, whereas intensive identifying clauses always have definite Identifieds, and (b) the order of the roles is fixed. These grammatical differences might suggest that exemplifying clauses should be treated as a subtype of characterizing clauses. However, more careful consideration reveals that if this were the case there would be a crucial difference from all characterizing clause types: The order of roles would be invariably Attribute^Carrier, as against the otherwise predominant Carrier^Attribute order. Furthermore, the way in which these clauses were used in their textual context was to provide further examples of particular categories under discussion. This is the sense in which they are "identifying"; they pick out certain items from a larger class of (potential) referents or referent classes, as do decoding intensive identifying clauses.

3.1.3. Naming clauses

I call the third type "naming" because one of the NPs provides a name, a designation, for the other, referential NP. Such clauses always involve the association of Identified and Token, and Identifier and Value. I encountered this type of clause a number of times in learning Gooniyandi, especially when my teachers pointed out things to me in picture books or in the environment and named them. For example:

> *ngirndaji labawoo jiga*
> this   white   flower
> "This is a white flower."   (18)

And (19) illustrates a pattern that I have been told was used in Gooniyandi language classes in the Fitzroy Crossing State School in 1985 to teach the children body part terms.

> *ngirndaji ngarragi marla*
> this   my   hand
> "This is my hand."   (19)

However, naming identifying clauses are apparently not restricted to circumstances of teaching non-speakers the names of objects. They are also used in identifying personal names and relationship terms to be used between individuals—see example (8).

These clauses are distinguished initially on intuitive-functional grounds. What they do is establish associations between non-linguistic referent entities and linguistic designations for them. They do not establish associations between alternative designations for an object, as do intensive identifying clauses, in which both NPs are (presumed) cognitively significant to the hearer, and so capable of being understood to refer to something. In other words, the second NP in naming Identifying clauses, the name, is used as a representative of itself; it has no "mental referent" (Fawcett 1980:90)—no sense, if you will. Two main things distinguish naming clauses from other identifying clauses, justifying the identification of the covert subtype. Firstly, the order of the phrases appears to be fixed; the clauses are always encoding. Secondly, alone among identifying clauses, naming clauses have situation clause agnates in which there is an inherent Identifier and an inherent Identified. This agnate clause involves the verbal lexeme *goowaj-* "call (by) name":

> *nginyji goowajgingga ngoombarna*
> you   I:call:you   husband
> "I call you 'husband'."   (20)

It should be noted, however, that naming clauses have alternative interpretations as intensive identifying clauses, where both phrases are used referentially (cf. Kuno & Wongkhomthong (1981:89), and Halliday (1994:129), who treats corresponding clauses in English as a subtype of intensive identifying clauses). For example, (8) might be used to identify the speaker as the individual whose name is mentioned.

3.2. Characterizing Clauses

Whereas identifying clauses identify an entity in terms of an alternative designation, characterizing clauses "characterize" an entity, in terms of a property, quality, location, use, and so forth. For example, (7) above characterizes the meat referred to by the first NP as rotten; it does not serve to identify the meat. As has already been mentioned, in characterizing clauses the Carrier almost always precedes the Attribute. I will now discuss in order the three main types of characterizing clauses.

3.2.1. Intensive characterizing clauses
Examples of intensive characterizing clauses include (7) and (9) above. The Attribute is normally realized by an NP that consists of a Qualifier only; sometimes the NP has an Entity, but pre-Entity roles are never realized (see above). Consequently, to each characterizing clause there usually corresponds a single NP consisting of the same words in the same order, in which the Qualifier of the NP corresponds to the Attribute of the clause. For example, to (7) there corresponds the NP [*ngirndaji maa thoowoorndoo*] "this rotten meat." This lack of contrast at the level of form has led some linguists to suggest that verbless clauses in other Australian languages resembling Gooniyandi in this respect consist of just single NPs—for instance, Dixon (1972:71). There are a number of arguments against this hypothesis as regards Gooniyandi. Firstly, propositional modifiers (which include markers of negation (e.g. *mangarri* "no, not"), probability (e.g. *yiganyi* "uncertain"), and so on) mark the nexus between the two constituents by their position:

ngirndaji gili   mangarri binyidi
this   same not   hard
"This is not hard (ground)."   (21)

Secondly, reversal of the order of the two joined constituents does not have a semantic effect identical to that of reordering the constituents of the corresponding NP (see McGregor 1990a:267–274). And thirdly, only the Attribute, and not the whole characterizing clause may be "verbalized" (see below).

Informally, a large number of different attributive relations may be distinguished, including size, shape, color, appearance, age, value, texture, sex, and so forth. This range is almost identical with the range of relations found between the Entity and its Qualifier in the NP. The main difference is that determiners and number words, which often function as Qualifiers, do not occur as Attributes.

3.2.2. Circumstantial characterizing clauses

A circumstantial attribute provides an extrinsic qualification of a thing in terms of its relationship to other things or places in the world. The Attribute, that is, is conflated with a circumstantial role, and so is realized by PPs or adverbials, rather than by NPs. However, it should be noted that there is considerable formal overlap between the expression classes that realize circumstantial and intensive Attributes, and many clause-forms are potentially ambiguous. For instance:

niyaji goornboo jiginya -ngarri
this   woman   child   -COMIT   (22)

is ambiguous between the two senses "This woman is with child" (i.e. is pregnant) (intensive), and "This woman has a child" (circumstantial). The first, intensive reading arises if jiginyangarri realizes the Qualifier role in the NP realizing the Attribute, in which case it belongs to an expression class that includes badiji "pregnant," nyamani "big," and so forth. The second, circumstantial reading arises when the PP jiginya-ngarri directly realizes the clausal role of Attribute, when it belongs to an expression class that includes tharra-ngarri (dog-COMIT) "with a dog," and so forth.

The five types of circumstantial characterizing clause are distinguished by the postposition that occurs on the NP functioning as Attribute; the circumstantial roles correspond with those found in other clause types (McGregor 1990a:338–353). I deal with the five types in order.

3.2.2.1. Locational. Here a location is attributed of an entity; the clause asserts that the entity is at a particular location. The Attribute may be realized by a LOC PP, by a locational adverbial, or by a complex the two (McGregor 1990a:287–289). Examples of the three possibilities in order are:

ngarragi tharra ngirndaji -ya
my   dog   this   -LOC
"My dog is here."   (23)

garndiwirri girli   warlibirri baabirri
two   same river   below
"The two rivers are below (the surface of the billabong—i.e.
                                    backwater lagoon)."   (24)

ngarragi ngaarri gilirni -ya   babaabirri
my   stone   grass -LOC inside
"My money is in the grass."   (25)

Locational characterizing clauses are not common. The preferred
pattern is for locations to be attributed of entities within situation
clauses, and this presumably correlates with the rarity of locative
expressions as Qualifiers in NPs.

3.2.2.2. Purpose.   This type attributes to an entity another
entity or process with which it is implicated as a purpose, function,
or beneficiary. Purposive Attributes are realized by DAT PPs:

thangarla   moonyjoo -yoo ligirr -woo
toothbrush tooth   -DAT clean -DAT
"A toothbrush is for cleaning teeth."   (26)

Unlike locational Attributes, purposive Attributes always occur in
characterizing clauses, and purposive expressions (DAT PPs) are often found as Qualifiers in NPs (see also below section 4).

Purposive Attributes are sometimes formally indistinguishable
from possessive Attributes (see section 3.2.3 below). However, the
distinction always shows up when the beneficiary/possessor is a
personal pronoun. The pronoun (in oblique form) must be followed
by the DAT postposition in purposive Attributes, as shown in (27),
but not in possessive Attributes.

riwi   mangarri ngarragi -yoo -miya yarrangi
camp not   my   -DAT -only our
boojoo -yoo -nyali
finish -DAT -REP
"This place is not only mine, it belongs to all of us."   (27)

3.2.2.3. Associative.   The associative Attribute ascribes to an
entity an association with another entity and is realized by a COMIT
PP. An example is the second sense of (22) above. Clauses with an
associative Attribute generally translate into English as "*x* has *y*," or
"*x* is with *y*."

3.2.2.4. Comparative.   In this case the attributive relation
takes the form of a comparison, and the Attribute is realized by a

phrase in constituency with the enclitic *-jangi* SEM(blative). For example:

goornboo ngoorroo yoowooloo -jangi
woman   that   man   -SEM
"That woman is like a man."   (28)

3.2.2.5. Source.   The source Attribute ascribes an origin to an entity, and is realized by an ABL PP:

nganyi *liyarnali   -nhingi*
I   from: west -ABL
"I'm from the west."   (29)

niyaji yoowooloo mooloorrja -nhingi
this   man   [place]   -ABL
"This man is from Mulurrja."   (30)

3.2.3. Possessive characterizing clauses

In this type an item is characterized by the property of being someone's possession. The Attribute is realized by an NP with a Qualifier realized by an oblique pronoun, or by a DAT PP. An example is:

Butcher ngaloowinyi Lanis -joo
[name]   son   [name] -DAT
"Butcher is Lanis's son /a son of Lanis."   (31)

Granted that there is no need to distinguish a class of possessive identifying clauses in Gooniyandi; it may seem surprising that I should set up a distinct class of possessive characterizing clauses. My reason for doing so is that possessive characterizing clauses contrast with intensive and circumstantial characterizing clauses in terms of the expression class of the Attribute; whereas, in intensive clauses the Qualifier in the Attribute NP is always a nominal, in possessive clauses it is frequently a pronominal. In circumstantial clauses the Attribute is realized by a PP or adverbial; in possessive clauses it is realized by an NP.

4. ATTRIBUTION AND IDENTIFICATION
IN SITUATION CLAUSES

This section turns to attribution and identification in verbal situation clauses (see section 2.2). The discussion is divided into three subsections. In the first I discuss clauses of "being," in which the

Process refers to a mode of being or existence of an entity. In the second I look briefly at clauses in which the Attribute is conflated with the Process. Then in the third subsection, I begin an investigation of attribution and identification in other clause types.

4.1. Processes of "Being"

There is a class of situation clauses that have an inherent Attribute, in addition to a single inherent participant, and an inherent Process.[5] The inherent participant is an Actor/Medium (McGregor 1990a:323), and this participant is usually the Carrier, as in (32). However, this is not always the case in Gooniyandi (unlike English—see Halliday 1967/8:61), and sometimes the Carrier is conflated with a non-participant Medium, the Range (McGregor 1990a:332–336). Example (33), for instance, which has an ellipsed Actor/Medium (the speaker—see McGregor 1985), has as well a non-participant Medium, the hand, and it is the latter entity that is located.

Carrier		Attribute	Process
ngarragi	*ngaboo*	*gambi*	*bagiri*
my	father	sick	he:lies
"My father is sick."			

(32)

Attribute	Carrier	Process
biliganyi	*marla*	*bagingi*
middle	hand	I:lay
"My hand only went halfway (i.e. when I reached up to the cupboard)."		

(33)

---

[5]For example, the Attribute *gambi* "sick" in (32) is inherent. For, although it could be ellipsed if it conveyed given information (see example (36) below), if it did not occur, and was not given, the resulting clause *ngarragi ngaboo bagiri* would mean, "My father is lying down" (cf. Hasan 1972:7). (The arguments immediately below demonstrate that the Process is inherent.)

I will refer to these as clauses (or processes) of "being," for reasons that will become clear shortly. Unlike other situation clauses, constituent order in "being" clauses is relatively fixed: The Carrier almost always precedes the Attribute, which almost always precedes the Process, as the examples in this section demonstrate. It is possible to identify the following grammatically distinct types:

(I)   intensive
(II) circumstantial
(a) locative
(b) extent
(c) associative

All of these have an inherent Attribute and an inherent Carrier. As has already been mentioned, there are no processes of "being" corresponding to identifying clauses.

Three main verbs fill the Process role in clauses of "being": *bagi-* "lie," *warang-* "sit," and *wara-* "stand." I will now argue that these verbals carry significant semantic content in "being" clauses, which are, furthermore, grammatically distinct from verbless characterizing clauses. The two types are NOT synonymous, and the VP is not an optional place-marking copula. The verbal type makes reference to a situation, which is a mode of "being" or existence of the Medium/Carrier, concomitant with its carrying the Attribute; in the verbless type the Carrier is characterized by its possession of the Attribute (see section 4). The arguments are as follows.

Firstly, the choice of verbal is meaningful. If the Carrier remains in a particular posture throughout the duration of the time it has the Attribute, the choice between the verbs of stance goes as follows (cf. Goddard 1985:38, Simpson 1983:402):

bagi-   "lie" occurs if the entity adopts a reclining or horizontal position, or has significantly greater extent horizontally than vertically.

warang-   "sit" occurs if the posture is a sitting one, or where the body as a whole adopts neither a horizontal nor a vertical orientation, and has roughly comparable horizontal and vertical extents.

wara-   "stand" occurs when the position is vertical, that is, when there is significantly greater vertical than horizontal extent, or where a significant part of the entity has vertical orientation.

Of the three verbs, *bagi-* "lie" appears to be the least marked one semantically, and is used when the entity adopts no particular postural mode, and is completely inactive in an abstract or intangible situation of "being." For example:

Billi marnawa   bagiwirri
Bill   his:brother they:lay
"He and Bill were brothers."   (34)

bagi- "lie," that is, appears to have a general existential sense—existence in anything but an upright or sitting posture.

Secondly, the expression class that realizes the role of Attribute differs somewhat depending on whether the clause is verbal or verbless. There are principled tendencies relating the type of attribute to one or the other clause type as the most common mode of expression. In general, the more "concrete" and "alienable" an Attribute is, the more it can be construed as an aspect of the mode of being of the Carrier, and the more likely it is that the attributing clause will be verbal. For example, locative and associative circumstantial Attributes are quite concrete and alienable, and they usually occur in situation clauses. On the other hand, if the quality is so inherent as to be inseparable from an entity, it is unlikely to contribute to the mode of being of the entity. Thus qualities such as color, size, and shape are infrequent as Attributes in situation clauses; they normally occur only when there has been a change in that quality. Likewise when the Attribute is another entity that is related to the Carrier either as a more abstract type of "circumstance," such as purpose, source/origin, comparison, or possession—clearly such Attributes cannot affect the mode of being of the Carrier in any significant way, and are never (to the best of my knowledge) found in Attributive "being" clauses. In between these limits there are a number of descriptive Attributes of qualities, which are neither inalienable, nor extrinsic to the object. These are the ones that commonly occur in both situation and relational clauses. If, on the other hand, Attributes are considered in terms of their characterizing potential, exactly the same pattern emerges: Locational, extent, and associative circumstances characterize an entity least, while inner defining qualities and extrinsic uses, likenesses, and so forth characterize an entity most, leaving the same residue of more accidental alienable qualities.

These two criteria justify my claim that the verbs of stance do not function as mere copulas, but as Processes in a distinct clause type, which refers to a mode of "being." I will now describe the five sub-types of Attributive "being" clauses.

4.1.1. Intensive

All that needs to be added regarding this type is that it allows at least two other verbal lexemes to realize the Process in addition to the three verbs of posture—which adds further support to my claim that the verb carries significant semantic content. The verb *ward-* "go" may occur when motion is the typical characteristic of the Carrier associated with its possession of the Attribute. For example, stockmen typically move about in the course of their work:

stockmanloondi   now niyaji -nhingi nganyi
I:became:a:stockman then this   -ABL   I
stockman wardngi
stockman I:went
"I became a stockman then; after that I was a stockman." (35)

However, it should be noted that the chioce of *ward-* "go" is determined by the speaker's perspective on the state of affairs, and is not strictly governed by properties of the referent situation. Although hunting as much as stockwork surely always involves significant movement, the verb *bagi-* "lie" was chosen in (36).

ngamoo bagingi
before   I:lay
"I used to be (a good hunter)."   (36)

Unlike (35), this does not come from a narrative, but was used by the speaker in casual conversation, in reference to a former ability of his.

The second verb that occurs in "being" clauses is *waba-* "smell, stink." In attributing the quality of rottenness of meat (especially), this verb is always used, rather than a stance verb. It is principally for this reason—that clauses such as (37) with the verb *waba-* "smell, stink" correspond to characterizing clauses such as (7) above—that I take these to be "being" clauses.

ngirndaji maa thoowoorndoo wabaari
this   meat rotten   it:stinks
"This meat is rotten."   (37)

4.1.2. Circumstantial

There do not exist Attributive circumstantial clauses of "being" corresponding to each type of circumstantial characterizing clauses, and there is an additional type that occurs in the former but not the latter.

4.1.2.1. Locative.   An example is B's reply in the following exchange:

A: ngoonyi -ya   ngaanggi garingi
   which   -LOC your   wife
B: babligaj -ja   warangji
   pub   -LOC she:sat
A: "Where's your wife?"
B: "She was at the pub."   (38)

4.1.2.2. Extent.   In this type, the Attribute indicates the extent of the Carrier, and it is typically realized by an ALL PP, or by an Adverbial. An example is:

(baali) danggi   -yirra bagiri
(road) Giekie:Gorge -ALL   it:lies
"(This road) goes to Giekie Gorge."   (39)

4.1.2.3. Associative.   An example is (40), in which the birds are claimed to be in a condition of having names.

jirigi yingi -ngarri bagiri
bird   name -COMIT it:lies
"The birds have names."   (40)

4.2. Attributive Processes

An Attribute may be conflated with the Process in a situation clause. That is, the expression for the Attribute, a nominal, also realizes the role of Process within the verbal complex. The following types are distinguishable:

(I)   intensive
(II)   circumstantial
(a) locative
(b) associative

4.2.1. Intensive

Clauses of this type may be either Intransitive, with just a Carrier/ Medium; Transitive, with a Causer/Agent, and a Carrier/Medium; or Reflexive/Reciprocal, with a Causer/Agent and a Carrier/Medium. Apparently the Carrier never conflates with the Agent in Reflexive/Reciprocal clauses, but the non-participant Medium in clauses such as (43) below is inherent. Examples of the three transitivity types are, respectively:

nganyi nyamani -loondi
I   big   -I:got
"I got/became big."   (41)

nganyi -ngga jiginya binarrig   -miila
I   -ERG child   knowledgeable -I:repeatedly:extend:it
"I'm teaching the child."   (42)

marla doomoo -wingarni
hand   clench -he:will:do:it:to:himself
"He will clench his fist."   (43)

What is the semantic difference between this mode of expression and expression by a "being" clause? The most obvious contrast is suggested by the pair of clauses in (35), where the Attributive Process clause refers to the process of entering the state, whereas the "being" clause refers to the condition of being in that state. However, this contrast does not account for all of the possibilities. Consider the following pair:

ngirrinyjila warangjirri
hungry   we:sat
"We were hungry."   (44)

nganyi ngirrinyjila -ngiri
I   hungry   -I:am
"I'm stinking hungry." (speaker's gloss)   (45)

These examples suggest that the contrast may depend on the degree to which the Attribute affects the Carrier. Where the Attribute is conflated with the Process, the Carrier is most affected, and is an Undergoer (see McGregor 1990a:327); in clauses of "being," it is less affected, and merely an Actor/Medium in a state. This also accounts for the inchoative/stative contrast: In processes of change the Carrier is clearly more deeply affected than in continuous states.

4.2.2. Circumstantial

Examples (46) and (47) illustrate the two types of circumstantial Attributive Process—locative and associative—respectively.

mirri   laandi   -wawoondi
sun   high   -it:will:be:getting
"The sun will be getting high."   (46)

marnba   moodoo   -ngarri   -loondi
bum   pimple   -COMIT   -I:got
"I got a pimple on my bum."   (47)

Unlike the intensive subtype, the circumstantial subtype shows very restricted transitivity options: All examples are Intransitive.

4.3. Processes of Action

There is no space in this chapter to give a full account of attribution and identification in other clause types. Accordingly, I will content myself with identifying the major types without going into detailed discussion. First, attribution and identification which is closely tied up in the situation must be distinguished from attribution and identification that is independent of the situation (cf. Halliday 1967/8:62, Nichols 1978:114). It is convenient to refer to the first type as SECONDARY PREDICATION, following Nichols (1978). The second type, by contrast, is characterizable in terms of the syntagmatic relations between the nominal phrases: They form PHRASE COMPLEXES with one another. I will consider the two possibilities in turn.

4.3.1. Secondary predication

Here, the secondary predication and the associated roles are normally optional. They are inherent only in the few clause types that have an Agent that establishes the relationship through his/her actions. As far as I am aware, identification occurs only with the verb goowaj- "call by name," as in (20). There is an inherent Identifier (the name), Identified (the thing named, and Goal), and Agent/Designator, which establishes the naming relationship. Inherent attribution occurs with the verb *yood-* "put," which in this context translates as "make:"

yoodbidi   maja
they:put:him boss
"They made him boss."   (48)

Here there are two inherent participant roles, both of whose realizing expressions are ellipsed, Carrier/Goal and Attributor/Agent; there is also an inherent Attribute, which is not ellipsed.

Elsewhere, secondary predication appears to always be attributive. The Carrier usually conflates with a participant role, Actor or Goal, occasionally with a non-participant Agent (Instrument) or Medium (Range), as in (51) below. As in characterizing and "being" clauses, the Carrier typically precedes the Attribute. Both intensive and circumstantial Attributes occur.

4.3.1.1. Intensive Attributes. Four types may be distinguished, depending on the way in which the Carrier and Attribute are related via the situation (for more detailed discussion and further examples see McGregor 1990a:353–360):

1. *Descriptive*, in which a quality or state is attributed of an entity as it is involved in the situation:

tharra -ngga girranginbini yoowa
dog   -ERG he:ran:me   fear
"The dog chased me frightened."   (49)

boolba -ngarri -nyali mooyoo bagiri
things -COMIT -REP   sleep   he:lies
"He sleeps still dressed."   (50)

2. *Resultative*, where the quality, condition, or state is acquired by the entity as a result of the situation. For example:

thaawoori gajngarni   jabiyabi
beard   I:cut:myself short
"I cut my beard short."   (51)

What distinguishes resultative from descriptive secondary predication is that only the former has agnates in which the attribute is realized by an ALL PP, and agnate biclausal modes of expression in which the attribute appears in a "being" clause. The remaining two types are distinguished on informal grounds, and I am presently unable to cite supporting formal evidence.

3.   *Conditional*, which indicates a condition of the entity when the situation took place. For example:

barngiyirri   maroowa
we:returned murderer
"We returned murderers."   (52)

It is not always easy to distinguish conditional Attributes from descriptive Attributes; the difference lies in the degree of involvement of the Attribute in the situation, which is least for conditional Attributes.

4.   *Capacity*, which indicates the role of the participant as he or she enacts the situation:

ngoolyoongoolyoo -ngga gajlimi
"cutter"   -ERG I:cut:him
"As a circumcisor I cut him."   (53)

4.3.1.2. Circumstantial Attributes.   In situation clauses other than clauses of "being," the only circumstantial Attributes are locational. These ascribe a location to the Medium (typically a Goal) as it is involved in the situation; they do not locate the entire situation. Locational Attributes usually occur in clauses of transfer and holding:

manyi mirra -ya   thirrangga
food   head -LOC she:carries:it:on:her:head
"She carries the food on her head."   (54)

4.3.2. Phrase complexes

These are complex units (Halliday 1961, Huddleston 1965) consisting of phrases, related together (among other possible ways) as Carrier to Attribute, or Identified to Identifier. The relationship is established by the speaker in order to facilitate the interpretation of the utterance and is totally independent of the situation. The two phrases of the complex are either contiguous (juxtaposed), or discontinuous. (For a more detailed discussion of these options, see McGregor forthcoming.)

4.3.2.1. Identification.   There are two types: intensive, and "that is." In the latter, one of the phrases, the second, lists the members of the first. Examples are, respectively:

yaanya gardiya   welfare ngarragi jaliji
other   white:person welfare my   friend

Fitzroy -ngarna bijngarningarra
Fitzroy dweller   he:came:up:to:me
"Another white man, my friend from Welfare in Fitzroy Cross-
ing, came up to me." (55)

garanyi doownga fortyfour twentytwo shotgun yoowarni
rifle   he:got:it forty:four twenty:two shotgun one
garndiwangoorroo
many
"He took rifles: a forty-four callibre, a twenty-two calibre, a shotgun, lots (of rifles)." (56)

It will be noted that intensive identification in situation clauses
does not correspond exactly to intensive identification in identifying
clauses: In the former the Identified entity is frequently indefinite,
whereas it is invariably definite in identifying clauses. Furthermore,
the identifying relation "that is" does not occur in identifying
clauses. These differences are due to the fact that the identification
is secondary in situation clauses.

4.3.2.2. Attribution. Attribution within phrase complexes
seems to be always intensive, as in

gamba joomoo laandi bagiri/ ngarranggarni
water   soak   up   it:lies dreamtime
-nhingi gamba/
-ABL   water
"There was a soak up (from where he was), one with dreamtime
associations." (57)

5. MORE ON THE CONTRAST BETWEEN
RELATIONAL AND SITUATION CLAUSES

In section 4.1 it was argued that there is a grammatical contrast
between verbal attributive "being" clauses and verbless characterizing clauses in Gooniyandi, and that the verbs of stance are not
optional and meaningless place-fillers whose presence is governed
by formal grammatical factors. It would seem to be impossible to
write formal rules based solely on morpho-syntactic factors that correctly predict when to insert a VP into a clause. Where available, the
choice between use and non-use of a verb of stance is meaningful.

I have suggested that the grammatical difference between verbless
and verbal clauses corresponds to a SEMANTIC difference—that between LOGICAL versus EXPERIENTIAL meaning. Relational clauses ex-

press "relationships" between entities, or an entity and a quality, which are imputed by the speaker, or, less commonly, sometimes by a participant in the referent situation. Experiential meaning is carried by the constituent nominal phrases and their roles in the clause, not by the clausal construction itself. Situational clauses refer to real or imaginary situations, which are, in the case of attributive "being" situations, modes of existence of an entity concomitant with its possession of the Attribute. This contrast accounts for the skewing in the distribution of types of attribute in relational versus "being" clauses noted above. (Compare also the skewings found between verbal and verbless existential clauses, which depend on the degree of abstractness of the existent (McGregor 1988:177).) To better illuminate the nature of the contrast, consider these near minimal pairs:

gilbarli   dijbari bagiyi
I:found:it broken it:lay
"I found it (i.e. a knife) broken."   (58)

manyi goolyingi langa yijgawoo
food   I:tasted:it salty   bad
"I tasted the food; it was salty, and no good."   (59)

Although the temporal relation between the condition and the process is parallel for (58) and (59), there is an important difference. In (58) the knife was found in a condition, whereas in (59) the food was tasted and determined to be in a certain condition. The Attribute is clearly one imputed by the speaker (who is also the taster); the food was not tasted in its mode of "being." Consider also the exchange of (38): Speaker A requests a location of the hearer's wife, an association between his wife and a location. Speaker B replies with a verbal situation clause, and not a relational clause; this is presumably because he is not willing to commit himself to an association because he is unsure—he knew that she was at one stage at the pub, but she may have since left (in keeping with this interpretation, note also the choice of tense: past, rather than present). Another example is provided by (40), which occurred in a text describing birds and followed a clause that made reference to the fact that in the past people gave names to the birds. Thus (40) refers to the situation resulting from the action of people in the past (cf. McGregor 1988:177); the speaker is describing a situation, rather than making a logical connection of possession between birds and their names.

To summarize, the speaker may (in many, but not all instances) choose to treat an Attribute as a characteristic of the Carrier, or alternatively as an aspect of its mode of "being." This is a real choice, determined by the way in which the speaker decides to represent the referent reality. In a sense, the choice of a characterizing clause allows a narrator to move out of his or her role of recounting events, and to place his or her own—or by implication, a referent participant's—interpretation or comments on the entities belonging to the referent world. A very similar semantic contrast underlies the opposition between verbal and verbless existential clauses: Verbal existential clauses refer to situations of existence; verbless existential clauses indicate or point to an existent. This should, I hope, clarify the difference in Gooniyandi between logical and experiential meaning. Logical meaning, it must be noted, is not so much concerned with the distinctions of formal logic (which was, of course, not developed in Gooniyandi culture), but with connections made by speakers between things, or between things and qualities.

A similar distinction has been made by Benveniste between "being" and logical relationships (although he does not make it clear whether the verbal notion he refers to is purely existential and appropriate only to existential assertions):

> What matters is to see clearly that there is no connection, either by nature or by necessity, between the verbal notion of 'to exist, to be really there' and the function of the 'copula.' One need not ask how it happens that the verb "to be" can be lacking or omitted. This is to reason in reverse: the real question should be the opposite, how is it that there is a verb "to be" which gives verbal expression and lexical consistency to a logical relationship in an assertive utterance.
>
> (Benveniste 1960/71:163)

Gooniyandi thus makes a natural and important semantic distinction that is confused in languages such as English, which treat logical-type "connections" as processes. This then is the single most important difference between relational clauses in English and Gooniyandi. In English, clause rank logical relations are treated as processes, whereas in Gooniyandi they are treated separately, as relationships. It is tempting to speculate furthermore, in an attempt to answer the question raised by Benveniste, that the move toward verbal representation of logical relationships in English (and perhaps other European languages as well) is an aspect of a more general move toward concretization and objectification, which has been part and parcel of the development of Western thought. What I am suggesting is that the representation of relationships as processes

parallels, and is another manifestation of the move toward representation of processes as entities, which seems to be taking place in
many registers of English, scientific and non-scientific.

Finally, the presence/absence of a VP correlates in an iconic way
with the experiential/logical opposition (cf. McGregor 1988:180–
181). Tense marking would be redundant in clauses that merely
state relationships imputed by the speaker, and likewise redundant
would be the verbally located distinctions of mood (factive and subjunctive in Gooniyandi) and mode (potential, desiderative, and definite), which modify, respectively, the proposition expressed and the
likelihood of occurrence of the situation. Secondly, in relational
clauses there is no one and nothing being or doing anything, nor is
there any action to affect anyone. This refines the observations of
some linguists (see section 1 above) that time is irrelevant to verbless clauses: Time is not irrelevant because or when it is predictable
or given, but rather is irrelevant when a *relationship* is being imputed between things (cf. Kuno & Wongkhomthong 1981:95–6).

6. SUMMARY AND CONCLUSIONS

In this chapter I have given a reasonably full description of Attribution and Identification in Gooniyandi clauses within a systemic-
functional framework. One notable omission has been a discussion
of clefts and pseudo-clefts. This is because in Gooniyandi they are
expressed not in terms of relational clauses (as in English), but in
situation clauses, which involve phrasal discontinuity and fracturing. There is no space in this chapter to discuss this interesting area
of Gooniyandi grammar (but see McGregor 1989, forthcoming).

The description has taken seriously Halliday's dictum of meaning
as choice, which appears in the title of this festschrift. Not only are
functional categories established only when there are clear grammatical reasons for doing so—crucially that there is some "reflex at
the level of form" (Fawcett 1987:178, Martin 1986:46, 1987:18ff)—
but they are also established *whenever* there is a contrast at the level
of form. The latter assumption has enabled us to identify an important functional opposition between verbal and verbless translation
equivalents of English relational clauses, where the overwhelming
majority of linguists implicitly assume the universality of a category
of relational clause (under whatever name they use, formal or functional in orientation) essentially coterminous with the set of English
relational clauses. The partial system network of Figure 10.2 summarizes the functional categories I have established for attribution
and identification in Gooniyandi clauses (note that phrase com-

plexes have not been included, as these are not relevant to the grammar of the clause).

I have two comments to make on this network. Firstly, by comparison with the networks systemicists generally like to draw, the network I have proposed is highly irregular and repetitious. Similar, but not precisely the same, distinctions are made within the various subtypes, and to redraw the network as a consolidated network (Fawcett 1987:159) would involve considerable wiring problems once beyond the second level of delicacy, making the network very hard to interpret. As I have shown, the skewings follow as consequences of the semantic contrasts between the less delicate options, especially the logical/experiential contrast. This raises an important problem (cf. Firth in Palmer 1968:24, 99): How can terms in the different systems be given the same labels when manifestly they belong to quite different paradigmatic sets? My answer is that the terms of different systems may, indeed *must be*, identified if there is no formal difference between them (cf. McGregor 1986b); in other words, if the same realization rule applies to each (Fawcett, personal communication).

Secondly, I have proposed that there is a primary grammatical distinction within the class of clauses that translate English rela-

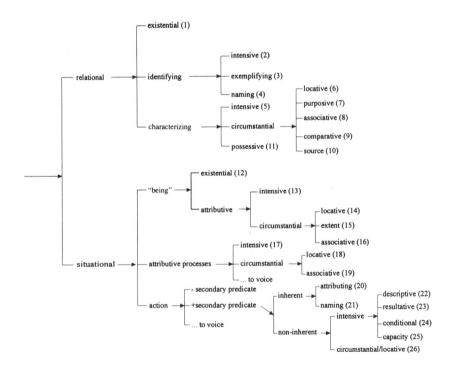

(1) *laandi girili -ya*
up   tree -LOC
garndiwangoorroo jirigi
many   bird
'In the tree are many birds.'

(2) *ngarragi riwi   ngirndaji*
my   country this
'This is my country.'

(3) *yaanya gawi gooloomangarri*
other   fish   catfish
'Another fist is the catfish.'

(4) *nganyi Nyibayarri*
I   [name]
'I am Nyibayarri.'

(5) *nginyji jimandi*
you   good
'You're good?'

(6) *ngoonyi -ya   ngaanggi yamadi*
which -LOC our   vessel
'Where is your car?'

(7) *diwinyi wayandi jard -goo*
tinder fire   light -DAT
Tinder is for lighting fires.'

(8) *nganyi garingi -ngarri*
I   wife   -COMIT
'I have a wife.'

(9) *banganyja   laba*
white:cockatoo white:coctatoo
-jangi -nyali
-SEM -REP
'The white cockatoo of the
banganyja species is just like
the ordinary white cockatoo.'

(10) *nganyi liyarnali -nhingi*
I   from:west -ABL
'I'm from the west.'

(11) *Butcher ngaloowinyi Lanis -joo*
[name] son   [name] -DAT
'Butcher is Lanis' son.'

(12) *girili -ya jirigi waranggiri*
tree -LOC bird it:sits
'There's a bird in the tree.'

(13) *laba   lawagoomarna*
white:cockatoo white
'The white cockatoo is white.'

(14) *ngoorri   -ya   warangji*
that   -LOC he:sat
'He was there.'

(15) *baali danggi   -yirra bagiri*
road Giekie:Gorge -ALL   it:lies
'The road goes to Giekie Gorge.'

(16) *jirigi yingi -ngarri bagiri*
bird name -COMIT it:lies
'The birds have names.'

(17) *nganyi boolgany -goowangiri*
I   old:man -I:am:getting
'I';m getting old.'

(18) *mirri laandi -wawoondi*
sun up   -it:will:be:getting
'The sun will be getting high.'

(19) *marnba moodoo -ngarri -loondi*
bum   pimple   -COMIT -I:got
'I got a pimple on my bum.'

(20) *yoodbidi   maja*
they:put:him boss
'They made him boss.'

(21) *gardiya   -ngga goowajgoorra*
white:person -ERG   they:call:it
Spinifex Yard
Spinifex:Yard
'Whites call it "Spinifex Yard".'

(22) *tharra -ngga girranginbini yoowa*
dog   -ERG he:ran:me   fear
'The dog chased me frightened.'

(23) *goorromba gajgajla boorna*
paper   I:cut:it piece
'I cut the paper to pieces.'

(24) *bijngarni   jimandi*
he:emerged good
'He arrived well.'

(25) *ngoorroo warrgoomgiri stockman*
that   he:works   stockman
'That (man) works as a stockman.'

(26) *gamba galinyjawila bucket -ja*
water I:will:carry:it bucket -LOC
'I'll carry the water in a bucket.'

Figure 10.2. Attribution and identification categories in Gooniyandi

tional clauses between verbless relational and verbal situation clauses. Thus relational clauses form a significantly smaller, though by no means less important, category in Gooniyandi than they do in English. Evidence for this grammatical contrast has already been given. It might be suggested, however, that the verbal/verbless distinction is not primary, and that the network of Figure 10.2 could be redrawn with [relational] encompassing the expected range of subtypes; in this view, the verbal/verbless (or experiential/logical) distinction would be secondary. Can any evidence be adduced for this alternative? One possibility is Fawcett's (1987) suggestion that the presence of the roles Carrier and Attribute in a clause defines English relational clauses. However, whereas a meaning opposition can be associated with the presence/absence of a VP, there is no apparent meaning opposition underlying the presence/absence of an Attribute, consistent across the range of clause types—and Fawcett (1987) does not suggest one for English. The same criticism applies to the criterion of presence of an inherent Attribute and Carrier (cf. Hasan 1972:7). As there seems to be no other grammatical reason to group together the translation equivalents of English relational clauses, my case is adequately justified.

Even within situation clauses I have not attempted to group together types that would translate English relational clauses. Distinctions between clause types have been made depending on the roles with which the Carrier and Attribute are conflated. In "being" clauses the Carrier is conflated with a participant or corresponding inner role (McGregor 1985:215), and in attributive processes, the Attribute is conflated with the Process. I have thus gone further than Halliday (1994:135), who does not identify systematic meaning contrasts between Circumstance as attribute, Circumstance as process, and so forth, but regards them all as subtypes of relational clauses. My reasons are that different subsystems and voice options are involved for the two types, and that there is no apparent meaning constant underlying the two groups.

Systemic linguistics, as is well known, places primacy on paradigmatic relations, regarding syntagmatic relations as secondary and derivative. This means that a complete systemic description of clauses in a given language will be in terms of the possible roles, and combination and conflation of roles. The discussion of this paper calls to question the adequacy of this view (cf. Butler 1985:92–93). For, purely in terms of the roles, their conflations and combinations, it would be impossible to distinguish in any meaningful way between predication of attributes within situation clauses (secondary predication), and phrase complexes. In the former, the Attribute is related to the Carrier through the process; in the latter, it is not.

This needs to be accounted for somewhere within the grammar, perhaps in some sort of dependency notation such as that suggested by Hudson (1976, 1984) Furthermore, there is an obvious connection between phrase complexes and verbless clauses, both functionally (in both the relationships belong to the logical component), and syntactically (the two constituents are juxtaposed), which must be accounted for in syntagmatic terms (McGregor 1990b). This recalls—and suggests qualifications to—Halliday's observation that: "The logical component is distinct from the other three [i.e. experiential, textual and interpersonal (W.McG)] in that all logical meanings, and only logical meanings, are expressed through the structure of 'unit complexes'" (Halliday 1978:130).

REFERENCES

Austin, P. (1981) *A grammar of Diyari, South Australia*. Cambridge, UK: Cambridge University Press.

Benveniste, E. (1960/71) The linguistic functions of 'to be' and 'to have'. In Benveniste, E. (1971) *Problems in general linguistics*. Translated by Meek, M. Coral Gables, Florida: University of Miami Press. 163–179.

Butler, C. (1985) *Systemic linguistics: theory and applications*. London: Batsford.

Dixon, R.M.W. (1972) *The Dyirbal language of North Queensland*. Cambridge, UK: Cambridge University Press.

Dixon, R.M.W. (1977) *A grammar of Yidiny*. Cambridge, UK: Cambridge University Press.

Fawcett, R. (1980) *Cognitive linguistics and social interaction*. Heidelberg, Germany: Groos.

Fawcett, R. (1987) The semantics of clause and verb for relational processes in English. In Halliday, M.A.K. & Fawcett, R. eds., *New developments in systemic linguistics, Volume 1: theory and description*. London: Frances Pinter. 130–183.

Goddard, C. (1985) *A grammar of Yankunytjatjara*. Alice Springs: Institute for Aboriginal Development.

Halliday, M.A.K. (1961) Categories of the theory of grammar. *Word* 17. 241–92.

Halliday, M.A.K. (1967/8) Notes on transitivity and theme in English. Parts 1, 2 & 3. *Journal of Linguistics* 3. 37–81, 199–244, and 4. 179–215.

Halliday, M.A.K. (1970) Language structure and language function. In Lyons, J. ed., *New horizons in linguistics*. Harmondsworth: Penguin. 140–165.

Halliday, M.A.K. (1973) *Explorations in the functions of language*. London: Arnold.

Halliday, M.A.K. (1978) *Language as social semiotic: the social interpretation of language and meaning*. London: Arnold.

Halliday, M.A.K. (1994) *An introduction to functional grammar*. Second edition. London: Arnold.

Hasan, R. (1972) The verb 'be' in Urdu. In Verhaar, J. ed., *The verb 'be' and its synonyms.* Dordrecht, Holland: Reidel. 1–63.

Heath, J. (1984) *Functional grammar of Nunggubuyu.* Canberra, Australia: Australian Institute of Aboriginal Studies.

Huddleston, R. (1965) Rank and depth. *Language* 41. 574–86.

Huddleston, R. (1984) *Introduction to the grammar of English.* Cambridge, UK: Cambridge University Press.

Hudson, R.A. (1976) *Arguments for a non-transformational grammar.* Chicago: The University of Chicago Press.

Hudson, R.A. (1984) *Word grammar.* Oxford, England: Basil Blackwell.

Kuno, S. & Wongkhomthong, P. (1981) Characterizational and identificational sentences in Thai. *Studies in language* 5. 65–109.

Lyons, J. (1968) *Introduction to theoretical linguistics.* Cambridge, UK: Cambridge University Press.

Martin, J. (1986) Transitivity in Tagalog: a functional interpretation of case. Manuscript.

Martin, J. (1987) Meaning of features in systemic linguistics. In Halliday, M.A.K. & Fawcett, R. eds., *New developments in systemic linguistics, Volume 1: theory and description.* London: Frances Pinter. 14–40.

McGregor, W.B. (1985) Body parts in Kuniyanti clause grammar. *Australian Journal of Linguistics* 5. 209–232.

McGregor, W.B. (1986a) Discourse function of intonation in Kuniyanti. *Australian Review of Applied Linguistics* 9. 136–49.

McGregor, W.B. (1986b) Formulating the meaning of closed class items. Unpublished manuscript of paper given to Semantics Workshop, ALS Conference, Adelaide, Australia, August 1986.

McGregor, W.B. (1988) Existential clauses in Gooniyandi: a systemic-functional description. *Papers in Australian linguistics,* No.17. Canberra, Australia: Pacific Linguistics. 167–184.

McGregor, W.B. (1989) Phrase fracturing in Gooniyandi. In Maracz, L. & Muysken, P. (eds), *Configurationality: the typology of asymmetries.* Dordrecht, Holland: Foris. 207–222.

McGregor, W.B. (1990a) *A functional grammar of Gooniyandi.* Amsterdam, Holland: John Benjamins.

McGregor, W.B. (1990b) The metafunctional hypothesis and syntagmatic relations. *Occasional Papers in Systemic Linguistics* 4. 5–50.

McGregor, W.B. (forthcoming.) Discontinuous nominal expressions in Gooniyandi: a functional account. To appear in *Functions of Language.*

Nichols, J. (1978) Secondary predicates. *Berkely Linguistics Society* 4. 114–127.

Palmer, F. (1968) *Selected papers of J.R. Firth, 1952–59.* London: Longman.

Simpson, J. (1983) *Aspects of Warlpiri morphology and syntax.* MIT: PhD thesis.

Tsunoda, T. (1981) *The Djaru language of Kimberley, Western Australia.* Canberra, Australia: Pacific Linguistics.

Part II
Below the Clause

A:
Time and Tense

11

TENSE in English Seen Through Systemic-functional Theory

Christian Matthiessen

Department of Linguistics
University of Sydney

The purpose of this chapter is to locate Halliday's (e.g. 1976, 1985) interpretation of TENSE in the overall interpretation of English and to say something about why it is located where it is.[1] The strategy will be to do this systemically by looking at TENSE through the fundamental dimensions that make up the overall semiotic space of language in context according to systemic-functional theory—in particular, rank, metafunctional diversification, and stratification. The theory enables us to locate any interpretation within a particular metafunction and at a particular rank; and it allows us to look at grammatically as well as semantically, and also paradigmatically as well as syntagmatically. That is: we locate TENSE within the overall system by shunting along its dimensions to find that intersection which provides the most powerful generalizations about the tense system.

---

[1] The chapter is based on a longer version with a more detailed discussion of other interpretations of tense in English and a section on situation specific semantics of English tense. I owe my understanding of how tense is organized to Michael Halliday; this paper would have been impossible without his work. I am greatly indebted to John Bateman for many helpful comments on an earlier version.

Furthermore, we can use the theory to argue about the interpretation because we can look at alternative interpretations in terms of the dimensions of the theory. The theory enables us to say what the interpretation is and it also enables us to say how it might be otherwise: given a particular location along the dimensions of the system, we can explore alternative placements along one or more of the dimensions. Any interpretation cast in terms of systemic-functional theory carries with it the potential for a number of arguments for or against it, although these may remain implicit in any given *presentation* of the interpretation. For example, Halliday interprets TENSE in terms of the logical metafunction, but what properties would it have if it were interpersonal instead? When we say that tense is logical, we have said that it is like other logical resources in certain respects, both systemically and structurally; but we have also said that it is unlike experiential, interpersonal, and textual resources in some equally fundamental ways. My chapter is an attempt to draw attention to, and make explicit, some of the consequences of locating the interpretation of TENSE in the grammar in the way Halliday does. We could write a similar companion paper for any of the areas discussed in his *Introduction to Functional Grammar*.

First, however, I will relate Halliday's interpretation of TENSE to others. Again, I will use systemic-functional theory to do this by looking at the alternative interpretations that have been proposed through the prism of systemic theory.

1. BACKGROUND: PERSPECTIVES ON TENSE

1.1. The Model Embodied in Traditional Grammar

The people in this book **might be going to have lived** *a long, long time from now* in Northern California. (Le Guin, Always Coming home)

The example above falls outside the traditional model of tense that has been applied to English; reflecting this tradition, Chatman (1978: 80) characterized the English tense system as follows:

The English tense system is not particularly rich, but it is capable of indicating without the aid of adverbs at least four temporal stages of events: (1) an earliest, by the past perfect, (2) a subsequent period, by the preterite (or past progressive), (3) a still later period, by the present (or present progressive), and (4) a latest, by the future (or the simple future or present progressive functioning as future. Let us refer to the narrative periods as "anterior time," "past time," "present time," and "future time."

What Chatman commented on is, in fact, not the English tense system but the most common of the **traditional models** of it, which is not particularly rich and certainly not rich enough for an interpretation of tense in English. As the quote from Chatman illustrates, the traditional model is typically coupled with a notion of *linear time*. It is closely associated with the Latin five-tense model of tense, which Lily took over from Donatus and Priscian in the 16th century; he recognized the following tenses (cf. Michael, 1970):

Pluperfect	had loved
Perfect	have loved
Imperfect	loved, did love
Present	love, do love
Future	will/shall love

English tense has changed considerably more than have the versions of Lily's descriptive model of it developed since his time. The traditional model has had a tremendous staying power. We find new theoretical versions of the old, traditional Latinate description. It is, for example, possible to trace it through the work of Reichenbach (1947), who takes it (only expanded by a future perfect) as the traditional model of tense, Hornstein's (1977, 1981) use of Reichenbach's work, and other related work in formal and computational linguistics. We find new theoretical versions of the traditional Latinate description, which illustrates Halliday's (1985: xxxiv) observation about linguistics in this century: "Twentieth century linguistics has produced an abundance of new theories, but it has tended to wrap old descriptions up inside them; what are needed now are new descriptions."

1.2. Breaks with the Traditional Model: Reductions and Expansions

There have, of course, been a number of breaks with the Latin interpretation of tense in English. I will mention two types; one is a reduction of the Latinate five-tense model and the other is an expansion. The two positions and the examples of proponents mentioned here are shown in Figure 11.1.

The critical dimension for locating the interpretation of the tense system is thus the rank scale. We can think of the two positions as

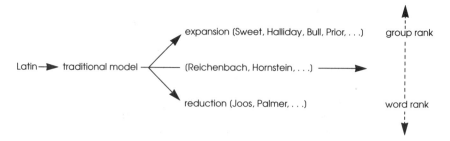

Figure 11.1. The traditional model and two later alternatives.

drawing different conclusions from the traditional model of tense. These different conclusions are reasonable if we think of the traditional model as being a description borrowed from Latin that does not follow from the application of the method of traditional grammar to English: traditional grammar developed as a word-based grammar and syntax grew out of the attempt to explain different word forms. There is a built-in tension between method and descriptive model. The reductionist approach seizes upon the word-based *method* of traditional grammar (and of certain modern structural approaches) and revises the interpretation of tense so that it is based on the structure of the verb. The expansionist position does not follow the word-based method of traditional grammar but instead it focuses on the *descriptive model* taken over from Latin, i.e. the list of tenses we find in the traditional model, which is based on the verbal group (at least implicitly), and recognizes that this traditional description has to be expanded to fit modern English. I will review the two positions briefly.[2]

1.2.1. Reduced model of tense

The reductionist position is based on a morphological interpretation of tense as a word rank system. Although this is a break with the Latinate model, it is not a break with the method of traditional grammar: it represents a continuation of the traditional word-based approach. Priestley (1768) argued against a future tense in particu-

---

[2]There is, of course, an extensive body of work on tense, including work within formal linguistics on the structure of semantic interpretations and models of time and events, work within computational linguistics on the modelling of temporal organization, work on tense in a typological perspective (e.g. by Comrie, 1985, and Dahl, 1985,) and work within functional linguistics on tense and discourse. It is impossible to review this work or do justice to it within the space of the present discussion.

lar; he put the case against it in the following way (quoted in Michael, 1970: 405):

The only natural rule for the use of technical terms to express time, &c. is to apply them to distinguish the different modifications of words; . . . A little reflection may, I think, suffice to convince any person, that we have no more business with a *future tense* in our language, than we do with the whole system of Latin moods and tenses; because we have no modification of our verbs to correspond with it.

At the same time, Priestley recognized compound forms such as *shall have been loving*, a kind of compound present tense. Modern writers tend to opt for the reduction and introduce aspect and/or phase as alternatives to tense. Modern versions of the reduction of the traditional model are exemplified by Joos (1964: e.g. 120) and Palmer (1974): the interpretation is morphologically grounded— tense is analyzed at word rank, which means that the three-term system past/present/future is reduced to the two-term system past/present because there is a past suffix but no future suffix; and the perfect and pluperfect tenses are reinterpreted as combinations of tense and phase, while the "compound" tenses with *be -ing* are analyzed as combinations of tense and aspect.

1.2.2. Expanded model of tense

The expansionist approach breaks with the traditional model to account for examples that fall outside this model. For example, the notions of compound tenses and the distinction between primary and secondary tenses have been used; we find them both in Sweet (1900). More recently, we find the expansionist position proposed both in logic and in linguistics.

In logic, Prior's work on temporal logic is—by implication—an expansion of the traditional model of English tense. Indeed, Prior (1967) clearly recognized and demonstrated that Reichenbach's (1947) formalization and revision of the traditional model was insufficient for English. It is interesting that Prior's insight has not been reflected in Hornstein's (1977, 1981) adaptation of Reichenbach.

In linguistics, Halliday's (1976, 1985) interpretation proposed within the general framework of a systemic-functional approach to language can be seen as a systematic generalization of the expansion of the traditional model.[3] It is systematic both in the internal

---

[3]Halliday first sorted out the English tense system in the 1950s in collaborative work with Jeffrey Ellis on tense and aspect systems in different languages.

analysis of the system of tense and in the way in which he showed how the tense system and the structures through which selections from it are realized manifest general principles we find in the grammar of English. This gives us the basis for exploring and evaluating TENSE in relation to other systems such as MODALITY and ASPECT in aspect languages. He locates TENSE at the rank of *group* rather than the lower rank of *word* thus bringing into focus not only forms of single verbs but *chains* of verbs;[4] and he locates it within the *logical* mode of the ideational metafunction thus allowing him to build a *serial* mode of tense to replace the traditional linear one. Outside systemic-functional linguistics, Bull's (1963) work on tense also represents a clear break with the traditional model. He also arrives at an interpretation of tense that allows for series of temporal re-orientations rather than linear arrangements relative to a single temporal anchor.

Halliday's description of tense is, I think, one of his many significant contributions to a fresh understanding of how English grammar works. It is important to emphasize that he developed the account to cope not only with written English but also with casual, unself-conscious spoken English, where the need for a re-evaluation of the account of English tense becomes very clear (cf. Halliday, 1979b, 1992). Very little of the discussion of tense seems to take account of this expansion of the database of tense. In teaching Halliday's interpretation of English tense, I've often found that the image students have of tense is one oriented toward writing (as was traditional grammar, of course); and they are often surprised at the complexity of examples taken from speech or corpora of spoken English. Examples of such complexity are less likely to turn up in written English, elicited examples, or in consciously constructed examples. Detailed accounts of Halliday's interpretation of English tense are available in Halliday (1976) and Halliday (1985). I will only give a brief summary here—enough to contrast it with the traditional model and to allow us to examine it from the various vantage point offered by systemic-functional theory.

1.3. Halliday's Interpretation

Halliday interprets tense at group rank rather than word rank. Consequently, it is not restricted to the alternation *does : did*, but

---

4It is a general property of functional interpretations that systems that have traditionally been approached from word-rank where their reactances may be most overt and thus exposed to analysis have had to be "up-ranked": this has happened with both VOICE and TRANSITIVITY, for example.

can take into account sequences such as *will do, is doing, have done, will have done, will be going to do, will be going to be doing, will be doing to have been doing,* and so on. That is, interpreting tense at group rank rather than word rank makes it possible to expand the traditional model. (As we will see in Section 2, the principle behind the organization of these sequences is the logical metafunction.) It makes it possible to interpret TENSE as a resource for construing a temporal series between the interpersonal "now" of speaking and the time of the occurrence of the process as a temporal event. The interpretation is based on two basic principles:

1. The tense system is 'past/present/future'; and
2. it is systemically recursive: repeated selections can be made from the same system. We can call this a **serial model** of tense.

The TENSE grammar based on these two systems is shown in Figure 11.2 (where X and Y are successive pairs of hypotactically related functions: α β; β γ, . . .). In this fragment of the verbal group system network, there are two simultaneous systems to the left, FINITENESS ('finite/nonfinite') and TENSE RECURSION ('secondary/no secondary'). Let's focus on the case when the feature 'finite' in the FINITENESS system holds and consider 'temporal' within the DEICTICITY system ('temporal/modal').[5] The feature 'temporal' leads to the system TENSE TYPE ('past/present/future').

The system TENSE TYPE ('past/present/future') can be reached either from the selection of 'temporal' in DEICTICITY (number (i) in Figure 11.2) or from the selection of 'secondary tense' in the system of TENSE RECURSION (numbered (ii) in Figure 11.2). When it is reached from 'temporal', it gives us the opposition 'past/present/future" for primary tense and when it is reached from 'secondary tense', it gives us the same opposition for secondary tense. The system TENSE TYPE can thus be instantiated as one or more system tokens by means of the selection of higher order tense, 'secondary tense,' from the system TENSE RECURSION. Each time we decide to loop back by selecting a higher order tense, we instantiate a new token of the same system type. The first time we select in the TENSE RECURSION system, the higher order tense is second order (secondary in an instantial sense), the second time, it is third order (tertiary), and so on. In this description, there is thus an agnation between

---

[5]The full paradigm that includes nonfinite as well as modal finite is presented in Halliday (1976, 1985). I will return to the option 'modal' in Section 4.1.

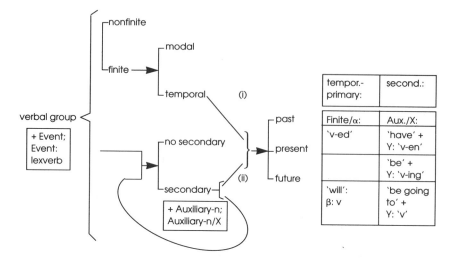

Figure 11.2.   Logical TENSE potential.

primary and secondary tenses based on logical ordering. (For further discussion of the issues involved in the interpretation of such logical systems, see Bateman (1989) and Matthiessen & Bateman (1991).)

The first time we choose tense, we choose primary tense and get the traditional alternation:

Table 11.1

primary tense	
past	walked: did walk
present	walk(s); do(es) walk
future	will walk

The point of Halliday's model is that English tense allows us to expand the first choice; it allows us to choose again: in addition to the primary tense selection, we can make a secondary one, realized by one of the auxiliaries *have -en* (past), *be -ing* (present), and *be going to* (future; also *be about to*). If the primary tense selection is past, one of the options is not to have a secondary tense, which results in the simple past; but we can also choose to have a secondary tense, in which case it may be past, present, or future:

Table 11.2

primary tense	secondary tense	
past	—	walked; did walk
	past	had walked
	present	was walking
	future	was going to walk

Halliday's further point is that we can now choose again, and again, and again: the secondary tense selection is systemically recursive. Here is a paradigm for primary past, with two repetitions of secondary selections, called secondary and tertiary for convenience.[6]

The most convenient way of naming these tense selections is to start with the last selection and work toward the first (e.g., Halliday, 1985: 177). This indicates the systemic environment in which a given tense selection has been made; for example, (primary:) past, (secondary:) future—*was going to walk*—is called future-in-past; and (primary:) past, (secondary:) future, (tertiary:) past—*was going to have walked*—is called past-in-future-in-present.

Halliday (e.g., 1985: 179) identifies three "stop rules" that prevent certain complex tenses; combinations prevented by the stop rules appear in shaded cells in the table on p. 447. If the secondary tense selection is "present," additional selections are unlikely, hence the absence of tertiary tenses in the table. (It is possible to go beyond the limits the stop rules set; for example, although two secondary futures can in principle be ruled out, there are two secondary futures in the following example from casual conversation: *Are you going to be definitely going to be in Australia for six more months?*)

2. GRAMMATICAL PERSPECTIVES ON TENSE

I have just sketched Halliday's interpretation of TENSE in English against the background of other approaches, and we can now view the system against the background of the overall system of English. That is, we can examine its location along the various dimensions that construe the overall semiotic space of language in context.

---

[6]That is, I use the term *secondary* both for the term in the general recursively enterable TENSE RECURSION system and for the first instantiation of that term in this system. The meaning intended will always be clear from context.

primary	secondary			tertiary		example
past	no secondary					walked
	secondary	past		no tertiary		had walked
				tertiary	past	had had walked
					present	had been walking
					future	had been going to walk
		present		no tertiary		was walking
		future		no tertiary		was going to walk
				tertiary	past	was going to have walked
					present	was going to be walking
					future	was going to be going to walk

Figure 11.3.   Sample paradigm of tense selections.

TENSE is placed globally in terms of stratification and metafunctional diversification and locally, within the lexicogrammatical stratum, in terms of rank in Figure 11.4. Locally we can also place it in terms of delicacy.

1. **Stratification:** Stratally, TENSE is a content system; and, within content, it is a lexicogrammatical system. Since the two content systems, [discourse] semantics and lexicogrammar, are related in a natural rather than arbitrary or conventional way (e.g., Halliday, 1985), the organization of TENSE is semantically motivated: In particular, the system of tense construes serial time as will be illustrated below in Section 3.

2. **Metafunctional diversification:** Metafunctionally, TENSE is an ideational system—a system for construing our experience of time; within the ideational metafunction, it is, more specifically, logical rather than experiential. This means that it is a recursive system and that selections are by realized means of verbs organized into interdependency structures.

3. **Rank:** In terms of the rank scale, TENSE is a group system rather than a clause or word system; more specifically, it is a verbal group system. This means that its environment "above" at clause rank includes centrally PROCESS TYPE

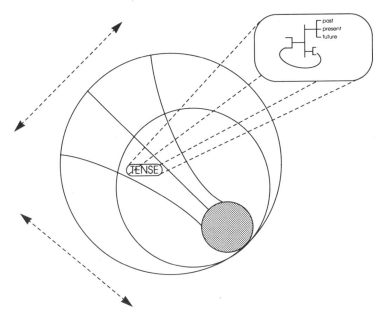

Figure 11.4. TENSE located within language in context.

and that its realizational domain "below" is not just a single verb but groups of verbs.

4. **Delicacy:** In terms of delicacy, TENSE is a grammatical system rather than a lexical one: it is a grammaticalization of temporal relations. This means, among other things, that it is realized through auxiliaries and that these verbs are much more generalized than their lexical homonyms *go, have.*

The interpretation of TENSE as an ideational system has important implications for variation according to contextual variables. In particular, it means that registerial variation will correlate with different field values in the first instance. For instance, we can expect both probabilistic differences in the tense system and attendant differences in the semantics of tense depending on whether the social activity of the field involves predicting events not yet experienced, fictionalizing recalled experience or generalizing particularized experience. In addition, since TENSE is interpreted as logical within the ideational, it is possible that it will be sensitive to the mode distinction between writing and speaking, in some way similar to complexing. The contextual implications are, then, significantly different from those of a system such as MODALITY, located within the interpersonal.

Although I have not tried to show this in Figure 11.4, TENSE is also located with respect to the three types of semiotic histories, semohistories, identified in Halliday (1989): phylogenesis, ontogenesis, and logogenesis. For instance, it is important to see TENSE as an evolving system in the history of the system—one that has to be interpreted in a different way from a few hundred years ago; and it is important to explore the development of instantial tense systems as texts unfold. These dimensions will be taken up again in Section 6, with particular focus on the contrast between three-term and two-term interpretations of the English (primary) tense system.

TENSE, like any linguistic system, is thus located somewhere along the various dimensions that construe the general system: it is an elaboration of the system at the intersection of these dimensions. It has properties that are specific to this systemic elaboration; but it also has a number of general properties it "inherits" from its systemic location. In what follows I will begin by focussing on TENSE within the grammatical system, and I will explore its location at the intersection of group rank and the logical metafunction in the first instance.

2.1. Tense within the Grammar of English

Let's focus on the lexicogrammatical stratum in Figure 11.4 and view it according to rank and metafunction. We can thus locate TENSE within the grammar of English by means of Halliday's function-rank matrix (cf. for example, Halliday, 1970; Matthiessen, 1995: Ch. 2). TENSE is an ideational functional region; more specifically, it's a logical one. It is a group region—more specifically a verbal group region. The TENSE cell in the function-rank map of the grammar is thus located by "logical" and "verbal group" as in Figure 11.5. It appears in boldface; the other systems that constitute its immediate or more distant systemic neighborhood will be discussed later.

The table in Figure 11.5 enables us to relate TENSE to various neighbors in the grammatical system, and this throws additional light on alternative interpretations of TENSE: If we shunted our interpretation of TENSE along one of the dimensions, it would mean that it was more like some other systems and less like others. If we stay within the logical subtype of the ideational metafunction, but shift from the simple verbal group to (hypotactic) verbal group complexes, we find various systems with temporal implications—in particular projection, temporal phase and temporal modulation (e.g., *plan to do, begin to do, begin by doing*); and these systems are, in turn, related to clause complexes. If we stay within the verbal group,

	ideational			interpersonal	textual
	logical		experiential		
clause		PROJECTION		CIRCUMSTANCE: location, extent, frequency	MODALITY	CONJUNCTION: textual sequence, simultaneity
group — nominal | verbal — complexes (all ranks)		PHASE etc.	**TENSE**		MODALITY	
word						

Figure 11.5.   The location of TENSE in the grammatical interpretation.

but shift to the interpersonal metafunction, we find the interpersonal neighbor of TENSE, namely, MODALITY (e.g., *can/ will/ must do*). If we shift to clause rank and the experiential subtype of the ideational metafunction, we find circumstantial resources for specifying temporal location, extent and frequency (e.g., *do on Monday, for many hours, every Tuesday*). At clause rank, we can move to the interpersonal metafunction and consider modality but, within COMMENT, interpersonal assessments of time (e.g., *still, already, yet*). And we can move to the textual metafunction, where we find the resources of conjunction (e.g., *later, meanwhile*).

Such an exploration of the system as a whole thus also shows how time and temporal relations are dispersed in the grammatical system according to the metafunctions: construed ideationally within TENSE and circumstantial TRANSITIVITY (location, extent, frequency), enacted interpersonally within COMMENT and MODALITY (usuality), and presented discoursally within CONJUNCTION (temporal conjunction). The comprehensive exploration also embodies the important principle that any alternative interpretation that rejects part of the tense system—for instance, future *will, be going to*—has to locate these rejected parts somewhere, within some other system.

2.2. Halliday's Interpretation within the Set of Alternative Ones

We have seen that the function-rank matrix locates TENSE in the overall interpretation of English. It also allows us to explore alternative interpretations by locating them in relation to Halliday's interpretation. I will focus on the family of reductionist interpretations of

		ideational		interpersonal	textual
		logical	experiential		
clause	complexes	PROJECTION	CIRCUMSTANCE: location, extent, frequency	MODALITY	CONJUNCTION: textual sequence, simultaneity
group (verbal)	complexes	PHASE etc.	[TENSE]	MODALITY	
word (nominal)			TENSE / PHASE / ASPECT → [MODALITY]		

Figure 11.6.   Halliday's interpretation of TENSE and the reductionist position.

TENSE (see section 1.2.1 above) because it contrasts fundamentally with Halliday's expansionist approach. The relationship between the two approaches is set out in the function-rank matrix in Figure 11.6.

The reductionist position can be characterized in relation to Halliday's by the following shifts. If we shift from "logical" to "experiential" and from group rank to word rank, we get a multivariate model of specific components—tense, phase, and aspect—rather than a univariate model of one generalized tense resource. If we stay at word rank but shift to the interpersonal metafunction, we get an interpretation of all or part of primary tense as a modality.[7] The two word-based interpretations are likely to co-occur. The different interpretations are diagrammed in Figure 11.7 for *will have been walking* (+ means future, − means past, and 0 means present).

2.3. Alternative Interpretations and Other Systems in the Grammar

The basis for the reductionist interpretation of TENSE is the view from word rank rather than group rank: if we look at the verb from word rank, primary tense future as well as secondary tenses tend to fall outside the reduced notion of tense as the opposition between

---

[7]The various alternative proposals that take all or part of primary tense to be a modality or secondary tense to be a phase or an aspect do not, of course, make the metafunctional assignments I have suggested. However, if we interpret English in functional terms, these assignments are the metafunctional consequences. The proposal that tense is a modality is often based on a philosophical foundation and a philosophical conception of modality; but when we look at modality from a functional perspective, we find that it is an interpersonal resource and that tense as a modality would thus also be interpersonal (cf. Section 4 below).

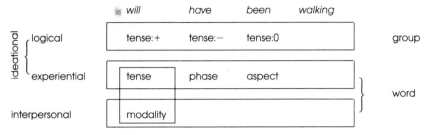

Figure 11.7. Alternative Interpretations of tense.

past and present (non-past) because primary future and secondary tenses do not operate in the verb system where the past suffix *-ed* contrasts with the absence of a suffix or with *-(e)s* (as in *work-ed* : *work-(s)*). Once the different rank bases of the interpretations have been established, it is the notion of metafunction that will help us characterize the differences between the interpretations: the reductionist position implies that tense is experiential and/or interpersonal. Metafunction will help us see the alternative interpretations in the light of the different systems in the grammar, thus bringing together the perspectives of Sections 2.1 and 2.2. In particular:

1. if TENSE were an experiential resource together with PHASE and ASPECT, it would be like temporal CIRCUM-STANCE in the experiential clause grammar; and
2. If TENSE or part of it were a modality, it would be an interpersonal resource in the grammar of English.

These two implications will be discussed in Sections 3 and 4. There are no alternative interpretations of TENSE that take it to be a textual resource, but we can still ask how it relates to temporal conjunction within the grammar (Section 5). I will now follow the table in Figure 11.5 from left to right: ideational (Section 3), interpersonal (Section 4), and textual (Section 5). Finally, I will review the primary tense system and the status of *will* as a realization of primary future taking a variety of dimensions into consideration.

3. TENSE AND METAFUNCTION: IDEATIONAL

As we have seen, Halliday interprets TENSE as an ideational resource. It follows from this that is a resource for *construing* time. This observation may seem self-evident, but it is important to keep in mind that it contrasts with two alternative metafunctional interpretations. We could interpret TENSE as an interpersonal resource or as a textual resource—either as an enactment of time forming part of the speaker's interaction with the listener (as modality is) or as a strategy for presenting messages (as conjunction, including temporal conjunction, is). I will return to these two metafunctions in Sections 4 and 5, but I will elaborate the ideational interpretation of TENSE first. I will explore what the consequences of locating TENSE in our interpretation of English in the logical part of grammar rather than the experiential one.

3.1. Two Ideational Models: Logical versus Experiential

As an ideational resource, TENSE could in principle be organized either experientially or logically, because the experiential and logical metafunctions are subtypes of the ideational one. The two alternative interpretations lead to different predictions about TENSE; a logical interpretation will predict *serial tense* as a representation of *serial time*, whereas an experiential interpretation will predict a non-serial model of component parts such as tense, phase, and aspect.[8] I will compare the two ideational models, and I will identify some of the advantages with the logical interpretation. The first two are grammar-internal considerations; the third is a semantic one:

1. **From a paradigmatic point of view:** The logical interpretation predicts that the tense system is systemically recursive (the logical mode of paradigmatic organization), whereas the experiential interpretation does not reflect this serial principle underlying tense (Section 3.1.1).

2. **From a syntagmatic point of view:** The logical interpretation predicts that tense is organized as a univariate interdependency structure (the logical mode of syntagmatic organization)—realized as a sequence of verb forms, each dependent in form on the preceding choice. In contrast, the experiential interpretation wrongly predicts constituents in a multivariate configuration, for example, Tense + Phase + Aspect (Section 3.1.2).

3. **From a semantic point of view:** The logical interpretation predicts that tense represents some kind of serial time,

---

[8]The choice between a serial tense model and a model that is based on tense, phase, and aspect depends on whether we interpret the verbal group at group rank or from below, at word rank (cf. Figure 11.6). Looked at from word rank, primary and secondary tense look different. Looked at from group rank, they can be seen to be links in the same tense series.

whereas the experiential interpretation wrongly predicts componential time of the kind we find represented in the temporal circumstances of the clause (Time + Duration + Frequency) (Section 3.1.3).

3.1.1. The TENSE system: a recursive logical system

The systemic potential of tense must be recursive in a logical interpretation; there must be a loop in the network, allowing for repeated tense selections from the same type of options. In other words, we would predict a serial model of tense with iterative series of tense selections. This is the model described in Section 1.3 above: the logical system of TENSE RECURSION in Figure 11.2 allows for repeated selections.

The logical interpretation thus brings out the recursive principle behind tense in English. It predicts that a primary tense selection may be followed by a secondary one, which may be followed by a repeated secondary one, and so on. See Table 11.3.

In contrast, if TENSE was experiential, its systemic potential would not be recursive as the logical system of Figure 11.2, but it would be "multivariate": each system would have a unique set of features, differentiating systems as different types. Interpretations that distinguish between tense and aspect (perfect and progressive) or tense, phase (perfect), and aspect (progressive) illustrate the experiential differentiation of system types. For example, there could be three simultaneous systems, as in Figure 11.8.

While the logical interpretation brings out the recursive principle behind tense, experiential interpretations assume a fixed number of components, which is a problem. The usual experiential description of TENSE, PHASE, and ASPECT (or, TENSE, PERFECT, and PROGRESSIVE) fails to include examples such as *will have been going to be working* or *will have been going to have been working*. Thus, although there is a corresponding experiential descrip-

Table 11.3

future	**will** work
past-in-future	will **have** worked
future-in-past-in-future	will have **been going** to work
past-in-future-in-past-in-future	will have been going to **have** work**ed**
present-in-past-in-future-in-past-in-future	will have been going to have **been** work**ing**

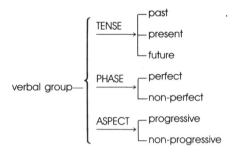

Figure 11.8. Experiential tense potential.

tion of the logical analysis of the first example in Figure 11.9, there is no experiential provision for the tertiary (third-order) future in the second example nor for the tertiary future and the quartenary past in the third example.

It is obviously possible to add an experiential system and a multi-variate function to deal with examples such as the one discussed above. However, such an approach would entirely miss the point, which is that tense is recursive, and we cannot predict a fixed number of experiential categories. Consider, for example, *will have been going to have been working, will be going to have been working,* and *is going to have been working.* That is, the logical interpretation brings out the systemic implications of the implicate order embodied in the tense system of English, whereas the experiential interpretation can only capture the explicate order made manifest in traditional examples of tense (cf. Butt, 1987, on different kinds of order).

Another problem is that the experiential systems in Figure 11.8 are simultaneous and thus unordered in relation to one another, just as, for example, the circumstantial systems of TIME (temporal location), DURATION (temporal extent), and FREQUENCY are in the

primary future	secondary past	tertiary future	quarternary past	quinary present	will have been going to have been doing
future tense	*perfect phase*	?	?	*progressive aspect*	

Figure 11.9. Problem with experiential analysis (in italics) relative to logical one.

primary future	secondary past	tertiary present			will have been doing
future tense	perfect phase	progressive aspect			
primary future	secondary past	tertiary future	quartenary present		will have been going to be doing
future tense	perfect phase	?	progressive aspect		

Figure 11.9. *(Continued)*

clause grammar. In contrast, the logical system tokens that instantiate the system type in Figure 11.2 are ordered with respect to one another. We will see that this ordering is important both for tense structure and for tense semantics.

3.1.2. TENSE structure: a logical interdependency structure

Since tense is a logical resource, the structure generated must be of the logical kind (i.e., it must be a univariate inter-dependency chain (series)), which is linearly recursive (Halliday, 1965, 1979a).[9] For example, the sequence *will have been working* has the following structural interpretation: α (*will*) → β (*have*) → γ (*been*) → δ (*working*).

Halliday's logical interpretation of tense explains two structural facts without any problems: both dependency in verbal forms and the sequence of auxiliaries reflect the logical ordering iconically. In the example *will have been going to be working* the form of each dependent verb is determined by the verb on which it is dependent. Thus, *will* is followed by the base form *have*; *have* is followed by the v-en form of *be*; *be going to* is followed by the base form *be*; and *be* is followed by the v-ing form of *work*. The form dependencies are diagrammed in Figure 11.10.

In a similar way, the sequence of verbs reflects the logical ordering

---

[9]That is, as a logical resource, TENSE must be organized according to the same general principles as complexes of various units, such as clause complexes, nominal group complexes, and verbal group complexes; and also according to the same general principles, such as modification in the nominal group. Logical tense structure is hypotactic rather than paratactic, which is true of group structures in general.

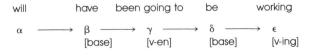

Figure 11.10. Form dependency and sequence.

of tense choices: α: primary (*will*—) ^ β: secondary (*have -en*) ^ γ: tertiary (*be going to*—) ^ δ: quartenary (*be -ing*) ^ ε: event (*work*). In the experiential interpretation, the structure generated would not be an interdependency structure, but rather a multivariate constituency structure, where each constituent has a unique value type.[10] Experiential interpretations posit a fixed number of multivariate constituents: each auxiliary would be a unique part of the whole group. We can state the maximal structure generated by the experiential potential as follows: Tense ^ Phase ^ Aspect ^ Event, as in Tense (*will*) Phase (*have*) Aspect (*been*) Event (*writing*). There are thus logical tense structures for which the experiential model has no equivalents (cf. Figure 11.10 above), as shown in Figure 11.11.

An experiential interpretation of tense leaves the two facts explained in terms of the logical structure above unexplained: (i) the dependency of verbal forms in the verbal group structure; and (ii) the sequence of functions in the group. For instance, in the structure Tense + Phase + Aspect, why should the form of the auxiliary realizing Aspect depend on the previous auxiliary? And why is the sequence Tense ^ Phase ^ Aspect and not Aspect ^ Tense ^ Phase or any other sequence?

3.1.3. At the semantic stratum: serial time

We have seen that the two ideational modes of representation, the logical and the experiential subtypes, differ significantly as models of tense within the grammar. We find the same kind of differences at the semantic stratum: the logical and experiential subtypes of the ideational metafunction "semanticize" our experience of reality in different ways and interpretations cast in terms of them yield different conceptions of time. The logical interpretation of tense in the grammar correctly predicts a serial logico-semantic organization of time: a verbal parallel to the nominal logic of classification in the

---

[10]That is, as an experiential resource, TENSE would display the kind of organization we find in TRANSITIVITY in the clause (e.g., Process + Actor + Goal + Time + Duration). See Section 3.2.2 below.

will	have	been going to	be	working

α ⟶	β ⟶	γ ⟶	δ ⟶	ε
	[base]	[v-en]	[base]	[v-ing]

Tense	Phase	?	Aspect	Event

Figure 11.11.   TENSE and the two modes of ideational structure.

nominal group. In contrast, the experiential interpretation would predict an experiential organization of time where Tense, Phase, and Aspect make unique and independent semantic contributions.

The logical interpretation of TENSE has the advantage that it allows us to capture the fact that tense represents serial time (i.e., chains of temporal relations betweens pairs of times). Each tense selection corresponds to a temporal link in such a chain. Primary tense simply represents the first link in a chain that may consist of more links. The logical interpretation constitutes the generalization and revision of Reichenbach's (1947) tense model needed to take account of examples that fall outside his account, such as *will have been going to tell, had been going to be writing, will have been going to be working,* and so on. Thus, if we want to express the following temporal relations: $t_0 < t_1 > t_2 < t_3$, the English tense resources will readily handle this task (see Figure 11.12).

In the example above, we have three reference times. The primary one is the time of speaking (t_0). Secondary tense gives us the second-

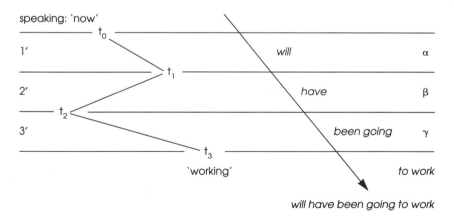

Figure 11.12.   Serial time expressed by serial tense.

ary reference time (t_1), and the next tense selection gives us the tertiary reference time (t_2):

primary reference time	secondary reference time	tertiary reference time	. . .
t_0	t_1	t_2	t_3

TENSE thus construes a path or chain between the interpersonally enacted time of speaking—'now' in the dialogic center of the interpersonal universe—and the ideationally construed time of the occurrence of the Event. The motivation for higher-order reference times is very clear in examples such as the following (each new tense selection is made in the environment of the previous one):

- **present-in-past-in-present**

A: So when is this thing scheduled to produce results, Frank?
B: Oh, it'**s been producing** results for a long time

(Svartvik & Quirk, 1980, 482)

- **present-in-future-in-present**

Yes, but he couldn't arrange for possible timetabling because the timetables of these students is not worked out until well into the term, until they know what they're doing, you see. They never know in the long vac or in the summer what they **are going to be doing** the next year.

(Svartvik & Quirk, 1980, 839)

- **present-in-past-in-past**

when I'**d been teaching** apprentices at Vauxhall I could have gone straight there but I just couldn't get there

(Svartvik & Quirk, 1980, 511)

- **future-in-past**

and she **was going to lend** me this thing but perhaps she's forgotten that I asked her

(Svartvik & Quirk, 1980, 801)

The secondary present typically construes a relation of simultaneity between the current reference time and the time of the occurrence of the event, usually involving time inclusion (cf. Matthiessen, 1984). This usually has the effect of narrowing the temporal focus from the unbounded one of the simple present: *he's watching the evening news: he watches the evening news; the ice is melting in the sun: ice melts in the sun*). With process types other than material, the narrowing may mean focusing on the beginning phase of the occurrence of the event rather than the whole event (as in Halliday's, 1985: 109, example: *I feel I'm knowing the city for the first time—* 'getting to know').

The problem for the experiential interpretation of tense is that it does not predict that the resources of tense represent serial time. Rather, experiential interpretations posit independent semantic components: for instance, time deixis (past vs. non-past; past vs. present vs. future; and so on), completion (completed vs. non-completed; or completive vs. non-completive), and continuity (continuous vs. non-continuous, imperfective vs. non-imperfective, and so on). Thus an experiential interpretation fails to capture the seriality of time chains such as the one diagrammed above in Figure 11.12.

To conclude the comparison, we have, then, two broadly different types of TENSE interpretation, logical interpretations and experiential ones. As should be clear from the preceding presentation, it makes a significant difference in the interpretation of TENSE where we locate it in the metafunctional space. The two alternative ideational interpretations of TENSE are summarized in the table in Figure 11.13.

(i) system	(ii) structure	(iii) meaning
logical	$\alpha \longrightarrow \beta \longrightarrow \gamma \longrightarrow \delta$ *will have been writing*	serial time
experiential		Tense	Perfect	Progressive	Event | *will have been writing*	time deixis completion continuity

Figure 11.13. Experiential and logical interpretations contrasted.

3.2. Beyond TENSE

Having seen how the two types of ideational interpretations of TENSE, the logical and the experiential models, differ, we can now look beyond TENSE. First, I will touch on logical parallels to TENSE in verbal group complexes: the logical interpretation of TENSE in the simple verbal group relates it to systems within the logical component in complex verbal groups. Then, I will turn to the experiential complement to the "logic" of time embodied in tense—circumstances of time in the clause.

3.2.1. Logical parallels

An important argument in favor of Halliday's interpretation of tense in terms of the logical organization of the verbal group is that it shows how tense is related in various ways to logically organized hypotactic complexes of verbal groups (such as *begin to work, want to work, seem to work*) and also of clauses (such as *he said that he made a mistake*) *within the same logical metafunction*. In contrast, an experiential interpretation would not bring out the parallels.[11] I will look briefly at (i) verbal group complexes and (ii) projecting clause complexes.

3.2.1.1. TENSE in the verbal group and verbal group complex systems. Halliday's (1985: 255–269) interpretation shows that various tenses have logical "neighbours" in hypotactic complexes of verbal groups—see Figure 11.5 above; and it also shows how they can be derived from verbal group complexes by simplification from verbal group complex to verbal group. The general principle is, I think, that the simple verbal group can be related to the complex one as a "simplified" replay. Thus, TENSE in the simple verbal group relates to expansions and projections in complexes, which express a number of meanings over and above temporal relationships embodied in 'past/present/future'. For example, the projecting hypotactic verbal group complex *want → to work* can be related to the simplex *will → work*.[12] The former is a combination of two groups related

---

[11]The observation about the unit of logical resources in the grammar can also be contrasted with Hornstein's (1977, 1981) isolation of purported universal time structures, without any attempt to identify the general principles of organization within the logical metafunction.

[12]See, for instance, examples of expanding verbal group complexes and tenses in the simple verbal group: *try to do/succeed in dong* (extending verbal group complex)—*have done* (secondary past) and *keep doing* (elaborating verbal group complex)—*be doing* (secondary present).

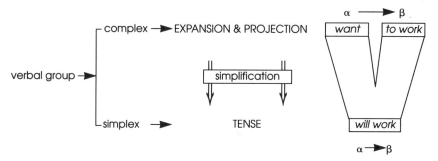

Figure 11.14a.   Complex verbal group and tense in simplex.

		α	β	TENSE	COMPLEX
expansion	elaboration	be	doing	present	*keep doing*
	extension	have	done	past	*try to do, succeed in doing*
projection		be going to	do	future	*intend to do*
		will	do	future	*want to do*

Figure 11.14b.   TENSE and related systems in verbal group hypotactic complexing.

through projection, *want* and *work*, while the latter is a combination of an auxiliary and a lexical verb, but the general relationship of hypotactic interdependency is the same (see Figure 11.14a).

Each group in the complex may have its own internal organization, for instance, (group α:) *has wanted* → (group β:) *to be working*. The parallels for primary and secondary tenses identified by Halliday (1985: Sections 7.A.4 and 7.A.6) are summarized in the table in Figure 11.14b.

It is interesting to note the relation between expansion and 'past/present' on the one hand and projection and 'future' on the other (cf. again Section 6.10 below).

3.2.1.2. Projection and sequent tenses.   As we have seen, the logico-semantic relation of projection combines verbal groups into complex verbal groups. It also combines clauses into clause complexes, again within the logical subcomponent of the ideational metafunction.[13] When the projection is hypotactic and the verbal

---

[13]Similarly, expansion figures in clause complexes as well as in verbal group complexes and temporal expansions (more specifically, temporal enhancements) are relevant to the topic of tense selections. However, I will not discuss them here.

group of the projecting clause is past, the tense selection in the projected clause is affected by the tense selection in the projecting clause. The principle is the same as we have seen in operation in projecting verbal group complexes: the projecting part projects a reference time into the projected part. The exact consequences depend on whether the projection is imperative or indicative.

1. **Imperative projections**—projections of proposals—are temporally similar to the projecting verbal group complexes discussed in the previous section: the projecting clause projects a time following the time of projection; for example (the symbol | | marks the clause boundary within the clause complex):

we told him | | to act quickly
we promised him | | to pick him up at noon
they wanted | | him to drop the inquiry
and after all the company wants | | people to invest in it

(Svartvik & Quirk, 1980, 426)

The projected clause is typically nonfinite and usually doesn't select for secondary tense.

2. In **indicative projections**—projections of propositions—the projecting clause projects a secondary time of speaking into the projected clause. That is, the time of projecting becomes a secondary reference time for the tense selection in the projected clause. The primary reference time is the time of speaking, as always. Thus, if the president says *I followed the spirit of the law* with a simple past, it is reported as a past-in-past:

The president said || that he had followed the spirit of the law.

The temporal relations for the projecting clause and the projected clause are diagrammed in Figure 11.15. Both have the same primary time of reference, t_0, the time of speaking, in relation to which the president's verbalization is past. In the projected clause, t_1 is the secondary reference time, which is the projected time of speaking—the time of the president's verbalization.

3.2.2. Experiential neighbors

Experiential interpretations that differentiate tense, perfect phase (aspect), and progressive aspect (cf. Figure 11.8) are currently very common. I have argued that the logical interpretation is to be preferred. We can see this also when we examine the representation

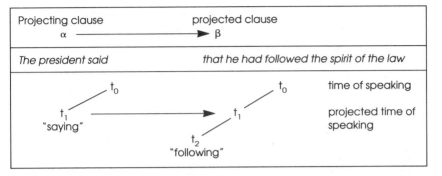

Figure 11.15.   Projection of time in clause complex.

of time in the clause (as opposed to the verbal group; cf. the table in Figure 11.5), where the model is experiential rather than logical: a composite phenomenon is decomposed into its component parts—the process, the participants involved, and attendant circumstances of time, place, and so on. While time is represented as a chain of temporal relations in the verbal group, time is analyzed into components in the clause—Frequency, Extent (in time: duration), and Location (in time). The clause grammar of circumstances does not specify the temporal relationship between these different components,[14] but they may be inferred from the tense selections in the verbal group, whose task it is to specify temporal relations. Different tense selections may thus lead to different interpretations of what times the temporal components of the clause apply to.

For example, in the clause *we will work for a long time next Wednesday,* we are given as distinct components: (i) the extent of the period of working (*for a long time*)—its duration—and (ii) the location of the time of working (*next Wednesday*). Consider now two different tense selections for the verbal group: (a) a simple future tense and (b) a complex tense selection, such as future-in-past.

(a) Given the selection of a simple future tense they can be con-

---

[14]Other circumstances are similar in this respect: they specify circumstantial components of the process configuration represented by the clause, but they do not indicate how these relate to the other components. For example, a spatial circumstance of destination may specify the destination of Medium and Agent or Medium alone (cf. *they drove me down to Ensenada, I drove down to Ensenada* and *they sent the package down to Ensenada*). Similarly, with a circumstance of place: cf. *we met him in the bar, we left him in the bar, we saw him in the bar, we called to him in the bar.* Experiential constituency structure does not specify scoping relations.

strued as applying to the same time, the time of working. (b) Where the tense selection is more complex, the two circumstances need not apply to the same time, because there is nothing in the experiential constituent structure to indicate any temporal relationship between the two.[15] For example, in the clause *we will have worked here for a long time next Wednesday*, we again have two circumstances of time, Extent and Location, but the verbal group realizing the Process has a secondary tense selection; it is past-in-future. The Extent is *for a long time* and it represents the extent of the period of working—its duration—and the Location is *next Wednesday* and it names a temporal location in the future specified by the primary present, which is not the same as the time of working. The two examples just discussed thus both have Extent and Location as elements of clause structure but have different verbal group structures; they are diagrammed in Figure 11.16.

Circumstances of time explicitly construe location, extent, and frequency in time. Nuclear TRANSITIVITY—the Process and participants directly involved in it—is in the first instance concerned with construing the configurational organization of our experience of "goings-on"; but the different domains of this experience and the nature of the participants have temporal implications. This is reflected in the attempts by linguists and philosophers of language (many of them drawing on Vendler, 1967—e.g., Dowty 1979, Foley & van Valin 1984) to set up temporally based typologies of events or verbs, discussed in terms of aktionsart or lexical aspect. In spite of

---

[15]If there are several temporal adjuncts, they may be ordered so that they mirror the serial ordering of the verbal group; see Halliday (1985: 182). For instance, in an example already cited, *Oh, it's been producing results for a long time*, we have a present-in-past-in-present verbal group and a circumstance of Extent (duration) in the clause representing the extent of the pastness, 'for a long time'. We can add a reference to the primary present, 'now', after the Extent: *Oh, it's been producing results for a long time now*. Similarly, we can add a reference to the time of the third-order present, say a specification of frequency of the producing, 'daily', before the Extent: *Oh, it's been producing results daily for a long time now*. These additions give us *daily—for a long time—now*, i.e., Frequency ∧ Extent ∧ Location. In itself, this is just a multivariate sequence, but in the context of the tense selection, the interpretation of the sequence is built up to mirror the serial ordering of the tense selections: tertiary present ~ Frequency (*daily*), secondary past ~ Extent (*for a long time*), and primary present ~ Location (*now*). If the tense selection is changed, so is the interpretation of the ordering of the temporal adjuncts. For example, if the tense selection is simplified to present-in-present, *Oh, it's producing results daily for a long time now*, both Frequency and Extent refer to the production: its occurrence is frequent and its extent is long when it occurs.

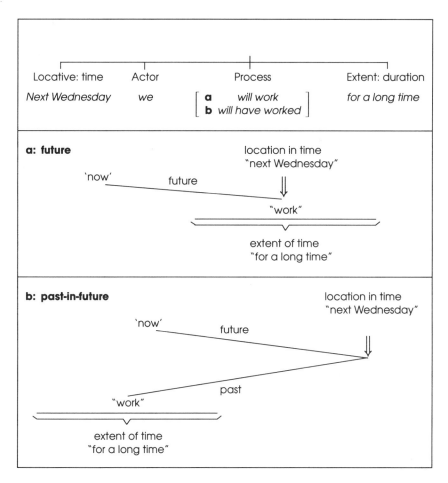

Figure 11.16.   Simple and complex tense selection and circumstances of time.

this substantial body of work, it is, in fact, not possible to base typologies of temporal profiles on verbs because the temporal profile is a function also of the nature and quantity of participants (see Halliday & Matthiessen, forthcoming, for discussion). To give just one example, *Henry climbed Mount Everest* is an event with a clear end-point, but *Henry climbs mountains* and *People climb Mount Everest every once in a while* are not events with end-points but rather activities. The PROCESS TYPES Halliday has identified in the English transitivity system are based, in the first instance, on considerations of the configuration of Process + participants (i.e. on nuclear TRANSITIVITY) rather than isolated events or verbs. And different types of configuration have different temporal implications—at least by default. Therefore, it stands to reason that this ideational system shows interaction with TENSE. Indeed, Halliday (1985) shows that the unmarked representation of present time varies across the process types: material clauses are present-in-present (e.g., *They're mending the neighbour's fence*) whereas the other process types are simple present (e.g., *They think/ say (he's mending the fence); he's a carpenter*). For example, the marked present tense in the environment of a mental clause is the present-in-present and it may be selected to indicate the inception of occurrence: *I'm believing him less and less.* Other marked tense selections are also interpretable in the environment of a particular process type. For instance, the simple past together with *ever* is used with mental clauses where we would expect to find a past-in-present: *Did you ever hear such a lot of rubbish?* Similarly, future time reference may, under certain conditions, be achieved by means of the simple present or the present-in-present; but this option is much more restricted than in other Germanic languages, at least German and Swedish, and the restrictions relate to PROCESS TYPE. The simple present can be used as a kind of implicit future-in-present typically with certain material processes whose temporal profile is such that the process includes both a phase of possible planning, scheduling or the like (i.e., projection of future occurrence) and a phase of actual occurrence: *we dine at 7; our flight leaves at 22:35; the play opens in December.*

3.3. Ideational Time: Experiential Components and Logical Series

We have, then, two ideational modes of explicitly representing time.[16] One is the logical mode of the verbal group. It construes time as *temporal relations* that may form time series—serial time. There are three highly generalized temporal relations, namely, past, present, and future, and they may be instantiated repeatedly in a verbal group to construct a time series.

The other is the experiential mode of the clause. It construes time multivariately in terms of the *component parts* of the occurrence of a process—frequency (*Last year we went there **every other week** for two days*), extent in time (*Last year we went there every other*

---

[16]Cf. Ehrich (1987), who distinguishes four types of temporal meaning, two of which are relational time, coded by tense, and positional time, coded by "temporal adverbs."

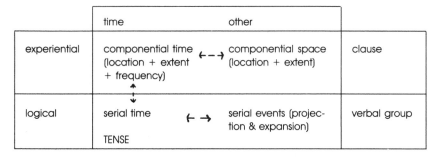

	time	other	
experiential	componential time ←–→ (location + extent + frequency)	componential space (location + extent)	clause
logical	serial time ←→ TENSE	serial events (projection & expansion)	verbal group

Figure 11.17. Ideational time.

week for two days), and location in time (*Last year* we went there every other week for two days).

The two ideational modes relate time systematically to other categories in different ways. As we saw in Section 3.2, the logical interpretation relates tense to projection and expansion in hypotactic verbal group complexes; complex tenses such as *will have been doing* are related to complexes such as *want to succeed in keeping doing*. In contrast, the experiential model of time relates it systematically to space.[17] The categories of extent and location apply to ordinary space as well as to temporal space (cf. Halliday, 1985: 138): *for an hour / a mile, in the morning / kitchen,* and so forth. The two ideational construals of time are summarized in Figure 11.17.

4. TENSE AND METAFUNCTION: INTERPERSONAL

We have seen how a logical interpretation of tense differs from an experiential one; the two make different claims about the ideational construal of time. Turning to the interpersonal metafunction, we can first ask what claims an interpersonal interpretation of tense would make and how it would contrast with the logical interpretation.

The question of how TENSE differs from interpersonal resources is of general interest; but it is also motivated by a particular inter-

---

[17]This is not to deny the connection between tense and space; cf. *be going to do* and 'be at doing': see e.g., Traugott (1978). However, there is no spatial system equivalent to tense in English—there is no system of serial space (other than paths constructed by means of the general resources of complexing—*from Sydney via Canberra to Melbourne*).

pretation of TENSE, which links it to MODALITY, either the tense system as a whole (tense as a kind of modality) or only the term 'future' (the reductionist position; cf. Figure 11.7). When we consider MODALITY from the point of view of English in the light of a metafunctional theory rather than philosophy, we see that it is an interpersonal resource (Halliday, 1985), so it follows that if TENSE or part of it were a type of modality, it too would be interpersonal. I will review the contrast between a three-term tense system with a future tense and a two-term one without a future tense in relation to a range of considerations. Here I will focus on the metafunctional implications.

As in the discussion of the two alternative ideational interpretations of TENSE, I will explore the logical interpretation of TENSE in relation to the interpersonal metafunction from three points of view: paradigmatic, semantic, and syntagmatic.

1. **From a paradigmatic point of view:** (a) As a logical resource, TENSE is metafunctionally differentiated from the interpersonal resource of MODALITY. If TENSE were interpersonal, it would be like MODALITY or it would actually be a type of MODALITY instead, as has sometimes been suggested. TENSE would be an aspect of the interaction between speaker and listener—time as a category of interaction, interpersonally enacted rather than ideationally construed.[18] (b) Since TENSE is a logical resource, we predict that it should interact with other ideational resources such as PROCESS TYPE and CIRCUMSTANTIATION within the clause. If it were interpersonal, TENSE would instead interact with interpersonal resources such as MOOD & KEY, MODALITY, and POLARITY. (c) If TENSE were an interpersonal resource, we could expect it to offer the interpersonal metaphorical alternatives MODALITY provides.

---

[18]There are two types of such "interpersonal time," both realized congruently with the Mood element: First are interpersonal mood Adjuncts in the clause enacting expectations and assessments in the domain of time—*he hasn't arrived yet; the mail is here already.* These are related to other interpersonal expectations and assessments such as *he hasn't arrived completely, the mail is actually here.* Second is usuality as a modal assessment (modal Finite *would, could,* etc.; or modal Adjunct *sometimes, often, always,* etc.). Usuality is related to probability as a kind of modalization: *The mail is usually/probably here.*

2. **From a semantic point of view:** The ideational and inter-personal metafunctions are sensitive to different aspects of context—field and tenor, respectively (Halliday, 1978; Halliday & Hasan, 1985). Since TENSE is an ideational resource, it is used to represent temporal relations according to the field of discourse and is not affected by the tenor of the relationship between speaker and listener. An interpersonal interpretation would predict that the reasons for choosing tenses were affected by the tenor of the relationship between speaker and listener.

3. **From a syntagmatic point of view:** Since it is a logical resource, TENSE is realized by interdependency structures (as in Figure 11.10 above). If it were interpersonal, it would have the potential for being realized prosodically.

I will start with the paradigmatic considerations.

4.1. Paradigmatic considerations

4.1.1. Tense and modality: alternation

Tense and modality of the subtype modalization (indicative modality, Halliday, 1985; sometimes called epistemic modality) are alternative types of deicticity: this opposition is represented by the DEICTICITY system in Figure 11.2 above. Halliday (1970) describes the alternation as follows:

> The function of the finiteness in the verb is to relate what is being said to the "speaker-now," both by allowing options of mood and by giving a reference point either in time or in the speaker's judgment. Hence the finite element always combines with one or other of the two categories that serve to provide the reference point, namely primary tense and modality; but they cannot both function in this way at the same time. This fact that primary tense and modality are both realized by 'anomalous finites' reflects the similarity between them; they are both 'deictic' in the extended sense, and differ merely in the type of deixis involved—'at the time at which I am speaking' or 'in my opinion'.

Tense and modality are, then, different ways of relating to the speaker-now. The choice of 'modal' displaces primary tense in the verbal group, and in this respect tense, is related to modality in the verbal group. That is, they are related as deictic categories through which the validity of a proposition can be argued. However, they are not related as modal categories; the feature 'temporal' does not itself have a modal value.[19] Although 'temporal' may mean cate gorically yes or no rather than an intermediate degree (modality), this only happens if there is no other expression of modality outside the Finite. When a modal Adjunct is present, it is this Adjunct that determines the modality value even if 'temporal' is selected. For instance, the following example is 'temporal,' but also expresses the modal values 'median' and 'probability' by means of the modal Adjunct *probably:*

Camptosaurus **probably** provided many a fine meal for the fierce Allosaurus.

(Dinosaurs)

I was jolly glad it was an innocuous conversation; we're **probably** being recorded now.

(Svartvik & Quirk, 1980, 506)

Thus, the choice of the feature 'temporal' does not by itself indicate a modal stance on the part of the speaker, which is exactly what we would expect from an ideational category: ideational construals of experience can be enacted interpersonally in different ways. Rather, 'temporal' is simply another way of relating to speaker-now.

Secondary tense selections reveal the ideational way in which 'temporal' relates to speaker-now. The choice of a primary tense term is merely the first link in the temporal chain between 'now' and the occurrence of the event; the selection of the next, secondary tense will then relate to this choice. In other words, the secondary tense selection is just a repeated choice from the same kind of system. In contrast, a secondary tense selection in the context of 'modal' DEICTICITY (instead of 'temporal') will not relate to the modalization but will instead express the temporal relation the primary tense displaced from the Finite cannot express. In other words, the secondary tense selection is a choice from a different kind of system. For instance, the pastness of the first example below is expressed by a secondary past when the feature modal is chosen, rather than a primary one as in the second example:

[This small hunter] may **have** used its smaller forelimbs for grasping its food.

(Dinosaurs)

---

[19]The situation is comparable to deixis in the nominal group. The Deictic may be either a demonstrative determiner or a possessive one, which means that demonstratives and possessives can both serve as deictic categories, but not that one is a subtype of the other.

[It] probably used its short front feet for hunting and eating.

(Dinosaurs)

The tendency to relate TENSE to MODALITY is particularly strong in the area of futurity. The temporal *will* and the modal *will* are, of course, similar in several respects: they have the same negative and contracted forms, *won't* and *'ll*, for example. These similarities can be captured straightforwardly at word rank by positing only one auxiliary verb *will*, not two (see further Section 6.2 below). The distinction between temporal and modal *will* is a property of the group, not of the word. For instance, they differ according to their metafunctional location in the system: modal *will* is agnate with interpersonal metaphors of modality whereas temporal *will* is not. I will return to the distinction between temporal and modal *will* in Section 6 below.

4.1.2. Interactions within metafunctions

If tense was an interpersonal resource, we would expect it to interact with interpersonal systems such as MOOD, MODALITY, and POLARITY. These systems interact in various ways with one another but not with TENSE; I will point to a few brief examples of the relevant interactions.

(i) The reason for choosing negative POLARITY depends on the MOOD environment in which the choice is made. If the environment is yes/no (polarity) interrogative, there is a special reason; in other MOOD environments, the issue is whether a negative polarity value is to be expressed or not. When the clause is a yes/no interrogative one, the issue is whether the speaker wants to express a positive expectation as to the value of the polarity, in which case negative is chosen, or whether he/she wants to remain neutral, in which case positive is chosen. For instance, in the first of the following examples, A says something like 'I expect it is Peel . . . don't you agree?' by choosing negative polarity in the yes/no interrogative:

A: **Isn't** it Peel who's always having rows with Doyen? "I think it is Peel"
B: I don't know what he is doing now, but he was always very colourful.

(Svartvik & Quirk, 1980, 171)

A: "I take care of all the playthings that children have loved. When they are old and worn out and the children don't need them anymore, I come and take them away with me and turn them into Real."
B: "**Wasn't** I real before?" asked the little Rabbit. "I thought I was."

(Williams, 1987)

Since they are both interpersonal resources, MOOD and PO-LARITY can combine to form interpersonal categories. The features 'yes/no interrogative' and 'negative' together define the category of 'non-assertive' (cf. Quirk, et al. 1972: 54), relevant to the selection between **some** and **any;** and 'interrogative' and 'negative' provide the environment in which the operator *do* may be used. There is also a constraint on the exclamative type of declarative clauses with respect to POLARITY: they have to be positive. Furthermore, MOOD and POLARITY together express speech functional categories such as denial (declarative and negative), contradiction (declarative + polarity reversed from the original claim), and prevention (imperative + negative). For further discussion of "negation" and speech function, see Givón (1979).

(ii) MODALITY also interacts with MOOD. The MOOD environment affects the orientation of a modal selection. In a declarative, the modal choice typically expresses the speaker's angle—his/her permission or will or assessment of possibility—but in a yes/no interrogative, the listener's angle is elicited. Thus, for example, *Can I take the car?* means 'Will you permit me to take the car?' and the response *Yes you can* means 'Yes, I will permit you to take the car.' *Will that be Henry at the door now?* means 'Do you think that's Henry at the door now?' In British English, modal *shall* differs predictably from temporal *shall* in this respect; modal: *Shall I turn off the oven?* 'Would you like me to turn off the oven?' (as an offer)— temporal: *Shall I still be here this time next year?* Furthermore, the distribution of èxpressions of possibility depends on the mood selection. While possibility can be expressed by either *may* or *can* in a non-yes/no environment, only *can* occurs in yes/no interrogative clauses.

We can see, then, that interpersonal resources interact with each other in a number of ways. In contrast, TENSE shows this kind of interaction with the ideational resource of TRANSITIVITY rather than with interpersonal regions: see Section 3.2 above.

4.2. Semantic Considerations

The semantics of TENSE is of a logical kind rather than of an interpersonal kind. As we have seen (cf. Figure 11.12 above), the terms of the TENSE system represent alternative temporal relations; and since they represent relations, they can be "serialized." TENSE resembles other logical resources such as modification in the nominal group in this respect. In contrast, interpersonal meanings tend to be scalar; for example, the terms within the resources of MODALITY stand for values on a scale—either the middle part of the scale (median: 'probable') or the outer parts (low: 'possible' or high: 'necessary'). Thus modal *will* is median on this scale, whereas temporal *will* does not have a scalar value: see further Section 6. There is another type of semantic difference between logical and interpersonal types of meaning in general and between TENSE and MODALITY in particular: interpersonal meanings tend to be associated with the act of meaning as a whole, and this is reflected in the way they are realized as prosodies (cf. Section 4.3 below).

We can also see the semantic difference between TENSE and interpersonal resources such as MODALITY in their orientation toward context. Interpersonal choices are influenced by the tenor of the relationship between speaker and listener (e.g., Halliday, 1978). We can see this clearly with modal choices; for instance, possibility may be used to achieve politeness: a speaker slides down the modal scale to enact a deferential positioning below the listener (cf. Butler, 1982). In contrast, tense choices are influenced by the field of discourse rather than by tenor. There is one apparent type of exception, but it turns out to be an affirmation of the principle of the correlation between interpersonal choices and tenor rather than an exception to it. Although projecting clauses normally serve ideationally to quote or report what somebody has said or thought, they may be brought into interpersonal service by means of interpersonal metaphors, in which case the verbal group of the projecting clause may select primary past to achieve politeness or deference rather than for any strictly temporal reasons (cf. the neutral: oblique contrast with modalizations in general: *will : would; can : could*)—*I thought you might like some tea; I was hoping you would join us; I was wondering if I could use your car; I wanted to ask you whether . . .* , and so on.

4.3. Syntagmatic Realization

As we have seen, TENSE and other logical resources are realized by interdependency structures (see e.g., Figure 11.10). In contrast, interpersonal features tend to be realized prosodically, as shown by Halliday (1979a) and further discussed in Poynton (1990) and in Matthiessen (1990). Consequently, if TENSE or some part of it was interpersonal, it would have the potential for prosodic realization, but it does not. The clearest example of prosody as a mode of realization may come from the region of KEY, which is a resource for expressing variations on the speech functions related to certainty and uncertainty. Selections are realized prosodically by tones (i.e., into-

tone 1 (falling):

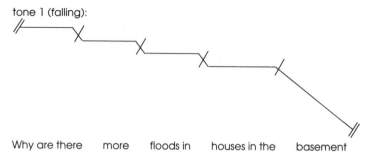

Why are there   more   floods in   houses in the   basement

Figure 11.18. Prosodic realization.

nation contours). The example in Figure 11.18, taken from Halliday (1985b: 54), illustrates the principle; it is a wh-interrogative clause and has tone 1 (falling), which is the unmarked tone for wh-interrogatives.

The melody runs throughout the tone group realizing the clause; it is, in other words, a prosody. POLARITY is related to KEY and is realized in a similar way, although it is realized by particular items rather than the pitch prosody (what we might call a grammatical prosody: see further Matthiessen, 1990). If the feature 'negative' is chosen, the Finite is negative and any subsequent polarity items (non-specific determiners, pronouns, etc.) also reflect the choice of negative polarity. That is, a negative prosody runs through the clause starting with Finite. The "non-standard" example in Figure 11.19, taken from Labov (1970), illustrates the principle, as does its standard equivalent.

MODALITY is again similar in its potential for prosodic realization. A modal selection characterizes the clause as a whole and may be realized by a modal auxiliary as Finite, a modal Adjunct, and a metaphorical form such as *I think;* these may be used individually, as in the following example of a disagreement:

A: Oh, well. That's **surely** debatable.
B: **I don't think** it's debatable. No.

(Svartvik & Quirk, 1980, 443)

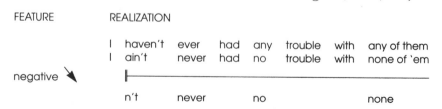

Figure 11.19. Polarity prosody.

Or they may be used together to create a modal prosody as in the following examples:

A: No, I only meant that maps must have existed.
B: Oh, maps **must** have existed, **certainly**.

(Svartvik & Quirk, 1980, 441)

He **could** have produced them from scratch **presumably**.

(Svartvik & Quirk, 1980, 450)

No. **I think probably** there **might** be lots of copies of texts.

(Svartvik & Quirk, 1980, 809)

Halliday (1970) discusses the prosodic realization of MODALITY:

> There is thus no single place in the clause where modality is located. It is a strand running prosodically through the clause . . . ; and this effect is further enhanced by the fact that . . . it may be realized also by the intonation contour, or tone.

Interpersonal sequences such as *n't . . . never . . . no . . . none, n't . . . ever . . . any . . . any, and I think . . . probably . . . might* may look superficially similar to a sequence such as *will . . . have . . . been going . . . to build;* but they are built on quite different principles. The first is an interpersonal prosody and is an ongoing realization of the same selection (negative and possibility, respectively, in the examples). The second is an interdependency structure and is a repeated realization of repeated selections (future, past, and future in the example). There are a number of specific consequences of these differences.

1. Because the prosody reflects one selection, it need not be present as a whole to express it as long as the negative item associated with Finite is present:

I have**n't** always had the same trouble with all of them.

Conversely, the expression of the prosody may be further extended without additional polarity choices in the clause:

I have**n't ever** had **any** trouble with **any** of them, in **any** way, **anywhere** we've worked together.

In contrast, the tense selection underlying *will . . . have . . . been going . . . to build* can only be expressed by the whole chain; and we could only add links if we made additional tense selections.

2. While the items in the negative prosody are not dependent on one another, either in terms of form or constraints on the range of alternatives, the verbs in the logical interdependency chain are dependent on one another; the form of each new verb expanding the tense series is determined by the previous choice (cf. Figure 11.10 above).

3. Moreover, because the polarity items in *I haven't ever had any trouble with any of them* are not ordered logically, their relative sequence is not fixed. For example, the temporal Adjunct can be thematized, with the concomitant reversal of Subject and Finite typical of clauses with negative themes (where the negativity is a feature of the clause rather than the thematic constituent alone):

Never have I had **any** trouble with **any** of them.

In contrast, the sequence in *will . . . have . . . been going . . . to build* reflects the logical ordering of the tense series and cannot normally be changed.

5. TENSE AND METAFUNCTION: TEXTUAL

When TENSE is interpreted as a modality, it is linked, by implication, to the interpersonal metafunction. As we have seen, an interpersonal interpretation does not bring out the principles embodied in the resources of TENSE, and we can turn to the textual metafunction to ask the same kind of question again—what does a textual interpretation of TENSE entail? There are no interpretations in the literature that would imply a textual interpretation comparable to the interpersonal interpretation implied by the modal analysis of it. However, we can still examine TENSE from a textual angle by comparing it with temporal CONJUNCTION.[20] CONJUNCTION is the

---

[20]Researchers have also, of course, explored parallels between REFERENCE (a textual resource) and TENSE in accounts of temporal reference times and also parallels between nominal and verbal deixis. I will not discuss these here—except to note that TENSE is different from REFERENCE in one fundamental respect: it is not a resource for establishing and tracking events or times in a discourse. As soon as we need to track an event, we have to nominalize it in one way or another—we have to reify through grammatical metaphor so that it can be manipulated in discourse as if it were a thing.

textual resource for presenting rhetorical (conjunctive) relations that hold between units of text (Halliday & Hasan, 1976; Martin, 1992; Halliday, 1985: Ch. 9); temporal conjunctive relations include those expressed by *then, later, subsequently, afterwards; immediately, meanwhile, simultaneously; earlier, before, previously.*

If TENSE was textual, its basic function ought to be to express time relations within a text, between clauses, just as temporal conjunctions such as *later, afterwards, immediately,* and *meanwhile* do. However, as we have seen, TENSE construes a temporal chain linking the time of speaking to the time of the Event, in one or more steps. The reference time of primary tense is the time of speaking, 'now', but the reference time of secondary tense is another time, related to the time of speaking by the primary tense selection. For any given tense selection, this secondary reference time may have been established previously in the text. Consequently, secondary tense can also come to serve to express temporal relations in the text, just as temporal conjunctions do. For instance, in the following examples, anteriority and posteriority are indicated conjunctively as well as by means of secondary tense selections:

anteriority:

The party was led by one of the greatest mountain men of his era, Joseph Walker, who <u>ten years earlier</u> **had explored** the region west of Salt Lake forcing a passage through the mountains to the coast.

(Stone, 1956, 55)

posteriority:

<u>The next time</u> he **would move** into California with a well-armed band of sixty-five to seventy trained men, to play a stormy, disputed, decisive role in it conquest.

(Stone, 1956, 60)

The examples illustrate correlations between 'earlier' and secondary past and between 'next time' and secondary future. Similar correlations are tabulated below.[21]

---

[21]The conjunctions in the table are non-structural, cohesive ones. We also find temporal conjunctive relations encoded in the logic of paratactic and hypotactic clause combining, of course—*while, when, before, since,* etc. I won't go into their interaction with tense selection here.

conjunction		tense
simple	complex	(secondary:)
anteriority	before, earlier, previously,	(terminal) until then, by this time, (interrupted) some time earlier	past
simultaneity	simultaneously, at the same time,	(durative) meanwhile, all this time,	present
posteriority — interruption		(interrupted) later, soon, after a time,	future
posteriority — sequence	then, next, subsequently, afterwards	(immediate) immediately, at once,	

Figure 11.20.   CONJUNCTION and SECONDARY TENSE.

6. THE THREE-TERM TENSE SYSTEM AND THE FULL RANGE OF DIMENSIONS

So far, I've focused on three fundamental dimensions of the linguistic system, namely, stratification, metafunction, and rank, using metafunction to organize the discussion of various possible interpretations of TENSE. However, at the outset of Section 2, I indicated that a full exploration of TENSE would bring in other dimensions as well; for instance, Figure 11.4 does not include potentiality. It is not possible to consider all of them for the whole tense system, so I will illustrate the principle with respect to the status of the primary future in English. Because it has come up in various contexts, this will also allow me to pull the points already made together.

Davidsen-Nielsen (1986) observes that most English grammarians currently recognize only two tenses: this is the reductionist position I introduced in Section 1.2. He is one of the few scholars who maintains that English has a future. His argument, like most arguments for or against the English future, hinges on the status of *will:* Can we or can't we distinguish between a modal and a temporal *will?* If we put this in terms of the interpretation of *will* in English, it is extremely important to take note of what angle on *will* is at issue—is it a word, a word form, or a gloss for a higher-ranking feature realized by the word *will?* In other words, we have to be absolutely clear about the dimensions of interpretation—rank, stratification, metafunctional diversification, and so on. In arguments about the English tense system, there is often slippage at this point.

6.1. The Dimensions to be Considered

The dimensions defining the overall semiotic space of language in context allow for a number of complementary perspectives and even though an exhaustive account needs to balance these different perspectives, one perspective is often prioritized as a vantage point for looking at some phenomenon. The choice of perspective is a way of foregrounding certain generalizations in the account; but there is typically a choice here—we have to select which generalizations to foreground, which perspective brings out the most powerful generalizations. Consequently, there is very often an alternative for which a number of arguments can be found. This is both a matter of variation in the system itself—static oscillation as well as dynamic change—and a matter of variation in observer perspective. The interpretation of the English primary tense system and future *will* either as a tense or as a modality is a good example. Figure 11.21

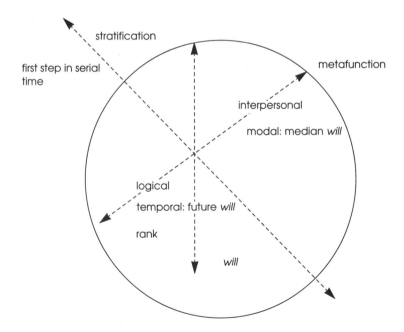

Figure 11.21. The dispersal of "will" in the linguistic system.

shows the interpretation of *will* relative to rank within the lex-icogrammatical system, metafunction within the content systems, and stratification of the content systems.

The diagram indicates that in the interpretation discussed here, there is one auxiliary *will* at word rank which realizes two different sets of features at group rank, with different metafunctional points of origin (logical—future; interpersonal—modal: median). It shows further that the group features have particular semantic interpreta-tions. There is thus ambiguity in the system: there are different realizational paths to the auxiliary *will*. However, whichever path we follow through the system, it is clear that information about *will* is dispersed in the system along that path. This is just the general principle that wherever we locate the interpretation of an item, a function, a system or some other category, it is related to other parts of the overall system along the various dimensions that make up the system. That is why any argument about a particular interpretation can never remain a local one; it has to be a global enterprise. Thus, if we look up the auxiliary *will* in the system, we will find that it realizes the Finite within a verbal group in two different paradigmat-ic environments, the temporal and the modal ones, and that, in addition, the features that constitute these environments realize different semantic features. (For the modal spread, cf. Halliday, 1976: 191, 202).

Here the dimension of axis is also critical: the interpretation is placed paradigmatically within the system, which shows contrasts and agnations; and systemic terms are realized syntagmatically. An-other dimension, potentiality, introduces semiotic time—the move between potential and instantial via instantiation. It is central to semohistory because it is the dimension that makes it possible to explore evolution in the system through instances. In addition to these dimensions, I will also discuss two dimensions that place the system as a whole relative to deeper perspectives—phylogenesis (diachrony), or the history of the system (in the species), and varia-tion across linguistic systems: typology. I will discuss the location of the interpretation of *will* along these various dimensions in the order I have introduced them here.

6.2. Rank

The rank scale is quite important in the grammatical interpretation of *will*. It provides us with the possible differentiation between the word *will* and its forms (*will, 'll, won't; would, 'd; wouldn't*) and higher-ranking terms realized by these. Halliday's analysis of future and modal *will* is not a word-rank analysis—it relates to group and

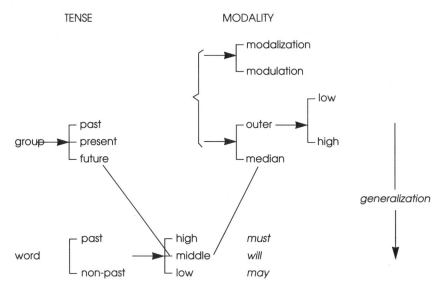

Figure 11.22.   Rank perspectives on *will*.

clause rank systems. At word rank, there seems to be no reason to differentiate two (or more) different types of *will*. In fact, in the word systems for the large computational systemic-functional grammar based on Halliday's work, we have only one *will* in the system network of the verb; this is one of the many areas we have developed in consultation with him. The situation can thus be diagrammed as in Figure 11.22 (cf. Martin & Matthiessen, 1992, on dimensions of agnation and rank).

Looked at from below, at word rank, there is only one feature, 'middle', realized by the word *will*. Looked at from above, there is one temporal environment in which the feature 'future' is realized by 'middle' and one modal environment in which the feature 'median' is realized by the preselection of 'middle'. (Note that this is a simplification of the general grammar; it is only intended to bring out the possibility of a differentiation between word rank, morphological, systems and higher-ranking ones.) The kind of diversification the analysis suggests for *will* as we move up the rank scale is a common feature of the grammatical system (in particular with grammatical items such as *be, do, have*), similar to the greater differentiation we find with moves up the linguistic strata. Conversely, generalization and neutralization is quite a regular aspect of the move down the rank scale precisely because lower-ranking units can serve in different higher-ranking systemic and structural environments. That is, in the move down the rank scale, units and their systems are de-

Table 11.4

form at word rank:	feature at group rank		
	primary 'future:' temporal *will*	median & modalization *will*	median & modulation *will*
will	—future tense realization	neutral	non-past
would		oblique (undertone / overtone)	past

contextualized—they are abstracted out of the grammatical system-ic and structural environments in which they serve at a higher rank. However, the environments accessible at the higher rank often contain information needed to resolve the ambiguity seen from the point of the lower-ranking unit concerning its higher-ranking environment (e.g., circumstantial features of temporal location, features of process type, features of subject person).[22]

At word rank, English does not have a three-term tense system. The relevant contrast realized morphemically is, for example, *look : looked*, which could be interpreted as 'present/past', but there are other possible systemic arrangements since the base form *look* is not restricted to the realization of the (non-third-person singular) present at group rank. However we interpret the contrast between *will* and *would* at word rank, it is clear that it realizes different group-rank systems: see Table 11.4.

The observation that *will* shows a tense contrast (*will/ would*) comparable to lexical verbs is thus an observation about word rank, not about group rank. Indeed, *would* can only be temporal if it is projected (*I will come : he said he would come*).[23]

The separation in rank in the interpretation is also important when we consider non-finite forms. The perspective from above allows us to recognize suppletion forms such as *be able to, be willing*

---

[22]It may, of course, be necessary to go beyond the immediate environment to re-solve an ambiguity—upwards to gain access to semantic and contextual informa-tion and "sideways" to consider the instantial information built up within the instantial system of the text at the relevant point in its history.

[23]We might also add the so-called author's *would* of prediction in the past (as in *twelve years later he would learn why they had rejected his offer*); but this would be a realization of future-in-past, alternating with *was going to*, not of pri-mary future. It thus contrasts with the past of modals realizing modulation, which is a simple past (as in *we asked him to help us, but he wouldn't* 'refused to').

Table 11.5

	unmarked		marked (negative, interrogative, focused)	
past	ran		did	run
present	runs		does	run
future	will (/shall)	run	will (/shall)	run

to. Therefore, here it is possible to recognize proportionalities such as *has to : can :: to have to : to be able to; did do : does do : will do :: have -en : be -ing : be going to*, which is precisely what the system network in Figure 11.2 above represents for the tense system. This doesn't automatically mean that they should be recognized; but because the grammar has evolved both word rank and group rank, these are interpretive possibilities. From above, it is thus possible to recognize greater formal similarity between 'past' and 'present' on the one hand and 'future' on the other, even for the primary tenses: see Table 11.5.

The separation of group and word rank systems is very important in evaluating evidence that has been put forward in favor of *will* as only modal in the grammar. Huddleston (e.g., 1984, 1991) is one of the linguists who has rejected the three-tense interpretation of English and argued that *will* belongs grammatically with the modals. One reason Huddleston (1991) cites for grouping *will* grammatically with the modals is that they share the following properties (Huddleston's number (86)):

i.   The modal operators have only tensed forms no base forms, not present or past participle;

ii. They are paradigmatically contrastive and cannot combine syntagmatically (other than in coordination): *She must win, She can swim, *She must can swim;* [syntactic, according to Huddleston]

iii. They show no person-number agreement with the subject;

iv. One of these verbs is required in the main clause of an unreal (remote) conditional construction. [syntactic, according to Huddleston]

Properties [i] and [iii] are straightforwardly morphological and are handled by the systemic treatment sketched above: at word rank, future *will* and modal *will* are realized by the same verb class. Note that from a higher ranking perspective, certain varieties do show a distinction in the realization of primary 'future' according to SUBJECT PERSON—in the environment of first person, the realization is *shall;* elsewhere, it is *will* (cf. Quirk et al., 1985: 213–4):

He'll be treated to lunch tomorrow.
We shall be treated to lunch tomorrow.

This is not the case with modal *will*. Huddleston suggests that properties [ii] and [iv] are syntactic, not morphological. As far as [ii] is concerned, that is a matter of perspective. One way of interpreting the situation is to say that *can, may, will,* and so forth, belong to a word class whose function potential is such that they can only serve as Finite; and this is true of *will* regardless of whether it is a realization of 'temporal' or 'modal: median' at a group rank—its function potential is the same. From the point of view of the group grammar, the realization of 'she must can swim' is *she must be able to swim;* the realization of 'she must will leave in a few hours' is *she must be going to leave in a few hours.* That is, looked at from above, we can recognize suppletion forms serving as non-finites (cf. above). In any case, [ii] presents absolutely no problem for Halliday's account.

As for [iv] ("One of these verbs is required in the main clause of an unreal (remote) conditional construction"), it is important to ask what "verb" means in this context—does the constraint apply to actual verb forms statable at word rank, or does it apply to verb uses statable at group rank? If the former was the case, it would be a straightforward argument in favor of one type of *will;* but, if the latter is the case, the crucial issue is whether temporal and modal *will* both satisfy the constraint. The former is not the case and we can probe the second case: see Table 11.6.

That is, the simple future realized by *will* is not possible in this environment; rather, a modal oblique *would* is required (with pastness indicated by secondary 'past'). Huddleston is perfectly right that this is a syntactic constraint—but it is precisely one that does not involve future *will* any more than it does the simple past or present: all three primary tenses are excluded from this unreal environment. Consequently, [iv] is not at all a reason for saying that future *will* belongs grammatically with the modals from the point of view of group or clause grammar. On the contrary, it is one piece of evidence against that view. The general interpretive principle is that we need a theory that sorts out the overall semiotic space in such a way that we can locate relevant systemic information very precisely

Table 11.6

	future	modal
past time reference	*if he had been there yesterday, we will know	if he had been there yesterday, we **would** *have* known
present time reference	*if he were there now, we will know	if he were there today, we **would** know
future time reference	*if he were there tomorrow, we will know	if he were there tomorrow, we **would** know

and apply constraints (e.g. in the form of preselections of systemic features) at the right point.

6.3. Metafunction

At group rank, the temporal interpretation of *will* and the modal one are aligned with different metafunctions. While finiteness or deicticity is grounded in the here and now that is enacted interpersonally in dialogue and the function Finite is interpersonal, TENSE and MODALITY relate to the here and now in metafunctionally different ways—logically and interpersonally, respectively. Just based on this differentiation, we can make certain predictions about the two types of *will*. From a logical point of view, temporal *will* should have properties such as the following (cf. Section 3.1 above):

1. Its agnation set should be related to the logical ordering of the system of TENSE; more specifically, we should expect an agnation between first order future and second order future and this is precisely what we find (see Section further 6.5 below): *(the journey) will take : is going to take (five hours)*.

2. Semantically, it should be the first link in the serialization of time construed by TENSE in English; and if there is no secondary tense, the relationship between the time of speaking, 'now', and the time of the occurrence of the (ideational) process should be one of precedence. This is indeed what we find (see Section 6.4 below).

3. Syntagmatically in the grammar, the logical ordering in semantics should be realized by increasing dependency in the verbal group, from α onwards, and it is (see Figures 11.10 and 11.12 above).

In contrast, from an interpersonal point of view, modal *will* should have properties associated with interpersonal systems in general such as POLARITY and COMMENT. We can focus on the *will* of modalization—probability rather than of modulation because this is the one that is closest to future *will:*

1. Its agnation set should be related to the prosodic spread of MODALIZATION in the grammar of English; more specifically, we should expect to find an agnation between *will* and mental clauses of metaphorical modality (*I think; do you think;* etc.), but also modal Adjuncts (*probably, presumably, predictably,* etc.) and modal Attributes (*[it is] probable, likely,* etc.)—and quite possibly also options in KEY. I showed in Section 4.3 that this is what we find for modal *will* but not for temporal *will.* See also Section 6.5 below.

2. Semantically, it should not be the first link in temporal serialization—the need to realize temporal relations is pushed onto secondary tense in the absence of primary tense; rather, it should be an interpersonal "coloring" of the clause as a whole as an interactive move (cf. Halliday, 1979a). Cf. Section 4.1.1, and see further Section 6.5.

3. Syntagmatically in the grammar, the interpersonal coloring should be reflected in the potential for a modal prosody—what Halliday (1976: 194) called concord. This happens in examples such as ***I think*** *that* ***will probably*** *be the postman,* where the modalization is strung out like a prosodic pitch movement or like "double negation." (Note that the situation is different with modulation.) I contrasted TENSE and MODALITY in Section 4.3 above; see also Section 6.5.

These are examples of the kind of systematic differences that a metafunctionally differentiating theory embodies: temporal and modal *will* are clearly distinct along metafunctional lines. The general interpretive principle is that we explore to see if differences are motivated by reference to the system in general.

6.4. Stratification

The particularly central aspect of stratification in this context is the bifurcation of content into two systems—content 1 and content 2, or semantics and lexicogrammar. When we approach the phenomena from above (stratally speaking), from semantics, it is the construal of serial time that stands out with respect to *will* as a future tense; that is, it can mark the first temporal relation in a series of temporal relations. For instance, see Figure 11.12 above.

This is quite different from a modal example such as *That will be Henry calling to invite us to his party* or, to consider a version comparable to our example above, *That will have been Henry calling to invite us to his party.* Here the first temporal move away from the NOW of speaking, t0, is the secondary 'past,' realized by *have . . . -en.* It is related to *That was probably Henry,* whereas *he will already have arrived by then* is not related to *he probably already arrived by then.* In *That will have been Henry,* the modality relates the proposition to the actual of here and now through probability rather than time. The temporal serialization is reflected grammatically in the sequence of Adjuncts of time, according to Halliday (1985: 182). For instance, *He will have arrived two hours before us tomorrow.* In contrast, modal *will* can be expanded prosodically, as in *I think that will probably have been Henry.*

6.5. Axis

6.5.1. Paradigmatic organization and agnation

Adopting the paradigmatic perspective of the systemic organization of content, we can ask what are agnate alternatives to examples of *will.* This means taking the relevant systemic descriptions of TENSE (see Figure 11.2 above) and MODALITY (see Halliday, 1985: Section 10.4, and the systemic representation of his description in Matthiessen, 1995: Section 5.5) in their systemic environments to work out what the consequences in agnation are. For instance, according to the systemic description in Figure 11.2, temporal *will* is agnate with *be going to* as primary to secondary—*it'll rain : it's going to rain.* Agnation does not of course mean synonymy—nor does glossing based on agnation; and grammatical agnation can be expected to be semantically justified.

Systemically, future *will* and modal: modalization and median *will* turn out to be quite different with respect to agnation. If modal and temporal *will* were actually the same—that is, if temporal *will* could be assimilated with modal *will*—they should have the same agnation sets, not different ones. For instance, the contrast between a simple present clause and one with *will* should be parallel, as has

Table 11.7

		That will be Henry	We will leave tomorrow
three-tense system		modal: modalization & median	temporal: future
two-tense system		modal: modalization & median	modal: modalization & median
logical	secondary future	≠ *That's going to be Henry*	~ **We are going to leave tomorrow**
interpersonal	modal Adjunct (i) congruent	~ **That's probably Henry**	≠ *We probably leave tomorrow*
	modal Adjunct (ii) metaphorical	~ **I think that's Henry**	≠ *I think we leave tomorrow*
	oblique version	~ **That would be Henry**	≠ *We would leave tomorrow*

sometimes been suggested, so that the following proportionality should obtain:

That is Henry : That will be Henry
::
We leave tomorrow : We will leave tomorrow

But how parallel are these two sets actually? Once we probe the agnation sets for the second member of each pair, we find that they are quite distinct: see Table 11.7.

That is, *That will be Henry* is agnate with versions with modal Adjuncts and it has an oblique version, but it is not agnate with the secondary future, whereas *We will leave tomorrow* has no modal agnates and no oblique version, but it is agnate with the secondary future. Here is a text example that suggests the agnation:

And I'll invite Lulu this afternoon. Oh, this **is going to** cheer Stanley up. It **will.** He's been down in the dumps lately. (Pinter, The Birthday Party)

And here there is a proportionality with the past:[24]

---

[24]One interesting semantic difference is, however, that the proportionality does not hold with a specific temporal Locative: *It's going to be cloudy tomorrow* is fine, but *it has been cloudy yesterday* is not.

we'll leave   : we're going to leave ::
we left : we have left

There are not, however, any agnate realizations involving modal Adjuncts. The situation is the reverse with modal *will*.
One interpretation of the pattern that emerges from the table above is precisely that the contrasts between the pairs *That's Henry : That'll be Henry* and *We leave tomorrow : We will leave tomorrow* should not be handled in parallel ways. The agnation patterns and alternative versions are in fact drawn along lines predicted by Halliday's three-term analysis with a future *will* rather than the reductionist two-term analysis with only a modal *will*.
Now, if we make the two examples exactly parallel except for an addition of a future circumstantial Location, we can see a further differentiation concerning a version with the simple present: see Table 11.8.
And if we probe the difference with a first person Subject, where *shall* is the marker of the simple 'future' in certain varieties of English, the following picture emerges: see Table 11.9.
That is, in first person, the two examples are actually formally distinct in certain varieties of English as already noted earlier.
The relevant modal interpretation of *will* is 'modalization: probability and median'. If we expand the paradigmatic focus to take in not only the median but also the outer modalities ('high/low') along the scale of probability and intersect these with semantically past, present and future time reference throughout the modal agnation set, the following picture emerges: see Tables 11.10-12.
That is, when the modality is expressed in the Finite, there is a verbal contrast between PAST and NON-PAST—*may/must have been : may / must be*. However, when the modality is expressed elsewhere, thus freeing up the Finite for tense, the finite contrast is 'past/present/future'—the 'future' tense shows up in reference to future time and it combines equally with high and low probability. This is what Halliday's account predicts: there is no contradiction

Table 11.8

	That will be Henry	That'll be Henry tomorrow
three-term	modal: modalization & median	temporal: future
two-term	modal: modalization & median	modal: modalization & median
simple present	*That's Henry* (non-modal version)	*?? That's Henry tomorrow*

Table 11.9

	Ah, I'll (probably) be the one she means	Ah, I'll be the one she means
three-term	modal	temporal: future
two-term	modal	modal
will	√	√
shall		√ Ah, I shall be the one she means

Table 11.10
Reference to Past Time.

modality expressed in	high	low
Finite	That must have been Henry yesterday	That may have been Henry yesterday
modal Adjunct (i): congruent	That was surely Henry yesterday	That was possibly Henry yesterday
modal Adjunct (ii): metaphorical projecting α clause	I'm sure that was Henry yesterday	I guess that was Henry yesterday
modal Attribute	It's certain that that was Henry yesterday	It's possible that that was Henry yesterday

Table 11.11
Reference to Present Time.

modality expressed in	high	low
Finite	That must be Henry now	That may be Henry now
modal Adjunct (i): congruent	That's surely Henry now	That's possibly Henry now
modal Adjunct (ii): metaphorical projecting α clause	I'm sure that's Henry now	I guess that's Henry now
modal Attribute	It's certain that that's Henry now	It's possible that that's Henry now

Table 11.12
Reference to Future Time.

modality expressed in	high	low
Finite	That must be Henry tomorrow	That may be Henry tomorrow
modal Adjunct (i): congruent	That'll surely be Henry tomorrow	That'll possibly be Henry now
modal Adjunct (ii): metaphorical projecting α clause	I'm sure that'll be Henry tomorrow	I guess that'll be Henry tomorrow
modal Attribute	It's certain that that'll be Henry tomorrow	It's possible that that'll be Henry tomorrow

Table 11.13

modality expressed in	past time reference	present time reference	future time reference
Finite	That'll have been Henry yesterday	That'll be Henry now	**That'll be Henry tomorrow**
modal Adjunct: congruent	That was probably Henry yesterday	That's probably Henry now	That'll probably be Henry tomorrow
modal Adjunct: metaphorical projecting α clause	I think that was Henry yesterday	I think that's Henry now	I think that'll be Henry tomorrow
modal Attribute	It's probable that that was Henry yesterday	It's probable that that's Henry now	It's probable that that'll be Henry tomorrow

between 'future' tense and 'high' or 'low' probability—it combines with probability in the same way as 'past' and 'present' do. If *will* was only a realization of modality, one would have to explain (i) why it can combine with modalities of other values without contradiction and (ii) why it shows up precisely in the environment where we can expect a future tense.

Now, what about median probability in the full paradigm set out for high and low probability above? This is the picture (again with only variants of a single example): see Table 11.13. The whole column of future time reference is clearly of interest; but the critical cell in the table is the one at the Finite row—*That'll be Henry tomorrow.* There are at least four possibilities:

1. It is unambiguous—it can only be a realization of 'modalization: median and probability'.
2. It is unambiguous—it can only be a realization of 'future' tense.
3. It is ambiguous—it can be a realization of either 1 or 2.
4. It is a neutralization of 1 and 2.

The two most likely ones are 3 and 4. The choice between them will clearly not decide between a modal interpretation with one *will* and Halliday's modal versus temporal interpretation with two *wills;* but it will be one piece of the puzzle. If it turns out to be 3, this is clearly an argument in favor of Halliday's analysis; if it is 4, it is compatible with either interpretation. More specifically, according to the modal interpretation, the different possibilities would presumably never arise—they would be seen as an artefact of Halliday's three-tense interpretation. It's clearly not easy to decide, and because various considerations are involved, I will leave the issue open for now. I can just note that if those varieties that alternate between *will* and *shall* in future time reference make a distinction between

I will be the one she recognizes tomorrow—'probably'

and

I shall be the one she recognizes tomorrow

we would have an indication that there can in fact be an ambiguity—possibility 3 above.

The discussion of paradigmatic agnation above is not intended to present conclusive evidence for the three-term system with a temporal *will.* Rather, it is intended to indicate how the systemic description of the grammar gives us the foundation for a systematic exploration of the implications in agnation for the two different interpretations of primary tense and *will.* As far as the examples presented here go, it seems very clear that we can recognize a temporal *will* within a three-term primary tense system. However, on the one hand, we need to make sure that we have systematically tested all the relevant systemic variables. In a comprehensive grammar, it is very hard to do this manually: we need to be able to generate paradigms of examples computationally (for instance, in order to intersect PROCESS TYPE, LOCATION, MOOD TYPE, MOOD PERSON, and other systems that may be relevant). On the other hand, we need to relate the systemic potential to naturally occurring examples that instantiate it (cf. Halliday, 1991). Both these considerations indicate that we have to treat individual examples (constructed or natural) with caution, whether we use them as examples or counter-examples: we have to ask where they are located relative to the relevant systemic variables, and we have to ask how representative they are in probabilistic terms.

6.5.2. Syntagmatic organization

The observations above have focused on the paradigmatic axis. From a syntagmatic point of view, *will* as Finite can also combine with the Adjuncts:

it'll be fine tomorrow : I think it'll probably be fine tomorrow

(1)

that'll be Henry : I think that'll probably be Henry   (2)

However, there is a significant difference between (1) and (2); they do not constitute a proportionality. With the temporal *will* in (1), the modal Adjuncts realize an additional feature of modality—additional, that is, to the temporal ordering that *will* construes. With modal *will* in (2), the effect is different—it is prosodic. The difference is quite principled and it is metafunctional in origin (cf. Sections 4 and 6.4 above).

6.6. Potentiality

Potentiality refers to the relation between the general systemic potential and the discoursal instance. It is the dimension that makes it possible to relate extensive samples of naturally occurring texts to the system—to generalize from texts to the system and then to use the system as a hypothesis about what we can expect to find in text. The relationship is crucial in tracking changes in the system; and it can be construed quantitatively in terms of the relationship between systemic probability and text frequency. Halliday and James (1993) offer this perspective on primary TENSE. It is also, as already noted above, one way we have of weighing the significance of individual, possibly constructed examples: How do they, as instances, generalize relative to the systemic potential? Also, it is one central way in which differences across registers are realized—the three-term primary tense system 'past/present/future' is implicated precisely when there is temporal variation in the field, as in the contrast between the social activities of narrating and forecasting. This is brought out when writers "play with" the system. For example:

> Once upon a time there **will** be a little girl called Uncumber. Uncumber **will** have a younger brother called Sulpice, and they **will** live with their parents in a house in the middle of the woods. There **will** be no windows in the house, because there **will** be nothing to see outside except the forest. While inside there **will** be all kinds of interesting things—strange animals, processions, jewels, battles, mazes, convolutions of pure shapes and pure colours—which *materialise* in the air at will, solid and brilliant and almost touchable. For this **will** be in the good new days a long, long while ahead, and it **will** be like that in people's houses then.
>
> (Michael Frayn, 1968, A Very Private Life, London: Collins)

Now, this kind of deployment of the system arguably depends precisely on the interpretation of *will* at group rank as 'future' in the system 'past/present/future.' We can make sense of the effect in terms of a dramatic change in the setting of the probabilities of the primary tense terms: 'future' takes over from 'past' as the narrative norm.

6.7. Phylogenesis

Language is a dynamic open system, and any subsystem such as TENSE is also open and dynamic: the tense potential evolves through countless instantiations in various semiotic environments, and it can "import" from, or "export" to, other subsystems. We know that tense systems may expand by "importing" from the domains of modality and motion (cf. Fleishman, 1982, and Traugott, 1978): lexical or grammatical items from other domains become systemic within TENSE as realizations, which means among other things that they enter into new agnation sets. In English, the use of *will* has gained ground over the present in the representation of future time. The meaning of the contrast between 'past' and 'present' has thus changed over the centuries. In Old English, for example, the distinction was really PAST versus NON-PAST (according to, for instance, Jespersen, 1931, and Strang, 1970). The simple present was the normal way of expressing futurity. Since that time, the range of future uses of the simple present has decreased; in Middle English "analytic forms were steadily on the increase" (Fridén, 1948: 20). Thus, the simple present of Old English has given ground to other ways of expressing futurity; it has also been restricted through the emergence of the present-in-present. In our interpretation of the Modern English tense system, we need to represent it so that it takes the phylogenetic trajectory into account. Somewhere in the overall system of English, the tense system has changed from 'past/present'. Now, one way of interpreting this is to see it as the emergence of a future tense in English, with a temporal *will* split off from modal *will*—a departure from certain other languages with Germanic roots. This would be consistent with the interpretation of the evolution of the English tense system as one of gradual elaboration to the point of its present richness, with a primary 'past/present/future' and a recursive secondary tense option. (This would also, at the same time, be a metafunctional shift from the interpersonal into the logical subtype of the ideational metafunction.) I am not at all saying that this is the only possible interpretation; what I am saying is that somewhere in the overall interpretation it is necessary to reflect the evolution of the system in such a way that the forward trajectory is brought out. This is one perspective Halliday's account is intended to address.

6.8. Register Variation

The tense system is variable over time, but it is also subject to "static oscillation," both dialectal and registerial. I am only concerned with register variation here. Different contexts are characterized by different field, tenor, and mode values and these correspond to different registers of the linguistic system; that is, differentiation within context is realized by variation within language. Since semantics is the linguistic interface to context, it is the locus of register variation in the first instance; but because semantics is naturally related to lexicogrammar, this second content stratum is also subject to register variation. Different contexts thus deploy TENSE in semantically different ways and these differences are projected onto TENSE itself within lexicogrammar (see Figure 11.23). At the semantic stratum, register variation tends to be noticed in the form of special uses, such as the dramatic present in (oral) narrative, the simple present of demonstration, the simple present in newspaper headlines. However, these are just part of the general principle of semantic adaptation to different context types. At the lexicogrammatical stratum, this adaptation shows up in register-specific systemic probabilities,

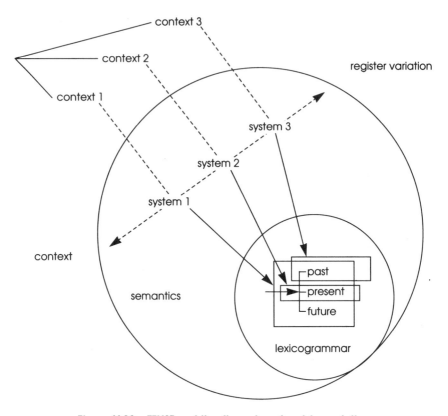

Figure 11.23.   TENSE and the dimension of register variation.

for instance, within primary tense. For example, in narrative registers, the primary past is much more likely than either the present or
the future; in procedural registers, the present is the most likely
selection; and in forecasts, the primary tense system is skewed toward the future. The limiting case is when the probability of one
term is 1 or 0: the register uses only a subpotential of the three-term
potential. Here the primary future may be excluded, but it may also
be foregrounded as the systemic norm in forecasting and planning.

Caffarel (1990, 1992) has described register variation within the
French tense system and also explored different theoretical alternatives for relating the general tense potential to register-specific
ones. Her study shows very clearly how registers vary in how much
of the overall tense potential take up and which options they favor
for elaboration. (For a review of the issues, see also Matthiessen,
1993.)

6.9. Typology

Typology is, among other things, a way of profiling the tense system of a language against languages with other tense systems, against languages with aspectual construals of time, against languages that may have yet other alternatives (as suggested by Whorf's interpretation of Hopi)—that is, locating it somewhere in the overall semiotic space of language in general. The interpretation of a given language should bring out the integrity of its own system in terms that are not borrowed from other languages (Martin, 1983; Matthiessen, Nanri & Zeng, 1991); but as a second step, it should also as far as possible locate the language within the overall systemic space, say of lexicogrammatical construals of time.

The analysis with future *will* takes into account the typological difference between modern English and languages such as Swedish and, indeed, earlier forms of English itself, where the distribution of the simple present was significantly different from that of modern English. Now, if we don't assume that a tense language necessarily has a future tense, the Swedish primary tense system would at least be a strong candidate for a two-term interpretation, 'past/present,' rather than a three-term one (cf. for example, Thorell, 1973). One way of bringing out the sharp difference between Modern English and Swedish in the construal of future time would be to interpret English as a three-term system, 'past/present/future'. That would align it more closely with French at this point (cf. Caffarel, 1990). And, it would also contrast it with languages with a greater number of primary contrasts construing not only location relative to the 'now' of speaking, but also relative temporal distance, as in certain languages spoken in Africa (cf. Comrie, 1985; Welmers, 1973).

6.10. Balance

How do these various dimensions stack up against one another in the balance between a three-term (primary) tense system with *will* (/ *shall*) as a realization of the term 'future' alongside modal uses of *will* and an exclusively modal interpretation?

To flesh out an argument that one would consider reasonably convincing from a systemic-functional point of view, we would need a substantial monograph: I would not claim that the indications I have presented above amount to overwhelming evidence—such situations are rare in any case in language, which abounds in partially contradictory tendencies. One important question is thus whether contradictions are in any sense accommodated within the system itself—in some sense resolved because of its multidimensionality. I have already suggested that the dimensionality in rank is precisely what allows the grammar to have it more than one way—a three-term tense system at group rank and a different system of verb forms at word rank. Similarly, with the metafunctions, it is perfectly possible that there are areas of overlap or regions where systems assigned to different metafunctions show similarities. It is also possible that semantic features such as time or cause may be organized into the systems of more than one metafunction (as we find, e.g. with temporal conjunctions and temporal circumstances—textual and ideational: experiential time, respectively).

Thus, if we consider temporal: future *will* and modal: median and modalization: probability *will* from a topological point of view (see Martin & Matthiessen, 1992), we can explore the semantic space construed by TENSE (ideational, logical) and the semantic space enacted by MODALITY and organize our interpretation in such a way that it shows the affinity between 'future' and 'median' probability (see Figure 11.24). Modality and tense are on different metafunctional planes—any given example is located within both planes; but there is a crossover area between the two. This can be hard to bring out typologically in a system network (see Martin & Matthiessen, 1992), although the topological closeness is, in a sense, symbolized by the lower-ranking realization *will*, where the ideational and interpersonal come together—but such difficulties are of a general, systemic kind. The closeness would be reflected, for instance, in the distribution of temporal *will* and modalization *will* in, for instance, clauses of logical and temporal conditioning, where both are unusual.

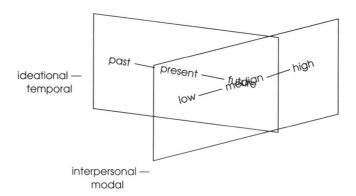

Figure 11.24. **Semantic distance among different categories of TENSE and MODALITY.**

If we relate the future within the simple verbal group to projection within hypotactic verbal group complexes (see Section 3.2.1.1 above), we can interpret the crossover point between the two meta-functional planes as one of projection. By another step in agnation, modality is related to projection through interpersonal metaphor—ideational projection such as *I think/ guess/ believe* comes to stand for interpersonal modality (see Halliday, 1985: Section 10.4; cf. also Matthiessen, 1991, on metaphor as a metafunctional interface). As already noted, this is also the environment in which the primary past can come to take on the modal value of obliqueness (*I thought, I just wanted, I was wondering* → . . .).

7. CONCLUSION

I suggested at the outset of the discussion that systemic theory can be used as a resource for enriching our interpretation of TENSE in English. It enables us to locate the interpretation in the overall system of English in its context: I have discussed the consequences of locating TENSE where Halliday has put it in terms of the various dimensions of language in context construed by systemic theory. I have compared and contrasted it at two levels—with other resources within the grammar and with alternative interpretations. The two perspectives have been shown to be mutually relevant in the sense that alternative interpretations often make TENSE more or less like other grammatical resources such as MODALITY.

Let me summarize the discussion of the grammar of TENSE in relation to other temporal resources set out in the table in Figure 11.5. TENSE is a grammatical resource for construing temporal relations serially. Other resources concerned with time complement it in ways that depend on their location in the grammatical system.

1. **Within the clause.** We find experiential Adjuncts (i.e. circumstances) expressing time: location in time, extent in time (duration), and frequency of the occurrence of the process. Together with TENSE, they constitute the ideational resources for construing time (cf. Figure 11.16 above). We also find an interpersonal angle on time in the clause, usuality as a type of modality and assessments of temporal expectations.

2. **Between clauses.** We find textual Adjuncts (i.e. conjuncts) presenting temporal relations: temporal conjuncts of precedence, simultaneity, and so forth. Temporal conjuncts

are cohesive devices; they do not create grammatical structure but serve to signal temporal relations in text. They are, however, related to the expression of temporal relations in clause complexes (organized by the logical function). In both cases, we find temporal relations that are text-internal (endophoric, as it were) and go beyond a single clause.

The systems mentioned are resources for expressing times or temporal relations. As such, they constitute the grammatical context in which a tense selection is made. For instance, a speaker may select a circumstantial time specification as well as a tense. In addition, a tense selection is made in the context of the selection of a particular kind of event in the taxonomy of events. For example, secondary present may be chosen in the context of a transitional event (as in *We're approaching L.A.*) or in the context of a durative event (as in *I'm liking Henry less and less*).

However, there is also another kind of context in which a tense selection is made—the higher-level semiotic context realized by language, with the semantic system as the interface. This is the source of register variation—of different versions of TENSE within the one general system. At this point in the system, we are quite a distance both from a word-based approach taking as its point of departure forms such as *do, did, will* and from a meaning-based approach (such as we might find in notional or communicative grammar) taking as its point of departure the meaning 'time', as it has been lexicalized within the ideational system of English. TENSE is part of a much more complex system—one where meaning is dispersed along dimensions such as metafunctional diversification, rank and register variation and items are drawn into multiple service along these dimensions. To interpret TENSE systemically means, then, both to locate it somewhere in the overall system and to reveal the global implications of this location.

REFERENCES

Bateman, J. (1989) Dynamic systemic-functional grammar: A new frontier. *Word.* 401–2: 263–286.

Bull, W. (1963) *Time, tense and the verb.* Berkeley, CA: University of California Press.

Butler, C. (1982) The directive function of the English modals. Ph.D. dissertation, University of Nottingham.

Butt, D. (1987) *Randomness, order and the latent patterning of text.* In Birch & O'Toole (eds), *Functions of Style.* London: Pinter.

Caffarel, A. (1990) *Mediating between grammar and context: A bi-stratal exploration of the semantics of French tense.* B.A. Honors thesis, Department of Linguistics, University of Sydney.

Caffarel, A. (1992) Context projected onto semantics and the consequences for grammatical selection. *Language Sciences* 92.4.

Chatman, S. (1978) *Story and discourse: Narrative structure in fiction and film.* Ithaca, NY: Cornell University Press.

Close, R. (1979) *Will* in *if-* clauses. In S. Greenbaum, G. Leech & J. Svartvik (eds.), *Studies in English linguistics for Randolph Quirk.* London: Longman.

Comrie, B. (1985) *Tense.* Cambridge, MA: Cambridge University Press.

Dahl, Ö. (1985). *Tense and aspect systems.* Oxford: Blackwell.

Davidsen-Nielsen, N. (1986) Has English a future? In I. Lindblad & M. Ljung (eds.), *Proceedings from the Third Nordic Conference for English Studies.* Haesselby, Sept. 25–27, 1986. Stockholm: Almqvist & Wiksell International. pp. 53–59.

Dowty, D. (1979). *Word meaning and Montague Grammar.* Dordrecht, The Netherlands: Reidel.

Ehrich, E. (1987) The generation of tense. In G. Kempen (ed.), *Natural language generation. New results in Artificial Intelligence, psychology and linguistics.* Dordrecht, The Netherlands: Martinus Nijhoff Publishers.

Fleishman, S. (1982) *The future in thought and language.* Cambridge, UK: Cambridge University Press.

Foley, W.A. & R.D. van Valin. (1984). *Functional syntax and universal grammar.* Cambridge, UK: Cambridge University Press.

Fridén, G. (1948) *Studies on the tenses of the English verb from Chaucer to Shakespeare with special reference to the late sixteenth century.* Ph.D. dissertation, Uppsala University.

Givón, T. (1979) *Understanding grammar.* New York: Academic Press.

Halliday, M.A.K. (1965) *Types of structure.* Working Paper for the O.S.T.I. Programme in the Linguistic Properties of Scientific English. Reprinted in M.A.K. Halliday & J.R. Martin (eds.), 1981, *Readings in systemic linguistics.* London: Batsford.

Halliday, M.A.K. (1967/8) Notes on transitivity and theme in English. *Journal of Linguistics.* V. 3(1) 37–81, 3(2) 199–244, 4(2) 179–215.

Halliday, M.A.K. (1970) Functional diversity in language, as seen from a consideration of modality and mood in English. *Foundations of Language,* Vol. 6(3) 327–51.

Halliday, M.A.K. (1973) *Explorations in the functions of language.* London: Edward Arnold.

Halliday, M.A.K. (1976) *System and function in language: Selected papers,* ed. G. Kress. London: Oxford University Press.

Halliday, M.A.K. (1978) *Language as social semiotic: The social interpretation of language and meaning.* London: Edward Arnold.

Halliday, M.A.K. (1979a) Modes of meaning and modes of saying. In Allerton, D.J., E. Carney, and D. Holdcroft (eds), *Function and Context in Linguistic Analysis: Essays Offered to William Haas.* Cambridge: Cambridge University Press.

Halliday, M.A.K. (1979b) On being teaching. In S. Greenbaum, G. Leech & J. Svartvik (eds.), *Studies in English linguistics for Randolph Quirk.* London: Longman.

Halliday, M.A.K. (1985) An *introduction to functional grammar.* London: Edward Arnold.

Halliday, M.A.K. (1985b) *Spoken and written language.* Geelong Vic.: Deakin University Press.

Halliday, M.A.K. (1991) Corpus studies and probabilistic grammar. In K. Aijmer & B. Altenberg (eds.), *English corpus linguistics: Studies in Honour or Jan Svartvik.* London: Longman.

Halliday, M.A.K. (1992) The history of a sentence: An essay in social semiotics. In Vita Fortunati (ed.), *Bologna, la cultura italiana e le letterature straniere moderne.* Volume terzo. Ravenna: Longo Editore. pp. 29–45.

Halliday, M.A.K. & R. Hasan. (1976) *Cohesion in English.* London: Longman.

Halliday, M.A.K. & R. Hasan. (1985). *Language, context and text: aspects of language in a social-semiotic perspective.* Geelong, Vic.: Deakin University Press.

Halliday, M.A.K. & Z.L. James. (1993) A quantitative study of polarity and primary tense in the English finite clause. In J.M. Sinclair, M. Hoey & G. Fox (eds.), *Techniques of description.* London: Routledge. pp. 32–66.

Halliday, M.A.K. & C. Matthiessen. (forthcoming). *Construing experience: a language-based approach to cognition.* Berlin: de Gruyter.

Hopper, P. & S. Thompson. (1980) Transitivity in grammar and discourse. *Language* 56: 251–99.

Hopper, P. & S. Thompson (eds.). (1982) Studies in transitivity. *Syntax and semantics,* Vol. 15. New York: Academic Press.

Hornstein, N. (1977) Towards a theory of tense. *Linguistic Inquiry,* Vol. 8: 521–58.

Hornstein, N. (1981) The study of meaning in natural language: three approaches to tense. In N. Hornstein & D. Lightfoot (eds.), *Explanation in linguistics: The logical problem of language acquisition.* London: Longman.

Huddleston, R. (1984) *Introduction to the Grammar of English.* Cambridge: Cambridge University Press.

Huddleston, R. (1991) Further remarks on Halliday's functional grammar: a reply to Matthiessen and Martin. *Occasional Papers in Systemic Linguistics* 5: 75–130.

Jespersen, O. (1931) *Modern English Grammar, Part V.* London: Edward Arnold.

Joos, M. (1964) *The English verb.* Madison: University of Wisconsin Press.

Labov, W. (1970) Negative attraction and negative concord. In Labov, *Lan-*

guage in the inner city: Studies in the Black English Vernacular. Philadelphia: The University of Pennsylvania Press.

Lily, W. (1549) *A shorte introduction of grammar.*

Martin, J.R. (1983) *Participant identification in English, Tagalog and Kate.* Australian Journal of Linguistics 3(1) 45–74.

Martin, J.R. (1992). *English text: system and structure.* Amsterdam: Benjamins.

Martin, J.R. & C. Matthiessen. (1992) Systemic typology and topology. In F. Christie (ed.), *Literacy in Social Processes.* Centre for Studies of Language in Education, Darwin, NT

Matthiessen, C. (1984) *Choosing tense in English.* USC, ISI/RR-84–143.

Matthiessen, C. (1990) *Metafunctional complementarity and harmony.* Department of Linguistics, University of Sydney.

Matthiessen, C. (1991) Language on language: the grammar of semiosis. *Social Semiotics,* 1(2).

Matthiessen, C. (1993) Register in the round. In M. Ghadessy (ed.), *Register analysis: Theory and practice.* London: Pinter.

Matthiessen, C. (1995) *Lexicogrammatical cartography: English systems.* Tokyo: International Language Sciences Publishers.

Matthiessen, C. & J. Bateman. (1991) *Text Generation and Systemic Linguistics: Experiences from English and Japanese.* London: Pinter.

Matthiessen, C., K. Nanri & Zeng Licheng. (1991) *Multilingual resources in text generation: Ideational focus.* In Proceedings of the 2nd Japan-Australia Symposium on Natural Language Processing, Japan, October 1991.

Michael, I. (1970) *English grammatical categories and the tradition to 1800.* Cambridge: Cambridge University Press.

Palmer, F.R. (1974) *The English verb.* London: Longman.

Poynton, C. (1990) *Address and the Semiotics of Social Relations: A systemic-functional account of address forms and practices in Australian English.* Ph.D. Thesis. Department of Linguistics, University of Sydney.

Prior, A. (1967) *Past, present and future.* London: Oxford University Press.

Quirk, R., S. Greenbaum, G. Leech, & J. Svartvik. (1972) *A Grammar of Contemporary English.* London: Longman.

Quirk, R., S. Greenbaum, G. Leech, & J. Svartvik. (1985) *A Comprehensive Grammar of the English Language.* London: Longman.

Reichenbach, H. (1947) *Elements of Symbolic Logic.* New York: Macmillan.

Stone, I. (1956) *Men to match my mountains. The monumental saga of the winning of America's Far West.* New York: Berkeley.

Strang, B. (1970) *A history of English.* London: Methuen.

Svartvik J. & R. Quirk. (1980) *A corpus of English conversation.* Lund: C.W.K. Gleerup.

Sweet, H. (1900) *New English Grammar.* Oxford: Clarendon Press.

Thorell, O. (1973) *Svensk grammatik.* Stockholm: Esselte Studium.

Traugott, E. (1978) On the expression of spatio-temporal relations in language. In J. Greenberg, C. Ferguson & E. Moravcsik (eds.), *Universals of Human Language III: Word formation*. Stanford: Stanford University Press.

Vendler, Z. (1967) *Linguistics in Philosophy*. Ithaca, NY: Cornell University Press.

Welmers, W. (1973) *African language structures*. Berkeley, CA: California University Press.

Williams, M. (1987) *The Velveteen Rabbit*. Abridged from the original. New York: Platt & Munk.

12

Toward a Systemic Approach to Tense and Aspect in Polish*

Nigel Gotteri

University of Sheffield, England

Time and tense are related, but rarely stand in a direct relationship
to each other. Even the most highly developed tense and aspect system expresses only a limited number of potential features, leaving
others unexpressed or expressed by some other means, the most
obvious means being time adjuncts. Thus, for example, relationships in time typically expressed by choice of perfect or continuous
forms in English are not readily expressed in Polish by choice of verb
or verb form. If it is important to express them, recourse is made to
adverbs like już "already, now" and właśnie "just." Ultimately, one
would hope to start from reference to time and constituency in time,
and to end with verb form choices and all the different elements that
allow speakers to choose to refer to time in a particular way on a
particular occasion. In the meantime, the question of aspect—and
the special way in which tenses interact with it—in Slavic languages
is one to which systemic methods clearly should be applied. The
starting-point for this paper is the range of forms that imperfective
and perfective verbs put at the speaker's disposal; this is the "para-
dox of formal systemic-functional grammar."

*Earlier versions of material in this paper appeared in *Sheffield Working Papers
in Language and Linguistics* (1984: 72–78), in a number of subsequent conference papers, and in lectures given in April and May 1995 at the Teacher Training
College of Foreign Languages in Bydgoszcz, Poland.

"Few parts of a language-system illustrate better than its aspect-system the validity of the structuralist slogan <u>Tout se tient</u> ('Everything hangs together')," according to Lyons (1977:714). Also, few parts illustrate better the potential usefulness of the systemic notion of interrelated ranges or <u>systems</u> of choices. I say potential usefulness, rather than actual usefulness in many cases, precisely because of the way in which everything hangs together; useful though it may be in the long run, better to keep quiet until you've got it right. This chapter claims no more than to be a preliminary survey of the edifice of Polish verb systems, a first attempt to see what hangs together and how.

1. FORMAL CHOICES

A Polish verb has few simple personal forms. In fact, apart from three special Imperative forms that need not concern us further here, there are just six Present forms. All other personal forms are composites. In addition to personal forms, there are fully inflecting Passive Participles; verbs of imperfective aspect also have fully inflecting Active Participles. There are Past Active Participles that are used in forming composite non-Present tenses. It is convenient also to associate Verbal Nouns in -ie with the paradigms of the verbs from which they are formed, because they retain the aspect of the motivating verb. Mention should also be made of four non-inflecting forms, two of them Adverbs. First, each verb has a Verbal Adverb. Second, verbs of imperfective aspect may have a Participial Adverb, an adverb formed by regular means from the Active Participle. The other two forms are the Infinitive and an Impersonal Past form in -o, which latter need not concern us further here.

(In addition to these simple forms of lexical verbs, two further kinds of element contribute to complexes that are traditionally regarded as coming within the verb paradigm: First, the mobile personal endings that contribute chiefly to Past forms and, second, two particles, one of which carries a conditional meaning and the other of which is optative or imperative.)

The range of simple forms is displayed as a taxonomic network in Figure 12.1.

The network does not include Past, Pluperfect, Conditional or periphrastic Future forms (verbs of imperfective aspect only) because these are all composites. The Past is made up from Past Active Participle and mobile personal ending, and the Present Conditional is composed of Past Active Participle, conditional particle and mobile

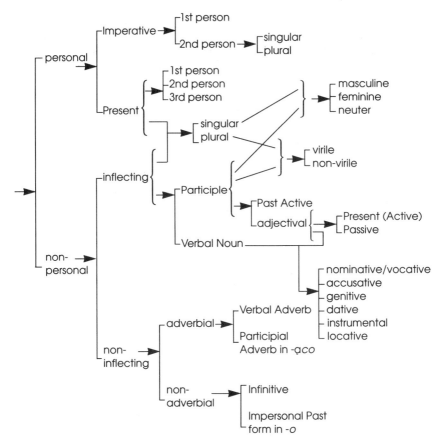

Figure 12.1. Taxonomy of simple forms of the Polish verb, displayed as a network.
Braces (curly brackets) represent conjunctions, and square brackets ([and]) represent disjunctions. Thus, $\begin{smallmatrix} a- \\ b- \end{smallmatrix}\} \to [\begin{smallmatrix} c \\ d \end{smallmatrix}$ represents "if both a and b, then either c or d." Also, $\begin{smallmatrix} a \\ b \end{smallmatrix}] \to [\begin{smallmatrix} c \\ d \end{smallmatrix}$ represents "if a or b, then either c or d"

personal ending. The rare, but possibly not quite extinct, Pluperfect and the quite common Past Conditional resemble the Past tense and the Present Conditional, but with the addition of a Past Active Participle of the verb być "be" to emphasize remoteness. The periphrastic Future of verbs of imperfective aspect is with personal (Future) forms of być and EITHER Infinitive OR Past (sic) Active Participle, the futurity of the personal forms overruling the pastness of the Active Participle.

The range of constructions with a claim to the title of Passive is greater than many grammars and textbooks of the language suggest. The most obvious ones involve być "be," bywać "be" (frequentative), zostawać "become" and its perfective partner zostać. These combine with Passive Participles, of perfective verbs in the case of zostawać/zostać, and of verbs of either aspect in the case of być and bywać.

2. SEMANTIC CHOICES

In Gotteri (1987) I labelled taxonomic networks like Figure 12.1 bogus and networks that set out to show ranges of semantic choices real. It is suggested in that paper that I have as yet no real network to offer for the Polish verb. The present chapter is partly an attempt to remedy that lack. What semantic choices are there? Traditional treatments would suggest the following outline, diagrammed systematically:

Figure 12.2. Traditional outline for Aspect.

or alternatively:

Figure 12.3. Traditional outline for Tense.

A certain rather obvious arbitrariness in the choice between the two formulations above, with aspect and tense as the broader (less delicate) choices respectively, suggests the rewiring in Figure 12.4, in order to restore equality between tense and aspect. The formulation in Figure 12.4 takes a step further the view that the tense system for perfective verbs offers a choice between past and non-past, rather than between past and future or (as has also been suggested) past and present.

These three diagrams encapsulate well-established grammar-book-type explanations of the meanings of the main tense forms. Figure 12.2 has the virtue that aspect is made a broader choice, matched by the formal choice of an imperfective or a perfective verb. Figure 12.3 is more in keeping with the (possibly rather translation-based or, worse

Figure 12.4.   Equality between Aspect and Tense.

still, anglocentric) notion that one does not have to worry about choice of aspect in the present because only imperfective verbs have a Present form with present meaning. Clearly this widespread view of the meanings of Polish verb forms assumes a close form-meaning correlation and is inclined to be strongly influenced by the received names of forms. (Tense names are very seductive; they flash their eyes at you and you forget your reservations.) Perhaps I can now refine my view of the semantic choices a little. Aspect is widely treated as a kind of privative opposition, with perfective aspect summing up the process concerned in terms of such things as completeness, beginning, end or result and seeing it as a single homogeneous whole, and imperfective aspect simply does not suggest any such summing up. The aspect system, seen thus, becomes:

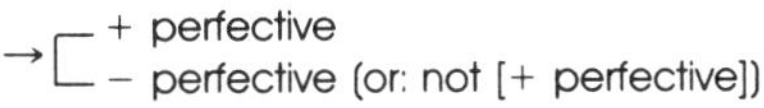

$$\rightarrow \begin{cases} + \text{ perfective} \\ - \text{ perfective (or: not [+ perfective])} \end{cases}$$

Figure 12.5.   Aspect system.

Let us now hypothesize, following Gotteri (1983) on Bulgarian, that the semantic feature realized by Past forms is something more like distance, [+ distance] in our metalanguage being tentatively glossed as "non-actual, non-present, remote in relation to time of utterance or some other process." The first semantic-tense choice becomes:

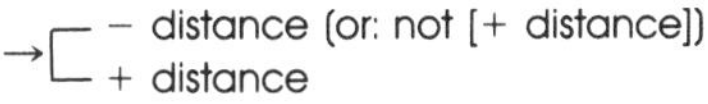

$$\rightarrow \begin{cases} - \text{ distance (or: not [+ distance])} \\ + \text{ distance} \end{cases}$$

Figure 12.6.   Semantic-tense choice.

If [+ perfective] has not been chosen, then not choosing [+ distance] imposes an obligation to choose further between present and future, the future of imperfective verbs (see above) being expressed periphrastically. It would not be surprising if the extra formal bulk of the future of verbs of imperfective aspect were to realize extra semantic complexity. Let us therefore assume that there is a further privative opposition:

$$\rightarrow \begin{cases} + \text{ future} \\ - \text{ future (or: not [+ future])} \end{cases}$$

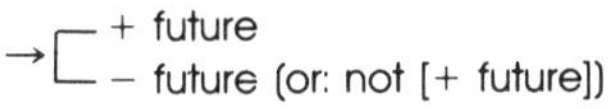

Figure 12.7.   Further privative opposition.

The semantic ("real") network to account for the meaning choices expressed by Past, Present and Future (Active) forms of Polish verbs now looks like this:

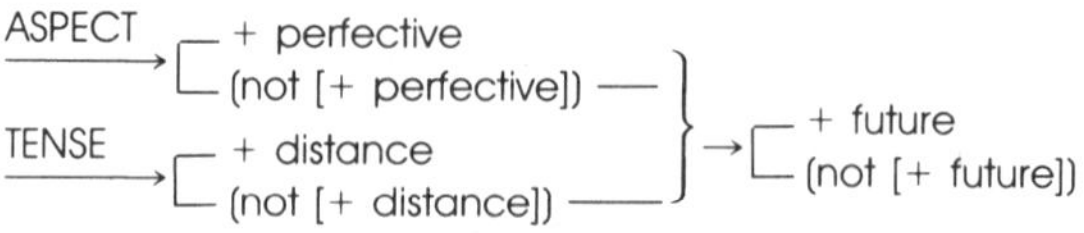

ASPECT ⟶ ┌ + perfective
         └ (not [+ perfective]) ──┐
                                  ├ ⟶ ┌ + future
TENSE ⟶ ┌ + distance   │   └ (not [+ future])
        └ (not [+ distance]) ─────┘

Figure 12.8. Semantic network.

Figure 12.8 is a consolidated network in which repetition of systems is avoided. One might unravel it into a displayed network like Figure 12.9:

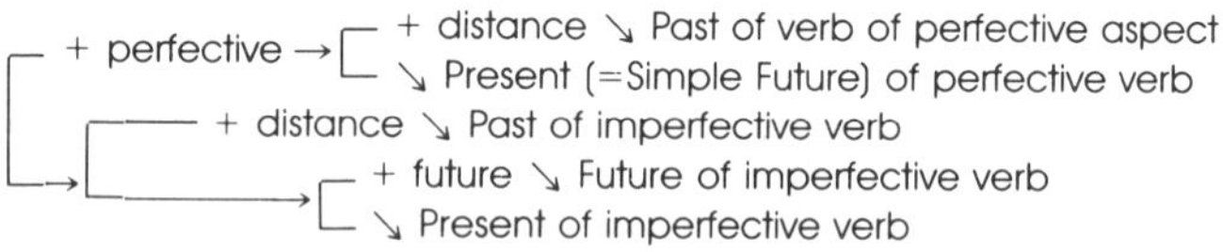

┌ + perfective ⟶ ┌ + distance ↘ Past of verb of perfective aspect
│   └ ↘ Present (=Simple Future) of perfective verb
│   ┌────── + distance ↘ Past of imperfective verb
└⟶ ┌┘   ⟶ ┌ + future ↘ Future of imperfective verb
               └ ↘ Present of imperfective verb

Figure 12.9. Displayed network.

Notice that the assumption that the oppositions so far are privative ones has allowed us quietly to drop the negative (not +) features, because, for example, the choice of an imperfective verb simply realizes a semantic choice of silence on the matter of summing up the process.

The diagonal arrows here are a conventional way of indicating formal realizations of meaning choices. This information can be made more legible for many purposes if it is presented as a list of forms with their semantic glosses, as at Figure 12.10.

3. DELICACY AND NON-FINITE VERB FORMS

The consolidated network (systems not repeated) in Figure 12.4 covers only the simple finite forms and the periphrastic Future of imperfective verbs, which allows tense and aspect systems to be simultaneous. If the semantics of non-finite forms is brought into the picture, aspect,

Present of perfective verb	[+perfective]
Past of perfective verb	[+perfective, +distance]
Past of imperfective verb	[+distance]
Future of imperfective verb	[+future]
Present of imperfective verb	Ø

Figure 12.10. Forms with their semantic glosses.

as Slavists might expect, begins to emerge as the broader or more fundamental (less delicate) system:

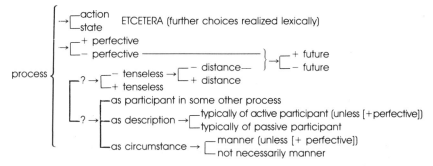

Figure 12.11.   Network with non-finite forms included.

According to the scheme that now incorporates non-finite forms, the list in Figure 12.10 of forms with glosses can be supplemented by the following:

Infinitive of imperfective verb	[+ tenseless]
Infinitive of perfective verb	[+ perfective, + tenseless]
Verbal Noun of imperfective verb	[as participant in some other process]
Verbal Noun of perfective verb	[+ perfective, as participant in some other process]
Present Participle of imperfective verb	[as description typically of an active participant]
Passive Participle of imperfective verb	[as description typically of a passive participant]
Passive Participle of perfective verb	[+ perfective, as description typically of a passive participant]
Verbal Adverb of imperfective verb	[as circumstance (not necessarily manner)]
Verbal Adverb of perfective verb	[+ perfective, as circumstance]
Participial Adverb of imperfective verb	[as manner circumstance]

Figure 12.12.   Forms with glosses.

Figures 12.10 and 12.12 are, of course, lists of selection expressions, with realizations listed on their left. The reversal of the usual order of meaning choice followed by formal realization raises questions about the kind of exercise being conducted here, to which I now turn.

4. THE PARADOX OF FORMAL SYSTEMIC— FUNCTIONAL GRAMMAR (SFG)

The exercise so far may appear paradoxical, in that the techniques of a functional school of linguistics, in a version that gives priority to semantics, are being used to account for a set of data delimited formally. That is, with few exceptions, our data for semantic classification are the simple forms of the Polish verb. The few exceptions are items that, though composite, may still be regarded as basic tense forms. (Imperative forms, Pluperfects and Conditionals have been ignored for reasons of space.) No apology is offered for this save the following two points: (a) discussions of tense and aspect frequently make points that are strongly suggestive of a systemic approach, at least to a systemicist, so one might as well come out of the closet and try to formulate and possibly adapt some of these points in one's own overtly systemic way, and (b) the alternative to delimiting one's data in this way seems to be to embark on a global and frankly unmanageable investigation of how Poles talk about processes, situations, the world, the universe and everything.

5. COMPOSITE FORMS AND CONSTRUCTIONS WITH MORE THAN ONE VERB

Composite forms such as Conditionals not yet treated may be seen as representing the addition of further semantic choices to our existing network(s). Constructions involving modals and the various passive constructions may be regarded as representing more than one pass through the network. For example, mam to zrobić "I am supposed to do that (literally: I-have that to-do)" would represent two passes through the network, yielding glosses as follows:

mam	1st person singular Present form of mieć "have," a verb of imperfective aspect	Ø
zrobić	Infinitive of zrobić "do," a verb of perfective aspect	[+ perfective + tenseless]

Figure 12.13. Two passes through the network.

As an example of a passive construction, byli otoczeni "they were surrounded" would yield the following two glosses:

byli	3rd person virile plural Past form of the verb być "be," of imperfective aspect (= virile plural form of Past Active Participle)	[+ distance]
otoczeni	virile plural form of Passive Participle of the verb otoczyć "surround," a verb of perfective aspect	[+ perfective, as description typically of a passive participant]

Figure 12.14. Passive construction.

6. SEMANTICS AND PRAGMATICS

In sketching preliminary hypotheses regarding the semantics of verb forms in Polish, I have concentrated exclusively on what semantic rights speakers have as they make their formal choices. A study of the pragmatics of verbal usage would be concerned with the significance of a particular choice in a particular utterance. A Present form of an imperfective verb, for example, although semantically blank as far as tense and aspect are concerned (cf. Gotteri 1983), might be an extremely significant choice when used by a particular speaker on a particular occasion where there might be good reason to expect some other non-blank form.

Because much in context is left to pragmatics, semantics as discussed here can be highly abstract. I would also suggest that many semantic features might best be described apophatically, or in negative terms. With what view of a situation is this verb incompatible? How can this form never be used? For example, perfective verbs in Polish are widely regarded as marked, in relation to their unmarked imperfective counterparts. They have no present active participle, they have no compound future tenses, they do not combine with phase verbs; semantically, they are unable to view the duration of a process from the inside, they view a process as a box that you are not allowed to open. All these are negative characteristics, or can at least most easily be defined in negative terms.

REFERENCES

Gotteri, N. (1983) "A note on Bulgarian verb systems." *MALS Journal*, New Series. 8: 49–60.

Gotteri, N. (1987) "When is a system network not a system network? And is that a fair question? Fragments from an ongoing discussion." *Occasional Papers in Systemic Linguistics*. 1: 5–14.

Lyons, J. (1977) *Semantics* (Volume Two). Cambridge, UK: Cambridge University Press.

13

Discourse–Pragmatic Distinctions of the Past-in-Present in English and Spanish*

Angela Downing

Departamento de Filología Inglesa
Universidad Complutense, Madrid

1. INTRODUCTION

Parallel forms exist in English and Spanish, as also in German, Italian and French among other languages (Comrie 1976, Dahl 1985) for what in systemic grammar is called the "past-in-present" (Halliday 1994), otherwise known in English as the present perfect. In Spanish several terms have been used, among which the most transparent is "ante-present" (Bello 1928). In British English and Peninsular Spanish, a distinction is maintained in both the written and the spoken modes between the meaning conveyed by the past-in-present and that conveyed by the past tense. Unlike French, therefore, the Spanish past-in-present has not wholly taken over the

---

*The following paper represents a small token of my indebtedness to Michael Halliday, who has opened up new perspectives on the relation between language and what we can do through language.

functions of the past in the spoken mode, that is, in Dahl's characterization, the perfect has not become perfective (1985:139).[1]

The distinction between past-in-present and past is based, in principle for both these standard varieties under consideration, on the conceptualization of the event in relation to the time-sphere in which it is located by the speaker. The time-sphere of the past-in-present is anterior to and extending up to the point of reference, which is taken here to be utterance time.[2] The time-sphere of the past tense is past time but separated from the present. Events located within the time-sphere of the past-in-present are typically seen to maintain some psychological link with the present. This is the notion that has been developed as "current relevance" or "present relevance" and by some "factor present at S" or "aftermath" (Fenn 1987), where S equals "point of speech," following Reichenbach (1947). As Fenn points out, this "factor present at S" has often been erroneously diagnosed in terms of real aftermath, whereas in fact, it can only be inferred from specific contexts, and then not always unambiguously. It must be evaluated therefore not merely in semantic terms, but with some discourse-pragmatic evaluation. I will claim that the problem with present relevance for English is that it over-predicts; for Spanish, however, it does not. Voicing dissatisfaction with both the term and the concept of current relevance, McCoard (1978) has asked why, if this concept is all it is meant to be, we cannot say in English "I have been born in Bristol/in 1940," or "Gutenberg has invented printing," since these facts appear to be of undoubted relevance to the speaker's present or to humanity in general. As McCoard points out, "Even great real-world relevance is not by itself sufficient to promote many examples to acceptability," (1978:45). This is certainly true of English, but not, I will maintain, of Spanish.

When located within the time-sphere of the past, events are seen as not having a psychological link with the present. The past tense (or tenses in the case of Spanish) are used in both British English and Peninsular Spanish "to sever the link between the event and the present moment" (Butt & Benjamin 1989:210).

So, although the past-in-present views the "pastness" of an event as an element of present time, the past tense seems to relate an event either to the context of its occurrence, or simply to the past in general, as distinct from the present (Fenn 1987:214).

---

[1] I wish to thank Isabel López-Varela for her help in preparing the illustrations.

[2] The point of reference can also be future time (Bauer 1969:190), but this is irrelevant to the present purpose.

In both British English and Peninsular Spanish, the past-in-present is the marked choice. There has to be some motivation for its use. Nevertheless, the problem remains of specifying in what contexts and why the past-in-present is acceptable in Spanish but its equivalent sounds odd, ungrammatical even, in English.

One factor said to be associated with the past time-sphere is the unrepeatability of the event. According to this, events that are unrepeatable, that is uniquely situated in the past, such as being born or dying, at least when predicated of one individual, are not usually expressed by the past-in-present in English.

Nevertheless, even events such as being born can sometimes be assigned to a present time-sphere, by virtue of plurality and/or iterativity as in (1) and (3), as well as metaphor, as in (2):

We've been born into a century of unprecedented change.

(1)

We've died with Christ. We've risen with Christ. We've been born again. (8773)   (2)

A number of people have invented printing devices.   (3)

In all such cases, the time-sphere is still open, since other participants may repeat the process.

For some analysts, indefiniteness of location within the time-sphere appears to be criterial for events expressed by the past-in-present, as opposed to the definiteness of location, at least by implication, of events expressed by the past. It is well known that this difference can be reinforced by the addition of adjuncts of non-specific time, such as *ever, recently* and *yet* for the past-in-present, and adverbials of specific time such as *yesterday, two months ago, last year* for the past[3]. In English, questions and subordinate clauses with *when* also serve to establish a definite location in time, and are therefore incompatible with the past-in-present as in (4) and (5):

*When have they arrived?   (4)

---

[3]*Ever* can also be used with reference to any of a series of specific occasions in the past, as in, "*Did you ever see Schofield act in 'King Lear'?*"

*I wasn't at home when they have arrived.   (5)

In utterances where *when* refers to a future event the time-sphere is, obviously, still open and the past-in-present is a coherent choice ("When you've finished, hand it in"). Upholders of the indefiniteness criterion claim that the past-in-present is used when the meanings of anteriority and indefiniteness are present in the speaker's mind even though no adjunct accompanies the verb (Alarcos 1978; Downing & Locke 1992:375; Kilby 1984:28; Leech 1971:36), and this notion of "indefinite time" involves and is prior to current relevance. Conversely, when the past is used, the event is thought of as located at a definite time, even though this is not made explicit. This does not mean, as Fenn (1988:165) rightly points out, that definiteness is to be equated with "clearly identified" in the sense that the time of the event is known or being referred to as such. With both past-in-present and past, "the act is predicated as having occurred within a particular span of time. But exactly at what point is of no consequence, even in the past tense sequence" (1988:164).

The problem has given rise to an ever more refined terminology. Fenn introduces the term "occurrence focus" for "reference to the act or the manner in which it proceeded" (1987:169). It is therefore a certain occurrence focus that locates an event occurring "yesterday" as a whole in the past, as in, "We had pizza for lunch yesterday," making the past tense obligatory; an event located in "today" may be seen either as a whole in the past, as in "We had pizza again for lunch today," since the timespan that includes lunch is now over, or in relation to speech time as in "We've had pizza again/*twice already today*," said at suppertime, since the timespan is still open.

Fenn adapts Dinsmore's (1981) formulation of a restrictive rule on the perfect in English in terms of "linear specification," characterized as any element locating an event in time explicitly or implicitly (in Fenn 1987:167): "The present perfect cannot be used if the time of the event is linearly specified (either explicitly or implicitly) for a time not connected to the present."

More interesting than this restrictive rule in itself is the reported suggestion that presupposition is the means by which the time of an event is implicitly specified. For instance, in *Harry has been in Borneo*, "He has enjoyed it a lot," the second clause is unacceptable in English because "at the point at which it is uttered the occurrence of the event of Harry's being in Borneo is presupposed as past, and the event described by the second sentence must be simultaneous to the event of Harry's being in Borneo" (in Fenn 1987:167).

The same would apply to such predications as having been born in a particular place or year. This event is necessarily presupposed in English as pertaining to a past time severed from the present. It is here that the close resemblance between English and Spanish in the meaning and use of the present perfect breaks down, because in Peninsular Spanish the equivalent of both the above sentences could be expressed by the past-in-present. ("Harry ha estado en Borneo. Le ha gustado.")

Intuitively, one would agree with Butt & Benjamin (1989:209) that "Spanish usually uses the present perfect wherever English does,[4] but the reverse is not true: The Spanish perfect often requires translation by the English simple Past."

2. AIMS AND HYPOTHESES

The first aim in this study is to test the implication in Butt and Benjamin's informal claim, namely that the Spanish past-in-present must be more frequent in Spanish than in English if it often requires translation by the English past. Once having established that this is in fact the case, an attempt is made to account for the greater use of the past-in-present in Spanish. Finally, given that the use of the past-in-present is a construal of experience, a way of categorizing reality, within the choices offered by a specific language, the choice of the past-in-present will be situated within the range of options available in this area to the two standard varieties of English and Spanish.

The present hypothesis is four-fold:

1. That the past-in-present in Spanish will have a higher frequency of occurrence than its equivalent form in English.
2. That for English, but not for Spanish, a past time-sphere blocks the use of the past-in-present.
3. That other factors may also intervene to block the use of the past-in-present in English.
4. That the best option as equivalent to some instances of the Spanish past-in-present is not necessarily the past in English.

---

[4]An exception is the so-called "perfect of persistent situation" described in 4.1.

	NUMBER OF WORDS	NUMBER OF TOKENS OF PAST-IN-PRESENT
SPANISH CORPUS	137.214	1.232
ENGLISH CORPUS	144.650	250

Figure 13.1. Database and Tokens.

3. DATABASE AND METHOD

The corpus of spoken Spanish comprising twenty-five "dialogues" (137,214 words), published under the title *El habla de la ciudad de Madrid* (Esgueva & Cantarero 1981), was scanned for tokens of the past-in-present.[5] Only finite indicative forms were considered (i.e. non-finite and subjunctive forms were excluded and the total number of tokens yielded was 1,232).[6]

A similar stretch of text from Svartvik and Quirk (1980), chosen at random and comprising 144,650 words was scanned for purposes of comparison. The number of tokens found was 250.

The first hypothesis to be tested would therefore appear to be confirmed: The past-in-present is more frequently used in Spanish than in English.

Out of the 1,232 examples comprising the Spanish database, many were found to be anomalous when translated into English with the past-in-present. These occurrences were then classified according to the following features:

1. presence of a past-time adverbial;
2. past time established by presupposition, even though no adverbial was present;

---

[5]Computerized with permission of the C.S.I.C. Most of the illustrations used derive from the two corpora described in section 3. Each of the illustrations is followed by a reference number.

It is perhaps an oversimplification to equate the Spanish of educated Madrid speakers with a national standard.

[6]Only one example containing the 2nd person plural form *habeis* + participle was found, and this was not relevant to the discussion.

3. process type (i.e. material, mental, relational and verbal). The first two of this set of features were chosen as criterial in establishing a past time-sphere. The third is central to the systemic-functional approach. In a fourth section, particular attention was centred on processes of being and certain mental processes, because these appeared to be likely areas of differentiation, on the basis of personal observation of spoken English and Spanish.

4. CLASSIFICATION AND DISCUSSION

4.1. Past-in-Present + Past-Time Adverbial or Conjunction

In the Spanish database, 89 tokens of the Spanish past-in-present accompanied by an indicator of past-time were found. These indicators included past-time adverbials such as *ayer* (*yesterday*) as in (6), *hace unos años* (*a few years ago*) as in (7), *al año siguiente* (*the following year*) as in (8), dates or national holidays, which refer to recent events as in (9) and others that refer to more distant events as in (10).

ayer hemos pensado hacer esto (3876)
*yesterday we've thought of doing that   (6)

una hermana que ha muerto hace unos años . . . (6931)
*a sister who has died some years ago   (7)

A lo mejor al año siguiente se han matriculado en el
último curso. (11063)
*Perhaps the following year they have signed on for the
final course   (8)

Ha sido un poco antes de Reyes (4114)
*It has been just before the Epiphany   (9)

hemos sido embajadores el año treinta y uno, treinta
y dos y treinta y tres de la República en Chile (6497)
*We've been embassadors to Chile in the years
(nineteen) thirty- one, thirty-two and thirty-three of
the Republic   (10)

Similarly, and again unlike English, *esta mañana* (*this morning*) can be used together with the past-in-present in Spanish not only when the time-sphere is still open (i.e. it is still morning) but when the "morning time-sphere" is now closed, such as happens when speaking in the evening. In (11) a student complains late in the day about the lack of buses:

Esta mañana he tenido que subir la cuesta a todo meter,
y aquí . . . y luego por las tardes aquí . . . (3861)
*This morning I've had to rush up the hill, and here . . .
and then in the afternoon/evening here . . .   (11)

Of the 89 occurrences with past-time expressions with the past-in-present, 35 occur with *cuando* ("when") as a conjunction, as in (12), or *cuándo* ("when") as an interrogative adverb, as in (13) (i.e. 39.3% of the 89 examples) and 2.8% of the total number of occurrences of the past-in-present in the Spanish corpus:

¿Has mirado tú la. . . . cuando hemos empezado?
*Have you looked at your . . . when we have started?
(11066)   (12)

¿Cuándo han terminado la carrera? (7376)
*When have they finished their degree?   (13)

The past-time signals that occur in these instances are not to be dismissed as "afterthoughts" such as occur occasionally in spontaneous conversation in English, in which the time expression is added after the main clause has been completed and will predictably occupy a separate tone group. No such instances were yielded by the present database. An invented example is suggested in (14):

Yes, I've already seen it, about a month ago.   (14)

The examples in this section confirm that a past-time sphere, signalled by a past-time adverbial or the conjunction *cuando*, is compatible with the past-in-present in Spanish. In English, on the other hand, the notion of aftermath or relevance to the present is more limited.

Needless to say, *cuando*, *cuándo* and *when* are not tied exclusively to past time, because they can introduce both habitual and prospective time-spheres as well as past. For a strictly past time-sphere, in Spanish as in English, the past tense would be used

	SPANISH PAST-IN-PRESENT + PAST TIME ADVERBIAL	SPANISH PAST-IN-PRESENT + *CUANDO* AS A CONJ/INTERROGATIVE ADV.
TOKENS	89	35
PERCENTAGE	7.1%	2.8%

Figure 13.2. Past-in-present + past-time markers in Spanish.

(*llegué/arrived; terminaron/did they finish*). The fact that the past is not used in these instances in Spanish indicates that the event represented by the past-in-present is felt to be in some way within the aftermath phase rather than relegated exclusively to past-time. According to Alarcos, this is because the event is felt to be situated at some indeterminate moment in the period leading up to the present (1978:26), in a time-sphere shared with the present rather than alien to it (1994:166).

How exactly the aftermath is to be interpreted will depend on both the context and the predication itself. Traditionally, four types of possible meaning of the perfect have been distinguished (Comrie 1976, Dahl 1985, MacCawley 1971), although it must be recognized that not all languages with the perfect form have the full range of these meanings, while in some languages there are distinct forms for some of these meanings (Comrie 1976:56). The meanings as specified by Comrie are as follows: perfect of result, as in "John has arrived," implying that John is still here; experiential perfect, which indicates that the situation has held at least once during some time in the past leading up to the present as in "Have you seen Almodóvar's latest film?"; perfect of persistent situation, which appears to be characteristic of English "I've shopped there for years" and finally perfect of recent past as in "Have you heard the news? The Government has fallen," similar to MacCawley's (1971) notion of "hot news perfect." As Comrie points out, English clearly distinguishes the experiential perfect from the perfect of result by means of *be* and *go* respectively, as in "Bill has been to America" and "Bill has gone to America." To this the use of *ever* might be added as an indicator of the experiential perfect. Otherwise, with other processes, this distinction is not always easy to draw in English.

Nor is it easy to distinguish between the meaning of recent past and that of result. Both the process type in terms of boundedness, and the participants in the discourse-setting are influential in conditioning meaning. *Change*, for instance, may be either gradual or sudden. Predicated of traffic lights, it would be a momentary event which, together with the past-in-present as in (15) will yield a meaning of "hot news," but of which there is clearly a result: They are now a different color (cf. Downing & Locke 1992:377):

The traffic lights have changed. Let's go!   (15)

For Spanish likewise, it proves difficult to establish the borderline between recency and result. This is partly due to the fact that recent events are likely to be felt as having results, and partly because what counts as "recent" in Spanish is more elastic than in English. Recency may be arguably attributed to the events in (12) *¿Has mirado tu. . . .cuando hemos empezado?*; but recency would seem to be an implausible interpretation in some of the tokens reflected in the following sections, such as (16b) and (19).

Just as the notion of recency needs to be applied with great flexibility to the dilucidation of the meanings of the past-in-present in Spanish, a similar flexibility must accompany that of result. It is not, as in English, only the direct results of a prior event that can be evoked by the past-in-present, as in "I've lost my keys" (They are still lost). Any sort of effect, whether of material consequences or purely subjective, affective even, can be evoked by the past-in-present in Spanish (Alarcos 1978, Bello 1928). Conversely, that effect will be absent if the past form is used. As an illustration, compare the following two examples, provided by native speakers. The first situates the boyfriend's death within the aftermath, in which the speaker still feels the effects of the event, and the second presents it more objectively, at a distance:

Mi novio ha muerto el año pasado
*My boyfriend has died last year   (16a)

Mi novio murió el año pasado
My boyfriend died last year   (16b)

A similar consciousness of the event may be attributed to many of the corpus examples in later sections.

Finally, a difference between Spanish and English can be detected in the so-called perfect of persistent situation, which is particularly clear with unbounded processes. In English such processes would be understood as continuing up to and including speech time, and many would require a time adverbial. Thus:

I've lived in London for years   (17)

would be taken to mean that I still live in London. In Spanish, on the other hand, the past-in-present would situate the living in London as an "antepresent" with present relevance, no doubt of an experiential or affective nature, but the living in London would have ceased. According to Moreno Cabrera, the time-sphere of the present in Spanish is obligatorily closed by the limits of the present, which I understand to be speech time (1991:298). Examples (18) and (19) illustrate this and also the fact that this rather subtle difference makes for frequent cross-cultural misunderstanding:

*Me ha hablado usted que ha estado cinco meses en
Londres.* (2241)
You have told me that *you have been in London for five
months. (the interviewee is no longer in London)   (18)

*En la calle Serrano hemos vivido muchos años. . . . Y luego
mis padres hicieron una casa en Serrano, esquina
General Oraá, y allí hemos vivido hasta que nos vinimos
ya para ésta de aquí.* (5865)
In Serrano street we have lived for many years. . . . And
then my parents built a house in Serrano, on the corner
of General Oraá, and *we've lived there until we came
to this one here.   (19)

To express persistence up to and including speech-time, Spanish, like many other languages, uses the present, either preceded or followed by time specification (*Hace cinco meses que estoy en Londres. Estoy/vivo en Londres desde hace cinco meses*). There is also available a progressive combination with *llevar* as in *Llevo cinco meses viviendo aquí.*

4.2. Past-time Established by Presupposition

When a past time-sphere is presupposed, there may be no time adverbial at all, as in (20), or there may be a time adverbial somewhere in the previous discourse, as in (21) and (22).

*la verdad es que sí, . . . he nacido en Madrid . . . pero mi
familia no es de Madrid* (8907)
Yes, indeed, *I've been born in Madrid . . . but my parents
aren't from Madrid   (20)

estábamos tranquilamente viendo la televisión después
de comer y hemos oído la sirena, asustados porque ha
sido al lado de casa y ha pasado al . . . nada en el medio
de la calle (10144)
We were watching television after lunch and *we've
heard the siren, alarmed because it *has been just by
the house and it *has gone past in the middle of the
street   (21)

hasta el punto que . . . una vecina. . . . .nos ha preguntado
a nosotros de balcón a balcón que qué pasaba, que si
se veía humo o no se veía: y hemos dicho que no, que
en absoluto (10151)
*And a neighbor has asked us, from one balcony to
another, what was happening, if you could see smoke or
not, and we've answered that there wasn't any   (22)

In (21) and (22), the hearing of the ambulance, the happening and
the asking all occurred in the past time-sphere established in the
previous co-text by the imperfect *estábamos viendo la televisión*
and by the time circumstance *después de comer*.

In (23) the event belongs to a past time-sphere, because the person referred to (Oscar Wilde) is no longer alive:

Y ha muerto aquí en Madrid (6483)
*And he has died here in Madrid   (23)

Again we find that the communicative motivation for bringing the
event into the time-sphere of the present is subjective, emotive even,
because the speaker had been talking enthusiastically of Oscar
Wilde and in (23) contrives to unite a temporal with a spatial proximity in referring to the fact that Oscar Wilde died in Madrid. This
use can be viewed in terms of appropriateness (Givón 1984:282);
that is, in this context the speaker feels that it is less appropriate to
relate the event in question merely as a past event; and this is a
discourse-pragmatic valuation, not purely semantic. The point is,
however, that in English, relevance to the present, however desirable
and "appropriate," is blocked by presupposition of pastness. In
Spanish, by contrast, appropriateness is the stronger factor.

I next turn to a further factor, related to discourse coherence, that
has incidence on the frequency of the past-in-present in Spanish as
opposed to English. This I have called "chaining."

4.3. "Chaining" in Spanish

In clauses with predicated themes and thematic equatives (cleft and pseudo-cleft sentences, respectively) the verbs of both clauses are put into the past-in-present in Spanish, forming what I will call a chaining:

> *lo que me ha pasado estos días de atrás ha sido que no me dormía* (5920)
> What has happened to me these days *has been that I wasn't getting to sleep   (24)

This phenomenon also occurs in clause complexes and with relative clauses as qualifiers of nominal groups. Example (25) illustrates chaining in paratactically related clauses, while in (26) and (27) the clauses are hypotactically related. In (28) chaining occurs between a main clause and a qualifier of a nominal group:

> *Han sido dos meses y medio..o algo así en . . . aquí en la Diputación y ha sido . . . ha sido favorable, positivo el balance.* (796)
> It has been two months and a half . . . or something like that . . . here in the regional council and the result has been favorable, positive.   (25)

> *Cuando han estado aquí han dicho que ellos se tratan con otro planeta* (1419)
> *When they have been here they have said that they have dealings with another planet   (26)

> *Este año hemos estado en Gijón, el sitio que menos me ha gustado de todos, por cierto* (770)
> This year we've been to Gijón, *the place I have least liked, incidentally   (27)

> *¿Cuál ha sido el bicho, el animal que más le ha entusiasmado?* (4640)
> *Which has been the creature, the animal that you've got most excited about?   (28)

This phenomenon presumably derives from the conditions examined in 4.2. and 4.3. Because a past-time adverbial or conjunction does not necessarily enforce a past time-sphere, and likewise because pastness via presupposition is no impediment to visualizing a past event as having present relevance, a series of past-in-present forms may be used to express a sequence of events or a complex event expressed by a complex unit.

4.4. Process Types and the Past-in-Present

All main process types occur with the past-in-present in Spanish.

- *Material processes* as in (29) in which the subject of conversation is the bus:

  A. *¿El 45 has cogido?*
  B. *No, el 34.* (9887)
  *Have you caught the (number) 45?
  No, the 34. (29)

- *Transitional material processes* as in (30)

  Una hermana que ha muerto hace unos años (6931)
  *A sister who has died some years ago (30)

- *Mental processes* of cognition and affectivity as in (31) and (32) respectively:

  se veía allí un ambiente de frivolidad y de, de amor libre . . . He entendido bastante (2253)
  One could detect an atmosphere of frivolity and . . . free love . . . *I have understood quite (well) (31)

  Lo que creo es que las monjas han querido actualizar la enseñanza y dar una enseñanza correspondiente al mundo de hoy (5640)
  What I think is that the nuns *have wished to bring their teaching up to date and provide teaching in line with present needs (32)

- *Relational processes* as in (33):

  Inf. *¿Guerra y Paz? ¡Qué bueno ha sido eso!* (6640)
  Mod. *¡Qué programa más bueno!, ¿verdad?*
  Inf. *War and Peace?* *How good that has been!
  Mod. What a good programme! eh? (or wasn't it?) (33)

- *Verbal processes*, as in (34):

  Cuando lo he dicho (11264)
  *When I've said so (34)

In the remainder of this section I will explore a little further the combination of past-in-present with verbs of being, thinking and liking in Spanish, because these verbs provide occurrences that sound most unfamiliar to an English ear. Excluded are instances involving plurality and/or iterativity, because the addition of these factors projects the event into an open time-sphere, as seen in section 1, in which case occurrences of the past-in-present are acceptable in English.

4.4. Unbounded Processes and the Past-in-Present

An outline was sketched in Downing & Locke (1992) of the meaning of the present perfect in combination with verb and situation types considered in terms of duration, boundedness and agentivity (cf. Bauer 1970, Brinton 1988). It was suggested (cf. Kilby 1984) that at least some unbounded durative situations are typically incompatible with the perfect in English unless accompanied by a time adverbial of extent or frequency. In systemic-functional grammar, such situations overlap with relational processes or mental processes as in (35) and (36), respectively:

*It has belonged to my mother.   (35)

*I've known him.   (36)

Such processes are homogeneous in that they do not imply change of state or event as in (37) and (38) in which the past-in-present is normal in English:

I've been ill.   (37)

It's been marvellous.   (38)

The addition of a time adverbial to the English equivalents (35) and (36) permits the "persistent present" interpretation as in (39), whereas pluralization/iterativity evoke an iterative "experiential" interpretation, as in (40) and (41), also acceptable in English:

I've known him for years.   (39)

It has belonged to my mother, my sister, my aunt—
practically every member of the family.   (40)

I've known a lot like him.   (41)

Brinton (1988), however, claims that without durative adverbials unbounded processes are "experiential," referring to a situation that has occurred once or repeatedly before the present. This seems to imply that *all* such unbounded processes in combination with the past-in-present will a) be acceptable without an adverbial, and b) will be acceptable referring to both single events and iterative events signalled by pluralization. Because iterativity and plurality have been shown to make for compatibility with the past-in-present, I proceeded to examine non-iterative, non-plural occurrences of state predications in the Spanish and English databases. Taking the Spanish corpus as starting point, on the grounds that the past-in-present has been shown to be more frequent in Spanish than in English, the frequency of the past-in-present was checked in construals of being, of knowing, thinking and liking.

4.4.1. Being

In Spanish, the construal of being is shared between *ser*, denoting inherent identity or nature, and also location of events, and *estar*, denoting transitory states or location. *Ser* and *estar* together, in combination with the past-in-present, yielded 124 examples, 10% of the total occurrences of this verb form. This compares with 20 occurrences of *be* + past-in-present in the English database, representing 8% of the total number of occurrences of this form in the English corpus selection.

In the Spanish data, examples with *ser* numbered 82 (6.6% of the total), almost doubling those with *estar* (42, 3.3% of the total). The distribution of identifying, attributive and circumstantial complementation types of these verbs is as follows:

4.4.1.1. Ser. *Attributive*

Realized by indefinite NG, as in (42) the total number was 24 (1.9%)

BEING

SPANISH ser/estar	ser	estar	ENGLISH be
TOKENS	124	82	42	20
PERCENTAGE	10%	6.6%	3.3%	8%

Figure 13.3. Processes of being + past-in-present.

Te empiezas a pensar que aquello ha sido una persona
(1797) (referring to a dissection)
You begin to think that *that has been a person   (42)

Realized by AdjG, as in (43) the total number was 10 (0.8%)

Ha sido sumamente tranquilo. (864)
It has been extremely quiet.   (43)

Identifying, realized by a definite NG, totalled 30 (2.4%)

Me parece que ha sido él. (12838)
*I think it has been him.   (44)

¿Cuál ha sido para usted el bicho, el animal que más
le ha entusiasmado? (4640)
*Which has been the creature, the animal that you've
been most keen on?   (45)

Circumstantial, 15 (1.2%)

Si no ha sido a los catorce o a los nueve ha sido a los
dieciocho (2070) (within the frame of falling in love)
*If it hasn't been at fourteen (years old) or at nine,
it's been at eighteen   (46)

4.4.1.2. Estar.   *Transitory location*, as in (47), totalled 31 (2.5%),
almost three times more frequent than *transitory state* totalling 11
(0.8%) illustrated in (48):

Este año he estado en Alemania
This year I've been to Germany   (47)

¿Y qué tal tiempo tuvieron este año?
Este año ha estado bastante bien. (4217)
And what kind of weather did you have this year?
This year it has been quite good.   (48)

4.5. Mental Processes

The next step was to search the databases for non-iterative non-
plural mental processes. Occurrences in the Spanish data were
found with the verbs *creer* (believe, think), *parecer* (seem), *oír* (hear),
gustar (like) and *entusiasmar* ("fill with enthusiasm") used roughly
as equivalent to "enjoy" but with Recipient Indirect Object. In addition, *querer* in the senses of "love" and of "volition" occurred, which

MENTAL PROCESSES		
Spanish	88 tokens	7.1%
English	--------------	--------

	Cognition	Perception	Affectivity
OCCURRENCES	12	42	34
PERCENTAGE	09%	33%	27%

Figure 13.4.   Non-iterative mental processes.

despite their plural subjects still proved difficult to parallel in English. In sum, the past-in-present in Spanish is able to co-occur with processes of cognition, perception, affectivity and volition. The total number was 88 (7.1% of the total).

In the LLC database, no occurrences of the past-in-present were found with *know, seem, like, love* or *enjoy*. One instance was found with *think* and one with *understand*, but both occurred with the frequency adverb *always* and are consequently irrelevant to the present discussion.

The Spanish instances are represented by the following examples:

Claro, se ha creído que le venía un muñeco para Reyes.
(4113)
*Of course, she has thought/believed she was getting
a doll for Christmas. (referring to the arrival of a
new brother)   (49)

*Pues a mí concretamente el casamiento de Jacqueline
me ha parecido bastante normal.* (404)
*Personally, Jacqueline's marriage has seemed quite
normal to me.   (50)

*Estábamos tranquilamente viendo la televisión después
de comer, y hemos oído la sirena.* (10146)
*We were peacefully seeing the televisión after lunch
and we've heard the siren.   (51)

La región es maravillosa, me ha gustado mucho
(3538)
*The region is beautiful, I've liked it a lot   (52)

Ahora ya leo muy poco, aunque ya, pero vamos, sí,
a mí me ha gustado leer. (5633)
Now I don't read much, although, well, yes, *I have
liked reading   (53)

Los bosques . . . me han entusiasmado. Me ha parecido
preciosísimo. Y he disfrutado mucho y los días que he
hecho excursiones largas . . . ha hecho hasta sol. (3531)
*I've loved the woods. It has all seemed beautiful to
me. And I've enjoyed it a lot and the days we've gone
on long trips it has even been sunny.   (54)

La pintura me ha entusiasmado. (6857)
*I've been very keen on painting.   (55)

Este año hemos estado en Gijón, el sitio que menos me
ha gustado de todos, por cierto (770)   (56)
This year we have been to Gijón, *the place I have
liked best, incidentally.

To judge from the illustrations provided in discussions on the past-
in-present, it appears to be implicitly assumed that the natural construal of an unbounded process or state is limited to two options: a)
iterative as in, "I've lived in many countries," which would be classed
as the experiential perfect; or b) lasting up to the present as in, "I've
always lived here," which would be the perfect of persistent situation,
also called the continuative perfect. But, as the examples in the
previous section show, it is also possible to visualize unbounded
processes that continue in the past for an unspecified period within
the time frame of the present but without continuing to speech time
and without iterativity. Or rather, it is easier to visualize these in
Spanish, because they do occur, expressed by the past-in-present,
whereas in English, for mental processes and some meanings of *be* at
least, the past-in-present sounds odd. A more natural choice would
sometimes be *used to + infinitive*. This is not to say that this construction provides a direct equivalent in meaning of the Spanish
past-in-present; it does not. Whereas the past-in-present in Spanish
is an "act of attribution of psychological proximity" (McCoard
1978:137), *used to + infinitive* centers on the discontinued nature of
the anterior state. The psychological proximity is lost. The only other
choice in English is the past, with its more definite associations.
Spanish, with its much richer system, can distinguish between a
perfective and imperfective past state as well as an anterior state. The

Table 13.1.
Past Choices in English and Spanish.

	English	Spanish
Past	I liked it.	Me gustó, (*past perfective*) Me gustaba, (*past imperfective*)
Used to + infinitive	I used to like it.	
Past-in-present	I have liked it.	Me ha gustado.

choices of both languages, discounting combinations with the progressive, can be set out as seen in Table 13.1.

Examples from the Spanish corpus for which *used to +inf.* could be an approximate equivalent include the following:

yo he sido hija única, pero ahora ya no (4553)
I used to be an only child, but I am no longer.   (57)

¿El diario EL Sol?, pues ha sido uno de los diarios más importantes de España. (6497)
The daily *El Sol*? It used to be one of the most
important daily newspapers in Spain.   (58)

5. CONCLUSIONS

This study has led to certain conclusions regarding the distribution of the past-in-present in spoken British English and spoken Peninsular Spanish that serve to confirm the hypotheses presented above in Section 2:

1. Although both of these standard varieties of English and Spanish are able to make a distinction between a wholly past time-sphere and a time-sphere that includes utterance time, the past-in-present has a far higher frequency of occurrence in Spanish than in English. This is primarily a result of the following factors or a combination of them:

a. For Spanish, the psychological link with utterance time that is a necessary condition for the use of the past-in-present takes precedence over any other factor. Present relevance may be felt, and the past-in-present felt to be consequently more appropriate than the past, not only when direct results of the past event are noticeable, but when any subjective or affective connection is felt to be present. As a result of this flexibility, the past-in-present can be used when a past time-sphere is either specified or presupposed.

For English there is a stricter assignation of the event to the past, anchored there contextually by the specification of time or place, or by presupposition, and this appears to take precedence in English.

b.   Recency is one contextual factor that triggers the choice of the past-in-present in Spanish. There appears to be no restriction on the process-type involved. Furthermore, the data show that the psychological attribution of recency is interpreted with great flexibility in Spanish; authentic data prove that it is not restricted, as is sometimes suggested (Butt and Benjamin 1989, Dahl 1985), to events occurring since midnight.

c.   Consequently, the speaker of Spanish is able to visualize an event both as past and at the same time as having a psychological link with the present. In discourse, two events that were partially overlapping in real time can be presented differently, according to the relevance or otherwise of each to the present, as in (59), where being educated is presented as having current relevance, but doing a degree in music has not such relevance. In English, presupposition of pastness would make for the past tense in both.

> *Se ha educado en colegios de religiosas. Realizó la carrera de piano y canto en el Conservatorio de Madrid.* (885)
> *She has been educated at a convent school. She studied the piano and singing at the Madrid Conservatorio. (59)

For English, on the contrary, the assignation of an event to a past time-sphere takes precedence and blocks the use of the past-in-present. The speaker of English, therefore, must choose between a past or a present time-sphere, but this choice is considerably restricted by process type.

Apparently the one situation in which Spanish does not use the past-in-present when English does is to express persistence to the present. Like other languages, Spanish uses the present and has available certain variations.

d.   In English, once the event is established as past, any other event occurring simultaneously with it or within the timespan of the first will be counted as past, via presupposition. In spoken Spanish, on the contrary, a series of consecutive events can be presented by means of the past-in-present in a clause chaining sequence.

e. In Spanish, furthermore, other grammatical constructions containing more than one clause (clefts, pseudo-clefts, nominal groups with embedded clauses as qualifiers) are able to maintain a "chaining" of past-in-present forms that would be ungrammatical in English.

f. In Spanish, processes of being and mental processes of cognition, perception and affectivity can be expressed, via the past-in-present, as anterior states occurring at an indefinite time in the past. This hardly occurs in English, which tends to view states and mental processes either as stretching up to the present or as iterative.

2. Not all occurrences of the Spanish past-in-present have as equivalent a past in English, however. The present may be the choice for a state that is still operative as in, "It's a girl"; (cf. Spanish *Ha sido niña* or "The region is beautiful"—"I love it" (*La región es preciosa, me ha encantado*)) or as at the end of television news bulletins "That's all for today" (cf. Spanish *Esto ha sido todo por hoy.*)

3. Certain non-iterative mental processes that do not persist up to the present are much less frequently expressed by the past-in-present in English than they are in Spanish. These include verbs of knowing, believing, belonging, liking and loving. Here a natural choice in English would appear to be *used to + infinitive*, as in, "I used to like reading" rather than "I've liked reading" (Spanish *Me ha gustado la lectura*), "I used to be keen on painting" rather than "I've liked painting" (cf. *Me ha entusiasmado la pintura*).

In such cases the past-in-present in English tends to be a marked form, receiving the intonation nucleus that in this case signals marked positive polarity and anteriority ("I HAVE liked reading"). Once again, Spanish is able to situate the state as psychologically closer although implicitly distant in time.

4. The aim of this study has been to show how the interplay of the various factors discussed here help to explain the greater distribution of the past-in-present in Spanish as compared with English. This is seen to be a consequence of the psychological difference in the construal of experience in this area between the two languages. To sum up, pastness in the present is felt to be appropriate for subjective rather than objective reasons, and is grammaticalized in the spoken language to a far greater extent in Spanish than it is in English.

REFERENCES

Alarcos Llorach, E. (1994) *Gramática de la lengua española*. Madrid, Spain: Espasa-Calpe

Alarcos Llorach, E. (1978) *Estudios de Gramática Funcional del Español*. Madrid, Spain: Gredos

Bauer, G. (1970) The English "Perfect" reconsidered. *Journal of Linguistics* 6, 189–197

Bello, A. (1928) *Gramática de la Lengua Castellana*. Repreducción de la versión sin anotaciones. Madrid, Spain: EDAF Universitaria, 1984

Brinton, L. (1988) *The Development of English Aspectual Systems*. Cambridge, England: Cambridge University Press

Butt, J. & Benjamin, C. (1989) *A New Grammar of Modern Spanish*. London: Edward Arnold

Comrie, Bernard (1976) *Aspect*. Cambridge, England: Cambridge University Press

Dahl, Östen (1985) *Tense and Aspect Systems*. Oxford, England: Blackwell

Dinsmore, J. (1981) Tense choice and time specification in English. *Linguistics, 19:* 475–494

Downing, A. & Locke, P. (1992) *A University Course in English Grammar*. Hemel Hempstead: Prentice-Hall

Esgueva, M. & Cantarero, M., eds. (1981) *El habla de la ciudad de Madrid. Materiales para su estudio*. Madrid, Spain: Consejo Superior de Investigaciones Científicas

Fenn, P. (1987) *A Semantic and Pragmatic Examination of the English Perfect*. Tübingen, Germany: Gunter Narr Verlag

Givón, T. (1984) *Syntax: A functional-typological introduction*. vol.I. Amsterdam/Philadelphia: John Benjamins

Halliday, M.A.K. (1994) *An Introduction to Functional Grammar*. Second edition. London: Edward Arnold

Kilby, D. (1984) *Descriptive Syntax and the English Verb*. London: Croom Helm

Leech, G. (1971) *Meaning and the English Verb*. London: Longman

McCawley, J.D. (1971) Tense and time reference in English. In C.J. Fillmore and D.T. Langendoen, eds. *Studies in Linguistic Semantics*. New York: Holt, Rinehart & Winston, 96–113

McCoard, R.W. (1978) *The English Perfect: Tense-choice and pragmatic awareness*. Amsterdam: North-Holland

Moreno Cabrera, J.C. (1991) *Curso Universitario de Lingüística General*. Tomo I: Teoría de la gramática y sintaxis general. Madrid, Spain: Editorial Síntesis

Reichenbach, H. (1947) *Elements of Symbolic Logic*. New York: Macmillan

Svartvik, J. & R. Quirk, eds. (1980) *A Corpus of English Conversation*. Lund: Gleerup

B:
Lexis and the
Nominal Group

14
Cultural Classification and System Networks: A Systemic Functional Approach to Lexis

Gordon H. Tucker

University of Wales
College of Cardiff

1. INTRODUCTION

When observers and critics of systemic functional linguistics examine the body of statements that expound the theoretical principles in which the tradition is grounded, they unsurprisingly turn first to the seminal writings of Michael Halliday. Whatever diversity currently exists among systemic models of language—a diversity that bears witness to the healthiness and resilience of the tradition itself—it is not difficult to find in some original idea of Halliday's the seeds from which this or that contemporary model has grown.

It is such an idea that has led to the work I will discuss here. And yet, unlike many others, it is an idea that has received relatively little attention until quite recently, perhaps simply because it concerns the treatment of lexis. Not that lexis has been neglected in the linguistics of the last two decades, but it conveniently has been seen as different from syntax, both within the systemic tradition and outside it, especially within the Chomskyan paradigm. And, as any student of modern linguistics will be aware, syntax has tended to dominate scholarly thinking in the discipline.

In the light of present-day systemic thinking, with its increased semantic orientation, one might be tempted to consider as visionary Halliday's (1961) view of lexis:

> The grammarian's dream is (and must be, such is the nature of grammar) of constant territorial expansion. He would like to turn the whole of linguistic form into grammar, hoping to show that lexis can be defined as "most delicate grammar." The exit to lexis would then be closed, and all exponents ranged in systems. No description has yet been made so delicate that we can test whether there really comes a place where increased delicacy yields no further systems.
>
> (Halliday, 1961:267)

But he immediately expresses caution: "For the moment it seems better to treat lexical relations [. . . .] as on a different level, and to require a different theory to account for them" (1961:267). And consequently, there is a shift of attention, especially to the phenomenon of collocation, and to the search for an alternative theory to account for lexis. Halliday does not abandon the grammarian's dream, however, since in a discussion with Herman Parret in 1974, he states:

> The lexical system is not something that is fitted in afterwards to a set of slots defined by the grammar. The lexicon—if I may go back to a definition I used many years ago—is simply the most delicate grammar. In other words, there is only one network of lexicogrammatical options. And as these become more and more specific, they tend more and more to be realized by the choice of lexical item rather than by the choice of a grammatical structure. But it is still part of a single grammatical system.
>
> (Halliday 1974)

The task that remains to be done is to make explicit how lexis might be organized along the lines suggested by Halliday above. Attempts have been made, although, perhaps inevitably in theoretical linguistics, they are fragmentary and exemplificatory, suggestive of how one might proceed in a full-scale, explicit model of language. Work by Berry (1977), Fawcett (1980:151–4), Hasan (1987), and Cross (1993) develops the notion of "most delicate grammar" in such a way and reference will be made to them later.

There is one difference, however, between the above-mentioned approaches to "lexis as most delicate grammar" and the approach adopted in the Cardiff Grammar discussed here. The latter constitutes the heart of a large computational grammar of English (see Fawcett 1988a; Fawcett and Tucker 1990; and Fawcett, Tucker and

Lin 1993). Also, a large grammar demands a lexical resource of considerable size, unless it is restricted by a high degree of domain and register specificity—as has often been the case in computational natural language systems. While the work described in detail here cannot extend beyond exemplification, in the Cardiff Grammar it is substantially and explicitly implemented to meet the objectives laid down in the design of the system. At the time of writing, the grammar described below handles over 1,000 lexical senses and should increase to well over 3,000 in the coming year.

Within computational linguistics, natural language processing (NLP) has always presented a challenge to linguistic theories. Not that any degree of success in computational implementation necessarily validates a particular theory, but certainly the lack of it cannot augur well for the theory concerned. And, although linguistic theories do not always claim to have computational usefulness, they are often used in computational linguistics projects, even when they do not. Kaplan and Bresnan's (1982) lexical functional grammar and Gazdar et al.'s generalized phrase structure grammar especially (Gazdar et al. 1985) are prominent theories that are commonly drawn upon for NLP. Systemic functional linguistics, despite the criticism that it lacks the precise mathematical formalism of other theories (although see Patten 1984 and 1988), currently provides the linguistic basis for several major machine grammars, among which are the NIGEL grammar of the PENMAN Project at ISI, University of Southern California and the University of Sydney (Mann and Matthiessen 1983/85, Matthiessen and Bateman 1991) and the Cardiff Grammar of the COMMUNAL Project at the University of Wales College of Cardiff, to which this discussion specifically refers.[1] Furthermore, especially within the branch of computational linguistics known as *natural language generation*, systemic functional grammar, due in great part to the importance that it attributes to "choice" in language, has recently achieved considerable prominence.

The modelling of lexis as "most delicate grammar" in the COMMUNAL natural language system can be seen as the first attempt to put into practice Michael Halliday's "grammarian's dream." External constraints imposed upon the NIGEL grammar led to the adoption of a more "conventional" lexicon (see Cumming 1986a and 1986b

---

[1]COMMUNAL stands for COnvivial Man-Machine Understanding through NAtural Language. Research in COMMUNAL is supported by grants from the the Speech Research Unit at DRA Malvern under contracts nos. ER1/9/4/2181/23 and CB/FRN/9/4/2072 /068/CSM.

and Matthiessen 1987a for the reasons for this choice), whereas COMMUNAL has had free rein to explore the full implications of a systemic functional approach to lexis. One other noteworthy attempt to model lexis computationally in this way is Cross's HORACE, a register-based model of lexis implemented in the framework of the NIGEL grammar (Cross 1993).

This chapter will begin with a brief commentary on the traditional or "standard" approach to lexis in linguistic theory. Sections 2 and 3 will then provide some justification for treating lexis as "most delicate grammar" and finally, sections 4 to 7 discuss the lexical phenomena to be accounted for and possible ways of representing such phenomena through system networks.

2. APPROACHES TO LEXIS

It is not difficult to see lexis as on the fringe of the grammatical system. Where else at the level of form is there such a clear connection with what is popularly thought of as "meaning," and where else are there items that have little or no structure beyond a rigid concatenation of morphemes? Lexis is traditionally an area of language that has to do with "content." Words or items that have less content are referred to as "grammatical" or "functional" words, words that are often considered to express meaning chiefly through their place in structure. It is through "content" words that language makes contact with the "real" world of things and events and with their representation in the human mind.

It should not be surprising that traditionally in linguistic theory we find the view of lexis as a separate component with its own organization and own kind of meaning—a view, moreover, that has gone virtually unchallenged. After all, throughout the history of literacy, there have been reference books that deal with grammatical structures (grammars) and those that deal with words and their meanings (dictionaries and thesauri). One interesting observation on thesauri, however, is that they are organized on the basis of related meanings, a type of organization with which a systemic functional approach to lexis has much in common (cf. Matthiessen 1990). In the era of Chomskyan linguistics we find formal representations of language modelled on the basis of the separation of syntax and lexicon. One of the only significant differences between a dictionary and a lexicon in such theories appears to be that the lexicon, as

Chomsky described it, is "an unordered list of all lexical formatives" (Chomsky 1965:84), the traditional alphabetical ordering disappearing presumably on the grounds that it has no grammatical or semantic significance.

There is no doubt that, in more recent work in the Chomskyan tradition, the lexicon has become far more central. However, the fact remains that lexically oriented models such as lexical functional grammar do not give more attention than Chomsky did to the semantics of words, but rather emphasize the syntactic potential of lexical "formatives," in order to free the syntactic component proper from the idiosyncratic syntactic behavior that such "formatives" exhibit.

Many prominent theories are still mainly concerned with syntax, and the difference between syntactic well-formedness and semantic acceptability has continued to be emphasized. Indeed, despite the considerable contribution to lexical semantics that has been made by Levin and collaborators on the MIT Lexicon Project (working within Chomsky's government and binding theory), the ultimate aim of this research is expressed by Levin herself as follows: "Ideally, the idea is to arrive at a classification (of syntactically relevant semantic classes of predicates) on purely syntactic grounds, with the hope that this classification would receive semantic support" (Levin 1985:2).

Other major contributions to lexical semantics, such as Jackendoff's work on semantic structure (1983, 1990) and Pustejovsky's theory of *qualia structure* (Pustejovsky 1991), insightful though they undoubtedly are, are also located within the "syntax and lexicon" approach and closely related to the "generative" tradition in general.

Thus it was the syntactic preoccupation of Chomskyan and neo-Chomskyan theory that established the separation of syntax and semantics in that research paradigm. It is logical, therefore, to expect that another starting point is needed in order to come up with another way of seeing things. One such possible starting point would be a semantically oriented theory of language. And it is the semantic orientation of systemic functional grammars, I believe, that permits another interpretation of the role of lexis. Moreover, if such grammars wish to remain consistent with the theoretical principles on which they are developed, they *must* attempt to find another interpretation. The following section examines the case for trying the approach of "lexis as most delicate grammar" within systemic functional grammar.

3. LEXIS AND SYSTEMIC FUNCTIONAL GRAMMAR

Michael Halliday's "grammarian's dream" in 1961 was set in the context of scale and category grammar. The semantically oriented system network had not yet come into its own. Had this been the case, the intervening years between that time and the present might have brought greater progress in the realization of the "dream." And it was perhaps his abandonment of "the grammarian's dream" (quoted above) "for the moment" that led systemicists away from this approach to lexis. The particular aspect of lexis that seemed to suggest a different approach was collocation. With collocation, a term inherited from Firth (Firth 1957:114 ff.), there is an attempt to draw a parallel in lexical relations with the already well-recognized concept of syntactic relations—that is, the syntagmatic relations that are thought to hold between lexical items. As there are already syntactic relations to account for the grammatical classes of lexical items (e.g. *common noun* as the *head* of a *nominal group*) collocational relations must refer essentially to the *sense* of items.

Berry (1977:51–76) perhaps goes further than others to develop the parallel between lexis and structure on the basis of collocational phenomena. Her discussion relates the collocational categories of lexical *cluster* and *set* to grammatical *classes* and *cross-classes* respectively, and she attempts to set up a rank scale for lexis on the same basis as the rank scale for structure. The parallel often breaks down, however, or raises problems, as in the case of the lack of coextensiveness between grammatical and lexical units. As we shall see, the way forward lies, not in relating grammar and lexis at the level of form, but, through the system networks at the level of meaning potential (i.e. semantics).

The collocates of a lexical item, and the clusters they form, are revealed through the statistical analysis of text. Collocation is based on the strong probability of lexical co-occurrence, which can only be established through extensive corpus linguistic investigation. The claim is that over large stretches of text collocational relations will "fall out," and indeed are central to recognizing each lexical item as a "unique class." They tell us little, however, about lexical structure or sequence, unlike units and classes of grammatical structure.

There is a sense in which collocation is fundamental to a systemic functional approach to lexis, indeed in which it contributes to the clarification of the notion of "lexis as most delicate grammar." The inherent challenge in this notion is to range all lexicogrammatical choices into systems. At the more delicate end of certain parts of the system network, systems will consist of features realized in lexical items. The justification for the composition of systems will depend to a great extent on our ability to capture the way in which such features share a common linguistic context and yet differ, one from the other, in a sense that can be considered "grammatical." It is here that the collocational properties of lexical items shed light on the nature of such systems. The results of corpus linguistic investigation, in terms of both lexical collocation and grammatical behavior associated with individual lexical items, will ultimately be instrumental in deciding the shape of "lexical" system networks, in determining how closely related features in a system can be said to be "grammatically" distinguished.

The goal of the "grammarian's dream" of "lexis as most delicate grammar" is therefore to treat lexis in the same way as structure, that is, as part of one unified system network representing the meaning potential of the language. Such a network, with its rightmost systems concerning the realization of the more delicate distinctions in meaning in individual lexical items, begins, I believe, to reflect Halliday's original notion of "most delicate grammar."

What is of utmost importance here is that we are dealing with the organization of *meanings*, irrespective of whether their realization is in structure or in lexical items. This is surely what is implied by Halliday's habit of treating grammatical features as choices between meanings, as is clearly shown in Halliday (1994), and by his adoption of the term "lexicogrammar." Any other interpretation would make it difficult to understand what Halliday himself intended by "only one network of lexicogrammatical options" (Halliday 1978).

4. SOME JUSTIFICATION FOR LEXICAL SYSTEM NETWORKS

4.1. Justification Relating to Alternative Approaches

Before exploring the system network approach to lexis, we should first consider possible objections and subsequently offer a justification for proceeding along this course. Justification for the traditional lexicon approach, it should be noted, is simply assumed and not explicitly provided by those who adopt it.

If we propose to capture the sense of a lexical item by a set of features chosen from a "lexical" system network, it may be argued that we are simply providing an alternative representation to a lexi-

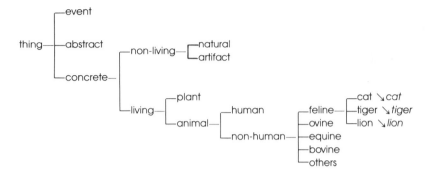

Figure 14.1.   A simplified system network including the sense/item for *cat*.

cal entry in a lexicon, which is itself specified by a set of features. Butler, in fact, commenting on Berry's lexical network, suggests that it is no more than a formalization of the familiar componential approach to lexical meaning (Butler 1985:134). Figure 14.1, for example, shows a simplified network from which one can select the more delicate features realized in *cat*. In a lexical entry approach this would be presented as in Figure 14.2.

Although the semantic features represented in both are similar, the system network shows what is not chosen as well as what is. The lexical entry only does this tacitly. This is why Chomsky (1965:83) provides a "branching diagram" to clarify features in the lexical entry, a diagram that in some respects resembles a system network. In fact, what the features in a lexical entry correspond to is a *selection expression* in systemic functional grammar, that is, the list of semantic features that have been selected by reference to the system network. We therefore need both the system network (to specify the potential) and the selection expression (for any actual formal item).

Secondly, it might be suggested that the system network approach may be said to be no more than a poor relation of such representations as the *semantic net* (cf. Brachman 1979) or the

CAT:
    [[+ thing]
    [+ concrete]
    [+ living]
    [+ animal]
    [+ feline]
    [+ cat]]

Figure 14.2.   Part of a lexical entry for the item *cat*.

conceptual dependency notation (Schank 1972) The system network has a different function, however, which is that of specifying all and only those meanings available to speakers through the linguistic resource. Moreover, a system network is accompanied by realization rules on certain features that specify the structure in which the meanings are realized. These differences are important ones. The system network is a formalism for representing *linguistically* realized meanings. Semantic nets, conceptual dependency notation and other forms of conceptual modelling, on the other hand, belong in the field of *artificial intelligence* (AI). Although they have been used to provide a semantic or conceptual representation for use in natural language processing, they are not essentially linguistic in nature.

A system network approach to lexis is concerned with lexical *choice*, with what is available in the lexical resource of the language. It is therefore not simply concerned with a direct mapping between concepts and lexical items, but with how concepts may be expressed linguistically in context. This involves providing for exploitation of the lexical resource for textual cohesion (cf. Halliday and Hasan 1976, Martin 1992), for choices in register, and for the expression of meanings relating to the interpersonal metafunction of language (cf. Matthiessen 1990).

4.2. Systemic Functional Theory and the Primacy of Choice

If one is justified in proposing the "lexis as most delicate grammar" approach as an alternative to lexical entries in a lexicon, the prinhcipal justification derives from the central philosophy of modern systemic functional linguistics itself, that is the notion of *choice*.

Systemicists have always insisted on the primacy of choice of paradigmatic relations. If the primacy of choice is an accepted starting point, then *chain* (syntagmatic relations) is to be explained as a consequence of choice. This does not invalidate the mass of enquiry into the nature of syntactic structure, nor the search for linguistic universals of a structural kind. Neither is it incompatible with the belief that cognitive or neural structures constrain the structural possibilities of language. Such are the "raw materials" of the mind and are not, I believe, essentially different from the constraints of human physiology in the production of contrastive units of sound (cf. Chomsky's notion of universal grammar (1981:3–15) and the constraints it places on possible grammars as "biological endowment").

4.3. Linguistic Meaning versus Conceptual Meaning

The notion of choice is closely linked with meaning and meaningful-ness. Also, systemic functional grammar is a semantically oriented theory of language that makes statements about how speakers can mean by exploiting the resource, in the form of a lexicogrammar of options that they have available to them as members of a speech community. When we investigate meaning and its realization through language, however, we must inevitably consider the problem of the boundary between semantics (in this case lexical semantics) and conceptual structure. I would argue that the linguist should not be overly concerned with that part of conceptual or mental organization that is not directly expressible or communicable through language, for that is no longer the domain of linguistics. And if semantics is to be understood as the organization of linguistic meaning, then it can be argued that linguistic theory should be concerned primarily with the kinds of meaning that the language system makes available.

This view is clearly not shared by all researchers, especially in the field of artificial intelligence. As Woods (1975:37) points out, "There is a great deal of misunderstanding on this point (the scope of se-mantics) among computational linguists and psychologists." Other scholars claim that, especially in the case of lexical semantics, lan-guage-independent conceptual structure must be developed prior to the development of a linguistic lexicon. Such a position is held by Nirenburg and Raskin, who assert that, in the context of natural language processing for a particular "subworld," "The first (lexicon) to be built must be the subworld concept lexicon," and that, "The availability of such a lexicon is a *sine qua non* for any subsequent lexical work in NLP." (Nirenburg and Raskin 1987:277). This is clearly not the semantics that is associated with system networks, where the principle of motivating a semantic feature by its "reflex in form" is a central concern (see Fawcett 1974–76/81:157 and 1980:101, Martin, 1987:16). And if we maintain that lexical items, as well as syntax, are part of the level of form, then semantic features in this part of the network too must be motivated by their reflex in form and not by whatever conceptual structure may be thought to exist independently of language.

The separation of conceptual structure and linguistic meaning does not imply denying the existence of some (partially) language-independent conceptual organization. It is rather a question of the criteria to be used in each of the two. Unlike the theoretical or de-scriptive linguist, the computational linguist working within the field of artificial intelligence is faced with the problem of what aspects of knowledge and belief to model and where, in terms of "components," to model them. One consequence of this is that the lexicogrammatical component need not bear the burden of all aspects of what has been considered to be "meaning." One case in point is the location of "selectional restrictions," or in systemic functional terms, the tendency of Processes in the TRANSITIVITY system to "prefer" Agents and Affected Entities, for example, with certain semantic characteristics, such as [human] or [animal]. Within generative linguistics, the inclusion of such phenomena has already been questioned. As Horrocks points out:

> The features in terms of which the selectional restrictions are stated seem to have more to do with semantics than syntax, and indeed could only be regarded as having syntactic import in a theory which required the syntax and lexicon together to generate all the grammatical sentences of a language, and no non-sentences, without assistance from other components.
>
> (Horrocks 1987:36)

In terms of a global computational model, such aspects of "semantics" may find a more appropriate place in the representation of beliefs about "events," rather than being the direct responsibility of the lexicogrammar.

4.4. Lexis and the Prepackaging of Meanings

There are of course differences between lexis and structure, but essentially it is a difference of form. At the semantic level it is one that, like many linguistic phenomena, constitutes a cline. The meanings that are realized through structure exploit (at least in English) the order and the presence (or absence) of syntagmatically related items. The meanings realized through lexis exploit the meaning-carrying potential of the single item. One aspect of their complexity is that they can be seen as a kind of "portmanteau" realization—as the term is used in morphology—bearing atoms that cannot be syntactically isolated. And they are different from structural items in the complexity of semantic load that they carry. Yet the difference, again, is not a clear-cut one. Lexical items are the realization of relatively long lists of semantic features (even in the simplified network in Figure 14.1). They allow us to prepackage bundles of meaning for easy access and processing. This complexity of features relieves the communicative load, and without this resource I would be forced into limitless periphrastic expressions, using more primitive items (in the extreme case, perhaps, the thirteen primitives proposed by Wierzbicka (1980:10)).

What grammatical and lexical items share, however, is the ability to realize meaning by contrasting paradigmatically with some other item in a given context. This brings me back to the system and the system network, which is the central theoretical formalism for expressing semantic choice through paradigmatic relations.

It would be easy to argue here that words are simply representations of a deeper conceptual structure, and that the reflex in form of the items themselves in no way indicates the organization that lies behind them. This would take the organization out of the sphere of language, with an arbitrary set of forms attached to the conceptual entities. Again I must emphasize that a decision to represent lexical senses in network form does not negate the argument for any assumed form of conceptual organization that might be proposed. The semantics of language simply isn't directly concerned with what organization is like at a non-linguistic level. This is a crucial point and the thrust of the argument for a system network approach to lexical semantics as well. A system network is a formalism for representing all the possible meanings available to language users, meanings that may or may not be in a one-to-one relationship with elements of conceptual organization.

4.5. The Open-Endedness of Lexis

Lexical classes are open-ended and subject to constant modification. This may be an inconvenient complication for linguistic theory, but it is a fact of language and must be handled within the theory. It is not simply a matter that can be left to be accounted for by sociolinguistics and/or historical linguistics. If new lexical items, or the re-definition of existing items, are constantly being introduced into a language—not least of all in registers such as those used by linguists—then we have to find ways of building them into the overall network. The same change and development over time occurs in syntax, although at a considerably slower rate, and this gives the impression that structures are more permanent. Lexis is inconvenient because it represents the most varying and idiosyncratic part of the grammar. Any *model* we build is inevitably the model of one language user; it is not, and cannot be, a representation of Saussurean "langue," however eclectic or idealized we attempt to make it. In the case of the grammatical structure of a language, it is easier to make the assumption that it represents by and large a common meaning potential of a speech community. However, this is not the case with lexis. Every individual has a different lexical resource from other speakers, often varying by several thousand words. This point is also made by Martin who claims that: "Speaking a language involves a mastery of next to all its closed systems but only those open systems that are relevant to the experience of the speaker" (Martin 1981:8). All we can hope to model is some kind of ideal user's lexical organization, and at the same time, to provide a mechanism for adding new lexical acquisitions. The system network already provides a framework of related senses. Thus, like the thesaurus, it provides an environment for locating new senses. Clearly, the feature constituency of certain more delicate systems may need to undergo modification as new senses are introduced or as items take on different senses with time. However, this is in the nature of systems themselves; they change to reflect a different linguistic "slicing up of the semantic cake." System networks, therefore, offer a good starting point for modelling the open-endedness of lexis.

5. LEXICAL PHENOMENA TO BE HANDLED

Before discussing in detail the organization of the lexical system network, it is useful to summarize the lexical phenomena to be accounted for. I take these to be at least:

1. *the grammar of words:* their lexical classes in terms of the relations they enter into with other elements in the grammar (e.g. "noun," "adjective") and the grammatical consequences of words (e.g. clausal complementation with verbs like *dislike, like, hate, want,* etc., or prepositions governed by adjectives).
2. *experiential lexical choice:* the "sense" of items (their dictionary definitions)—including lexical relations such as synonymy, hyponymy (e.g., *dog/spaniel*), meronymy (e.g., *arm/hand/finger*) and opposites (e.g., *true/false, husband/wife*) (see Cruse (1986) for a comprehensive account of such phenomena).
3. *affective lexical choice:* one aspect of their interpersonal meaning (e.g., *fantastic, terrific*)
4. *textual lexical choice:* the informational load of the word
5. *the collocational behavior of the word* (e.g., *dog, tail, wag*)

The discussion in section 4.2 drew attention to the question of where to handle the various aspects of lexical meaning. This has important consequences for the role of the system network in providing a place for all aspects of what has gone under the name of "lexical semantics." The selection of features in any system must be motivated by reference to other components in the overall system, such as the belief representation, discourse grammar, etc. Thus, whereas the system network has the responsibility for expressing the lexical potential of the language, it is not by simply representing this potential systemically that all the problems of expressing lexical relations are automatically resolved. A system, for example, may include options that are senses of *co-hyponyms* (e.g., *spaniel, alsatian* and *boxer), co-meronyms* (e.g., *window* and *wall*) or one of the large class of *opposites* (e.g., *groove* and *ridge*); see Cruse (1986). All such relations can be expressed in system network form, but the nature of a particular relation must depend on reference to other aspects of belief in the global system. This constitutes a limitation on the explanatory power of a system network representation of lexical relations, but it does not invalidate the approach. Such relations, given the paradigmatic nature of systems, are still expressed as options in meaning determined by context.

It would be misleading to claim that for every lexical sense/item in the Cardiff Grammar there exists a full specification of all the aspects of lexis listed above. What I can say at this point in the exploration and development of this approach is that, in our view, none of the phenomena appears to pose insurmountable problems.

I will illustrate the discussion with part of the system network that deals with the lexical realization of *Things* as *nouns,* rather than attempt to cover the lexical realization of "Processes," especially since the latter has already been given extensive coverage in all the lexical semantic literature. Hasan (1987), especially, has made a significant contribution to modelling lexis as "most delicate grammar" in one area of material Processes, and Cross's work also concentrates on material Processes of "transformation" (Cross 1993). The Cardiff Grammar itself already has a well-developed TRANSITIVITY network handling several hundred verb senses relating to material, mental and relational Processes, including substantial coverage of mental Process complementation types. Fawcett's approach to relational processes was extensively described in Fawcett (1987) and the COMMUNAL approach to complementation is described in Fawcett's contribution to this volume.

Firstly, I will briefly describe how, in the Cardiff Grammar, features in the network for Things, which are realized through nominal group structure, lead on to more delicate systems whose features are realized in lexis. Given the framework of natural language generation, the following description assumes a *process* orientation rather than a *synoptic* one. In other words, we are approaching the system network and realization rules—which, viewed synoptically, represent the meaning potential of the language—from the point of view of "generating" language, of "instantiating" the potential. As process, the system network is *entered* and then *traversed,* and the realization rules that pertain to features in systems are *applied* in the course of generation.

6. LEXICAL SYSTEM NETWORKS FOR THING IN THE CARDIFF GRAMMAR

6.1. The Cultural Classification of Things

In Fawcett and Tucker's Cardiff Grammar, the lexical resource available as nouns is represented in a subnetwork within the system network for Thing.[2] The network for Thing is entered in order to generate meanings realized through the structure of the nominal group. Functions served by nominal groups include filling: (a) Participant Roles (e.g. *the little boy* cried); (b) certain types of Circumstantial Role (e.g. I saw him *last week*); (c) the completive element of prepositional groups (e.g. on *the table*), and so forth. One feature option in the network is [cultural classification potential], which allows the class of Thing to be referred to by a common noun expounding the head of the nominal group. This option is dependent on the prior choice of the feature [outsider]; an "outsider" is a "third person" referred to in the ongoing speech event. If the referent Thing is either the speaker or the addressee, the feature [interactant] will be selected whose realization is always a first or second person pronoun.

As Fawcett has suggested (1980:211), meanings realized as common nouns represent the "*cultural classification*" of Things as expressed in a language. Similarly, within the TRANSITIVITY system and

---

[2]Some confusion may arise from reference to parts of the overall network as either a **subnetwork** or as a **network** (e.g. "the network for Thing.") The Cardiff Grammar, in fact, treats the parts of the network that are realized through difference structures, such as the clause, nominal group, and so forth, effectively as separate networks. All these major areas of the lexicogrammar can also be seen to form one unified network, with an initial system for "entity" having the features [situation], [thing], [quality] and [quantity].

the system network for "Quality" the "cultural classification for Processes and Qualities is realized by verbs and adjectives/adverbs respectively."

If the option [cultural classification] is selected in the network for Thing, we enter the "lexical" subnetwork. From this point onward, any path through the network will lead to realization in lexis. Now, with the exception of nouns with clearly differentiated grammatical behavior, such as *mass* and *count* nouns, the distinction between one noun and another tends to reflect what might be seen as a purely semantic classification.[3] The network itself seems to resemble a form of taxonomy, with systems and their features derived from the kind of semantic relations traditionally discussed in lexical semantics (cf. Cruse 1986). For example, the feature [living] is the entry condition to another system, as shown above in Figure 14.1.

This raises two related problems. Firstly, what has such a system to do with "most delicate grammar?" Secondly, how do we justify the features in each lexical system—and indeed the overall design of the network? We are, after all, concerned with open set lexical classes whose members, in grammatical terms at least, are not distinguished by their behavior within the unit in which they occur. It is precisely for the lack of formal justification for semantic features that Butler criticizes Fawcett's 1980 account of such lexical networks (Butler 1985:134).

---

[3]It will be observed that the network for "cultural classification of Thing," as illustrated in Figure 14.1, does not make an initial distinction on the basis of the features [mass] and [count]. Although this distinction is fundamental to noun senses and, as I indicated, has grammatical consequences, especially in terms of the potential for quantification, if such a system is entered early in the traversal of the network it leads to two problems in particular. Firstly, certain closely related senses would be separated. An example of this is [furniture], realized by the **mass** noun *furniture*, and its hyponyms, such as [table], [chair], [bed] and so forth, which are realized by the **count** nouns *table, chair, bed*, and so forth. Secondly, a number of Thing senses are realized both as a count and as a mass noun (e.g. vegetables such as *potato, cabbage, onion* etc.) that may be treated as separate countable entities, or—especially in their culinary sense—as a substance. Making an initial or early "cut" in the system network in terms of mass/count would therefore involve considerable duplication, and, again, would lead to the complete separation of the two clearly related senses.

The current version of the Cardiff Grammar makes the features [mass] and [count] dependent on the choice of a particular sense. In this way the choice, for example, of [potato] in its "individual entity" sense will lead automatically to the feature [count], whereas [potato] in its "substance" sense will to the feature [mass]. Thus [potato] appears only once in the network and the respective potential for quantification is "controlled" by the consequent addition of either [count] and [mass] to the selection expression.

The answers to these questions lie both in the nature of co-occurrence within the context and in the lexical semantic relations that hold in a consistent way between features in a system and between systems in the network. We thus set up the hypothesis that there is a relationship between the semantically oriented nature of features in a system and the grammatical and lexical behavior associated with such features. In terms of lexical and structural co-occurrence, we will expect features in a system to have properties in common that are not shared by features in other systems, yet at the same time to exhibit "more delicate" properties that establish them as unique lexical senses. The ultimate validity of such a hypothesis can only be demonstrated as a result of extensive corpus linguistic investigation of the behavior of each lexical item. Moreover, the more we learn of such behavior, the greater will become our ability to model the organization of lexis in the grammar. Great emphasis therefore falls on the initial establishment of lexical networks according to semantic criteria, and it is this aspect of the "cultural classification of Things" that is discussed below.

6.2. Criteria for Lexical System Networks

The nature of classification of the lexical system network is closely related to our perception and classification of phenomena in the world of our experience. It is primarily through language that we make sense of the "external world." It would thus be surprising to find that the general organization of Things in a system network was greatly different from any ontological approach to classification. The difference will lie, as I have said, in the fact that the system network in concerned with making explicit the linguistic resource and, here in particular, the lexical resource.

The design of lexical system networks, as with ontologies, is influenced by ideas in concept categorization, especially: (a) Rosch's work on prototypes (Rosch 1978; cf. Lakoff 1987); and (b) theories of knowledge and knowledge representation, such as Dahlgren's theory of naive semantics (Dahlgren 1988) and Jackendoff's work on semantics and cognition (Jackendoff 1983, 1990). Another fundamental source of insight, and particularly relevant given the linguistic context, is the kind of relational information about word senses encoded in dictionary definitions. Considerable work has been carried out on machine readable dictionaries, such as LDOCE (Proctor 1987), with the aim of uncovering underlying taxonomies and other lexical semantic relations (Wilks et al. 1989, Boguraev and Briscoe 1989). The following discussion deals with some of the considerations taken in the development of the lexical system network for Thing.

Two major categories of Thing, artifacts and living things, appear to be appropriately describable in terms of ISA (or ISAKINDOF) and ISPARTOF relationships, as they are sometimes referred to in the AI literature. They correspond roughly with lexical semantic relations of hyponymy and meronymy respectively. The two types are confirmed by our own intuitions, by entailment tests for the expressions (Leech 1970) and by evidence from dictionary definitions; for example, a "coach," is a kind of "public transport road vehicle," which is a kind of "road vehicle," which is a kind of "vehicle," which is a kind of "artifact," is a kind of "non-living object," which is a kind of "object," which is a kind of "concrete thing," which is a kind of "thing." It should be remembered we are dealing with semantic features such as [public transport road vehicle] rather than lexical items that expound them. This is the specification of features in the network, not of lexical items. Not all features that we need in the network are accompanied by realization rules that lead to lexical items. Features to the left-hand side of the network will reflect broad classificatory divisions, for which there may or may not be a reflex in lexis. It is the basic level categories (Rosch 1978), which are predominantly lexicalized.

How, then, can we establish which non-terminal features to include in the network? One important aid is the fact that in very many cases there is indeed a lexical item realizing a superordinate sense. The fact that the corresponding lexical item may be a register-specific term is immaterial. Examples include *artifact* and *vehicle* for the list of features just mentioned. Consider also items such as *cetacean* and *sibling*. Wherever there exists a lexical item that realizes a superordinate term, the network must provide both for: (a) its realization as such—which implies that the term leads directly to a lexical item—and (b) the possibility of more delicate systems in the network if a more specific term is required. The potential to lexify at a superordinate level, even though the referent has been identified as a basic level category, is of obvious importance with aspects of textuality, such as cohesion. The referent to be expressed may be a *dog*, yet it can be referred to, especially in a subsequent reference, as the *animal*. This problem of how to avoid following the network into the more delicate categories is solved in the Cardiff Grammar by use of the "as such" feature. Thus, for example, when the feature [tool] is reached in the subnetwork for artifacts, the set of features selected (up to and including this feature) can be realized as the item *tool* at this level of delicacy. If a more delicate degree of lexical specification,

Figure 14.3.   General versus more delicate lexical choice in the Cardiff Grammar.

such as *hammer,* is required, traversal of the network continues until a system containing the corresponding feature [hammer] is reached. The initial system, with the feature [tool] as an entry condition, contains two features as shown in Figure 14.3. The feature [tool as such] bears a realization rule that causes the head of the nominal group to be expounded by the item *tool.* In this case, the traversal of this network is complete. The feature [tool specified] has no realization rule, but is the entry condition to a system containing more delicate options, and these typically either have a realization in form or are in contrast with a feature that does.

A second major problem is the following: What are the criteria on which we decide between two or more systems, each of which might claim to be the main system dependent on a feature? In other words, in terms of the lexical system network, how do we establish more delicate systems? One of the central problems in classification is that there is more than one way to classify a set of entities. Let us take the example of *whale.* A whale is an "animal," and is further classifiable as an "animal that lives in the sea," and/or as a "large animal," as a "fishlike animal" and/or as a "mammal." Whales are also "hunted by man" for the products that can be derived from their carcasses. They are on the whole "harmless to humans" rather than being "dangerous." Any of these categorizations could be used as criteria for the design of the system network. One might therefore construct a network based on systems with features such as [sea living animal] versus [land living animal], or with [mammal] versus [fish], or with [wild animal] versus [domestic animal], and so forth. Each would produce very different results in the overall shape and organization of the network. What this suggests is that entities are cross-classified in as many ways as humans decide to set up culturally significant or useful classification systems. Artifacts, for example, tend to be classified predominantly according to their function—and yet they can also be classified according to their physical appearance, size, weight, and so forth. One criterion may be dominant in one situation and another dominant in a different one. When someone is asked to fetch a *screwdriver,* it is not the function that allows identification, but its shape and appearance.

6.3. Cross-classification

One drawback, therefore, of using a single system network is that it forces one to select as "dominant" one type of contrast at any given degree of delicacy. Yet it is precisely the criteria for identifying the dominant type that is the issue here. We could, of course, construct the network with a number of simultaneously entered systems—one for size, one for appearance, one for behavior, one for zoological classification, and so forth, which in some way all mapped into one another (to realize a unique item such as *whale*). System networks lend themselves equally to this approach and indeed those proposed by Berry (1977), Hasan (1987) and Cross (1993) all adopt it. Cross-classification can be easily introduced into system networks by using the "AND" relationship. In this way, a single entry condition can require a number of systems to be entered in parallel, and features can be selected from each one. In Berry's illustration (1977:62), reproduced in Figure 14.4 below, in order to reach the feature [bull], for example, the "ANIMALHOOD" system, [human] versus [non-human], the "SEX" system, [differentiated] versus [non-differentiated] and the "MATURITY" system, [adult] versus [youthful], must all be entered simultaneously.

However, there is one inherent danger in the extensive use of simultaneous or parallel systems. Since a feature from each of a number of parallel systems must be selected, the network is suggesting that there is some formal outcome to *every possible combination* of selected features. It is often the case, however, that not all combinations result in a lexical item, that certain paths through the

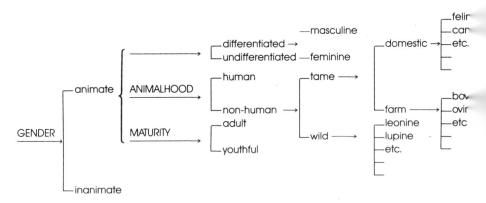

Figure 14.4. Berry's system network for "gender systems."

network, as is the case in Cross's network for "material processes of transformation" (Cross 1993:211), produce selection expressions for which there is no realization. Such networks, it would seem, do not adhere to the principle that systems and features be motivated by some "reflex in form." We cannot simply treat such cases as "lexical gaps," because it is hard in practice to draw networks that can be traversed without yielding a result. If this happens the network must be re-drawn.

Lexical gaps clearly exist in languages, but I would suggest that it is not the responsibility of the system network to make them explicit. Rosch (1978) has pointed that not all features recognized in conceptual categorization combine freely with one another to produce existing categories, and that, moreover, such features do not exist independently of one another in cognitive structures. Similarly, not all combinations of semantic features in a system network will combine into bundles realized by some lexical item. The solution to this dilemma is to provide for constraints to be placed on the co-selection of features from systems in parallel. This may be achieved by some marking notation (e.g., as discussed by Martin (1987), or by the use of "elaborated networks" as discussed by Fawcett (1988b)). In the latter case, relevant systems are repeated every time they are applicable, rather than being represented as across-the-board parallel systems. In this way, systems such as SEX DIFFERENTIATION would appear whenever some feature or set of features was cross-classified in this way to produce different lexical items. But note that it would not be sufficient to redesign the network in order to group together all features that are entry conditions to this system. Such a grouping would, in fact, cut across other important categorizations. Both ducks and cattle are distinguished lexically according to sex, yet they would be separated primarily in terms of their membership of the class of birds and of mammals respectively. A third method would be to make entry to the SEX DIFFERENTIATION system dependent on features denoting just those animals that require this distinction. In COMMUNAL we use the last two techniques; they are, in a sense, formal equivalents of each other.

We have still left unanswered the question of semantic criteria for lexical system membership. Class membership in cognitive psychology is at the heart of Rosch's prototype theory (Rosch 1978). Essentially, Rosch's theory is cognitive rather than linguistic, but it is still relevant here. It refutes the classical approach to classification in which entities are included in or excluded from class membership on the basis of possession of a certain number of characteristics or properties. A frequently used example is the classification of birds.

One central characteristic that birds have is that they fly, yet penguins and emus, for example, do not have the faculty of flight and are still members of the class "birds." The basis of Rosch's theory is that people work with typical—or prototypical—examples of class members. Sparrows are therefore more typical members of the class of birds than are penguins or emus. Experiments by Ashcraft (1976) and Rosch (1978) suggested also that subjects have an awareness of the relationship between an entity and its characteristics, in terms of being able to rate these according to how typical they are of the entity. Dahlgren's (1988) work on "naive semantics" exploited this kind of knowledge by representing features of objects as probabilistic features.

In the long term, therefore, it would be possible to construct classifications, and consequently system networks, based on the natural and naive beliefs that speakers have of entities. Such an approach would provide us with lists of typical characteristics of entities on which basis they could be classified. There is, however, a high degree of agreement in the kinds of taxonomies that are found in the various literatures. Much of the organization of the Cardiff Grammar network derives from the intuitive responses of co-researchers, from the insights of the literatures cited, and with the corroboration of shared linguistic classification encoded in dictionaries. The LDOCE definition for *hammer* (Proctor 1987), for example, is the following: "A tool with a heavy head, for driving nails into wood, or for striking things to break them or move them." Within such a definition we have information that allows us to classify *hammer* in the superordinate category *tool*, and further specification that allows a more delicate sub-classification in terms of function (for driving nails into wood or striking things) and in terms of physical form (with a heavy head). The important decision remains that of which criteria to select as a basis for the classification. It is here that cognitive research into typical characteristics of entities may throw some light on the problem. In the case of *hammer*, as with artifacts in general, function appears to be the major criterion in most situations. Artifacts come into being precisely because of their function. This leaves *shape, size, color,* and so forth, as less central characteristics.

Since the grammar of the language requires knowledge of such peripheral characteristics—a Process type may require an Affected entity with the characteristic "moveable"—this information must be available somewhere. Yet it seems counter-intuitive to cross-classify in the systemic network (as discussed above) all objects that are moveable. It seems reasonable to posit, at some other level, a *concep-*

tual ontology of entities, events, and so forth as part of the belief representation of a system, whether in human or artificial intelligence. And it is here that knowledge of the characteristics of entities, especially of the peripheral and encyclopaedic kind, can be represented. In such a way, the system network is freed of the burden of being required to represent all characteristics of entities.

7. THE RELATIONSHIP BETWEEN THE SEMANTICS OF LEXIS AND HIGHER CONCEPTS

Systems have been referred to as choice points (Matthiessen and Bateman 1991:89). In one sense, it is the very nature of a system to indicate which features can be selected in a given context. Thus in generation, the network is traversed and a feature is chosen from each system encountered. Systems do not tell us, however, which feature to choose or how to choose it; they simply offer us the linguistically possible alternatives. Any system that uses a systemic functional grammar to produce text must also provide for means of making the choices. In both the NIGEL Grammar and the Cardiff Grammar, features in systems are selected by decisions in "higher" components in the overall model. Systemic choice is motivated by a large number of elements that constitute various aspects of the text plan. They will include: the message content (usually represented in some "logical form"), general and local beliefs, knowledge of the addressee, and knowledge of discourse, and so forth. It is the role of the lexicogrammar to provide for the "unification" of all these various aspects of meaning and belief in the structure of the language.

Lexical choice must be motivated in the same way. There will therefore be a "mapping" between the ontology of concepts, from which the text plan will select the referents that are to be expressed, and the lexical system network, which makes available appropriate lexical items for the expression of the required referents. The congruent ideational realization in lexis is likely to correspond with a concept in the ontology. Thus, in many cases the selection of a conceptual referent will predetermine a feature in the network and with it a specific lexical item. As I pointed out above, in most respects the ontology of entities and the system network will be similar and often identical. It is not, however, simply a case of automatically realizing a concept with the equivalent lexical item in the network. Lexical items are selected according to interpersonal and textual criteria as well. As section 7.3 illustrates, these metafunctions will influence the choice of lexis in terms of degree of formality, register specificity, expressive and attitudinal content and textual organization such as recoverability of referent. Each lexical item, therefore, will ultimately be a conflation of functions from each of the three metafunctions.

8. HANDLING LEXICAL PHENOMENA IN THE NETWORK

8.1. Lexis and Structure

Lexical choice both depends on and determines structural and further lexical choice. The grammatical class to which a lexical item belongs is established by the place of each lexical subnetwork in the larger system network. Nouns, for example, are exponents of features selected within the system network for Thing. The element of structure that they expound and the element's role in the structure of the nominal group are determined by the systems and realization rules found in this network. Here also, lexical features interact with the NUMBER and MASS/COUNT systems, which determine their eventual morphology and grammatical behavior. Thus, the *selection expression* or list of features selected in the choice of a particular lexical item will contain all aspects of its grammatical and structural "inheritance." In this sense, such a selection expression resembles the feature list for a lexical entry as used in the "lexicon" approach to lexis in the "formal linguistics" tradition.

Let us consider verb senses for a moment. These too are a type of *cultural classification*, in that they express the meaning potential for referring to the types of Process (in a broad sense that includes "states" as well as "actions") available to a member of a culture through his/her language. The complex structural ramifications of lexical choice for Processes expounded by *Main verbs* are fully specified in the system network for TRANSITIVITY. The subnetwork is organized in such a way that selection of a Process type determines selection of the Participant Roles associated with it, their potential to be realized overtly or to be left unrealized (i.e. "covert"). The potential thematic ordering of Participant Roles through options in VOICE and/or THEME is also a consequence of selection of a Process type. The grammar of Processes, their "sub-categorization," is therefore fully expressed by the interaction and interdependency between systems in the TRANSITIVITY network.

It should be made clear, at this point, that the system network is only responsible for specifying what meanings are possible through different structural configurations associated with lexical choice.

The elements of structure themselves, their potential place in the structure of a unit and the place they occupy as the result of systemic choice are determined by the potential structure associated with each, and the realizations rules on certain features in the network. The potential structure is a list of all elements that may be components of a unit or class of unit, related to one another by the allocation of a numbered place in structure to each one. Wherever an element may be located in more than one place in structure, as in the case of many clause elements such as Complements, Adjuncts and the Operator, it is the realization rules that allocate the numbered place. Insertion of the various elements of structure in their appropriate place is the responsibility of the realization rules. The structural properties of lexically and grammatically realized senses are therefore only fully specified by reference to the system network, the realization rules, and the potential structure.[4]

8.2. Lexical Semantic Relations

The expression of lexical semantic relations in the network has already been mentioned briefly. Much of the lexical network for Thing reflects the relation of hyponymy, and to a lesser extent that of meronymy (which is illustrated in Figure 14.5). Other relations, such as the several kinds of oppositeness (cf. Cruse 1986) are also readily expressible within systems. Features are related in terms of being members of a set that is expressed by the entry condition to a system or to the system label. As members of a set, they are in a relationship with the entry condition and also with one another. The concept of a systemic relationship is broader than any of the the above relations, and so a system network can be used to represent any and all of them.

I should emphasize, however, that the system network notation alone does not magically resolve all the complexities discussed in the literature of lexical semantics. Such feature labelling as [whole human] and [part human] simply indicates the presence of choice, a choice that involves the difference between senses related hyponymically or meronymically. The motivation for such choice, as we

---

[4]It should be pointed out that a **potential structure** can only be specified "in advance" in the case of units that have fixed structure. Wherever an element of structure may occupy more than one place in a unit—as is the case with a number of elements in the clause (e.g. Complements, Adjuncts and the Operator)—the element will be placed by a separate rule as a consequence of the selection of a feature that determines the placement.

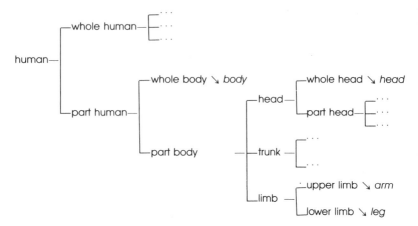

Figure 14.5. A simplified system network showing part-whole relations.

have seen, will be found elsewhere in the overall system; in the case of meanings realized as nouns, it is the concept ontology that is largely responsible for making such relations explicit. Their representation in the system network is, as we have seen, concerned with making the senses available as lexical items and specifying the lexicogrammatical consequences of choices involving such relations.

A different kind of problem is raised by the interpretation of the verb *finish* in the sentence:

I've finished the book. (1)

Interpreting the sense of *finish* depends to some extent on the semantics of *book*. If we do know how books relate to Processes—here, by being read or written—then we cannot recover the unrealized process in the utterance. Pustejovsky's theory of *qualia structure* is one approach to lexical semantics that addressed this kind of problem. Pustejovsky refers to the role that the item *book* takes on as "logical metonymy." This, therefore, is another lexical semantic relation to be accounted for. In his approach, part of the semantics of *book* specifies what the artifact is used for, its *telic role* (Pustejovsky 1991:425ff). Now, although the sense realized by *book* will be located appropriately in the network, in close proximity and related to other similar verbal artifacts, the "telic role" associated with one or more such artifacts will ultimately be established by reference to the concept ontology. It is the concept in the ontology, and not the feature in the system network, to which is attached a list of relevant attributes.

The linguistic consequences of the choice of a lexical item, however, are fully the responsibility of the system network. Once again, it is necessary to consider carefully the extent to which the lexicogrammar should be asked to account for certain "semantic" phenomena. Freeing the lexicogrammar of such phenomena does not weaken the linguistic theory. It is rather a question of redistributing the phenomena, or perhaps of redrawing the boundary between "conceptual" and "linguistic" semantics.

8.3. Register and Lexis

I referred briefly in section 7 to the textual and interpersonal influence on lexical choice, which is also discussed in Matthiessen (1990). If lexical networks are to be sensitive to such concerns, the choice of appropriate items must be made available. Thus, when a choice in the TENOR system (affecting the degree of formality of the intended text) is made, this must interact with lexis wherever the lexical potential allows the degree of formality to be expressed. For example, the "Quality" sense that might be glossed as [overcome by alcohol] can be expressed formally as *intoxicated*, less formally as *drunk*, and even less formally as *sloshed*. The feature [overcome by alcohol], in experiential terms, is neutral, whereas the three lexical items differ in interpersonal terms. In such cases the formalism of system networks and realization rules offer two methods of representing this potential. In the first, the features [formal] and [overcome by alcohol] may constitute a joint entry condition to a single-feature system (if there is only one formal lexical item available) that yields a feature [intoxicated], which is expounded by the item *intoxicated*. The feature [consultative] will also constitute a similar joint entry condition with [overcome by alcohol] to yield the feature [drunk] and the item *drunk*. Finally, the features [casual] and [overcome by alcohol] lead to the feature [sloshed] and the item *sloshed*. This system is shown in Figure 14.6.

In the second method, which is the approach adopted in the Cardiff Grammar, the lexical choice is expressed in the realization rule on [overcome by alcohol] by the use of conditions on application of the rule. Such a rule takes the form:

(feature) overcome by alcohol: (condition 1) if [formal] then (operation) a < "intoxicated"
(= the apex is expounded by -), (condition 2) if [consultative] then (operation) a < "drunk,"
(condition 3) if [casual] then (operation) a < "sloshed"

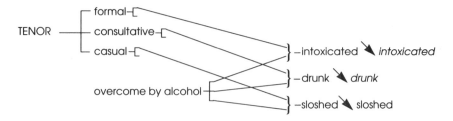

Figure 14.6.   Interpersonal lexical differences modelled as joint entry conditions involving the TENOR system.

It might seem that these alternative approaches are in fact notational variants, with the choice of one or the other determined by whether one prefers greater complexity in the network or in the realization rules. The first approach, however, involves creating extra features that are not in any systemic relationship; the features [intoxicated], [drunk] and [sloshed] are not options in a system, because they have different entry conditions.

There seems no good reason why interpersonally and textually determined variants should not appear in close proximity in the same network. This applies equally to register- determined lexis. If register is seen as restricting the lexicogrammatical potential according to the activity of the speaker, then this can be achieved by the interaction of parallel systems or by the influence of a choice at some more abstract or "higher" level such as {field = electronics}. This would have the effect of resetting the networks and preferring lexical and structurally features appropriate to this field. The alternative to this would be to posit entirely separate networks for register-determined lexis, a solution that appears implausible in that it suggests that choice of register determines lexical choice in an absolute way. The solution presented here, once again, supports Halliday's view of language potential as "only one network of lexicogrammatical options."

8.4. Collocation

I introduced the problem of handling collocation in section 3, and a fuller discussion of the approach being developed in the Cardiff Grammar to this aspect of the behavior of words is found in Tucker (in press). What seems most fruitful in the examination of collocation is the light that it sheds on the nature of each lexical item as a unique grammatical class. The set of lexical items that collocate with a given item (its collocational cluster) is likely to be unique, and it can be considered to be an essential part of the individual behavior of the item. Knowing the collocates of a word does not, however, enable us to predict, as we can with grammatical classes, which lexical items will co-occur at the same time. It seems to me that the collocational "cohesiveness" varies along a cline. The occurrence of *sour* with *milk* in the context of "going bad" is strongly predicted. So are the kinds of superlatives like *faintest* and *slightest* that are found in the context *I haven't the . . . idea* (see Tucker, in press). Other collocates, established on the basis of strong probability of co-occurrence over large sample of text, are less predictable. For example, Berry gives possible members of the cluster for dog as *growl*, *wag* and *tail*. Although these would by no means exhaust cluster membership, it is perfectly plausible to find *dog* occurring without any member from the cluster of its collocates. The more "cohesive" the collocation, the greater is the likelihood that other lexicogrammatical factors, beyond pure lexical co-occurrence, are involved. The collocation of *dog, wag* and *tail*, for example involves the relations, expressed through the TRANSITIVITY system, of the Participant Roles of Agent and Affected, and a material Process. This approach to collocational phenomena is also proposed in Martin (1992) where the relations between such lexical items are considered to be examples of what he terms "nuclear relations." In terms of "selectional restrictions" or "preferences," the verb *wag* will prefer *dog* as an Agent and *tail* as an Affected entity. Similarly, whenever *milk* is modified by a Quality of Thing expressing "gone bad," the item *sour* is the almost certain candidate; *rancid* would not do, since it is used exclusively to modify substances such as *butter* and *oil*.

The extent to which the lexicogrammar can or should be responsible for the whole range of lexical co-occurrence is still an issue to be resolved. At the more "adhesive" end of the cline, where the co-occurrence of two lexical items is all but compulsory, the system network and realization rules are able to express the relationship. This is achieved by the use of *preferences rules*, which determine feature selection between passes through the networks. Thus, for example, when the complex process realized by *haven't the . . . idea* has been selected, a preferences rule will constrain selection in the network for Quality to those lexical systems and features that are expounded exclusively by items such as *slightest, faintest, foggiest*, and so forth (See Tucker, in press, for a fuller account).

Expressing co-occurrence phenomena through "preferences," which are statements of probability of occurrence, seems to me to capture the essence of collocation. Also, as Hasan (1987:188) emphasizes, unlike the "selectional restrictions" of early generative grammar, such statements do not attempt to specify well- or ill-formedness, but rather express the expectation of certain semantic features. A speaker may "override" a preference as expressed in the lexicogrammar, without the automatic consequence of ill-formedness, and the hearer, who shares the same lexicogrammar is able to interpret the utterance by comparing what was in fact selected with what was expected.

In my view, then, the real value of the collocations that can be established by corpus linguistic investigation lies in the insights they offer to how preferences are to be expressed in two or more passes through the network, in those "most delicate" parts that are realized lexically. In the last example given above, the strict collocation of this small set of adjectives with the noun *idea* suggests that they are related systemically, that they constitute a system of closely related meanings in a given context. Thus, in the Cardiff Grammar, we do not model collocation at the level of form; instead, we use the phenomenon to model the semantics behind it, in terms of organization the system network, which, in turn gives rise to lexical co-occurrence through the statements of probabilities associated with feature selection.

9. CONCLUSION

The discussion in this chapter has ranged over a large number of issues raised in the treatment of lexis—without, however, exhausting it. Neither has it given full accounts of how the various aspects of lexis are handled in a systemic approach. There are still many questions unanswered, as indeed there are aspects of the behavior of lexical items to be uncovered by the mass of research that is now being carried out in the field of corpus linguistics and the automatic extraction of lexical information from machine-readable sources. But I have suggested that our experience in the COMMUNAL Project suggests strongly that there are highly promising ways forward in most of these within systemic functional theory, and that such a way forward is consonant with Halliday's original, imaginative notion of "lexis as most delicate grammar."

"Constructing the dictionary out of the grammar" as Michael Halliday explains his purpose as a grammarian (Halliday 1991), is a long and arduous task. When we enter the domain of lexically realized meanings, we embark on the description of the unique behavior of tens of thousands of items. We are required to leave behind the comfortable generalizations that, starting from the grammatical end of language, we initially encounter. Systemic functional linguistics entrusts the task of explaining language to its central formalism, the system network. The purpose of this chapter has been to demonstrate that even in the case of lexis and lexical relations the system network—always in close association with its related realization rules—has impressive explanatory power.

As the COMMUNAL Project progresses, more of these matters will be implemented and developed, and on a larger scale. What I have tried to demonstrate here is that the system network is far more than merely a strong candidate as a means of representing lexical semantics in a unifying way. And it has the additional advantage of permitting the treatment of lexis to remain consistent with the general theoretical principles of systemic functional linguistics, so providing a unified theory of language.

REFERENCES

Ashcraft, M.H. (1976) "Property norms for typical and atypical items from 17 categories: a description and discussion." *Memory and Cognition* 6(3):227–232.

Berry, M. (1977) *Introduction to systemic linguistics, Vol 2: Levels and links*. London: Batsford.

Bobrow, Daniel G. and Collins, Allan (eds.) (1975) *Representation and understanding: Studies in cognitive science*. London: Academic Press.

Boguraev, Bran and Briscoe, Ted (1989) *Computational lexicography for natural language programming*. London: Longman.

Brachman, R.J. (1979) "On the epistemological status of semantic networks" in Findler, N. (ed.), *Associative networks: Representations and use of knowledge by computer*. New York: Academic Press.

Butler, C.S. (1985) Systemic linguistics: Theory and application. London: Batsford.

Chomsky, Noam (1965) *Aspects of the theory of syntax*. Cambridge, MA: MIT Press.

Chomsky, Noam (1981) *Lectures on government and binding*. Dordrecht, Holland/Riverton, NJ: Foris.

Cross, M. (1993) "Collocation in computer modelling of lexis as most delicate grammar," in M. Ghadessy (Ed.) *Register analysis: Theory and practice*. London: Pinter.

Cruse, D. (1986) *Lexical semantics*. Cambridge: Cambridge University Press.

Cumming, Susanna (1986a) *Design of a master lexicon*. ISI Research Report. Marina Del Rey: University of Southern California.

Cumming, Susanna (1986b) *The lexicon in text generation*. USC/ISI report. Marina Del Rey: University of Southern California.

564   Tucker

Dahlgren, Kathleen (1988) *Naive semantics for natural language under-standing.* Boston: Kluwer.

Fawcett, R.P. (1974–6/81) "Some proposals for systemic syntax." Cardiff, Wales: The Polytechnic of Wales. (First published in MALS Journal).

Fawcett, R.P. (1980) *Cognitive linguistics and social interaction: Towards an integrated model of a systemic functional grammar and the other components of an interacting mind.* Heidelberg, Germany: Julius Groos and Exeter University.

Fawcett, R.P. (1987) "The semantics of clause and verb for relational processes in English," In Halliday and Fawcett (Eds.), *New developments in systemic linguistics.* London: Pinter.

Fawcett, R.P. (1988a) "Language Generation as Choice in Social Interaction," in Zock and Sabah (Eds.), *Advances in natural language generation.* London: Pinter.

Fawcett, R.P. (1988b) "What makes a good system network good?" In Benson, James and Greaves, William (1988) *Systemic functional approaches to discourse.* Norwood, NJ: Ablex.

Fawcett, R.P. and Tucker, G.H. (1990) "Demonstration of GENESIS: A very large, semantically based systemic functional grammar." In *Procs of 13th International Conference on Computational Linguistics,* Vol 1. pp. 47–49.

Fawcett, R.P., Tucker, G.H. and Lin, Y. (1993) "The role of realization in realization: How a systemic grammar works." in H. Horacek M. Zock (ed.) *From planning to realization in natural language generation.* London: Pinter.

Firth, J.R. (1957) *Papers in linguistics 1934–1951.* London: Oxford University Press.

Gazdar, G., Klein, E., Pullum, G.K. and Sag, I. (1985) *Generalized phrase structure grammar.* Oxford, England: Blackwell.

Halliday, M.A.K. (1961) "Categories of the theory of grammar." In *Word 17:241–92.*

Halliday, M.A.K. (1978) *Language as social semiotic: The social interpretation of language and meaning.* London: Arnold.

Halliday, M.A.K. (1991) "Language as system and language as instance: the corpus as a theoretical construct," in J.Svartvik (ed.) *Directions in Corpus Linguistics.* Proceedings of the Nobel Symposium 82, Stockholm (1991). Berlin, Germany: Mouton de Gruyter.

Halliday, M.A.K. (1994) (2nd Edition) *An introduction to functional grammar.* London: Arnold.

Halliday, M.A.K. and Fawcett, R.P. (eds.) (1987) *New developments in systemic linguistics, Vol 1: Theory and description.* London: Frances Pinter.

Halliday, M.A.K. and Hasan, R. (1976) *Cohesion in English.* London: Longman.

Halliday, M.A.K. and Martin, J.R. (1981) (eds.) *Readings in systemic linguistics.* London: Batsford.

Hasan, R. (1987) "The grammarian's dream: lexis as most delicate grammar," in Halliday and Fawcett (Eds.), *New developments in systemic linguistics, Vol. 1.* London: Pinter.

Horrocks, Geoffrey (1987) *Generative grammar.* London: Longman.

Jackendoff, Ray (1983) *Semantics and cognition.* Cambridge, MA: MIT Press

Jackendoff, Ray (1990) *Semantic structures.* Cambridge, MA: MIT Press.

Kaplan, R.M. and Bresnan, J. (1982) "Lexical functional grammar: A formal system for grammatical representation" in Bresnan, J. (ed.) 1982. *The mental representation of grammatical relations.* Cambridge, MA: MIT Press.

Lakoff, George (1987) *Women, fire, and dangerous things: What categories reveal about the mind.* Chicago: University of Chicago Press.

Leech, Geoffrey (1970) "On the theory and practice of semantic testing." In *Lingua,* 24. 343–64.

Levin, Beth (1985) "Lexical semantics in review: an introduction," in Levin, Beth (ed.) (1985) *Lexical semantics in review, No. 1.* Lexical Project Working Papers, Center for Cognitive Studies, MIT, Cambridge, MA.

Mann, W.C. and Matthiessen, Christian (1983/85) "Demonstration of the Nigel text generation computer program," in Benson, J.D., and Greaves, W.S. (eds.) (1985) *Systemic perspectives on discourse, Vol 1: Selected theoretical papers from the Ninth International Systemic Workshop.* Norwood, NJ: Ablex.

Martin, J. R. (1981) *Lexical cohesion.* Sydney, Australia: The University of Sydney.

Martin, J. R. (1987) "The meaning of features in systemic linguistics," in Halliday and Fawcett (Eds.), *New developments in systemic linguistics, Vol. 1.* London: Pinter.

Martin, J.R. (1992) *English Text: System and structure.* Philadelphia: John Benjamins.

Matthiessen, Christian (1987a) "Semantics for a systemic grammar: The chooser and inquiry framework" in Benson, James D., Cummings, Michael J. and Greaves, William S. (eds.) (1987) *Linguistics in a systemic perspective.* Amsterdam: John Benjamins.

Matthiessen, Christian (1987b) "Notes on the organization of the environment of a text generation program" in Kempen, Gerard (ed.) (1987) *Natural Language Generation.* Dordrecht, Holland: Martinus Nijhof.

Matthiessen, C.M.I.M. (1990) "Lexico(grammatical) choice in text generation" in C.L. Paris, W.R. Swartout and W.C. Mann (eds.) *Natural language generation in artificial intelligence and computational linguistics.* Dordrecht, Holland: Kluwer Academic Publishers.

Matthiessen, Christian M.I.M. and Bateman John A. (1991) *Text Generation and Systemic functional linguistics: Experiences from English and Japanese.* London: Pinter.

Nirenburg, Sergei and Raskin, Victor (1987) "The subworld concept lexicon and the lexicon management system" in *Computational Linguistics, Volume 13, numbers 3–4*.

Patten, Terry. (1984) *Planning and systemic text generation: A conflation.* DAI working paper No.166. Edinburgh: University of Edinburgh.

Patten, Terry (1988) *Systemic text generation as problem solving.* Cambridge: Cambridge University Press.

Proctor, Paul, (Ed.) (1987) *Longman Dictionary of Contemporary English* (New edition). London: Longman.

Pustejovsky, James (1991) "The generative lexicon." in *Computational Linguistics, Vol. 17, No. 4.*

Rosch, E. (1978) "Principles of categorization." In Rosch E. and Lloyd, B.B. (eds.) *Cognition and categorization.* Hillsdale, NJ: Lawrence Erlbaum.

Schank, R.C. (1972) "Conceptual dependency: A theory of natural language understanding." In *Cognitive Psychology* 3, 552–631.

Tucker, Gordon H. (1989) "Natural language generation with a systemic functional grammar," in *Laboratorio degli studi linguistici, 1989/1.* Università degli studi di Camerino.

Tucker, Gordon H. (in press) "So grammarians haven't the faintest idea: Reconciling lexis-oriented and grammar-oriented approaches to language." In R. Hasan, D. Butt and C. Cloran (Eds) *Functional descriptions: Language form and linguistic theory.* Amsterdam: Benjamins.

Wierzbicka, Anna (1980) *Lingua mentalis: The semantics of natural language.* Sydney, Australia: Academic Press.

Wilks, Y., Fass, D., Guo, C., McDonald, J., Plate, T. and Slator, B. (1989) "A tractable machine dictionary as a resource for computational semantics." In Boguraev, Bran and Bricoe, Ted (1989).

Woods, William A. (1975) "What's in a link: Foundations for semantic networks," in Bobrow and Collins (Eds.), *Representation and understanding: Studies in cognitive science.* London: Academic Press.

Zock, Michael and Sabah, Gérard (eds.) (1988) *Advances in natural language generation: An interdisciplinary perspective. Volumes 1 and 2.* London: Pinter.

15

"NGp of NGp" Constructions: A Functional-Structural Study*

V. Prakasam

*Central Institute of English
and Foreign Languages
Hyderabad, India*

Michael Halliday's theorizing about the structure of language, starting from his study of Chinese (1956), has always been from a comprehensive viewpoint—rejecting nothing as irrelevant to a serious, holistic study of language and its use. This has been a great asset to systemicists. Indeed, many of the later insights of Speech Act theories and Pragmatics could easily be built into his comprehensive view of language and linguistics. My personal discussions with him in Hyderabad (1968) and later in London (1970) have helped me to develop a useful and healthy attitude toward linguistics.

1. INTRODUCTION

In this chapter I wish to study, from a functional-structural point of view, those nominal groups that have what I will call an "of NGp"

---

*I am very grateful to Dr. Robin Fawcett for his valuable comments and suggestions, which have led to a thorough revision of the paper. I have immensely benefited from the points discussed by Sinclair in his *Corpus, Concordance, Collocation* (1991), especially in shaping my own arguments in this regard.

constituent. The point of departure will be the distinction made by Halliday between "Head" and "Thing" in his discussion of the nominal group in *Introduction to Functional Grammar* (1994, henceforth IFG). I will not consider all "of-constructions," but only certain representative examples, of which I will study the experiential and logical structures. I will not touch on all the "of-constructions" that enter into clause structure, for example, *(think) of someone; (be aware) of something; (accuse someone) of something.* (For a detailed study of all these expressions see Sinclair, 1991; also *Collins Cobuild English Grammar* 1990 and *Collins Cobuild English Language Dictionary* 1991.) I will use the expression "NGp of NGp" because it is not in principle a noun but a nominal group that precedes and follows the item *of,* and in many cases a full group occurs.

"Thing" is one of the nominal group functions reflecting experiential structure, and it specifies *a class of things* (Halliday, 1994:181). Thing is considered the semantic core of the nominal group (p. 189). The elements that co-occur with Thing are: Deictic, Numerative, Epithet, Classifier, Qualifier. This type of structure is called "a multivariate structure": a constellation of elements each having a distinct function with respect to the whole (p. 193). "Head" is one of the nominal group functions reflecting its logical structure, and it is this structure that reflects the relationship of sub-categorization (p. 191). The other elements that co-occur with Head are the premodifier and postmodifier. The logical analysis expresses the recursive aspect of the modifying relation, giving us a univariate structure (i.e. a structure generated by the recurrence of the same function (p. 193)).

Let's have a look at the example given by Halliday for the two types of analysis (p. 191), shown in Fig. 15.1 on p. 569.

Halliday asserted that Thing and Head do not coincide in all structures, for instance, in the case of nominal groups involving a measure of something (p. 195). See, for example, Fig. 15.2.

Now that we have reminded ourselves of the framework for the

Numerative	Thing

A   pack   of cards

Modifier ·	Head	Postmodifier
β	α	β

Figure 15.2.

	those	two	splendid	old	electric	trains	with pantographs
Experiential	Deictic	Numerative	**Epithet**		Classifier	Thing	Qualifier
			Attitude	Quality			
			Premodifier			Head	Postmodifier
Logical	ζ	e	δ	γ	β	α	β

FIGURE 15.1

nominal group in IFG, we can go on to consider the "NGp of NGp" constructions that are the focus of this chapter. For a detailed study of "N's N" (genitive) structures and "N of NP" (possessive) structures see Hawkins (1980), Jespersen (1961), and Lyons (1986). I will not discuss the points made by them systematically, but some of their views will be covered in the discussion of the experiential and logical structures. For comparable studies of "of-NGp" constructions, see Fawcett (1980), Renouf and Sinclair (1991), Sinclair (1991).

Fawcett (1980) treated "of" in these nominal groups as "selector." His views in this regard deserve full quotation:

> The essential concept . . . in understanding the relationships that the various "determiners" that may co-occur in a nominal group have with each other and with what follows them is that of SELECTION. That is, just as in *seven of those girls* the item *seven* selects a stated quantity from the particular set of girls identified by *those girls*, so *seven* in *seven girls* selects a stated quantity from the whole class of girls. The only difference between the types of selection in the two cases is that in the second case the semantic relationship of "selection" is made overt by using the item *of*.
>
> (Fawcett 1980:203)

Sinclair's views on of give us a different dimension: "The function of of is to introduce a second noun as a potential head word" (Sinclair 1991:85)

The analysis of different nominal groups offered here tries to capture that potential in "of-phrase." Sinclair rightly said: "A grammatical account (of of) will concentrate on the status of the head-word, the distinction between single and double heads, and the indeterminate cases." (Sinclair 1991:98)

Interestingly and appropriately, Sinclair and Halliday, like Fawcett, question the prepositional status of of:

> In most of its contexts of use of is functioning not as minor Process/Predicator but rather as a structure marker in the nominal group (cf. to as structure marker in the verbal group). Hence of phrases occur as clause elements only in two cases: (1) as circumstance of Matter, e.g. Of George Washington it is said that he never told a lie, (2) as one of a cluster of circumstances expressing a sense of 'source', all ultimately deriving from abstract Locative 'from': died/was cured of cancer, accused/convicted/acquitted of murder, and so on.
>
> (Halliday 1994:213)

Sinclair presented a corpus view of of as follows:

> Prepositions are principally involved in combining with following nouns to produce prepositional phrases which function as adjuncts in

clauses. This is not anything like the main role of of, which combines with preceding nouns to produce elaborations of the nominal group. . . .

It is not unreasonable to expect that quite a few of the very common words in a language are so unlike the others that they should be considered as unique, one-member word class. If that status is granted to of, then there is no substantial difference between a dictionary entry for the word and a section of a grammar devoted to it. The one-member class is the place where grammar and lexis join.

(Sinclair 1991:82–83)

The statistical study of Renouf and Sinclair (1991:128–143) confirms the observation that "of-phrases" are found more in the structure of a nominal group than in the structure of a clause.

2. EQUATIVE AND DEICTIC CONSTRUCTIONS

Let us now take up a few nominal groups and study their functional-structural configuration. Look at the following:

The Kingdom of Nepal   (1)

The King of Nepal   (2)

I wish to suggest that (1) expresses an equative relationship, where "of" is appositively linking "Nepal" to "Kingdom," the latter specifying the referential value of the former. Examples (3b) and (3c) are offered in support of this claim, and so of the analysis in Figure 15.3.

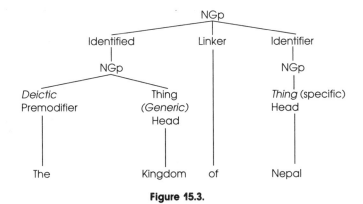

Figure 15.3.

I visited the Kingdom of Nepal in 1956.   (3a)

I visited the Kingdom in 1956.   (3b)

I visited Nepal in 1956.   (3c)

*I visited Nepal's Kingdom in 1956.   (3d)

The unacceptability of (3d) reflects the inadmissibility of the following bracketing:

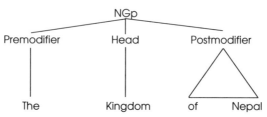

[△ is used to show that the structure is not analyzed.]

Figure 15.4.

Example (3b) is opaque; it needs contextualization to get the correct interpretation.
    Now let us compare (3a) to (3d) with (4a) to (4d):

I had an audience with the King of Nepal.   (4a)

I had an audience with the King.   (4b)

I had an audience with Nepal's King.   (4c)

*I had an audience with Nepal.   (4d)

Example (4b) needs contextualization for correct interpretation, whereas (4d) is unacceptable. Any analysis of (2) should reflect this kind of relationship, as is shown in Fig. 15.5 (p. 573).
    The analysis captures the fact that the possessive can in some cases appear as a premodifier.

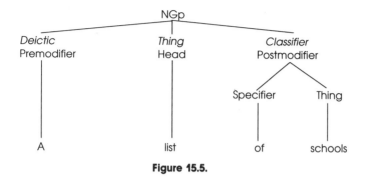

Figure 15.5.

3. DEFINITE AND INDEFINITE DETERMINERS

Consider the following:

A list of schools   (5)

A number of schools   (6)

The number of schools   (7)

Structurally, these expressions can be represented as follows:

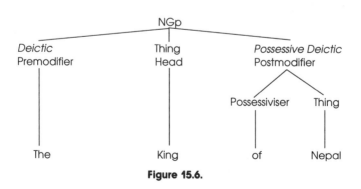

Figure 15.6.

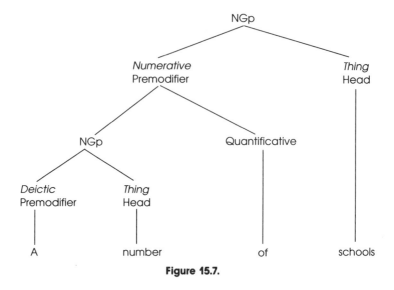

Figure 15.7.

The following is the analysis of (6) if one follows Fawcett (1980:204):

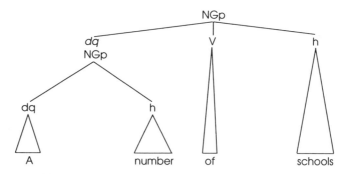

Key: dq = quantifying determiner
     h = head
     v = selector (always expounded by *of*, phonologically /əv/, hence v)

Figure 15.8.

(His analysis of (5) involved a nominal group that fills a different determiner, namely the representational determiner, but I will not discuss that proposal further here.)

However, I want to suggest that if (6) is given a definite article, it invites an analysis different from (6) with an indefinite article (see Figure 15.9). For Fawcett, the analysis would be the same as for (6)

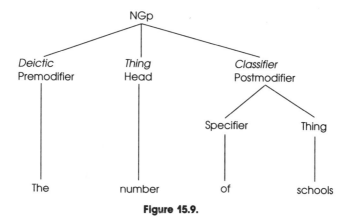

Figure 15.9.

(with a deictic determiner (dd) expounded by the replacing the quantifying determiner (dq), expounded by a).

Now compare (8), (9) and (10) with (5), (6) and (7) respectively:

I gave him a list of schools to be inspected, and he lost it.

(8)

He inspected a number of schools, and found their functioning satisfactory.

(9)

The number of schools he inspected is much below the target.

(10)

Thus the pronominalization of the subsequent reference indicates clearly what the true referent of the antecedent nominal group is. Also consider the following:

There are a number of schools in Patiala.

(11)

The number of schools in Patiala is too small.

(12)

What Sinclair said in this regard is this: "The identification of head-word is the first step in describing a nominal group. It is reasonable to expect the headword of a nominal group to be the principal reference point to the physical world" (Sinclair 1991:86–87). Sinclair seems to have expected "Head" and "Thing" to coincide most of the time. They do, but not always—certainly not with "of-phrases" in the Nominal Group. It may be that it is in order to avoid this clash of

"Head" and "Thing" that we have alternative expressions (Collins Cobuild English Grammar:112):

two teas for "two cups of tea"   (13)

two sugars for "two spoonfuls of sugar"   (14)

4. POSSESSIVES, CONSTITUTIVES AND EPITHETS

The logical structure of a given set of nominal groups may be iso-morphic, but the groups' experiential structures may differ. This is what happens when we take possessive postmodifier and classifier postmodifier constructions. Look at the following:

The legs of a table   (15)

The idols of five metals   (16)

Example (16) may sound odd but, like the archaic "a calf of gold" that occurs in Biblical language, it is a common expression in the register of Indian religious texts or discussions, because the idols made of five metals are commonly found in Indian temples, and sometimes they are stolen and smuggled out to satisfy the sophisti-cated hunger of the lovers of antiques. The structures of (15) and (16) will be as follows:

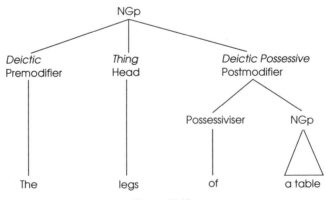

Figure 15.10.

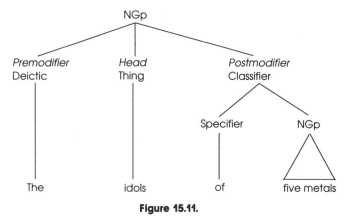

Figure 15.11.

The fact that the deictic possessive is not alternatively used as a premodifier genitive is generally attributed to its low rank in the scale of animacy (Jespersen 1961:324).

5. DOUBLE-HEADED NOMINALS

Consider the following:

The daughter of the King   (17)

The Church of England   (18)

I want to marry the daughter of the King, and for that I will have to impress him.   (19)

I have seen the daughter of the King, and I think I can't live without her.   (20)

I saw the daughter of the King, and I think they resemble each other quite a bit.   (21)

He is the Head of the Church of England.   (22a)

*He is the Head of England.   (22b)

?He is the Head of the Church.   (22c)

(22c) needs contextualization for correct interpretation. "Church of England" behaves more like a chemical compound that refers to a new thing. The analysis, then, for (17) and (18) will be as follows:

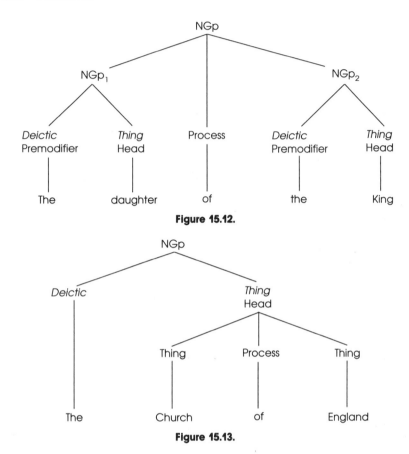

Figure 15.12.

Figure 15.13.

If "the" in (18) is to be treated as an inalienable part of Thing, the analysis will be different:

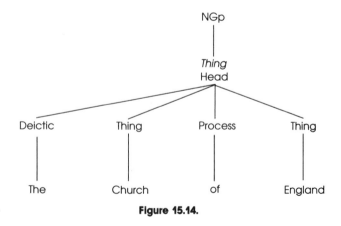

Figure 15.14.

Example (17) is of special significance because the constituent nouns can be anaphorically referred to either separately or together. If we bracket "of" with the second nominal, we may not be able to account for the freedom of the two nominals. This should be due to the fact that a relational nominal like "daughter" demands another nominal as an obligatory element either as an of-phrase or as a genitive. In this respect, (17) is different from (2) and (15). However, the fact that we can have the King's daughter might alternatively lead us to relate of with NGp_2 to yield a possessive postmodifier.

Let us now examine the following:

A scholar of extraordinary brilliance   (23)

A painter of unquestionable talent   (24)

Here, the "of-phrases" are considered to be qualifiers/postmodifiers. If we look at them carefully, we realize that the qualifiers are postposed epithets. This structure gives the noun in the "of-phrase" an unmarked tonic status. The structural analysis of (23) and (24) will be as follows:

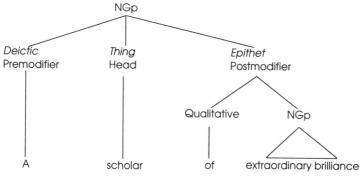

Figure 15.15.

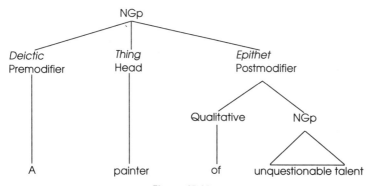

Figure 15.16.

6. MEASURE GROUPS

Examine the following:

A glass of wine   (25)

The glass of wine   (26)

Would you like to have a cup of <u>coffee</u> or a glass of <u>wine</u>?(27a)
I think I'd opt for the <u>former</u>.   (27b)

The glass of wine I left on the table is missing.   (28)

Example (28) refers to the "container" with its "contained," whereas (27a) refers to the "contained"; the reply in (27b) confirms this. The structural analysis reflecting these functional values will be as follows:

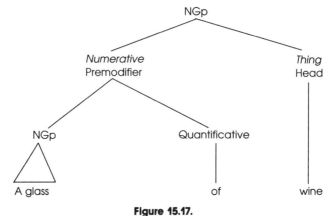

Figure 15.17.

Here "numerative" includes "measure" concept. (Alternatively, we could use the "higher" term "quantifier.")

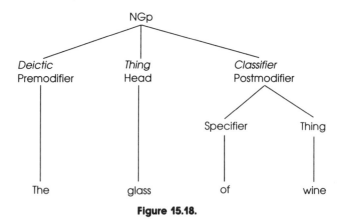

Figure 15.18.

Sometimes, however, (26) may attract the analysis of (25), when the "container" is salient:

The glass of wine you offered me yesterday would be very welcome today. (29)

We cannot attribute the difference between (25) and (26) only to the difference between a and the. Consider the following:

A wee bit of honey (30)

The wee bit of honey (31)

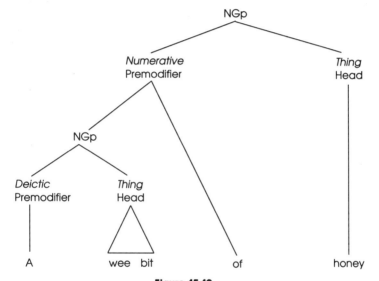

Figure 15.19.

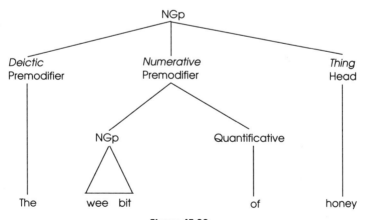

Figure 15.20.

Example (31) is different from (26) for obvious reasons: Wee̲ bit̲ refers to "smallness" of quantity in both (30) and (31), whereas gl̲ass in
(25) is "nonconcrete" and in (26) it is "concrete." In most measure
nominal groups the "concrete" rendering differs from the "nonconcrete" one where it has the meaning of "some:"

$$\text{There } \underline{\text{are}} \left\{ \begin{array}{c} \text{a pack of} \\ \text{some} \end{array} \right\} \underline{\text{cards}} \text{ on the table.} \qquad (32)$$

This i̲s only one pa̲ck; we need two packs for our game.

(33)

The difference also emanates from the "anyness" and "oneness" of "a."

7. CONCLUSION

The "NGp of NGp" constructions studied in this chapter are representative of only some of the possible patterns. The following points
emerge from the preceding discussion.

1. The coincidence or non-coincidence of "Head" and "Thing"
    depends on the discoursal context.
2. There is a certain amount of dynamism involved in the
    structuring of nominal groups; the same construction may
    invite different analyses. In this way, the nominal group
    structuration is similar to Given–New structuration of a
    clause (see Prakasam 1985:59–66).
3. Deictic possessives, classifiers and epithets can be post-
    modifiers in nominal groups with "of-phrases."
4. This study strengthens the desire expressed by Sinclair to
    give o̲f a one-member word class status. In the analyses
    presented here, of̲ is shown as process, linker, specifier,
    quantificative, possessive and qualificative. These are ex-
    periential terms. Grammatically, we can call o̲f a "pendent."

The Pendent we are talking of (o̲f) functions as a post-positional
element, a pre-positional element and an inter-positional element in
the process, giving us different points of salience—NGp_1 or NGp_2 or
both NGp_1 and NGp_2.

REFERENCES

Aijmer, K. & Berget Attenberg, (Eds.) (1991). *English Corpus Studies: Studies in honour of Ian Svartvik.* London: Longman.

Collins Cobuild English Grammar. (1990). (Editor-in-Chief: John Sinclair), New Delhi, India: Rupa & Co.

Collins Cobuild English Language Dictionary. (1991). (Editor-in-Chief: John Sinclair). New Delhi, India: Harper Collins India.

Fawcett, R.P. (1980). *Cognitive Linguistics and Social Interaction: towards an integrated model of a systemic functional grammar and the other components of a communicating mind.* Heidelberg, Germany: Julius Groos Verlag.

Halliday, M.A.K. (1956). "Grammatical Categories in Modern Chinese." *Transactions of the Philological Society 1956:* 177–224.

Halliday, M.A.K. (1994). *An Introduction to Functional Grammar.* (2nd edition) London: Edward Arnold.

Hawkins, R. (1980). "Towards an account of the possessive constructions: NP's N and the N of NP." *Journal of Linguistics.* 17:247–269.

Jespersen, O. (1961). *A Modern English Grammar on Historical Principles. Part VIII—Syntax.* London: George Allen and Unwin Ltd.

Lyons, C. (1986). "The Syntax of English Genitive Constructions." *Journal of Linguistics* 22:123–143.

Prakasam, V. (1985). *The Linguistic Spectrum.* Patiala, India: Punjabi University.

Renouf, A. & J.M. Sinclair. (1991). "Collocational Frameworks in English." In Aijmer and Attenberg. (Eds.) (1991):128–143.

Sinclair, J. (1991). *Corpus, Concordance, Collocation.* London: Oxford University Press.

Part III
Above the Clause

16

The Development of the Concept of Cohesive Harmony

Gerald Parsons

Department of English Studies
University of Nottingham
Nottingham, U.K.

1. INTRODUCTION

This paper owes much to Halliday's work in general and in particular to his work on functional relations (1985:101–157). In addition, it owes a great debt to his joint research with Hasan (Halliday and Hasan 1976) and Halliday and Hasan (1989). Halliday (1985:318) said, "For a text to be coherent, it must be cohesive." The purpose of the current research is to test this notion quantitatively by investigating if a significant correlation can be found between cohesion and coherence.

This research began as a dissertation in part-fulfillment of the requirements for an M.A. degree at the University of Nottingham in 1987. The dissertation was then modified and some of the results were given as a paper at the sixteenth International Systemic Congress in Helsinki in 1989. The research was then published as a monograph in 1990. The paper given at Helsinki has since appeared in a publication of a collection of some of the papers that were given at the Helsinki Congress (Parsons 1989).

An important conclusion from this research was that the use of Hasan's chain interaction method (Halliday and Hasan 1985:70) shows a statistically significant correlation exists between the relative coherence of the texts and the rank score recorded by informants, who judged the relative coherence of 16 texts, which were written by post-graduate electrical engineering students (Parsons 1990:163). Subsequent work has developed the chain interaction method and extended the concept of cohesive harmony so that a better explanation of the informants' perceptions has now been achieved.

The first part of this paper will give a brief theoretical background that will be followed by an account of the methodology used and a short summary of the author's work on this subject prior to the present study.

However, the main body of this paper will give an account of the way in which the chain interaction method has been developed and the significance this development has on our understanding of the concept of cohesive harmony and coherence. This will be achieved by developing the notion of *significant chains,* which was introduced toward the end of the Helsinki paper (Parsons 1989:425). This notion was developed in response to the observation that there seemed to be relationship between the number of longer interacting chains in a text and the text's perceived coherence.

2. THEORETICAL BACKGROUND

2.1. The Concept of Coherence

The concept of coherence seems to be a pre-theoretical notion, in that the lay person has an intuitive notion of what is meant by coherence, and a group of informants is often able to agree on the relative coherence of a series of texts. However, precise definitions of coherence are not readily available.

Lyons (1981:199) saw coherence as a phenomenon in which what is being said in one unit of text is considered as being relevant to what has been said in the immediately preceding unit. For de Beaugrande and Dressler (1981:13), coherence concerns the way in which the arrangement of ideas and relations "which underlie the surface text, are mutually accessible and relevant." They consider that "continuity of senses is the foundation of coherence." Halliday (1985:48) said a characteristic feature of a text is that it "hangs together." He explained this means that a particular point in a text has been conditioned by what has preceded it, which sets up "expectations and these are matched up with the expectations . . . that the reader or listener bring from the external sources." He considered that cohesion is an important feature of coherence.

Hasan (Halliday & Hasan 1985:94) considered that coherence involves the idea of unity and "that the patterns of language manifest or realize the existence of semantic bonds." She described the relative coherence of three sample texts and noted that the one that is markedly less coherent than the others has several unconnected grammatical subjects. The text lacks what she described as topical unity. She concluded that coherence that is an essential feature of a text is not an absolute property but is gradable and that a text's relative position in a group depends on the composition of the group. The examination of coherence "*involves the examination of cohesion*" (my italics). She considered that cohesion is an essential feature of a text. This is reinforced when she said "cohesion is the foundation upon which the edifice of coherence is built."

This view would not be unreservedly supported by other scholars. Brown and Yule (1983:204), for instance, gave examples of texts that display few if any markers of cohesive relations. They go on to show that cohesion alone is not necessarily a sufficient guarantee for the production of a text. It is possible to produce a contiguous series of sentences that are cohesive but in which no account has been taken of building a coherent series of events. A reader/listener would try and look for a coherent interpretation of a series of sentences if at all possible. The present study is based on the view that among a variety of text types there is a gradation dependent on the extent to which they rely upon cohesion to provide coherence. A useful contribution to this debate would be to investigate *quantitatively* the extent to which cohesion contributes to coherence.

2.2. The Measurement of Cohesion by Chain Interaction

It was in Hasan (1980) that she first investigated the inter-relationship between cohesion and coherence. This work eventually culminated in Halliday and Hasan (1985) in which an account of the relationship between cohesion and coherence was published. This research was reprinted in 1989, so that these two works are identical.

However, in 1984 Hasan published a similar paper in which she developed a method of measuring the relative cohesion of series of texts. In the 1985 article, she developed this work and called this method *chain interaction.* It is based on the recognition of cohesive chains within a text. The term *cohesive chain* refers to a semantic relationship between the members of the chain. There are three types of relationship: co-referentiality, co-classification and co-extension. Co-reference refers to identity of reference. The terms refer to the same item. Co-classification relates different members of the same class of thing, processes or circumstances (Halliday & Hasan 1985:74). The last term ties members that are in the same general field of meaning. This covers the semantic relations of synonymy, antonymy, hyponymy and the part—whole relationship of meronymy. These three types of meaning relation lead to two types of cohesive chain, known as identity and similarity chains. The relation between members of identity chains is that of co-reference, and members of similarity chains are connected by co-classification and co-extension.

It is quite possible for a text to have all or most of its lexical items or tokens entering into chains and still not be coherent. It is necessary to introduce a relation that is characteristic of those between the components of a message. This relation is chain interaction and brings together members of two or more distinct chains. A minimum requirement for chain interaction is that at least two members of one chain should stand in the same relation to at least two members of another chain. The relationships can be that of:

1. "actor–action" (for example, *girl ran*)
2. "action–acted–upon" (for example, *took wheels*)
3. "action and/or actor location (for example, *girl cycled Paris*)
4. "saying–text" (for example, *said words*)
5. "attribute–attributant" (for example, *shiny wheels*)

These relationships are based on Halliday (1985:101–157) (in recent work (Parsons 1995 in press), the present author has drawn heavily on the notions expressed by Halliday to accommodate functional relationships in the current data not described by Hasan above).

The concept of chain interaction takes the concept of cohesion further than counting the number of cohesive devices because it necessitates that at least two sentences or clauses should each contain at least two items belonging to two different chains. This will mean that "similar things are being said about similar phenomena in a coherent text" (Halliday & Hasan 1985:92).

The method consists of producing a lexical rendering of the text, followed by an inspection of the lexical tokens to realize two lists, one consisting of identity chains and the other of similarity chains. A lexical rendering is a reproduction of the text omitting the grammatical or "function" words such as articles, prepositions and conjunctions. It also involves the recovery of the referent in reference and the original item in ellipsis. Further inspection of the text enables the interacting chains to be located and to be represented schematically.

This procedure then results in the classification of the total lexical tokens into three groups. The first consists of *relevant tokens*, which enter into identity chains. The second divides relevant tokens into *central tokens*, which enter into chain interaction, and *non-central tokens*, which do not enter into chain interaction. The final group consists of *peripheral tokens*, which are the remaining tokens that do not enter into any kind of chain. A detailed step-by-step analysis of a text using this method may be found in Parsons (1990:48).

3. METHODOLOGY

A group of 16 post-graduate students in civil and electronic engineering were asked to write an account of "Coffee Growing." This was an exercise devised by Cooper (1979:10) and was so designed that all the writers were supplied with the same amount of information in the form of a flow diagram, so that the problem of disparate background knowledge was overcome. The exercise was the description of a process. This involves sequencing and therefore is particularly appropriate to a study of cohesion.

The view is held that coherence is a pre-theoretical notion; that is, readers have an intuitive understanding of the meaning of coherence and they can reach a general agreement on the relative coherence of a series text. An important feature of the current work was to ask a group of informants to judge the relative coherence of the texts and then to account for the informants' perceptions in linguistic terms.

The informants were asked to grade the texts for coherence. A grading scheme was devised that involved the informants placing the texts into five categories ranging from good to poor. Marks from one to five were given according to the category into which the text was placed by an informant.

4. COHESIVE HARMONY

Hasan (1984:218) put forward four hypotheses. The first is a general hypothesis and subsumes the others. It considers that ranking by cohesive harmony will match the ranking of texts on a cline of coherence judged by informants. The second emphasizes the importance of the percentage of central tokens that is seen as a measure of cohesive harmony, and claims that any text will be seen as coherent if it contains at least 50% central tokens (expressed with respect to total lexical tokens). The third claims that if two texts show no difference in cohesive harmony, variation in coherence will correlate with the number of breaks in the chain of interaction. Finally, she considered that all else being equal, the more coherent the text the higher will be the ratio of central tokens to peripheral (CT/PT) tokens.

In another paper (Halliday & Hasan 1985:94) she said that a text is more likely to be coherent if:

1. the ratio of relevant to peripheral tokens (RT/PT) is high
2. the ratio of central to non-central tokens (CT/nCT) is high
3. there are no breaks in the chain of interaction.

The sum of these three phenomena is described as cohesive harmony.

5. RESULTS

The application of statistical analysis to my results showed a significant correlation between the percentage central tokens (%CT) and the rank score resulting from the informant test. This correlation supports Hasan's first hypothesis, which relates ranking by cohesive harmony with coherence. It also lends support to the hypothesis, which emphasizes the importance of the %CT as a measure of cohesive harmony.

The statistical analysis involved the calculation of the correlation coefficient r, the value of which enables an assessment of the extent to which pairs of variables correlate. For 16 pairs of results, a value of r in excess of 0.426 indicates significance at the 5% level (if the sign associated with the correlation coefficient is negative, the two variables will have an inverse relationship). This means that there is a 95% chance that the variables correlate. This is often considered adequate for linguistic purposes.

Table 16.1 gives the correlation coefficients relating the informants' rank score and %CT, RT/PT, CT/nCT and CT/PT.

TABLE 16.1
Correlation Coefficients for the Ratios

variable	r-value
%CT	0.427
RT/PT	0.214
CT/nCT	0.223
CT/PT	0.320

Table 16.1 shows that apart from %CT, the correlation coefficient is too low for significant correlation, thus throwing doubt on the remainder of Hasan's concept of cohesive harmony. The overall conclusion at this stage is that the %CT analysis emphasizes the crucial role of central tokens as a predictor of coherence, and the lack of correlation for the ratios RT/PT, CT/nCT, and CT/PT with coherence suggests that the concept of cohesive harmony needs modifying.

Having given a very brief account of the background to this research, I will now give an outline of the development of the chain interaction method and the concept of cohesive harmony.

6. THE ORGANIZATIONAL FEATURES OF CENTRAL TOKENS

6.1. Introduction

The previous section emphasized the crucial role that central tokens play in contributing to textual cohesion and coherence. The remainder of this paper will be concerned with the significance of their organization as reflected in the schematic diagrams. It will therefore be useful to give an example of one of these diagrams taken from the data. Figure 16.1 gives the schematic diagram for text C, which was

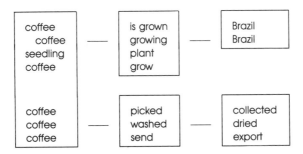

Figure 16.1.   Text C—Schematic Diagram Representing the Interacting Chains.

judged by the informants to be relatively low in the ranking for coherence. This judgement was confirmed by the analysis.

It will be noticed that there are five interacting chains that, reading from left to right, have 7, 4, 2, 3 and 3 items respectively. This diagram is one of the simplest, those for most of the remaining texts are much more complex with as many as 15 interacting chains. There seemed to be a tendency for the more coherent texts to have a larger number of longer interacting chains than the less coherent texts. It was decided therefore to investigate whether there was a relationship between the number of long chains and the coherence of the texts.

It was first necessary to define exactly what is meant by a long chain. It was decided that a long chain was one that was longer than the average for the population under consideration, and it was measured in terms of the number of central tokens associated with each chain. This was done by calculating the average chain length for each text and then finding the overall average for all the texts. The value was found to be 3.13, and so it was decided a long chain should be one that contained four or more tokens and that these chains should be called *significant chains* and that the tokens should be called *significant tokens*. At this stage in the work, it was decided to use the notation (S4) to represent a significant token in a text, therefore the expression %S4 represents the ratio of significant tokens to total lexical tokens expressed as a percentage. The significance of the number four is that it represents the minimum number of central tokens that need to be in an interacting chain for them to be described as significant tokens. This means that an extension of Hasan's taxonomy has been proposed so that central tokens are now to be divided into *significant central tokens (S4)* and *non-significant central tokens (nS4)*. The latter are central tokens that do not occur in long chains and so for the present purpose are all the central tokens occurring in 2- and 3-membered chains. There are 19 central tokens in Fig. 16.1, of which 11 are significant tokens. The calculation of %S4 will therefore not include the 8 central tokens occurring in the 2- and 3-membered chains.

6.2. An Examination of the Relationship between Coherence and Significant Chains

Because %CT correlates with coherence, a way of testing whether significant chains make a greater contribution to coherence would be to compare the correlation coefficient relating the percentage significant tokens (%S4) and rank score to that relating %CT and rank score.

Having introduced the notion of significant tokens and chains and outlined a possible line of enquiry, it would now seem appropriate to consider certain hypotheses.

6.2.1. Hypotheses.   *Four hypotheses will be considered:*

1. *Significant chains play a special role in contributing to coherence.*

For this hypothesis to be true, the correlation coefficient relating %ST and rank score will have to be higher than the equivalent one relating %CT and rank score.

2. *The higher the percentage of significant tokens, the more coherent will be the text as perceived by informants.*

This hypothesis is parallel to Hasan's hypothesis, which relates %CT and coherence and will be tested in the same way as hypothesis 1. If significant chains do make a special contribution to coherence, it would seem plausible that there will be a correlation between %ST and coherence.

3. *The higher the ratio of significant to peripheral tokens, the more coherent will be the text as perceived by informants.*

This is equivalent to Hasan's hypothesis, which relates the ratio CT/PT to coherence. Although a significant correlation was not found to exist between CT/PT and coherence, it seems likely that the correlation coefficient relating S4/PT will at any rate be higher if hypotheses 1 and 2 are found to be valid.

4. *The higher the ratio of significant tokens to non-significant tokens, the more coherent will be the text as perceived by informants.*

This is equivalent to Hasan's hypothesis which relates CT/nCT to coherence. Similar comments apply to this hypothesis as applied to hypothesis 3. These hypotheses will now be tested.

6.3. Testing the Hypotheses

The number of significant tokens associated with each text was found by inspecting the appropriate diagram and counting the number of tokens in chains with four or more central tokens. The %S4 was then obtained with respect to the total lexical tokens.

The number of non-significant tokens was obtained by deducting the number of significant tokens from the total number of central

TABLE 16.2
Comparison of the Correlation
Coefficients for the above Hypotheses
with those of Hasan's Concept of
Cohesive Harmony

%S4	0.538
%CT	0.427
S4/PT	0.459
CT/PT	0.320
S4/nS4	0.304
CT/nCT	0.223

tokens. Table 16.2 gives a comparison of the correlation coefficients for the above hypotheses with those of Hasan's concept of cohesive harmony.

A noticeable item of interest is that in all cases there is a greater correspondence between the informants' perception and the results for the significant tokens than those for the central tokens. Even though no significant correlation exists between the CT/PT and rank score, the value of $r = 0.459$ for S4/PT and rank score is significant at the 5.0% level and 2.5% for %S4. In the latter case, a value of $r = 0.497$ is sufficient to show correlation at the 2.5% level; therefore, there is at least a 97.5 chance that the variables correlate. In the light of these results, the decision to extend Hasan's taxonomy of central tokens seems to have been justified. Although the fourth hypothesis was found not to be valid (the value of r was less than 0.426), even so the r value is higher than the corresponding value for CT/nCT.

This approach has been to increase the delicacy of the analysis. The term is being used here in the sense that it is used by systemic linguists. The scale of delicacy determines the degree of detail in the analysis or the "fineness of the distinction in meaning" (Berry 1975:177). This manifests itself in the development of the classification of lexical tokens.

It would appear that the informants are perceiving those texts that have central tokens organized into long chains to be more coherent than those in which the tokens are organized mainly in short chains. The former are highly valued for their coherent properties, not just because they are highly cohesive in terms of chain interaction, but also because they have a larger number of long chains. Hasan, after noting that a high number lexical tokens entering into cohesive chains does not "necessarily lead to coherence" (Halliday & Hasan 1985:91), goes on to postulate the need for chain interaction that is a relation that brings together components of two or more distinct chains. It is now suggested on the basis of the above results that chain interaction alone does not necessarily result in the most coherent texts, but that interaction that involves long chains is more likely to lead to greater coherence. Hasan said that in a coherent text, "one says similar kinds of things about similar phenomena" (Halliday & Hasan 1985:92). The extent to which this happens may be judged by the extent to which chain interaction takes place. The existence of a number of long interacting chains indicates a larger amount of interaction that is likely to lead to a coherent text in which there are more occurrences "when one is saying similar things about similar phenomena." The importance of this for an understanding of coherence is that it is a feature of which an informant may be subconsciously aware when evaluating a text for its coherent properties. It is likely that a complex of factors contribute to the informants' evaluations and that some dominate over others dependent on the text.

A question that arises from the results is the reason why the informants should find texts with long chains to be more coherent. At this stage, we can only speculate about the reasons. A possible explanation is that the existence of long chains provides a relatively unvarying feature to a text that causes it to be more easily read. Although this is speculative, one aspect of this question can be investigated, and that is whether there is a point beyond which an increase in chain length ceases to be favorably evaluated by informants. This will form the subject of the next section.

7. AN INVESTIGATION INTO THE EFFECT UPON COHERENCE OF CHAINS WITH OVER FOUR TOKENS

In view of the above results, the next step was to investigate the extent to which this approach could be developed by progressively increasing the value of the number of lexical tokens that constitutes a long chain from four to five and then six. The notation was on the same basis as before. The symbol S5 has a similar meaning to that of S4 and refers to the number of central tokens in chains with five or more central tokens. This means that %S5 for a text is the ratio of the total number of central tokens in chains containing five or more tokens to lexical tokens expressed as a percentage. This is the sum of the central tokens in chains with five, six or more tokens and excludes those central tokens in chains containing four or less. (It will soon be shown that this method was developed even further by

TABLE 16.3
Correlation Coefficients for the S5, S4,
and CT Analyses

%S5	0.586
%S4	0.538
%CT	0.427
S5/PT	0.553
S4/PT	0.459
CT/PT	0.320
S5/nS5	0.502
S4/nS4	0.304
CT/nCT	0.223

examining chains with six or more central tokens (S6) and chains with three or more central tokens (S3).)

The method used was exactly the same as before with a parallel series of hypotheses. Table 16.3 shows the results for the %S5 analyses and, for convenience, simultaneously includes the results from Table 16.2.

There are two interesting points emerging from the table. The first is that the results for the S5 analyses give the best interpretation of the informants' perceptions, and the CT analyses give results that accord less well. The second is that the analyses involving percentages give a better interpretation than those involving the ratio of interacting tokens to peripheral tokens, which in turn give better results than the ratios involving non-significant tokens. This is interesting because it is something that will need to be explained as the theory is developed.

The higher correlation coefficients for the S5 analyses (all of which are significant at the 2.5% level) justify increasing the delicacy of the chain interaction method by dividing S4 tokens into S5 and non-S5 (ns5) tokens. Some of the S4 tokens will be in chains containing five or more members. These are the S5 tokens and are the ones that are being considered when an S5 analysis is being undertaken.

Figure 16.2 shows the extension that is being proposed. The choices at a fork are mutually exclusive in that it is not possible for a central token, for instance, to be simultaneously a central token and a non-significant token.

In the light of the above results, it is now proposed to modify Hasan's concept of cohesive harmony by replacing the %CT by %S5. This means that %S5 is seen as a measure of cohesive harmony. Again, ranking by cohesive harmony will match the ranking of texts

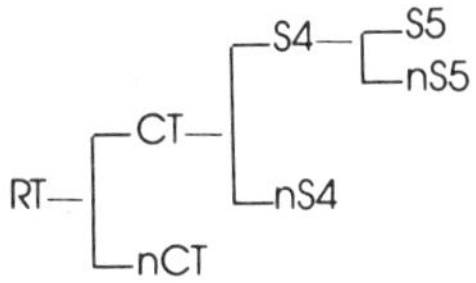

Figure 16.2. Diagram showing the Taxonomy of Relevant Tokens.

on a cline of coherence. Furthermore, because the ratios S5/PT and S5/nS5 both significantly correlate with coherence, it is proposed to incorporate them into the revised concept of cohesive harmony.

The above proposal is only justified if it can be shown that the consideration of chains that contain six or more central tokens or even seven or more do not result in higher correlation coefficients than those for the S5 analyses. Another possibility that has to be considered is whether the results for a C3 analysis produce a higher correlation coefficient than for the S5 analysis.

The same method as before was used by counting the tokens in chains with six or more members. The analysis of chains containing over three members was called the C3 analysis because many of the chains only had three members and so did not qualify to be called long chains.

The results are shown in Table 16.4. It can be seen that a peak had been reached with chains containing five or more members. None of the analyses significantly correlate with coherence. This means that the proposal to modify Hasan's concept of cohesive harmony by replacing %CT by %S5 and to incorporate S5/PT and S5/nS5 into the concept is justified. The correlations coefficients for these ratios are higher than the corresponding ratios for the analyses CT, C3, S4, S6 and S7.

It had previously been proposed that a possible explanation for the reason that texts with long chains are evaluated to be more coherent is that the long chains provide a relatively unvarying feature to a text, enabling it to be more easily read. It now seems that there is a limit beyond which this hypothesis cannot be taken. It appears that a text can be too cohesive, and that beyond a certain point, an informant ceases to evaluate a text favorably, possibly be

TABLE 16.4
Correlation Coefficients for S6 and C3 Analyses

%S6	0.307		%S3	0.381
S6/PT	0.285		C3/PT	0.361
S6/nS6	0.325		C3/nC3	−0.068

cause it lacks lexical and structural variety. A similar view has been expressed by Perera (1984:251). It is likely that there is a balance between a text being too cohesive and being not cohesive enough and that a writer needs to steer a course between not making a text insufficiently cohesive and making it too cohesive. This a possible reason why the C3 analysis provided a lower cut-off point.

Of course, the above hypotheses are only conjecture, but the way to a better understanding of coherence is found by advancing hypotheses and ascertaining that extent to which they correspond to the experimental data. Eventually, as the research proceeds, the need to accept, reject or modify the hypothesis gradually becomes clear.

The results show that long chains appear to play a special role in contributing to the informants' perceptions of coherence.

8. FUTURE RESEARCH

The results of this research are interesting in that there is quantitative evidence supporting the notion expressed by Hasan that "an examination of coherence involves an examination of cohesion" (1984:184). A feature of research is that it often presents new questions to be answered and new areas for investigation.

A question revealed by the present research is why the CT analysis provides a better explanation of the informants' perception than the C3 analysis when the results arising from the examination of significant tokens would suggest the reverse?

Another area for investigation is the extent and way in which the ratios contribute to textual coherence. It may well be that the contribution of cohesion to coherence is an interplay of these ratios. A question that follows naturally from this one is the extent to which cohesion is contributing to coherence compared with other possible factors such as thematic progression.

It would also be interesting to know if other examples of the same data would corroborate the results, and also if the results are generally applicable to other genres.

The answers to some of these questions will form the subject of further research (Parsons 1985, in press).

REFERENCES

Berry, M.H. (1975). *An Introduction to Systemic Linguistics*. London: Batsford

Brown, G. & G. Yule (1983). *Discourse Analysis.* Cambridge, MA: Cambridge University Press.

Cooper, J. (1979). *Think and Link.* London: Arnold.

de Beaugrande, R. & W.U. Dressler (1981). *Introduction to Text Linguistics.* London: Longman.

Halliday, M.A.K. (1985). *An Introduction to Functional Grammar.* London: Edward Arnold.

Halliday, M.A.K. & R. Hasan (1976). *Cohesion in English.* London: Longman.

Halliday, M.A.K. & R. Hasan (1985). *Language Context and Text: Aspects of Languages in a Social Semiotic Perspective.* Victoria: Deakin University.

Hasan, R. (1980). *Coherence and cohesive harmony.* Revised version of a talk given at the meeting of the International Reading Association, St. Louis, MO.

Hasan, R. (1984). "Coherence and Cohesive Harmony," in Flood, J. (ed.) *Understanding Reading Comprehension Delaware.* International Reading Association.

Lyons, J. (1981). *Language Meaning and Context.* London: Fontana.

Parsons, G. (1989). *The relations between cohesion and coherence.* A paper given at the Sixteenth International Systemic Congress Helsinki published in *Trends in Linguistics* (ed., Ventola, E.) Berlin: de Gruyter.

Parsons, G. (1990). *Cohesion and Coherence: Scientific Texts.* Nottingham: University of Nottingham.

Parsons, G. (1995). *Measuring Cohesion in English Texts: The Relationship between Cohesion and Coherence.* PhD Thesis University of Nottingham: English Department.

Perera, K. (1984). *Children's Writing and Reading: Analysing Classroom Language.* Oxford: Blackwell.

Part IV
Across Languages

17

A Fragment of a Multilingual Transfer Component and its Relation to Discourse Knowledge*

Erich Steiner

Universität des Saarlandes in Saarbrüken
Germany

1. INTRODUCTION

My *goals* in this paper will be the following:

- to re-emphasize the fact that grammatical information is distributed over *ranks*, rather than locally complete. This should prepare the way for an easier integration of grammatical knowledge and discourse knowledge into one model;

*This paper is a slightly extended version of my earlier "A fragment of a multilingual transfer component and its relations to discourse knowledge" in Wiebke Ramm (ed.) (1994) *Text and Context in Machine Translation: Aspects of Discourse Representation and Discourse Processing*. Studies in Machine Translation and Natural Language Processing. Vol. 6. Office for Official Publications of the European Communities. I am very grateful to the publisher for giving permission to reprint this paper. Some of the ideas outlined here were developed in the course of ESPRIT basic research project 6665 DANDELION.

- to explore the notion of a *multilingual grammar fragment,* looking at the word-rank IMPERATIVE in four languages;
- to explore one possibility of *generalization* from existing fragments by *unification,* looking at the clause rank IMPERATIVE for three of the languages above;
- to attempt a first *abstraction* from the resulting multilingual grammar fragment, illustrating a first move toward a semantic representation of those parts of our grammar fragment that, intuitively, do not strictly belong to the area of IMPERATIVE; and
- to attempt a specification of the place of multilingual fragments in a system architecture incorporating discourse knowledge.

Motivations for an interest in the areas just indicated include the following:

- for many purposes, a clarification of the notion of *translational equivalent* would be helpful. In particular, and especially for a modelling of human translation, it is clearly not the case that the best translational equivalent is something like a *governor-complement-modifier* structure with as little as possible structural transfer;
- for the teaching of translation to humans, it is very desirable to have a model of what is the information relevant for a particular area of the structure of the languages involved. The description of only monolingual grammar fragments without a clear model of how to relate them translationally is unsatisfactory;
- the notion of a *multilingual grammar fragment* has been evoked repeatedly in recent work on multilingual text generation (Matthiessen and Bateman, 1991; Bateman *et al.,* 1992; Zajac, 1990). The models discussed there as a basis for creating multilingual fragments (type unification) could provide one important way of talking about *generalization* of grammar fragments; and
- intuitively, one would like to be able to define a level of information one step *abstracted* from grammar, something more *semantic, knowledge-based, or functional* than grammar itself. Models in this area include the *Penman Upper Model* (cf. Bateman *et al.,* 1990) and Nirenburg et al.'s (1992) *Tam-*

erlan representations for so-called *knowledge-based ma-chine translation.*

A major theoretical background to my remarks here is Halliday's (1985) An Introduction to Functional Grammar. The notion of "generalization," which I will be suggesting in the first part of my paper here is, within a Hallidayan framework, an intra-level one between grammar fragments of different languages. The notion of "abstraction," on the other hand, which I will be discussing in the later parts, is an inter-level one between a number of grammar fragments of one or several languages on the one hand, and between a "semantic" level, on the other. One motivation for my remarks is to explore some thoughts arising out of a Hallidayan notion of lexicogrammar for a representation of meaning shared by different languages, although not being in an any sense "universal."

What I am proposing in the remarks to follow is outside the core of what would normally be called *discourse for machine translation*, in that I will not directly address classical discourse questions such as inter sentential coreference, thematic progression, background-ing and foregrounding, or *consecutio temporum* in discourse. It is hoped, though, that I can at least add to knowledge relevant to dis-course representations because:

- the properties addressed in our semantic components are often relevant to discourse, rather than to isolated sen-tences,
- the process of abstraction from grammar (Figures 17.14 to 17.16) potentially makes us independent of grammatical ranks,
- the features of texts addressed in our semantic component are translationally relevant, especially for stretches of dis-course beyond the clause.

2. GRAMMATICAL INFORMATION IS DISTRIBUTED OVER RANKS

In this section, I want to look at the information about the MOOD type of a sentence, in order to illustrate the fact that the information relevant for the assignment of a clause to a MOOD type is, even within grammar, distributed over different ranks. I will be *monolingual and multi-rank* in my perspective, whereas in the next section, my perspective will become *multilingual and monorank.*

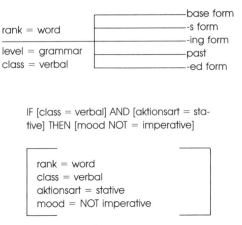

Figure 17.1. Mood on word rank: English

Figure 17.1 outlines mood on word rank for English, also stating a candidate constraint. However, even that constraint, which, being a negative constraint involving one sub-class of verbs only, is quite weak, because there are verbs, often classified as stative, which violate it (cf. my sample sentences (3) and (4) later on). For Figure 17.1 and the following figures, it may be useful to consult Section 9 of this chapter on some notational conventions.

It follows quite clearly that English, in contrast to, say Russian or Latin, does not really have a category of MOOD on that rank.

Figure 17.2 outlines mood on group-rank for English. Again, almost all realizations have the base form of the syntactic head. A possible constraint for identifying a group as IMPERATIVE in English would be so loose as to be of little classificatory value.

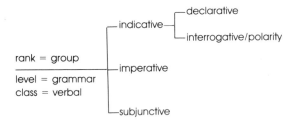

Note: Almost all realizations of the features in Figure 17.2 have as a realization the base form of the syntactic head verb.

Figure 17.2. Mood on group rank: English

A candidate constraint:
IF [groupmood = imperative]
THEN
[class = verbal] AND [head = baseform] AND [lex-verb = base OR -ing OR -ed] AND [tense = present OR present perfect] AND [aktionsart = NOT stative]

```
┌                                          ┐
  groupmood = imperative
  class = verbal
  aktionsart = NOT stative
  head = base form
  lex-verb = base OR -ing OR -ed
  tense = present OR present perfect
└                                          ┘
```

In Figure 17.2 an example for an [imperative] with [present perfect tense] is a sentence such as *Have this done by tomorrow.*

Figure 17.3 outlines the imperative on clause rank for English. As for the constraints, we already have all the constraints from the word- and group ranks, and now we can add two further ones, involving the role of the *Subject* and the formation of *tags*.
Selected realization statements:

Feature	Realization
politeness, yes	lexicalize with "please" in positions x or y
urgency, yes	add tag with "shall/will"
emphasis, yes	"do"—insertion

Selective constraints:

```
┌                                  ┐
  clausemood = imperative
  class = main
  subj = non obligatory
  tag = [head = "will/shall"]
└                                  ┘
```

These constraints are combined with the constraints in Figures 17.1 and 17.2.

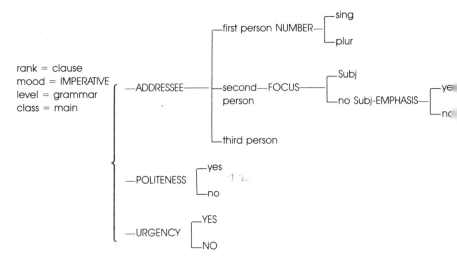

Figure 17.3.   Imperative on clause rank: English

With respect to the material contained in Figures 17.1 to 17.3, I want to illustrate one particular way in which information is distributed over language. I would also like to emphasize the fact that the information relevant *for translation* is not localized in one place, for example, the *head* of the constructions involved here. To the extent that this is true more generally, it is an important property of linguistic elements, both for a formal and for a non-formal model of translation.

Another observation that is interesting in my clause level account of the English [imperative] is that I have included here the types of [urgency] and [politeness], following descriptive grammars. Although these are clearly relevant for an account of various forms of imperative sentences in English, they are, on the other hand, not only relevant for that area, nor do they share the same types of typical realizations that are traditionally associated with the [imperative]. They are thus candidates for the *semantic abstractions*, in that case into an *interaction base* to be discussed later on.

3. WHAT IS A MULTILINGUAL GRAMMAR FRAGMENT FOR A GIVEN RANK: THE EXAMPLE OF WORD-RANK IMPERATIVES

Assume we are looking at English (E), German (G), Russian (R), and Spanish (S). The phenomenon we are interested in is one type of

IMPERATIVE, namely the imperative directed at the addressee in the discourse situation. Note that for these four languages, there are at least two further types of imperatives, one involving the speaker (let's. . .), and the other the imperative directed at a third person (Russian *pusst* + *indicative* of verb, German *edel sei der Mensch, hilfreich und gut*). The ranks at which the phenomenon can be described are different ones for the languages involved. In particular, not all of the languages make the distinction at all ranks (E not having a unique imperative at word rank, for example), and even for those that do, they make different distinctions. The following distinctions, for example, appear to be made at word rank:

- The number of different realizations at work rank are S(4), G(3), R(2), E(1) (Cf. Figures 17.4–17.6). For the Russian case, I am not, at this point, counting the use of the post-fix *-ka* expressing a mild request, as well as the use of *-te* in the case of requests with speaker inclusion, where it expresses either politeness, or the fact of more than one addressee.
- The number of unique (i.e., unambiguously "imperative") realizations at word rank are R(2), S(1), G(1), E(0).
- A system network for the maximum number of distinctions (S) looks as follows:

imperative $\Rightarrow f_1$ (a $\vee$ b) $\wedge f_2$ (c $\vee$ d).

A functional gloss for the features would be:

imperative $\Rightarrow$ NUMBER (singular $\vee$ plural) $\wedge$ RELATIONSHIP (near $\vee$ far), (i.e., intimate or distant).

Figure 17.7 contains the realizations in the four languages concerned as sub-types of the maximum number of grammatical distinctions.

- The same distinctions may be made for some combination of languages, but in different *dependencies*. Whereas, for example, even on word rank Spanish allows the *intimate vs. distant* option for both singular and plural, German and Russian have only one form for the [polite] option, one that does not formally distinguish between [singular and plural] *on word rank*. German furthermore requires the insertion of the *Sie* Subject for the polite variant, but this is a question to be handled on clause rank.

Quite clearly, only Spanish makes all of these distinctions at work rank, and the maximum number of unambiguously *imperative* distinctions at word rank is made in Russian (2). Figures 17.4 to 17.6 illustrate our point. Figure 17.7 illustrates the relationships between the grammatical types distinguished by our features and the morphological realizations in the four languages involved.

In Figure 17.7a, the four types introduced are all characterized through the attributes NUMBER and RELATIONSHIP as discussed above, or POLITENESS, which is used instead of RELATIONSHIP in Figures 17.4 to 17.6. In the next section, I will use SOCIAL DISTANCE as a more transparent term for the same feature. *Near, far, sing, pl* are all

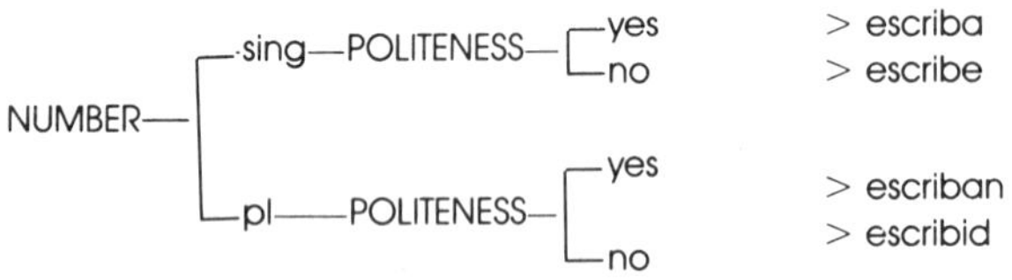

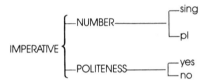

A more economical, *consolidated* version of the network is as follows:

Figure 17.4. The [imperative] on word rank in Spanish

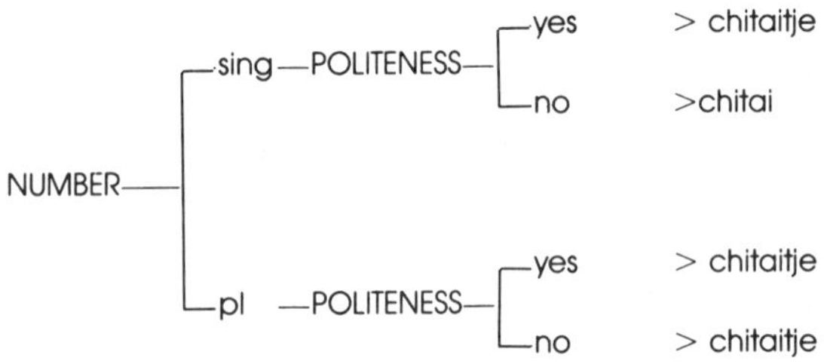

Figure 17.5. The [imperative] on word rank in Russian

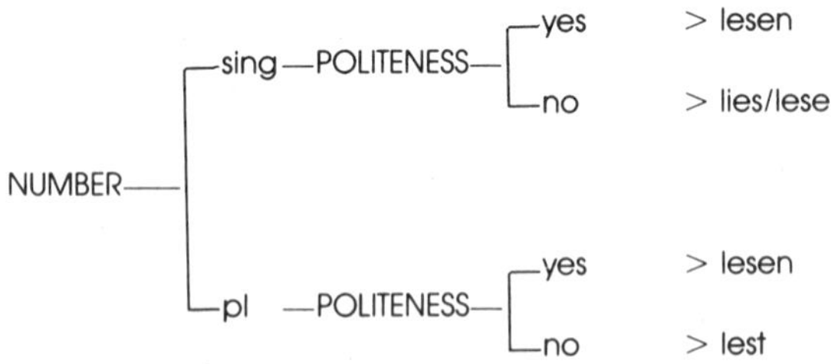

Figure 17.6. The [imperative] on word rank in German

atomic features. Declaration of language specific subtypes in Figure 17.7b; prefixes S, G, R, E, are used for the languages concerned, letters after these mark the morphological realizations:

T [1]: near,sing
T [2]: near,pl
T [3]: far,sing
T [4]: far,pl

Figure 17.7a.   Definition of Types

T (S_e,T[1]),T (S_a,T[3]),
T (S_{an},T[4]),T (S_{id},T[2]),
T ($G_{,,}$[1]),T (G_{en},T[3]),
T (G_{en},T[4]),T (G_t,T[2]),
T (R_t,T[1]),T (R_{ite},T[2]),
T (R_{ite},T[3]),T (R_{ite},T[4]),
T (E_0,T[1]),T (E_0,T[2]),
T (E_0,T]3]),T (E_0,T[4]).

Figure 17.7b.   Definition of Subtypes

Figure 17.7c illustrates these definitions and declarations.

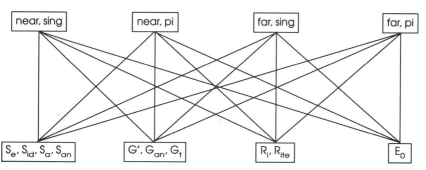

Figure 17.7c.   Word-rank realization of imperatives as "sub-types" of a multilingual fragment

I will now turn to the question of what is a multilingual fragment, and in what sense.

4. A GRAMMATICAL GENERALIZATION: UNIFICATION OF (CLAUSE RANK) GRAMMAR FRAGMENTS

I leave the rank of *group* out of account here, although obviously it is a relevant rank for a language that, for example, realizes one type of imperative by the insertion of an element of the verbal group. The particles -*ka*, -*te* in Russian, which I have mentioned before, would be an example if they were not analyzed as parts of the verb they are attached to. At clause rank, then, a grammatical feature such as [imperative] generalizes an entire set of constraints on clauses, constraints involving all or some of constituent structure, linear precedence (order), lexical insertion, morphology, voice, aspect, tense. The networks for *commands/imperatives* of our four languages at clause rank are different from each other in the same way as those on word rank, only in much more complicated ways. In particular, it is not a necessary condition for a clause to be [imperative], that the word mood becomes [imperative]. For German and Russian, the verb-imperative, where it is the unique one (cf. above) may be a sufficient condition (i.e., it may percolate upwards). Let us look at clause rank networks in Figures 17.3, 17.8, and 17.9.

In Figure 17.8, the system with the name NEAR is continued from the more comprehensive system immediately above. The bottom two systems together with the [plural] option have a zero realization in German. The [urgency, yes] option is realized by particle insertion (*doch*) and similar devices.

In Figure 17.9a the [urgency, yes] type is realized either by [+/-conjunctive mood], although this is not a mood option on word rank in Russian, or the [+/-bij = infinitive] option, or by [+ perfective aspect] in the verb, where that is possible.

The TENOR options have to do with the insertion of *pusst versus -da*.

Given such a state of affairs, what is a *generalization* of these grammar fragments? A frequently given answer is that what generalizes these fragments is another network, or alternative form of knowledge representation, at a *functional/semantic* level of language. In the case of my example, this would normally be rated as part of some *interaction base* (cf. Matthiessen and Bateman, 1991, pp. 213ff]. It would furthermore be stated that there are complex pre-selection relationships that map these two levels onto each other. This answer is a relevant one, and maybe even the best one, provided one defines the *complex mapping relationships/realizations* with sufficient clarity. I would like first, though, to look at a different generalization, a generalization across languages and across ranks, but within the level of grammar. This leads me into the area of *multilingual fragments*, and only through there into semantics.

A possible candidate operation for generalizing grammar fragments from different languages might be *unification* in the classical sense.

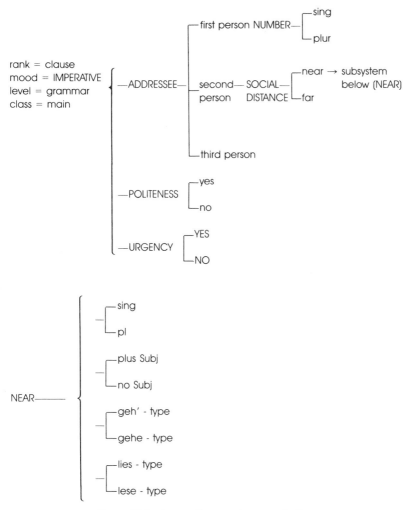

Figure 17.8.   Imperative on clause rank: German

There are, then, two questions:

* Will unification between some given group of grammar fragments succeed? In the case of the same feature in different
languages with contradicting dependent features, for example, there would be difficulties, as far as we can see at the
moment. We would in any case always obtain a fragment

Bitte
Type
Aufforderung (cont. network ADDRESSEE, 17.9b)
Verbot
Warnung
Kommando
URGENCY
yes
no
POLITENESS
yes
no

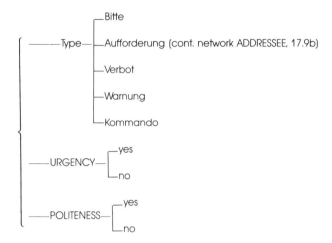

Figure 17.9a. Imperative on clause rank: Russian

TYPE = Aufforderung
ADDRESSEE
first person REGISTER (cf. Figure 17.9c)
second person
SOCIAL DISTANCE
near
sing
pl
far
third person
TENOR
neutral
ceremonious

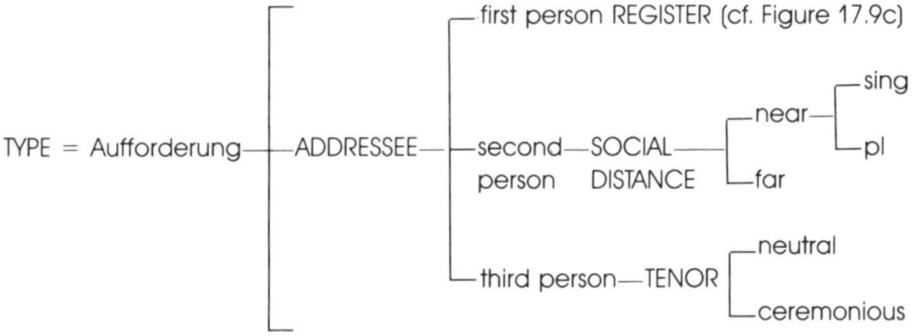

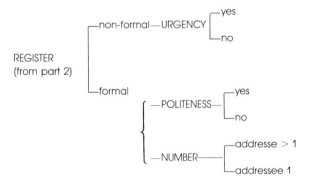

Figure 17.9b. Imperative on clause rank: Russian

REGISTER (from part 2)
non-formal
URGENCY
yes
no
formal
POLITENESS
yes
no
NUMBER
addresse > 1
addressee 1

Figure 17.9c.

allowing all the non-contradictory distinctions made in any one of the languages. Is that what we want, intuitively?

- How, precisely, is a unification of the grammar fragments different from an abstraction into a semantic/functional level?

Possibly, unification in its usual definition is not what we ultimately want as a description of the generalization even of grammar fragments, because it prevents generalizations that we want, as in the case of, for example,:

$$(S1 \ (a \lor b \ (c \lor d))) \land (S2 \ (a \ (c \lor d) \lor b \ (e \lor f))))$$

(cf. Figure 17.10)

Is this just a problem of the naming of features (i.e., using different attribute names in the case just given would solve the problem in one way). The point is, though, that I want an explicit way to describe, maybe formalize, what I mean by *generalization*. This I believe to be true both of generalization of monolingual grammar fragments into multilingual grammar fragments, and of the generalization of (a) grammar fragment(s) in one language into its semantic/functional counterpart.

In attempting a unification of the three grammar fragments in Figures 17.3, 17.8, 17.9, we notice the following:

- Unification will yield a unified fragment that copies finer distinctions from the monolingual fragments into the corresponding places of the more generalized grammar. This presupposes that there is no contradiction between features, otherwise unification will fail.
- For the fragments to unify at all in a meaningful way, the grammar writers of the monolingual fragments need to ensure cross-linguistic consistency in naming of features, wherever this seems intuitively necessary. Otherwise, no unification will result.
- In the ADDRESSEE system, there is a fairly massive clash of features at first sight. However, one could write the monolingual fragments in such a way as to ensure the possibility of unification, by re-arranging dependencies and naming of features accordingly. We do insist, though, that in a realistic enterprise of grammar writing in a multilingual context, the fact remains that different descriptive grammars have very different

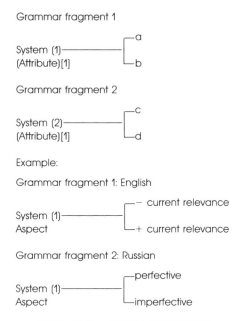

Grammar fragment 1

System (1)————————— a
(Attribute)[1]   b

Grammar fragment 2

System (2)————————— c
(Attribute)[1]   d

Example:

Grammar fragment 1: English

System (1)————————— – current relevance
Aspect   + current relevance

Grammar fragment 2: Russian

System (1)————————— perfective
Aspect   imperfective

Figure 17.10.   Failures of unification.

terminologies, and it always takes a process of human revision of feature names and attributes to make fragments available to unification. So far in the history of linguistics, grammars in different languages have never been written in one single model and with one single terminology, and this will remain true for some time to come, which is of particular relevance in distributed grammar engineering.

The resulting multilingual grammar fragment would look as in Figure 17.11. Strictly speaking, I have ignored the problem here that in a unification of our fragments as they are now, the ADDRESSEE system would be doubled in the resulting multilingual system, once being dependent on TYPE, as in Figure 17.11, but also being a system on the same level of delicacy as TYPE. This problem could be avoided in various ways, for example first copying the TYPE system into German and English, but I want to illustrate the problem here of simply working on the basis of available descriptive grammars. Figure 17.11 in this one respect, contains the result of unification of the slightly homogenized versions of our monolingual fragments.

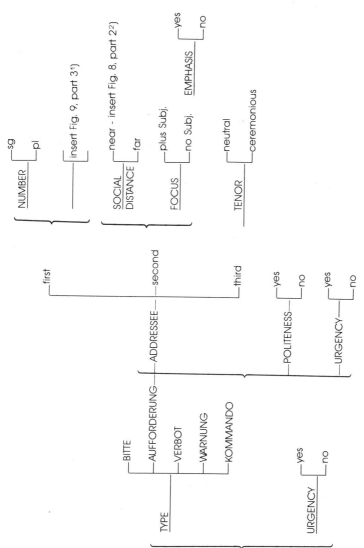

Figure 17.11. An exploratory multilingual fragment

NUMBER — sg / pl

— insert Fig. 9, part 3[1])

SOCIAL DISTANCE — near - insert Fig. 8, part 2[2]) / far

FOCUS — plus Subj. / no Subj.

EMPHASIS — yes / no

TENOR — neutral / ceremonious

TYPE — BITTE / AUFFORDERUNG — ADDRESSEE — first / second / third — VERBOT / WARNUNG / KOMMANDO

POLITENESS — yes / no

URGENCY — yes / no

URGENCY — yes / no

In our exploratory multilingual fragment in Figure 17.11, systems such as TENOR, FOCUS, REGISTER, SOCIAL DISTANCE have lexicogrammatical realizations in one language, but realizations in discourse only in some others. It is at these points that even a grammar-based account, such as we have been following it up to here, clearly shows the necessity of taking into account semantic abstractions and realizations in discourse. It is therefore to these areas that I will be moving in what follows.

5. A SEMANTIC ABSTRACTION 1: A SKETCH OF A FRAGMENT OF AN INTERACTION SEMANTICS

I will at this point come back to the other possibility for *abstraction* mentioned above, which is that of not attempting *unification* of grammar fragments, but rather that of relating grammar fragments to a semantic level.

The observation that I am starting from in this case is that our grammar fragments encode what seems intuitively very different types of information under the general label of IMPERATIVE, thus unnecessarily complicating the fragments. These different types of information include information about:

- formality
- number of addressees
- politeness
- ceremonious versus non-ceremonious language
- Subject insertion
- mildness versus hardness of a request

There would seem to be two different types of disadvantage to incorporating all these very different types of information into one grammatical area:

- my grammar fragments are overloaded with many different types of rather incoherent information, and one might be forced to include even more, and more idiosyncratic types.
- I am repeating information in my grammars of imperative here, which seems to occur elsewhere in the language as well.

If I took out all the intuitively non-central information from my networks, I would be left with increasingly leaner versions of our imperative network (cf. Figures 17.12, 17.13).

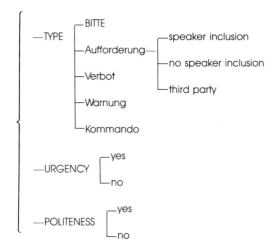

Figure 17.12.   A lean grammatical network (1)

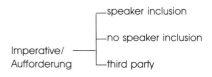

Figure 17.13.   A lean grammatical network (2)

As it turns out, the other types of information can now be integrated in a network for a more semantically oriented *interaction semantics*, or for the *tenor of discourse* (Figure 17.14).

The features under [speaker attitude] will now lead to a grammatical realization only in conjunction and disjunction with features from other networks, as shown in Figure 17.15.

In Figure 17.15, a feature [distance] from our interaction semantics occurs in very different areas of the grammar, and potentially even different languages, as a constraint. Formal interpretations of our informal feature structures here are those of constraint based formalisms for natural language processing, as, for example, in (Bateman *et al.*, 1992; Zajac, 1992). As is usual in Systemic theory, in my

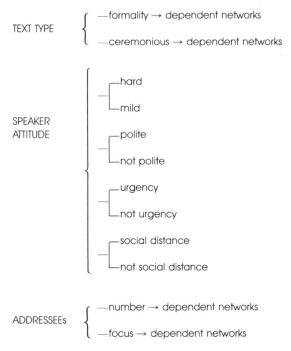

TEXT TYPE { —formality → dependent networks
—ceremonious → dependent networks

SPEAKER
ATTITUDE
— [—hard
—mild
— [—polite
—not polite
— [—urgency
—not urgency
— [—social distance
—not social distance

ADDRESSEEs { —number → dependent networks
—focus → dependent networks

Figure 17.14.   Interpersonal and textual information factored out of imperatives

constraints I capture the fact that a functional category such as [speaker attitude] is not only relevant to one particular grammatical system, such as the [imperative], but that it has implications across the system of a language.

6. A SEMANTIC ABSTRACTION 2: A FRAGMENT OF AN AKTIONSART SEMANTICS

Some remarks on the interaction between *aktionsart* and other areas of systemic grammar can be found in Stei·ier (1991a). I owe the following examples in particular to Dowty and Bolinger (Dowty, 1991, p. 560).

In my constraints on the [imperative] mentioned in our section on the imperative in English, I made use of a constraint that restricts imperatives to *stative* verbs. Examples (1) and (2) below illustrate this point:

```
┌─────                 ─────┐
  speaker attitude : distance
  Aufforderung : no speaker
               inclusion
  language : German
  ┌──────────────────────┐
  |German sub-grammer|
└─────                 ─────┘
```

```
┌─────                 ─────┐
  speaker attitude : distance
  statement : indicative
  language : German
  ┌──────────────────────┐
  |German sub-grammer|
└─────                 ─────┘
```

```
┌─────                 ─────┐
  speaker attitude : distance
  class : nominal
  head : lex"Dame"
  language : German
  ┌──────────────────────┐
  |German sub-grammer|
└─────                 ─────┘
```

Figure 17.15.   Constraints and realization

*Resemble your father.   (1)

*Be fat.   (2)

Both (1) and (2) are ungrammatical; yet, it is quite clear that there
are sub-classes of stative verbs that allow the imperative, as shown
in (3) and (4) below:

Sit in the garden.   (3)

Stand in the corner.   (4)

Are there, then, different types of statives? More importantly, in my present context, do I want to use the *stativity* constraint as part of a *mood network*, differentiating imperatives from non-imperatives? I would like to argue here that there is a semantic/functional distinction involved, relevant to very different areas of the grammar of English, and thus again better covered in a unified way in a semantic abstraction.

Examples (5) to (7) show that it is not only the imperative that interacts with stativity, but that there are other constructions as well, and, in fact, I am not here exhausting their number for English.

She caught a glimpse of the dancer nude.   (5)
*She caught a glimpse of the statue nude.

They took the vote with the chairman absent.   (6)
*They took the vote with the chairman arrogant.

The rowboat is lying on the river bank.   (7)
*New Orleans is lying on the river bank.

My point here is that, rather than duplicate a grammatical aktionsarten sub-system in various areas of grammar (mood, clause final adjective adjuncts, with-complements, progressive aspect, tenses, number. . .), I could have it as one semantic system, headed by something like *property of ascription*, and having the two dependent features (accidental, essential). This would then have to be linked to the various grammatical sub-systems in which it plays a role. Note that we can then use that same system to control, say, the Spanish *ser* versus *estar* opposition, or one aspect of the German *sein* versus *haben* distinction in complex tenses.

7. THE PLACE OF MULTILINGUAL FRAGMENTS IN A DISCOURSE ORIENTED ARCHITECTURE

I want to give an outline of the place of transfer components of the type explored here. They would conceivably be modules in the following contexts:

- They could show, in the process of human translations, which are functionally adequate translations between a number of languages.

- They could take the place of traditional transfer components in machine translation systems, treating traditional transfer as inferencing over types.
- They could serve as grammars in multilingual text generation and discourse-oriented machine translation.

7.1. Human Translation

Human translators, in the course of their training, usually acquire grammatical knowledge of the languages they deal with. This knowledge can be represented in the form as in our Figures 17.3, 17.8, and 17.9. It is common to all those sharing a professional interest in language (i.e., there is nothing that would belong in a model of translation specifically, rather than, say, a model of language teaching, or text production). A translator will then add to that knowledge, at least, his/her case-by-case knowledge about which grammatical features and constructions are translational equivalents for any given language pair or triple. Something more specifically *multilingual* and *translational* comes into play when people develop knowledge or potentials for action as represented in the exploratory multilingual fragment in Figure 17.11. Knowledge of that type overstates the potential of any single one of the languages concerned, but it only postulates distinctions that are made by at least one of the languages—and thus have to be translated when they occur in texts. My claim here is that anyone translating imperatives between English, Russian, and German will somehow have to have command of the knowledge expressed in Figure 17.11. It is, among other factors, one of the properties of this fragment that it will predict in which cases a translator will have to actively search for creative translations. My fragment predicts, for example, that Russian makes relatively fine *register* distinctions in the case of *Aufforderung-type* imperatives of the sub-class SPEAKER INCLUSION, which would be largely neutralized both in English and German (cf. Bell, 1991; Hatim and Mason, 1990, for an account of *register* in translation studies). This means that these constructions do receive a translation, but one having fewer distinctive features than the original—something occasionally referred to as *undertranslation* in the literature. It is here that a translator will now have to look *outside* the system of imperative of the target language for ways to express meanings encoding URGENCY, POLITENESS, NUMBER OF ADDRESSEES— and this, indeed, seems to be what a good translator does.

The solution just sketched indicates that, ultimately, I should be looking toward more functional and semantic fragments of the type of Figures 17.12 to 17.14. As we have already seen in this brief discussion of these, languages differ greatly as to where in their linguistic systems they make a certain distinction (such as distinctions concerning FORMALITY, CEREMONIOUSNESS, MILDNESS, POLITENESS, URGENCY, SOCIAL DISTANCE, NUMBER, FOCUS, to name only those seen in Figure 17.14). What happens in a translation is, accordingly, not a maximally *equivalent* transfer within a restricted grammatical area, but rather a transfer of functional values that mutually constrain each other in such ways as to always yield grammatical realizations in the languages concerned.

Let us look at one of the classical cases of translation, so-called *undertranslation* in the case of translating from a relatively finely differentiating language into a less finely differentiating language for some area of grammar. As an example, I will discuss the translation of sentences such as (8) to (11) below from German into English:

Lies das Buch. (8)

Lese das Buch. (9)

Gehe nach Hause. (10)

Geh' nach Hause. (11)

I want to show here that as long as I rely on multilingual fragments arrived at by purely grammatical unification, as in Figure 17.11 above, I will obtain the neutralizing translations *Read the book* for both (8) and (9), and *Go home* for both (10) and (11). This follows automatically from defining monolingual realizations as sub-types of our generalized multilingual grammar fragment, an example of which I gave in Figure 17.7 above for word rank. No additional mechanisms or processes, I believe, need to be postulated.

For ease of reference, I repeat the relevant part of our system for imperatives on clause rank in German and English here, pointing out again that this system necessarily is part of the relevant portion of the unified grammar fragment in Figure 17.11:

English only has the grammatical options of Subject insertion available where German allows a four-fold distinction as shown above. However, I want a model that allows a so-called *creative solution* to the problem of *undertranslation*, and the beginnings of such

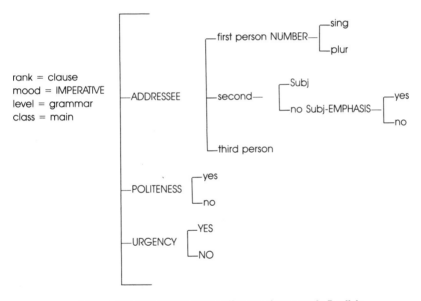

Part of the imperative on clause rank for German

Figure 17.3 (repeated): Imperative on clause rank: English

a model can be found in the multilingual fragments I have discussed in Figure 17.14 above. Assume that, instead of the *intra grammar generalization* by unification, I have created part of an *interaction base and text base,* as shown in the networks in Figure 17.14. In that case, our German options of [text type, colloquial], which is roughly what is expressed by sentences such as (9) and (11) (cf.

Engel, 1988, p. 427), are no longer sub-types of [imperatives], as which they would indeed only allow translation into the more general *default* grammatical type, but rather they are now subtypes of textual options in *formality*. As such, they do have English functional equivalents. English realizations of the [colloquial] option include *vocatives, particles, tag questions, contractions, lexical choice, intonation,* and I can now choose one of those to avoid undertranslation where necessary. Sentence (11), for example, can now become any of (11a)–(11d) in English:

Geh' nach Hause.   (11)

Go home, Jack. (if that is the name of the addressee)   (11a)

Just go home.   (11b)

Go home, won't you.   (11c)

Do go home.   (11d)

Quite clearly, each of the possibilities in (11a) to (11d) realizes meanings besides [colloquial], and it can be seen as the particular capability of the professional rather than the untrained translator that s/he will be able to consciously manipulate each of the corresponding choices.

Am I, in representing multilingual information in the way outlined here, making strong claims about *psychological processes* during translation and/or about specific *methods for teaching translation?* The answer is initially negative, certainly for the first part of our question, and partly also for the second: The information that I am using here derives from descriptive standard grammars, and these do not usually make any strong claims for psychological reality. Furthermore, unification and factoring out as abstraction are only formal methods of merging monolingual information into multilingual knowledge, and any quick and spectacular claim for psychological reality would have a weak foundation. Where I am making a somewhat stronger claim follows.

Any approach addressing psychologically real processes during translation will have to include as a central component the knowledge that I am postulating here. It may be represented in very different ways, but a model without a clear way of modelling this knowledge seems to me very difficult to imagine. As a way of teaching the translationally relevant contrastive knowledge, the representation of multilingual knowledge that I suggest here may be a reasonable candidate fairly directly. However, questions of teaching methodology must be given a decisive place. Whatever my methodological considerations may be here, though, my claim is again that knowledge of that type is a relevant and necessary part of teaching human translation. For those who might claim that knowledge of this type belongs within *foreign language teaching* rather than translation (a claim that might conceivably be formulated within a position as in Stolze (1992, p. 64) or as in Vermeer and Witte (1990, pp. 135ff), the difficulty for me seems to be essentially that they are pushing outside of translation theory a large area of knowledge and potential application that will become increasingly relevant in the near future, and, second, that it is simply a highly controversial claim that students of translation enter their training with a full command of their foreign languages already given. The teaching of translation and foreign language teaching simply cannot be that strictly separated, whatever the speculative feasibility of such a separation.

Let me come back to the claim that the opposition between *transfer-based* and *interlingua-based approaches* to translation theory loses much of its force within a context of representing multilingual information as above: I would like to suggest in a bit more detail that the approach suggested here resolves the old debate between transfer and interlingua in models both of machine translation (cf. Allegranza *et al.*, 1991; Nirenberg *et al.*, 1992) and human translation (cf. Newmark, 1988; Snell-Hornby, 1986; Wilss, 1982 and many others):

- What I am proposing here is clearly not based on any assumptions about a universal interlingua. The categories that I have identified for my grammatical and semantic networks are all categories that are structurally encoded in the lexicogrammar of at least one of the languages that are in the sample of our analysis. There is no way in which a category would turn up here, only because it is encoded in some other language outside my sample, or because it is postulated by some other theory about human cognition, perception, interaction or whatever. Such independent motivation would be welcome, but would not be decisive for our formulation here. It is guaranteed, on the other hand, that any category that is relevant to at least one of our languages is included in the categories of our multilingual fragment.

• My approach is not a conventional transfer-based approach, in that it does not rely on case-by-case transfer rules. There is no stipulation at all that the pairing of, say, types of [imperatives] between two or more languages will be an interesting, sufficient, or even elegant way of thinking about translation. Quite clearly, the very structure of my representations is geared toward the fact that translational equivalents will have to be sought by using one's knowledge in very different areas of grammar and semantics in individual cases of translation.

7.2. Machine Translation

I will now move on to a brief characterization of the place various types of grammar fragments could find in a *machine translation architecture*. In earlier work, as in Steiner (1990, 1991b), I indicated types of problems and types of solutions that would motivate such an architecture. Here I want to concentrate on the role of grammar fragments in such an architecture. The next section will focus on ways of representing discourse knowledge.

The discussion will focus on two alternative possibilities: In *case 1* it will be assumed that an MT architecture contains multilingual grammar fragments of the type introduced in Figure 17.11. In *case 2*, the assumption will be the incorporation of more semantic modules of the type illustrated in Figure 17.14.

• **Case 1:** Assume that I have, for a given group of languages, monolingual grammar fragments of the type of Figures 17.3, 17.8, 17.9, and that I unify them into a multilingual grammar fragment of the type in Figure 17.11. Then, such a fragment could be used in parsing any of the languages of the former monolingual fragments. How, though, can I use the multilingual fragment for generation of the text in a target language different from the source language? One way would be that of using prefixes coding the language on features and/or systems in the grammar (cf. on the use of such prefixes [Bateman *et al.*, 1991; Zajac, 1990]). This would allow to set language parameters, as it were, whereby MT simply becomes analysis in some source language and re-generation in some target language. There are, of course, several remaining problems. One is that of *(computational) complexity*, the other that of using a maximally unified linguistic theory, which allows consistency in feature naming (distributed grammar engineering). The first problem is being worked on in various places, the second can be overcome, as is shown in the experience of large scale multilingual work as in *Eurotra* (Durand *et al.*, 1991). Of special significance may be the fact that, in the way indicated, we do not need a separate transfer component, but what used to be *transfer* now simply falls out of specifying correct monolingual grammatical sub-types of a multilingual grammar fragment.

*   **Case 2:** Assume that instead of a unification of grammar fragments as above, I use *lean grammar fragments* as in Figures 17.12 and 17.13, and *interpersonal and textual knowledge* of the type of Figure 17.14, expressed as an *interaction base* and a *text base* (Halliday, 1982; Matthiessen and Bateman, 1991). There is, then, a different modularization of linguistic knowledge, using the notion of *language function* as a modularizing principle. The formal problems and solutions would essentially be as in case 1 above, provided I can formulate the connection between the semantics and the grammar in a declarative way. An example is given in the following: Assume I add to the semantic text semantics and interaction semantics yet another system, say [orientation] as in Figure 17.16 (Halliday, 1984).

Then, a selection expression from that network with the features

[ORIENTATION, DEMAND, COMMAND, POLITE, NUMBER1, NOT SOCIAL DISTANCE]

might result in sentences (12) to (14) below:

Could you, please, leave (E).   (12)

Geh' bitte (G).   (13)

Ty by poshjol (R).   (14)

Only (13) realizes this with the help of a grammatical imperative, whereas (12) has a grammatical [interrogative] plus a lexical marker *please*, and (14) has what is often termed a Russian [conjunctive], a particle plus a past verb form. This is to say, out of our generations, only the German one actually enters the grammatical network of [imperative] or [Aufforderung], whereas the English and Russian

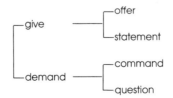

Figure 17.16.   An interaction fragment.

ones do not on the grammatical level. My selection expression above is, of course, restricted only to those features absolutely needed in the present context.

7.3. Discourse Knowledge

In this section, I will first discuss a general form of representation for the types of information in discourse that I am working with. Next, I will be looking at the example of a little discourse represented in such a way, and finally I will suggest rudimentary semantic bases for the example discussed.

Assume, I represent discourse as an (ordered) set of feature descriptions (FD) of sentences (clause complexes) (for a more detailed description of this approach, see Steiner (1991a, pp. 84ff)). Feature descriptions of various ranks are linked through rhetorical relations. Feature descriptions at clause rank are linked through clause combining relations (Halliday, 1985) to form clause complexes. FDs of various ranks are again linked through means of cohesion, for example, co-reference, ellipsis, substitution, lexical cohesion (cf. Halliday and Hasan, 1976). Rhetorical Relations are a sub-class of relations from the three semantic bases.

The general picture then looks as follows:

FD1

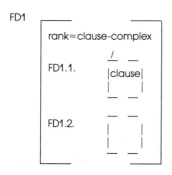

FD2

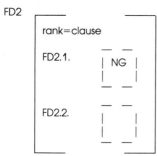

FD1 and FD2 would be related through a rhetorical relation, FD 1.1 and FD 2.1. through, say, an anaphoric reference, FD 1.2 and FD 2.1 through, say, lexical cohesion, and FD 1.2 and FD 2.2 through, say, ellipsis. Realizations of such a piece of discourse should be obvious. Note that the shorthand forms of discourse representation segments here represent the *structural* aspect of discourse representation, something much more fully developed in frameworks such as DISCOURSE REPRESENTATION THEORY (Asher, 1993; Kamp and Reyle, 1993). Staying in line with the functional approach followed here, I will continue to investigate the *systemic-* or *classification-angle.*

In the representation below, I am giving examples of representations of two little texts in the so-called *sentence planning language* SPL of PENMAN (Kasper, 1989). SPL essentially gives feature descriptions with types. Another potentially interesting formalism would be TFS (cf. Zajac, 1990). These representations illustrate how a functionally motivated *semantic* representation abstracts away from language specific syntactic facts while preserving a controlled linkage to syntax.

The first sample text is the following:

Die elektronischen Wörterbücher, die das Ziel des EDR sind, werden Wörterbücher auf Computern, mit Computern und für Computer sein.   (15)

The electronic dictionaries that are the aim of EDR will be dictionaries in computers, with computers, and for computers.

```
(A1/classificatory
    :speechact (spact1/assertion
                        :polarity (polarity1/positive))
    :speech-act-id (speechact/speech-act
        :speaking-time-id (speakingtime/time
            :time-in-relation-to-speaking-time-id speaking-time
            :time-in-relation-id (speakingtime
                            eventtime
                            speakingtime) eventtime
            :preced-q (speakingtime eventtime) precedes))
    :event-time (eventtime/time
                        :precede-q (eventtime speakingtime) notprecedes)
    :speakerassessment (modality1/. . .
    :obligation (modality2/. . .
    :theme-id A11
    :mood-id A11
    :diathesis activization
```

```
:g-attribuant (A11/entity
              :name voerterbuch
              :identifiability-q identifiable
              :singularity-q nonsingular
              :multiplicity-q multiple
              :property-ascription (A111/elektronisch
                      . . .)
              :g-relation (A112/g-identifying
                      :speechact
                      :polarity
                      :g-attribuant (A1111/die
                          . . .)
                      :g-identifier (A1112/Ziel
                          . . .)))
:g-classifier (A12/entity
              :name voerterbuch
              :identifiability-q nonidentifiable
              :multiplicity-q multiple
              :singularity-q nonsingular
              :relations ((A121/local
                      . . .)
                      (A122/accompaniment
                      . . .)
                      (A123/beneficiary
                      . . .))))
```

A second example, involving some co-reference, follows below (I am indebted to Christa Hauenschild for the example):

Adam steigt in seinen Wagen. Er fährt mit 100 gegen die Mauer.
Adam gets into his car. He drives at 100 kms/hr against the wall.   (16)

Terms from the Upper Model, the text base, and the interaction base are taken from the fragments following after the representation.

Sentence 1:

```
(A1/directional
    :direction_type into
    :speechact (spact1/assertion
                :polarity (polarity1/positive))
```

:speech-act-id (speechact/speech-act
  :speaking-time-id (speakingtime/time
    :time-in-relation-to-speaking-time-id speaking-time
    :time-in-relation-id (speakingtime
      eventtime
      speakingtime) eventtime
    :preced-q (speakingtime eventtime) notprecedes))
:event-time (eventtime/time
            :precede-q (eventtime speakingtime) notprecedes
:speakerassessment (modality1/. . .
                    :modality positive)
:obligation (modality2/. . .
             :deonticvalue neutral)
:theme-id A11
:mood-id A11
:diathesis activization
:g-agent_attribuant (A11/human
                    :name Adam
                    :identifiability-q identifiable
                    :singularity-q singular
                    :multiplicity-q nonmultiple)
:g-location (A12/direction
            :relation in
            :domain (A121/entity
                    :name wagen
                    :identifiability-q identifiable
                    :singularity-q singular
                    :multiplicity-q nonmultiple
                    :identification-type possessive
                                         (person. . .
                                         gender. . .
                                         number. . .))))

Sentence 2:

(A1/directional
  :direction_type against
  :speechact (spact1/assertion
              :polarity (polarity1/positive))
  :speech-act-id (speechact/speech-act
    :speaking-time-id (speakingtime/time
      :time-in-relation-to-speaking-time-id speaking-time
      :time-in-relation-id (speakingtime

```
                    eventtime
                    speakingtime) eventtime
        :preced-q (speakingtime eventtime) notprecedes))
        :event-time (eventtime/time
                    :precede-q (eventtime speakingtime) notprecedes)
        :speakerassessment (modality1/. . .
                            :modality positive)
        :obligation (modality2/. . .
                            :deonticvalue neutral)
        :theme-id A11
        :mood-id A11
        :diathesis activization
        :g-agent_attribuant (A11/human
                            :identifiability-q identifiable
                            :singularity-q singular
                            :multiplicity-q nonmultiple
                            :reference_type coreference
                            :person third_party
                            :number singular
                            :gender masculine)
        :g-location (A12/direction
                            :relation against
                            :domain (A121/entity
                                    :name mauer
                                    :identifiability-q identifiable
                                    :singularity-q singular
                                    :multiplicity-q nonmultiple
                                    :identification-type default))
        :g-manner (A13/
                            :relation with
                            :domain velocity))
```

The following rudimentary *Upper Model* is an inheritance hierarchy (original ideas from Bateman, Halliday, Matthiessen). *Special-
ize* links a sub-class to its class. *Restriction* expresses properties of a
class. *Role,* where it is used, expresses as special type of restriction,
a role restriction.

```
specialize(entity, phenomenon)
specialize(process, phenomenon)
specialize)quality, phenomenon)
specialize(relation, phenomenon)
specialize(metaphenomenon, phenomenon)
```

specialize(action, process)
specialize(relational, process)
specialize(mental, process)
specialize(communication, process)

restriction(perspective, process)
specialize(aktionsart, perspective)
specialize(diathesis, perspective)

role(agent_attribuant, relational)
role(location, relational)
specialize(direction, location)
specialize(locational, relational)
specialize(directional, locational)
restriction(direction_type, directional)
specialize(in, direction_type)
specialize(against, direction_type)

specialize(identification, relation)
specialize(possession, identification)
restriction(number, identification)
restriction(person, identification)
restriction(gender, identification)
specialize(deixis, identification)
specialize(default, identification) (e.g., "the")

specialize(manner, relation)

The following rudimentary *interaction-base* contains the concepts used in my representations above. It will then have to be augmented by the components I developed in the earlier parts of this paper:

relationship $\Rightarrow$ interpersonal OR speaker_assessment
interpersonal $\Rightarrow$ initiating OR responding (cf. Halliday, 1984)
interpersonal $\Rightarrow$ giving OR demanding
interpersonal $\Rightarrow$ goods_&_services OR information
= $\Rightarrow$ speech_acts etc.

speaker_assessment $\Rightarrow$ modality
speaker assessment $\Rightarrow$ emotional_assessment
modality $\Rightarrow$ deontic OR epistemic
epistemic $\Rightarrow$ positive OR verycertain OR probably OR possible OR negative

The following is a rudimentary *text-base*.

structuring ⇒ grounding
grounding ⇒ focussing
grounding ⇒ thematizing
grounding ⇒ ranking
grounding ⇒ taxis
taxis ⇒ parataxis OR hypotaxis

restriction(given, focussing)
restriction(new, focussing)
restriction(theme, thematizing)
restriction(rheme, thematizing)
restriction(head, ranking)
restriction(argument, ranking)
restriction(modifier, ranking)

reference ⇒ coreference
reference ⇒ noncoreference

What I have been trying to bring out in my remarks about discourse knowledge here is that providing a way of abstracting away from grammatical categories to functional and semantic categories is helpful to get access to knowledge relevant to discourse rather than to isolated sentences only. My focus in these remarks has not been on discourse problems such as the *part-of* relation between events and situations, but rather on problems such as *focus, identifiability, formality* and so forth. I hope to have illustrated how the approach advocated here opens the door to considerations of that kind.

8. CONCLUSION

As was pointed out in the introduction, the thoughts offered here are mainly thoughts about ways of generalizing and abstracting from grammar fragments in several languages. They could, hopefully, be relevant to multilingual work in general, more specifically translation, and hopefully also machine translation and the representation of discourse knowledge. Within the last field, they could help to pave the way towards dealing with linguistic information beyond the clause by freeing us in a controlled way from the grammatical rank scale. Quite clearly, though, there is still a long way to go from such fragmentary remarks to a concrete MT architecture.

9. NOTATIONAL CONVENTION

In my rendering of Russian realizations, I am using here occasionally a latinized spelling that is not checked against official regulations of latinization for Russian.

REFERENCES

Allegranza, V., S. Krauwer, & E. Steiner. (eds.) (1991). *Machine Translation Special Issues on Eurotra*. Vol. 6 No. 5, 6. Dordrecht, Germany: Reidel.

Asher, N. (1993). *Reference to abstract objects in discourse*. Dordrecht: Kluwer.

Bateman, J.A., R.T. Kasper, J.D. Moore, & R.A. Whitney. (1990). A general organization of knowledge for natural language processing: the PENMAN upper model. Technical report, USC/Information Sciences Institute, Marina del Rey, California.

Bateman, J.A., C.M.I.M. Matthiessen, K. Nanri, & L. Zeng. (1991). The reuse of linguistic resources across languages in multilingual generation components. In *Proceedings of the 1991 International Joint Conference on Artificial Intelligence, Sydney, Australia*, volume 2, pages 966–971. Morgan Kaufmann.

Bateman, J.A., M. Emele, & S. Momma. (1992). The nondirectional representation of Systemic Functional Grammars and Semantics as Typed Feature Structures. In *Proceedings of COLING-92*, volume III, pages 916–920.

Bateman, J.A. (1992). The theoretical status of ontologies in natural language processing. In Susanne Preuß and Birte Schmitz (eds.) *Text Representation and Domain Modelling—ideas from linguistics and AI*, pp. 50–99. KIT-Report 97, Technische Universität Berlin, May 1992. (Papers from KIT-FAST Workshop, Technical University Berlin, October 9th–11th 1991).

Bell, R.T. (1991). *Translation and translating*. London: Longman.

Dowty, D. (1991). Thematic proto roles and argument selection. *Language*, 67(4).

Durand, J., P. Bennett, V. Allegranza, F. van Eynde, L. Humphreys, P. Schmidt, & E. Steiner. (1991). The EUROTRA linguistic specifications: An overview. *Machine Translation*, 6(2).

Engel, U. (1988). *Deutsche Grammatik*. Heidelberg: Groos.

Fawcett, R. (1980). *Cognitive linguistics and social interaction*. Heidelberg: Groos.

Halliday, M.A.K. (1982). How is a text like a clause? In Sture Allen (ed.) *Text Processing*. Stockholm: Almqvist and Wiksell.

Halliday, M.A.K. (1984). Language as code and language as behaviour. In Fawcett R., M.A.K. Halliday, S. Lamb, and A. Makkai, (Eds.) *The semiotics of culture and language, Vols. 1 and 2*. London: Frances Pinter.

Halliday, M.A.K. (1985). *An introduction to functional grammar*. London: Edward Arnold.

Halliday, M.A.K. & R. Hasan. (1976). *Cohesion in English*. London: Longman.

Hatim, B.,& I. Mason. (1990). *Discourse and the translator*. London: Longman.

Kameyama, M., R. Ochitani, & S. Peters. (1991). Resolving translation mismatches with information flow. In *Annual Meeting of the Association of Computational Linguistics*, pp. 193–200, Berkeley, CA: Association of Computational Linguistics.

Kamp, H., & U. Reyle. (1993). *From discourse to logic*. Dordrecht, Kluwer.

Kasper, R.T. (1989). A flexible interface for linking applications to PENMAN's sentence generator. In *Proceedings of the DARPA workshop on speech and natural language*.

Matthiessen, C.M.I.M., & J.A. Bateman. (1991). *Text generation and systemic-functional linguistics: Experiences from English and Japanese*. London: Frances Pinter.

Newmark, P. (1988). *A textbook of translation*. New York: Prentice Hall.

Nirenburg, S., J. Carbonell, M. Tomita, & K. Goodman. (1992). *Machine Translation: A knowledge-based approach*. San Mateo, CA: Morgan Kaufmann Publishers.

Sharp, R. (1991). Cat-2: a formalism for multilingual machine translation. *Machine Translation*, 6(1,2).

Snell-Hornby, M. (1986). *Übersetzungswissenschaft—eine Neuorientierung*. Tübingen: Gunter Narr.

Steiner, E. (1990). Aspects of a functional grammar for machine translation. In *Proceedings of the Third International Conference on Theoretical and Methodological Issues in Machine Translation*, Linguistic Research Center, University of Texas at Austin.

Steiner, E. (1991a). *A functional perspective on language, action, and interpretation*. Berlin: Mouton de Gruyter.

Steiner, E. (1991b). Structural and lexical information in a functional approach to machine translation. In *Proceedings of the International Conference on Current Issues in Computational Linguistics*, Universiti Sains, Penang, Malaysia.

Stolze, R. (1992). *Hermeneutisches Übersetzen*. Tübingen, Germany: Gunter Narr.

Vermeer, H.J., & H. Witte. (1990). Mögen sie Zistrosen. *Textcon Text Beiheft 3*.

Wilss, W. (1982). *The Science of Translation*. Tübingen, Germany: Gunter Narr.

Zajac, R. (1990). A relational approach to translation. In *Proceedings of the Third International Conference on Theoretical and Methodological Issues in Machine Translation*, Linguistic Research Center, University of Texas at Austin.

Zajac, R. (1992). Inheritance and constraint-based grammar formalisms. *Computational Linguistics. Special Issue on Inheritance: I. 1992*. 159–182, 18(2).

Author Index

Subject Index